HOLY BIBLE

NEW TESTAMENT

- For Additional Resources -
www.timetorevive.com
1-877-265-1605

Life Bible Study, LLC is a Christian Publisher serving churches and
Christian communities in order to advance the Gospel of Jesus Christ,
making disciples as we go.

Life Bible Study, LLC
5184 Caldwell Mill Road Suite 204-221
Hoover, AL 35244

For additional copies or quantity orders please call:
1-877-265-1605 or order online at
www.lifebiblestudy.org/timetorevive

New American Standard Bible (NASB)
Copyright © 1960, 1962, 1963, 1968, 1971, 1972, 1973, 1975, 1977, 1995
by The Lockman Foundation
A Corporation Not for Profit, La Habra, California
All Rights Reserved (2d)
www.lockman.org

1 2 3 4 5 / 21 20 19 18 17
Printed in China

CONTENTS

FOREWORD

Scriptural Promise

The grass withers, the flower fades, but the word of our God stands forever. Isaiah 40:8

The New American Standard Bible has been produced with the conviction that the words of Scripture as originally penned in the Hebrew, Aramaic, and Greek were inspired by God. Since they are the eternal Word of God, the Holy Scriptures speak with fresh power to each generation, to give wisdom that leads to salvation, that men may serve Christ to the glory of God.

The purpose of the Editorial Board in making this translation was to adhere as closely as possible to the original languages of the Holy Scriptures, and to make the translation in a fluent and readable style according to current English usage.

The Fourfold Aim of The Lockman Foundation

1. These publications shall be true to the original Hebrew, Aramaic, and Greek.

2. They shall be grammatically correct.

3. They shall be understandable.

4. They shall give the Lord Jesus Christ His proper place, the place which the Word gives Him; therefore, no work will ever be personalized.

Preface to The *New American Standard Bible*

In the history of English Bible translations, the King James Version is the most prestigious. This time-honored version of 1611, itself a revision of the Bishops' Bible of 1568, became the basis for the English Revised Version appearing in 1881 (New Testament) and 1885 (Old Testament). The American counterpart of this last work was published in 1901 as the American Standard Version. The ASV, a product of both British and American scholarship, has been highly regarded for its scholarship and accuracy. Recognizing the values of the American Standard Version, the Lockman Foundation felt an urgency to preserve these and other lasting values of the ASV by incorporating recent discoveries of Hebrew and Greek textual sources and by rendering it into more current English. Therefore, in 1959 a new translation project was launched, based on the time-honored principles of translation of the ASV and KJV. The result is the New American Standard Bible.

Translation work for the NASB was begun in 1959. In the preparation of this work numerous other translations have been consulted along with the linguistic tools and literature of biblical scholarship. Decisions about English renderings were made by consensus of a team composed of educators and pastors. Subsequently, review and evaluation by other Hebrew and Greek scholars outside the Editorial Board were sought and carefully considered.

The Editorial Board has continued to function since publication of the complete Bible in 1971. This edition of the NASB represents revisions and refinements recommended over the last several years as well as thorough research based on modern English usage.

Principles of Translation

MODERN ENGLISH USAGE: The attempt has been made to render the grammar and terminology in contemporary English. When it was felt that the word-for-word literalness was unacceptable to the modern reader, a change was made in the direction of a more current English idiom. In the instances where this has been done, the more literal rendering has been indicated in the notes. There are a few exceptions to this procedure. In particular, frequently "And" is not translated at the beginning of sentences because of differences in style between ancient and modern writing. Punctuation is a relatively modern invention, and ancient writers often linked most of their sentences with "and" or other connectives. Also, the Hebrew idiom "answered and said" is sometimes reduced to "answered" or "said" as demanded by the context. For current English the idiom "it came about that" has not been translated in the New Testament except when a major transition is needed.

HEBREW TEXT: In the present translation the latest edition of Rudolf Kittel's BIBLIA HEBRAICA has been employed together with the most recent light from lexicography, cognate languages, and the Dead Sea Scrolls.

HEBREW TENSES: Consecution of tenses in Hebrew remains a puzzling factor in translation. The translators have been guided by the requirements of a literal translation, the sequence of tenses, and the immediate and broad contexts.

THE PROPER NAME OF GOD IN THE OLD TESTAMENT: In the Scriptures, the name of God is most significant and understandably so. It is inconceivable to think of spiritual matters without a proper designation for the Supreme Deity. Thus the most common name for the Deity is God, a translation of the original Elohim. One of the titles for God is Lord, a translation of Adonai. There is yet another name which is particularly assigned to God as His special or proper name, that is, the four letters YHWH (Exodus 3:14 and Isaiah 42:8). This name has not been pronounced by the Jews because of reverence for the great sacredness of the divine name. Therefore, it has been consistently translated LORD. The only exception to this translation of YHWH is when it occurs in immediate proximity to the word Lord, that is, Adonai. In that case it is regularly translated GOD in order to avoid confusion.

It is known that for many years YHWH as been transliterated as Yahweh, however no complete certainty attaches to this pronunciation.

GREEK TEXT: Consideration was given to the latest available manuscripts with a view to determining the best Greek text. In most instances the 26th edition of Eberhard Nestle's NOVUM TESTAMENTUM GRAECE was followed.

GREEK TENSES: A careful distinction has been made in the treatment of the Greek aorist tense (usually translated as the English past, "He did") and the Greek imperfect tense (normally rendered either as English past progressive, "He was doing"; or, if inceptive, as "He began to do" or "He started to do"; or else if customary past, as "He used to do"). "Began" is italicized if it renders an imperfect tense, in order to distinguish it from the Greek verb for "begin." In some contexts the difference between the Greek imperfect and the English past is conveyed better by the choice of vocabulary or by other words in the context, and in such cases the Greek imperfect may be rendered as a simple past tense (e.g. "had an illness for many years" would be preferable to "was having an illness for many years" and would be understood in the same way).

On the other hand, not all aorists have been rendered as English pasts ("He did"), for some of them are clearly to be rendered as English perfects ("He has done"), or even as past perfects ("He had done"), judging from the context in which they occur. Such aorists have been rendered as perfects or past perfects in this translation.

As for the distinction between aorist and present imperatives, the translators have usually rendered these imperatives in the customary manner, rather than attempting any such fine distinction as "Begin to do!" (for the aorist imperative), or, "Continually do!" (for the present imperative).

As for sequence of tenses, the translators took care to follow English rules rather than Greek in translating Greek presents, imperfects and aorists. Thus, where English says, "We knew that he was doing," Greek puts it, "We knew that he does"; similarly, "We knew that he had done" is the Greek, "We knew that he did." Likewise, the English, "When he had come, they met him," is represented in Greek by: "When he came, they met him." In all cases a consistent transfer has been made from the Greek tense in the subordinate clause to the appropriate tense in English.

In the rendering of negative questions introduced by the particle *me-* (which always expects the answer "No") the wording has been altered from a mere, "Will he not do this?" to a more accurate, "He will not do this, will he?"

Editorial Board, THE LOCKMAN FOUNDATION

EXPLANATION OF GENERAL FORMAT

NOTES AND CROSS REFERENCES are not used in this edition.

PERSONAL PRONOUNS are capitalized when pertaining to Deity.

ITALICS are used in the text to indicate words which are not found in the original Hebrew, Aramaic, or Greek but implied by it. Italics are used in the marginal notes to signify alternate readings for the text. Roman text in the marginal alternate readings is the same as italics in the Bible text.

ALL CAPS in the New Testament are used in the text to indicate Old Testament quotations or obvious references to Old Testament texts. Variations of Old Testament wording are found in New Testament citations depending on whether the New Testament writer translated from a Hebrew text, used existing Greek or Aramaic translations, or paraphrased the material. It should be noted that modern rules for the indication of direct quotation were not used in biblical times thus the ancient writer would use exact quotations or references to quotation without specific indication of such. Also see **THE PROPER NAME OF GOD IN THE OLD TESTAMENT** under *Principles of Translation*.

ASTERISKS are used to mark verbs that are historical presents in the Greek which have been translated with an English past tense in order to conform to modern usage. The translators recognized that in some contexts the present tense seems more unexpected and unjustified to the English reader than a past tense would have been. But Greek authors frequently used the present tense for the sake of heightened vividness, thereby transporting their readers in imagination to the actual scene at the time of occurrence. However, the translators felt that it would be wise to change these historical presents to English past tenses.

[ ] = In text, brackets indicate words possibly not in the original writings.

MATTHEW

The Genealogy of Jesus the Messiah

1 The record of the genealogy of Jesus the Messiah, the son of David, the son of Abraham:

2 Abraham was the father of Isaac, Isaac the father of Jacob, and Jacob the father of ᵃJudah and his brothers. ³Judah was the father of Perez and Zerah by Tamar, Perez was the father of Hezron, and Hezron the father of Ram. ⁴Ram was the father of Amminadab, Amminadab the father of Nahshon, and Nahshon the father of Salmon. ⁵Salmon was the father of Boaz by Rahab, Boaz was the father of Obed by Ruth, and Obed the father of Jesse. ⁶Jesse was the father of David the king.

David was the father of Solomon by ᵇBathsheba who had been the wife of Uriah. ⁷Solomon was the father of Rehoboam, Rehoboam the father of Abijah, and Abijah the father of Asa. ⁸Asa was the father of Jehoshaphat, Jehoshaphat the father of Joram, and Joram the father of Uzziah ⁹Uzziah was the father of Jotham, Jotham the father of Ahaz, and Ahaz the father of Hezekiah. ¹⁰Hezekiah was the father of Manasseh, Manasseh the father of Amon, and Amon the father of Josiah. ¹¹Josiah became the father of Jeconiah and his brothers, at the time of the deportation to Babylon.

12 After the deportation to Babylon: Jeconiah became the father of Shealtiel, and Shealtiel the father of Zerubbabel. ¹³Zerubbabel was the father of Abihud, Abihud the father of Eliakim, and Eliakim the father of Azor. ¹⁴Azor was the father of Zadok, Zadok the father of Achim, and Achim the father of Eliud. ¹⁵Eliud was the father of Eleazar, Eleazar the father of Matthan, and Matthan the father of Jacob. ¹⁶Jacob was the father of Joseph the husband of Mary, by whom Jesus was born, who is called the Messiah.

17 So all the generations from Abraham to David are fourteen generations; from David to the deportation to Babylon, fourteen generations; and from the deportation to Babylon to the Messiah, fourteen generations.

Conception and Birth of Jesus

18 Now the birth of Jesus Christ

ᵃ **1:2** Gr *Judas*; names of people in the Old Testament are given in their Old Testament form; ᵇ **1:6** Lit her of Uriah was as follows: when His mother Mary had been betrothed to Joseph, before they came together she was found to be with child by the Holy Spirit. ¹⁹And Joseph her husband, being a righteous man and not wanting to disgrace her, planned ᵃto send her away secretly. ²⁰But when he had considered this, behold, an angel of the Lord appeared to him in a dream, saying, "Joseph, son of David, do not be afraid to take Mary as your wife; for the Child who has been ᵇconceived in her is of the Holy Spirit. ²¹She will bear a Son; and you shall call His name Jesus, for He will save His people from their sins." ²²Now all this took place to fulfill what was spoken by the Lord through the prophet: ²³"BEHOLD, THE VIRGIN SHALL BE WITH CHILD AND SHALL BEAR A SON, AND THEY SHALL CALL HIS NAME IMMANUEL," which translated means, "GOD WITH US." ²⁴And Joseph awoke from his sleep and did as the angel of the Lord commanded him, and took *Mary* as his wife, ²⁵ᶜbut kept her a virgin until she gave birth to a Son; and he called His name Jesus.

The Visit of the Magi

2 Now after Jesus was born in Bethlehem of Judea in the days of Herod the king, ᵈmagi from the east arrived in Jerusalem, saying, ²"Where is He who has been born King of the Jews? For we saw His star in the east and have come to worship Him." ³When Herod the king heard *this,* he was troubled, and all Jerusalem with him. ⁴Gathering together all the chief priests and scribes of the people, he inquired of them where the Messiah was to be born. ⁵They said to him, "In Bethlehem of Judea; for this is what has been written by the prophet:

⁶'AND YOU, BETHLEHEM, LAND OF JUDAH,

ARE BY NO MEANS LEAST AMONG THE LEADERS OF JUDAH;

FOR OUT OF YOU SHALL COME FORTH A RULER

WHO WILL SHEPHERD MY PEOPLE ISRAEL.' "

7 Then Herod secretly called the magi and determined from them the exact time the star appeared. ⁸And he sent them to Bethlehem and said, "Go and search carefully for the Child; and when you have found *Him,* report to me, so that I too may come and worship Him." ⁹After hearing the king, they went their way; and the star, which they had seen in the east, went on before them until it came and stood over *the place* where the Child was. ¹⁰When they saw the star, they rejoiced exceedingly with great joy. ¹¹After coming into the house they saw the Child with Mary His mother; and they

---

ᵃ **1:19** Or *to divorce her;* ᵇ **1:20** Lit *begotten;* ᶜ **1:25** Lit *and was not knowing her;* ᵈ **2:1** A caste of wise men specializing in astronomy, astrology, and natural science fell to the ground and worshiped Him. Then, opening their treasures, they presented to Him gifts of gold, frankincense, and myrrh. [12]And having been warned *by God* in a dream not to return to Herod, the magi left for their own country by another way.

The Flight to Egypt

13 Now when they had gone, behold, an angel of the Lord *appeared to Joseph in a dream and said, "Get up! Take the Child and His mother and flee to Egypt, and remain there until I tell you; for Herod is going to search for the Child to destroy Him."

14 So Joseph got up and took the Child and His mother while it was still night, and left for Egypt. [15]He remained there until the death of Herod. *This was* to fulfill what had been spoken by the Lord through the prophet: "OUT OF EGYPT I CALLED MY SON."

Herod Slaughters Babies

16 Then when Herod saw that he had been tricked by the magi, he became very enraged, and sent and slew all the male children who were in Bethlehem and all its vicinity, from two years old and under, according to the time which he had determined from the magi. [17]Then what had been spoken through Jeremiah the prophet was fulfilled:

[18]"A VOICE WAS HEARD IN RAMAH,
WEEPING AND GREAT MOURNING,
RACHEL WEEPING FOR HER CHILDREN;
AND SHE REFUSED TO BE COMFORTED,
BECAUSE THEY WERE NO MORE."

19 But when Herod died, behold, an angel of the Lord *appeared in a dream to Joseph in Egypt, and said, [20]"Get up, take the Child and His mother, and go into the land of Israel; for those who sought the Child's life are dead." [21]So Joseph got up, took the Child and His mother, and came into the land of Israel. [22]But when he heard that Archelaus was reigning over Judea in place of his father Herod, he was afraid to go there. Then after being warned *by God* in a dream, he left for the regions of Galilee, [23]and came and lived in a city called Nazareth. *This was* to fulfill what was spoken through the prophets: "He shall be called a Nazarene."

The Preaching of John the Baptist

3 Now in those days John the Baptist *came, preaching in the wilderness of Judea, saying, [2]"Repent, for the kingdom of heaven is at hand." [3]For this is the one referred to by Isaiah the prophet

when he said,
"THE VOICE OF ONE CRYING IN
  THE WILDERNESS,
'MAKE READY THE WAY OF THE
  LORD,
MAKE HIS PATHS STRAIGHT!' "
⁴Now John himself had a garment of camel's hair and a leather belt around his waist; and his food was locusts and wild honey. ⁵Then Jerusalem was going out to him, and all Judea and all the district around the Jordan; ⁶and they were being baptized by him in the Jordan River, as they confessed their sins.

7 But when he saw many of the Pharisees and Sadducees coming for baptism, he said to them, "You brood of vipers, who warned you to flee from the wrath to come? ⁸Therefore bear fruit in keeping with repentance; ⁹and do not suppose that you can say to yourselves, 'We have Abraham for our father'; for I say to you that from these stones God is able to raise up children to Abraham. ¹⁰The axe is already laid at the root of the trees; therefore every tree that does not bear good fruit is cut down and thrown into the fire.

11 "As for me, I baptize you ᵃwith water for repentance, but He who is coming after me is mightier than I, and I am not fit to remove His sandals; He will baptize you with the Holy Spirit and fire. ¹²His winnowing fork is in His hand, and He will thoroughly clear His threshing floor; and He will gather His wheat into the barn, but He will burn up the chaff with unquenchable fire."

The Baptism of Jesus

13 Then Jesus *arrived from Galilee at the Jordan *coming* to John, to be baptized by him. ¹⁴But John tried to prevent Him, saying, "I have need to be baptized by You, and do You come to me?" ¹⁵But Jesus answering said to him, "Permit *it* at this time; for in this way it is fitting for us to fulfill all righteousness." Then he *permitted Him. ¹⁶After being baptized, Jesus came up immediately from the water; and behold, the heavens were opened, and he saw the Spirit of God descending as a dove *and* lighting on Him, ¹⁷and behold, a voice out of the heavens said, "This is ᵇMy beloved Son, in whom I am well-pleased."

The Temptation of Jesus

4 Then Jesus was led up by the Spirit into the wilderness to be tempted by the devil. ²And after He had fasted forty days and forty nights, He ᶜthen became hungry. ³And the tempter came and said to Him, "If You are the Son of God, command that these stones become bread." ⁴But He answered

---

ᵃ **3:11** The Gr here can be translated *in, with* or *by;* ᵇ **3:17** Or *My Son, the Beloved;* ᶜ **4:2** Lit *later became;* or *afterward became* and said, "It is written, 'MAN SHALL NOT LIVE ON BREAD ALONE, BUT ON EVERY WORD THAT PROCEEDS OUT OF THE MOUTH OF GOD.' "

5 Then the devil *took Him into the holy city and had Him stand on the pinnacle of the temple, [6]and *said to Him, "If You are the Son of God, throw Yourself down; for it is written,

'HE WILL COMMAND HIS AN-
      GELS CONCERNING YOU';
and
'ON *their* HANDS THEY WILL
      BEAR YOU UP,
SO THAT YOU WILL NOT STRIKE
      YOUR FOOT AGAINST A
      STONE.' "

[7]Jesus said to him, "On the other hand, it is written, 'YOU SHALL NOT PUT THE LORD YOUR GOD TO THE TEST.' "

8 Again, the devil *took Him to a very high mountain and *showed Him all the kingdoms of the world and their glory; [9]and he said to Him, "All these things I will give You, if You fall down and worship me." [10]Then Jesus *said to him, "Go, Satan! For it is written, 'YOU SHALL WORSHIP THE LORD YOUR GOD, AND SERVE HIM ONLY.' " [11]Then the devil [a]left Him; and behold, angels came and *began* to minister to Him.

Jesus Begins His Ministry

12 Now when Jesus heard that John had been taken into custody, He withdrew into Galilee; [13]and leaving Nazareth, He came and settled in Capernaum, which is by the sea, in the region of Zebulun and Naphtali. [14]*This was* to fulfill what was spoken through Isaiah the prophet:

[15]"THE LAND OF ZEBULUN AND
      THE LAND OF NAPHTALI,
BY THE WAY OF THE SEA,
      BEYOND   THE   JOR-
      DAN,   GALILEE   OF   THE
      [a]GENTILES—
[16]"THE PEOPLE WHO WERE SIT-
      TING IN DARKNESS SAW A
      GREAT LIGHT,
AND THOSE WHO WERE SIT-
      TING IN THE LAND AND
      SHADOW OF DEATH,
UPON   THEM   A   LIGHT
      DAWNED."

17 From that time Jesus began to preach and say, "Repent, for the kingdom of heaven is at hand."

The First Disciples

18 Now as Jesus was walking by the Sea of Galilee, He saw two brothers, Simon who was called Peter, and Andrew his brother, casting a net into the sea; for they were fishermen. [19]And He *said to them, "Follow Me, and I will make you fishers of men." [20]Immediately they left their nets and followed Him. [21]Going on from there He

---

[a] **4:15** Lit *nations*, usually non-Jewish

saw two other brothers, James the *son* of Zebedee, and John his brother, in the boat with Zebedee their father, mending their nets; and He called them. ²²Immediately they left the boat and their father, and followed Him.

Ministry in Galilee

23 Jesus was going throughout all Galilee, teaching in their synagogues and proclaiming the gospel of the kingdom, and healing every kind of disease and every kind of sickness among the people.

24 The news about Him spread throughout all Syria; and they brought to Him all who were ill, those suffering with various diseases and pains, demoniacs, epileptics, paralytics; and He healed them. ²⁵Large crowds followed Him from Galilee and *the* Decapolis and Jerusalem and Judea and *from* beyond the Jordan.

The Sermon on the Mount; The Beatitudes

5 When Jesus saw the crowds, He went up on the mountain; and after He sat down, His disciples came to Him. ²He opened His mouth and *began* to teach them, saying,

3 "Blessed are the poor in spirit, for theirs is the kingdom of heaven.

4 "Blessed are those who mourn, for they shall be comforted.

5 "Blessed are the ᵃgentle, for they shall inherit the earth.

6 "Blessed are those who hunger and thirst for righteousness, for they shall be satisfied.

7 "Blessed are the merciful, for they shall receive mercy.

8 "Blessed are the pure in heart, for they shall see God.

9 "Blessed are the peacemakers, for they shall be called sons of God.

10 "Blessed are those who have been persecuted for the sake of righteousness, for theirs is the kingdom of heaven.

11 "Blessed are you when *people* insult you and persecute you, and falsely say all kinds of evil against you because of Me. ¹²Rejoice and be glad, for your reward in heaven is great; for in the same way they persecuted the prophets who were before you.

Disciples and the World

13 "You are the salt of the earth; but if the salt has become tasteless, how can it be made salty *again?* It is no longer good for

ᵃ **5:5** Or humble, meek

anything, except to be thrown out and trampled under foot by men.

14 "You are the light of the world. A city set on a hill cannot be hidden; ¹⁵nor does *anyone* light a lamp and put it under a basket, but on the lampstand, and it gives light to all who are in the house. ¹⁶Let your light shine before men in such a way that they may see your good works, and glorify your Father who is in heaven.

17 "Do not think that I came to abolish the Law or the Prophets; I did not come to abolish but to fulfill. ¹⁸For truly I say to you, until heaven and earth pass away, not the smallest letter or stroke shall pass from the Law until all is accomplished. ¹⁹Whoever then annuls one of the least of these commandments, and teaches others *to do* the same, shall be called least in the kingdom of heaven; but whoever keeps and teaches *them,* he shall be called great in the kingdom of heaven.

20 "For I say to you that unless your righteousness surpasses *that* of the scribes and Pharisees, you will not enter the kingdom of heaven.

Personal Relationships

21 "You have heard that the ancients were told, 'YOU SHALL NOT COMMIT MURDER' and 'Whoever commits murder shall be ᵃliable to the court.' ²²But I say to you that everyone who is angry with his brother shall be guilty before the court; and whoever says to his brother, ᵇ'You good-for-nothing,' shall be guilty before ᶜthe supreme court; and whoever says, 'You fool,' shall be guilty *enough to go* into the ᵈfiery hell. ²³Therefore if you are presenting your offering at the altar, and there remember that your brother has something against you, ²⁴leave your offering there before the altar and go; first be reconciled to your brother, and then come and present your offering. ²⁵Make friends quickly with your opponent at law while you are with him on the way, so that your opponent may not hand you over to the judge, and the judge to the officer, and you be thrown into prison. ²⁶Truly I say to you, you will not come out of there until you have paid up the last ᵉcent.

27 "You have heard that it was said, 'YOU SHALL NOT COMMIT ADULTERY'; ²⁸but I say to you that everyone who looks at a woman with lust for her has already committed adultery with her in his heart. ²⁹If your right eye makes you stumble, tear it out and throw it from you; for it is better for you to lose one of the parts of your body, than for your whole body to

ᵃ **5:21** Or *guilty before;* ᵇ **5:22** Or *empty-head;* Gr *Raka (Raca)* fr Aram *reqa;* ᶜ **5:22** Lit *the Sanhedrin;* ᵈ **5:22** Lit *Gehenna of fire;* ᵉ **5:26** Lit *quadrans* (equaling two mites); i.e. 164 of a daily wage be thrown into hell. [30]If your right hand makes you stumble, cut it off and throw it from you; for it is better for you to lose one of the parts of your body, than for your whole body to go into hell.

31 "It was said, 'WHOEVER SENDS HIS WIFE AWAY, LET HIM GIVE HER A CERTIFICATE OF DIVORCE'; [32]but I say to you that everyone who divorces his wife, except for *the* reason of unchastity, makes her commit adultery; and whoever marries a divorced woman commits adultery.

33 "Again, you have heard that the ancients were told, 'YOU SHALL NOT MAKE FALSE VOWS, BUT SHALL FULFILL YOUR VOWS TO THE LORD.' [34]But I say to you, make no oath at all, either by heaven, for it is the throne of God, [35]or by the earth, for it is the footstool of His feet, or by Jerusalem, for it is THE CITY OF THE GREAT KING. [36]Nor shall you make an oath by your head, for you cannot make one hair white or black. [37]But let your statement be, 'Yes, yes' *or* 'No, no'; anything beyond these is of evil.

38 "You have heard that it was said, 'AN EYE FOR AN EYE, AND A TOOTH FOR A TOOTH.' [39]But I say to you, do not resist an evil person; but whoever slaps you on your right cheek, turn the other to him also. [40]If anyone wants to sue you and take your [a]shirt, let him have your [b]coat also. [41]Whoever forces you to go one mile, go with him two. [42]Give to him who asks of you, and do not turn away from him who wants to borrow from you.

43 "You have heard that it was said, 'YOU SHALL LOVE YOUR NEIGHBOR and hate your enemy.' [44]But I say to you, love your enemies and pray for those who persecute you, [45]so that you may be sons of your Father who is in heaven; for He causes His sun to rise on *the* evil and *the* good, and sends rain on *the* righteous and *the* unrighteous. [46]For if you love those who love you, what reward do you have? Do not even the tax collectors do the same? [47]If you greet only your brothers, what more are you doing *than others*? Do not even the Gentiles do the same? [48]Therefore you are to be perfect, as your heavenly Father is perfect.

Giving to the Poor and Prayer

6 "Beware of practicing your righteousness before men to be noticed by them; otherwise you have no reward with your Father who is in heaven.

2 "So when you give to the poor, do not sound a trumpet before

[a] **5:40** Lit *tunic*; i.e. a garment worn next to the body; [b] **5:40** Lit *cloak*; i.e. an outer garment

you, as the hypocrites do in the synagogues and in the streets, so that they may be honored by men. Truly I say to you, they have their reward in full. ³But when you give to the poor, do not let your left hand know what your right hand is doing, ⁴so that your giving will be in secret; and your Father who sees *what is done* in secret will reward you.

5 "When you pray, you are not to be like the hypocrites; for they love to stand and pray in the synagogues and on the street corners so that they may be seen by men. Truly I say to you, they have their reward in full. ⁶But you, when you pray, go into your inner room, close your door and pray to your Father who is in secret, and your Father who sees *what is done* in secret will reward you.

7 "And when you are praying, do not use meaningless repetition as the Gentiles do, for they suppose that they will be heard for their many words. ⁸So do not be like them; for your Father knows what you need before you ask Him.

9 "Pray, then, in this way:
'Our Father who is in heaven,
Hallowed be Your name.
¹⁰'Your kingdom come.
Your will be done,
On earth as it is in heaven.

¹¹'Give us this day our daily bread.
¹²'And forgive us our debts, as we also have forgiven our debtors.
¹³'And do not lead us into temptation, but deliver us from evil. [For Yours is the kingdom and the power and the glory forever. Amen.']
¹⁴For if you forgive others for their transgressions, your heavenly Father will also forgive you. ¹⁵But if you do not forgive others, then your Father will not forgive your transgressions.

Fasting; The True Treasure; Wealth (Mammon)

16 "Whenever you fast, do not put on a gloomy face as the hypocrites *do,* for they neglect their appearance so that they will be noticed by men when they are fasting. Truly I say to you, they have their reward in full. ¹⁷But you, when you fast, anoint your head and wash your face ¹⁸so that your fasting will not be noticed by men, but by your Father who is in secret; and your Father who sees *what is done* in secret will reward you.

19 "Do not store up for yourselves treasures on earth, where moth and rust destroy, and where thieves break in and steal. ²⁰But store up for yourselves treasures in heaven, where neither moth nor rust destroys, and where thieves do not break in or steal; ²¹for

where your treasure is, there your heart will be also.

22 "The eye is the lamp of the body; so then if your eye is clear, your whole body will be full of light. [23]But if your eye is bad, your whole body will be full of darkness. If then the light that is in you is darkness, how great is the darkness!

24 "No one can serve two masters; for either he will hate the one and love the other, or he will be devoted to one and despise the other. You cannot serve God and [a]wealth.

The Cure for Anxiety

25 "For this reason I say to you, do not be worried about your life, *as to* what you will eat or what you will drink; nor for your body, *as to* what you will put on. Is not life more than food, and the body more than clothing? [26]Look at the birds of the air, that they do not sow, nor reap nor gather into barns, and *yet* your heavenly Father feeds them. Are you not worth much more than they? [27]And who of you by being worried can add a *single* hour to his life? [28]And why are you worried about clothing? Observe how the lilies of the field grow; they do not toil nor do they spin, [29]yet I say to you that not even Solomon in all his glory clothed himself like one

of these. [30]But if God so clothes the grass of the field, which is *alive* today and tomorrow is thrown into the furnace, *will He* not much more *clothe* you? You of little faith! [31]Do not worry then, saying, 'What will we eat?' or 'What will we drink?' or 'What will we wear for clothing?' [32]For the Gentiles eagerly seek all these things; for your heavenly Father knows that you need all these things. [33]But seek first His kingdom and His righteousness, and all these things will be added to you.

34 "So do not worry about tomorrow; for tomorrow will care for itself. Each day has enough trouble of its own.

Judging Others

7 "Do not judge so that you will not be judged. [2]For in the way you judge, you will be judged; and by your standard of measure, it will be measured to you. [3]Why do you look at the speck that is in your brother's eye, but do not notice the log that is in your own eye? [4]Or how can you say to your brother, 'Let me take the speck out of your eye,' and behold, the log is in your own eye? [5]You hypocrite, first take the log out of your own eye, and then you will see clearly to take the speck out of your brother's eye.

[a] **6:24** Gr *mamonas*, for Aram *mamon* (mammon), i.e. wealth, etc., personified as an object of worship

6 "Do not give what is holy to dogs, and do not throw your pearls before swine, or they will trample them under their feet, and turn and tear you to pieces.

Prayer and the Golden Rule

7 "Ask, and it will be given to you; seek, and you will find; knock, and it will be opened to you. ⁸For everyone who asks receives, and he who seeks finds, and to him who knocks it will be opened. ⁹Or what man is there among you who, when his son asks for a loaf, will give him a stone? ¹⁰Or if he asks for a fish, he will not give him a snake, will he? ¹¹If you then, being evil, know how to give good gifts to your children, how much more will your Father who is in heaven give what is good to those who ask Him!

12 "In everything, therefore, treat people the same way you want them to treat you, for this is the Law and the Prophets.

The Narrow and Wide Gates

13 "Enter through the narrow gate; for the gate is wide and the way is broad that leads to destruction, and there are many who enter through it. ¹⁴For the gate is small and the way is narrow that leads to life, and there are few who find it.

A Tree and Its Fruit

15 "Beware of the false prophets, who come to you in sheep's clothing, but inwardly are ravenous wolves. ¹⁶You will know them by their fruits. Grapes are not gathered from thorn *bushes* nor figs from thistles, are they? ¹⁷So every good tree bears good fruit, but the bad tree bears bad fruit. ¹⁸A good tree cannot produce bad fruit, nor can a bad tree produce good fruit. ¹⁹Every tree that does not bear good fruit is cut down and thrown into the fire. ²⁰So then, you will know them by their fruits.

21 "Not everyone who says to Me, 'Lord, Lord,' will enter the kingdom of heaven, but he who does the will of My Father who is in heaven *will enter.* ²²Many will say to Me on that day, 'Lord, Lord, did we not prophesy in Your name, and in Your name cast out demons, and in Your name perform many miracles?' ²³And then I will declare to them, 'I never knew you; DEPART FROM ME, YOU WHO PRACTICE LAWLESSNESS.'

The Two Foundations

24 "Therefore everyone who hears these words of Mine and acts on them, may be compared to a wise man who built his house on the rock. ²⁵And the rain fell, and the floods came, and the winds blew and slammed against that house;

and *yet* it did not fall, for it had been founded on the rock. ²⁶Everyone who hears these words of Mine and does not act on them, will be like a foolish man who built his house on the sand. ²⁷The rain fell, and the floods came, and the winds blew and slammed against that house; and it fell—and great was its fall."

28 When Jesus had finished these words, the crowds were amazed at His teaching; ²⁹for He was teaching them as *one* having authority, and not as their scribes.

Jesus Cleanses a Leper; The Centurion's Faith

8 When Jesus came down from the mountain, large crowds followed Him. ²And a leper came to Him and bowed down before Him, and said, "Lord, if You are willing, You can make me clean." ³Jesus stretched out His hand and touched him, saying, "I am willing; be cleansed." And immediately his leprosy was cleansed. ⁴And Jesus *said to him, "See that you tell no one; but go, show yourself to the priest and present the offering that Moses commanded, as a testimony to them."

5 And when Jesus entered Capernaum, a centurion came to Him, imploring Him, ⁶and saying, "Lord, my servant is lying

paralyzed at home, fearfully tormented." ⁷Jesus *said to him, "I will come and heal him." ⁸But the centurion said, "Lord, I am not worthy for You to come under my roof, but just say the word, and my servant will be healed. ⁹For I also am a man under authority, with soldiers under me; and I say to this one, 'Go!' and he goes, and to another, 'Come!' and he comes, and to my slave, 'Do this!' and he does *it.*" ¹⁰Now when Jesus heard *this,* He marveled and said to those who were following, "Truly I say to you, I have not found such great faith with anyone in Israel. ¹¹I say to you that many will come from east and west, and ªrecline *at the table* with Abraham, Isaac and Jacob in the kingdom of heaven; ¹²but the sons of the kingdom will be cast out into the outer darkness; in that place there will be weeping and gnashing of teeth." ¹³And Jesus said to the centurion, "Go; it shall be done for you as you have believed." And the servant was healed that *very* moment.

Peter's Mother-in-law and Many Others Healed

14 When Jesus came into Peter's home, He saw his mother-in-law lying sick in bed with a fever. ¹⁵He touched her hand, and the fever left her; and she got up and waited on Him. ¹⁶When evening came, they brought to Him many who

ª **8:11** Or *dine*

were demon-possessed; and He cast out the spirits with a word, and healed all who were ill. ¹⁷*This was* to fulfill what was spoken through Isaiah the prophet: "HE HIMSELF TOOK OUR INFIRMITIES AND CARRIED AWAY OUR DISEASES."

Discipleship Tested

18 Now when Jesus saw a crowd around Him, He gave orders to depart to the other side *of the sea.* ¹⁹Then a scribe came and said to Him, "Teacher, I will follow You wherever You go." ²⁰Jesus *said to him, "The foxes have holes and the birds of the air *have* nests, but the Son of Man has nowhere to lay His head." ²¹Another of the disciples said to Him, "Lord, permit me first to go and bury my father." ²²But Jesus *said to him, "Follow Me, and allow the dead to bury their own dead."

23 When He got into the boat, His disciples followed Him. ²⁴And behold, there arose a great storm on the sea, so that the boat was being covered with the waves; but Jesus Himself was asleep. ²⁵And they came to *Him* and woke Him, saying, "Save *us,* Lord; we are perishing!" ²⁶He *said to them, "Why are you afraid, you men of little faith?" Then He got up and rebuked the winds and the sea, and it became perfectly calm. ²⁷The

men were amazed, and said, "What kind of a man is this, that even the winds and the sea obey Him?"

Jesus Casts Out Demons

28 When He came to the other side into the country of the Gadarenes, two men who were demon-possessed met Him as they were coming out of the tombs. *They were* so extremely violent that no one could pass by that way. ²⁹And they cried out, saying, "What business do we have with each other, Son of God? Have You come here to torment us before the time?" ³⁰Now there was a herd of many swine feeding at a distance from them. ³¹The demons *began* to entreat Him, saying, "If You *are going to* cast us out, send us into the herd of swine." ³²And He said to them, "Go!" And they came out and went into the swine, and the whole herd rushed down the steep bank into the sea and perished in the waters. ³³The herdsmen ran away, and went to the city and reported everything, including what had happened to the demoniacs. ³⁴And behold, the whole city came out to meet Jesus; and when they saw Him, they implored Him to leave their region.

A Paralytic Healed

9 Getting into a boat, Jesus crossed over *the sea* and came to His own city.

2 And they brought to Him a paralytic lying on a bed. Seeing their faith, Jesus said to the paralytic, "Take courage, son; your sins are forgiven." ³And some of the scribes said to themselves, "This *fellow* blasphemes." ⁴And Jesus knowing their thoughts said, "Why are you thinking evil in your hearts? ⁵Which is easier, to say, 'Your sins are forgiven,' or to say, 'Get up, and walk'? ⁶But so that you may know that the Son of Man has authority on earth to forgive sins"— then He *said to the paralytic, "Get up, pick up your bed and go home." ⁷And he got up and went home. ⁸But when the crowds saw *this,* they were awestruck, and glorified God, who had given such authority to men.

Matthew Called

9 As Jesus went on from there, He saw a man called Matthew, sitting in the tax collector's booth; and He *said to him, "Follow Me!" And he got up and followed Him.

10 Then it happened that as Jesus was reclining *at the table* in the house, behold, many tax collectors and sinners came and were dining with Jesus and His disciples. ¹¹When the Pharisees saw *this,* they said to His disciples, "Why is your Teacher eating with the tax collectors and sinners?" ¹²But when Jesus heard *this,* He said, "*It is* not those who are healthy who need a physician, but those who are sick. ¹³But go and learn what this means: 'I DESIRE COMPASSION, ^aAND NOT SACRIFICE,' for I did not come to call the righteous, but sinners."

The Question about Fasting

14 Then the disciples of John *came to Him, asking, "Why do we and the Pharisees fast, but Your disciples do not fast?" ¹⁵And Jesus said to them, "The attendants of the bridegroom cannot mourn as long as the bridegroom is with them, can they? But the days will come when the bridegroom is taken away from them, and then they will fast. ¹⁶But no one puts a patch of unshrunk cloth on an old garment; for the patch pulls away from the garment, and a worse tear results. ¹⁷Nor do *people* put new wine into old wineskins; otherwise the wineskins burst, and the wine pours out and the wineskins are ruined; but they put new wine into fresh wineskins, and both are preserved."

Miracles of Healing

18 While He was saying these things to them, a *synagogue* official came and bowed down before Him, and said, "My daughter has just died; but come and lay Your

^a **9:13** l.c. more than

hand on her, and she will live." [19]Jesus got up and *began* to follow him, and *so did* His disciples.

20 And a woman who had been suffering from a hemorrhage for twelve years, came up behind Him and touched the fringe of His cloak; [21]for she was saying to herself, "If I only touch His garment, I will get well." [22]But Jesus turning and seeing her said, "Daughter, take courage; your faith has made you well." At once the woman was made well.

23 When Jesus came into the official's house, and saw the flute-players and the crowd in noisy disorder, [24]He said, "Leave; for the girl has not died, but is asleep." And they *began* laughing at Him. [25]But when the crowd had been sent out, He entered and took her by the hand, and the girl got up. [26]This news spread throughout all that land.

27 As Jesus went on from there, two blind men followed Him, crying out, "Have mercy on us, Son of David!" [28]When He entered the house, the blind men came up to Him, and Jesus *said to them, "Do you believe that I am able to do this?" They *said to Him, "Yes, Lord." [29]Then He touched their eyes, saying, "It shall be done to you according to your faith." [30]And their eyes were opened. And Jesus sternly warned them: "See that no one knows *about this!*" [31]But they went out and spread the news about Him throughout all that land.

32 As they were going out, a mute, demon-possessed man was brought to Him. [33]After the demon was cast out, the mute man spoke; and the crowds were amazed, *and were* saying, "Nothing like this has ever been seen in Israel." [34]But the Pharisees were saying, "He casts out the demons by the ruler of the demons."

35 Jesus was going through all the cities and villages, teaching in their synagogues and proclaiming the gospel of the kingdom, and healing every kind of disease and every kind of sickness.

36 Seeing the people, He felt compassion for them, because they were distressed and dispirited like sheep without a shepherd. [37]Then He *said to His disciples, "The harvest is plentiful, but the workers are few. [38]Therefore beseech the Lord of the harvest to send out workers into His harvest."

The Twelve Disciples; Instructions for Service

10 Jesus summoned His twelve disciples and gave them

authority over unclean spirits, to cast them out, and to heal every kind of disease and every kind of sickness.

2 Now the names of the twelve apostles are these: The first, Simon, who is called Peter, and Andrew his brother; and James the son of Zebedee, and John his brother; ³Philip and Bartholomew; Thomas and Matthew the tax collector; James the son of Alphaeus, and Thaddaeus; ⁴Simon the Zealot, and Judas Iscariot, the one who betrayed Him.

5 These twelve Jesus sent out after instructing them: "Do not go in *the* way of *the* Gentiles, and do not enter *any* city of the Samaritans; ⁶but rather go to the lost sheep of the house of Israel. ⁷And as you go, preach, saying, 'The kingdom of heaven is at hand.' ⁸Heal *the* sick, raise *the* dead, cleanse *the* lepers, cast out demons. Freely you received, freely give. ⁹Do not acquire gold, or silver, or copper for your money belts, ¹⁰or a bag for *your* journey, or even two coats, or sandals, or a staff; for the worker is worthy of his support. ¹¹And whatever city or village you enter, inquire who is worthy in it, and stay at his house until you leave *that city.* ¹²As you enter the house, give it your greeting. ¹³If the house is worthy, give it your *blessing of* peace. But if it is not worthy, take back your *blessing of* peace. ¹⁴Whoever does not receive you, nor heed your words, as you go out of that house or that city, shake the dust off your feet. ¹⁵Truly I say to you, it will be more tolerable for *the* land of Sodom and Gomorrah in the day of judgment than for that city.

A Hard Road before Them

16 "Behold, I send you out as sheep in the midst of wolves; so be shrewd as serpents and innocent as doves. ¹⁷But beware of men, for they will hand you over to *the* courts and scourge you in their synagogues; ¹⁸and you will even be brought before governors and kings for My sake, as a testimony to them and to the Gentiles. ¹⁹But when they hand you over, do not worry about how or what you are to say; for it will be given you in that hour what you are to say. ²⁰For it is not you who speak, but *it is* the Spirit of your Father who speaks in you.

21 "Brother will betray brother to death, and a father *his* child; and children will rise up against parents and cause them to be put to death. ²²You will be hated by all because of My name, but it is the one who has endured to the end who will be saved.

23 "But whenever they persecute you in one city, flee to the next; for truly I say to you, you will not finish *going through* the cities of Israel until the Son of Man comes.

The Meaning of Discipleship

24 "A disciple is not above his teacher, nor a slave above his master. **25**It is enough for the disciple that he become like his teacher, and the slave like his master. If they have called the head of the house Beelzebul, how much more *will they malign* the members of his household!

26 "Therefore do not fear them, for there is nothing concealed that will not be revealed, or hidden that will not be known. **27**What I tell you in the darkness, speak in the light; and what you hear *whispered* in *your* ear, proclaim upon the housetops. **28**Do not fear those who kill the body but are unable to kill the soul; but rather fear Him who is able to destroy both soul and body in hell. **29**Are not two sparrows sold for a ªcent? And *yet* not one of them will fall to the ground apart from your Father. **30**But the very hairs of your head are all numbered. **31**So do not fear; you are more valuable than many sparrows.

32 "Therefore everyone who confesses Me before men, I will also confess him before My Father

ª**10:29** Gr *assarion*, the smallest copper coin

who is in heaven. **33**But whoever denies Me before men, I will also deny him before My Father who is in heaven.

34 "Do not think that I came to bring peace on the earth; I did not come to bring peace, but a sword. **35**For I came to SET A MAN AGAINST HIS FATHER, AND A DAUGHTER AGAINST HER MOTHER, AND A DAUGHTER-IN-LAW AGAINST HER MOTHER-IN-LAW; **36**and A MAN'S ENEMIES WILL BE THE MEMBERS OF HIS HOUSEHOLD.

37 "He who loves father or mother more than Me is not worthy of Me; and he who loves son or daughter more than Me is not worthy of Me. **38**And he who does not take his cross and follow after Me is not worthy of Me. **39**He who has found his life will lose it, and he who has lost his life for My sake will find it.

The Reward of Service

40 "He who receives you receives Me, and he who receives Me receives Him who sent Me. **41**He who receives a prophet in *the* name of a prophet shall receive a prophet's reward; and he who receives a righteous man in the name of a righteous man shall receive a righteous man's reward. **42**And whoever in the name of a disciple gives to one of these little ones even a cup of cold water to drink, truly I say to you, he shall not lose his reward."

John's Questions

11 When Jesus had finished giving instructions to His twelve disciples, He departed from there to teach and preach in their cities.

2 Now when John, while imprisoned, heard of the works of Christ, he sent *word* by his disciples ³and said to Him, "Are You the Expected One, or shall we look for someone else?" ⁴Jesus answered and said to them, "Go and report to John what you hear and see: ⁵*the* BLIND RECEIVE SIGHT and *the* lame walk, *the* lepers are cleansed and *the* deaf hear, *the* dead are raised up, and *the* POOR HAVE THE GOSPEL PREACHED TO THEM. ⁶And blessed is he who does not take offense at Me."

Jesus' Tribute to John

7 As these men were going *away,* Jesus began to speak to the crowds about John, "What did you go out into the wilderness to see? A reed shaken by the wind? ⁸But what did you go out to see? A man dressed in soft *clothing?* Those who wear soft *clothing* are in kings' palaces! ⁹But what did you go out to see? A prophet? Yes, I tell you, and one who is more than a prophet.

¹⁰This is the one about whom it is written,

'BEHOLD, I SEND MY MESSENGER
    AHEAD OF YOU,
WHO WILL PREPARE YOUR WAY
    BEFORE YOU.'

¹¹Truly I say to you, among those born of women there has not arisen *anyone* greater than John the Baptist! Yet the one who is least in the kingdom of heaven is greater than he. ¹²From the days of John the Baptist until now the kingdom of heaven suffers violence, and violent men take it by force. ¹³For all the prophets and the Law prophesied until John. ¹⁴And if you are willing to accept *it,* John himself is Elijah who was to come. ¹⁵He who has ears to hear, let him hear.

16 "But to what shall I compare this generation? It is like children sitting in the market places, who call out to the other *children,* ¹⁷and say, 'We played the flute for you, and you did not dance; we sang a dirge, and you did not mourn.' ¹⁸For John came neither eating nor drinking, and they say, 'He has a demon!' ¹⁹The Son of Man came eating and drinking, and they say, 'Behold, a gluttonous man and a drunkard, a friend of tax collectors and sinners!' Yet wisdom is vindicated by her deeds."

The Unrepenting Cities

20 Then He began to denounce the

cities in which most of His miracles were done, because they did not repent. ²¹"Woe to you, Chorazin! Woe to you, Bethsaida! For if the miracles had occurred in Tyre and Sidon which occurred in you, they would have repented long ago in sackcloth and ashes. ²²Nevertheless I say to you, it will be more tolerable for Tyre and Sidon in *the* day of judgment than for you. ²³And you, Capernaum, will not be exalted to heaven, will you? You will descend to Hades; for if the miracles had occurred in Sodom which occurred in you, it would have remained to this day. ²⁴Nevertheless I say to you that it will be more tolerable for the land of Sodom in *the* day of judgment, than for you."

Come to Me

25 At that time Jesus said, "I praise You, Father, Lord of heaven and earth, that You have hidden these things from *the* wise and intelligent and have revealed them to infants. ²⁶Yes, Father, for this way was well-pleasing in Your sight. ²⁷All things have been handed over to Me by My Father; and no one knows the Son except the Father; nor does anyone know the Father except the Son, and anyone to whom the Son wills to reveal *Him.*

28 "Come to Me, all who are weary and heavy-laden, and I will give you rest. ²⁹Take My yoke upon you and learn from Me, for I am gentle and humble in heart, and YOU WILL FIND REST FOR YOUR SOULS. ³⁰For My yoke is easy and My burden is light."

Sabbath Questions

12 At that time Jesus went through the grainfields on the Sabbath, and His disciples became hungry and began to pick the heads *of grain* and eat. ²But when the Pharisees saw *this,* they said to Him, "Look, Your disciples do what is not lawful to do on a Sabbath." ³But He said to them, "Have you not read what David did when he became hungry, he and his companions, ⁴how he entered the house of God, and they ate the consecrated bread, which was not lawful for him to eat nor for those with him, but for the priests alone? ⁵Or have you not read in the Law, that on the Sabbath the priests in the temple break the Sabbath and are innocent? ⁶But I say to you that something greater than the temple is here. ⁷But if you had known what this means, 'I DESIRE COMPASSION, AND NOT A SACRIFICE,' you would not have condemned the innocent.

Lord of the Sabbath

⁸For the Son of Man is Lord of the Sabbath."

9 Departing from there, He went into their synagogue. [10]And a man *was there* whose hand was withered. And they questioned Jesus, asking, "Is it lawful to heal on the Sabbath?"—so that they might accuse Him. [11]And He said to them, "What man is there among you who has a sheep, and if it falls into a pit on the Sabbath, will he not take hold of it and lift it out? [12]How much more valuable then is a man than a sheep! So then, it is lawful to do good on the Sabbath." [13]Then He *said to the man, "Stretch out your hand!" He stretched it out, and it was restored to normal, like the other. [14]But the Pharisees went out and conspired against Him, *as to* how they might destroy Him.

15 But Jesus, aware of *this,* withdrew from there. Many followed Him, and He healed them all, [16]and warned them not to tell who He was. [17]*This was* to fulfill what was spoken through Isaiah the prophet:

[18]"BEHOLD, MY SERVANT WHOM I HAVE CHOSEN;
MY BELOVED IN WHOM MY SOUL is WELL-PLEASED;
I WILL PUT MY SPIRIT UPON HIM,
AND HE SHALL PROCLAIM JUSTICE TO THE GENTILES.
[19]"HE WILL NOT QUARREL, NOR CRY OUT;

NOR WILL ANYONE HEAR HIS VOICE IN THE STREETS.
[20]"A BATTERED REED HE WILL NOT BREAK OFF,
AND A SMOLDERING WICK HE WILL NOT PUT OUT,
UNTIL HE LEADS JUSTICE TO VICTORY.
[21]"AND IN HIS NAME THE GENTILES WILL HOPE."

The Pharisees Rebuked

22 Then a demon-possessed man *who was* blind and mute was brought to Jesus, and He healed him, so that the mute man spoke and saw. [23]All the crowds were amazed, and were saying, "This man cannot be the Son of David, can he?" [24]But when the Pharisees heard *this,* they said, "This man casts out demons only by Beelzebul the ruler of the demons."

25 And knowing their thoughts Jesus said to them, "Any kingdom divided against itself is laid waste; and any city or house divided against itself will not stand. [26]If Satan casts out Satan, he is divided against himself; how then will his kingdom stand? [27]If I by Beelzebul cast out demons, by whom do your sons cast *them* out? For this reason they will be your judges. [28]But if I cast out demons by the Spirit of God, then the kingdom of God has come upon you. [29]Or how can anyone enter the strong man's house and carry off his property, unless he first binds the strong *man*? And then he will plunder his house.

The Unpardonable Sin

³⁰He who is not with Me is against Me; and he who does not gather with Me scatters.

31 "Therefore I say to you, any sin and blasphemy shall be forgiven people, but blasphemy against the Spirit shall not be forgiven. ³²Whoever speaks a word against the Son of Man, it shall be forgiven him; but whoever speaks against the Holy Spirit, it shall not be forgiven him, either in this age or in the *age* to come.

Words Reveal Character

33 "Either make the tree good and its fruit good, or make the tree bad and its fruit bad; for the tree is known by its fruit. ³⁴You brood of vipers, how can you, being evil, speak what is good? For the mouth speaks out of that which fills the heart. ³⁵The good man brings out of *his* good treasure what is good; and the evil man brings out of *his* evil treasure what is evil. ³⁶But I tell you that every careless word that people speak, they shall give an accounting for it in the day of judgment. ³⁷For by your words you will be justified, and by your words you will be condemned."

The Desire for Signs

38 Then some of the scribes and Pharisees said to Him, "Teacher, we want to see a sign from You." ³⁹But He answered and said to them, "An evil and adulterous generation craves for a sign; and *yet* no sign will be given to it but the sign of Jonah the prophet; ⁴⁰for just as JONAH WAS THREE DAYS AND THREE NIGHTS IN THE BELLY OF THE SEA MONSTER, so will the Son of Man be three days and three nights in the heart of the earth. ⁴¹The men of Nineveh will stand up with this generation at the judgment, and will condemn it because they repented at the preaching of Jonah; and behold, something greater than Jonah is here. ⁴²*The* Queen of *the* South will rise up with this generation at the judgment and will condemn it, because she came from the ends of the earth to hear the wisdom of Solomon; and behold, something greater than Solomon is here.

43 "Now when the unclean spirit goes out of a man, it passes through waterless places seeking rest, and does not find *it*. ⁴⁴Then it says, 'I will return to my house from which I came'; and when it comes, it finds *it* unoccupied, swept, and put in order. ⁴⁵Then it goes and takes along with it seven other spirits more wicked than itself, and they go in and live there;

and the last state of that man becomes worse than the first. That is the way it will also be with this evil generation."

Changed Relationships

46 While He was still speaking to the crowds, behold, His mother and brothers were standing outside, seeking to speak to Him. [47]Someone said to Him, "Behold, Your mother and Your brothers are standing outside seeking to speak to You." [48]But Jesus answered the one who was telling Him and said, "Who is My mother and who are My brothers?" [49]And stretching out His hand toward His disciples, He said, "Behold My mother and My brothers! [50]For whoever does the will of My Father who is in heaven, he is My brother and sister and mother."

Jesus Teaches in Parables

13 That day Jesus went out of the house and was sitting by the sea. [2]And large crowds gathered to Him, so He got into a boat and sat down, and the whole crowd was standing on the beach.

3 And He spoke many things to them in parables, saying, "Behold, the sower went out to sow; [4]and as he sowed, some *seeds* fell beside the road, and the birds came and ate them up. [5]Others fell on the rocky places, where they did not have much soil; and immediately they sprang up, because they had no depth of soil. [6]But when the sun had risen, they were scorched; and because they had no root, they withered away. [7]Others fell among the thorns, and the thorns came up and choked them out. [8]And others fell on the good soil and *yielded a crop, some a hundredfold, some sixty, and some thirty. [9]He who has ears, let him hear."

An Explanation

10 And the disciples came and said to Him, "Why do You speak to them in parables?" [11]Jesus answered them, "To you it has been granted to know the mysteries of the kingdom of heaven, but to them it has not been granted. [12]For whoever has, to him *more* shall be given, and he will have an abundance; but whoever does not have, even what he has shall be taken away from him. [13]Therefore I speak to them in parables; because while seeing they do not see, and while hearing they do not hear, nor do they understand. [14]In their case the prophecy of Isaiah is being fulfilled, which says,

'YOU WILL KEEP ON HEARING, BUT WILL NOT UNDERSTAND;
YOU WILL KEEP ON SEEING, BUT WILL NOT PERCEIVE;
[15]FOR THE HEART OF THIS PEOPLE HAS BECOME DULL,

WITH THEIR EARS THEY
    SCARCELY HEAR,
AND THEY HAVE CLOSED
    THEIR EYES,
OTHERWISE THEY WOULD SEE
    WITH THEIR EYES,
HEAR WITH THEIR EARS,
AND UNDERSTAND WITH
    THEIR HEART AND RETURN,
AND I WOULD HEAL THEM.'
[16]But blessed are your eyes, because they see; and your ears, because they hear. [17]For truly I say to you that many prophets and righteous men desired to see what you see, and did not see *it,* and to hear what you hear, and did not hear *it.*

The Sower Explained

[18]"Hear then the parable of the sower. [19]When anyone hears the word of the kingdom and does not understand it, the evil *one* comes and snatches away what has been sown in his heart. This is the one on whom seed was sown beside the road. [20]The one on whom seed was sown on the rocky places, this is the man who hears the word and immediately receives it with joy; [21]yet he has no *firm* root in himself, but is *only* temporary, and when affliction or persecution arises because of the word, immediately he falls away. [22]And the one on whom seed was sown among the thorns, this is the man who hears the word, and the worry of the world and the deceitfulness of wealth choke the word, and it becomes unfruitful. [23]And the one on whom seed was sown on the good soil, this is the man who hears the word and understands it; who indeed bears fruit and brings forth, some a hundredfold, some sixty, and some thirty."

Tares among Wheat

24 Jesus presented another parable to them, saying, "The kingdom of heaven may be compared to a man who sowed good seed in his field. [25]But while his men were sleeping, his enemy came and sowed [a]tares among the wheat, and went away. [26]But when the wheat sprouted and bore grain, then the tares became evident also. [27]The slaves of the landowner came and said to him, 'Sir, did you not sow good seed in your field? How then does it have tares?' [28]And he said to them, 'An enemy has done this!' The slaves *said to him, 'Do you want us, then, to go and gather them up?' [29]But he *said, 'No; for while you are gathering up the tares, you may uproot the wheat with them. [30]Allow both to grow together until the harvest; and in the time of the harvest I will say to the reapers, "First gather up the tares and bind them in bundles to burn them up; but gather the wheat into my barn." ' "

[a] **13:25** Or *darnel,* a weed resembling wheat

The Mustard Seed

31 He presented another parable to them, saying, "The kingdom of heaven is like a mustard seed, which a man took and sowed in his field; [32]and this is smaller than all *other* seeds, but when it is full grown, it is larger than the garden plants and becomes a tree, so that THE BIRDS OF THE AIR come and NEST IN ITS BRANCHES."

The Leaven

33 He spoke another parable to them, "The kingdom of heaven is like leaven, which a woman took and hid in three pecks of flour until it was all leavened."

34 All these things Jesus spoke to the crowds in parables, and He did not speak to them without a parable. [35]*This was* to fulfill what was spoken through the prophet:
"I WILL OPEN MY MOUTH IN PARABLES;
I WILL UTTER THINGS HIDDEN SINCE THE FOUNDATION OF THE WORLD."

The Tares Explained

36 Then He left the crowds and went into the house. And His disciples came to Him and said, "Explain to us the parable of the tares of the field." [37]And He said, "The one who sows the good seed is the Son of Man, [38]and the field is the world; and *as for* the good seed, these are the sons of the kingdom; and the tares are the sons of the evil *one;* [39]and the enemy who sowed them is the devil, and the harvest is the end of the age; and the reapers are angels. [40]So just as the tares are gathered up and burned with fire, so shall it be at the end of the age. [41]The Son of Man will send forth His angels, and they will gather out of His kingdom all stumbling blocks, and those who commit lawlessness, [42]and will throw them into the furnace of fire; in that place there will be weeping and gnashing of teeth. [43]Then THE RIGHTEOUS WILL SHINE FORTH AS THE SUN in the kingdom of their Father. He who has ears, let him hear.

Hidden Treasure

44 "The kingdom of heaven is like a treasure hidden in the field, which a man found and hid *again;* and from joy over it he goes and sells all that he has and buys that field.

A Costly Pearl

45 "Again, the kingdom of heaven is like a merchant seeking fine pearls, [46]and upon finding one pearl of great value, he went and sold all that he had and bought it.

A Dragnet

47 "Again, the kingdom of heaven is like a dragnet cast into the sea, and gathering *fish* of every kind; ⁴⁸and when it was filled, they drew it up on the beach; and they sat down and gathered the good *fish* into containers, but the bad they threw away. ⁴⁹So it will be at the end of the age; the angels will come forth and take out the wicked from among the righteous, ⁵⁰and will throw them into the furnace of fire; in that place there will be weeping and gnashing of teeth.

51 "Have you understood all these things?" They *said to Him, "Yes." ⁵²And Jesus said to them, "Therefore every scribe who has become a disciple of the kingdom of heaven is like a head of a household, who brings out of his treasure things new and old."

Jesus Revisits Nazareth

53 When Jesus had finished these parables, He departed from there. ⁵⁴He came to His hometown and *began* teaching them in their synagogue, so that they were astonished, and said, "Where *did* this man *get* this wisdom and *these* miraculous powers? ⁵⁵Is not this the carpenter's son? Is not His mother called Mary, and His brothers, James and Joseph and Simon and Judas? ⁵⁶And His sisters, are they not all with us? Where then *did* this man *get* all these things?" ⁵⁷And they took offense at Him. But Jesus said to them, "A

prophet is not without honor except in his hometown and in his *own* household." ⁵⁸And He did not do many miracles there because of their unbelief.

John the Baptist Beheaded

14At that time Herod the tetrarch heard the news about Jesus, ²and said to his servants, "This is John the Baptist; he has risen from the dead, and that is why miraculous powers are at work in him."

3 For when Herod had John arrested, he bound him and put him in prison because of Herodias, the wife of his brother Philip. ⁴For John had been saying to him, "It is not lawful for you to have her." ⁵Although Herod wanted to put him to death, he feared the crowd, because they regarded John as a prophet.

6 But when Herod's birthday came, the daughter of Herodias danced before *them* and pleased Herod, ⁷so *much* that he promised with an oath to give her whatever she asked. ⁸Having been prompted by her mother, she *said, "Give me here on a platter the head of John the Baptist." ⁹Although he was grieved, the king commanded *it* to be given because of his oaths, and because of his dinner guests. ¹⁰He sent and had John beheaded

in the prison. ¹¹And his head was brought on a platter and given to the girl, and she brought it to her mother. ¹²His disciples came and took away the body and buried it; and they went and reported to Jesus.

Five Thousand Fed

13 Now when Jesus heard *about John,* He withdrew from there in a boat to a secluded place by Himself; and when the people heard *of this,* they followed Him on foot from the cities. ¹⁴When He went ashore, He saw a large crowd, and felt compassion for them and healed their sick.

15 When it was evening, the disciples came to Him and said, "This place is desolate and the hour is already late; so send the crowds away, that they may go into the villages and buy food for themselves." ¹⁶But Jesus said to them, "They do not need to go away; you give them *something* to eat!" ¹⁷They *said to Him, "We have here only five loaves and two fish." ¹⁸And He said, "Bring them here to Me." ¹⁹Ordering the people to sit down on the grass, He took the five loaves and the two fish, and looking up toward heaven, He blessed *the food,* and breaking the loaves He gave them to the disciples, and the disciples *gave them* to the crowds, ²⁰and they all ate

and were satisfied. They picked up what was left over of the broken pieces, twelve full baskets. ²¹There were about five thousand men who ate, besides women and children.

Jesus Walks on the Water

22 Immediately He made the disciples get into the boat and go ahead of Him to the other side, while He sent the crowds away. ²³After He had sent the crowds away, He went up on the mountain by Himself to pray; and when it was evening, He was there alone. ²⁴But the boat was already ᵃa long distance from the land, battered by the waves; for the wind was contrary. ²⁵And in the ᵇfourth watch of the night He came to them, walking on the sea. ²⁶When the disciples saw Him walking on the sea, they were terrified, and said, "It is a ghost!" And they cried out in fear. ²⁷But immediately Jesus spoke to them, saying, "Take courage, it is I; do not be afraid."

28 Peter said to Him, "Lord, if it is You, command me to come to You on the water." ²⁹And He said, "Come!" And Peter got out of the boat, and walked on the water and came toward Jesus. ³⁰But seeing the wind, he became frightened, and beginning to sink, he cried out, "Lord, save me!" ³¹Immediately Jesus stretched out His hand

ᵃ**14:24** Lit *many stadia from*; a stadion was about 600 feet or about 182 meters; ᵇ**14:25** I.e. 3–6 a.m.

and took hold of him, and *said to him, "You of little faith, why did you doubt?" ³²When they got into the boat, the wind stopped. ³³And those who were in the boat worshiped Him, saying, "You are certainly God's Son!"

34 When they had crossed over, they came to land at Gennesaret. ³⁵And when the men of that place recognized Him, they sent *word* into all that surrounding district and brought to Him all who were sick; ³⁶and they implored Him that they might just touch the fringe of His cloak; and as many as touched *it* were cured.

Tradition and Commandment

15 Then some Pharisees and scribes *came to Jesus from Jerusalem and said, ²"Why do Your disciples break the tradition of the elders? For they do not wash their hands when they eat bread." ³And He answered and said to them, "Why do you yourselves transgress the commandment of God for the sake of your tradition? ⁴For God said, 'HONOR YOUR FATHER AND MOTHER,' and, 'HE WHO SPEAKS EVIL OF FATHER OR MOTHER IS TO BE PUT TO DEATH.' ⁵But you say, 'Whoever says to *his* father or mother, "Whatever I have that would help you has been given *to God*," ⁶he is not to honor his father or his mother[a].' And *by this* you invalidated the word of God for the sake of your tradition. ⁷You hypocrites, rightly did Isaiah prophesy of you:

⁸"THIS PEOPLE HONORS ME WITH THEIR LIPS,

BUT THEIR HEART IS FAR AWAY FROM ME.

⁹"BUT IN VAIN DO THEY WORSHIP ME,

TEACHING AS DOCTRINES THE PRECEPTS OF MEN.' "

10 After Jesus called the crowd to Him, He said to them, "Hear and understand. ¹¹*It is* not what enters into the mouth *that* defiles the man, but what proceeds out of the mouth, this defiles the man."

12 Then the disciples *came and *said to Him, "Do You know that the Pharisees were offended when they heard this statement?" ¹³But He answered and said, "Every plant which My heavenly Father did not plant shall be uprooted. ¹⁴Let them alone; they are blind guides [b]of the blind. And if a blind man guides a blind man, both will fall into a pit."

The Heart of Man

15 Peter said to Him, "Explain the parable to us." ¹⁶Jesus said, "Are you still lacking in understanding also? ¹⁷Do you not understand that everything that goes into the mouth passes into the stomach, and is eliminated? ¹⁸But the

---

[a] **15:6** I.e. by supporting them with it; [b] **15:14** Later mss add *of the blind*

things that proceed out of the mouth come from the heart, and those defile the man. [19]For out of the heart come evil thoughts, murders, adulteries, fornications, thefts, false witness, slanders. [20]These are the things which defile the man; but to eat with unwashed hands does not defile the man."

The Syrophoenician Woman

21 Jesus went away from there, and withdrew into the district of Tyre and Sidon. [22]And a Canaanite woman from that region came out and *began* to cry out, saying, "Have mercy on me, Lord, Son of David; my daughter is cruelly demon-possessed." [23]But He did not answer her a word. And His disciples came and implored Him, saying, "Send her away, because she keeps shouting at us." [24]But He answered and said, "I was sent only to the lost sheep of the house of Israel." [25]But she came and *began* to bow down before Him, saying, "Lord, help me!" [26]And He answered and said, "It is not good to take the children's bread and throw it to the dogs." [27]But she said, "Yes, Lord; but even the dogs feed on the crumbs which fall from their masters' table." [28]Then Jesus said to her, "O woman, your faith is great; it shall be done for you as you wish." And her daughter was healed at once.

Healing Crowds

29 Departing from there, Jesus went along by the Sea of Galilee, and having gone up on the mountain, He was sitting there. [30]And large crowds came to Him, bringing with them *those who were* lame, crippled, blind, mute, and many others, and they laid them down at His feet; and He healed them. [31]So the crowd marveled as they saw the mute speaking, the crippled restored, and the lame walking, and the blind seeing; and they glorified the God of Israel.

Four Thousand Fed

32 And Jesus called His disciples to Him, and said, "I feel compassion for the people, because they have remained with Me now three days and have nothing to eat; and I do not want to send them away hungry, for they might faint on the way." [33]The disciples *said to Him, "Where would we get so many loaves in *this* desolate place to satisfy such a large crowd?" [34]And Jesus *said to them, "How many loaves do you have?" And they said, "Seven, and a few small fish." [35]And He directed the people to sit down on the ground; [36]and He took the seven loaves and the fish; and giving thanks, He broke them and started giving them to the disciples, and the disciples *gave them* to the people. [37]And they all ate and were satisfied, and

they picked up what was left over of the broken pieces, seven large baskets full. ³⁸And those who ate were four thousand men, besides women and children.

39 And sending away the crowds, Jesus got into the boat and came to the region of Magadan.

Pharisees Test Jesus

16 The Pharisees and Sadducees came up, and testing Jesus, they asked Him to show them a sign from heaven. ²But He replied to them, "When it is evening, you say, '*It will be* fair weather, for the sky is red.' ³And in the morning, '*There will be* a storm today, for the sky is red and threatening.' Do you know how to discern the appearance of the sky, but cannot *discern* the signs of the times? ⁴An evil and adulterous generation seeks after a sign; and a sign will not be given it, except the sign of Jonah." And He left them and went away.

5 And the disciples came to the other side *of the sea,* but they had forgotten to bring *any* bread. ⁶And Jesus said to them, "Watch out and beware of the leaven of the Pharisees and Sadducees." ⁷They began to discuss *this* among themselves, saying, "*He said that* because we did not bring *any* bread." ⁸But Jesus, aware of this, said, "You men of little faith, why do you discuss among yourselves that you have no bread? ⁹Do you not yet understand or remember the five loaves of the five thousand, and how many baskets *full* you picked up? ¹⁰Or the seven loaves of the four thousand, and how many large baskets *full* you picked up? ¹¹How is it that you do not understand that I did not speak to you concerning bread? But beware of the leaven of the Pharisees and Sadducees." ¹²Then they understood that He did not say to beware of the leaven of bread, but of the teaching of the Pharisees and Sadducees.

Peter's Confession of Christ

13 Now when Jesus came into the district of Caesarea Philippi, He was asking His disciples, "Who do people say that the Son of Man is?" ¹⁴And they said, "Some *say* John the Baptist; and others, Elijah; but still others, Jeremiah, or one of the prophets." ¹⁵He *said to them, "But who do you say that I am?" ¹⁶Simon Peter answered, "You are the Christ, the Son of the living God." ¹⁷And Jesus said to him, "Blessed are you, Simon Bar-jona, because flesh and blood did not reveal *this* to you, but My Father who is in heaven. ¹⁸I also say to you that you are Peter, and upon this rock I will build My church; and the gates of Hades will not overpower it. ¹⁹I will give you the

keys of the kingdom of heaven; and whatever you bind on earth shall have been bound in heaven, and whatever you loose on earth shall have been loosed in heaven." ²⁰Then He warned the disciples that they should tell no one that He was the Christ.

Jesus Foretells His Death

21 From that time Jesus began to show His disciples that He must go to Jerusalem, and suffer many things from the elders and chief priests and scribes, and be killed, and be raised up on the third day. ²²Peter took Him aside and began to rebuke Him, saying, "God forbid *it*, Lord! This shall never happen to You." ²³But He turned and said to Peter, "Get behind Me, Satan! You are a stumbling block to Me; for you are not setting your mind on God's interests, but man's."

Discipleship Is Costly

24 Then Jesus said to His disciples, "If anyone wishes to come after Me, he must deny himself, and take up his cross and follow Me. ²⁵For whoever wishes to save his life will lose it; but whoever loses his life for My sake will find it. ²⁶For what will it profit a man if he gains the whole world and forfeits his soul? Or what will a man give in exchange for his soul? ²⁷For the Son of Man is going to come in the glory of His Father with His angels, and WILL THEN REPAY EVERY MAN ACCORDING TO HIS DEEDS.

28 "Truly I say to you, there are some of those who are standing here who will not taste death until they see the Son of Man coming in His kingdom."

The Transfiguration

17 Six days later Jesus *took with Him Peter and James and John his brother, and *led them up on a high mountain by themselves. ²And He was transfigured before them; and His face shone like the sun, and His garments became as white as light. ³And behold, Moses and Elijah appeared to them, talking with Him. ⁴Peter said to Jesus, "Lord, it is good for us to be here; if You wish, I will make three tabernacles here, one for You, and one for Moses, and one for Elijah." ⁵While he was still speaking, a bright cloud overshadowed them, and behold, a voice out of the cloud said, "This is My beloved Son, with whom I am well-pleased; listen to Him!" ⁶When the disciples heard *this,* they fell face down to the ground and were terrified. ⁷And Jesus came to *them* and touched them and said, "Get up, and do not be afraid." ⁸And lifting up their eyes, they saw no one except Jesus Himself alone.

9 As they were coming down from the mountain, Jesus commanded them, saying, "Tell the vision to no one until the Son of Man has risen from the dead." ¹⁰And His disciples asked Him, "Why then do the scribes say that Elijah must come first?" ¹¹And He answered and said, "Elijah is coming and will restore all things; ¹²but I say to you that Elijah already came, and they did not recognize him, but did to him whatever they wished. So also the Son of Man is going to suffer at their hands." ¹³Then the disciples understood that He had spoken to them about John the Baptist.

The Demoniac

14 When they came to the crowd, a man came up to Jesus, falling on his knees before Him and saying, ¹⁵"Lord, have mercy on my son, for he is a lunatic and is very ill; for he often falls into the fire and often into the water. ¹⁶I brought him to Your disciples, and they could not cure him." ¹⁷And Jesus answered and said, "You unbelieving and perverted generation, how long shall I be with you? How long shall I put up with you? Bring him here to Me." ¹⁸And Jesus rebuked him, and the demon came out of him, and the boy was cured at once.

19 Then the disciples came to Jesus privately and said, "Why could we not drive it out?" ²⁰And He *said to them, "Because of the littleness of your faith; for truly I say to you, if you have faith the size of a mustard seed, you will say to this mountain, 'Move from here to there,' and it will move; and nothing will be impossible to you. ²¹ᵃ[But this kind does not go out except by prayer and fasting."]

22 And while they were gathering together in Galilee, Jesus said to them, "The Son of Man is going to be delivered into the hands of men; ²³and they will kill Him, and He will be raised on the third day." And they were deeply grieved.

The Tribute Money

24 When they came to Capernaum, those who collected the ᵇtwo-drachma *tax* came to Peter and said, "Does your teacher not pay the two-drachma *tax*?" ²⁵He *said, "Yes." And when he came into the house, Jesus spoke to him first, saying, "What do you think, Simon? From whom do the kings of the earth collect customs or polltax, from their sons or from strangers?" ²⁶When Peter said, "From strangers," Jesus said to him, "Then the sons are exempt. ²⁷However, so that we do not offend them, go to the sea and throw in a hook, and take the first fish that comes up; and when you open its mouth, you

ᵃ **17:21** Early mss do not contain this v; ᵇ **17:24** Equivalent to two denarii or two days' wages, paid as a temple tax will find [a]a shekel. Take that and give it to them for you and Me."

Rank in the Kingdom

18 At that time the disciples came to Jesus and said, "Who then is greatest in the kingdom of heaven?" [2]And He called a child to Himself and set him before them, [3]and said, "Truly I say to you, unless you are converted and become like children, you will not enter the kingdom of heaven. [4]Whoever then humbles himself as this child, he is the greatest in the kingdom of heaven. [5]And whoever receives one such child in My name receives Me; [6]but whoever causes one of these little ones who believe in Me to stumble, it would be better for him to have a heavy millstone hung around his neck, and to be drowned in the depth of the sea.

Stumbling Blocks

7 "Woe to the world because of *its* stumbling blocks! For it is inevitable that stumbling blocks come; but woe to that man through whom the stumbling block comes!

8 "If your hand or your foot causes you to stumble, cut it off and throw it from you; it is better for you to enter life crippled or lame, than to have two hands or two feet and be cast into the eternal fire. [9]If your eye causes you to stumble,

pluck it out and throw it from you. It is better for you to enter life with one eye, than to have two eyes and be cast into the fiery hell.

10 "See that you do not despise one of these little ones, for I say to you that their angels in heaven continually see the face of My Father who is in heaven. [11b][For the Son of Man has come to save that which was lost.]

Ninety-nine Plus One

12 "What do you think? If any man has a hundred sheep, and one of them has gone astray, does he not leave the ninety-nine on the mountains and go and search for the one that is straying? [13]If it turns out that he finds it, truly I say to you, he rejoices over it more than over the ninety-nine which have not gone astray. [14]So it is not *the* will of your Father who is in heaven that one of these little ones perish.

Discipline and Prayer

15 "If your brother sins[c], go and show him his fault in private; if he listens to you, you have won your brother. [16]But if he does not listen *to you,* take one or two more with you, so that BY THE MOUTH OF TWO OR THREE WITNESSES EVERY FACT MAY BE CONFIRMED. [17]If he refuses to listen to them, tell it to the church; and if he refuses

[a] **17:27** Lit *standard coin,* which was a shekel; [b] **8:11** Early mss do not contain this v; [c] **18:15** Late mss add *against you*

to listen even to the church, let him be to you as a Gentile and a tax collector. ¹⁸Truly I say to you, whatever you bind on earth shall have been bound in heaven; and whatever you loose on earth shall have been loosed in heaven.

19 "Again I say to you, that if two of you agree on earth about anything that they may ask, it shall be done for them by My Father who is in heaven. ²⁰For where two or three have gathered together in My name, I am there in their midst."

Forgiveness

21 Then Peter came and said to Him, "Lord, how often shall my brother sin against me and I forgive him? Up to seven times?" ²²Jesus *said to him, "I do not say to you, up to seven times, but up to seventy times seven.

23 "For this reason the kingdom of heaven may be compared to a king who wished to settle accounts with his slaves. ²⁴When he had begun to settle *them,* one who owed him ^aten thousand talents was brought to him. ²⁵But since he did not have *the means* to repay, his lord commanded him to be sold, along with his wife and children and all that he had, and repayment to be made. ²⁶So the slave fell *to the ground* and prostrated himself before him, saying, 'Have patience with me and I

will repay you everything.' ²⁷And the lord of that slave felt compassion and released him and forgave him the debt. ²⁸But that slave went out and found one of his fellow slaves who owed him a hundred ^bdenarii; and he seized him and *began* to choke *him,* saying, 'Pay back what you owe.' ²⁹So his fellow slave fell *to the ground* and *began* to plead with him, saying, 'Have patience with me and I will repay you.' ³⁰But he was unwilling and went and threw him in prison until he should pay back what was owed. ³¹So when his fellow slaves saw what had happened, they were deeply grieved and came and reported to their lord all that had happened. ³²Then summoning him, his lord *said to him, 'You wicked slave, I forgave you all that debt because you pleaded with me. ³³Should you not also have had mercy on your fellow slave, in the same way that I had mercy on you?' ³⁴And his lord, moved with anger, handed him over to the torturers until he should repay all that was owed him. ³⁵My heavenly Father will also do the same to you, if each of you does not forgive his brother from your heart."

Concerning Divorce

19 When Jesus had finished these words, He departed from Galilee and came into the region of Judea beyond the Jordan;

---

^a**18:24** A talent was worth more than fifteen years' wages of a laborer; ^b**18:24** The denarius was a day's wages

²and large crowds followed Him, and He healed them there.

3 *Some* Pharisees came to Jesus, testing Him and asking, "Is it lawful *for a man* to divorce his wife for any reason at all?" ⁴And He answered and said, "Have you not read that He who created *them* from the beginning MADE THEM MALE AND FEMALE, ⁵and said, 'FOR THIS REASON A MAN SHALL LEAVE HIS FATHER AND MOTHER AND BE JOINED TO HIS WIFE, AND THE TWO SHALL BECOME ONE FLESH'? ⁶So they are no longer two, but one flesh. What therefore God has joined together, let no man separate." ⁷They *said to Him, "Why then did Moses command to GIVE HER A CERTIFICATE OF DIVORCE AND SEND *her* AWAY?" ⁸He *said to them, "Because of your hardness of heart Moses permitted you to divorce your wives; but from the beginning it has not been this way. ⁹And I say to you, whoever divorces his wife, except for immorality, and marries another woman commits adultery."

10 The disciples *said to Him, "If the relationship of the man with his wife is like this, it is better not to marry." ¹¹But He said to them, "Not all men *can* accept this statement, but *only* those to whom it has been given. ¹²For there are eunuchs who were born that way from their mother's womb; and there are eunuchs who were made eunuchs by men; and there are *also* eunuchs who made themselves eunuchs for the sake of the kingdom of heaven. He who is able to accept *this,* let him accept *it.*"

Jesus Blesses Little Children

13 Then *some* children were brought to Him so that He might lay His hands on them and pray; and the disciples rebuked them. ¹⁴But Jesus said, "Let the children alone, and do not hinder them from coming to Me; for the kingdom of heaven belongs to such as these." ¹⁵After laying His hands on them, He departed from there.

The Rich Young Ruler

16 And someone came to Him and said, "Teacher, what good thing shall I do that I may obtain eternal life?" ¹⁷And He said to him, "Why are you asking Me about what is good? There is *only* One who is good; but if you wish to enter into life, keep the commandments." ¹⁸*Then* he *said to Him, "Which ones?" And Jesus said, "YOU SHALL NOT COMMIT MURDER; YOU SHALL NOT COMMIT ADULTERY; YOU SHALL NOT STEAL; YOU SHALL NOT BEAR FALSE WITNESS; ¹⁹HONOR YOUR FATHER AND MOTHER; and YOU SHALL LOVE

YOUR NEIGHBOR AS YOUR-SELF." ²⁰The young man *said to Him, "All these things I have kept; what am I still lacking?" ²¹Jesus said to him, "If you wish to be complete, go *and* sell your possessions and give to *the* poor, and you will have treasure in heaven; and come, follow Me." ²²But when the young man heard this statement, he went away grieving; for he was one who owned much property.

²³ And Jesus said to His disciples, "Truly I say to you, it is hard for a rich man to enter the kingdom of heaven. ²⁴Again I say to you, it is easier for a camel to go through the eye of a needle, than for a rich man to enter the kingdom of God." ²⁵When the disciples heard *this*, they were very astonished and said, "Then who can be saved?" ²⁶And looking at *them* Jesus said to them, "With people this is impossible, but with God all things are possible."

The Disciples' Reward

²⁷ Then Peter said to Him, "Behold, we have left everything and followed You; what then will there be for us?" ²⁸And Jesus said to them, "Truly I say to you, that you who have followed Me, in the regeneration when the Son of Man will sit on His glorious throne, you also shall sit upon twelve thrones, judging the twelve tribes of Israel.

²⁹And everyone who has left houses or brothers or sisters or father or mother ^aor children or farms for My name's sake, will receive many times as much, and will inherit eternal life. ³⁰But many *who are* first will be last; and *the* last, first.

Laborers in the Vineyard

20 "For the kingdom of heaven is like a landowner who went out early in the morning to hire laborers for his vineyard. ²When he had agreed with the laborers for a ^bdenarius for the day, he sent them into his vineyard. ³And he went out about the ^cthird hour and saw others standing idle in the market place; ⁴and to those he said, 'You also go into the vineyard, and whatever is right I will give you.' And *so* they went. ⁵Again he went out about the ^dsixth and the ninth hour, and did the same thing. ⁶And about the ^eeleventh *hour* he went out and found others standing *around;* and he *said to them, 'Why have you been standing here idle all day long?' ⁷They *said to him, 'Because no one hired us.' He *said to them, 'You go into the vineyard too.'

⁸ "When evening came, the owner of the vineyard *said to his foreman, 'Call the laborers and pay them their wages, beginning with the last *group* to the first.' ⁹When those *hired* about the eleventh

^a**19:29** One early ms adds *or wife*; ^b**20:2** The denarius was a day's wages; ^c**20:3** I.e. 9 a.m.; ^d**20:5** I.e. noon and 3 p.m.; ^e**20:6** I.e. 5 p.m.

hour came, each one received a [a]denarius. [10]When those *hired* first came, they thought that they would receive more; but each of them also received a denarius. [11]When they received it, they grumbled at the landowner, [12]saying, 'These last men have worked *only* one hour, and you have made them equal to us who have borne the burden and the scorching heat of the day.' [13]But he answered and said to one of them, 'Friend, I am doing you no wrong; did you not agree with me for a denarius? [14]Take what is yours and go, but I wish to give to this last man the same as to you. [15]Is it not lawful for me to do what I wish with what is my own? Or is your eye envious because I am generous?' [16]So the last shall be first, and the first last."

Death, Resurrection Foretold

17 As Jesus was about to go up to Jerusalem, He took the twelve *disciples* aside by themselves, and on the way He said to them, [18]"Behold, we are going up to Jerusalem; and the Son of Man will be delivered to the chief priests and scribes, and they will condemn Him to death, [19]and will hand Him over to the Gentiles to mock and scourge and crucify *Him,* and on the third day He will be raised up."

Preferment Asked

20 Then the mother of the sons of Zebedee came to Jesus with her sons, bowing down and making a request of Him. [21]And He said to her, "What do you wish?" She *said to Him, "Command that in Your kingdom these two sons of mine may sit one on Your right and one on Your left." [22]But Jesus answered, "You do not know what you are asking. Are you able to drink the cup that I am about to drink?" They *said to Him, "We are able." [23]He *said to them, "My cup you shall drink; but to sit on My right and on *My* left, this is not Mine to give, but it is for those for whom it has been prepared by My Father."

24 And hearing *this,* the ten became indignant with the two brothers. [25]But Jesus called them to Himself and said, "You know that the rulers of the Gentiles lord it over them, and *their* great men exercise authority over them. [26]It is not this way among you, but whoever wishes to become great among you shall be your servant, [27]and whoever wishes to be first among you shall be your slave; [28]just as the Son of Man did not come to be served, but to serve, and to give His life a ransom for many."

Sight for the Blind

29 As they were leaving Jericho, a large crowd followed Him. [30]And two blind men sitting by the road,

[a] **20:9** The denarius was a day's wages

hearing that Jesus was passing by, cried out, "Lord, have mercy on us, Son of David!" [31]The crowd sternly told them to be quiet, but they cried out all the more, "Lord, Son of David, have mercy on us!" [32]And Jesus stopped and called them, and said, "What do you want Me to do for you?" [33]They *said to Him, "Lord, *we want* our eyes to be opened." [34]Moved with compassion, Jesus touched their eyes; and immediately they regained their sight and followed Him.

The Triumphal Entry

21 When they had approached Jerusalem and had come to Bethphage, at the Mount of Olives, then Jesus sent two disciples, [2]saying to them, "Go into the village opposite you, and immediately you will find a donkey tied *there* and a colt with her; untie them and bring them to Me. [3]If anyone says anything to you, you shall say, 'The Lord has need of them,' and immediately he will send them." [4]This took place to fulfill what was spoken through the prophet:

[5]"SAY TO THE DAUGHTER OF ZION,
'BEHOLD YOUR KING IS COMING TO YOU,
GENTLE, AND MOUNTED ON A DONKEY,
EVEN ON A COLT, THE FOAL OF A BEAST OF BURDEN.' "

[6]The disciples went and did just as Jesus had instructed them, [7]and brought the donkey and the colt, and laid their coats on them; and He sat on the coats. [8]Most of the crowd spread their coats in the road, and others were cutting branches from the trees and spreading them in the road. [9]The crowds going ahead of Him, and those who followed, were shouting,
"Hosanna to the Son of David;
BLESSED IS HE WHO COMES IN THE NAME OF THE LORD;
Hosanna in the highest!"

[10]When He had entered Jerusalem, all the city was stirred, saying, "Who is this?" [11]And the crowds were saying, "This is the prophet Jesus, from Nazareth in Galilee."

Cleansing the Temple

12 And Jesus entered the temple and drove out all those who were buying and selling in the temple, and overturned the tables of the money changers and the seats of those who were selling doves. [13]And He *said to them, "It is written, 'MY HOUSE SHALL BE CALLED A HOUSE OF PRAYER'; but you are making it a ROBBERS' DEN."

14 And *the* blind and *the* lame came to Him in the temple, and He healed them. [15]But when the chief priests and the scribes saw the wonderful things that He had done, and the children who were shouting in the temple, "Hosanna to the Son of David," they became indignant [16]and said to Him, "Do You hear what these *children* are saying?" And Jesus *said to them, "Yes; have you never read, 'OUT OF THE MOUTH OF INFANTS AND NURSING BABIES YOU HAVE PREPARED PRAISE FOR YOURSELF'?" [17]And He left them and went out of the city to Bethany, and spent the night there.

The Barren Fig Tree

18 Now in the morning, when He was returning to the city, He became hungry. [19]Seeing a lone fig tree by the road, He came to it and found nothing on it except leaves only; and He *said to it, "No longer shall there ever be *any* fruit from you." And at once the fig tree withered.

20 Seeing *this,* the disciples were amazed and asked, "How did the fig tree wither *all* at once?" [21]And Jesus answered and said to them, "Truly I say to you, if you have faith and do not doubt, you will not only do what was done to the fig tree, but even if you say to this mountain, 'Be taken up and cast into the sea,' it will happen. [22]And all things you ask in prayer, believing, you will receive."

Authority Challenged

23 When He entered the temple, the chief priests and the elders of the people came to Him while He was teaching, and said, "By what authority are You doing these things, and who gave You this authority?" [24]Jesus said to them, "I will also ask you one thing, which if you tell Me, I will also tell you by what authority I do these things. [25]The baptism of John was from what *source,* from heaven or from men?" And they *began* reasoning among themselves, saying, "If we say, 'From heaven,' He will say to us, 'Then why did you not believe him?' [26]But if we say, 'From men,' we fear the people; for they all regard John as a prophet." [27]And answering Jesus, they said, "We do not know." He also said to them, "Neither will I tell you by what authority I do these things.

Parable of Two Sons

28 "But what do you think? A man had two sons, and he came to the first and said, 'Son, go work today in the vineyard.' [29]And he answered, 'I will not'; but afterward he regretted it and went. [30]The man came to the second and said the same thing; and he answered, 'I *will,* sir'; but he did not go. [31]Which of the two did the will of his father?" They *said, "The first." Jesus *said to them, "Truly I say to you that the tax collectors and prostitutes will get into the kingdom of God before you.

[32]For John came to you in the way of righteousness and you did not believe him; but the tax collectors and prostitutes did believe him; and you, seeing *this,* did not even feel remorse afterward so as to believe him.

Parable of the Landowner

33 "Listen to another parable. There was a landowner who PLANTED A VINEYARD AND PUT A WALL AROUND IT AND DUG A WINE PRESS IN IT, AND BUILT A TOWER, and rented it out to vine-growers and went on a journey. [34]When the harvest time approached, he sent his slaves to the vine-growers to receive his produce. [35]The vine-growers took his slaves and beat one, and killed another, and stoned a third. [36]Again he sent another group of slaves larger than the first; and they did the same thing to them. [37]But afterward he sent his son to them, saying, 'They will respect my son.' [38]But when the vine-growers saw the son, they said among themselves, 'This is the heir; come, let us kill him and seize his inheritance.' [39]They took him, and threw him out of the vineyard and killed him. [40]Therefore when the owner of the vineyard comes, what will he do to those vine-growers?" [41]They *said to Him, "He will bring those wretches to a wretched end, and will rent out the vineyard to other vine-growers who will pay him the proceeds at the *proper* seasons."

42 Jesus *said to them, "Did you never read in the Scriptures,

'THE STONE WHICH THE BUILDERS REJECTED,
THIS BECAME THE CHIEF CORNER *stone*;
THIS CAME ABOUT FROM THE LORD,
AND IT IS MARVELOUS IN OUR EYES'?

[43]Therefore I say to you, the kingdom of God will be taken away from you and given to a people, producing the fruit of it. [44]And he who falls on this stone will be broken to pieces; but on whomever it falls, it will scatter him like dust."

45 When the chief priests and the Pharisees heard His parables, they understood that He was speaking about them. [46]When they sought to seize Him, they feared the people, because they considered Him to be a prophet.

Parable of the Marriage Feast

22 Jesus spoke to them again in parables, saying, [2]"The kingdom of heaven may be compared to a king who gave a wedding feast for his son. [3]And he sent out his slaves to call those who had been invited to the wedding feast, and they were unwilling to come. [4]Again he sent out other slaves saying, 'Tell those who have been invited, "Behold, I have prepared my dinner; my oxen and my fattened livestock are *all* butchered and everything is ready; come to the wedding feast." ' ⁵But they paid no attention and went their way, one to his own farm, another to his business, ⁶and the rest seized his slaves and mistreated them and killed them. ⁷But the king was enraged, and he sent his armies and destroyed those murderers and set their city on fire. ⁸Then he *said to his slaves, 'The wedding is ready, but those who were invited were not worthy. ⁹Go therefore to the main highways, and as many as you find *there,* invite to the wedding feast.' ¹⁰Those slaves went out into the streets and gathered together all they found, both evil and good; and the wedding hall was filled with dinner guests.

11 "But when the king came in to look over the dinner guests, he saw a man there who was not dressed in wedding clothes, ¹²and he *said to him, 'Friend, how did you come in here without wedding clothes?' And the man was speechless. ¹³Then the king said to the servants, 'Bind him hand and foot, and throw him into the outer darkness; in that place there will be weeping and gnashing of teeth.' ¹⁴For many are called, but few *are* chosen."

Tribute to Caesar

15 Then the Pharisees went and plotted together how they might trap Him in what He said. ¹⁶And they *sent their disciples to Him, along with the Herodians, saying, "Teacher, we know that You are truthful and teach the way of God in truth, and defer to no one; for You are not partial to any. ¹⁷Tell us then, what do You think? Is it lawful to give a poll-tax to Caesar, or not?" ¹⁸But Jesus perceived their malice, and said, "Why are you testing Me, you hypocrites? ¹⁹Show Me the coin *used* for the poll-tax." And they brought Him a denarius. ²⁰And He *said to them, "Whose likeness and inscription is this?" ²¹They *said to Him, "Caesar's." Then He *said to them, "Then render to Caesar the things that are Caesar's; and to God the things that are God's." ²²And hearing *this,* they were amazed, and leaving Him, they went away.

Jesus Answers the Sadducees

23 On that day *some* Sadducees (who say there is no resurrection) came to Jesus and questioned Him, ²⁴asking, "Teacher, Moses said, 'IF A MAN DIES HAVING NO CHILDREN, HIS BROTHER AS NEXT OF KIN SHALL MARRY HIS WIFE, AND RAISE UP CHILDREN FOR HIS BROTHER.' ²⁵Now there were seven brothers with us; and the first married and died, and

having no children left his wife to his brother; [26]so also the second, and the third, down to the seventh. [27]Last of all, the woman died. [28]In the resurrection, therefore, whose wife of the seven will she be? For they all had *married* her."

[29] But Jesus answered and said to them, "You are mistaken, not understanding the Scriptures nor the power of God. [30]For in the resurrection they neither marry nor are given in marriage, but are like angels in heaven. [31]But regarding the resurrection of the dead, have you not read what was spoken to you by God: [32]'I AM THE GOD OF ABRAHAM, AND THE GOD OF ISAAC, AND THE GOD OF JACOB'? He is not the God of the dead but of the living." [33]When the crowds heard *this*, they were astonished at His teaching.

[34] But when the Pharisees heard that Jesus had silenced the Sadducees, they gathered themselves together. [35]One of them, [a]a lawyer, asked Him *a question*, testing Him, [36]"Teacher, which is the great commandment in the Law?" [37]And He said to him, " 'YOU SHALL LOVE THE LORD YOUR GOD WITH ALL YOUR HEART, AND WITH ALL YOUR SOUL, AND WITH ALL YOUR MIND.' [38]This is the great and foremost commandment. [39]The second is like it, 'YOU SHALL LOVE YOUR NEIGHBOR AS YOURSELF.' [40]On these two commandments depend the whole Law and the Prophets."

[41] Now while the Pharisees were gathered together, Jesus asked them a question: [42]"What do you think about the Christ, whose son is He?" They *said to Him, "*The son* of David." [43]He *said to them, "Then how does David in the Spirit call Him 'Lord,' saying,

[44]'THE LORD SAID TO MY LORD,
"SIT AT MY RIGHT HAND,
UNTIL I PUT YOUR ENEMIES BENEATH YOUR FEET" '?

[45]If David then calls Him 'Lord,' how is He his son?" [46]No one was able to answer Him a word, nor did anyone dare from that day on to ask Him another question.

Pharisaism Exposed

23 Then Jesus spoke to the crowds and to His disciples, [2]saying: "The scribes and the Pharisees have seated themselves in the chair of Moses; [3]therefore all that they tell you, do and observe, but do not do according to their deeds; for they say *things* and do not do *them*. [4]They tie up heavy burdens and lay them on men's shoulders, but they themselves are unwilling to move them with *so much as* a finger. [5]But they do all their

[a] **22:35** I.e. an expert in the Mosaic Law

deeds to be noticed by men; for they broaden their ªphylacteries and lengthen the tassels *of their garments.* ⁶They love the place of honor at banquets and the chief seats in the synagogues, ⁷and respectful greetings in the market places, and being called Rabbi by men. ⁸But do not be called Rabbi; for One is your Teacher, and you are all brothers. ⁹Do not call *anyone* on earth your father; for One is your Father, He who is in heaven. ¹⁰Do not be called leaders; for One is your Leader, *that is,* Christ. ¹¹But the greatest among you shall be your servant. ¹²Whoever exalts himself shall be humbled; and whoever humbles himself shall be exalted.

Eight Woes

13 "But woe to you, scribes and Pharisees, hypocrites, because you shut off the kingdom of heaven from people; for you do not enter in yourselves, nor do you allow those who are entering to go in. ¹⁴ᵇ[Woe to you, scribes and Pharisees, hypocrites, because you devour widows' houses, and for a pretense you make long prayers; therefore you will receive greater condemnation.]

15 "Woe to you, scribes and Pharisees, hypocrites, because you travel around on sea and land to make one proselyte; and when he becomes one, you make him twice as much a son of hell as yourselves.

16 "Woe to you, blind guides, who say, 'Whoever swears by the temple, *that* is nothing; but whoever swears by the gold of the temple is obligated.' ¹⁷You fools and blind men! Which is more important, the gold or the temple that sanctified the gold? ¹⁸And, 'Whoever swears by the altar, *that* is nothing, but whoever swears by the offering on it, he is obligated.' ¹⁹You blind men, which is more important, the offering, or the altar that sanctifies the offering? ²⁰Therefore, whoever swears by the altar, swears *both* by the altar and by everything on it. ²¹And whoever swears by the temple, swears *both* by the temple and by Him who dwells within it. ²²And whoever swears by heaven, swears *both* by the throne of God and by Him who sits upon it.

23 "Woe to you, scribes and Pharisees, hypocrites! For you tithe mint and dill and cummin, and have neglected the weightier provisions of the law: justice and mercy and faithfulness; but these are the things you should have done without neglecting the others. ²⁴You blind guides, who strain out a gnat and swallow a camel!

25 "Woe to you, scribes and Pharisees, hypocrites! For you clean the

ª **23:5** I.e. small cases containing Scripture texts worn on the left arm and forehead for religious purposes; ᵇ**23:14** This v not found in early mss outside of the cup and of the dish, but inside they are full of robbery and self-indulgence. ²⁶You blind Pharisee, first clean the inside of the cup and of the dish, so that the outside of it may become clean also.

27 "Woe to you, scribes and Pharisees, hypocrites! For you are like whitewashed tombs which on the outside appear beautiful, but inside they are full of dead men's bones and all uncleanness. ²⁸So you, too, outwardly appear righteous to men, but inwardly you are full of hypocrisy and lawlessness.

29 "Woe to you, scribes and Pharisees, hypocrites! For you build the tombs of the prophets and adorn the monuments of the righteous, ³⁰and say, 'If we had been *living* in the days of our fathers, we would not have been partners with them in *shedding* the blood of the prophets.' ³¹So you testify against yourselves, that you are sons of those who murdered the prophets. ³²Fill up, then, the measure *of the guilt* of your fathers. ³³You serpents, you brood of vipers, how will you escape the sentence of hell?

34 "Therefore, behold, I am sending you prophets and wise men and scribes; some of them you will kill and crucify, and some of them

you will scourge in your synagogues, and persecute from city to city, ³⁵so that upon you may fall *the guilt of* all the righteous blood shed on earth, from the blood of righteous Abel to the blood of Zechariah, the son of Berechiah, whom you murdered between the temple and the altar. ³⁶Truly I say to you, all these things will come upon this generation.

Lament over Jerusalem

37 "Jerusalem, Jerusalem, who kills the prophets and stones those who are sent to her! How often I wanted to gather your children together, the way a hen gathers her chicks under her wings, and you were unwilling. ³⁸Behold, your house is being left to you desolate! ³⁹For I say to you, from now on you will not see Me until you say, 'BLESSED IS HE WHO COMES IN THE NAME OF THE LORD!' "

Signs of Christ's Return

24 Jesus came out from the temple and was going away when His disciples came up to point out the temple buildings to Him. ²And He said to them, "Do you not see all these things? Truly I say to you, not one stone here will be left upon another, which will not be torn down."

3 As He was sitting on the Mount of Olives, the disciples came

to Him privately, saying, "Tell us, when will these things happen, and what *will be* the sign of Your coming, and of the end of the age?"

4 And Jesus answered and said to them, "See to it that no one misleads you. ⁵For many will come in My name, saying, 'I am the Christ,' and will mislead many. ⁶You will be hearing of wars and rumors of wars. See that you are not frightened, for *those things* must take place, but *that* is not yet the end. ⁷For nation will rise against nation, and kingdom against kingdom, and in various places there will be famines and earthquakes. ⁸But all these things are *merely* the beginning of birth pangs.

9 "Then they will deliver you to tribulation, and will kill you, and you will be hated by all nations because of My name. ¹⁰At that time many will fall away and will betray one another and hate one another. ¹¹Many false prophets will arise and will mislead many. ¹²Because lawlessness is increased, most people's love will grow cold. ¹³But the one who endures to the end, he will be saved. ¹⁴This gospel of the kingdom shall be preached in the whole world as a testimony to all the nations, and then the end will come.

Perilous Times

15 "Therefore when you see the ABOMINATION OF DESOLATION which was spoken of through Daniel the prophet, standing in the holy place (let the reader understand), ¹⁶then those who are in Judea must flee to the mountains. ¹⁷Whoever is on the housetop must not go down to get the things out that are in his house. ¹⁸Whoever is in the field must not turn back to get his cloak. ¹⁹But woe to those who are pregnant and to those who are nursing babies in those days! ²⁰But pray that your flight will not be in the winter, or on a Sabbath. ²¹For then there will be a great tribulation, such as has not occurred since the beginning of the world until now, nor ever will. ²²Unless those days had been cut short, no life would have been saved; but for the sake of the elect those days will be cut short. ²³Then if anyone says to you, 'Behold, here is the Christ,' or 'There *He is*,' do not believe *him*. ²⁴For false Christs and false prophets will arise and will show great signs and wonders, so as to mislead, if possible, even the elect. ²⁵Behold, I have told you in advance. ²⁶So if they say to you, 'Behold, He is in the wilderness,' do not go out, *or,* 'Behold, He is in the inner rooms,' do not believe *them*. ²⁷For just as the lightning comes from the east and flashes even to the west, so

will the coming of the Son of Man be. ²⁸Wherever the corpse is, there the vultures will gather.

The Glorious Return

29 "But immediately after the tribulation of those days THE SUN WILL BE DARKENED, AND THE MOON WILL NOT GIVE ITS LIGHT, AND THE STARS WILL FALL from the sky, and the powers of the heavens will be shaken. ³⁰And then the sign of the Son of Man will appear in the sky, and then all the tribes of the earth will mourn, and they will see the SON OF MAN COMING ON THE CLOUDS OF THE SKY with power and great glory. ³¹And He will send forth His angels with A GREAT TRUMPET and THEY WILL GATHER TOGETHER His elect from the four winds, from one end of the sky to the other.

Parable of the Fig Tree

32 "Now learn the parable from the fig tree: when its branch has already become tender and puts forth its leaves, you know that summer is near; ³³so, you too, when you see all these things, recognize that He is near, *right* at the door. ³⁴Truly I say to you, this generation will not pass away until all these things take place. ³⁵Heaven and earth will pass away, but My words will not pass away.

36 "But of that day and hour no one knows, not even the angels of heaven, nor the Son, but the Father alone. ³⁷For the coming of the Son of Man will be just like the days of Noah. ³⁸For as in those days before the flood they were eating and drinking, marrying and giving in marriage, until the day that Noah entered the ark, ³⁹and they did not understand until the flood came and took them all away; so will the coming of the Son of Man be. ⁴⁰Then there will be two men in the field; one will be taken and one will be left. ⁴¹Two women *will be* grinding at the mill; one will be taken and one will be left.

Be Ready for His Coming

42 "Therefore be on the alert, for you do not know which day your Lord is coming. ⁴³But be sure of this, that if the head of the house had known at what time of the night the thief was coming, he would have been on the alert and would not have allowed his house to be broken into. ⁴⁴For this reason you also must be ready; for the Son of Man is coming at an hour when you do not think *He will.*

45 "Who then is the faithful and sensible slave whom his master put in charge of his household to give them their food at the proper time? ⁴⁶Blessed is that slave whom his master finds so doing when he comes. [47]Truly I say to you that he will put him in charge of all his possessions. [48]But if that evil slave says in his heart, 'My master is not coming for a long time,' [49]and begins to beat his fellow slaves and eat and drink with drunkards; [50]the master of that slave will come on a day when he does not expect *him* and at an hour which he does not know, [51]and will cut him in pieces and assign him a place with the hypocrites; in that place there will be weeping and gnashing of teeth.

Parable of Ten Virgins

25 "Then the kingdom of heaven will be comparable to ten virgins, who took their lamps and went out to meet the bridegroom. [2]Five of them were foolish, and five were prudent. [3]For when the foolish took their lamps, they took no oil with them, [4]but the prudent took oil in flasks along with their lamps. [5]Now while the bridegroom was delaying, they all got drowsy and *began* to sleep. [6]But at midnight there was a shout, 'Behold, the bridegroom! Come out to meet *him.*' [7]Then all those virgins rose and trimmed their lamps. [8]The foolish said to the prudent, 'Give us some of your oil, for our lamps are going out.' [9]But the prudent answered, 'No, there will not be enough for us and you *too;* go instead to the dealers and buy *some* for yourselves.' [10]And while they were going away to make the purchase, the bridegroom came, and those who were ready went in with him to the wedding feast; and the door was shut. [11]Later the other virgins also came, saying, 'Lord, lord, open up for us.' [12]But he answered, 'Truly I say to you, I do not know you.' [13]Be on the alert then, for you do not know the day nor the hour.

Parable of the Talents

14 "For *it is* just like a man *about* to go on a journey, who called his own slaves and entrusted his possessions to them. [15]To one he gave five talents, to another, two, and to another, one, each according to his own ability; and he went on his journey. [16]Immediately the one who had received the five talents went and traded with them, and gained five more talents. [17]In the same manner the one who *had received* the two *talents* gained two more. [18]But he who received the one *talent* went away, and dug *a hole* in the ground and hid his master's money.

19 "Now after a long time the master of those slaves *came and *settled accounts with them. [20]The one who had received the five talents came up and brought five more talents, saying, 'Master, you entrusted five talents to me. See, I have gained five more talents.' [21]His master said to him, 'Well done, good and faithful slave. You were faithful with a few things, I will put you in charge of many things; enter into the joy of your master.'

22 "Also the one who *had received* the two talents came up and said, 'Master, you entrusted two talents to me. See, I have gained two more talents.' [23]His master said to him, 'Well done, good and faithful slave. You were faithful with a few things, I will put you in charge of many things; enter into the joy of your master.'

24 "And the one also who had received the one talent came up and said, 'Master, I knew you to be a hard man, reaping where you did not sow and gathering where you scattered no *seed*. [25]And I was afraid, and went away and hid your talent in the ground. See, you have what is yours.'

26 "But his master answered and said to him, 'You wicked, lazy slave, you knew that I reap where I did not sow and gather where I scattered no *seed*. [27]Then you ought to have put my money in the bank, and on my arrival I would have received my *money* back with interest. [28]Therefore take away the talent from him, and give it to the one who has the ten talents.'

29 "For to everyone who has, *more* shall be given, and he will have an abundance; but from the one who does not have, even what he does have shall be taken away. [30]Throw out the worthless slave into the outer darkness; in that place there will be weeping and gnashing of teeth.

The Judgment

31 "But when the Son of Man comes in His glory, and all the angels with Him, then He will sit on His glorious throne. [32]All the nations will be gathered before Him; and He will separate them from one another, as the shepherd separates the sheep from the goats; [33]and He will put the sheep on His right, and the goats on the left.

34 "Then the King will say to those on His right, 'Come, you who are blessed of My Father, inherit the kingdom prepared for you from the foundation of the world. [35]For I was hungry, and you gave Me *something* to eat; I was thirsty, and you gave Me *something* to drink; I was a stranger, and you invited Me in; [36]naked, and you clothed Me; I was sick, and you visited Me; I was in prison, and you came to Me.' [37]Then the righteous will answer Him, 'Lord, when did we see You hungry, and feed You, or thirsty, and give You *something* to drink? [38]And when did we see You a stranger, and invite You in, or naked, and clothe You? ³⁹When did we see You sick, or in prison, and come to You?' ⁴⁰The King will answer and say to them, 'Truly I say to you, to the extent that you did it to one of these brothers of Mine, *even* the least *of them,* you did it to Me.'

41 "Then He will also say to those on His left, 'Depart from Me, accursed ones, into the eternal fire which has been prepared for the devil and his angels; ⁴²for I was hungry, and you gave Me *nothing* to eat; I was thirsty, and you gave Me nothing to drink; ⁴³I was a stranger, and you did not invite Me in; naked, and you did not clothe Me; sick, and in prison, and you did not visit Me.' ⁴⁴Then they themselves also will answer, 'Lord, when did we see You hungry, or thirsty, or a stranger, or naked, or sick, or in prison, and did not take care of You?' ⁴⁵Then He will answer them, 'Truly I say to you, to the extent that you did not do it to one of the least of these, you did not do it to Me.' ⁴⁶These will go away into eternal punishment, but the righteous into eternal life."

The Plot to Kill Jesus

26 When Jesus had finished all these words, He said to His disciples, ²"You know that after two days the Passover is coming,

and the Son of Man is *to be* handed over for crucifixion."

3 Then the chief priests and the elders of the people were gathered together in the court of the high priest, named Caiaphas; ⁴and they plotted together to seize Jesus by stealth and kill Him. ⁵But they were saying, "Not during the festival, otherwise a riot might occur among the people."

The Precious Ointment

6 Now when Jesus was in Bethany, at the home of Simon the leper, ⁷a woman came to Him with an alabaster vial of very costly perfume, and she poured it on His head as He reclined *at the table.* ⁸But the disciples were indignant when they saw *this,* and said, "Why this waste? ⁹For this *perfume* might have been sold for a high price and *the money* given to the poor." ¹⁰But Jesus, aware of this, said to them, "Why do you bother the woman? For she has done a good deed to Me. ¹¹For you always have the poor with you; but you do not always have Me. ¹²For when she poured this perfume on My body, she did it to prepare Me for burial. ¹³Truly I say to you, wherever this gospel is preached in the whole world, what this woman has done will also be spoken of in memory of her."

Judas's Bargain

14 Then one of the twelve, named Judas Iscariot, went to the chief priests ¹⁵and said, "What are you willing to give me to betray Him to you?" And they weighed out thirty pieces of silver to him. ¹⁶From then on he *began* looking for a good opportunity to betray Jesus.

17 Now on the first *day* of Unleavened Bread the disciples came to Jesus and asked, "Where do You want us to prepare for You to eat the Passover?" ¹⁸And He said, "Go into the city to a certain man, and say to him, 'The Teacher says, "My time is near; I *am* to keep the Passover at your house with My disciples." ' " ¹⁹The disciples did as Jesus had directed them; and they prepared the Passover.

The Last Passover

20 Now when evening came, Jesus was reclining *at the table* with the twelve disciples. ²¹As they were eating, He said, "Truly I say to you that one of you will betray Me." ²²Being deeply grieved, they each one began to say to Him, "Surely not I, Lord?" ²³And He answered, "He who dipped his hand with Me in the bowl is the one who will betray Me. ²⁴The Son of Man *is to* go, just as it is written of Him; but woe to that man by whom the Son of Man is betrayed! It would have been good for that man if he had

not been born." ²⁵And Judas, who was betraying Him, said, "Surely it is not I, Rabbi?" Jesus *said to him, "You have said *it* yourself."

The Lord's Supper Instituted

26 While they were eating, Jesus took *some* bread, and after a blessing, He broke *it* and gave *it* to the disciples, and said, "Take, eat; this is My body." ²⁷And when He had taken a cup and given thanks, He gave *it* to them, saying, "Drink from it, all of you; ²⁸for this is My blood of the covenant, which is poured out for many for forgiveness of sins. ²⁹But I say to you, I will not drink of this fruit of the vine from now on until that day when I drink it new with you in My Father's kingdom."

30 After singing a hymn, they went out to the Mount of Olives.

31 Then Jesus *said to them, "You will all fall away because of Me this night, for it is written, 'I WILL STRIKE DOWN THE SHEPHERD, AND THE SHEEP OF THE FLOCK SHALL BE SCATTERED.' ³²But after I have been raised, I will go ahead of you to Galilee." ³³But Peter said to Him, "*Even* though all may fall away because of You, I will never fall away." ³⁴Jesus said to him, "Truly I say to you that this *very* night, before a rooster crows, you will deny Me three times." ³⁵Peter *said to Him, "Even if I have to die with You, I will not deny You." All the disciples said the same thing too.

The Garden of Gethsemane

36 Then Jesus *came with them to a place called Gethsemane, and *said to His disciples, "Sit here while I go over there and pray." ³⁷And He took with Him Peter and the two sons of Zebedee, and began to be grieved and distressed. ³⁸Then He *said to them, "My soul is deeply grieved, to the point of death; remain here and keep watch with Me."

39 And He went a little beyond *them,* and fell on His face and prayed, saying, "My Father, if it is possible, let this cup pass from Me; yet not as I will, but as You will." ⁴⁰And He *came to the disciples and *found them sleeping, and *said to Peter, "So, you *men* could not keep watch with Me for one hour? ⁴¹Keep watching and praying that you may not enter into temptation; the spirit is willing, but the flesh is weak."

42 He went away again a second time and prayed, saying, "My Father, if this cannot pass away unless I drink it, Your will be done." ⁴³Again He came and found them sleeping, for their eyes were heavy. ⁴⁴And He left them again,

and went away and prayed a third time, saying the same thing once more. ⁴⁵Then He *came to the disciples and *said to them, "Are you still sleeping and resting? Behold, the hour is at hand and the Son of Man is being betrayed into the hands of sinners. ⁴⁶Get up, let us be going; behold, the one who betrays Me is at hand!"

Jesus' Betrayal and Arrest

47 While He was still speaking, behold, Judas, one of the twelve, came up accompanied by a large crowd with swords and clubs, *who came* from the chief priests and elders of the people. ⁴⁸Now he who was betraying Him gave them a sign, saying, "Whomever I kiss, He is the one; seize Him." ⁴⁹Immediately Judas went to Jesus and said, "Hail, Rabbi!" and kissed Him. ⁵⁰And Jesus said to him, "Friend, *do* what you have come for." Then they came and laid hands on Jesus and seized Him.

51 And behold, one of those who were with Jesus reached and drew out his sword, and struck the slave of the high priest and cut off his ear. ⁵²Then Jesus *said to him, "Put your sword back into its place; for all those who take up the sword shall perish by the sword. ⁵³Or do you think that I cannot appeal to My Father, and He will at once put at My disposal more than twelve

[a]legions of angels? [54]How then will the Scriptures be fulfilled, *which say* that it must happen this way?"

55 At that time Jesus said to the crowds, "Have you come out with swords and clubs to arrest Me as *you would* against a robber? Every day I used to sit in the temple teaching and you did not seize Me. [56]But all this has taken place to fulfill the Scriptures of the prophets." Then all the disciples left Him and fled.

Jesus before Caiaphas

57 Those who had seized Jesus led Him away to Caiaphas, the high priest, where the scribes and the elders were gathered together. [58]But Peter was following Him at a distance as far as the courtyard of the high priest, and entered in, and sat down with the officers to see the outcome.

59 Now the chief priests and the whole Council kept trying to obtain false testimony against Jesus, so that they might put Him to death. [60]They did not find *any,* even though many false witnesses came forward. But later on two came forward, [61]and said, "This man stated, 'I am able to destroy the temple of God and to rebuild it in three days.' " [62]The high priest stood up and said to Him, "Do You not answer? What is it that these

men are testifying against You?" [63]But Jesus kept silent. And the high priest said to Him, "I adjure You by the living God, that You tell us whether You are the Christ, the Son of God." [64]Jesus *said to him, "You have said it *yourself*; nevertheless I tell you, hereafter you will see THE SON OF MAN SITTING AT THE RIGHT HAND OF POWER, and COMING ON THE CLOUDS OF HEAVEN."

65 Then the high priest tore his robes and said, "He has blasphemed! What further need do we have of witnesses? Behold, you have now heard the blasphemy; [66]what do you think?" They answered, "He deserves death!"

67 Then they spat in His face and beat Him with their fists; and others slapped Him, [68]and said, "Prophesy to us, You Christ; who is the one who hit You?"

Peter's Denials

69 Now Peter was sitting outside in the courtyard, and a servant-girl came to him and said, "You too were with Jesus the Galilean." [70]But he denied *it* before them all, saying, "I do not know what you are talking about." [71]When he had gone out to the gateway, another *servant-girl* saw him and *said to those who were there, "This man was with Jesus of Nazareth." [72]And

[a] **26:53** A legion equaled 6,000 troops

again he denied *it* with an oath, "I do not know the man." [73]A little later the bystanders came up and said to Peter, "Surely you too are *one* of them; for even the way you talk gives you away." [74]Then he began to curse and swear, "I do not know the man!" And immediately a rooster crowed. [75]And Peter remembered the word which Jesus had said, "Before a rooster crows, you will deny Me three times." And he went out and wept bitterly.

Judas's Remorse

27 [1]Now when morning came, all the chief priests and the elders of the people conferred together against Jesus to put Him to death; [2]and they bound Him, and led Him away and delivered Him to Pilate the governor.

[3] Then when Judas, who had betrayed Him, saw that He had been condemned, he felt remorse and returned the thirty pieces of silver to the chief priests and elders, [4]saying, "I have sinned by betraying innocent blood." But they said, "What is that to us? See *to that* yourself!" [5]And he threw the pieces of silver into the temple sanctuary and departed; and he went away and hanged himself. [6]The chief priests took the pieces of silver and said, "It is not lawful to put them into the temple treasury, since it is the price of blood." [7]And they conferred together and with the money bought the Potter's Field as a burial place for strangers. [8]For this reason that field has been called the Field of Blood to this day. [9]Then that which was spoken through Jeremiah the prophet was fulfilled: "AND THEY TOOK THE THIRTY PIECES OF SILVER, THE PRICE OF THE ONE WHOSE PRICE HAD BEEN SET by the sons of Israel; [10]AND THEY GAVE THEM FOR THE POTTER'S FIELD, AS THE LORD DIRECTED ME."

Jesus before Pilate

[11] Now Jesus stood before the governor, and the governor questioned Him, saying, "Are You the King of the Jews?" And Jesus said to him, "*It is as* you say." [12]And while He was being accused by the chief priests and elders, He did not answer. [13]Then Pilate *said to Him, "Do You not hear how many things they testify against You?" [14]And He did not answer him with regard to even a *single* charge, so the governor was quite amazed.

[15] Now at *the* feast the governor was accustomed to release for the people *any* one prisoner whom they wanted. [16]At that time they were holding a notorious prisoner, called Barabbas. [17]So when the people gathered together, Pilate said to them, "Whom do you want

me to release for you? Barabbas, or Jesus who is called Christ?" ¹⁸For he knew that because of envy they had handed Him over.

19 While he was sitting on the judgment seat, his wife sent him *a message,* saying, "Have nothing to do with that righteous Man; for last night I suffered greatly in a dream because of Him." ²⁰But the chief priests and the elders persuaded the crowds to ask for Barabbas and to put Jesus to death. ²¹But the governor said to them, "Which of the two do you want me to release for you?" And they said, "Barabbas." ²²Pilate *said to them, "Then what shall I do with Jesus who is called Christ?" They all *said, "Crucify Him!" ²³And he said, "Why, what evil has He done?" But they kept shouting all the more, saying, "Crucify Him!"

24 When Pilate saw that he was accomplishing nothing, but rather that a riot was starting, he took water and washed his hands in front of the crowd, saying, "I am innocent of this Man's blood; see *to that* yourselves." ²⁵And all the people said, "His blood shall be on us and on our children!" ²⁶Then he released Barabbas for them; but after having Jesus scourged, he handed Him over to be crucified.

Jesus Is Mocked

27 Then the soldiers of the governor took Jesus into the Praetorium and gathered the whole *Roman* cohort around Him. ²⁸They stripped Him and put a scarlet robe on Him. ²⁹And after twisting together a crown of thorns, they put it on His head, and a reed in His right hand; and they knelt down before Him and mocked Him, saying, "Hail, King of the Jews!" ³⁰They spat on Him, and took the reed and *began* to beat Him on the head. ³¹After they had mocked Him, they took the *scarlet* robe off Him and put His *own* garments back on Him, and led Him away to crucify Him.

32 As they were coming out, they found a man of Cyrene named Simon, whom they pressed into service to bear His cross.

The Crucifixion

33 And when they came to a place called Golgotha, which means Place of a Skull, ³⁴they gave Him wine to drink mixed with gall; and after tasting *it,* He was unwilling to drink.

35 And when they had crucified Him, they divided up His garments among themselves by casting lots. ³⁶And *sitting* down, they *began* to keep watch over Him there. ³⁷And above His head they put up the charge against Him which read, "THIS IS JESUS THE KING OF THE JEWS."

38 At that time two robbers *were crucified with Him, one on the right and one on the left. [39]And those passing by were hurling abuse at Him, wagging their heads [40]and saying, "You who *are going to* destroy the temple and rebuild it in three days, save Yourself! If You are the Son of God, come down from the cross." [41]In the same way the chief priests also, along with the scribes and elders, were mocking *Him* and saying, [42]"He saved others; He cannot save Himself. He is the King of Israel; let Him now come down from the cross, and we will believe in Him. [43]HE TRUSTS IN GOD; LET GOD RESCUE *Him* now, IF HE DELIGHTS IN HIM; for He said, 'I am the Son of God.' " [44]The robbers who had been crucified with Him were also insulting Him with the same words.

45 Now from the [a]sixth hour darkness fell upon all the land until the [b]ninth hour. [46]About the ninth hour Jesus cried out with a loud voice, saying, "ELI, ELI, LAMA SABACHTHANI?" that is, "MY GOD, MY GOD, WHY HAVE YOU FORSAKEN ME?" [47]And some of those who were standing there, when they heard it, *began* saying, "This man is calling

for Elijah." [48]Immediately one of them ran, and taking a sponge, he filled it with sour wine and put it on a reed, and gave Him a drink. [49]But the rest *of them* said, "Let us see whether Elijah will come to save Him."[c] [50]And Jesus cried out again with a loud voice, and yielded up His spirit. [51]And behold, the veil of the temple was torn in two from top to bottom; and the earth shook and the rocks were split. [52]The tombs were opened, and many bodies of the saints who had fallen asleep were raised; [53]and coming out of the tombs after His resurrection they entered the holy city and appeared to many. [54]Now the centurion, and those who were with him keeping guard over Jesus, when they saw the earthquake and the things that were happening, became very frightened and said, "Truly this was the Son of God!"

55 Many women were there looking on from a distance, who had followed Jesus from Galilee while ministering to Him. [56]Among them was Mary Magdalene, and Mary the mother of James and Joseph, and the mother of the sons of Zebedee.

Jesus Is Buried

57 When it was evening, there came a rich man from Arimathea, named Joseph, who himself had

[a]**27:45** I.e. 12 noon; [b]**27:45** I.e. 3 p.m.; [c]**27:49** Some early mss read *And another took a spear and pierced His side, and there came out water and blood* (cf John 19:34)

also become a disciple of Jesus. [58]This man went to Pilate and asked for the body of Jesus. Then Pilate ordered it to be given *to him.* [59]And Joseph took the body and wrapped it in a clean linen cloth, [60]and laid it in his own new tomb, which he had hewn out in the rock; and he rolled a large stone against the entrance of the tomb and went away. [61]And Mary Magdalene was there, and the other Mary, sitting opposite the grave.

62 Now on the next day, the day after the preparation, the chief priests and the Pharisees gathered together with Pilate, [63]and said, "Sir, we remember that when He was still alive that deceiver said, 'After three days I *am to* rise again.' [64]Therefore, give orders for the grave to be made secure until the third day, otherwise His disciples may come and steal Him away and say to the people, 'He has risen from the dead,' and the last deception will be worse than the first." [65]Pilate said to them, "You have a guard; go, make it *as* secure as you know how." [66]And they went and made the grave secure, and along with the guard they set a seal on the stone.

Jesus Is Risen!

28 Now after the Sabbath, as it began to dawn toward the first *day* of the week, Mary Magdalene and the other Mary came to look at the grave. [2]And behold, a severe earthquake had occurred, for an angel of the Lord descended from heaven and came and rolled away the stone and sat upon it. [3]And his appearance was like lightning, and his clothing as white as snow. [4]The guards shook for fear of him and became like dead men. [5]The angel said to the women, "Do not be afraid; for I know that you are looking for Jesus who has been crucified. [6]He is not here, for He has risen, just as He said. Come, see the place where He was lying. [7]Go quickly and tell His disciples that He has risen from the dead; and behold, He is going ahead of you into Galilee, there you will see Him; behold, I have told you."

8 And they left the tomb quickly with fear and great joy and ran to report it to His disciples. [9]And behold, Jesus met them and greeted them. And they came up and took hold of His feet and worshiped Him. [10]Then Jesus *said to them, "Do not be afraid; go and take word to My brethren to leave for Galilee, and there they will see Me."

11 Now while they were on their way, some of the guard came into the city and reported to the chief priests all that had happened.

¹²And when they had assembled with the elders and consulted together, they gave a large sum of money to the soldiers, ¹³and said, "You are to say, 'His disciples came by night and stole Him away while we were asleep.' ¹⁴And if this should come to the governor's ears, we will win him over and keep you out of trouble." ¹⁵And they took the money and did as they had been instructed; and this story was widely spread among the Jews, *and is* to this day.

The Great Commission

16 But the eleven disciples proceeded to Galilee, to the mountain which Jesus had designated. ¹⁷When they saw Him, they worshiped *Him;* but some were doubtful. ¹⁸And Jesus came up and spoke to them, saying, "All authority has been given to Me in heaven and on earth. ¹⁹Go therefore and make disciples of all the nations, baptizing them in the name of the Father and the Son and the Holy Spirit, ²⁰teaching them to observe all that I commanded you; and lo, I am with you always, even to the end of the age."

MARK

Preaching of John the Baptist

1 The beginning of the gospel of Jesus Christ, the Son of God.

2 As it is written in Isaiah the prophet:
"BEHOLD, I SEND MY MESSEN-
    GER AHEAD OF YOU,
WHO WILL PREPARE YOUR WAY;
³THE VOICE OF ONE CRYING IN
    THE WILDERNESS,
'MAKE READY THE WAY OF THE
    LORD,

MAKE HIS PATHS STRAIGHT.' "
⁴John the Baptist appeared in the wilderness ªpreaching a baptism of repentance for the forgiveness of sins. ⁵And all the country of Judea was going out to him, and all the people of Jerusalem; and they were being baptized by him in the Jordan River, confessing their sins. ⁶John was clothed with camel's hair and *wore* a leather belt around his waist, and his diet was locusts and wild honey. ⁷And he

ª**1:4** Or proclaiming

was preaching, and saying, "After me One is coming who is mightier than I, and I am not fit to stoop down and untie the thong of His sandals. [8]I baptized you [a]with water; but He will baptize you with the Holy Spirit."

The Baptism of Jesus

9 In those days Jesus came from Nazareth in Galilee and was baptized by John in the Jordan. [10]Immediately coming up out of the water, He saw the heavens opening, and the Spirit like a dove descending upon Him; [11]and a voice came out of the heavens: "You are My beloved Son, in You I am well-pleased."

12 Immediately the Spirit *impelled Him to go out into the wilderness. [13]And He was in the wilderness forty days being tempted by Satan; and He was with the wild beasts, and the angels were ministering to Him.

Jesus Preaches in Galilee

14 Now after John had been taken into custody, Jesus came into Galilee, preaching the gospel of God, [15]and saying, "The time is fulfilled, and the kingdom of God is at hand; repent and believe in the gospel."

16 As He was going along by the Sea of Galilee, He saw Simon and Andrew, the brother of Simon, casting a net in the sea; for they were fishermen. [17]And Jesus said to them, "Follow Me, and I will make you become fishers of men." [18]Immediately they left their nets and followed Him. [19]Going on a little farther, He saw James the son of Zebedee, and John his brother, who were also in the boat mending the nets. [20]Immediately He called them; and they left their father Zebedee in the boat with the hired servants, and went away to follow Him.

21 They *went into Capernaum; and immediately on the Sabbath He entered the synagogue and began to teach. [22]They were amazed at His teaching; for He was teaching them as one having authority, and not as the scribes. [23]Just there was a man in their synagogue with an unclean spirit; and he cried out, [24]saying, "What business do we have with each other, Jesus [b]of Nazareth? Have You come to destroy us? I know who You are—the Holy One of God!" [25]And Jesus rebuked him, saying, "Be quiet, and come out of him!" [26]Throwing him into convulsions, the unclean spirit cried out with a loud voice and came out of him. [27]They were all amazed, so that they debated among themselves, saying, "What is this? A new teaching with authority!

[a]1:8 The Gr here can be translated in, with or by; [b]1:24 Lit the Nazarene

He commands even the unclean spirits, and they obey Him." [28]Immediately the news about Him spread everywhere into all the surrounding district of Galilee.

Crowds Healed

29 And immediately after they came out of the synagogue, they came into the house of Simon and Andrew, with James and John. [30]Now Simon's mother-in-law was lying sick with a fever; and immediately they *spoke to Jesus about her. [31]And He came to her and raised her up, taking her by the hand, and the fever left her, and she [a]waited on them.

32 When evening came, after the sun had set, they *began* bringing to Him all who were ill and those who were demon-possessed. [33]And the whole city had gathered at the door. [34]And He healed many who were ill with various diseases, and cast out many demons; and He was not permitting the demons to speak, because they knew who He was.

35 In the early morning, while it was still dark, Jesus got up, left *the house,* and went away to a secluded place, and was praying there. [36]Simon and his companions searched for Him; [37]they found Him, and *said to Him, "Everyone is looking for You." [38]He

*said to them, "Let us go somewhere else to the towns nearby, so that I may preach there also; for that is what I came for." [39]And He went into their synagogues throughout all Galilee, preaching and casting out the demons.

40 And a leper *came to Jesus, beseeching Him and falling on his knees before Him, and saying, "If You are willing, You can make me clean." [41]Moved with compassion, Jesus stretched out His hand and touched him, and *said to him, "I am willing; be cleansed." [42]Immediately the leprosy left him and he was cleansed. [43]And He sternly warned him and immediately sent him away, [44]and He *said to him, "See that you say nothing to anyone; but go, show yourself to the priest and offer for your cleansing what Moses commanded, as a testimony to them." [45]But he went out and began to proclaim it freely and to spread the news around, to such an extent that Jesus could no longer publicly enter a city, but [b]stayed out in unpopulated areas; and they were coming to Him from everywhere.

The Paralytic Healed

2 When He had come back to Capernaum several days afterward, it was heard that He was at home. [2]And many were gathered together, so that there was

1:31 Or served; **1:45** Lit was

no longer room, not even near the door; and He was speaking the word to them. ³And they *came, bringing to Him a paralytic, carried by four men. ⁴Being unable to get to Him because of the crowd, they removed the roof above Him; and when they had dug an opening, they let down the pallet on which the paralytic was lying. ⁵And Jesus seeing their faith *said to the paralytic, "ᵃSon, your sins are forgiven." ⁶But some of the scribes were sitting there and reasoning in their hearts, ⁷"Why does this man speak that way? He is blaspheming; who can forgive sins but God alone?" ⁸Immediately Jesus, aware in His spirit that they were reasoning that way within themselves, *said to them, "Why are you reasoning about these things in your hearts? ⁹Which is easier, to say to the paralytic, 'Your sins are forgiven'; or to say, 'Get up, and pick up your pallet and walk'? ¹⁰But so that you may know that the Son of Man has authority on earth to forgive sins"—He *said to the paralytic, ¹¹"I say to you, get up, pick up your pallet and go home." ¹²And he got up and immediately picked up the pallet and went out in the sight of everyone, so that they were all amazed and were glorifying God, saying, "We have never seen anything like this."

¹³ And He went out again by the seashore; and all the people were coming to Him, and He was teaching them.

Levi (Matthew) Called

¹⁴As He passed by, He saw Levi the *son* of Alphaeus sitting in the tax booth, and He *said to him, "Follow Me!" And he got up and followed Him.

¹⁵ And it *happened that He was reclining *at the table* in his house, and many tax collectors and sinners were dining with Jesus and His disciples; for there were many of them, and they were following Him. ¹⁶When the scribes of the Pharisees saw that He was eating with the sinners and tax collectors, they said to His disciples, "Why is He eating and drinking with tax collectors and sinners?" ¹⁷And hearing *this,* Jesus *said to them, "*It is* not those who are healthy who need a physician, but those who are sick; I did not come to call the righteous, but sinners."

¹⁸ John's disciples and the Pharisees were fasting; and they *came and *said to Him, "Why do John's disciples and the disciples of the Pharisees fast, but Your disciples do not fast?" ¹⁹And Jesus said to them, "While the bridegroom is with them, the attendants of the bridegroom cannot fast, can

ᵃ**2:5** Lit *child*

they? So long as they have the bridegroom with them, they cannot fast. ²⁰But the days will come when the bridegroom is taken away from them, and then they will fast in that day.

21 "No one sews a patch of unshrunk cloth on an old garment; otherwise the patch pulls away from it, the new from the old, and a worse tear results. ²²No one puts new wine into old wineskins; otherwise the wine will burst the skins, and the wine is lost and the skins *as well*; but *one puts* new wine into fresh wineskins."

Question of the Sabbath

23 And it happened that He was passing through the grainfields on the Sabbath, and His disciples began to make their way along while picking the heads *of grain*. ²⁴The Pharisees were saying to Him, "Look, why are they doing what is not lawful on the Sabbath?" ²⁵And He *said to them, "Have you never read what David did when he was in need and he and his companions became hungry; ²⁶how he entered the house of God in the time of Abiathar *the* high priest, and ate the consecrated bread, which is not lawful for *anyone* to eat except the priests, and he also gave it to those who were with him?" ²⁷Jesus said to them, "The Sabbath was made for

man, and not man for the Sabbath. ²⁸So the Son of Man is Lord even of the Sabbath."

Jesus Heals on the Sabbath

3 He entered again into a synagogue; and a man was there whose hand was withered. ²They were watching Him *to see* if He would heal him on the Sabbath, so that they might accuse Him. ³He *said to the man with the withered hand, "Get up and come forward!" ⁴And He *said to them, "Is it lawful to do good or to do harm on the Sabbath, to save a life or to kill?" But they kept silent. ⁵After looking around at them with anger, grieved at their hardness of heart, He *said to the man, "Stretch out your hand." And he stretched it out, and his hand was restored. ⁶The Pharisees went out and immediately *began* conspiring with the Herodians against Him, *as to* how they might destroy Him.

7 Jesus withdrew to the sea with His disciples; and a great multitude from Galilee followed; and *also* from Judea, ⁸and from Jerusalem, and from Idumea, and beyond the Jordan, and the vicinity of Tyre and Sidon, a great number of people heard of all that He was doing and came to Him. ⁹And He told His disciples that a boat should stand ready for Him because of the crowd, so that they

would not crowd Him; ¹⁰for He had healed many, with the result that all those who had afflictions pressed around Him in order to touch Him. ¹¹Whenever the unclean spirits saw Him, they would fall down before Him and shout, "You are the Son of God!" ¹²And He earnestly warned them not to tell who He was.

The Twelve Are Chosen

13 And He *went up on the mountain and *summoned those whom He Himself wanted, and they came to Him. ¹⁴And He appointed twelve, so that they would be with Him and that He *could* send them out to preach, ¹⁵and to have authority to cast out the demons. ¹⁶And He appointed the twelve: Simon (to whom He gave the name Peter), ¹⁷and James, the *son* of Zebedee, and John the brother of James (to them He gave the name Boanerges, which means, "Sons of Thunder"); ¹⁸and Andrew, and Philip, and Bartholomew, and Matthew, and Thomas, and James the son of Alphaeus, and Thaddaeus, and Simon the Zealot; ¹⁹and Judas Iscariot, who betrayed Him.

20 And He *came ^ahome, and the crowd *gathered again, to such an extent that they could not even eat a meal. ²¹When His own ^bpeople heard *of this,* they went out to take custody of Him; for they

were saying, "He has lost His senses." ²²The scribes who came down from Jerusalem were saying, "He is possessed by Beelzebul," and "He casts out the demons by the ruler of the demons." ²³And He called them to Himself and began speaking to them in parables, "How can Satan cast out Satan? ²⁴If a kingdom is divided against itself, that kingdom cannot stand. ²⁵If a house is divided against itself, that house will not be able to stand. ²⁶If Satan has risen up against himself and is divided, he cannot stand, but he is finished! ²⁷But no one can enter the strong man's house and plunder his property unless he first binds the strong man, and then he will plunder his house.

28 "Truly I say to you, all sins shall be forgiven the sons of men, and whatever blasphemies they utter; ²⁹but whoever blasphemes against the Holy Spirit never has forgiveness, but is guilty of an eternal sin"— ³⁰because they were saying, "He has an unclean spirit."

31 Then His mother and His brothers *arrived, and standing outside they sent *word* to Him and called Him. ³²A crowd was sitting around Him, and they *said to Him, "Behold, Your mother and Your brothers are outside looking for You." ³³Answering them, He *said, "Who are My mother and

^a**3:20** Lit *into a house;* ^b**3:21** Or *kinsmen*

My brothers?" ³⁴Looking about at those who were sitting around Him, He *said, "Behold My mother and My brothers! ³⁵For whoever does the will of God, he is My brother and sister and mother."

Parable of the Sower and Soils

4 He began to teach again by the sea. And such a very large crowd gathered to Him that He got into a boat in the sea and sat down; and the whole crowd was by the sea on the land. ²And He was teaching them many things in parables, and was saying to them in His teaching, ³"Listen *to this!* Behold, the sower went out to sow; ⁴as he was sowing, some *seed* fell beside the road, and the birds came and ate it up. ⁵Other *seed* fell on the rocky *ground* where it did not have much soil; and immediately it sprang up because it had no depth of soil. ⁶And after the sun had risen, it was scorched; and because it had no root, it withered away. ⁷Other *seed* fell among the thorns, and the thorns came up and choked it, and it yielded no crop. ⁸Other *seeds* fell into the good soil, and as they grew up and increased, they yielded a crop and produced thirty, sixty, and a hundredfold." ⁹And He was saying, "He who has ears to hear, let him hear."

10 As soon as He was alone, His followers, along with the twelve,

began asking Him *about* the parables. ¹¹And He was saying to them, "To you has been given the mystery of the kingdom of God, but those who are outside get everything in parables, ¹²so that WHILE SEEING, THEY MAY SEE AND NOT PERCEIVE, AND WHILE HEARING, THEY MAY HEAR AND NOT UNDERSTAND, OTHERWISE THEY MIGHT RETURN AND BE FORGIVEN."

Explanation

13 And He *said to them, "Do you not understand this parable? How will you understand all the parables? ¹⁴The sower sows the word. ¹⁵These are the ones who are beside the road where the word is sown; and when they hear, immediately Satan comes and takes away the word which has been sown in them. ¹⁶In a similar way these are the ones on whom seed was sown on the rocky *places,* who, when they hear the word, immediately receive it with joy; ¹⁷and they have no *firm* root in themselves, but are *only* temporary; then, when affliction or persecution arises because of the word, immediately they fall away. ¹⁸And others are the ones on whom seed was sown among the thorns; these are the ones who have heard the word, ¹⁹but the worries of the ᵃworld, and the deceitfulness of riches, and the desires for other things enter in and

ᵃ**4:19** Or *age*

choke the word, and it becomes unfruitful. [20]And those are the ones on whom seed was sown on the good soil; and they hear the word and accept it and bear fruit, thirty, sixty, and a hundredfold."

21 And He was saying to them, "A lamp is not brought to be put under a basket, is it, or under a bed? Is it not *brought* to be put on the lampstand? [22]For nothing is hidden, except to be revealed; nor has *anything* been secret, but that it would come to light. [23]If anyone has ears to hear, let him hear." [24]And He was saying to them, "Take care what you listen to. By your standard of measure it will be measured to you; and more will be given you besides. [25]For whoever has, to him *more* shall be given; and whoever does not have, even what he has shall be taken away from him."

Parable of the Seed

26 And He was saying, "The kingdom of God is like a man who casts seed upon the soil; [27]and he goes to bed at night and gets up by day, and the seed sprouts and grows—how, he himself does not know. [28]The soil produces crops by itself; first the blade, then the head, then the mature grain in the head. [29]But when the crop permits, he immediately puts in the sickle, because the harvest has come."

Parable of the Mustard Seed

30 And He said, "How shall we apicture the kingdom of God, or by what parable shall we present it? [31]*It is* like a mustard seed, which, when sown upon the soil, though it is smaller than all the seeds that are upon the soil, [32]yet when it is sown, it grows up and becomes larger than all the garden plants and forms large branches; so that THE BIRDS OF THE bAIR can NEST UNDER ITS SHADE."

33 With many such parables He was speaking the word to them, so far as they were able to hear it; [34]and He did not speak to them without a parable; but He was explaining everything privately to His own disciples.

Jesus Stills the Sea

35 On that day, when evening came, He *said to them, "Let us go over to the other side." [36]Leaving the crowd, they *took Him along with them in the boat, just as He was; and other boats were with Him. [37]And there *arose a fierce gale of wind, and the waves were breaking over the boat so much that the boat was already filling up. [38]Jesus Himself was in the stern, asleep on the cushion; and they *woke Him and *said to Him, "Teacher, do You not care that we are perishing?" [39]And He got up and rebuked the wind and said to

a**4:30** Lit *compare*; b**4:32** Or *sky*

the sea, "Hush, be still." And the wind died down and it became perfectly calm. ⁴⁰And He said to them, "Why are you afraid? Do you still have no faith?" ⁴¹They became very much afraid and said to one another, "Who then is this, that even the wind and the sea obey Him?"

The Gerasene Demoniac

5 They came to the other side of the sea, into the country of the Gerasenes. ²When He got out of the boat, immediately a man from the tombs with an unclean spirit met Him, ³and he had his dwelling among the tombs. And no one was able to bind him anymore, even with a chain; ⁴because he had often been bound with shackles and chains, and the chains had been torn apart by him and the shackles broken in pieces, and no one was strong enough to subdue him. ⁵Constantly, night and day, he was screaming among the tombs and in the mountains, and gashing himself with stones. ⁶Seeing Jesus from a distance, he ran up and bowed down before Him; ⁷and shouting with a loud voice, he *said, "What business do we have with each other, Jesus, Son of the Most High God? I implore You by God, do not torment me!" ⁸For He had been saying to him, "Come out of the man, you unclean spirit!" ⁹And He was asking him, "What is

your name?" And he *said to Him, "My name is Legion; for we are many." ¹⁰And he *began* to implore Him earnestly not to send them out of the country. ¹¹Now there was a large herd of swine feeding nearby on the mountain. ¹²*The demons* implored Him, saying, "Send us into the swine so that we may enter them." ¹³Jesus gave them permission. And coming out, the unclean spirits entered the swine; and the herd rushed down the steep bank into the sea, about two thousand *of them;* and they were drowned in the sea.

14 Their herdsmen ran away and reported it in the city and in the country. And *the people* came to see what it was that had happened. ¹⁵They *came to Jesus and *observed the man who had been demon-possessed sitting down, clothed and in his right mind, the very man who had had the "legion"; and they became frightened. ¹⁶Those who had seen it described to them how it had happened to the demon-possessed man, and *all* about the swine. ¹⁷And they began to implore Him to leave their region. ¹⁸As He was getting into the boat, the man who had been demon-possessed was imploring Him that he might accompany Him. ¹⁹And He did not let him, but He *said to him, "Go home to your people and report to

them *what great things the Lord has done for you, and *how* He had mercy on you." ²⁰And he went away and began to proclaim in Decapolis what great things Jesus had done for him; and everyone was amazed.

Miracles and Healing

21 When Jesus had crossed over again in the boat to the other side, a large crowd gathered around Him; and so He stayed by the seashore. ²²One of the synagogue officials named Jairus *came up, and on seeing Him, *fell at His feet ²³and *implored Him earnestly, saying, "My little daughter is at the point of death; *please* come and lay Your hands on her, so that she will get well and live." ²⁴And He went off with him; and a large crowd was following Him and pressing in on Him.

25 A woman who had had a hemorrhage for twelve years, ²⁶and had endured much at the hands of many physicians, and had spent all that she had and was not helped at all, but rather had grown worse— ²⁷after hearing about Jesus, she came up in the crowd behind *Him* and touched His cloak. ²⁸For she thought, "If I just touch His garments, I will get well." ²⁹Immediately the flow of her blood was dried up; and she felt in her body that she was healed of her affliction. ³⁰Immediately Jesus, perceiving in Himself that the power *proceeding* from Him had gone forth, turned around in the crowd and said, "Who touched My garments?" ³¹And His disciples said to Him, "You see the crowd pressing in on You, and You say, 'Who touched Me?' " ³²And He looked around to see the woman who had done this. ³³But the woman fearing and trembling, aware of what had happened to her, came and fell down before Him and told Him the whole truth. ³⁴And He said to her, "Daughter, your faith has made you well; go in peace and be healed of your affliction."

35 While He was still speaking, they *came from the *house of* the synagogue official, saying, "Your daughter has died; why trouble the Teacher anymore?" ³⁶But Jesus, overhearing what was being spoken, *said to the synagogue official, "Do not be afraid *any longer,* only believe." ³⁷And He allowed no one to accompany Him, except Peter and James and John the brother of James. ³⁸They *came to the house of the synagogue official; and He *saw a commotion, and *people* loudly weeping and wailing. ³⁹And entering in, He *said to them, "Why make a commotion and weep? The child has not died, but is asleep." ⁴⁰They *began* laughing at Him. But putting

*5:19 Or everything that

them all out, He *took along the child's father and mother and His own companions, and *entered *the room* where the child was. [41]Taking the child by the hand, He *said to her, "Talitha kum!" (which translated means, "Little girl, I say to you, get up!"). [42]Immediately the girl got up and *began* to walk, for she was twelve years old. And immediately they were completely astounded. [43]And He gave them strict orders that no one should know about this, and He said that *something* should be given her to eat.

Teaching at Nazareth

6 Jesus went out from there and *came into His hometown; and His disciples *followed Him. [2]When the Sabbath came, He began to teach in the synagogue; and the many listeners were astonished, saying, "Where did this man *get* these things, and what is *this* wisdom given to Him, and such miracles as these performed by His hands? [3]Is not this the carpenter, the son of Mary, and brother of James and Joses and Judas and Simon? Are not His sisters here with us?" And they took offense at Him. [4]Jesus said to them, "A prophet is not without honor except in his hometown and among his *own* relatives and in his *own* household." [5]And He could do no miracle there except that He

laid His hands on a few sick people and healed them. [6]And He wondered at their unbelief.

And He was going around the villages teaching.

The Twelve Sent Out

7 And He *summoned the twelve and began to send them out in pairs, and gave them authority over the unclean spirits; [8]and He instructed them that they should take nothing for *their* journey, except a mere staff—no bread, no bag, no money in their belt— [9]but *to* wear sandals; and *He added,* "Do not put on two [a]tunics." [10]And He said to them, "Wherever you enter a house, stay there until you leave town. [11]Any place that does not receive you or listen to you, as you go out from there, shake the dust off the soles of your feet for a testimony against them." [12]They went out and preached that *men* should repent. [13]And they were casting out many demons and were anointing with oil many sick people and healing them.

John's Fate Recalled

14 And King Herod heard *of it,* for His name had become well known; and *people* were saying, "John the Baptist has risen from the dead, and that is why these miraculous powers are at work in Him." [15]But others were saying, "He is Elijah."

[a]**6:9** Or inner garments

And others were saying, "*He is* a prophet, like one of the prophets *of old.*" ¹⁶But when Herod heard *of it,* he kept saying, "John, whom I beheaded, has risen!"

17 For Herod himself had sent and had John arrested and bound in prison on account of Herodias, the wife of his brother Philip, because he had married her. ¹⁸For John had been saying to Herod, "It is not lawful for you to have your brother's wife." ¹⁹Herodias had a grudge against him and wanted to put him to death and could not *do so;* ²⁰for Herod was afraid of John, knowing that he was a righteous and holy man, and he kept him safe. And when he heard him, he was very perplexed; but he used to enjoy listening to him. ²¹A strategic day came when Herod on his birthday gave a banquet for his lords and military commanders and the leading men of Galilee; ²²and when the daughter of Herodias herself came in and danced, she pleased Herod and his dinner guests; and the king said to the girl, "Ask me for whatever you want and I will give it to you." ²³And he swore to her, "Whatever you ask of me, I will give it to you; up to half of my kingdom." ²⁴And she went out and said to her mother, "What shall I ask for?" And she said, "The head of John the Baptist." ²⁵Immediately she came in a hurry to the king and asked, saying, "I want you to give me at once the head of John the Baptist on a platter." ²⁶And although the king was very sorry, *yet* because of his oaths and because of his dinner guests, he was unwilling to refuse her. ²⁷Immediately the king sent an executioner and commanded *him* to bring *back* his head. And he went and had him beheaded in the prison, ²⁸and brought his head on a platter, and gave it to the girl; and the girl gave it to her mother. ²⁹When his disciples heard *about this,* they came and took away his body and laid it in a tomb.

30 The apostles *gathered together with Jesus; and they reported to Him all that they had done and taught. ³¹And He *said to them, "Come away by yourselves to a secluded place and rest a while." (For there were many *people* coming and going, and they did not even have time to eat.) ³²They went away in the boat to a secluded place by themselves.

Five Thousand Fed

³³*The people* saw them going, and many recognized *them* and ran there together on foot from all the cities, and got there ahead of them. ³⁴When Jesus went ashore, He saw a large crowd, and He felt compassion for them because they were like sheep without a shepherd;

and He began to teach them many things. [35]When it was already quite late, His disciples came to Him and said, "This place is desolate and it is already quite late; [36]send them away so that they may go into the surrounding countryside and villages and buy themselves something to eat." [37]But He answered them, "You give them *something* to eat!" And they *said to Him, "Shall we go and spend two hundred [a]denarii on bread and give them *something* to eat?" [38]And He *said to them, "How many loaves do you have? Go look!" And when they found out, they *said, "Five, and two fish." [39]And He commanded them all to sit down by groups on the green grass. [40]They sat down in groups of hundreds and of fifties. [41]And He took the five loaves and the two fish, and looking up toward heaven, He blessed *the food* and broke the loaves and He kept giving *them* to the disciples to set before them; and He divided up the two fish among them all. [42]They all ate and were satisfied, [43]and they picked up twelve full baskets of the broken pieces, and also of the fish. [44]There were five thousand men who ate the loaves.

Jesus Walks on the Water

45 Immediately Jesus made His disciples get into the boat and go ahead of *Him* to the other side to Bethsaida, while He Himself was sending the crowd away. [46]After bidding them farewell, He left for the mountain to pray.

47 When it was evening, the boat was in the middle of the sea, and He was alone on the land. [48]Seeing them straining at the oars, for the wind was against them, at about the fourth watch of the night He *came to them, walking on the sea; and He intended to pass by them. [49]But when they saw Him walking on the sea, they supposed that it was a ghost, and cried out; [50]for they all saw Him and were terrified. But immediately He spoke with them and *said to them, "Take courage; it is I, do not be afraid." [51]Then He got into the boat with them, and the wind stopped; and they were utterly astonished, [52]for they had not gained any insight from the *incident of* the loaves, but their heart was hardened.

Healing at Gennesaret

53 When they had crossed over they came to land at Gennesaret, and moored to the shore. [54]When they got out of the boat, immediately *the people* recognized Him, [55]and ran about that whole country and began to carry here and there on their pallets those who were sick, to the place they heard He was. [56]Wherever He entered villages, or cities, or countryside,

*6:37 The denarius was equivalent to one day's wage

they were laying the sick in the market places, and imploring Him that they might just touch the fringe of His cloak; and as many as touched it were being cured.

Followers of Tradition

7 The Pharisees and some of the scribes gathered around Him when they had come from Jerusalem, [2]and had seen that some of His disciples were eating their bread with impure hands, that is, unwashed. [3](For the Pharisees and all the Jews do not eat unless they carefully wash their hands, *thus* observing the traditions of the elders; [4]and *when they come* from the market place, they do not eat unless they cleanse themselves; and there are many other things which they have received in order to observe, such as the washing of cups and pitchers and copper pots.) [5]The Pharisees and the scribes *asked Him, "Why do Your disciples not walk according to the tradition of the elders, but eat their bread with impure hands?" [6]And He said to them, "Rightly did Isaiah prophesy of you hypocrites, as it is written:

"THIS PEOPLE HONORS ME
    WITH THEIR LIPS,
BUT THEIR HEART IS FAR AWAY
    FROM ME.
[7]'BUT IN VAIN DO THEY WOR-
    SHIP ME,
TEACHING AS DOCTRINES THE
    PRECEPTS OF MEN.'
[8]Neglecting the commandment of God, you hold to the tradition of men."

[9] He was also saying to them, "You are experts at setting aside the commandment of God in order to keep your tradition. [10]For Moses said, 'HONOR YOUR FATHER AND YOUR MOTHER'; and, 'HE WHO SPEAKS EVIL OF FATHER OR MOTHER, IS TO BE PUT TO DEATH'; [11]but you say, 'If a man says to *his* father or *his* mother, whatever I have that would help you is Corban (that is to say, a given *to God*),' [12]you no longer permit him to do anything for *his* father or *his* mother; [13]*thus* invalidating the word of God by your tradition which you have handed down; and you do many things such as that."

The Heart of Man

[14] After He called the crowd to Him again, He *began* saying to them, "Listen to Me, all of you, and understand: [15]there is nothing outside the man which can defile him if it goes into him; but the things which proceed out of the man are what defile the man. [16b][If anyone has ears to hear, let him hear."]

[17] When he had left the crowd *and* entered the house, His disciples questioned Him about the parable.

---

a**7:11** Or *a gift, i.e. an offering;* b**7:16** Early mss do not contain this verse

[18] And He *said to them, "Are you so lacking in understanding also? Do you not understand that whatever goes into the man from outside cannot defile him, [19] because it does not go into his heart, but into his stomach, and is eliminated?" (*Thus He* declared all foods clean.) [20] And He was saying, "That which proceeds out of the man, that is what defiles the man. [21] For from within, out of the heart of men, proceed the evil thoughts, fornications, thefts, murders, adulteries, [22] deeds of coveting *and* wickedness, *as well as* deceit, sensuality, envy, slander, pride *and* foolishness. [23] All these evil things proceed from within and defile the man."

The Syrophoenician Woman

[24] Jesus got up and went away from there to the region of Tyre[a]. And when He had entered a house, He wanted no one to know *of it*; yet He could not escape notice. [25] But after hearing of Him, a woman whose little daughter had an unclean spirit immediately came and fell at His feet. [26] Now the woman was a [b]Gentile, of the Syrophoenician race. And she kept asking Him to cast the demon out of her daughter. [27] And He was saying to her, "Let the children be satisfied first, for it is not good to take the children's bread and throw it to the dogs." [28] But she answered and *said to Him, "Yes, Lord, *but* even the dogs under the table feed on the children's crumbs." [29] And He said to her, "Because of this answer go; the demon has gone out of your daughter." [30] And going back to her home, she found the child lying on the bed, the demon having left.

31 Again He went out from the region of Tyre, and came through Sidon to the Sea of Galilee, within the region of Decapolis. [32] They *brought to Him one who was deaf and spoke with difficulty, and they *implored Him to lay His hand on him. [33] Jesus took him aside from the crowd, by himself, and put His fingers into his ears, and after spitting, He touched his tongue *with the saliva;* [34] and looking up to heaven with a deep sigh, He *said to him, "Ephphatha!" that is, "Be opened!" [35] And his ears were opened, and the impediment of his tongue was removed, and he *began* speaking plainly. [36] And He gave them orders not to tell anyone; but the more He ordered them, the more widely they continued to proclaim it. [37] They were utterly astonished, saying, "He has done all things well; He makes even the deaf to hear and the mute to speak."

Four Thousand Fed

8 In those days, when there was again a large crowd and they had nothing to eat, Jesus called

7:24 Two early mss add *and Sidon*; [b]7:26 Lit Greek

His disciples and *said to them, ²"I feel compassion for the people because they have remained with Me now three days and have nothing to eat. ³If I send them away hungry to their homes, they will faint on the way; and some of them have come from a great distance." ⁴And His disciples answered Him, "Where will anyone be able *to find enough* bread here in *this* desolate place to satisfy these people?" ⁵And He was asking them, "How many loaves do you have?" And they said, "Seven." ⁶And He *directed the people to sit down on the ground; and taking the seven loaves, He gave thanks and broke them, and started giving them to His disciples to serve to them, and they served them to the people. ⁷They also had a few small fish; and after He had blessed them, He ordered these to be served as well. ⁸And they ate and were satisfied; and they picked up seven large baskets full of what was left over of the broken pieces. ⁹About four thousand were *there;* and He sent them away. ¹⁰And immediately He entered the boat with His disciples and came to the district of Dalmanutha.

¹¹The Pharisees came out and began to argue with Him, seeking from Him a sign from heaven, to test Him. ¹²Sighing deeply in His spirit, He *said, "Why does this generation seek for a sign? Truly I say to you, no sign will be given to this generation." ¹³Leaving them, He again embarked and went away to the other side.

¹⁴And they had forgotten to take bread, and did not have more than one loaf in the boat with them. ¹⁵And He was giving orders to them, saying, "Watch out! Beware of the leaven of the Pharisees and the leaven of Herod." ¹⁶They *began* to discuss with one another *the fact* that they had no bread. ¹⁷And Jesus, aware of this, *said to them, "Why do you discuss *the fact* that you have no bread? Do you not yet see or understand? Do you have a hardened heart? ¹⁸HAVING EYES, DO YOU NOT SEE? AND HAVING EARS, DO YOU NOT HEAR? And do you not remember, ¹⁹when I broke the five loaves for the five thousand, how many baskets full of broken pieces you picked up?" They *said to Him, "Twelve." ²⁰"When *I broke* the seven for the four thousand, how many large baskets full of broken pieces did you pick up?" And they *said to Him, "Seven." ²¹And He was saying to them, "Do you not yet understand?"

²²And they *came to Bethsaida. And they *brought a blind man to Jesus and *implored Him to touch him. ²³Taking the blind man by

the hand, He brought him out of the village; and after spitting on his eyes and laying His hands on him, He asked him, "Do you see anything?" ²⁴And he looked up and said, "I see men, for I see *them* like trees, walking around." ²⁵Then again He laid His hands on his eyes; and he looked intently and was restored, and *began* to see everything clearly. ²⁶And He sent him to his home, saying, "Do not even enter the village."

Peter's Confession of Christ

27 Jesus went out, along with His disciples, to the villages of Caesarea Philippi; and on the way He questioned His disciples, saying to them, "Who do people say that I am?" ²⁸They told Him, saying, "John the Baptist; and others *say* Elijah; but others, one of the prophets." ²⁹And He *continued* by questioning them, "But who do you say that I am?" Peter *answered and *said to Him, "You are the Christ." ³⁰And He warned them to tell no one about Him.

31 And He began to teach them that the Son of Man must suffer many things and be rejected by the elders and the chief priests and the scribes, and be killed, and after three days rise again. ³²And He was stating the matter plainly. And Peter took Him aside and began to rebuke Him. ³³But turning

around and seeing His disciples, He rebuked Peter and *said, "Get behind Me, Satan; for you are not setting your mind on ᵃGod's interests, but man's."

34 And He summoned the crowd with His disciples, and said to them, "If anyone wishes to come after Me, he must deny himself, and take up his cross and follow Me. ³⁵For whoever wishes to save his life will lose it, but whoever loses his life for My sake and the gospel's will save it. ³⁶For what does it profit a man to gain the whole world, and forfeit his soul? ³⁷For what will a man give in exchange for his soul? ³⁸For whoever is ashamed of Me and My words in this adulterous and sinful generation, the Son of Man will also be ashamed of him when He comes in the glory of His Father with the holy angels."

The Transfiguration

9And Jesus was saying to them, "Truly I say to you, there are some of those who are standing here who will not taste death until they see the kingdom of God after it has come with power."

2 Six days later, Jesus *took with Him Peter and James and John, and *brought them up on a high mountain by themselves. And He was transfigured before them; ³and

ᵃ**8:33** Lit *the things of God*

His garments became radiant and exceedingly white, as no launderer on earth can whiten them. ⁴Elijah appeared to them along with Moses; and they were talking with Jesus. ⁵Peter *said to Jesus, "Rabbi, it is good for us to be here; let us make three tabernacles, one for You, and one for Moses, and one for Elijah." ⁶For he did not know what to answer; for they became terrified. ⁷Then a cloud formed, overshadowing them, and a voice came out of the cloud, "This is My beloved Son, listen to Him!" ⁸All at once they looked around and saw no one with them anymore, except Jesus alone.

⁹ As they were coming down from the mountain, He gave them orders not to relate to anyone what they had seen, until the Son of Man rose from the dead. ¹⁰They seized upon that statement, discussing with one another what rising from the dead meant. ¹¹They asked Him, saying, *"Why is it* that the scribes say that Elijah must come first?" ¹²And He said to them, "Elijah does first come and restore all things. And *yet* how is it written of the Son of Man that He will suffer many things and be treated with contempt? ¹³But I say to you that Elijah has indeed come, and they did to him whatever they wished, just as it is written of him."

All Things Possible

14 When they came *back* to the disciples, they saw a large crowd around them, and *some* scribes arguing with them. ¹⁵Immediately, when the entire crowd saw Him, they were amazed and *began* running up to greet Him. ¹⁶And He asked them, "What are you discussing with them?" ¹⁷And one of the crowd answered Him, "Teacher, I brought You my son, possessed with a spirit which makes him mute; ¹⁸and whenever it seizes him, it slams him *to the ground* and he foams *at the mouth,* and grinds his teeth and stiffens out. I told Your disciples to cast it out, and they could not *do it."* ¹⁹And He *answered them and *said, "O unbelieving generation, how long shall I be with you? How long shall I put up with you? Bring him to Me!" ²⁰They brought the boy to Him. When he saw Him, immediately the spirit threw him into a convulsion, and falling to the ground, he *began* rolling around and foaming *at the mouth.* ²¹And He asked his father, "How long has this been happening to him?" And he said, "From childhood. ²²It has often thrown him both into the fire and into the water to destroy him. But if You can do anything, take pity on us and help us!" ²³And Jesus said to him, " 'If You can?' All things are possible to him who believes." [24]Immediately the boy's father cried out and said, "I do believe; help my unbelief." [25]When Jesus saw that a crowd was rapidly gathering, He rebuked the unclean spirit, saying to it, "You deaf and mute spirit, I command you, come out of him and do not enter him again." [26]After crying out and throwing him into terrible convulsions, it came out; and *the boy* became so much like a corpse that most *of them* said, "He is dead!" [27]But Jesus took him by the hand and raised him; and he got up. [28]When He came into *the* house, His disciples *began* questioning Him privately, "Why could we not drive it out?" [29]And He said to them, "This kind cannot come out by anything but prayer."

Death and Resurrection Foretold

30 From there they went out and *began* to go through Galilee, and He did not want anyone to know *about it.* [31]For He was teaching His disciples and telling them, "The Son of Man is to be [a]delivered into the hands of men, and they will kill Him; and when He has been killed, He will rise three days later." [32]But they did not understand *this* statement, and they were afraid to ask Him.

33 They came to Capernaum; and when He was in the house, He *began* to question them, "What

were you discussing on the way?" [34]But they kept silent, for on the way they had discussed with one another which *of them was* the greatest. [35]Sitting down, He called the twelve and *said to them, "If anyone wants to be first, he shall be last of all and servant of all." [36]Taking a child, He set him before them, and taking him in His arms, He said to them, [37]"Whoever receives one child like this in My name receives Me; and whoever receives Me does not receive Me, but Him who sent Me."

Dire Warnings

38 John said to Him, "Teacher, we saw someone casting out demons in Your name, and we tried to prevent him because he was not following us." [39]But Jesus said, "Do not hinder him, for there is no one who will perform a miracle in My name, and be able soon afterward to speak evil of Me. [40]For he who is not against us is [b]for us. [41]For whoever gives you a cup of water to drink because of your name as *followers* of Christ, truly I say to you, he will not lose his reward.

42 "Whoever causes one of these little ones who believe to stumble, it would be better for him if, with a heavy millstone hung around his neck, he had been cast into the sea. [43]If your hand ca

[a]9:31 Or *betrayed;* [b]9:40 Or on o

you to enter life crippled, than, having your two hands, to go into hell, into the unquenchable fire, [44a][where THEIR WORM DOES NOT DIE, AND THE FIRE IS NOT QUENCHED.] [45]If your foot causes you to stumble, cut it off; it is better for you to enter life lame, than, having your two feet, to be cast into hell, [46b][where THEIR WORM DOES NOT DIE, AND THE FIRE IS NOT QUENCHED.] [47]If your eye causes you to stumble, throw it out; it is better for you to enter the kingdom of God with one eye, than, having two eyes, to be cast into hell, [48]where THEIR WORM DOES NOT DIE, AND THE FIRE IS NOT QUENCHED.

[49] "For everyone will be salted with fire. [50]Salt is good; but if the salt becomes unsalty, with what will you make it salty *again*? Have salt in yourselves, and be at peace with one another."

Jesus' Teaching about Divorce

10 Getting up, He *went from there to the region of Judea and beyond the Jordan; crowds *gathered around Him again, and, according to His custom, He once more *began* to teach them.

2 *Some* Pharisees came up to Jesus, testing Him, and *began* to ques- ~~~~ ~~~~ lawful for

answered and said to them, "What did Moses command you?" [4]They said, "Moses permitted *a man* TO WRITE A CERTIFICATE OF DIVORCE AND SEND *her* AWAY." [5]But Jesus said to them, "Because of your hardness of heart he wrote you this commandment. [6]But from the beginning of creation, *God* MADE THEM MALE AND FEMALE. [7]FOR THIS REASON A MAN SHALL LEAVE HIS FATHER AND MOTHER,[c] [8]AND THE TWO SHALL BECOME ONE FLESH; so they are no longer two, but one flesh. [9]What therefore God has joined together, let no man separate."

10 In the house the disciples *began* questioning Him about this again. [11]And He *said to them, "Whoever divorces his wife and marries another woman commits adultery against her; [12]and if she herself divorces her husband and marries another man, she is committing adultery."

Jesus Blesses Little Children

13 And they were bringing children to Him so that He might touch them; but the disciples rebuked them. [14]But when Jesus saw this, He was indignant and said to them, "Permit the children to come to Me; do not hinder them; for the kingdom of God belongs to ~~~~ these. [15]Truly I say to you,

early mss; [b]**9:46** See v 44,

whoever does not receive the kingdom of God like a child will not enter it *at all.*" [16]And He took them in His arms and *began* blessing them, laying His hands on them.

The Rich Young Ruler

17 As He was setting out on a journey, a man ran up to Him and knelt before Him, and asked Him, "Good Teacher, what shall I do to inherit eternal life?" [18]And Jesus said to him, "Why do you call Me good? No one is good except God alone. [19]You know the commandments, 'DO NOT MURDER, DO NOT COMMIT ADULTERY, DO NOT STEAL, DO NOT BEAR FALSE WITNESS, Do not defraud, HONOR YOUR FATHER AND MOTHER.' " [20]And he said to Him, "Teacher, I have kept all these things from my youth up." [21]Looking at him, Jesus felt a love for him and said to him, "One thing you lack: go and sell all you possess and give to the poor, and you will have treasure in heaven; and come, follow Me." [22]But at these words he was saddened, and he went away grieving, for he was one who owned much property.

23 And Jesus, looking around, *said to His disciples, "How hard it will be for those who are wealthy to enter the kingdom of God!" [24]The disciples were amazed at His words. But Jesus *answered again and *said to them, "Children, how hard it is to enter the kingdom of God! [25]It is easier for a camel to go through the eye of a needle than for a rich man to enter the kingdom of God." [26]They were even more astonished and said to Him, "Then who can be saved?" [27]Looking at them, Jesus *said, "With people it is impossible, but not with God; for all things are possible with God."

28 Peter began to say to Him, "Behold, we have left everything and followed You." [29]Jesus said, "Truly I say to you, there is no one who has left house or brothers or sisters or mother or father or children or farms, for My sake and for the gospel's sake, [30]but that he will receive a hundred times as much now in the present age, houses and brothers and sisters and mothers and children and farms, along with persecutions; and in the age to come, eternal life. [31]But many *who are* first will be last, and the last, first."

Jesus' Sufferings Foretold

32 They were on the road going up to Jerusalem, and Jesus was walking on ahead of them; and they were amazed, and those who followed were fearful. And again He took the twelve aside and began to tell them what was going to happen to Him, [33]*saying,* "Behold, we are going up to Jerusalem, and the Son of Man will be ᵃdelivered to the chief priests and the scribes; and they will condemn Him to death and will hand Him over to the Gentiles. ³⁴They will mock Him and spit on Him, and scourge Him and kill *Him,* and three days later He will rise again."

35 James and John, the two sons of Zebedee, *came up to Jesus, saying, "Teacher, we want You to do for us whatever we ask of You." ³⁶And He said to them, "What do you want Me to do for you?" ³⁷They said to Him, "Grant that we may sit, one on Your right and one on *Your* left, in Your glory." ³⁸But Jesus said to them, "You do not know what you are asking. Are you able to drink the cup that I drink, or to be baptized with the baptism with which I am baptized?" ³⁹They said to Him, "We are able." And Jesus said to them, "The cup that I drink you shall drink; and you shall be baptized with the baptism with which I am baptized. ⁴⁰But to sit on My right or on *My* left, this is not Mine to give; but it is for those for whom it has been prepared."

41 Hearing *this,* the ten began to feel indignant with James and John. ⁴²Calling them to Himself, Jesus *said to them, "You know that those who are recognized as

rulers of the Gentiles lord it over them; and their great men exercise authority over them. ⁴³But it is not this way among you, but whoever wishes to become great among you shall be your servant; ⁴⁴and whoever wishes to be first among you shall be slave of all. ⁴⁵For even the Son of Man did not come to be served, but to serve, and to give His life a ransom for many."

Bartimaeus Receives His Sight

46 Then they *came to Jericho. And as He was leaving Jericho with His disciples and a large crowd, a blind beggar *named* Bartimaeus, the son of Timaeus, was sitting by the road. ⁴⁷When he heard that it was Jesus the Nazarene, he began to cry out and say, "Jesus, Son of David, have mercy on me!" ⁴⁸Many were sternly telling him to be quiet, but he kept crying out all the more, "Son of David, have mercy on me!" ⁴⁹And Jesus stopped and said, "Call him *here.*" So they *called the blind man, saying to him, "Take courage, stand up! He is calling for you." ⁵⁰Throwing aside his cloak, he jumped up and came to Jesus. ⁵¹And answering him, Jesus said, "What do you want Me to do for you?" And the blind man said to Him, "ᵇRabboni, *I want* to regain my sight!" ⁵²And Jesus said to him, "Go; your faith has made you well." Immediately he regained his

ᵃ**10:33** Or *betrayed;* ᵇ**10:51** I.e. My Master

sight and *began* following Him on the road.

The Triumphal Entry

11 As they *approached Jerusalem, at Bethphage and Bethany, near the Mount of Olives, He *sent two of His disciples, ²and *said to them, "Go into the village opposite you, and immediately as you enter it, you will find a colt tied *there,* on which no one yet has ever sat; untie it and bring it *here.* ³If anyone says to you, 'Why are you doing this?' you say, 'The Lord has need of it'; and immediately he will send it back here." ⁴They went away and found a colt tied at the door, outside in the street; and they *untied it. ⁵Some of the bystanders were saying to them, "What are you doing, untying the colt?" ⁶They spoke to them just as Jesus had told *them,* and they gave them permission. ⁷They *brought the colt to Jesus and put their coats on it; and He sat on it. ⁸And many spread their coats in the road, and others *spread* leafy branches which they had cut from the fields. ⁹Those who went in front and those who followed were shouting:

"Hosanna!

BLESSED IS HE WHO COMES IN THE NAME OF THE LORD;

¹⁰Blessed *is* the coming kingdom of our father David;

Hosanna in the highest!"

11 Jesus entered Jerusalem *and* *came* into the temple; and after looking around at everything, He left for Bethany with the twelve, since it was already late.

12 On the next day, when they had left Bethany, He became hungry. ¹³Seeing at a distance a fig tree in leaf, He went *to see* if perhaps He would find anything on it; and when He came to it, He found nothing but leaves, for it was not the season for figs. ¹⁴He said to it, "May no one ever eat fruit from you again!" And His disciples were listening.

Jesus Drives Money Changers from the Temple

15 Then they *came to Jerusalem. And He entered the temple and began to drive out those who were buying and selling in the temple, and overturned the tables of the money changers and the seats of those who were selling doves; ¹⁶and He would not permit anyone to carry merchandise through the temple. ¹⁷And He *began* to teach and say to them, "Is it not written, 'MY HOUSE SHALL BE CALLED A HOUSE OF PRAYER FOR ALL THE NATIONS'? But you have made it a ROBBERS' DEN.'" ¹⁸The chief priests and the scribes heard *this,* and *began* seeking how to destroy Him; for they were afraid of Him, for the whole crowd was astonished at His teaching.

19 When evening came, they would go out of the city.

20 As they were passing by in the morning, they saw the fig tree withered from the roots *up.* ²¹Being reminded, Peter *said to Him, "Rabbi, look, the fig tree which You cursed has withered." ²²And Jesus *answered saying to them, "Have faith in God. ²³Truly I say to you, whoever says to this mountain, 'Be taken up and cast into the sea,' and does not doubt in his heart, but believes that what he says is going to happen, it will be *granted* him. ²⁴Therefore I say to you, all things for which you pray and ask, believe that you have received them, and they will be *granted* you. ²⁵Whenever you stand praying, forgive, if you have anything against anyone, so that your Father who is in heaven will also forgive you your transgressions. ²⁶ᵃ[But if you do not forgive, neither will your Father who is in heaven forgive your transgressions."]

Jesus' Authority Questioned

27 They *came again to Jerusalem. And as He was walking in the temple, the chief priests and the scribes and the elders *came to Him, ²⁸and *began* saying to Him, "By what authority are You doing these things, or who gave You this authority to do these

things?" ²⁹And Jesus said to them, "I will ask you one question, and you answer Me, and *then* I will tell you by what authority I do these things. ³⁰Was the baptism of John from heaven, or from men? Answer Me." ³¹They *began* reasoning among themselves, saying, "If we say, 'From heaven,' He will say, 'Then why did you not believe him?' ³²But shall we say, 'From men'?"—they were afraid of the people, for everyone considered John to have been a real prophet. ³³Answering Jesus, they *said, "We do not know." And Jesus *said to them, "Nor will I tell you by what authority I do these things."

Parable of the Vine-growers

12 And He began to speak to them in parables: "A man PLANTED A VINEYARD AND PUT A WALL AROUND IT, AND DUG A VAT UNDER THE WINE PRESS AND BUILT A TOWER, and rented it out to ᵇvine-growers and went on a journey. ²At the *harvest* time he sent a slave to the vine-growers, in order to receive *some* of the produce of the vineyard from the vine-growers. ³They took him, and beat him and sent him away empty-handed. ⁴Again he sent them another slave, and they wounded him in the head, and treated him shamefully. ⁵And he sent another, and that one they killed; and *so with* many others,

ᵃ**11:26** Early mss do not contain this v; ᵇ**12:1** Or *tenant farmers,* also vv 2, 7, 9 beating some and killing others. ⁶He had one more *to send,* a beloved son; he sent him last *of all* to them, saying, 'They will respect my son.' ⁷But those vine-growers said to one another, 'This is the heir; come, let us kill him, and the inheritance will be ours!' ⁸They took him, and killed him and threw him out of the vineyard. ⁹What will the owner of the vineyard do? He will come and destroy the vine-growers, and will give the vineyard to others. ¹⁰Have you not even read this Scripture:

'THE STONE WHICH THE BUILDERS REJECTED,
THIS BECAME THE CHIEF CORNER *stone;*
¹¹THIS CAME ABOUT FROM THE LORD,
AND IT IS MARVELOUS IN OUR EYES'?"

12 And they were seeking to seize Him, and *yet* they feared the people, for they understood that He spoke the parable against them. And *so* they left Him and went away.

Jesus Answers the Pharisees, Sadducees and Scribes

13 Then they *sent some of the Pharisees and Herodians to Him in order to trap Him in a statement. ¹⁴They *came and *said to Him, "Teacher, we know that You are truthful and defer to no one; for You are not partial to any, but teach the way of God in truth. Is it lawful to pay a poll-tax to Caesar, or not? ¹⁵Shall we pay or shall we not pay?" But He, knowing their hypocrisy, said to them, "Why are you testing Me? Bring Me a ᵃdenarius to look at." ¹⁶They brought *one.* And He *said to them, "Whose likeness and inscription is this?" And they said to Him, "Caesar's." ¹⁷And Jesus said to them, "Render to Caesar the things that are Caesar's, and to God the things that are God's." And they were amazed at Him.

18 *Some* Sadducees (who say that there is no resurrection) *came to Jesus, and *began* questioning Him, saying, ¹⁹"Teacher, Moses wrote for us that IF A MAN'S BROTHER DIES and leaves behind a wife AND LEAVES NO CHILD, HIS BROTHER SHOULD MARRY THE WIFE AND RAISE UP CHILDREN TO HIS BROTHER. ²⁰There were seven brothers; and the first took a wife, and died leaving no children. ²¹The second one married her, and died leaving behind no children; and the third likewise; ²²and *so* all seven left no children. Last of all the woman died also. ²³In the resurrection, ᵇwhen they rise again, which one's wife will she be? For all seven had married her." ²⁴Jesus said to them, "Is this not the reason you are mistaken, that you do not understand the Scriptures or the power of God? ²⁵For when they

rise from the dead, they neither marry nor are given in marriage, but are like angels in heaven. ²⁶But regarding the fact that the dead rise again, have you not read in the book of Moses, in the *passage* about *the burning* bush, how God spoke to him, saying, 'I AM THE GOD OF ABRAHAM, AND THE GOD OF ISAAC, AND THE GOD OF JACOB'? ²⁷He is not the God of the dead, but of the living; you are greatly mistaken."

28 One of the scribes came and heard them arguing, and recognizing that He had answered them well, asked Him, "What commandment is the foremost of all?" ²⁹Jesus answered, "The foremost is, 'HEAR, O ISRAEL! THE LORD OUR GOD IS ONE LORD; ³⁰AND YOU SHALL LOVE THE LORD YOUR GOD WITH ALL YOUR HEART, AND WITH ALL YOUR SOUL, AND WITH ALL YOUR MIND, AND WITH ALL YOUR STRENGTH.' ³¹The second is this, 'YOU SHALL LOVE YOUR NEIGHBOR AS YOURSELF.' There is no other commandment greater than these." ³²The scribe said to Him, "Right, Teacher; You have truly stated that HE IS ONE, AND THERE IS NO ONE ELSE BESIDES HIM; ³³AND TO LOVE HIM WITH ALL THE HEART AND WITH ALL THE UNDERSTANDING AND WITH ALL THE STRENGTH, AND TO LOVE ONE'S NEIGHBOR AS HIMSELF, is much more than all burnt offerings and sacrifices." ³⁴When Jesus saw that he had answered intelligently, He said to him, "You are not far from the kingdom of God." After that, no one would venture to ask Him any more questions.

35 And Jesus *began* to say, as He taught in the temple, "How *is it that* the scribes say that the Christ is the son of David? ³⁶David himself said in the Holy Spirit,
'THE LORD SAID TO MY LORD,
"SIT AT MY RIGHT HAND,
UNTIL I PUT YOUR ENEMIES
    BENEATH YOUR FEET." '
³⁷David himself calls Him 'Lord'; so in what sense is He his son?" And the large crowd enjoyed listening to Him.

38 In His teaching He was saying: "Beware of the scribes who like to walk around in long robes, and *like* respectful greetings in the market places, ³⁹and chief seats in the synagogues and places of honor at banquets, ⁴⁰who devour widows' houses, and for appearance's sake offer long prayers; these will receive greater condemnation."

The Widow's Mite

41 And He sat down opposite the treasury, and *began* observing how the people were putting money into the treasury; and many rich people were putting in large sums. ⁴²A poor widow came and put in two small copper coins, which amount to a cent. ⁴³Calling His disciples to Him, He said to them, "Truly I say to you, this poor widow put in more than all the contributors to the treasury; ⁴⁴for they all put in out of their surplus, but she, out of her poverty, put in all she owned, all she had to live on."

Things to Come

13 As He was going out of the temple, one of His disciples *said to Him, "Teacher, behold ªwhat wonderful stones and what wonderful buildings!" ²And Jesus said to him, "Do you see these great buildings? Not one stone will be left upon another which will not be torn down."

3 As He was sitting on the Mount of Olives opposite the temple, Peter and James and John and Andrew were questioning Him privately, ⁴"Tell us, when will these things be, and what *will be* the sign when all these things are going to be fulfilled?" ⁵And Jesus began to say to them, "See to it that no one misleads you. ⁶Many will come in My name, saying, 'I am *He!*' and will mislead many. ⁷When you hear of wars and rumors of wars, do not be fright

things must take place; but *that is* not yet the end. ⁸For nation will rise up against nation, and kingdom against kingdom; there will be earthquakes in various places; there will *also* be famines. These things are *merely* the beginning of birth pangs.

9 "But be on your guard; for they will deliver you to *the* courts, and you will be flogged in *the* synagogues, and you will stand before governors and kings for My sake, as a testimony to them. ¹⁰The gospel must first be preached to all the nations. ¹¹When they arrest you and hand you over, do not worry beforehand about what you are to say, but say whatever is given you in that hour; for it is not you who speak, but *it is* the Holy Spirit. ¹²Brother will betray brother to death, and a father *his* child; and children will rise up against parents and have them put to death. ¹³You will be hated by all because of My name, but the one who endures to the end, he will be saved.

14 "But when you see the ABOMINATION OF DESOLATION standing where it should not be (let the reader understand), then those who are in Judea must flee to the mountains. ¹⁵The one who of his house; ¹⁶and the one who is in the field must not turn back to get his coat. ¹⁷But woe to those who are pregnant and to those who are nursing babies in those days! ¹⁸But pray that it may not happen in the winter. ¹⁹For those days will be a *time of* tribulation such as has not occurred since the beginning of the creation which God created until now, and never will. ²⁰Unless the Lord had shortened *those* days, no life would have been saved; but for the sake of the elect, whom He chose, He shortened the days. ²¹And then if anyone says to you, 'Behold, here is the Christ'; or, 'Behold, *He is* there'; do not believe *him*; ²²for false Christs and false prophets will arise, and will show signs and wonders, in order to lead astray, if possible, the elect. ²³But take heed; behold, I have told you everything in advance.

The Return of Christ

²⁴"But in those days, after that tribulation, THE SUN WILL BE DARKENED AND THE MOON WILL NOT GIVE ITS LIGHT, ²⁵AND THE STARS WILL BE FALLING from heaven, and the powers that are in the heavens will be shaken. ²⁶Then they will see THE SON OF MAN COMING IN CLOUDS, with great power and together His elect from the four winds, from the farthest end of the earth to the farthest end of heaven.

²⁸"Now learn the parable from the fig tree: when its branch has already become tender and puts forth its leaves, you know that summer is near. ²⁹Even so, you too, when you see these things happening, recognize that He is near, *right* at the door. ³⁰Truly I say to you, this ^ageneration will not pass away until all these things take place. ³¹Heaven and earth will pass away, but My words will not pass away. ³²But of that day or hour no one knows, not even the angels in heaven, nor the Son, but the Father *alone*.

³³"Take heed, keep on the alert; for you do not know when the *appointed* time will come. ³⁴*It is* like a man away on a journey, *who* upon leaving his house and putting his slaves in charge, *assigning* to each one his task, also commanded the doorkeeper to stay on the alert. ³⁵Therefore, be on the alert—for you do not know when the master of the house is coming, whether in the evening, at midnight, or when the rooster crows, or in the morning— ³⁶in case he should come suddenly and find you asleep. ³⁷What I say to you I say to all, 'Be alert!' "

Death Plot and Anointing

14 Now the Passover and Unleavened Bread were two days away; and the chief priests and the scribes were seeking how to seize Him by stealth and kill Him; ²for they were saying, "Not during the festival, otherwise there might be a riot of the people."

3 While He was in Bethany at the home of Simon the leper, and reclining *at the table,* there came a woman with an alabaster vial of very costly perfume of pure nard; *and* she broke the vial and poured it over His head. ⁴But some were indignantly *remarking* to one another, "Why has this perfume been wasted? ⁵For this perfume might have been sold for over three hundred ᵃdenarii, and *the money* given to the poor." And they were scolding her. ⁶But Jesus said, "Let her alone; why do you bother her? She has done a good deed to Me. ⁷For you always have the poor with you, and whenever you wish you can do good to them; but you do not always have Me. ⁸She has done what she could; she has anointed My body beforehand for the burial. ⁹Truly I say to you, wherever the gospel is preached in the whole world, what this woman has done will also be spoken of in memory of her."

10 Then Judas Iscariot, who was one of the twelve, went off to the chief priests in order to betray Him to them. ¹¹They were glad when they heard *this,* and promised to give him money. And he *began* seeking how to betray Him at an opportune time.

The Last Passover

12 On the first day of Unleavened Bread, when the Passover *lamb* was being sacrificed, His disciples *said to Him, "Where do You want us to go and prepare for You to eat the Passover?" ¹³And He *sent two of His disciples and *said to them, "Go into the city, and a man will meet you carrying a pitcher of water; follow him; ¹⁴and wherever he enters, say to the owner of the house, 'The Teacher says, "Where is My guest room in which I may eat the Passover with My disciples?" ' ¹⁵And he himself will show you a large upper room furnished *and* ready; prepare for us there." ¹⁶The disciples went out and came to the city, and found *it* just as He had told them; and they prepared the Passover.

17 When it was evening He *came with the twelve. ¹⁸As they were reclining *at the table* and eating, Jesus said, "Truly I say to you that one of you will betray Me—one who is eating with Me." ¹⁹They began to be grieved and to say to

ᵃ**14:5** The denarius was equivalent to a day's wages

Him one by one, "Surely not I?" ²⁰And He said to them, "*It is* one of the twelve, one who dips with Me in the bowl. ²¹For the Son of Man *is to* go just as it is written of Him; but woe to that man by whom the Son of Man is betrayed! *It would have been* good for that man if he had not been born."

The Lord's Supper

22 While they were eating, He took *some* bread, and after a blessing He broke *it,* and gave *it* to them, and said, "Take *it;* this is My body." ²³And when He had taken a cup *and* given thanks, He gave *it* to them, and they all drank from it. ²⁴And He said to them, "This is My blood of the covenant, which is poured out for many. ²⁵Truly I say to you, I will never again drink of the fruit of the vine until that day when I drink it new in the kingdom of God."

26 After singing a hymn, they went out to the Mount of Olives.

27 And Jesus *said to them, "You will all fall away, because it is written, 'I WILL STRIKE DOWN THE SHEPHERD, AND THE SHEEP SHALL BE SCATTERED.' ²⁸But after I have been raised, I will go ahead of you to Galilee." ²⁹But Peter said to Him, "*Even* though all may fall away, yet I will not." ³⁰And Jesus *said to him, "Truly I say to you, that this very night, before a rooster crows twice, you yourself will deny Me three times." ³¹But *Peter* kept saying insistently, "*Even* if I have to die with You, I will not deny You!" And they all were saying the same thing also.

Jesus in Gethsemane

32 They *came to a place named Gethsemane; and He *said to His disciples, "Sit here until I have prayed." ³³And He *took with Him Peter and James and John, and began to be very distressed and troubled. ³⁴And He *said to them, "My soul is deeply grieved to the point of death; remain here and keep watch." ³⁵And He went a little beyond *them,* and fell to the ground and *began* to pray that if it were possible, the hour might pass Him by. ³⁶And He was saying, "Abba! Father! All things are possible for You; remove this cup from Me; yet not what I will, but what You will." ³⁷And He *came and *found them sleeping, and *said to Peter, "Simon, are you asleep? Could you not keep watch for one hour? ³⁸Keep watching and praying that you may not come into temptation; the spirit is willing, but the flesh is weak." ³⁹Again He went away and prayed, saying the same words. ⁴⁰And again He came and found them sleeping, for their eyes were very heavy; and they did not know what to answer Him.

⁴¹And He *came the third time, and *said to them, "Are you still sleeping and resting? It is enough; the hour has come; behold, the Son of Man is being betrayed into the hands of sinners. ⁴²Get up, let us be going; behold, the one who betrays Me is at hand!"

Betrayal and Arrest

43 Immediately while He was still speaking, Judas, one of the twelve, *came up accompanied by a crowd with swords and clubs, *who were* from the chief priests and the scribes and the elders. ⁴⁴Now he who was betraying Him had given them a signal, saying, "Whomever I kiss, He is the one; seize Him and lead Him away under guard." ⁴⁵After coming, Judas immediately went to Him, saying, "Rabbi!" and kissed Him. ⁴⁶They laid hands on Him and seized Him. ⁴⁷But one of those who stood by drew his sword, and struck the slave of the high priest and cut off his ear. ⁴⁸And Jesus said to them, "Have you come out with swords and clubs to arrest Me, as *you would* against a robber? ⁴⁹Every day I was with you in the temple teaching, and you did not seize Me; but *this has taken place* to fulfill the Scriptures." ⁵⁰And they all left Him and fled.

51 A young man was following Him, wearing *nothing but* a linen sheet over *his* naked *body;* and they *seized him. ⁵²But he pulled free of the linen sheet and escaped naked.

Jesus before His Accusers

53 They led Jesus away to the high priest; and all the chief priests and the elders and the scribes *gathered together. ⁵⁴Peter had followed Him at a distance, right into the courtyard of the high priest; and he was sitting with the officers and warming himself at the fire. ⁵⁵Now the chief priests and the whole ªCouncil kept trying to obtain testimony against Jesus to put Him to death, and they were not finding any. ⁵⁶For many were giving false testimony against Him, but their testimony was not consistent. ⁵⁷Some stood up and *began* to give false testimony against Him, saying, ⁵⁸"We heard Him say, 'I will destroy this temple made with hands, and in three days I will build another made without hands.' " ⁵⁹Not even in this respect was their testimony consistent. ⁶⁰The high priest stood up *and came* forward and questioned Jesus, saying, "Do You not answer? What is it that these men are testifying against You?" ⁶¹But He kept silent and did not answer. Again the high priest was questioning Him, and saying to Him, "Are You the Christ, the Son of the Blessed *One?*" ⁶²And Jesus said, "I am; and you shall see THE SON OF

ª**14:55** Or *Sanhedrin*

MAN SITTING AT THE RIGHT HAND OF POWER, and COMING WITH THE CLOUDS OF HEAVEN." ⁶³Tearing his clothes, the high priest *said, "What further need do we have of witnesses? ⁶⁴You have heard the blasphemy; how does it seem to you?" And they all condemned Him to be deserving of death. ⁶⁵Some began to spit at Him, and to blindfold Him, and to beat Him with their fists, and to say to Him, "Prophesy!" And the officers received Him with slaps *in the face.*

Peter's Denials

⁶⁶ As Peter was below in the courtyard, one of the servant-girls of the high priest *came, ⁶⁷and seeing Peter warming himself, she looked at him and *said, "You also were with Jesus the Nazarene." ⁶⁸But he denied *it,* saying, "I neither know nor understand what you are talking about." And he went out onto the porch.ᵃ ⁶⁹The servant-girl saw him, and began once more to say to the bystanders, "This is *one* of them!" ⁷⁰But again he denied it. And after a little while the bystanders were again saying to Peter, "Surely you are *one* of them, for you are a Galilean too." ⁷¹But he began to curse and swear, "I do not know this man you are talking about!" ⁷²Immediately a rooster crowed a second time. And Peter remembered how

Jesus had made the remark to him, "Before a rooster crows twice, you will deny Me three times." And he began to weep.

Jesus before Pilate

15 Early in the morning the chief priests with the elders and scribes and the whole ᵃCouncil, immediately held a consultation; and binding Jesus, they led Him away and delivered Him to Pilate. ²Pilate questioned Him, "Are You the King of the Jews?" And He *answered him, "*It is as* you say." ³The chief priests *began* to accuse Him harshly. ⁴Then Pilate questioned Him again, saying, "Do You not answer? See how many charges they bring against You!" ⁵But Jesus made no further answer; so Pilate was amazed.

⁶ Now at *the* feast he used to release for them *any* one prisoner whom they requested. ⁷The man named Barabbas had been imprisoned with the insurrectionists who had committed murder in the insurrection. ⁸The crowd went up and began asking him *to do* as he had been accustomed to do for them. ⁹Pilate answered them, saying, "Do you want me to release for you the King of the Jews?" ¹⁰For he was aware that the chief priests had handed Him over because of envy. ¹¹But the chief priests stirred up the crowd

ᵃ**14:68** Later mss add *and a rooster crowed;* ᵇ**15:1** Or *Sanhedrin* *to ask* him to release Barabbas for them instead. ¹²Answering again, Pilate said to them, "Then what shall I do with Him whom you call the King of the Jews?" ¹³They shouted back, "Crucify Him!" ¹⁴But Pilate said to them, "Why, what evil has He done?" But they shouted all the more, "Crucify Him!" ¹⁵Wishing to satisfy the crowd, Pilate released Barabbas for them, and after having Jesus scourged, he handed Him over to be crucified.

Jesus Is Mocked

16 The soldiers took Him away into the palace (that is, the Praetorium), and they *called together the whole *Roman* ᵃcohort. ¹⁷They *dressed Him up in purple, and after twisting a crown of thorns, they put it on Him; ¹⁸and they began to acclaim Him, "Hail, King of the Jews!" ¹⁹They kept beating His head with a ᵇreed, and spitting on Him, and kneeling and bowing before Him. ²⁰After they had mocked Him, they took the purple robe off Him and put His *own* garments on Him. And they *led Him out to crucify Him.

21 They *pressed into service a passer-by coming from the country, Simon of Cyrene (the father of Alexander and Rufus), to bear His cross.

The Crucifixion

22 Then they *brought Him to the place Golgotha, which is translated, Place of a Skull. ²³They tried to give Him wine mixed with myrrh; but He did not take it. ²⁴And they *crucified Him, and *divided up His garments among themselves, casting lots for them *to decide* what each man should take. ²⁵It was the ᶜthird hour when they crucified Him. ²⁶The inscription of the charge against Him read, "THE KING OF THE JEWS."

27 They *crucified two robbers with Him, one on His right and one on His left. ²⁸ᵈ[And the Scripture was fulfilled which says, "And He was numbered with transgressors."] ²⁹Those passing by were hurling abuse at Him, wagging their heads, and saying, "Ha! You who *are going to* destroy the temple and rebuild it in three days, ³⁰save Yourself, and come down from the cross!" ³¹In the same way the chief priests also, along with the scribes, were mocking *Him* among themselves and saying, "He saved others; He cannot save Himself. ³²Let *this* Christ, the King of Israel, now come down from the cross, so that we may see and believe!" Those who were crucified with Him were also insulting Him.

33 When the ᵉsixth hour came, darkness fell over the whole land

---

ᵃ**15:16** Or *battalion;* ᵇ**15:19** Or *staff* (made of a reed); ᶜ**15:25** I.e. 9 a.m.; ᵈ**15:28** Early mss do not contain this v; ᵉ**15:33** I.e. noon until the [a]ninth hour. [34]At the ninth hour Jesus cried out with a loud voice, "ELOI, ELOI, LAMA SABACHTHANI?" which is translated, "MY GOD, MY GOD, WHY HAVE YOU FORSAKEN ME?" [35]When some of the bystanders heard it, they *began* saying, "Behold, He is calling for Elijah." [36]Someone ran and filled a sponge with sour wine, put it on a reed, and gave Him a drink, saying, "Let us see whether Elijah will come to take Him down." [37]And Jesus uttered a loud cry, and breathed His last. [38]And the veil of the temple was torn in two from top to bottom. [39]When the centurion, who was standing right in front of Him, saw the way He breathed His last, he said, "Truly this man was the Son of God!"

40 There were also *some* women looking on from a distance, among whom *were* Mary Magdalene, and Mary the mother of James the Less and Joses, and Salome. [41]When He was in Galilee, they used to follow Him and minister to Him; and *there were* many other women who came up with Him to Jerusalem.

Jesus Is Buried

42 When evening had already come, because it was the preparation day, that is, the day before the Sabbath, [43]Joseph of Arimathea came, a prominent member of the Council, who himself was waiting for the kingdom of God; and he gathered up courage and went in before Pilate, and asked for the body of Jesus. [44]Pilate wondered if He was dead by this time, and summoning the centurion, he questioned him as to whether He was already dead. [45]And ascertaining this from the centurion, he granted the body to Joseph. [46]Joseph bought a linen cloth, took Him down, wrapped Him in the linen cloth and laid Him in a tomb which had been hewn out in the rock; and he rolled a stone against the entrance of the tomb. [47]Mary Magdalene and Mary the *mother* of Joses were looking on *to see* where He was laid.

The Resurrection

16 When the Sabbath was over, Mary Magdalene, and Mary the *mother* of James, and Salome, bought spices, so that they might come and anoint Him. [2]Very early on the first day of the week, they *came to the tomb when the sun had risen. [3]They were saying to one another, "Who will roll away the stone for us from the entrance of the tomb?" [4]Looking up, they *saw that the stone had been rolled away, although it was extremely large. [5]Entering the tomb, they saw a young man sitting at the right, wearing a white robe;

15 33 I.e. 3 p.m.

and they were amazed. [6]And he *said to them, "Do not be amazed; you are looking for Jesus the Nazarene, who has been crucified. He has risen; He is not here; behold, *here is* the place where they laid Him. [7]But go, tell His disciples and Peter, 'He is going ahead of you to Galilee; there you will see Him, just as He told you.' " [8]They went out and fled from the tomb, for trembling and astonishment had gripped them; and they said nothing to anyone, for they were afraid.

9 [a][Now after He had risen early on the first day of the week, He first appeared to Mary Magdalene, from whom He had cast out seven demons. [10]She went and reported to those who had been with Him, while they were mourning and weeping. [11]When they heard that He was alive and had been seen by her, they refused to believe it.

12 After that, He appeared in a different form to two of them while they were walking along on their way to the country. [13]They went away and reported it to the others, but they did not believe them either.

The Disciples Commissioned
14 Afterward He appeared to the eleven themselves as they were reclining *at the table*; and He reproached them for their unbelief

and hardness of heart, because they had not believed those who had seen Him after He had risen. [15]And He said to them, "Go into all the world and preach the gospel to all creation. [16]He who has believed and has been baptized shall be saved; but he who has disbelieved shall be condemned. [17]These signs will accompany those who have believed: in My name they will cast out demons, they will speak with new tongues; [18]they will pick up serpents, and if they drink any deadly *poison,* it will not hurt them; they will lay hands on the sick, and they will recover."

19 So then, when the Lord Jesus had spoken to them, He was received up into heaven and sat down at the right hand of God. [20b]And they went out and preached everywhere, while the Lord worked with them, and confirmed the word by the signs that followed.]

[*And they promptly reported all these instructions to Peter and his companions. And after that, Jesus Himself sent out through them from east to west the sacred and imperishable proclamation of eternal salvation.*]

[a]**16:9** Later mss add vv 9-20; [b]**16:20** A few late mss and versions contain this paragraph, usually after v 8; a few have it at the end of ch

LUKE

Introduction

1 Inasmuch as many have undertaken to compile an account of the things accomplished among us, ²just as they were handed down to us by those who from the beginning were eyewitnesses and servants of the ^aword, ³it seemed fitting for me as well, having investigated everything carefully from the beginning, to write *it* out for you in consecutive order, most excellent Theophilus; ⁴so that you may know the exact truth about the things you have been taught.

Birth of John the Baptist Foretold

5 In the days of Herod, king of Judea, there was a priest named Zacharias, of the division of ^aAbijah; and he had a wife from the daughters of Aaron, and her name was Elizabeth. ⁶They were both righteous in the sight of God, walking blamelessly in all the commandments and requirements of the Lord. ⁷But they had no child, because Elizabeth was barren, and they were both advanced in years.

8 Now it happened *that* while he was performing his priestly service before God in the *appointed* order of his division, ⁹according to the custom of the priestly office, he was chosen by lot to enter the temple of the Lord and burn incense. ¹⁰And the whole multitude of the people were in prayer outside at the hour of the incense offering. ¹¹And an angel of the Lord appeared to him, standing to the right of the altar of incense. ¹²Zacharias was troubled when he saw *the angel,* and fear gripped him. ¹³But the angel said to him, "Do not be afraid, Zacharias, for your petition has been heard, and your wife Elizabeth will bear you a son, and you will give him the name John. ¹⁴You will have joy and gladness, and many will rejoice at his birth. ¹⁵For he will be great in the sight of the Lord; and he will drink no wine or liquor, and he will be filled with the Holy Spirit while yet in his mother's womb. ¹⁶And he will turn many of the sons of Israel back to the Lord their God. ¹⁷It is he who will go *as a forerunner* before Him in the spirit and power of Elijah, TO TURN THE HEARTS OF THE FATHERS BACK TO THE CHILDREN, and the disobedient to the attitude of the righteous, so as to make ready a people prepared for the Lord."

1:2 I.e. gospel; b1:5 Gr *Abia*

18 Zacharias said to the angel, "How will I know this *for certain?* For I am an old man and my wife is advanced in years." ¹⁹The angel answered and said to him, "I am Gabriel, who stands in the presence of God, and I have been sent to speak to you and to bring you this good news. ²⁰And behold, you shall be silent and unable to speak until the day when these things take place, because you did not believe my words, which will be fulfilled in their proper time."

21 The people were waiting for Zacharias, and were wondering at his delay in the temple. ²²But when he came out, he was unable to speak to them; and they realized that he had seen a vision in the temple; and he kept making signs to them, and remained mute. ²³When the days of his priestly service were ended, he went back home.

24 After these days Elizabeth his wife became pregnant, and she kept herself in seclusion for five months, saying, ²⁵"This is the way the Lord has dealt with me in the days when He looked *with favor* upon *me,* to take away my disgrace among men."

Jesus' Birth Foretold

26 Now in the sixth month the angel Gabriel was sent from God to a city in Galilee called Nazareth, ²⁷to a virgin engaged to a man whose name was Joseph, of the descendants of David; and the virgin's name was Mary. ²⁸And coming in, he said to her, "Greetings, favored one! The Lord *is* with you." ²⁹But she was very perplexed at *this* statement, and kept pondering what kind of salutation this was. ³⁰The angel said to her, "Do not be afraid, Mary; for you have found favor with God. ³¹And behold, you will conceive in your womb and bear a son, and you shall name Him Jesus. ³²He will be great and will be called the Son of the Most High; and the Lord God will give Him the throne of His father David; ³³and He will reign over the house of Jacob forever, and His kingdom will have no end." ³⁴Mary said to the angel, "How can this be, since I am a virgin?" ³⁵The angel answered and said to her, "The Holy Spirit will come upon you, and the power of the Most High will overshadow you; and for that reason the holy Child shall be called the Son of God. ³⁶And behold, even your relative Elizabeth has also conceived a son in her old age; and she who was called barren is now in her sixth month. ³⁷For nothing will be impossible with God." ³⁸And Mary said, "Behold, the [a]bondslave of the Lord; may it be done to me according to your word." And the angel departed from her.

[a]**1:38** I.e. female slave

Mary Visits Elizabeth

39 Now at this time Mary arose and went in a hurry to the hill country, to a city of Judah, ⁴⁰and entered the house of Zacharias and greeted Elizabeth. ⁴¹When Elizabeth heard Mary's greeting, the baby leaped in her womb; and Elizabeth was filled with the Holy Spirit. ⁴²And she cried out with a loud voice and said, "Blessed *are* you among women, and blessed *is* the fruit of your womb! ⁴³And how has it *happened* to me, that the mother of my Lord would come to me? ⁴⁴For behold, when the sound of your greeting reached my ears, the baby leaped in my womb for joy. ⁴⁵And blessed *is* she who believed that there would be a fulfillment of what had been spoken to her by the Lord."

The Magnificat

46 And Mary said:

"My soul exalts the Lord,
⁴⁷And my spirit has rejoiced in
    God my Savior.
⁴⁸"For He has had regard for the
    humble state of His bondslave;
For behold, from this time on
    all generations will count me
    blessed.
⁴⁹"For the Mighty One has done
    great things for me;
And holy is His name.
⁵⁰"AND HIS MERCY IS
    UPON GENERATION
    AFTER GENERATION

TOWARD THOSE WHO FEAR
    HIM.
⁵¹"He has done mighty deeds with
    His arm;
He has scattered *those who were*
    proud in the thoughts of their
    heart.
⁵²"He has brought down rulers
    from *their* thrones,
And has exalted those who were
    humble.
⁵³"HE HAS FILLED THE HUNGRY
    WITH GOOD THINGS;
And sent away the rich
    empty-handed.
⁵⁴"He has given help to Israel His
    servant,
In remembrance of His mercy,
⁵⁵As He spoke to our fathers,
To Abraham and his descendants
    forever."

56 And Mary stayed with her about three months, and *then* returned to her home.

John Is Born

57 Now the time had come for Elizabeth to give birth, and she gave birth to a son. ⁵⁸Her neighbors and her relatives heard that the Lord had displayed His great mercy toward her; and they were rejoicing with her.

59 And it happened that on the eighth day they came to circumcise the child, and they were going to call him Zacharias, after his father. ⁶⁰But his mother answered and said, "No indeed; but he shall be called John." ⁶¹And they said to her, "There is no one among your relatives who is called by that name." ⁶²And they made signs to his father, as to what he wanted him called. ⁶³And he asked for a tablet and wrote as follows, "His name is John." And they were all astonished. ⁶⁴And at once his mouth was opened and his tongue *loosed*, and he *began* to speak in praise of God. ⁶⁵Fear came on all those living around them; and all these matters were being talked about in all the hill country of Judea. ⁶⁶All who heard them kept them in mind, saying, "What then will this child *turn out to* be?" For the hand of the Lord was certainly with him.

Zacharias's Prophecy

67 And his father Zacharias was filled with the Holy Spirit, and prophesied, saying:
⁶⁸"Blessed *be* the Lord God of Israel,
For He has visited us and accomplished redemption for His people,
⁶⁹And has raised up a horn of salvation for us
In the house of David His servant—
⁷⁰As He spoke by the mouth of His holy prophets from of old—
⁷¹Salvation FROM OUR ENEMIES, And FROM THE HAND OF ALL WHO HATE US;
⁷²To show mercy toward our fathers,
And to remember His holy covenant,
⁷³The oath which He swore to Abraham our father,
⁷⁴To grant us that we, being rescued from the hand of our enemies,
Might serve Him without fear,
⁷⁵In holiness and righteousness before Him all our days.
⁷⁶"And you, child, will be called the prophet of the Most High;
For you will go on BEFORE THE LORD TO PREPARE HIS WAYS;
⁷⁷To give to His people *the* knowledge of salvation
By the forgiveness of their sins,
⁷⁸Because of the tender mercy of our God,
With which the Sunrise from on high will visit us,
⁷⁹TO SHINE UPON THOSE WHO SIT IN DARKNESS AND THE SHADOW OF DEATH,
To guide our feet into the way of peace."
80 And the child continued to grow and to become strong in spirit, and he lived in the deserts until the day of his public appearance to Israel.

Jesus' Birth in Bethlehem

2 Now in those days a decree went out from Caesar Augustus, that a census be taken of all ªthe inhabited earth. ²This was the

ª**2:1** I.e. the Roman empire

first census taken while [a]Quirinius was governor of Syria. [3]And everyone was on his way to register for the census, each to his own city. [4]Joseph also went up from Galilee, from the city of Nazareth, to Judea, to the city of David which is called Bethlehem, because he was of the house and family of David, [5]in order to register along with Mary, who was engaged to him, and was with child. [6]While they were there, the days were completed for her to give birth. [7]And she gave birth to her firstborn son; and she wrapped Him in cloths, and laid Him in a manger, because there was no room for them in the inn.

[8] In the same region there were *some* shepherds staying out in the fields and keeping watch over their flock by night. [9]And an angel of the Lord suddenly stood before them, and the glory of the Lord shone around them; and they were terribly frightened. [10]But the angel said to them, "Do not be afraid; for behold, I bring you good news of great joy which will be for all the people; [11]for today in the city of David there has been born for you a Savior, who is [b]Christ the Lord. [12]This *will be* a sign for you: you will find a baby wrapped in cloths and lying in a manger." [13]And suddenly there appeared with the angel a multitude of the heavenly host praising God and saying,

[14]"Glory to God in the highest,
And on earth peace among men
    [c]with whom He is pleased."
[15] When the angels had gone away from them into heaven, the shepherds *began* saying to one another, "Let us go straight to Bethlehem then, and see this thing that has happened which the Lord has made known to us." [16]So they came in a hurry and found their way to Mary and Joseph, and the baby as He lay in the manger. [17]When they had seen this, they made known the statement which had been told them about this Child. [18]And all who heard it wondered at the things which were told them by the shepherds. [19]But Mary treasured all these things, pondering them in her heart. [20]The shepherds went back, glorifying and praising God for all that they had heard and seen, just as had been told them.

Jesus Presented at the Temple

[21] And when eight days had passed, before His circumcision, His name was *then* called Jesus, the name given by the angel before He was conceived in the womb.

[22] And when the days for their purification according to the law of Moses were completed, they brought Him up to Jerusalem to present Him to the Lord [23](as it is written in the Law of the Lord,

[a]2:2 Gr Kyrenios; [b]2:11 I.e. Messiah; c2:14 Lit *of good pleasure*; or *of good will*

"EVERY *firstborn* MALE THAT OPENS THE WOMB SHALL BE CALLED HOLY TO THE LORD"), [24]and to offer a sacrifice according to what was said in the Law of the Lord, "A PAIR OF TURTLEDOVES OR TWO YOUNG PIGEONS."

25 And there was a man in Jerusalem whose name was Simeon; and this man was righteous and devout, looking for the consolation of Israel; and the Holy Spirit was upon him. [26]And it had been revealed to him by the Holy Spirit that he would not see death before he had seen the Lord's Christ. [27]And he came in the Spirit into the temple; and when the parents brought in the child Jesus, to carry out for Him the custom of the Law, [28]then he took Him into his arms, and blessed God, and said,
[29]"Now Lord, You are releasing Your bond-servant to depart in peace,
According to Your word;
[30]For my eyes have seen Your salvation,
[31]Which You have prepared in the presence of all peoples,
[32]A LIGHT OF REVELATION TO THE GENTILES,
And the glory of Your people Israel."
33 And His father and mother were amazed at the things which were being said about Him. [34]And Simeon blessed them and said to Mary His mother, "Behold, this *Child* is appointed for the fall and rise of many in Israel, and for a sign to be opposed— [35]and a sword will pierce even your own soul—to the end that thoughts from many hearts may be revealed."

36 And there was a prophetess, Anna the daughter of Phanuel, of the tribe of Asher. She was advanced in years and had lived with *her* husband seven years after her marriage, [37]and then as a widow to the age of eighty-four. She never left the temple, serving night and day with fastings and prayers. [38]At that very moment she came up and *began* giving thanks to God, and continued to speak of Him to all those who were looking for the redemption of Jerusalem.

Return to Nazareth

39 When they had performed everything according to the Law of the Lord, they returned to Galilee, to their own city of Nazareth. [40]The Child continued to grow and become strong, increasing in wisdom; and the grace of God was upon Him.

Visit to Jerusalem

41 Now His parents went to Jerusalem every year at the Feast of the Passover. [42]And when He became twelve, they went up *there* according to the custom of the Feast;

⁴³and as they were returning, after spending the full number of days, the boy Jesus stayed behind in Jerusalem. But His parents were unaware of it, ⁴⁴but supposed Him to be in the caravan, and went a day's journey; and they *began* looking for Him among their relatives and acquaintances. ⁴⁵When they did not find Him, they returned to Jerusalem looking for Him. ⁴⁶Then, after three days they found Him in the temple, sitting in the midst of the teachers, both listening to them and asking them questions. ⁴⁷And all who heard Him were amazed at His understanding and His answers. ⁴⁸When they saw Him, they were astonished; and His mother said to Him, "Son, why have You treated us this way? Behold, Your father and I have been anxiously looking for You." ⁴⁹And He said to them, "Why is it that you were looking for Me? Did you not know that I had to be in My Father's *house?*" ⁵⁰But they did not understand the statement which He had made to them. ⁵¹And He went down with them and came to Nazareth, and He continued in subjection to them; and His mother treasured all *these* things in her heart.

⁵² And Jesus kept increasing in wisdom and stature, and in favor with God and men.

John the Baptist Preaches

3 Now in the fifteenth year of the reign of Tiberius Caesar, when Pontius Pilate was governor of Judea, and Herod was tetrarch of Galilee, and his brother Philip was tetrarch of the region of Ituraea and Trachonitis, and Lysanias was tetrarch of Abilene, ²in the high priesthood of Annas and Caiaphas, the word of God came to John, the son of Zacharias, in the wilderness. ³And he came into all the district around the Jordan, preaching a baptism of repentance for the forgiveness of sins; ⁴as it is written in the book of the words of Isaiah the prophet,

"THE VOICE OF ONE CRYING IN
   THE WILDERNESS,
'MAKE READY THE WAY OF THE
   LORD,
MAKE HIS PATHS STRAIGHT.
⁵'EVERY RAVINE WILL BE
   FILLED,
AND EVERY MOUNTAIN AND
   HILL WILL BE BROUGHT
   LOW;
THE CROOKED WILL BECOME
   STRAIGHT,
AND THE ROUGH ROADS
   SMOOTH;
⁶AND ALL FLESH WILL SEE THE
   SALVATION OF GOD.'"

7 So he *began* saying to the crowds who were going out to be baptized by him, "You brood of vipers, who warned you to flee from the wrath to come? ⁸Therefore bear fruits in

keeping with repentance, and do not begin to say to yourselves, 'We have Abraham for our father,' for I say to you that from these stones God is able to raise up children to Abraham. [9]Indeed the axe is already laid at the root of the trees; so every tree that does not bear good fruit is cut down and thrown into the fire."

10 And the crowds were questioning him, saying, "Then what shall we do?" [11]And he would answer and say to them, "The man who has two tunics is to share with him who has none; and he who has food is to do likewise." [12]And *some* tax collectors also came to be baptized, and they said to him, "Teacher, what shall we do?" [13]And he said to them, "Collect no more than what you have been ordered to." [14]*Some* soldiers were questioning him, saying, "And *what about* us, what shall we do?" And he said to them, "Do not take money from anyone by force, or accuse *anyone* falsely, and be content with your wages."

15 Now while the people were in a state of expectation and all were wondering in their hearts about John, as to whether he was the Christ, [16]John answered and said to them all, "As for me, I baptize you with water; but One is coming who is mightier than I, and I am not fit to untie the thong of His sandals; He will baptize you with the Holy Spirit and fire. [17]His winnowing fork is in His hand to thoroughly clear His threshing floor, and to gather the wheat into His barn; but He will burn up the chaff with unquenchable fire."

18 So with many other exhortations he preached the gospel to the people. [19]But when Herod the tetrarch was reprimanded by him because of Herodias, his brother's wife, and because of all the wicked things which Herod had done, [20]Herod also added this to them all: he locked John up in prison.

Jesus Is Baptized

21 Now when all the people were baptized, Jesus was also baptized, and while He was praying, heaven was opened, [22]and the Holy Spirit descended upon Him in bodily form like a dove, and a voice came out of heaven, "You are My beloved Son, in You I am well-pleased."

Genealogy of Jesus

23 When He began His ministry, Jesus Himself was about thirty years of age, being, as was supposed, the son of Joseph, the son of Eli, [24]the son of Matthat, the son of Levi, the son of Melchi, the son of Jannai, the son of Joseph, [25]the son of Mattathias, the son of

Amos, the son of Nahum, the son of Hesli, the son of Naggai, ²⁶the son of Maath, the son of Mattathias, the son of Semein, the son of Josech, the son of Joda, ²⁷the son of Joanan, the son of Rhesa, the son of Zerubbabel, the son of Shealtiel, the son of Neri, ²⁸the son of Melchi, the son of Addi, the son of Cosam, the son of Elmadam, the son of Er, ²⁹the son of Joshua, the son of Eliezer, the son of Jorim, the son of Matthat, the son of Levi, ³⁰the son of Simeon, the son of Judah, the son of Joseph, the son of Jonam, the son of Eliakim, ³¹the son of Melea, the son of Menna, the son of Mattatha, the son of Nathan, the son of David, ³²the son of Jesse, the son of Obed, the son of Boaz, the son of Salmon, the son of Nahshon, ³³the son of Amminadab, the son of Admin, the son of Ram, the son of Hezron, the son of Perez, the son of Judah, ³⁴the son of Jacob, the son of Isaac, the son of Abraham, the son of Terah, the son of Nahor, ³⁵the son of Serug, the son of Reu, the son of Peleg, the son of Heber, the son of Shelah, ³⁶the son of Cainan, the son of Arphaxad, the son of Shem, the son of Noah, the son of Lamech, ³⁷the son of Methuselah, the son of Enoch, the son of Jared, the son of Mahalaleel, the son of Cainan, ³⁸the son of Enosh, the son of Seth, the son of Adam, the son of God.

The Temptation of Jesus

4 Jesus, full of the Holy Spirit, returned from the Jordan and was led around by the Spirit in the wilderness ²for forty days, being tempted by the devil. And He ate nothing during those days, and when they had ended, He became hungry. ³And the devil said to Him, "If You are the Son of God, tell this stone to become bread." ⁴And Jesus answered him, "It is written, 'MAN SHALL NOT LIVE ON BREAD ALONE.' "

5 And he led Him up and showed Him all the kingdoms of the world in a moment of time. ⁶And the devil said to Him, "I will give You all this domain and its glory; for it has been handed over to me, and I give it to whomever I wish. ⁷Therefore if You worship before me, it shall all be Yours." ⁸Jesus answered him, "It is written, 'YOU SHALL WORSHIP THE LORD YOUR GOD AND SERVE HIM ONLY.' "

9 And he led Him to Jerusalem and had Him stand on the pinnacle of the temple, and said to Him, "If You are the Son of God, throw Yourself down from here; ¹⁰for it is written,

'HE WILL COMMAND HIS AN-
    GELS CONCERNING YOU TO
    GUARD YOU,'
¹¹and,
'ON *their* HANDS THEY WILL

BEAR YOU UP,
SO THAT YOU WILL NOT STRIKE
YOUR FOOT AGAINST A
STONE.' "
¹²And Jesus answered and said to him, "It is said, 'YOU SHALL NOT PUT THE LORD YOUR GOD TO THE TEST.' "

13 When the devil had finished every temptation, he left Him until an opportune time.

Jesus' Public Ministry
14 And Jesus returned to Galilee in the power of the Spirit, and news about Him spread through all the surrounding district. ¹⁵And He *began* teaching in their synagogues and was praised by all.

16 And He came to Nazareth, where He had been brought up; and as was His custom, He entered the synagogue on the Sabbath, and stood up to read. ¹⁷And the book of the prophet Isaiah was handed to Him. And He opened the book and found the place where it was written,
¹⁸"THE SPIRIT OF THE LORD IS UPON ME,
BECAUSE HE ANOINTED ME TO PREACH THE GOSPEL TO THE POOR.
HE HAS SENT ME TO PROCLAIM RELEASE TO THE CAPTIVES,
AND RECOVERY OF SIGHT TO THE BLIND,
TO SET FREE THOSE WHO ARE OPPRESSED,
¹⁹TO PROCLAIM THE FAVORABLE YEAR OF THE LORD."
²⁰And He closed the book, gave it back to the attendant and sat down; and the eyes of all in the synagogue were fixed on Him. ²¹And He began to say to them, "Today this Scripture has been fulfilled in your hearing." ²²And all were speaking well of Him, and wondering at the gracious words which were falling from His lips; and they were saying, "Is this not Joseph's son?" ²³And He said to them, "No doubt you will quote this proverb to Me, 'Physician, heal yourself! Whatever we heard was done at Capernaum, do here in your hometown as well.' " ²⁴And He said, "Truly I say to you, no prophet is welcome in his hometown. ²⁵But I say to you in truth, there were many widows in Israel in the days of Elijah, when the sky was shut up for three years and six months, when a great famine came over all the land; ²⁶and yet Elijah was sent to none of them, but only to Zarephath, *in the land* of Sidon, to a woman who was a widow. ²⁷And there were many lepers in Israel in the time of Elisha the prophet; and none of them was cleansed, but only Naaman the Syrian." ²⁸And all *the people* in the synagogue were filled with rage as they heard these things; ²⁹and they

got up and drove Him out of the city, and led Him to the brow of the hill on which their city had been built, in order to throw Him down the cliff. ³⁰But passing through their midst, He went His way.

31 And He came down to Capernaum, a city of Galilee, and He was teaching them on the Sabbath; ³²and they were amazed at His teaching, for His message was with authority. ³³In the synagogue there was a man possessed by the spirit of an unclean demon, and he cried out with a loud voice, ³⁴"Let us alone! What business do we have with each other, Jesus of Nazareth? Have You come to destroy us? I know who You are—the Holy One of God!" ³⁵But Jesus rebuked him, saying, "Be quiet and come out of him!" And when the demon had thrown him down in the midst *of the people,* he came out of him without doing him any harm. ³⁶And amazement came upon them all, and they *began* talking with one another saying, "What is this message? For with authority and power He commands the unclean spirits and they come out." ³⁷And the report about Him was spreading into every locality in the surrounding district.

Many Are Healed

38 Then He got up and *left* the synagogue, and entered Simon's home. Now Simon's mother-in-law was suffering from a high fever, and they asked Him to help her. ³⁹And standing over her, He rebuked the fever, and it left her; and she immediately got up and waited on them.

40 While the sun was setting, all those who had any *who were* sick with various diseases brought them to Him; and laying His hands on each one of them, He was healing them. ⁴¹Demons also were coming out of many, shouting, "You are the Son of God!" But rebuking them, He would not allow them to speak, because they knew Him to be the Christ.

42 When day came, Jesus left and went to a secluded place; and the crowds were searching for Him, and came to Him and tried to keep Him from going away from them. ⁴³But He said to them, "I must preach the kingdom of God to the other cities also, for I was sent for this purpose."

44 So He kept on preaching in the synagogues of ªJudea.

The First Disciples

5 Now it happened that while the crowd was pressing around Him and listening to the word of God, He was standing by the lake of Gennesaret; ²and He saw two

ª**4:44** I.e. the country of the Jews (including Galilee)

boats lying at the edge of the lake; but the fishermen had gotten out of them and were washing their nets. ³And He got into one of the boats, which was Simon's, and asked him to put out a little way from the land. And He sat down and *began* teaching the people from the boat. ⁴When He had finished speaking, He said to Simon, "Put out into the deep water and let down your nets for a catch." ⁵Simon answered and said, "Master, we worked hard all night and caught nothing, but I will do as You say *and* let down the nets." ⁶When they had done this, they enclosed a great quantity of fish, and their nets *began* to break; ⁷so they signaled to their partners in the other boat for them to come and help them. And they came and filled both of the boats, so that they began to sink. ⁸But when Simon Peter saw *that,* he fell down at Jesus' feet, saying, "Go away from me Lord, for I am a sinful man!" ⁹For amazement had seized him and all his companions because of the catch of fish which they had taken; ¹⁰and so also *were* James and John, sons of Zebedee, who were partners with Simon. And Jesus said to Simon, "Do not fear, from now on you will be catching men." ¹¹When they had brought their boats to land, they left everything and followed Him.

The Leper and the Paralytic

12 While He was in one of the cities, behold, *there was* a man covered with leprosy; and when he saw Jesus, he fell on his face and implored Him, saying, "Lord, if You are willing, You can make me clean." ¹³And He stretched out His hand and touched him, saying, "I am willing; be cleansed." And immediately the leprosy left him. ¹⁴And He ordered him to tell no one, "But go and show yourself to the priest and make an offering for your cleansing, just as Moses commanded, as a testimony to them." ¹⁵But the news about Him was spreading even farther, and large crowds were gathering to hear *Him* and to be healed of their sicknesses. ¹⁶But Jesus Himself would *often* slip away to the wilderness and pray.

17 One day He was teaching; and there were *some* Pharisees and teachers of the law sitting *there,* who had come from every village of Galilee and Judea and *from* Jerusalem; and the power of the Lord was *present* for Him to perform healing. ¹⁸And *some* men *were* carrying on a bed a man who was paralyzed; and they were trying to bring him in and to set him down in front of Him. ¹⁹But not finding any *way* to bring him in because of the crowd, they went up on the roof and let him down

through the tiles with his stretcher, into the middle of the crowd, in front of Jesus. ²⁰Seeing their faith, He said, "Friend, your sins are forgiven you." ²¹The scribes and the Pharisees began to reason, saying, "Who is this *man* who speaks blasphemies? Who can forgive sins, but God alone?" ²²But Jesus, aware of their reasonings, answered and said to them, "Why are you reasoning in your hearts? ²³Which is easier, to say, 'Your sins have been forgiven you,' or to say, 'Get up and walk'? ²⁴But, so that you may know that the Son of Man has authority on earth to forgive sins,"—He said to the paralytic—"I say to you, get up, and pick up your stretcher and go home." ²⁵Immediately he got up before them, and picked up what he had been lying on, and went home glorifying God. ²⁶They were all struck with astonishment and *began* glorifying God; and they were filled with fear, saying, "We have seen remarkable things today."

Call of Levi (Matthew)

27 After that He went out and noticed a tax collector named Levi sitting in the tax booth, and He said to him, "Follow Me." ²⁸And he left everything behind, and got up and *began* to follow Him.

29 And Levi gave a big reception for Him in his house; and there was a great crowd of tax collectors and other *people* who were reclining *at the table* with them. ³⁰The Pharisees and their scribes *began* grumbling at His disciples, saying, "Why do you eat and drink with the tax collectors and sinners?" ³¹And Jesus answered and said to them, "*It is* not those who are well who need a physician, but those who are sick. ³²I have not come to call the righteous but sinners to repentance."

33 And they said to Him, "The disciples of John often fast and offer prayers, the *disciples* of the Pharisees also do the same, but Yours eat and drink." ³⁴And Jesus said to them, "You cannot make the attendants of the bridegroom fast while the bridegroom is with them, can you? ³⁵But *the* days will come; and when the bridegroom is taken away from them, then they will fast in those days." ³⁶And He was also telling them a parable: "No one tears a piece of cloth from a new garment and puts it on an old garment; otherwise he will both tear the new, and the piece from the new will not match the old. ³⁷And no one puts new wine into old wineskins; otherwise the new wine will burst the skins and it will be spilled out, and the skins will be ruined. ³⁸But new wine must be put into fresh wineskins. ³⁹And no one, after drinking old

wine wishes for new; for he says, 'The old is good *enough.*' "

Jesus Is Lord of the Sabbath

6 Now it happened that He was passing through *some* grainfields on a Sabbath; and His disciples were picking the heads of grain, rubbing them in their hands, and eating *the grain.* [2]But some of the Pharisees said, "Why do you do what is not lawful on the Sabbath?" [3]And Jesus answering them said, "Have you not even read what David did when he was hungry, he and those who were with him, [4]how he entered the house of God, and took and ate the ᵃconsecrated bread which is not lawful for any to eat except the priests alone, and gave it to his companions?" [5]And He was saying to them, "The Son of Man is Lord of the Sabbath."

6 On another Sabbath He entered the synagogue and was teaching; and there was a man there whose right hand was withered. [7]The scribes and the Pharisees were watching Him closely *to see* if He healed on the Sabbath, so that they might find *reason* to accuse Him. [8]But He knew what they were thinking, and He said to the man with the withered hand, "Get up and come forward!" And he got up and came forward. [9]And Jesus said to them, "I ask you, is it lawful to do good or to do harm on the Sabbath, to save a life or to destroy it?" [10]After looking around at them all, He said to him, "Stretch out your hand!" And he did *so;* and his hand was restored. [11]But they themselves were filled with rage, and discussed together what they might do to Jesus.

Choosing the Twelve

12 It was at this time that He went off to the mountain to pray, and He spent the whole night in prayer to God. [13]And when day came, He called His disciples to Him and chose twelve of them, whom He also named as apostles: [14]Simon, whom He also named Peter, and Andrew his brother; and James and John; and Philip and Bartholomew; [15]and Matthew and Thomas; James *the son* of Alphaeus, and Simon who was called the Zealot; [16]Judas *the son* of James, and Judas Iscariot, who became a traitor.

17 Jesus came down with them and stood on a level place; and *there was* a large crowd of His disciples, and a great throng of people from all Judea and Jerusalem and the coastal region of Tyre and Sidon, [18]who had come to hear Him and to be healed of their diseases; and those who were troubled with unclean spirits were being cured. [19]And all the people were trying to

ᵃ**6:4** Or *showbread;* lit *loaves of presentation*

touch Him, for power was coming from Him and healing *them* all.

The Beatitudes

20 And turning His gaze toward His disciples, He *began* to say, "Blessed *are* you *who are* poor, for yours is the kingdom of God. ²¹Blessed *are* you who hunger now, for you shall be satisfied. Blessed *are* you who weep now, for you shall laugh. ²²Blessed are you when men hate you, and ostracize you, and insult you, and scorn your name as evil, for the sake of the Son of Man. ²³Be glad in that day and leap *for joy,* for behold, your reward is great in heaven. For in the same way their fathers used to treat the prophets. ²⁴But woe to you who are rich, for you are receiving your comfort in full. ²⁵Woe to you who are well-fed now, for you shall be hungry. Woe *to you* who laugh now, for you shall mourn and weep. ²⁶Woe *to you* when all men speak well of you, for their fathers used to treat the false prophets in the same way.

²⁷ "But I say to you who hear, love your enemies, do good to those who hate you, ²⁸bless those who curse you, pray for those who mistreat you. ²⁹Whoever hits you on the cheek, offer him the other also; and whoever takes away your coat, do not withhold your shirt from him either. ³⁰Give to everyone who asks of you, and whoever takes away what is yours, do not demand it back. ³¹Treat others the same way you want them to treat you. ³²If you love those who love you, what credit is *that* to you? For even sinners love those who love them. ³³If you do good to those who do good to you, what credit is *that* to you? For even sinners do the same. ³⁴If you lend to those from whom you expect to receive, what credit is *that* to you? Even sinners lend to sinners in order to receive back the same *amount.* ³⁵But love your enemies, and do good, and lend, expecting nothing in return; and your reward will be great, and you will be sons of the Most High; for He Himself is kind to ungrateful and evil *men.* ³⁶Be merciful, just as your Father is merciful.

³⁷ "Do not judge, and you will not be judged; and do not condemn, and you will not be condemned; pardon, and you will be pardoned. ³⁸Give, and it will be given to you. They will pour into your lap a good measure—pressed down, shaken together, *and* running over. For by your standard of measure it will be measured to you in return."

39 And He also spoke a parable to them: "A blind man cannot guide a blind man, can he? Will they not both fall into a pit? ⁴⁰A pupil is not above his teacher; but everyone, after he has been fully trained, will be like his teacher. ⁴¹Why do you look at the speck that is in your brother's eye, but do not notice the log that is in your own eye? ⁴²Or how can you say to your brother, 'Brother, let me take out the speck that is in your eye,' when you yourself do not see the log that is in your own eye? You hypocrite, first take the log out of your own eye, and then you will see clearly to take out the speck that is in your brother's eye. ⁴³For there is no good tree which produces bad fruit, nor, on the other hand, a bad tree which produces good fruit. ⁴⁴For each tree is known by its own fruit. For men do not gather figs from thorns, nor do they pick grapes from a briar bush. ⁴⁵The good man out of the good treasure of his heart brings forth what is good; and the evil *man* out of the evil *treasure* brings forth what is evil; for his mouth speaks from that which fills his heart.

Builders and Foundations

46 "Why do you call Me, 'Lord, Lord,' and do not do what I say? ⁴⁷Everyone who comes to Me and hears My words and acts on them, I will show you whom he is like: ⁴⁸he is like a man building a house, who dug deep and laid a foundation on the rock; and when a flood occurred, the torrent burst against that house and could not shake it, because it had been well built. ⁴⁹But the one who has heard and has not acted *accordingly,* is like a man who built a house on the ground without any foundation; and the torrent burst against it and immediately it collapsed, and the ruin of that house was great."

Jesus Heals a Centurion's Servant

7 When He had completed all His discourse in the hearing of the people, He went to Capernaum.

2 And a centurion's slave, who was highly regarded by him, was sick and about to die. ³When he heard about Jesus, he sent some Jewish elders asking Him to come and save the life of his slave. ⁴When they came to Jesus, they earnestly implored Him, saying, "He is worthy for You to grant this to him; ⁵for he loves our nation and it was he who built us our synagogue." ⁶Now Jesus *started* on His way with them; and when He was not far from the house, the centurion sent friends, saying to Him, "Lord, do not trouble Yourself further, for I am not worthy for You to come under my roof; ⁷for this reason I did not even consider myself worthy to come to You, but *just* say the word, and my servant will be healed. ⁸For I also am a man placed under authority,

with soldiers under me; and I say to this one, 'Go!' and he goes, and to another, 'Come!' and he comes, and to my slave, 'Do this!' and he does it." [9]Now when Jesus heard this, He marveled at him, and turned and said to the crowd that was following Him, "I say to you, not even in Israel have I found such great faith." [10]When those who had been sent returned to the house, they found the slave in good health.

[11] Soon afterwards He went to a city called Nain; and His disciples were going along with Him, accompanied by a large crowd. [12]Now as He approached the gate of the city, a dead man was being carried out, the only son of his mother, and she was a widow; and a sizeable crowd from the city was with her. [13]When the Lord saw her, He felt compassion for her, and said to her, "Do not weep." [14]And He came up and touched the coffin; and the bearers came to a halt. And He said, "Young man, I say to you, arise!" [15]The dead man sat up and began to speak. And *Jesus* gave him back to his mother. [16]Fear gripped them all, and they *began* glorifying God, saying, "A great prophet has arisen among us!" and, "God has visited His people!" [17]This report concerning Him went out all over Judea and in all the surrounding district.

A Deputation from John

[18] The disciples of John reported to him about all these things. [19]Summoning two of his disciples, John sent them to the Lord, saying, "Are You the Expected One, or do we look for someone else?" [20]When the men came to Him, they said, "John the Baptist has sent us to You, to ask, 'Are You the Expected One, or do we look for someone else?' " [21]At that very time He cured many *people* of diseases and afflictions and evil spirits; and He gave sight to many *who were* blind. [22]And He answered and said to them, "Go and report to John what you have seen and heard: *the* BLIND RECEIVE SIGHT, *the* lame walk, *the* lepers are cleansed, and *the* deaf hear, *the* dead are raised up, *the* POOR HAVE THE GOSPEL PREACHED TO THEM. [23]Blessed is he who does not take offense at Me."

[24] When the messengers of John had left, He began to speak to the crowds about John, "What did you go out into the wilderness to see? A reed shaken by the wind? [25]But what did you go out to see? A man dressed in soft clothing? Those who are splendidly clothed and live in luxury are *found* in royal palaces! [26]But what did you go out to see? A prophet? Yes, I say to you, and one who is more than a prophet. [27]This is the one about

whom it is written,

'BEHOLD, I SEND MY MESSEN-
   GER AHEAD OF YOU,
WHO WILL PREPARE YOUR
   WAY BEFORE YOU.'

[28]I say to you, among those born of women there is no one greater than John; yet he who is least in the kingdom of God is greater than he." [29]When all the people and the tax collectors heard *this,* they acknowledged God's justice, having been baptized with the baptism of John. [30]But the Pharisees and the [a]lawyers rejected God's purpose for themselves, not having been baptized by John.

31 "To what then shall I compare the men of this generation, and what are they like? [32]They are like children who sit in the market place and call to one another, and they say, 'We played the flute for you, and you did not dance; we sang a dirge, and you did not weep.' [33]For John the Baptist has come eating no bread and drinking no wine, and you say, 'He has a demon!' [34]The Son of Man has come eating and drinking, and you say, 'Behold, a gluttonous man and a drunkard, a friend of tax collectors and sinners!' [35]Yet wisdom is vindicated by all her children."

36 Now one of the Pharisees was requesting Him to dine with him, and He entered the Pharisee's house and reclined *at the table.* [37]And there was a woman in the city who was a sinner; and when she learned that He was reclining *at the table* in the Pharisee's house, she brought an alabaster vial of perfume, [38]and standing behind *Him* at His feet, weeping, she began to wet His feet with her tears, and kept wiping them with the hair of her head, and kissing His feet and anointing them with the perfume. [39]Now when the Pharisee who had invited Him saw this, he said to himself, "If this man were a prophet He would know who and what sort of person this woman is who is touching Him, that she is a sinner."

Parable of Two Debtors

[40]And Jesus answered him, "Simon, I have something to say to you." And he replied, "Say it, Teacher." [41]"A moneylender had two debtors: one owed five hundred [b]denarii, and the other fifty. [42]When they were unable to repay, he graciously forgave them both. So which of them will love him more?" [43]Simon answered and said, "I suppose the one whom he forgave more." And He said to him, "You have judged correctly." [44]Turning toward the woman, He said to Simon, "Do you see this woman? I entered your house; you gave Me no water for My feet, but she has wet My feet with her tears

[a]**7:30** I.e. experts in the Mosaic Law; [b]**7:41** The denarius was equivalent to a day's wages

and wiped them with her hair. ⁴⁵You gave Me no kiss; but she, since the time I came in, has not ceased to kiss My feet. ⁴⁶You did not anoint My head with oil, but she anointed My feet with perfume. ⁴⁷For this reason I say to you, her sins, which are many, have been forgiven, for she loved much; but he who is forgiven little, loves little." ⁴⁸Then He said to her, "Your sins have been forgiven." ⁴⁹Those who were reclining *at the table* with Him began to say to themselves, "Who is this *man* who even forgives sins?" ⁵⁰And He said to the woman, "Your faith has saved you; go in peace."

Ministering Women

8 Soon afterwards, He *began* going around from one city and village to another, proclaiming and preaching the kingdom of God. The twelve were with Him, ²and *also* some women who had been healed of evil spirits and sicknesses: Mary who was called Magdalene, from whom seven demons had gone out, ³and Joanna the wife of Chuza, Herod's steward, and Susanna, and many others who were contributing to their support out of their private means.

Parable of the Sower

4 When a large crowd was coming together, and those from the various cities were journeying to Him, He spoke by way of a parable: ⁵"The sower went out to sow his seed; and as he sowed, some fell beside the road, and it was trampled under foot and the birds of the air ate it up. ⁶Other *seed* fell on rocky *soil,* and as soon as it grew up, it withered away, because it had no moisture. ⁷Other *seed* fell among the thorns; and the thorns grew up with it and choked it out. ⁸Other *seed* fell into the good soil, and grew up, and produced a crop a hundred times as great." As He said these things, He would call out, "He who has ears to hear, let him hear."

9 His disciples *began* questioning Him as to what this parable meant. ¹⁰And He said, "To you it has been granted to know the mysteries of the kingdom of God, but to the rest *it is* in parables, so that SEEING THEY MAY NOT SEE, AND HEARING THEY MAY NOT UNDERSTAND.

11 "Now the parable is this: the seed is the word of God. ¹²Those beside the road are those who have heard; then the devil comes and takes away the word from their heart, so that they will not believe and be saved. ¹³Those on the rocky *soil are* those who, when they hear, receive the word with joy; and these have no *firm* root;

they believe for a while, and in time of temptation fall away. [14]The *seed* which fell among the thorns, these are the ones who have heard, and as they go on their way they are choked with worries and riches and pleasures of *this* life, and bring no fruit to maturity. [15]But the *seed* in the good soil, these are the ones who have heard the word in an honest and good heart, and hold it fast, and bear fruit with perseverance.

Parable of the Lamp

[16] "Now no one after lighting a lamp covers it over with a container, or puts it under a bed; but he puts it on a lampstand, so that those who come in may see the light. [17]For nothing is hidden that will not become evident, nor *anything* secret that will not be known and come to light. [18]So take care how you listen; for whoever has, to him *more* shall be given; and whoever does not have, even what he thinks he has shall be taken away from him."

[19] And His mother and brothers came to Him, and they were unable to get to Him because of the crowd. [20]And it was reported to Him, "Your mother and Your brothers are standing outside, wishing to see You." [21]But He answered and said to them, "My mother and My brothers are these who hear the word of God and do it."

Jesus Stills the Sea

[22] Now on one of *those* days Jesus and His disciples got into a boat, and He said to them, "Let us go over to the other side of the lake." So they launched out. [23]But as they were sailing along He fell asleep; and a fierce gale of wind descended on the lake, and they *began* to be swamped and to be in danger. [24]They came to Jesus and woke Him up, saying, "Master, Master, we are perishing!" And He got up and rebuked the wind and the surging waves, and they stopped, and it became calm. [25]And He said to them, "Where is your faith?" They were fearful and amazed, saying to one another, "Who then is this, that He commands even the winds and the water, and they obey Him?"

The Demoniac Cured

[26] Then they sailed to the country of the Gerasenes, which is opposite Galilee. [27]And when He came out onto the land, He was met by a man from the city who was possessed with demons; and who had not put on any clothing for a long time, and was not living in a house, but in the tombs. [28]Seeing Jesus, he cried out and fell before Him, and said in a loud voice, "What business do we have with each other, Jesus, Son of the

Most High God? I beg You, do not torment me." ²⁹For He had commanded the unclean spirit to come out of the man. For it had seized him many times; and he was bound with chains and shackles and kept under guard, and *yet* he would break his bonds and be driven by the demon into the desert. ³⁰And Jesus asked him, "What is your name?" And he said, "Legion"; for many demons had entered him. ³¹They were imploring Him not to command them to go away into the abyss.

32 Now there was a herd of many swine feeding there on the mountain; and *the demons* implored Him to permit them to enter the swine. And He gave them permission. ³³And the demons came out of the man and entered the swine; and the herd rushed down the steep bank into the lake and was drowned.

34 When the herdsmen saw what had happened, they ran away and reported it in the city and *out* in the country. ³⁵*The people* went out to see what had happened; and they came to Jesus, and found the man from whom the demons had gone out, sitting down at the feet of Jesus, clothed and in his right mind; and they became frightened. ³⁶Those who had seen it reported to them how the man

who was demon-possessed had been made well. ³⁷And all the people of the country of the Gerasenes and the surrounding district asked Him to leave them, for they were gripped with great fear; and He got into a boat and returned. ³⁸But the man from whom the demons had gone out was begging Him that he might accompany Him; but He sent him away, saying, ³⁹"Return to your house and describe what great things God has done for you." So he went away, proclaiming throughout the whole city what great things Jesus had done for him.

Miracles of Healing

40 And as Jesus returned, the people welcomed Him, for they had all been waiting for Him. ⁴¹And there came a man named Jairus, and he was an official of the synagogue; and he fell at Jesus' feet, and *began* to implore Him to come to his house; ⁴²for he had an only daughter, about twelve years old, and she was dying. But as He went, the crowds were pressing against Him.

43 And a woman who had a hemorrhage for twelve years, and could not be healed by anyone, ⁴⁴came up behind Him and touched the fringe of His cloak, and immediately her hemorrhage stopped. ⁴⁵And Jesus said, "Who

is the one who touched Me?" And while they were all denying it, Peter said, "Master, the people are crowding and pressing in on You." 46But Jesus said, "Someone did touch Me, for I was aware that power had gone out of Me." 47When the woman saw that she had not escaped notice, she came trembling and fell down before Him, and declared in the presence of all the people the reason why she had touched Him, and how she had been immediately healed. 48And He said to her, "Daughter, your faith has made you well; go in peace."

49 While He was still speaking, someone *came from *the house of* the synagogue official, saying, "Your daughter has died; do not trouble the Teacher anymore." 50But when Jesus heard *this,* He answered him, "Do not be afraid *any longer;* only believe, and she will be made well." 51When He came to the house, He did not allow anyone to enter with Him, except Peter and John and James, and the girl's father and mother. 52Now they were all weeping and lamenting for her; but He said, "Stop weeping, for she has not died, but is asleep." 53And they *began* laughing at Him, knowing that she had died. 54He, however, took her by the hand and called, saying, "Child, arise!" 55And her spirit returned, and she got up immediately; and He gave orders for *something* to be given her to eat. 56Her parents were amazed; but He instructed them to tell no one what had happened.

Ministry of the Twelve

9 And He called the twelve together, and gave them power and authority over all the demons and to heal diseases. 2And He sent them out to proclaim the kingdom of God and to perform healing. 3And He said to them, "Take nothing for *your* journey, neither a staff, nor a bag, nor bread, nor money; and do not *even* have two tunics apiece. 4Whatever house you enter, stay there until you leave that city. 5And as for those who do not receive you, as you go out from that city, shake the dust off your feet as a testimony against them." 6Departing, they *began* going throughout the villages, preaching the gospel and healing everywhere.

7 Now Herod the tetrarch heard of all that was happening; and he was greatly perplexed, because it was said by some that John had risen from the dead, 8and by some that Elijah had appeared, and by others that one of the prophets of old had risen again. 9Herod said, "I myself had John beheaded; but who is this man about whom I

hear such things?" And he kept trying to see Him.

10 When the apostles returned, they gave an account to Him of all that they had done. Taking them with Him, He withdrew by Himself to a city called Bethsaida. ¹¹But the crowds were aware of this and followed Him; and welcoming them, He *began* speaking to them about the kingdom of God and curing those who had need of healing.

Five Thousand Fed

12 Now the day was ending, and the twelve came and said to Him, "Send the crowd away, that they may go into the surrounding villages and countryside and find lodging and get something to eat; for here we are in a desolate place." ¹³But He said to them, "You give them *something* to eat!" And they said, "We have no more than five loaves and two fish, unless perhaps we go and buy food for all these people." ¹⁴(For there were about five thousand men.) And He said to His disciples, "Have them sit down *to eat* in groups of about fifty each." ¹⁵They did so, and had them all sit down. ¹⁶Then He took the five loaves and the two fish, and looking up to heaven, He blessed them, and broke *them,* and kept giving *them* to the disciples to set before the people. ¹⁷And they all ate and were satisfied; and the broken pieces which they had left over were picked up, twelve baskets *full.*

18 And it happened that while He was praying alone, the disciples were with Him, and He questioned them, saying, "Who do the people say that I am?" ¹⁹They answered and said, "John the Baptist, and others *say* Elijah; but others, that one of the prophets of old has risen again." ²⁰And He said to them, "But who do you say that I am?" And Peter answered and said, "The Christ of God." ²¹But He warned them and instructed *them* not to tell this to anyone, ²²saying, "The Son of Man must suffer many things and be rejected by the elders and chief priests and scribes, and be killed and be raised up on the third day."

23 And He was saying to *them* all, "If anyone wishes to come after Me, he must deny himself, and take up his cross daily and follow Me. ²⁴For whoever wishes to save his life will lose it, but whoever loses his life for My sake, he is the one who will save it. ²⁵For what is a man profited if he gains the whole world, and loses or forfeits himself? ²⁶For whoever is ashamed of Me and My words, the Son of Man will be ashamed of him when He comes in His glory, and *the glory* of the Father and of the holy angels. ²⁷But I say to you truthfully, there are some of those standing here who will not taste death until they see the kingdom of God."

The Transfiguration

28 Some eight days after these sayings, He took along Peter and John and James, and went up on the mountain to pray. ²⁹And while He was praying, the appearance of His face became different, and His clothing *became* white *and* gleaming. ³⁰And behold, two men were talking with Him; and they were Moses and Elijah, ³¹who, appearing in glory, were speaking of His departure which He was about to accomplish at Jerusalem. ³²Now Peter and his companions had been overcome with sleep; but when they were fully awake, they saw His glory and the two men standing with Him. ³³And as these were leaving Him, Peter said to Jesus, "Master, it is good for us to be here; let us make three tabernacles: one for You, and one for Moses, and one for Elijah"—not realizing what he was saying. ³⁴While he was saying this, a cloud formed and *began* to overshadow them; and they were afraid as they entered the cloud. ³⁵Then a voice came out of the cloud, saying, "This is My Son, *My* Chosen One; listen to Him!" ³⁶And when the voice had spoken, Jesus was found alone. And

they kept silent, and reported to no one in those days any of the things which they had seen.

37 On the next day, when they came down from the mountain, a large crowd met Him. ³⁸And a man from the crowd shouted, saying, "Teacher, I beg You to look at my son, for he is my only *boy*, ³⁹and a spirit seizes him, and he suddenly screams, and it throws him into a convulsion with foaming *at the mouth*; and only with difficulty does it leave him, mauling him *as it leaves*. ⁴⁰I begged Your disciples to cast it out, and they could not." ⁴¹And Jesus answered and said, "You unbelieving and perverted generation, how long shall I be with you and put up with you? Bring your son here." ⁴²While he was still approaching, the demon slammed him *to the ground* and threw him into a convulsion. But Jesus rebuked the unclean spirit, and healed the boy and gave him back to his father. ⁴³And they were all amazed at the greatness of God.

But while everyone was marveling at all that He was doing, He said to His disciples, ⁴⁴"Let these words sink into your ears; for the Son of Man is going to be delivered into the hands of men." ⁴⁵But they did not understand this statement, and it was concealed from them so that they would not perceive it;

and they were afraid to ask Him about this statement.

The Test of Greatness

46 An argument started among them as to which of them might be the greatest. [47]But Jesus, knowing what they were thinking in their heart, took a child and stood him by His side, [48]and said to them, "Whoever receives this child in My name receives Me, and whoever receives Me receives Him who sent Me; for the one who is least among all of you, this is the one who is great."

49 John answered and said, "Master, we saw someone casting out demons in Your name; and we tried to prevent him because he does not follow along with us." [50]But Jesus said to him, "Do not hinder *him;* for he who is not against you is for you."

51 When the days were approaching for His ascension, He was determined to go to Jerusalem; [52]and He sent messengers on ahead of Him, and they went and entered a village of the Samaritans to make arrangements for Him. [53]But they did not receive Him, because He was traveling toward Jerusalem. [54]When His disciples James and John saw *this,* they said, "Lord, do You want us to command fire to come down from heaven and consume them?" [55]But He turned and rebuked them, [and said, "You do not know what kind of spirit you are of; [56]for the Son of Man did not come to destroy men's lives, but to save them."] And they went on to another village.

Exacting Discipleship

57 As they were going along the road, someone said to Him, "I will follow You wherever You go." [58]And Jesus said to him, "The foxes have holes and the birds of the air *have* nests, but the Son of Man has nowhere to lay His head." [59]And He said to another, "Follow Me." But he said, "Lord, permit me first to go and bury my father." [60]But He said to him, "Allow the dead to bury their own dead; but as for you, go and proclaim everywhere the kingdom of God." [61]Another also said, "I will follow You, Lord; but first permit me to say good-bye to those at home." [62]But Jesus said to him, "No one, after putting his hand to the plow and looking back, is fit for the kingdom of God."

The Seventy Sent Out

10 Now after this the Lord appointed seventy others, and sent them in pairs ahead of Him to every city and place where He Himself was going to come. [2]And He was saying to them, "The harvest is plentiful, but the laborers are few; therefore beseech the Lord of the harvest to send out laborers into His harvest. ³Go; behold, I send you out as lambs in the midst of wolves. ⁴Carry no money belt, no bag, no shoes; and greet no one on the way. ⁵Whatever house you enter, first say, 'Peace *be* to this house.' ⁶If a man of peace is there, your peace will rest on him; but if not, it will return to you. ⁷Stay in that house, eating and drinking what they give you; for the laborer is worthy of his wages. Do not keep moving from house to house. ⁸Whatever city you enter and they receive you, eat what is set before you; ⁹and heal those in it who are sick, and say to them, 'The kingdom of God has come near to you.' ¹⁰But whatever city you enter and they do not receive you, go out into its streets and say, ¹¹'Even the dust of your city which clings to our feet we wipe off *in protest* against you; yet be sure of this, that the kingdom of God has come near.' ¹²I say to you, it will be more tolerable in that day for Sodom than for that city.

13 "Woe to you, Chorazin! Woe to you, Bethsaida! For if the miracles had been performed in Tyre and Sidon which occurred in you, they would have repented long ago, sitting in sackcloth and ashes. ¹⁴But it will be more tolerable for Tyre and Sidon in the judgment than for you. ¹⁵And you, Capernaum, will not be exalted to heaven, will you? You will be brought down to Hades!

16 "The one who listens to you listens to Me, and the one who rejects you rejects Me; and he who rejects Me rejects the One who sent Me."

The Happy Results

17 The seventy returned with joy, saying, "Lord, even the demons are subject to us in Your name." ¹⁸And He said to them, "I was watching Satan fall from heaven like lightning. ¹⁹Behold, I have given you authority to tread on serpents and scorpions, and over all the power of the enemy, and nothing will injure you. ²⁰Nevertheless do not rejoice in this, that the spirits are subject to you, but rejoice that your names are recorded in heaven."

21 At that very time He rejoiced greatly in the Holy Spirit, and said, "I praise You, O Father, Lord of heaven and earth, that You have hidden these things from *the* wise and intelligent and have revealed them to infants. Yes, Father, for this way was well-pleasing in Your sight. ²²All things have been handed over to Me by My Father, and no one knows who the Son is except the Father, and who the Father is except the Son, and anyone to whom the Son wills to reveal *Him*."

23 Turning to the disciples, He said privately, "Blessed *are* the eyes which see the things you see, ²⁴for I say to you, that many prophets and kings wished to see the things which you see, and did not see *them*, and to hear the things which you hear, and did not hear *them*."

25 And a lawyer stood up and put Him to the test, saying, "Teacher, what shall I do to inherit eternal life?" ²⁶And He said to him, "What is written in the Law? How does it read to you?" ²⁷And he answered, "YOU SHALL LOVE THE LORD YOUR GOD WITH ALL YOUR HEART, AND WITH ALL YOUR SOUL, AND WITH ALL YOUR STRENGTH, AND WITH ALL YOUR MIND; AND YOUR NEIGHBOR AS YOURSELF." ²⁸And He said to him, "You have answered correctly; DO THIS AND YOU WILL LIVE." ²⁹But wishing to justify himself, he said to Jesus, "And who is my neighbor?"

The Good Samaritan

³⁰Jesus replied and said, "A man was going down from Jerusalem to Jericho, and fell among robbers, and they stripped him and beat him, and went away leaving him half dead. ³¹And by chance a priest was going down on that road, and when he saw him, he passed by on the other side. ³²Likewise a Levite also, when he came to the place and saw him, passed by on the other side. ³³But a Samaritan, who was on a journey, came upon him; and when he saw him, he felt compassion, ³⁴and came to him and bandaged up his wounds, pouring oil and wine on *them;* and he put him on his own beast, and brought him to an inn and took care of him. ³⁵On the next day he took out two ᵃdenarii and gave them to the innkeeper and said, 'Take care of him; and whatever more you spend, when I return I will repay you.' ³⁶Which of these three do you think proved to be a neighbor to the man who fell into the robbers' *hands?*" ³⁷And he said, "The one who showed mercy toward him." Then Jesus said to him, "Go and do the same."

Martha and Mary

38 Now as they were traveling along, He entered a village; and a woman named Martha welcomed Him into her home. ³⁹She had a sister called Mary, who was seated at the Lord's feet, listening to His word. ⁴⁰But Martha was distracted with all her preparations; and she came up *to Him* and said, "Lord, do You not care that my sister has left me to do all the serving

ᵃ**10:35** The denarius was equivalent to a day's wages

alone? Then tell her to help me." ⁴¹But the Lord answered and said to her, "Martha, Martha, you are worried and bothered about so many things; ⁴²but *only* one thing is necessary, for Mary has chosen the good part, which shall not be taken away from her."

Instruction about Prayer

11 It happened that while Jesus was praying in a certain place, after He had finished, one of His disciples said to Him, "Lord, teach us to pray just as John also taught his disciples." ²And He said to them, "When you pray, say:
ᵃ"Father, hallowed be Your name.
Your kingdom come.
³"Give us each day our daily bread.
⁴"And forgive us our sins,
For we ourselves also forgive everyone who is indebted to us.
And lead us not into temptation.' "
5 Then He said to them, "Suppose one of you has a friend, and goes to him at midnight and says to him, 'Friend, lend me three loaves; ⁶for a friend of mine has come to me from a journey, and I have nothing to set before him'; ⁷and from inside he answers and says, 'Do not bother me; the door has already been shut and my children and I are in bed; I cannot get up and give you *anything*.' ⁸I tell you, even though he will not get up and give him *anything* because he is his friend, yet because of his persistence he will get up and give him as much as he needs.

9 "So I say to you, ask, and it will be given to you; seek, and you will find; knock, and it will be opened to you. ¹⁰For everyone who asks, receives; and he who seeks, finds; and to him who knocks, it will be opened. ¹¹Now suppose one of you fathers is asked by his son for a fish; he will not give him a snake instead of a fish, will he? ¹²Or *if* he is asked for an egg, he will not give him a scorpion, will he? ¹³If you then, being evil, know how to give good gifts to your children, how much more will *your* heavenly Father give the Holy Spirit to those who ask Him?"

Pharisees' Blasphemy

14 And He was casting out a demon, and it was mute; when the demon had gone out, the mute man spoke; and the crowds were amazed. ¹⁵But some of them said, "He casts out demons by Beelzebul, the ruler of the demons." ¹⁶Others, to test *Him,* were demanding of Him a sign from heaven. ¹⁷But He knew their thoughts and said to them, "Any kingdom divided against itself is laid waste; and a house *divided* against itself falls. ¹⁸If Satan also is divided against himself, how will his kingdom stand? For you say that I cast out demons

---

ᵃ11:2 Later mss add phrases from Matt 6:9-13 to make the two passages closely similar by Beelzebul. ¹⁹And if I by Beelzebul cast out demons, by whom do your sons cast them out? So they will be your judges. ²⁰But if I cast out demons by the finger of God, then the kingdom of God has come upon you. ²¹When a strong *man,* fully armed, guards his own house, his possessions are undisturbed. ²²But when someone stronger than he attacks him and overpowers him, he takes away from him all his armor on which he had relied and distributes his plunder. ²³He who is not with Me is against Me; and he who does not gather with Me, scatters.

²⁴ "When the unclean spirit goes out of a man, it passes through waterless places seeking rest, and not finding any, it says, 'I will return to my house from which I came.' ²⁵And when it comes, it finds it swept and put in order. ²⁶Then it goes and takes *along* seven other spirits more evil than itself, and they go in and live there; and the last state of that man becomes worse than the first."

²⁷ While Jesus was saying these things, one of the women in the crowd raised her voice and said to Him, "Blessed is the womb that bore You and the breasts at which You nursed." ²⁸But He said, "On the contrary, blessed are those who hear the word of God and observe it."

The Sign of Jonah

²⁹ As the crowds were increasing, He began to say, "This generation is a wicked generation; it seeks for a sign, and *yet* no sign will be given to it but the sign of Jonah. ³⁰For just as Jonah became a sign to the Ninevites, so will the Son of Man be to this generation. ³¹The Queen of the South will rise up with the men of this generation at the judgment and condemn them, because she came from the ends of the earth to hear the wisdom of Solomon; and behold, something greater than Solomon is here. ³²The men of Nineveh will stand up with this generation at the judgment and condemn it, because they repented at the preaching of Jonah; and behold, something greater than Jonah is here.

³³ "No one, after lighting a lamp, puts it away in a cellar nor under a basket, but on the lampstand, so that those who enter may see the light. ³⁴The eye is the lamp of your body; when your eye is clear, your whole body also is full of light; but when it is bad, your body also is full of darkness. ³⁵Then watch out that the light in you is not darkness. ³⁶If therefore your whole body is full of light, with no dark part in

it, it will be wholly illumined, as when the lamp illumines you with its rays."

Woes upon the Pharisees

37 Now when He had spoken, a Pharisee *asked Him to have lunch with him; and He went in, and reclined *at the table*. ³⁸When the Pharisee saw it, he was surprised that He had not first ceremonially washed before the meal. ³⁹But the Lord said to him, "Now you Pharisees clean the outside of the cup and of the platter; but inside of you, you are full of robbery and wickedness. ⁴⁰You foolish ones, did not He who made the outside make the inside also? ⁴¹But give that which is within as charity, and then all things are clean for you.

42 "But woe to you Pharisees! For you pay tithe of mint and rue and every *kind of* garden herb, and *yet* disregard justice and the love of God; but these are the things you should have done without neglecting the others. ⁴³Woe to you Pharisees! For you love the chief seats in the synagogues and the respectful greetings in the market places. ⁴⁴Woe to you! For you are like concealed tombs, and the people who walk over *them* are unaware *of it*."

45 One of the ᵃlawyers *said to Him in reply, "Teacher, when You

ᵃ11:45 I.e. experts in the Mosaic Law

say this, You insult us too." ⁴⁶But He said, "Woe to you lawyers as well! For you weigh men down with burdens hard to bear, while you yourselves will not even touch the burdens with one of your fingers. ⁴⁷Woe to you! For you build the tombs of the prophets, and *it was* your fathers *who* killed them. ⁴⁸So you are witnesses and approve the deeds of your fathers; because it was they who killed them, and you build *their tombs*. ⁴⁹For this reason also the wisdom of God said, 'I will send to them prophets and apostles, and *some* of them they will kill and *some* they will persecute, ⁵⁰so that the blood of all the prophets, shed since the foundation of the world, may be charged against this generation, ⁵¹from the blood of Abel to the blood of Zechariah, who was killed between the altar and the house *of God*; yes, I tell you, it shall be charged against this generation.' ⁵²Woe to you lawyers! For you have taken away the key of knowledge; you yourselves did not enter, and you hindered those who were entering."

53 When He left there, the scribes and the Pharisees began to be very hostile and to question Him closely on many subjects, ⁵⁴plotting against Him to catch *Him* in something He might say.

God Knows and Cares

12 Under these circumstances, after so many thousands of people had gathered together that they were stepping on one another, He began saying to His disciples first *of all*, "Beware of the leaven of the Pharisees, which is hypocrisy. ²But there is nothing covered up that will not be revealed, and hidden that will not be known. ³Accordingly, whatever you have said in the dark will be heard in the light, and what you have whispered in the inner rooms will be proclaimed upon the housetops.

4 "I say to you, My friends, do not be afraid of those who kill the body and after that have no more that they can do. ⁵But I will warn you whom to fear: fear the One who, after He has killed, has authority to cast into hell; yes, I tell you, fear Him! ⁶Are not five sparrows sold for two cents? *Yet* not one of them is forgotten before God. ⁷Indeed, the very hairs of your head are all numbered. Do not fear; you are more valuable than many sparrows.

8 "And I say to you, everyone who confesses Me before men, the Son of Man will confess him also before the angels of God; ⁹but he who denies Me before men will be denied before the angels of God. ¹⁰And everyone who speaks a word against the Son of Man, it will be forgiven him; but he who blasphemes against the Holy Spirit, it will not be forgiven him. ¹¹When they bring you before the synagogues and the rulers and the authorities, do not worry about how or what you are to speak in your defense, or what you are to say; ¹²for the Holy Spirit will teach you in that very hour what you ought to say."

Covetousness Denounced

13 Someone in the crowd said to Him, "Teacher, tell my brother to divide the *family* inheritance with me." ¹⁴But He said to him, "Man, who appointed Me a judge or arbitrator over you?" ¹⁵Then He said to them, "Beware, and be on your guard against every form of greed; for not *even* when one has an abundance does his life consist of his possessions." ¹⁶And He told them a parable, saying, "The land of a rich man was very productive. ¹⁷And he began reasoning to himself, saying, 'What shall I do, since I have no place to store my crops?' ¹⁸Then he said, 'This is what I will do: I will tear down my barns and build larger ones, and there I will store all my grain and my goods. ¹⁹And I will say to my soul, "Soul, you have many goods laid up for many years *to come*; take your ease, eat, drink *and* be merry." ' ²⁰But God said to him,

'You fool! This *very* night your soul is required of you; and *now* who will own what you have prepared?' [21]So is the man who stores up treasure for himself, and is not rich toward God."

22 And He said to His disciples, "For this reason I say to you, do not worry about *your* life, *as to* what you will eat; nor for your body, *as to* what you will put on. [23]For life is more than food, and the body more than clothing. [24]Consider the ravens, for they neither sow nor reap; they have no storeroom nor barn, and *yet* God feeds them; how much more valuable you are than the birds! [25]And which of you by worrying can add a *single* [a]hour to his [b]life's span? [26]If then you cannot do even a very little thing, why do you worry about other matters? [27]Consider the lilies, how they grow: they neither toil nor spin; but I tell you, not even Solomon in all his glory clothed himself like one of these. [28]But if God so clothes the grass in the field, which is *alive* today and tomorrow is thrown into the furnace, how much more *will He clothe* you? You men of little faith! [29]And do not seek what you will eat and what you will drink, and do not keep worrying. [30]For all these things the nations of the world eagerly seek; but your Father knows that you need these things. [31]But seek His kingdom, and these things will be added to you. [32]Do not be afraid, little flock, for your Father has chosen gladly to give you the kingdom.

33 "Sell your possessions and give to charity; make yourselves money belts which do not wear out, an unfailing treasure in heaven, where no thief comes near nor moth destroys. [34]For where your treasure is, there your heart will be also.

Be in Readiness

35 "Be dressed in readiness, and *keep* your lamps lit. [36]Be like men who are waiting for their master when he returns from the wedding feast, so that they may immediately open *the door* to him when he comes and knocks. [37]Blessed are those slaves whom the master will find on the alert when he comes; truly I say to you, that he will gird himself *to serve,* and have them recline *at the table,* and will come up and wait on them. [38]Whether he comes in the [c]second watch, or even in the [d]third, and finds *them* so, blessed are those *slaves.*

39 "But be sure of this, that if the head of the house had known at what hour the thief was coming, he would not have allowed his house to be broken into. [40]You too, be ready; for the Son of Man

[a]**12:25** Lit *cubit* (approx 18 in.) ; [b]**12:25** Or *height;* [c]**12:38** I.e. 9 p.m. to midnight; [d]**12:38** I.e. midnight to 3 a.m.

is coming at an hour that you do not expect."

41 Peter said, "Lord, are You addressing this parable to us, or to everyone *else* as well?" ⁴²And the Lord said, "Who then is the faithful and sensible steward, whom his master will put in charge of his servants, to give them their rations at the proper time? ⁴³Blessed is that slave whom his master finds so doing when he comes. ⁴⁴Truly I say to you that he will put him in charge of all his possessions. ⁴⁵But if that slave says in his heart, 'My master will be a long time in coming,' and begins to beat the slaves, *both* men and women, and to eat and drink and get drunk; ⁴⁶the master of that slave will come on a day when he does not expect *him* and at an hour he does not know, and will cut him in pieces, and assign him a place with the unbelievers. ⁴⁷And that slave who knew his master's will and did not get ready or act in accord with his will, will receive many lashes, ⁴⁸but the one who did not know *it*, and committed deeds worthy of a flogging, will receive but few. From everyone who has been given much, much will be required; and to whom they entrusted much, of him they will ask all the more.

Christ Divides Men

49 "I have come to cast fire upon the earth; and how I wish it were already kindled! ⁵⁰But I have a baptism to undergo, and how distressed I am until it is accomplished! ⁵¹Do you suppose that I came to grant peace on earth? I tell you, no, but rather division; ⁵²for from now on five *members* in one household will be divided, three against two and two against three. ⁵³They will be divided, father against son and son against father, mother against daughter and daughter against mother, mother-in-law against daughter-in-law and daughter-in-law against mother-in-law."

54 And He was also saying to the crowds, "When you see a cloud rising in the west, immediately you say, 'A shower is coming,' and so it turns out. ⁵⁵And when *you see* a south wind blowing, you say, 'It will be a hot day,' and it turns out *that way*. ⁵⁶You hypocrites! You know how to analyze the appearance of the earth and the sky, but why do you not analyze this present time?

57 "And why do you not even on your own initiative judge what is right? ⁵⁸For while you are going with your opponent to appear before the magistrate, on *your* way *there* make an effort to settle with him, so that he may not drag you before the judge, and the judge turn you over to the officer, and the officer throw you into prison. ⁵⁹I say to you, you will not get out of there until you have paid the very last cent."

Call to Repent

13 Now on the same occasion there were some present who reported to Him about the Galileans whose blood Pilate had mixed with their sacrifices. ²And Jesus said to them, "Do you suppose that these Galileans were *greater* sinners than all *other* Galileans because they suffered this *fate?* ³I tell you, no, but unless you repent, you will all likewise perish. ⁴Or do you suppose that those eighteen on whom the tower in Siloam fell and killed them were *worse* culprits than all the men who live in Jerusalem? ⁵I tell you, no, but unless you repent, you will all likewise perish."

6 And He *began* telling this parable: "A man had a fig tree which had been planted in his vineyard; and he came looking for fruit on it and did not find any. ⁷And he said to the vineyard-keeper, 'Behold, for three years I have come looking for fruit on this fig tree without finding any. Cut it down! Why does it even use up the ground?' ⁸And he answered and said to him, 'Let it alone, sir, for this year too, until I dig around it and put in fertilizer; ⁹and if it bears fruit next year, *fine;* but if not, cut it down.' "

Healing on the Sabbath

10 And He was teaching in one of the synagogues on the Sabbath. ¹¹And there was a woman who for eighteen years had had a sickness caused by a spirit; and she was bent double, and could not straighten up at all. ¹²When Jesus saw her, He called her over and said to her, "Woman, you are freed from your sickness." ¹³And He laid His hands on her; and immediately she was made erect again and *began* glorifying God. ¹⁴But the synagogue official, indignant because Jesus had healed on the Sabbath, *began* saying to the crowd in response, "There are six days in which work should be done; so come during them and get healed, and not on the Sabbath day." ¹⁵But the Lord answered him and said, "You hypocrites, does not each of you on the Sabbath untie his ox or his donkey from the stall and lead him away to water *him?* ¹⁶And this woman, a daughter of Abraham as she is, whom Satan has bound for eighteen long years, should she not have been released from this bond on the Sabbath day?" ¹⁷As He said this, all His opponents were being humiliated; and the entire crowd was rejoicing over all the glorious things being done by Him.

Parables of Mustard
Seed and Leaven

18 So He was saying, "What is the kingdom of God like, and to what shall I compare it? ¹⁹It is like a mustard seed, which a man took and threw into his own garden; and it grew and became a tree, and THE BIRDS OF THE AIR NESTED IN ITS BRANCHES."

20 And again He said, "To what shall I compare the kingdom of God? ²¹It is like leaven, which a woman took and hid in three pecks of flour until it was all leavened."

Teaching in the Villages

22 And He was passing through from one city and village to another, teaching, and proceeding on His way to Jerusalem. ²³And someone said to Him, "Lord, are there *just* a few who are being saved?" And He said to them, ²⁴"Strive to enter through the narrow door; for many, I tell you, will seek to enter and will not be able. ²⁵Once the head of the house gets up and shuts the door, and you begin to stand outside and knock on the door, saying, 'Lord, open up to us!' then He will answer and say to you, 'I do not know where you are from.' ²⁶Then you will begin to say, 'We ate and drank in Your presence, and You taught in our streets'; ²⁷and He will say, 'I tell you, I do not know where you are from; DEPART FROM ME, ALL YOU EVILDOERS.' ²⁸In that place there will be weeping and gnashing of teeth when you see Abraham and Isaac and Jacob and all the prophets in the kingdom of God, but yourselves being thrown out. ²⁹And they will come from east and west and from north and south, and will recline *at the table* in the kingdom of God. ³⁰And behold, *some* are last who will be first and *some* are first who will be last."

31 Just at that time some Pharisees approached, saying to Him, "Go away, leave here, for Herod wants to kill You." ³²And He said to them, "Go and tell that fox, 'Behold, I cast out demons and perform cures today and tomorrow, and the third *day* I reach My goal.' ³³Nevertheless I must journey on today and tomorrow and the next *day;* for it cannot be that a prophet would perish outside of Jerusalem. ³⁴O Jerusalem, Jerusalem, *the city* that kills the prophets and stones those sent to her! How often I wanted to gather your children together, just as a hen *gathers* her brood under her wings, and you would not *have it!* ³⁵Behold, your house is left to you *desolate;* and I say to you, you will not see Me until *the time* comes when you say, 'BLESSED IS HE WHO COMES IN THE NAME OF THE LORD!' "

Jesus Heals on the Sabbath

14 It happened that when He went into the house of one of the leaders of the Pharisees on *the* Sabbath to eat bread, they were watching Him closely. [2]And there in front of Him was a man suffering from dropsy. [3]And Jesus answered and spoke to the lawyers and Pharisees, saying, "Is it lawful to heal on the Sabbath, or not?" [4]But they kept silent. And He took hold of him and healed him, and sent him away. [5]And He said to them, "Which one of you will have a son or an ox fall into a well, and will not immediately pull him out on a Sabbath day?" [6]And they could make no reply to this.

Parable of the Guests

[7] And He *began* speaking a parable to the invited guests when He noticed how they had been picking out the places of honor *at the table,* saying to them, [8]"When you are invited by someone to a wedding feast, do not take the place of honor, for someone more distinguished than you may have been invited by him, [9]and he who invited you both will come and say to you, 'Give *your* place to this man,' and then in disgrace you proceed to occupy the last place. [10]But when you are invited, go and recline at the last place, so that when the one who has invited you comes, he may say to you, 'Friend, move up higher'; then you will have honor in the sight of all who are at the table with you. [11]For everyone who exalts himself will be humbled, and he who humbles himself will be exalted."

[12] And He also went on to say to the one who had invited Him, "When you give a luncheon or a dinner, do not invite your friends or your brothers or your relatives or your rich neighbors, otherwise they may also invite you in return and *that* will be your repayment. [13]But when you give a reception, invite *the* poor, *the* crippled, *the* lame, *the* blind, [14]and you will be blessed, since they do not have *the means* to repay you; for you will be repaid at the resurrection of the righteous."

[15] When one of those who were reclining *at the table* with Him heard this, he said to Him, "Blessed is everyone who will eat bread in the kingdom of God!"

Parable of the Dinner

[16]But He said to him, "A man was giving a big dinner, and he invited many; [17]and at the dinner hour he sent his slave to say to those who had been invited, 'Come; for everything is ready now.' [18]But they all alike began to make excuses. The first one said to him, 'I have bought a piece of land and I need to go out and look at it; please

consider me excused.' [19]Another one said, 'I have bought five yoke of oxen, and I am going to try them out; please consider me excused.' [20]Another one said, 'I have married a wife, and for that reason I cannot come.' [21]And the slave came *back* and reported this to his master. Then the head of the household became angry and said to his slave, 'Go out at once into the streets and lanes of the city and bring in here the poor and crippled and blind and lame.' [22]And the slave said, 'Master, what you commanded has been done, and still there is room.' [23]And the master said to the slave, 'Go out into the highways and along the hedges, and compel *them* to come in, so that my house may be filled. [24]For I tell you, none of those men who were invited shall taste of my dinner.' "

Discipleship Tested

25 Now large crowds were going along with Him; and He turned and said to them, [26]"If anyone comes to Me, and does not [a]hate his own father and mother and wife and children and brothers and sisters, yes, and even his own life, he cannot be My disciple. [27]Whoever does not carry his own cross and come after Me cannot be My disciple. [28]For which one of you, when he wants to build a tower, does not first sit down and calculate

[a]**14:26** I.e. by comparison of his love for Me

the cost to see if he has enough to complete it? [29]Otherwise, when he has laid a foundation and is not able to finish, all who observe it begin to ridicule him, [30]saying, 'This man began to build and was not able to finish.' [31]Or what king, when he sets out to meet another king in battle, will not first sit down and consider whether he is strong enough with ten thousand *men* to encounter the one coming against him with twenty thousand? [32]Or else, while the other is still far away, he sends a delegation and asks for terms of peace. [33]So then, none of you can be My disciple who does not give up all his own possessions.

34 "Therefore, salt is good; but if even salt has become tasteless, with what will it be seasoned? [35]It is useless either for the soil or for the manure pile; it is thrown out. He who has ears to hear, let him hear."

The Lost Sheep

15 Now all the tax collectors and the sinners were coming near Him to listen to Him. [2]Both the Pharisees and the scribes *began* to grumble, saying, "This man receives sinners and eats with them."

3 So He told them this parable, saying, [4]"What man among you, if he has a hundred sheep and has

lost one of them, does not leave the ninety-nine in the open pasture and go after the one which is lost until he finds it? [5]When he has found it, he lays it on his shoulders, rejoicing. [6]And when he comes home, he calls together his friends and his neighbors, saying to them, 'Rejoice with me, for I have found my sheep which was lost!' [7]I tell you that in the same way, there will be *more* joy in heaven over one sinner who repents than over ninety-nine righteous persons who need no repentance.

The Lost Coin

8 "Or what woman, if she has ten silver coins and loses one coin, does not light a lamp and sweep the house and search carefully until she finds it? [9]When she has found it, she calls together her friends and neighbors, saying, 'Rejoice with me, for I have found the coin which I had lost!' [10]In the same way, I tell you, there is joy in the presence of the angels of God over one sinner who repents."

The Prodigal Son

11 And He said, "A man had two sons. [12]The younger of them said to his father, 'Father, give me the share of the estate that falls to me.' So he divided his wealth between them. [13]And not many days later, the younger son gathered everything together and went on a journey into a distant country, and there he squandered his estate with loose living. [14]Now when he had spent everything, a severe famine occurred in that country, and he began to be impoverished. [15]So he went and hired himself out to one of the citizens of that country, and he sent him into his fields to feed swine. [16]And he would have gladly filled his stomach with the pods that the swine were eating, and no one was giving *anything* to him. [17]But when he came to his senses, he said, 'How many of my father's hired men have more than enough bread, but I am dying here with hunger! [18]I will get up and go to my father, and will say to him, "Father, I have sinned against heaven, and in your sight; [19]I am no longer worthy to be called your son; make me as one of your hired men." ' [20]So he got up and came to his father. But while he was still a long way off, his father saw him and felt compassion *for him,* and ran and embraced him and kissed him. [21]And the son said to him, 'Father, I have sinned against heaven and in your sight; I am no longer worthy to be called your son.' [22]But the father said to his slaves, 'Quickly bring out the best robe and put it on him, and put a ring on his hand and sandals on his feet; [23]and bring the fattened calf, kill it, and let us eat and celebrate; [24]for this son of mine was dead and has come to life again; he was lost and has been found.' And they began to celebrate.

25 "Now his older son was in the field, and when he came and approached the house, he heard music and dancing. ²⁶And he summoned one of the servants and *began* inquiring what these things could be. ²⁷And he said to him, 'Your brother has come, and your father has killed the fattened calf because he has received him back safe and sound.' ²⁸But he became angry and was not willing to go in; and his father came out and *began* pleading with him. ²⁹But he answered and said to his father, 'Look! For so many years I have been serving you and I have never neglected a command of yours; and *yet* you have never given me a young goat, so that I might celebrate with my friends; ³⁰but when this son of yours came, who has devoured your wealth with prostitutes, you killed the fattened calf for him.' ³¹And he said to him, 'Son, you have always been with me, and all that is mine is yours. ³²But we had to celebrate and rejoice, for this brother of yours was dead and *has begun* to live, and *was* lost and has been found.' "

The Unrighteous Steward

16 Now He was also saying to the disciples, "There was a rich man who had a manager, and this *manager* was reported to him as squandering his possessions. ²And he called him and said to him, 'What is this I hear about you? Give an accounting of your management, for you can no longer be manager.' ³The manager said to himself, 'What shall I do, since my master is taking the management away from me? I am not strong enough to dig; I am ashamed to beg. ⁴I know what I shall do, so that when I am removed from the management people will welcome me into their homes.' ⁵And he summoned each one of his master's debtors, and he *began* saying to the first, 'How much do you owe my master?' ⁶And he said, 'A hundred measures of oil.' And he said to him, 'Take your bill, and sit down quickly and write fifty.' ⁷Then he said to another, 'And how much do you owe?' And he said, 'A hundred measures of wheat.' He *said to him, 'Take your bill, and write eighty.' ⁸And his master praised the unrighteous manager because he had acted shrewdly; for the sons of this age are more shrewd in relation to their own kind than the sons of light. ⁹And I say to you, make friends for yourselves by means of the ᵃwealth of unrighteousness, so that when it fails, they will receive you into the eternal dwellings.

ᵃ**16:9** Gr *mamonas*, for Aram *mamon* (mammon); i.e. wealth, etc., personified as an object of worship

10 "He who is faithful in a very little thing is faithful also in much; and he who is unrighteous in a very little thing is unrighteous also in much. ¹¹Therefore if you have not been faithful in the *use of* unrighteous wealth, who will entrust the true *riches* to you? ¹²And if you have not been faithful in *the use of* that which is another's, who will give you that which is your own? ¹³No servant can serve two masters; for either he will hate the one and love the other, or else he will be devoted to one and despise the other. You cannot serve God and wealth."

14 Now the Pharisees, who were lovers of money, were listening to all these things and were scoffing at Him. ¹⁵And He said to them, "You are those who justify yourselves in the sight of men, but God knows your hearts; for that which is highly esteemed among men is detestable in the sight of God.

16 "The Law and the Prophets *were proclaimed* until John; since that time the gospel of the kingdom of God has been preached, and everyone is forcing his way into it. ¹⁷But it is easier for heaven and earth to pass away than for one stroke of a letter of the Law to fail.

18 "Everyone who divorces his wife and marries another commits adultery, and he who marries one who is divorced from a husband commits adultery.

The Rich Man and Lazarus

19 "Now there was a rich man, and he habitually dressed in purple and fine linen, joyously living in splendor every day. ²⁰And a poor man named Lazarus was laid at his gate, covered with sores, ²¹and longing to be fed with the *crumbs* which were falling from the rich man's table; besides, even the dogs were coming and licking his sores. ²²Now the poor man died and was carried away by the angels to Abraham's bosom; and the rich man also died and was buried. ²³In Hades he lifted up his eyes, being in torment, and *saw Abraham far away and Lazarus in his bosom. ²⁴And he cried out and said, 'Father Abraham, have mercy on me, and send Lazarus so that he may dip the tip of his finger in water and cool off my tongue, for I am in agony in this flame.' ²⁵But Abraham said, 'Child, remember that during your life you received your good things, and likewise Lazarus bad things; but now he is being comforted here, and you are in agony. ²⁶And besides all this, between us and you there is a great chasm fixed, so that those who wish to come over from here to you will not be able, and *that* none may cross over from there to us.' ²⁷And he said, 'Then I beg you, father, that you send him to my father's house— ²⁸for I have five brothers—in order that he may warn them, so that they will not also come to this place of torment.' ²⁹But Abraham *said, 'They have Moses and the Prophets; let them hear them.' ³⁰But he said, 'No, father Abraham, but if someone goes to them from the dead, they will repent!' ³¹But he said to him, 'If they do not listen to Moses and the Prophets, they will not be persuaded even if someone rises from the dead.' "

Instructions

17 He said to His disciples, "It is inevitable that stumbling blocks come, but woe to him through whom they come! ²It would be better for him if a millstone were hung around his neck and he were thrown into the sea, than that he would cause one of these little ones to stumble. ³Be on your guard! If your brother sins, rebuke him; and if he repents, forgive him. ⁴And if he sins against you seven times a day, and returns to you seven times, saying, 'I repent,' forgive him."

5 The apostles said to the Lord, "Increase our faith!" ⁶And the Lord said, "If you had faith like a mustard seed, you would say to this mulberry tree, 'Be uprooted and be planted in the sea'; and it would obey you.

7 "Which of you, having a slave plowing or tending sheep, will say to him when he has come in from the field, 'Come immediately and sit down to eat'? ⁸But will he not say to him, 'Prepare something for me to eat, and *properly* clothe yourself and serve me while I eat and drink; and afterward you may eat and drink'? ⁹He does not thank the slave because he did the things which were commanded, does he? ¹⁰So you too, when you do all the things which are commanded you, say, 'We are unworthy slaves; we have done *only* that which we ought to have done.' "

Ten Lepers Cleansed

11 While He was on the way to Jerusalem, He was passing between Samaria and Galilee. ¹²As He entered a village, ten leprous men who stood at a distance met Him; ¹³and they raised their voices, saying, "Jesus, Master, have mercy on us!" ¹⁴When He saw them, He said to them, "Go and show yourselves to the priests." And as they were going, they were cleansed. ¹⁵Now one of them, when he saw that he had been healed, turned back, glorifying God with a loud voice, ¹⁶and he fell on his face at His feet, giving thanks to Him. And he was a Samaritan. ¹⁷Then

Jesus answered and said, "Were there not ten cleansed? But the nine—where are they? [18]Was no one found who returned to give glory to God, except this foreigner?" [19]And He said to him, "Stand up and go; your faith [a]has made you well."

20 Now having been questioned by the Pharisees as to when the kingdom of God was coming, He answered them and said, "The kingdom of God is not coming with signs to be observed; [21]nor will they say, 'Look, here it is!' or, 'There it is!' For behold, the kingdom of God is in your midst."

Second Coming Foretold

22 And He said to the disciples, "The days will come when you will long to see one of the days of the Son of Man, and you will not see it. [23]They will say to you, 'Look there! Look here!' Do not go away, and do not run after them. [24]For just like the lightning, when it flashes out of one part of the sky, shines to the other part of the sky, so will the Son of Man be in His day. [25]But first He must suffer many things and be rejected by this generation. [26]And just as it happened in the days of Noah, so it will be also in the days of the Son of Man: [27]they were eating, they were drinking, they were marrying, they were being given in marriage, until the day that Noah entered the ark, and the flood came and destroyed them all. [28]It was the same as happened in the days of Lot: they were eating, they were drinking, they were buying, they were selling, they were planting, they were building; [29]but on the day that Lot went out from Sodom it rained fire and brimstone from heaven and destroyed them all. [30]It will be just the same on the day that the Son of Man is revealed. [31]On that day, the one who is on the housetop and whose goods are in the house must not go down to take them out; and likewise the one who is in the field must not turn back. [32]Remember Lot's wife. [33]Whoever seeks to keep his life will lose it, and whoever loses his life will preserve it. [34]I tell you, on that night there will be two in one bed; one will be taken and the other will be left. [35]There will be two women grinding at the same place; one will be taken and the other will be left. [36b][Two men will be in the field; one will be taken and the other will be left."] [37]And answering they *said to Him, "Where, Lord?" And He said to them, "Where the body is, there also the vultures will be gathered."

Parables on Prayer

18 Now He was telling them a parable to show that at all times they ought to pray and not to lose heart, [2]saying, "In a certain

---

*[17:19] Lit has saved you; [b][17:36] Early mss do not contain this v

city there was a judge who did not fear God and did not respect man. ³There was a widow in that city, and she kept coming to him, saying, 'Give me legal protection from my opponent.' ⁴For a while he was unwilling; but afterward he said to himself, 'Even though I do not fear God nor respect man, ⁵yet because this widow bothers me, I will give her legal protection, otherwise by continually coming she will wear me out.' " ⁶And the Lord said, "Hear what the unrighteous judge *said; ⁷now, will not God bring about justice for His elect who cry to Him day and night, and will He delay long over them? ⁸I tell you that He will bring about justice for them quickly. However, when the Son of Man comes, will He find faith on the earth?"

The Pharisee and the Publican

9 And He also told this parable to some people who trusted in themselves that they were righteous, and viewed others with contempt: ¹⁰"Two men went up into the temple to pray, one a Pharisee and the other a tax collector. ¹¹The Pharisee stood and was praying this to himself: 'God, I thank You that I am not like other people: swindlers, unjust, adulterers, or even like this tax collector. ¹²I fast twice a week; I pay tithes of all that I get.' ¹³But the tax collector, standing some distance away, was even

unwilling to lift up his eyes to heaven, but was beating his breast, saying, 'God, be merciful to me, the sinner!' ¹⁴I tell you, this man went to his house justified rather than the other; for everyone who exalts himself will be humbled, but he who humbles himself will be exalted."

15 And they were bringing even their babies to Him so that He would touch them, but when the disciples saw it, they *began* rebuking them. ¹⁶But Jesus called for them, saying, "Permit the children to come to Me, and do not hinder them, for the kingdom of God belongs to such as these. ¹⁷Truly I say to you, whoever does not receive the kingdom of God like a child will not enter it *at all*."

The Rich Young Ruler

18 A ruler questioned Him, saying, "Good Teacher, what shall I do to inherit eternal life?" ¹⁹And Jesus said to him, "Why do you call Me good? No one is good except God alone. ²⁰You know the commandments, 'DO NOT COMMIT ADULTERY, DO NOT MURDER, DO NOT STEAL, DO NOT BEAR FALSE WITNESS, HONOR YOUR FATHER AND MOTHER.' " ²¹And he said, "All these things I have kept from *my* youth." ²²When Jesus heard *this*, He said to him, "One thing you

still lack; sell all that you possess and distribute it to the poor, and you shall have treasure in heaven; and come, follow Me." ²³But when he had heard these things, he became very sad, for he was extremely rich. ²⁴And Jesus looked at him and said, "How hard it is for those who are wealthy to enter the kingdom of God! ²⁵For it is easier for a camel to go through the eye of a needle than for a rich man to enter the kingdom of God." ²⁶They who heard it said, "Then who can be saved?" ²⁷But He said, "The things that are impossible with people are possible with God."

28 Peter said, "Behold, we have left our own *homes* and followed You." ²⁹And He said to them, "Truly I say to you, there is no one who has left house or wife or brothers or parents or children, for the sake of the kingdom of God, ³⁰who will not receive many times as much at this time and in the age to come, eternal life."

31 Then He took the twelve aside and said to them, "Behold, we are going up to Jerusalem, and all things which are written through the prophets about the Son of Man will be accomplished. ³²For He will be handed over to the Gentiles, and will be mocked and mistreated and spit upon, ³³and after they have scourged Him, they will kill Him; and the third day He will rise again." ³⁴But the disciples understood none of these things, and *the meaning of* this statement was hidden from them, and they did not comprehend the things that were said.

Bartimaeus Receives Sight

35 As Jesus was approaching Jericho, a blind man was sitting by the road begging. ³⁶Now hearing a crowd going by, he *began* to inquire what this was. ³⁷They told him that Jesus of Nazareth was passing by. ³⁸And he called out, saying, "Jesus, Son of David, have mercy on me!" ³⁹Those who led the way were sternly telling him to be quiet; but he kept crying out all the more, "Son of David, have mercy on me!" ⁴⁰And Jesus stopped and commanded that he be brought to Him; and when he came near, He questioned him, ⁴¹"What do you want Me to do for you?" And he said, "Lord, *I want* to regain my sight!" ⁴²And Jesus said to him, "Receive your sight; your faith has made you well." ⁴³Immediately he regained his sight and *began* following Him, glorifying God; and when all the people saw it, they gave praise to God.

Zaccheus Converted

19 He entered Jericho and was passing through. ²And there was a man called by the name of

Zaccheus; he was a chief tax collector and he was rich. ³Zaccheus was trying to see who Jesus was, and was unable because of the crowd, for he was small in stature. ⁴So he ran on ahead and climbed up into a sycamore tree in order to see Him, for He was about to pass through that way. ⁵When Jesus came to the place, He looked up and said to him, "Zaccheus, hurry and come down, for today I must stay at your house." ⁶And he hurried and came down and received Him gladly. ⁷When they saw it, they all *began* to grumble, saying, "He has gone to be the guest of a man who is a sinner." ⁸Zaccheus stopped and said to the Lord, "Behold, Lord, half of my possessions I will give to the poor, and if I have defrauded anyone of anything, I will give back four times as much." ⁹And Jesus said to him, "Today salvation has come to this house, because he, too, is a son of Abraham. ¹⁰For the Son of Man has come to seek and to save that which was lost."

Parable of Money Usage

11 While they were listening to these things, Jesus went on to tell a parable, because He was near Jerusalem, and they supposed that the kingdom of God was going to appear immediately. ¹²So He said, "A nobleman went to a distant country to receive a kingdom for himself, and *then* return. ¹³And he called ten of his slaves, and gave them ten ªminas and said to them, 'Do business *with this* until I come *back*.' ¹⁴But his citizens hated him and sent a delegation after him, saying, 'We do not want this man to reign over us.' ¹⁵When he returned, after receiving the kingdom, he ordered that these slaves, to whom he had given the money, be called to him so that he might know what business they had done. ¹⁶The first appeared, saying, 'Master, your mina has made ten minas more.' ¹⁷And he said to him, 'Well done, good slave, because you have been faithful in a very little thing, you are to be in authority over ten cities.' ¹⁸The second came, saying, 'Your mina, master, has made five minas.' ¹⁹And he said to him also, 'And you are to be over five cities.' ²⁰Another came, saying, 'Master, here is your mina, which I kept put away in a handkerchief; ²¹for I was afraid of you, because you are an exacting man; you take up what you did not lay down and reap what you did not sow.' ²²He *said to him, 'By your own words I will judge you, you worthless slave. Did you know that I am an exacting man, taking up what I did not lay down and reaping what I did not sow? ²³Then why did you not put my money in the bank, and having come, I would

ª**19:13** A mina is equal to about 100 days' wages

have collected it with interest?' ²⁴Then he said to the bystanders, 'Take the mina away from him and give it to the one who has the ten minas.' ²⁵And they said to him, 'Master, he has ten minas *already.*' ²⁶I tell you that to everyone who has, more shall be given, but from the one who does not have, even what he does have shall be taken away. ²⁷But these enemies of mine, who did not want me to reign over them, bring them here and slay them in my presence."

Triumphal Entry

28 After He had said these things, He was going on ahead, going up to Jerusalem.

29 When He approached Beth-phage and Bethany, near the mount that is called Olivet, He sent two of the disciples, ³⁰saying, "Go into the village ahead of *you;* there, as you enter, you will find a colt tied on which no one yet has ever sat; untie it and bring it *here.* ³¹If anyone asks you, 'Why are you untying it?' you shall say, 'The Lord has need of it.' " ³²So those who were sent went away and found it just as He had told them. ³³As they were untying the colt, its owners said to them, "Why are you untying the colt?" ³⁴They said, "The Lord has need of it." ³⁵They brought it to Jesus, and they threw their coats on the colt and put

Jesus *on it.* ³⁶As He was going, they were spreading their coats on the road. ³⁷As soon as He was approaching, near the descent of the Mount of Olives, the whole crowd of the disciples began to praise God joyfully with a loud voice for all the miracles which they had seen, ³⁸shouting:

"BLESSED IS THE KING WHO
    COMES IN THE NAME OF
    THE LORD;
Peace in heaven and glory in the
    highest!"

³⁹Some of the Pharisees in the crowd said to Him, "Teacher, rebuke Your disciples." ⁴⁰But Jesus answered, "I tell you, if these become silent, the stones will cry out!"

41 When He approached *Jeru-salem,* He saw the city and wept over it, ⁴²saying, "If you had known in this day, even you, the things which make for peace! But now they have been hidden from your eyes. ⁴³For the days will come upon you when your enemies will throw up a barricade against you, and surround you and hem you in on every side, ⁴⁴and they will level you to the ground and your children within you, and they will not leave in you one stone upon another, because you did not recognize the time of your visitation."

Traders Driven from the Temple

45 Jesus entered the temple and began to drive out those who were selling, ⁴⁶saying to them, "It is written, 'AND MY HOUSE SHALL BE A HOUSE OF PRAYER,' but you have made it a ROBBERS' DEN.'"

47 And He was teaching daily in the temple; but the chief priests and the scribes and the leading men among the people were trying to destroy Him, ⁴⁸and they could not find anything that they might do, for all the people were hanging on to every word He said.

Jesus' Authority Questioned

20 On one of the days while He was teaching the people in the temple and preaching the gospel, the chief priests and the scribes with the elders confronted *Him*, ²and they spoke, saying to Him, "Tell us by what authority You are doing these things, or who is the one who gave You this authority?" ³Jesus answered and said to them, "I will also ask you a question, and you tell Me: ⁴Was the baptism of John from heaven or from men?" ⁵They reasoned among themselves, saying, "If we say, 'From heaven,' He will say, 'Why did you not believe him?' ⁶But if we say, 'From men,' all the people will stone us to death, for they are convinced that John was

a prophet." ⁷So they answered that they did not know where *it came* from. ⁸And Jesus said to them, "Nor will I tell you by what authority I do these things."

Parable of the Vine-growers

9 And He began to tell the people this parable: "A man planted a vineyard and rented it out to vine-growers, and went on a journey for a long time. ¹⁰At the *harvest* time he sent a slave to the vine-growers, so that they would give him *some* of the produce of the vineyard; but the vine-growers beat him and sent him away empty-handed. ¹¹And he proceeded to send another slave; and they beat him also and treated him shamefully and sent him away empty-handed. ¹²And he proceeded to send a third; and this one also they wounded and cast out. ¹³The owner of the vineyard said, 'What shall I do? I will send my beloved son; perhaps they will respect him.' ¹⁴But when the vine-growers saw him, they reasoned with one another, saying, 'This is the heir; let us kill him so that the inheritance will be ours.' ¹⁵So they threw him out of the vineyard and killed him. What, then, will the owner of the vineyard do to them? ¹⁶He will come and destroy these vine-growers and will give the vineyard to others." When they heard it, they said, "May it never be!" [17]But Jesus looked at them and said, "What then is this that is written:

'THE STONE WHICH THE
    BUILDERS REJECTED,
THIS BECAME THE CHIEF COR-
    NER *stone*'?

[18]Everyone who falls on that stone will be broken to pieces; but on whomever it falls, it will scatter him like dust."

Tribute to Caesar

19 The scribes and the chief priests tried to lay hands on Him that very hour, and they feared the people; for they understood that He spoke this parable against them. [20]So they watched Him, and sent spies who pretended to be righteous, in order that they might catch Him in some statement, so that they *could* deliver Him to the rule and the authority of the governor. [21]They questioned Him, saying, "Teacher, we know that You speak and teach correctly, and You are not partial to any, but teach the way of God in truth. [22]Is it lawful for us to pay taxes to Caesar, or not?" [23]But He detected their trickery and said to them, [24]"Show Me a ªdenarius. Whose likeness and inscription does it have?" They said, "Caesar's." [25]And He said to them, "Then render to Caesar the things that are Caesar's, and to God the things that are God's." [26]And they were unable

ª**20:24** The denarius was a day's wages

to catch Him in a saying in the presence of the people; and being amazed at His answer, they became silent.

Is There a Resurrection?

27 Now there came to Him some of the Sadducees (who say that there is no resurrection), [28]and they questioned Him, saying, "Teacher, Moses wrote for us that IF A MAN'S BROTHER DIES, having a wife, AND HE IS CHILDLESS, HIS BROTHER SHOULD MARRY THE WIFE AND RAISE UP CHILDREN TO HIS BROTHER. [29]Now there were seven brothers; and the first took a wife and died childless; [30]and the second [31]and the third married her; and in the same way all seven died, leaving no children. [32]Finally the woman died also. [33]In the resurrection therefore, which one's wife will she be? For all seven had married her."

34 Jesus said to them, "The sons of this age marry and are given in marriage, [35]but those who are considered worthy to attain to that age and the resurrection from the dead, neither marry nor are given in marriage; [36]for they cannot even die anymore, because they are like angels, and are sons of God, being sons of the resurrection. [37]But that the dead are raised, even Moses showed, in the *passage about the burning* bush, where he calls the

Lord THE GOD OF ABRAHAM, AND THE GOD OF ISAAC, AND THE GOD OF JACOB. [38]Now He is not the God of the dead but of the living; for all live to Him." [39]Some of the scribes answered and said, "Teacher, You have spoken well." [40]For they did not have courage to question Him any longer about anything.

[41]Then He said to them, "How *is it that* they say [a]the Christ is David's son? [42]For David himself says in the book of Psalms,

'THE LORD SAID TO MY LORD,
"SIT AT MY RIGHT HAND,
[43]UNTIL I MAKE YOUR ENE-
   MIES A FOOTSTOOL FOR
   YOUR FEET." '
[44]Therefore David calls Him 'Lord,' and how is He his son?"

[45]And while all the people were listening, He said to the disciples, [46]"Beware of the scribes, who like to walk around in long robes, and love respectful greetings in the market places, and chief seats in the synagogues and places of honor at banquets, [47]who devour widows' houses, and for appearance's sake offer long prayers. These will receive greater condemnation."

The Widow's Gift

21 And He looked up and saw the rich putting their gifts into the treasury. [2]And He saw a poor widow putting in two small copper coins. [3]And He said, "Truly I say to you, this poor widow put in more than all *of them;* [4]for they all out of their surplus put into the offering; but she out of her poverty put in all that she had to live on."

[5]And while some were talking about the temple, that it was adorned with beautiful stones and votive gifts, He said, [6]"*As for* these things which you are looking at, the days will come in which there will not be left one stone upon another which will not be torn down."

[7]They questioned Him, saying, "Teacher, when therefore will these things happen? And what *will be* the sign when these things are about to take place?" [8]And He said, "See to it that you are not misled; for many will come in My name, saying, 'I am *He*,' and, 'The time is near.' Do not go after them. [9]When you hear of wars and disturbances, do not be terrified; for these things must take place first, but the end *does* not *follow* immediately."

Things to Come

[10]Then He continued by saying to them, "Nation will rise against nation and kingdom against kingdom, [11]and there will be great earthquakes, and in various places

plagues and famines; and there will be terrors and great signs from heaven.

12 "But before all these things, they will lay their hands on you and will persecute you, delivering you to the synagogues and prisons, bringing you before kings and governors for My name's sake. ¹³It will lead to an opportunity for your testimony. ¹⁴So make up your minds not to prepare beforehand to defend yourselves; ¹⁵for I will give you utterance and wisdom which none of your opponents will be able to resist or refute. ¹⁶But you will be betrayed even by parents and brothers and relatives and friends, and they will put *some* of you to death, ¹⁷and you will be hated by all because of My name. ¹⁸Yet not a hair of your head will perish. ¹⁹By your endurance you will gain your lives.

20 "But when you see Jerusalem surrounded by armies, then recognize that her desolation is near. ²¹Then those who are in Judea must flee to the mountains, and those who are in the midst of the city must leave, and those who are in the country must not enter the city; ²²because these are days of vengeance, so that all things which are written will be fulfilled. ²³Woe to those who are pregnant and to those who are nursing babies in those days; for there will be great distress upon the land and wrath to this people; ²⁴and they will fall by the edge of the sword, and will be led captive into all the nations; and Jerusalem will be trampled under foot by the Gentiles until the times of the Gentiles are fulfilled.

The Return of Christ

25 "There will be signs in sun and moon and stars, and on the earth dismay among nations, in perplexity at the roaring of the sea and the waves, ²⁶men fainting from fear and the expectation of the things which are coming upon the world; for the powers of the heavens will be shaken. ²⁷Then they will see THE SON OF MAN COMING IN A CLOUD with power and great glory. ²⁸But when these things begin to take place, straighten up and lift up your heads, because your redemption is drawing near."

29 Then He told them a parable: "Behold the fig tree and all the trees; ³⁰as soon as they put forth *leaves,* you see it and know for yourselves that summer is now near. ³¹So you also, when you see these things happening, recognize that the kingdom of God is near. ³²Truly I say to you, this generation will not pass away until all things take place. ³³Heaven and earth will pass away, but My words will not pass away.

34 "Be on guard, so that your hearts will not be weighted down with dissipation and drunkenness and the worries of life, and that day will not come on you suddenly like a trap; ³⁵for it will come upon all those who dwell on the face of all the earth. ³⁶But keep on the alert at all times, praying that you may have strength to escape all these things that arc about to take place, and to stand before the Son of Man."

37 Now during the day He was teaching in the temple, but at evening He would go out and spend the night on the mount that is called Olivet. ³⁸And all the people would get up early in the morning *to come* to Him in the temple to listen to Him.

Preparing the Passover

22 Now the Feast of Unleavened Bread, which is called the Passover, was approaching. ²The chief priests and the scribes were seeking how they might put Him to death; for they were afraid of the people.

3 And Satan entered into Judas who was called Iscariot, belonging to the number of the twelve. ⁴And he went away and discussed with the chief priests and officers how he might betray Him to them. ⁵They were glad and agreed to give him money. ⁶So he consented, and *began* seeking a good opportunity to betray Him to them apart from the crowd.

7 Then came the *first* day of Unleavened Bread on which the Passover *lamb* had to be sacrificed. ⁸And Jesus sent Peter and John, saying, "Go and prepare the Passover for us, so that we may eat it." ⁹They said to Him, "Where do You want us to prepare it?" ¹⁰And He said to them, "When you have entered the city, a man will meet you carrying a pitcher of water; follow him into the house that he enters. ¹¹And you shall say to the owner of the house, 'The Teacher says to you, "Where is the guest room in which I may eat the Passover with My disciples?" ' ¹²And he will show you a large, furnished upper room; prepare it there." ¹³And they left and found *everything* just as He had told them; and they prepared the Passover.

The Lord's Supper

14 When the hour had come, He reclined *at the table,* and the apostles with Him. ¹⁵And He said to them, "I have earnestly desired to eat this Passover with you before I suffer; ¹⁶for I say to you, I shall never again eat it until it is fulfilled in the kingdom of God." ¹⁷And when He had taken a cup *and* given thanks, He said, "Take this and share it among yourselves; [18]for I say to you, I will not drink of the fruit of the vine from now on until the kingdom of God comes." [19]And when He had taken *some* bread *and* given thanks, He broke it and gave it to them, saying, "This is My body which is given for you; do this in remembrance of Me." [20]And in the same way *He took* the cup after they had eaten, saying, "This cup which is poured out for you is the new covenant in My blood. [21]But behold, the hand of the one betraying Me is with Mine on the table. [22]For indeed, the Son of Man is going as it has been determined; but woe to that man by whom He is betrayed!" [23]And they began to discuss among themselves which one of them it might be who was going to do this thing.

Who Is Greatest

24 And there arose also a dispute among them *as to* which one of them was regarded to be greatest. [25]And He said to them, "The kings of the Gentiles lord it over them; and those who have authority over them are called 'Benefactors.' [26]But *it is* not this way with you, but the one who is the greatest among you must become like the youngest, and the leader like the servant. [27]For who is greater, the one who reclines *at the table* or the one who serves? Is it not the one who reclines *at the table?* But I am among you as the one who serves.

28 "You are those who have stood by Me in My trials; [29]and just as My Father has granted Me a kingdom, I grant you [30]that you may eat and drink at My table in My kingdom, and you will sit on thrones judging the twelve tribes of Israel.

31 "Simon, Simon, behold, Satan has demanded *permission* to sift you like wheat; [32]but I have prayed for you, that your faith may not fail; and you, when once you have turned again, strengthen your brothers." [33]But he said to Him, "Lord, with You I am ready to go both to prison and to death!" [34]And He said, "I say to you, Peter, the rooster will not crow today until you have denied three times that you know Me."

35 And He said to them, "When I sent you out without money belt and bag and sandals, you did not lack anything, did you?" They said, "*No*, nothing." [36]And He said to them, "But now, whoever has a money belt is to take it along, likewise also a bag, and whoever has no sword is to sell his coat and buy one. [37]For I tell you that this which is written must be fulfilled in Me, 'AND HE WAS NUMBERED WITH TRANSGRESSORS'; for that which refers to Me has *its* fulfillment." ³⁸They said, "Lord, look, here are two swords." And He said to them, "It is enough."

The Garden of Gethsemane

39 And He came out and proceeded as was His custom to the Mount of Olives; and the disciples also followed Him. ⁴⁰When He arrived at the place, He said to them, "Pray that you may not enter into temptation." ⁴¹And He withdrew from them about a stone's throw, and He knelt down and *began* to pray, ⁴²saying, "Father, if You are willing, remove this cup from Me; yet not My will, but Yours be done." ⁴³Now an angel from heaven appeared to Him, strengthening Him. ⁴⁴And being in agony He was praying very fervently; and His sweat became like drops of blood, falling down upon the ground. ⁴⁵When He rose from prayer, He came to the disciples and found them sleeping from sorrow, ⁴⁶and said to them, "Why are you sleeping? Get up and pray that you may not enter into temptation."

Jesus Betrayed by Judas

47 While He was still speaking, behold, a crowd *came,* and the one called Judas, one of the twelve, was preceding them; and he approached Jesus to kiss Him. ⁴⁸But Jesus said to him, "Judas, are you betraying the Son of Man with a kiss?" ⁴⁹When those who were around Him saw what was going to happen, they said, "Lord, shall we strike with the sword?" ⁵⁰And one of them struck the slave of the high priest and cut off his right ear. ⁵¹But Jesus answered and said, "Stop! No more of this." And He touched his ear and healed him. ⁵²Then Jesus said to the chief priests and officers of the temple and elders who had come against Him, "Have you come out with swords and clubs as you would against a robber? ⁵³While I was with you daily in the temple, you did not lay hands on Me; but this hour and the power of darkness are yours."

Jesus' Arrest

54 Having arrested Him, they led Him *away* and brought Him to the house of the high priest; but Peter was following at a distance. ⁵⁵After they had kindled a fire in the middle of the courtyard and had sat down together, Peter was sitting among them. ⁵⁶And a servant-girl, seeing him as he sat in the firelight and looking intently at him, said, "This man was with Him too." ⁵⁷But he denied *it,* saying, "Woman, I do not know Him." ⁵⁸A little later, another saw him and said, "You are *one* of them too!" But Peter said, "Man, I am not!" ⁵⁹After about an hour had passed, another man *began* to insist, saying,

"Certainly this man also was with Him, for he is a Galilean too." [60]But Peter said, "Man, I do not know what you are talking about." Immediately, while he was still speaking, a rooster crowed. [61]The Lord turned and looked at Peter. And Peter remembered the word of the Lord, how He had told him, "Before a rooster crows today, you will deny Me three times." [62]And he went out and wept bitterly.

[63] Now the men who were holding Jesus in custody were mocking Him and beating Him, [64]and they blindfolded Him and were asking Him, saying, "Prophesy, who is the one who hit You?" [65]And they were saying many other things against Him, blaspheming.

Jesus before the Sanhedrin

[66] When it was day, the [a]Council of elders of the people assembled, both chief priests and scribes, and they led Him away to their council *chamber,* saying, [67]"If You are the Christ, tell us." But He said to them, "If I tell you, you will not believe; [68]and if I ask a question, you will not answer. [69]But from now on THE SON OF MAN WILL BE SEATED AT THE RIGHT HAND of the power OF GOD." [70]And they all said, "Are You the Son of God, then?" And He said to them, "Yes, I am." [71]Then they said, "What further need do we have

[a]**22:66** Or Sanhedrin

of testimony? For we have heard it ourselves from His own mouth."

Jesus before Pilate

23 Then the whole body of them got up and brought Him before Pilate. [2]And they began to accuse Him, saying, "We found this man misleading our nation and forbidding to pay taxes to Caesar, and saying that He Himself is Christ, a King." [3]So Pilate asked Him, saying, "Are You the King of the Jews?" And He answered him and said, "*It is as* you say." [4]Then Pilate said to the chief priests and the crowds, "I find no guilt in this man." [5]But they kept on insisting, saying, "He stirs up the people, teaching all over Judea, starting from Galilee even as far as this place."

[6] When Pilate heard it, he asked whether the man was a Galilean. [7]And when he learned that He belonged to Herod's jurisdiction, he sent Him to Herod, who himself also was in Jerusalem at that time.

Jesus before Herod

[8] Now Herod was very glad when he saw Jesus; for he had wanted to see Him for a long time, because he had been hearing about Him and was hoping to see some sign performed by Him. [9]And he questioned Him at some length; but He answered him nothing.

[10]And the chief priests and the scribes were standing there, accusing Him vehemently. [11]And Herod with his soldiers, after treating Him with contempt and mocking Him, dressed Him in a gorgeous robe and sent Him back to Pilate. [12]Now Herod and Pilate became friends with one another that very day; for before they had been enemies with each other.

Pilate Seeks Jesus' Release

13 Pilate summoned the chief priests and the rulers and the people, [14]and said to them, "You brought this man to me as one who incites the people to rebellion, and behold, having examined Him before you, I have found no guilt in this man regarding the charges which you make against Him. [15]No, nor has Herod, for he sent Him back to us; and behold, nothing deserving death has been done by Him. [16]Therefore I will punish Him and release Him." [17a][Now he was obliged to release to them at the feast one prisoner.]

18 But they cried out all together, saying, "Away with this man, and release for us Barabbas!" [19](He was one who had been thrown into prison for an insurrection made in the city, and for murder.) [20]Pilate, wanting to release Jesus, addressed them again, [21]but they kept on calling out, saying, "Crucify, crucify Him!" [22]And he said to them the third time, "Why, what evil has this man done? I have found in Him no guilt *demanding* death; therefore I will punish Him and release Him." [23]But they were insistent, with loud voices asking that He be crucified. And their voices *began* to prevail. [24]And Pilate pronounced sentence that their demand be granted. [25]And he released the man they were asking for who had been thrown into prison for insurrection and murder, but he delivered Jesus to their will.

Simon Bears the Cross

26 When they led Him away, they seized a man, Simon of Cyrene, coming in from the country, and placed on him the cross to carry behind Jesus.

27 And following Him was a large crowd of the people, and of women who were mourning and lamenting Him. [28]But Jesus turning to them said, "Daughters of Jerusalem, stop weeping for Me, but weep for yourselves and for your children. [29]For behold, the days are coming when they will say, 'Blessed are the barren, and the wombs that never bore, and the breasts that never nursed.' [30]Then they will begin TO SAY TO THE MOUNTAINS, 'FALL ON US,' AND TO THE HILLS, 'COVER US.'

[a]**23:17** Early mss do not contain this v

³¹For if they do these things when the tree is green, what will happen when it is dry?"

32 Two others also, who were criminals, were being led away to be put to death with Him.

The Crucifixion

33 When they came to the place called The Skull, there they crucified Him and the criminals, one on the right and the other on the left. ³⁴But Jesus was saying, "Father, forgive them; for they do not know what they are doing." And they cast lots, dividing up His garments among themselves. ³⁵And the people stood by, looking on. And even the rulers were sneering at Him, saying, "He saved others; let Him save Himself if this is the Christ of God, His Chosen One." ³⁶The soldiers also mocked Him, coming up to Him, offering Him sour wine, ³⁷and saying, "If You are the King of the Jews, save Yourself!" ³⁸Now there was also an inscription above Him, "THIS IS THE KING OF THE JEWS."

39 One of the criminals who were hanged *there* was hurling abuse at Him, saying, "Are You not the Christ? Save Yourself and us!" ⁴⁰But the other answered, and rebuking him said, "Do you not even fear God, since you are under the same sentence of condemnation?

⁴¹And we indeed *are suffering* justly, for we are receiving what we deserve for our deeds; but this man has done nothing wrong." ⁴²And he was saying, "Jesus, remember me when You come in Your kingdom!" ⁴³And He said to him, "Truly I say to you, today you shall be with Me in Paradise."

44 It was now about the ᵃsixth hour, and darkness fell over the whole land until the ᵇninth hour, ⁴⁵because the sun was obscured; and the veil of the temple was torn in two. ⁴⁶And Jesus, crying out with a loud voice, said, "Father, INTO YOUR HANDS I COMMIT MY SPIRIT." Having said this, He breathed His last. ⁴⁷Now when the centurion saw what had happened, he *began* praising God, saying, "Certainly this man was innocent." ⁴⁸And all the crowds who came together for this spectacle, when they observed what had happened, *began* to return, beating their breasts. ⁴⁹And all His acquaintances and the women who accompanied Him from Galilee were standing at a distance, seeing these things.

Jesus Is Buried

50 And a man named Joseph, who was a member of the Council, a good and righteous man ⁵¹(he had not consented to their plan and action), *a man* from Arimathea,

ᵃ**23:44** I.e. noon; ᵇ**23:44** I.e. 3 p.m.

a city of the Jews, who was waiting for the kingdom of God; [52]this man went to Pilate and asked for the body of Jesus. [53]And he took it down and wrapped it in a linen cloth, and laid Him in a tomb cut into the rock, where no one had ever lain. [54]It was the preparation day, and the Sabbath was about to begin. [55]Now the women who had come with Him out of Galilee followed, and saw the tomb and how His body was laid. [56]Then they returned and prepared spices and perfumes.

And on the Sabbath they rested according to the commandment.

The Resurrection

24 But on the first day of the week, at early dawn, they came to the tomb bringing the spices which they had prepared. [2]And they found the stone rolled away from the tomb, [3]but when they entered, they did not find the body of the Lord Jesus. [4]While they were perplexed about this, behold, two men suddenly stood near them in dazzling clothing; [5]and as *the women* were terrified and bowed their faces to the ground, *the men* said to them, "Why do you seek the living One among the dead? [6]He is not here, but He has risen. Remember how He spoke to you while He was still in Galilee, [7]saying that the Son of

Man must be delivered into the hands of sinful men, and be crucified, and the third day rise again." [8]And they remembered His words, [9]and returned from the tomb and reported all these things to the eleven and to all the rest. [10]Now they were Mary Magdalene and Joanna and Mary the *mother* of James; also the other women with them were telling these things to the apostles. [11]But these words appeared to them as nonsense, and they would not believe them. [12]But Peter got up and ran to the tomb; stooping and looking in, he *saw the linen wrappings only; and he went away to his home, marveling at what had happened.

The Road to Emmaus

13 And behold, two of them were going that very day to a village named Emmaus, which was [a]about seven miles from Jerusalem. [14]And they were talking with each other about all these things which had taken place. [15]While they were talking and discussing, Jesus Himself approached and *began traveling with them. [16]But their eyes were prevented from recognizing Him. [17]And He said to them, "What are these words that you are exchanging with one another as you are walking?" And they stood still, looking sad. [18]One *of them,* named Cleopas, answered and said to Him, "Are You the only

[a]**24:13** Lit *60 stadia;* one stadion was about 600 ft

one visiting Jerusalem and unaware of the things which have happened here in these days?" ¹⁹And He said to them, "What things?" And they said to Him, "The things about Jesus the Nazarene, who was a prophet mighty in deed and word in the sight of God and all the people, ²⁰and how the chief priests and our rulers delivered Him to the sentence of death, and crucified Him. ²¹But we were hoping that it was He who was going to redeem Israel. Indeed, besides all this, it is the third day since these things happened. ²²But also some women among us amazed us. When they were at the tomb early in the morning, ²³and did not find His body, they came, saying that they had also seen a vision of angels who said that He was alive. ²⁴Some of those who were with us went to the tomb and found it just exactly as the women also had said; but Him they did not see." ²⁵And He said to them, "O foolish men and slow of heart to believe in all that the prophets have spoken! ²⁶Was it not necessary for the Christ to suffer these things and to enter into His glory?" ²⁷Then beginning with Moses and with all the prophets, He explained to them the things concerning Himself in all the Scriptures.

28 And they approached the village where they were going, and He acted as though He were going farther. ²⁹But they urged Him, saying, "Stay with us, for it is *getting* toward evening, and the day is now nearly over." So He went in to stay with them. ³⁰When He had reclined *at the table* with them, He took the bread and blessed *it,* and breaking *it,* He *began* giving *it* to them. ³¹Then their eyes were opened and they recognized Him; and He vanished from their sight. ³²They said to one another, "Were not our hearts burning within us while He was speaking to us on the road, while He was explaining the Scriptures to us?" ³³And they got up that very hour and returned to Jerusalem, and found gathered together the eleven and those who were with them, ³⁴saying, "The Lord has really risen and has appeared to Simon." ³⁵They *began* to relate their experiences on the road and how He was recognized by them in the breaking of the bread.

Other Appearances

36 While they were telling these things, He Himself stood in their midst and *said to them, "Peace be to you." ³⁷But they were startled and frightened and thought that they were seeing a spirit. ³⁸And He said to them, "Why are you troubled, and why do doubts arise in your hearts? ³⁹See My hands and My feet, that it is I Myself; touch

Me and see, for a spirit does not have flesh and bones as you see that I have." [40]And when He had said this, He showed them His hands and His feet. [41]While they still could not believe *it* because of their joy and amazement, He said to them, "Have you anything here to eat?" [42]They gave Him a piece of a broiled fish; [43]and He took it and ate *it* before them.

[44] Now He said to them, "These are My words which I spoke to you while I was still with you, that all things which are written about Me in the Law of Moses and the Prophets and the Psalms must be fulfilled." [45]Then He opened their minds to understand the Scriptures, [46]and He said to them, "Thus it is written, that the Christ would suffer and rise again from the dead the third day, [47]and that repentance for forgiveness of sins would be proclaimed in His name to all the nations, beginning from Jerusalem. [48]You are witnesses of these things. [49]And behold, I am sending forth the promise of My Father upon you; but you are to stay in the city until you are clothed with power from on high."

The Ascension

[50] And He led them out as far as Bethany, and He lifted up His hands and blessed them. [51]While He was blessing them, He parted from them and was carried up into heaven. [52]And they, after worshiping Him, returned to Jerusalem with great joy, [53]and were continually in the temple praising God.

JOHN

The Deity of Jesus Christ

1 In the beginning was the Word, and the Word was with God, and the Word was God. [2]He was in the beginning with God. [3]All things came into being through Him, and apart from Him nothing came into being that has come into being. [4]In Him was life, and the life was the Light of men. [5]The Light shines in the darkness, and the darkness did not [a]comprehend it.

The Witness John

[6] There [b]came a man sent from God, whose name was John. [7]He came as a witness, to testify about the Light, so that all might believe

[a]1:5 Or overpower; [b]1:6 Or came into being

through him. [8]He was not the Light, but *he came* to testify about the Light.

[9]There was the true Light[a] which, coming into the world, enlightens every man. [10]He was in the world, and the world was made through Him, and the world did not know Him. [11]He came to His [b]own, and those who were His own did not receive Him. [12]But as many as received Him, to them He gave the right to become children of God, *even* to those who believe in His name, [13]who were born, not of blood nor of the will of the flesh nor of the will of man, but of God.

The Word Made Flesh

[14]And the Word became flesh, and dwelt among us, and we saw His glory, glory as of the only begotten from the Father, full of grace and truth. [15]John *testified about Him and cried out, saying, "This was He of whom I said, 'He who comes after me has a higher rank than I, for He existed before me.' " [16]For of His fullness we have all received, and grace upon grace. [17]For the Law was given through Moses; grace and truth were realized through Jesus Christ. [18]No one has seen God at any time; the only begotten God who is in the bosom of the Father, He has explained *Him*.

The Testimony of John

[19]This is the testimony of John, when the Jews sent to him priests and Levites from Jerusalem to ask him, "Who are you?" [20]And he confessed and did not deny, but confessed, "I am not the Christ." [21]They asked him, "What then? Are you Elijah?" And he *said, "I am not." "Are you the Prophet?" And he answered, "No." [22]Then they said to him, "Who are you, so that we may give an answer to those who sent us? What do you say about yourself?" [23]He said, "I am A VOICE OF ONE CRYING IN THE WILDERNESS, 'MAKE STRAIGHT THE WAY OF THE LORD,' as Isaiah the prophet said."

[24]Now they had been sent from the Pharisees. [25]They asked him, and said to him, "Why then are you baptizing, if you are not the Christ, nor Elijah, nor the Prophet?" [26]John answered them saying, "I baptize [c]in water, *but* among you stands One whom you do not know. [27]*It is* He who comes after me, the thong of whose sandal I am not worthy to untie." [28]These things took place in Bethany beyond the Jordan, where John was baptizing.

[29]The next day he *saw Jesus coming to him and *said, "Behold, the Lamb of God who takes away the sin of the world! [30]This is He

[a]1:9 *Or which enlightens every person coming into the world;* [b]1:11 *Or own things, possessions, domain;*
[b]1:26 The Gr here can be translated *in, with* or *by*

on behalf of whom I said, 'After me comes a Man who has a higher rank than I, for He existed before me.' ³¹I did not recognize Him, but so that He might be manifested to Israel, I came baptizing ᵃin water." ³²John testified saying, "I have seen the Spirit descending as a dove out of heaven, and He remained upon Him. ³³I did not recognize Him, but He who sent me to baptize ᵇin water said to me, 'He upon whom you see the Spirit descending and remaining upon Him, this is the One who baptizes in the Holy Spirit.' ³⁴I myself have seen, and have testified that this is the Son of God."

Jesus' Public Ministry, First Converts

35 Again the next day John was standing with two of his disciples, ³⁶and he looked at Jesus as He walked, and *said, "Behold, the Lamb of God!" ³⁷The two disciples heard him speak, and they followed Jesus. ³⁸And Jesus turned and saw them following, and *said to them, "What do you seek?" They said to Him, "Rabbi (which translated means Teacher), where are You staying?" ³⁹He *said to them, "Come, and you will see." So they came and saw where He was staying; and they stayed with Him that day, for it was about the ᶜtenth hour. ⁴⁰One of the two who heard John *speak* and followed

Him, was Andrew, Simon Peter's brother. ⁴¹He *found first his own brother Simon and *said to him, "We have found the Messiah" (which translated means Christ). ⁴²He brought him to Jesus. Jesus looked at him and said, "You are Simon the son of John; you shall be called Cephas" (which is translated Peter).

43 The next day He purposed to go into Galilee, and He *found Philip. And Jesus *said to him, "Follow Me." ⁴⁴Now Philip was from Bethsaida, of the city of Andrew and Peter. ⁴⁵Philip *found Nathanael and *said to him, "We have found Him of whom Moses in the Law and *also* the Prophets wrote—Jesus of Nazareth, the son of Joseph." ⁴⁶Nathanael said to him, "Can any good thing come out of Nazareth?" Philip *said to him, "Come and see." ⁴⁷Jesus saw Nathanael coming to Him, and *said of him, "Behold, an Israelite indeed, in whom there is no deceit!" ⁴⁸Nathanael *said to Him, "How do You know me?" Jesus answered and said to him, "Before Philip called you, when you were under the fig tree, I saw you." ⁴⁹Nathanael answered Him, "Rabbi, You are the Son of God; You are the King of Israel." ⁵⁰Jesus answered and said to him, "Because I said to you that I saw you under the fig tree, do you believe? You

---

ᵃ**1:31** The Gr here can be translated *in, with or by;* ᵇ**1:33** The Gr here can be translated *in, with or by;* ᶜ**1:39** Perhaps 10 a.m. (Roman time) will see greater things than these." ⁵¹And He *said to him, "Truly, truly, I say to you, you will see the heavens opened and the angels of God ascending and descending on the Son of Man."

Miracle at Cana

2 On the third day there was a wedding in Cana of Galilee, and the mother of Jesus was there; ²and both Jesus and His disciples were invited to the wedding. ³When the wine ran out, the mother of Jesus *said to Him, "They have no wine." ⁴And Jesus *said to her, "Woman, what does that have to do with us? My hour has not yet come." ⁵His mother *said to the servants, "Whatever He says to you, do it." ⁶Now there were six stone waterpots set there for the Jewish custom of purification, containing twenty or thirty gallons each. ⁷Jesus *said to them, "Fill the waterpots with water." So they filled them up to the brim. ⁸And He *said to them, "Draw some out now and take it to the ᵃheadwaiter." So they took it to him. ⁹When the headwaiter tasted the water which had become wine, and did not know where it came from (but the servants who had drawn the water knew), the headwaiter *called the bridegroom, ¹⁰and *said to him, "Every man serves the good wine first, and when the people have drunk freely, then he serves the poorer wine;

ᵃ2:8 Or steward

but you have kept the good wine until now." ¹¹This beginning of His signs Jesus did in Cana of Galilee, and manifested His glory, and His disciples believed in Him.

12 After this He went down to Capernaum, He and His mother and His brothers and His disciples; and they stayed there a few days.

First Passover
Cleansing the Temple

13 The Passover of the Jews was near, and Jesus went up to Jerusalem. ¹⁴And He found in the temple those who were selling oxen and sheep and doves, and the money changers seated at their tables. ¹⁵And He made a scourge of cords, and drove them all out of the temple, with the sheep and the oxen; and He poured out the coins of the money changers and overturned their tables; ¹⁶and to those who were selling the doves He said, "Take these things away; stop making My Father's house a place of business." ¹⁷His disciples remembered that it was written, "ZEAL FOR YOUR HOUSE WILL CONSUME ME." ¹⁸The Jews then said to Him, "What sign do You show us as your authority for doing these things?" ¹⁹Jesus answered them, "Destroy this temple, and in three days I will raise it up." ²⁰The Jews then said, "It took forty-six years to build this temple, and

will You raise it up in three days?" [21]But He was speaking of the temple of His body. [22]So when He was raised from the dead, His disciples remembered that He said this; and they believed the Scripture and the word which Jesus had spoken.

[23] Now when He was in Jerusalem at the Passover, during the feast, many believed in His name, observing His signs which He was doing. [24]But Jesus, on His part, was not entrusting Himself to them, for He knew all men, [25]and because He did not need anyone to testify concerning man, for He Himself knew what was in man.

The New Birth

3 Now there was a man of the Pharisees, named Nicodemus, a ruler of the Jews; [2]this man came to Jesus by night and said to Him, "Rabbi, we know that You have come from God *as* a teacher; for no one can do these signs that You do unless God is with him." [3]Jesus answered and said to him, "Truly, truly, I say to you, unless one is born again he cannot see the kingdom of God."

[4] Nicodemus *said to Him, "How can a man be born when he is old? He cannot enter a second time into his mother's womb and be born, can he?" [5]Jesus answered,

"Truly, truly, I say to you, unless one is born of water and the Spirit he cannot enter into the kingdom of God. [6]That which is born of the flesh is flesh, and that which is born of the Spirit is spirit. [7]Do not be amazed that I said to you, 'You must be born again.' [8]The wind blows where it wishes and you hear the sound of it, but do not know where it comes from and where it is going; so is everyone who is born of the Spirit."

[9] Nicodemus said to Him, "How can these things be?" [10]Jesus answered and said to him, "Are you the teacher of Israel and do not understand these things? [11]Truly, truly, I say to you, we speak of what we know and testify of what we have seen, and you do not accept our testimony. [12]If I told you earthly things and you do not believe, how will you believe if I tell you heavenly things? [13]No one has ascended into heaven, but He who descended from heaven: the Son of Man. [14]As Moses lifted up the serpent in the wilderness, even so must the Son of Man be lifted up; [15]so that whoever [a]believes will in Him have eternal life.

[16] "For God so loved the world, that He gave His only begotten Son, that whoever believes in Him shall not perish, but have eternal life. [17]For God did not send the

[a]3:15 Or believes in Him will have eternal life

Son into the world to judge the world, but that the world might be saved through Him. [18]He who believes in Him is not judged; he who does not believe has been judged already, because he has not believed in the name of the only begotten Son of God. [19]This is the judgment, that the Light has come into the world, and men loved the darkness rather than the Light, for their deeds were evil. [20]For every one who does evil hates the Light, and does not come to the Light for fear that his deeds will be exposed. [21]But he who practices the truth comes to the Light, so that his deeds may be manifested as having been wrought in God."

John's Last Testimony

22 After these things Jesus and His disciples came into the land of Judea, and there He was spending time with them and baptizing. [23]John also was baptizing in Aenon near Salim, because there was much water there; and *people* were coming and were being baptized— [24]for John had not yet been thrown into prison.

25 Therefore there arose a discussion on the part of John's disciples with a Jew about purification. [26]And they came to John and said to him, "Rabbi, He who was with you beyond the Jordan, to whom you have testified, behold, He is baptizing and all are coming to Him." [27]John answered and said, "A man can receive nothing unless it has been given him from heaven. [28]You yourselves are my witnesses that I said, 'I am not the Christ,' but, 'I have been sent ahead of Him.' [29]He who has the bride is the bridegroom; but the friend of the bridegroom, who stands and hears him, rejoices greatly because of the bridegroom's voice. So this joy of mine has been made full. [30]He must increase, but I must decrease.

31 "He who comes from above is above all, he who is of the earth is from the earth and speaks of the earth. He who comes from heaven is above all. [32]What He has seen and heard, of that He testifies; and no one receives His testimony. [33]He who has received His testimony has set his seal to *this,* that God is true. [34]For He whom God has sent speaks the words of God; for He gives the Spirit without measure. [35]The Father loves the Son and has given all things into His hand. [36]He who believes in the Son has eternal life; but he who does not obey the Son will not see life, but the wrath of God abides on him."

Jesus Goes to Galilee

4 Therefore when the Lord knew that the Pharisees had heard that Jesus was making and baptizing more disciples than John ²(although Jesus Himself was not baptizing, but His disciples were), ³He left Judea and went away again into Galilee. ⁴And He had to pass through Samaria. ⁵So He *came to a city of Samaria called Sychar, near the parcel of ground that Jacob gave to his son Joseph; ⁶and Jacob's well was there. So Jesus, being wearied from His journey, was sitting thus by the well. It was about the ᵃsixth hour.

The Woman of Samaria

7 There *came a woman of Samaria to draw water. Jesus *said to her, "Give Me a drink." ⁸For His disciples had gone away into the city to buy food. ⁹Therefore the Samaritan woman *said to Him, "How is it that You, being a Jew, ask me for a drink since I am a Samaritan woman?" (For Jews have no dealings with Samaritans.) ¹⁰Jesus answered and said to her, "If you knew the gift of God, and who it is who says to you, 'Give Me a drink,' you would have asked Him, and He would have given you living water." ¹¹She *said to Him, "Sir, You have nothing to draw with and the well is deep; where then do You get that living water? ¹²You are not greater than our father Jacob, are You, who gave us the well, and drank of it himself and his sons and his cattle?" ¹³Jesus answered and said to her,

"Everyone who drinks of this water will thirst again; ¹⁴but whoever drinks of the water that I will give him shall never thirst; but the water that I will give him will become in him a well of water springing up to eternal life."

15 The woman *said to Him, "Sir, give me this water, so I will not be thirsty nor come all the way here to draw." ¹⁶He *said to her, "Go, call your husband and come here." ¹⁷The woman answered and said, "I have no husband." Jesus *said to her, "You have correctly said, 'I have no husband'; ¹⁸for you have had five husbands, and the one whom you now have is not your husband; this you have said truly." ¹⁹The woman *said to Him, "Sir, I perceive that You are a prophet. ²⁰Our fathers worshiped in this mountain, and you *people* say that in Jerusalem is the place where men ought to worship." ²¹Jesus *said to her, "Woman, believe Me, an hour is coming when neither in this mountain nor in Jerusalem will you worship the Father. ²²You worship what you do not know; we worship what we know, for salvation is from the Jews. ²³But an hour is coming, and now is, when the true worshipers will worship the Father in spirit and truth; for such people the Father seeks to be His worshipers. ²⁴God is spirit, and those who worship Him must

---

ᵃ4:6 Perhaps 6 p.m. Roman time or noon Jewish time

worship in spirit and truth." ²⁵The woman *said to Him, "I know that Messiah is coming (He who is called Christ); when that One comes, He will declare all things to us." ²⁶Jesus *said to her, "I who speak to you am *He.*"

27 At this point His disciples came, and they were amazed that He had been speaking with a woman, yet no one said, "What do You seek?" or, "Why do You speak with her?" ²⁸So the woman left her waterpot, and went into the city and *said to the men, ²⁹"Come, see a man who told me all the things that I *have* done; this is not the Christ, is it?" ³⁰They went out of the city, and were coming to Him.

31 Meanwhile the disciples were urging Him, saying, "Rabbi, eat." ³²But He said to them, "I have food to eat that you do not know about." ³³So the disciples were saying to one another, "No one brought Him *anything* to eat, did he?" ³⁴Jesus *said to them, "My food is to do the will of Him who sent Me and to accomplish His work. ³⁵Do you not say, 'There are yet four months, and *then* comes the harvest'? Behold, I say to you, lift up your eyes and look on the fields, that they are white for harvest. ³⁶Already he who reaps is receiving wages and is gathering fruit for life eternal; so that he who sows and he who reaps may rejoice together. ³⁷For in this *case* the saying is true, 'One sows and another reaps.' ³⁸I sent you to reap that for which you have not labored; others have labored and you have entered into their labor."

The Samaritans

39 From that city many of the Samaritans believed in Him because of the word of the woman who testified, "He told me all the things that I *have* done." ⁴⁰So when the Samaritans came to Jesus, they were asking Him to stay with them; and He stayed there two days. ⁴¹Many more believed because of His word; ⁴²and they were saying to the woman, "It is no longer because of what you said that we believe, for we have heard for ourselves and know that this One is indeed the Savior of the world."

43 After the two days He went forth from there into Galilee. ⁴⁴For Jesus Himself testified that a prophet has no honor in his own country. ⁴⁵So when He came to Galilee, the Galileans received Him, having seen all the things that He did in Jerusalem at the feast; for they themselves also went to the feast.

Healing a Nobleman's Son

46 Therefore He came again to

Cana of Galilee where He had made the water wine. And there was a royal official whose son was sick at Capernaum. [47]When he heard that Jesus had come out of Judea into Galilee, he went to Him and was imploring *Him* to come down and heal his son; for he was at the point of death. [48]So Jesus said to him, "Unless you *people* see signs and wonders, you *simply* will not believe." [49]The royal official *said to Him, "Sir, come down before my child dies." [50]Jesus *said to him, "Go; your son lives." The man believed the word that Jesus spoke to him and started off. [51]As he was now going down, *his* slaves met him, saying that his son was living. [52]So he inquired of them the hour when he began to get better. Then they said to him, "Yesterday at the [a]seventh hour the fever left him." [53]So the father knew that *it was* at that hour in which Jesus said to him, "Your son lives"; and he himself believed and his whole household. [54]This is again a second sign that Jesus performed when He had come out of Judea into Galilee.

The Healing at Bethesda

5 After these things there was a feast of the Jews, and Jesus went up to Jerusalem.

2 Now there is in Jerusalem by the sheep *gate* a pool, which is called in Hebrew Bethesda, having five porticoes. [3]In these lay a multitude of those who were sick, blind, lame, and withered, [b][waiting for the moving of the waters; [4]for an angel of the Lord went down at certain seasons into the pool and stirred up the water; whoever then first, after the stirring up of the water, stepped in was made well from whatever disease with which he was afflicted.] [5]A man was there who had been ill for thirty-eight years. [6]When Jesus saw him lying *there,* and knew that he had already been a long time *in that condition,* He *said to him, "Do you wish to get well?" [7]The sick man answered Him, "Sir, I have no man to put me into the pool when the water is stirred up, but while I am coming, another steps down before me." [8]Jesus *said to him, "Get up, pick up your pallet and walk." [9]Immediately the man became well, and picked up his pallet and *began* to walk.

Now it was the Sabbath on that day. [10]So the Jews were saying to the man who was cured, "It is the Sabbath, and it is not permissible for you to carry your pallet." [11]But he answered them, "He who made me well was the one who said to me, 'Pick up your pallet and walk.'" [12]They asked him, "Who is the man who said to you, 'Pick up *your pallet* and walk'?" [13]But the man who was healed did not know

[a]**4:52** Perhaps 7 p.m. Roman time or 1 p.m. Jewish time; [b]**5:3** Early mss do not contain the remainder of v 3, nor v 4

who it was, for Jesus had slipped away while there was a crowd in *that* place. ¹⁴Afterward Jesus *found him in the temple and said to him, "Behold, you have become well; do not sin anymore, so that nothing worse happens to you." ¹⁵The man went away, and told the Jews that it was Jesus who had made him well. ¹⁶For this reason the Jews were persecuting Jesus, because He was doing these things on the Sabbath. ¹⁷But He answered them, "My Father is working until now, and I Myself am working."

Jesus' Equality with God

¹⁸For this reason therefore the Jews were seeking all the more to kill Him, because He not only was breaking the Sabbath, but also was calling God His own Father, making Himself equal with God.

19 Therefore Jesus answered and was saying to them, "Truly, truly, I say to you, the Son can do nothing of Himself, unless *it is* something He sees the Father doing; for whatever the Father does, these things the Son also does in like manner. ²⁰For the Father loves the Son, and shows Him all things that He Himself is doing; and *the Father* will show Him greater works than these, so that you will marvel. ²¹For just as the Father raises the dead and gives them life, even so the Son also

gives life to whom He wishes. ²²For not even the Father judges anyone, but He has given all judgment to the Son, ²³so that all will honor the Son even as they honor the Father. He who does not honor the Son does not honor the Father who sent Him.

24 "Truly, truly, I say to you, he who hears My word, and believes Him who sent Me, has eternal life, and does not come into judgment, but has passed out of death into life.

Two Resurrections

²⁵Truly, truly, I say to you, an hour is coming and now is, when the dead will hear the voice of the Son of God, and those who hear will live. ²⁶For just as the Father has life in Himself, even so He gave to the Son also to have life in Himself; ²⁷and He gave Him authority to execute judgment, because He is *the* Son of Man. ²⁸Do not marvel at this; for an hour is coming, in which all who are in the tombs will hear His voice, ²⁹and will come forth; those who did the good *deeds* to a resurrection of life, those who committed the evil *deeds* to a resurrection of judgment.

30 "I can do nothing on My own initiative. As I hear, I judge; and My judgment is just, because I do not seek My own will, but the will of Him who sent Me.

31 "If I *alone* testify about Myself, My testimony is not true. [32]There is another who testifies of Me, and I know that the testimony which He gives about Me is true.

Witness of John

[33]You have sent to John, and he has testified to the truth. [34]But the testimony which I receive is not from man, but I say these things so that you may be saved. [35]He was the lamp that was burning and was shining and you were willing to rejoice for a while in his light.

Witness of Works

[36]But the testimony which I have is greater than *the testimony of* John; for the works which the Father has given Me to accomplish—the very works that I do—testify about Me, that the Father has sent Me.

Witness of the Father

[37]And the Father who sent Me, He has testified of Me. You have neither heard His voice at any time nor seen His form. [38]You do not have His word abiding in you, for you do not believe Him whom He sent.

Witness of the Scripture

[39a]You search the Scriptures because you think that in them you

ᵃ**5:39** Or (a command) *Search the Scriptures!*

have eternal life; it is these that testify about Me; [40]and you are unwilling to come to Me so that you may have life. [41]I do not receive glory from men; [42]but I know you, that you do not have the love of God in yourselves. [43]I have come in My Father's name, and you do not receive Me; if another comes in his own name, you will receive him. [44]How can you believe, when you receive glory from one another and you do not seek the glory that is from the *one and* only God? [45]Do not think that I will accuse you before the Father; the one who accuses you is Moses, in whom you have set your hope. [46]For if you believed Moses, you would believe Me, for he wrote about Me. [47]But if you do not believe his writings, how will you believe My words?"

Five Thousand Fed

6After these things Jesus went away to the other side of the Sea of Galilee (or Tiberias). [2]A large crowd followed Him, because they saw the signs which He was performing on those who were sick. [3]Then Jesus went up on the mountain, and there He sat down with His disciples. [4]Now the Passover, the feast of the Jews, was near. [5]Therefore Jesus, lifting up His eyes and seeing that a large crowd was coming to Him, *said to Philip, "Where are we to buy bread, so that these may eat?" [6]This He was saying to test him, for He Himself knew what He was intending to do. [7]Philip answered Him, "Two hundred [a]denarii worth of bread is not sufficient for them, for everyone to receive a little." [8]One of His disciples, Andrew, Simon Peter's brother, *said to Him, [9]"There is a lad here who has five barley loaves and two fish, but what are these for so many people?" [10]Jesus said, "Have the people sit down." Now there was much grass in the place. So the men sat down, in number about five thousand. [11]Jesus then took the loaves, and having given thanks, He distributed to those who were seated; likewise also of the fish as much as they wanted. [12]When they were filled, He *said to His disciples, "Gather up the leftover fragments so that nothing will be lost." [13]So they gathered them up, and filled twelve baskets with fragments from the five barley loaves which were left over by those who had eaten. [14]Therefore when the people saw the sign which He had performed, they said, "This is truly the Prophet who is to come into the world."

Jesus Walks on the Water

[15] So Jesus, perceiving that they were intending to come and take Him by force to make Him king, withdrew again to the mountain by Himself alone.

[16] Now when evening came, His disciples went down to the sea, [17]and after getting into a boat, they *started to* cross the sea to Capernaum. It had already become dark, and Jesus had not yet come to them. [18]The sea *began* to be stirred up because a strong wind was blowing. [19]Then, when they had rowed about three or four miles, they *saw Jesus walking on the sea and drawing near to the boat; and they were frightened. [20]But He *said to them, "It is I; do not be afraid." [21]So they were willing to receive Him into the boat, and immediately the boat was at the land to which they were going.

[22] The next day the crowd that stood on the other side of the sea saw that there was no other small boat there, except one, and that Jesus had not entered with His disciples into the boat, but *that* His disciples had gone away alone. [23]There came other small boats from Tiberias near to the place where they ate the bread after the Lord had given thanks. [24]So when the crowd saw that Jesus was not there, nor His disciples, they themselves got into the small boats, and came to Capernaum seeking Jesus. [25]When they found Him on the other side of the sea, they said to Him, "Rabbi, when did You get here?"

[a]**6:7** The denarius was equivalent to a day's wages

Words to the People

26 Jesus answered them and said, "Truly, truly, I say to you, you seek Me, not because you saw signs, but because you ate of the loaves and were filled. **27**Do not work for the food which perishes, but for the food which endures to eternal life, which the Son of Man will give to you, for on Him the Father, God, has set His seal." **28**Therefore they said to Him, "What shall we do, so that we may work the works of God?" **29**Jesus answered and said to them, "This is the work of God, that you believe in Him whom He has sent." **30**So they said to Him, "What then do You do for a sign, so that we may see, and believe You? What work do You perform? **31**Our fathers ate the manna in the wilderness; as it is written, 'HE GAVE THEM BREAD OUT OF HEAVEN TO EAT.' " **32**Jesus then said to them, "Truly, truly, I say to you, it is not Moses who has given you the bread out of heaven, but it is My Father who gives you the true bread out of heaven. **33**For the bread of God is ᵃthat which comes down out of heaven, and gives life to the world." **34**Then they said to Him, "Lord, always give us this bread."

35 Jesus said to them, "I am the bread of life; he who comes to Me will not hunger, and he who believes in Me will never thirst.

ᵃ**6:33** Or He who comes

36But I said to you that you have seen Me, and yet do not believe. **37**All that the Father gives Me will come to Me, and the one who comes to Me I will certainly not cast out. **38**For I have come down from heaven, not to do My own will, but the will of Him who sent Me. **39**This is the will of Him who sent Me, that of all that He has given Me I lose nothing, but raise it up on the last day. **40**For this is the will of My Father, that everyone who beholds the Son and believes in Him will have eternal life, and I Myself will raise him up on the last day."

Words to the Jews

41 Therefore the Jews were grumbling about Him, because He said, "I am the bread that came down out of heaven." **42**They were saying, "Is not this Jesus, the son of Joseph, whose father and mother we know? How does He now say, 'I have come down out of heaven'?" **43**Jesus answered and said to them, "Do not grumble among yourselves. **44**No one can come to Me unless the Father who sent Me draws him; and I will raise him up on the last day. **45**It is written in the prophets, 'AND THEY SHALL ALL BE TAUGHT OF GOD.' Everyone who has heard and learned from the Father, comes to Me. **46**Not that anyone has seen the Father, except the One who is from God;

He has seen the Father. ⁴⁷Truly, truly, I say to you, he who believes has eternal life. ⁴⁸I am the bread of life. ⁴⁹Your fathers ate the manna in the wilderness, and they died. ⁵⁰This is the bread which comes down out of heaven, so that one may eat of it and not die. ⁵¹I am the living bread that came down out of heaven; if anyone eats of this bread, he will live forever; and the bread also which I will give for the life of the world is My flesh."

52 Then the Jews *began* to argue with one another, saying, "How can this man give us *His* flesh to eat?" ⁵³So Jesus said to them, "Truly, truly, I say to you, unless you eat the flesh of the Son of Man and drink His blood, you have no life in yourselves. ⁵⁴He who eats My flesh and drinks My blood has eternal life, and I will raise him up on the last day. ⁵⁵For My flesh is true food, and My blood is true drink. ⁵⁶He who eats My flesh and drinks My blood abides in Me, and I in him. ⁵⁷As the living Father sent Me, and I live because of the Father, so he who eats Me, he also will live because of Me. ⁵⁸This is the bread which came down out of heaven; not as the fathers ate and died; he who eats this bread will live forever."

Words to the Disciples

⁵⁹These things He said in the synagogue as He taught in Capernaum.

60 Therefore many of His disciples, when they heard *this* said, "This is a difficult statement; who can listen to it?" ⁶¹But Jesus, conscious that His disciples grumbled at this, said to them, "Does this cause you to stumble? ⁶²*What* then if you see the Son of Man ascending to where He was before? ⁶³It is the Spirit who gives life; the flesh profits nothing; the words that I have spoken to you are spirit and are life. ⁶⁴But there are some of you who do not believe." For Jesus knew from the beginning who they were who did not believe, and who it was that would betray Him. ⁶⁵And He was saying, "For this reason I have said to you, that no one can come to Me unless it has been granted him from the Father."

Peter's Confession of Faith

66 As a result of this many of His disciples withdrew and were not walking with Him anymore. ⁶⁷So Jesus said to the twelve, "You do not want to go away also, do you?" ⁶⁸Simon Peter answered Him, "Lord, to whom shall we go? You have words of eternal life. ⁶⁹We have believed and have come to know that You are the Holy One of God." ⁷⁰Jesus answered them, "Did I Myself not choose you, the twelve, and *yet* one of you is a devil?" [71]Now He meant Judas *the son* of Simon Iscariot, for he, one of the twelve, was going to betray Him.

Jesus Teaches at the Feast

7 After these things Jesus was walking in Galilee, for He was unwilling to walk in Judea because the Jews were seeking to kill Him. [2]Now the feast of the Jews, the Feast of Booths, was near. [3]Therefore His brothers said to Him, "Leave here and go into Judea, so that Your disciples also may see Your works which You are doing. [4]For no one does anything in secret when he himself seeks to be *known* publicly. If You do these things, show Yourself to the world." [5]For not even His brothers were believing in Him. [6]So Jesus *said to them, "My time is not yet here, but your time is always opportune. [7]The world cannot hate you, but it hates Me because I testify of it, that its deeds are evil. [8]Go up to the feast yourselves; I do not go up to this feast because My time has not yet fully come." [9]Having said these things to them, He stayed in Galilee.

10 But when His brothers had gone up to the feast, then He Himself also went up, not publicly, but as if, in secret. [11]So the Jews were seeking Him at the feast and were saying, "Where is He?" [12]There was much grumbling among the crowds concerning Him; some were saying, "He is a good man"; others were saying, "No, on the contrary, He leads the people astray." [13]Yet no one was speaking openly of Him for fear of the Jews.

14 But when it was now the midst of the feast Jesus went up into the temple, and *began to* teach. [15]The Jews then were astonished, saying, "How has this man become learned, having never been educated?" [16]So Jesus answered them and said, "My teaching is not Mine, but His who sent Me. [17]If anyone is willing to do His will, he will know of the teaching, whether it is of God or *whether* I speak from Myself. [18]He who speaks from himself seeks his own glory; but He who is seeking the glory of the One who sent Him, He is true, and there is no unrighteousness in Him.

19 "Did not Moses give you the Law, and *yet* none of you carries out the Law? Why do you seek to kill Me?" [20]The crowd answered, "You have a demon! Who seeks to kill You?" [21]Jesus answered them, "I did one deed, and you all marvel. [22]For this reason Moses has given you circumcision (not because it is from Moses, but from the fathers), and on *the* Sabbath you circumcise a man. [23]If a man receives circumcision on *the* Sabbath so that the Law of Moses will not be broken, are you angry with Me because I made an entire man well on *the* Sabbath? [24]Do not judge according to appearance, but judge with righteous judgment."

25 So some of the people of Jerusalem were saying, "Is this not the man whom they are seeking to kill? [26]Look, He is speaking publicly, and they are saying nothing to Him. The rulers do not really know that this is the Christ, do they? [27]However, we know where this man is from; but whenever the Christ may come, no one knows where He is from." [28]Then Jesus cried out in the temple, teaching and saying, "You both know Me and know where I am from; and I have not come of Myself, but He who sent Me is true, whom you do not know. [29]I know Him, because I am from Him, and He sent Me." [30]So they were seeking to seize Him; and no man laid his hand on Him, because His hour had not yet come. [31]But many of the crowd believed in Him; and they were saying, "When the Christ comes, He will not perform more signs than those which this man has, will He?"

32 The Pharisees heard the crowd muttering these things about Him, and the chief priests and the Pharisees sent officers to seize Him. [33]Therefore Jesus said, "For a little while longer I am with you, then I go to Him who sent Me. [34]You will seek Me, and will not find Me; and where I am, you cannot come." [35]The Jews then said to one another, "Where does this man intend to go that we will not find Him? He is not intending to go to the Dispersion among the Greeks, and teach the Greeks, is He? [36]What is this statement that He said, 'You will seek Me, and will not find Me; and where I am, you cannot come'?"

37 Now on the last day, the great *day* of the feast, Jesus stood and cried out, saying, "If anyone is thirsty, let him come to Me and drink. [38]He who believes in Me, as the Scripture said, 'From his innermost being will flow rivers of living water.' " [39]But this He spoke of the Spirit, whom those who believed in Him were to receive; for the Spirit was not yet *given,* because Jesus was not yet glorified.

Division of People over Jesus
40 *Some* of the people therefore, when they heard these words, were saying, "This certainly is the Prophet." [41]Others were saying, "This is the Christ." Still others were saying, "Surely the Christ is not going to come from Galilee, is He? [42]Has not the Scripture said

that the Christ comes from the descendants of David, and from Bethlehem, the village where David was?" ⁴³So a division occurred in the crowd because of Him. ⁴⁴Some of them wanted to seize Him, but no one laid hands on Him.

45 The officers then came to the chief priests and Pharisees, and they said to them, "Why did you not bring Him?" ⁴⁶The officers answered, "Never has a man spoken the way this man speaks." ⁴⁷The Pharisees then answered them, "You have not also been led astray, have you? ⁴⁸No one of the rulers or Pharisees has believed in Him, has he? ⁴⁹But this crowd which does not know the Law is accursed." ⁵⁰Nicodemus (he who came to Him before, being one of them) *said to them, ⁵¹"Our Law does not judge a man unless it first hears from him and knows what he is doing, does it?" ⁵²They answered him, "You are not also from Galilee, are you? Search, and see that no prophet arises out of Galilee." ^{53a}[Everyone went to his home.

The Adulterous Woman

8 But Jesus went to the Mount of Olives. ²Early in the morning He came again into the temple, and all the people were coming to Him; and He sat down and *began* to teach them. ³The scribes and the Pharisees *brought a woman caught in adultery, and having set her in the center *of the court,* ⁴they *said to Him, "Teacher, this woman has been caught in adultery, in the very act. ⁵Now in the Law Moses commanded us to stone such women; what then do You say?" ⁶They were saying this, testing Him, so that they might have grounds for accusing Him. But Jesus stooped down and with His finger wrote on the ground. ⁷But when they persisted in asking Him, He straightened up, and said to them, "He who is without sin among you, let him *be the* first to throw a stone at her." ⁸Again He stooped down and wrote on the ground. ⁹When they heard it, they *began* to go out one by one, beginning with the older ones, and He was left alone, and the woman, where she was, in the center *of the court.* ¹⁰Straightening up, Jesus said to her, "Woman, where are they? Did no one condemn you?" ¹¹She said, "No one, Lord." And Jesus said, "I do not condemn you, either. Go. From now on sin no more."]

Jesus Is the Light of the World

12 Then Jesus again spoke to them, saying, "I am the Light of the world; he who follows Me will not walk in the darkness, but will have the Light of life." ¹³So the Pharisees said to Him, "You are testifying

^a**7:53** Later mss add the story of the adulterous woman, numbering it as John 7:53–8:11

about Yourself; Your testimony is not true." ¹⁴Jesus answered and said to them, "Even if I testify about Myself, My testimony is true, for I know where I came from and where I am going; but you do not know where I come from or where I am going. ¹⁵You judge according to the flesh; I am not judging anyone. ¹⁶But even if I do judge, My judgment is true; for I am not alone *in it*, but I and the Father who sent Me. ¹⁷Even in your law it has been written that the testimony of two men is true. ¹⁸I am He who testifies about Myself, and the Father who sent Me testifies about Me." ¹⁹So they were saying to Him, "Where is Your Father?" Jesus answered, "You know neither Me nor My Father; if you knew Me, you would know My Father also." ²⁰These words He spoke in the treasury, as He taught in the temple; and no one seized Him, because His hour had not yet come.

21 Then He said again to them, "I go away, and you will seek Me, and will die in your sin; where I am going, you cannot come." ²²So the Jews were saying, "Surely He will not kill Himself, will He, since He says, 'Where I am going, you cannot come'?" ²³And He was saying to them, "You are from below, I am from above; you are of this world, I am not of this world. ²⁴Therefore I said to you that you will die in your sins; for unless you believe that I am *He*, you will die in your sins." ²⁵So they were saying to Him, "Who are You?" Jesus said to them, "What have I been saying to you *from* the beginning? ²⁶I have many things to speak and to judge concerning you, but He who sent Me is true; and the things which I heard from Him, these I speak to the world." ²⁷They did not realize that He had been speaking to them about the Father. ²⁸So Jesus said, "When you lift up the Son of Man, then you will know that I am *He*, and I do nothing on My own initiative, but I speak these things as the Father taught Me. ²⁹And He who sent Me is with Me; He has not left Me alone, for I always do the things that are pleasing to Him." ³⁰As He spoke these things, many came to believe in Him.

The Truth Will Make You Free

31 So Jesus was saying to those Jews who had believed Him, "If you continue in My word, *then* you are truly disciples of Mine; ³²and you will know the truth, and the truth will make you free." ³³They answered Him, "We are Abraham's descendants and have never yet been enslaved to anyone; how is it that You say, 'You will become free'?"

34 Jesus answered them, "Truly, truly, I say to you, everyone who

commits sin is the slave of sin. [35]The slave does not remain in the house forever; the son does remain forever. [36]So if the Son makes you free, you will be free indeed. [37]I know that you are Abraham's descendants; yet you seek to kill Me, because My word has no place in you. [38]I speak the things which I have seen with *My* Father; therefore you also do the things which you heard from *your* father."

39 They answered and said to Him, "Abraham is our father." Jesus *said to them, "If you are Abraham's children, do the deeds of Abraham. [40]But as it is, you are seeking to kill Me, a man who has told you the truth, which I heard from God; this Abraham did not do. [41]You are doing the deeds of your father." They said to Him, "We were not born of fornication; we have one Father: God." [42]Jesus said to them, "If God were your Father, you would love Me, for I proceeded forth and have come from God, for I have not even come on My own initiative, but He sent Me. [43]Why do you not understand what I am saying? *It is* because you cannot hear My word. [44]You are of *your* father the devil, and you want to do the desires of your father. He was a murderer from the beginning, and does not stand in the truth because there is no truth in him. Whenever he speaks a lie, he speaks from his own *nature,* for he is a liar and the father of lies. [45]But because I speak the truth, you do not believe Me. [46]Which one of you convicts Me of sin? If I speak truth, why do you not believe Me? [47]He who is of God hears the words of God; for this reason you do not hear *them,* because you are not of God."

48 The Jews answered and said to Him, "Do we not say rightly that You are a Samaritan and have a demon?" [49]Jesus answered, "I do not have a demon; but I honor My Father, and you dishonor Me. [50]But I do not seek My glory; there is One who seeks and judges. [51]Truly, truly, I say to you, if anyone keeps My word he will never see death." [52]The Jews said to Him, "Now we know that You have a demon. Abraham died, and the prophets *also;* and You say, 'If anyone keeps My word, he will never taste of death.' [53]Surely You are not greater than our father Abraham, who died? The prophets died too; whom do You make Yourself out *to be?*" [54]Jesus answered, "If I glorify Myself, My glory is nothing; it is My Father who glorifies Me, of whom you say, 'He is our God'; [55]and you have not come to know Him, but I know Him; and if I say that I do not know Him, I will be a liar like you, but I do know Him and keep His word. [56]Your father Abraham

rejoiced to see My day, and he saw *it* and was glad." ⁵⁷So the Jews said to Him, "You are not yet fifty years old, and have You seen Abraham?" ⁵⁸Jesus said to them, "Truly, truly, I say to you, before Abraham was born, I am." ⁵⁹Therefore they picked up stones to throw at Him, but Jesus hid Himself and went out of the temple.

Healing the Man Born Blind

9 As He passed by, He saw a man blind from birth. ²And His disciples asked Him, "Rabbi, who sinned, this man or his parents, that he would be born blind?" ³Jesus answered, "*It was* neither *that* this man sinned, nor his parents; but *it was* so that the works of God might be displayed in him. ⁴We must work the works of Him who sent Me as long as it is day; night is coming when no one can work. ⁵While I am in the world, I am the Light of the world." ⁶When He had said this, He spat on the ground, and made clay of the spittle, and applied the clay to his eyes, ⁷and said to him, "Go, wash in the pool of Siloam" (which is translated, Sent). So he went away and washed, and came *back* seeing. ⁸Therefore the neighbors, and those who previously saw him as a beggar, were saying, "Is not this the one who used to sit and beg?" ⁹Others were saying, "This is he," *still* others were saying, "No, but

he is like him." He kept saying, "I am the one." ¹⁰So they were saying to him, "How then were your eyes opened?" ¹¹He answered, "The man who is called Jesus made clay, and anointed my eyes, and said to me, 'Go to Siloam and wash'; so I went away and washed, and I received sight." ¹²They said to him, "Where is He?" He *said, "I do not know."

Controversy over the Man

13 They *brought to the Pharisees the man who was formerly blind. ¹⁴Now it was a Sabbath on the day when Jesus made the clay and opened his eyes. ¹⁵Then the Pharisees also were asking him again how he received his sight. And he said to them, "He applied clay to my eyes, and I washed, and I see." ¹⁶Therefore some of the Pharisees were saying, "This man is not from God, because He does not keep the Sabbath." But others were saying, "How can a man who is a sinner perform such signs?" And there was a division among them. ¹⁷So they *said to the blind man again, "What do you say about Him, since He opened your eyes?" And he said, "He is a prophet."

18 The Jews then did not believe *it* of him, that he had been blind and had received sight, until they called the parents of the very one who had received his sight, ¹⁹and questioned them, saying, "Is this your son, who you say was born blind? Then how does he now see?" [20]His parents answered them and said, "We know that this is our son, and that he was born blind; [21]but how he now sees, we do not know; or who opened his eyes, we do not know. Ask him; he is of age, he will speak for himself." [22]His parents said this because they were afraid of the Jews; for the Jews had already agreed that if anyone confessed Him to be Christ, he was to be put out of the synagogue. [23]For this reason his parents said, "He is of age; ask him."

[24] So a second time they called the man who had been blind, and said to him, "Give glory to God; we know that this man is a sinner." [25]He then answered, "Whether He is a sinner, I do not know; one thing I do know, that though I was blind, now I see." [26]So they said to him, "What did He do to you? How did He open your eyes?" [27]He answered them, "I told you already and you did not listen; why do you want to hear it again? You do not want to become His disciples too, do you?" [28]They reviled him and said, "You are His disciple, but we are disciples of Moses. [29]We know that God has spoken to Moses, but as for this man, we do not know where He is from." [30]The man answered and said to them, "Well, here is an amazing thing, that you do not know where He is from, and *yet* He opened my eyes. [31]We know that God does not hear sinners; but if anyone is God-fearing and does His will, He hears him. [32]Since the beginning of time it has never been heard that anyone opened the eyes of a person born blind. [33]If this man were not from God, He could do nothing." [34]They answered him, "You were born entirely in sins, and are you teaching us?" So they put him out.

Jesus Affirms His Deity

[35] Jesus heard that they had put him out, and finding him, He said, "Do you believe in the Son of Man?" [36]He answered, "Who is He, Lord, that I may believe in Him?" [37]Jesus said to him, "You have both seen Him, and He is the one who is talking with you." [38]And he said, "Lord, I believe." And he worshiped Him. [39]And Jesus said, "For judgment I came into this world, so that those who do not see may see, and that those who see may become blind." [40]Those of the Pharisees who were with Him heard these things and said to Him, "We are not blind too, are we?" [41]Jesus said to them, "If you were blind, you would have no sin; but since you say, 'We see,' your sin remains.

Parable of the Good Shepherd

10 "Truly, truly, I say to you, he who does not enter by the door into the fold of the sheep, but climbs up some other way, he is a thief and a robber. ²But he who enters by the door is a shepherd of the sheep. ³To him the door-keeper opens, and the sheep hear his voice, and he calls his own sheep by name and leads them out. ⁴When he puts forth all his own, he goes ahead of them, and the sheep follow him because they know his voice. ⁵A stranger they simply will not follow, but will flee from him, because they do not know the voice of strangers." ⁶This figure of speech Jesus spoke to them, but they did not understand what those things were which He had been saying to them.

7 So Jesus said to them again, "Truly, truly, I say to you, I am the door of the sheep. ⁸All who came before Me are thieves and robbers, but the sheep did not hear them. ⁹I am the door; if anyone enters through Me, he will be saved, and will go in and out and find pasture. ¹⁰The thief comes only to steal and kill and destroy; I came that they may have life, and have *it* abundantly.

11 "I am the good shepherd; the good shepherd lays down His life for the sheep. ¹²He who is a hired hand, and not a shepherd, who is not the owner of the sheep, sees the wolf coming, and leaves the sheep and flees, and the wolf snatches them and scatters *them.* ¹³*He flees* because he is a hired hand and is not concerned about the sheep. ¹⁴I am the good shepherd, and I know My own and My own know Me, ¹⁵even as the Father knows Me and I know the Father; and I lay down My life for the sheep. ¹⁶I have other sheep, which are not of this fold; I must bring them also, and they will hear My voice; and they will become one flock *with* one shepherd. ¹⁷For this reason the Father loves Me, because I lay down My life so that I may take it again. ¹⁸No one has taken it away from Me, but I lay it down on My own initiative. I have authority to lay it down, and I have authority to take it up again. This commandment I received from My Father."

19 A division occurred again among the Jews because of these words. ²⁰Many of them were saying, "He has a demon and is insane. Why do you listen to Him?" ²¹Others were saying, "These are not the sayings of one demon-possessed. A demon cannot open the eyes of the blind, can he?"

Jesus Asserts His Deity

22 At that time the Feast of the

Dedication took place at Jerusalem; [23]it was winter, and Jesus was walking in the temple in the portico of Solomon. [24]The Jews then gathered around Him, and were saying to Him, "How long will You keep us in suspense? If You are the Christ, tell us plainly." [25]Jesus answered them, "I told you, and you do not believe; the works that I do in My Father's name, these testify of Me. [26]But you do not believe because you are not of My sheep. [27]My sheep hear My voice, and I know them, and they follow Me; [28]and I give eternal life to them, and they will never perish; and no one will snatch them out of My hand. [29a]My Father, who has given *them* to Me, is greater than all; and no one is able to snatch *them* out of the Father's hand. [30]I and the Father are one."

[31] The Jews picked up stones again to stone Him. [32]Jesus answered them, "I showed you many good works from the Father; for which of them are you stoning Me?" [33]The Jews answered Him, "For a good work we do not stone You, but for blasphemy; and because You, being a man, make Yourself out *to be* God." [34]Jesus answered them, "Has it not been written in your Law, 'I SAID, YOU ARE GODS'? [35]If he called them gods, to whom the word of God came (and the Scripture cannot be broken),

[36]do you say of Him, whom the Father sanctified and sent into the world, 'You are blaspheming,' because I said, 'I am the Son of God'? [37]If I do not do the works of My Father, do not believe Me; [38]but if I do them, though you do not believe Me, believe the works, so that you may know and understand that the Father is in Me, and I in the Father." [39]Therefore they were seeking again to seize Him, and He eluded their grasp.

[40] And He went away again beyond the Jordan to the place where John was first baptizing, and He was staying there. [41]Many came to Him and were saying, "While John performed no sign, yet everything John said about this man was true." [42]Many believed in Him there.

The Death and Resurrection of Lazarus

11 Now a certain man was sick, Lazarus of Bethany, the village of Mary and her sister Martha. [2]It was the Mary who anointed the Lord with ointment, and wiped His feet with her hair, whose brother Lazarus was sick. [3]So the sisters sent *word* to Him, saying, "Lord, behold, he whom You love is sick." [4]But when Jesus heard *this*, He said, "This sickness is not to end in death, but for the glory of God, so that the Son of God may be glorified by it." [5]Now

10:29 One early ms reads What My Father has given Me is greater than all

Jesus loved Martha and her sister and Lazarus. ⁶So when He heard that he was sick, He then stayed two days *longer* in the place where He was. ⁷Then after this He *said to the disciples, "Let us go to Judea again." ⁸The disciples *said to Him, "Rabbi, the Jews were just now seeking to stone You, and are You going there again?" ⁹Jesus answered, "Are there not twelve hours in the day? If anyone walks in the day, he does not stumble, because he sees the light of this world. ¹⁰But if anyone walks in the night, he stumbles, because the light is not in him." ¹¹This He said, and after that He *said to them, "Our friend Lazarus has fallen asleep; but I go, so that I may awaken him out of sleep." ¹²The disciples then said to Him, "Lord, if he has fallen asleep, he will recover." ¹³Now Jesus had spoken of his death, but they thought that He was speaking of literal sleep. ¹⁴So Jesus then said to them plainly, "Lazarus is dead, ¹⁵and I am glad for your sakes that I was not there, so that you may believe; but let us go to him." ¹⁶Therefore Thomas, who is called Didymus, said to *his* fellow disciples, "Let us also go, so that we may die with Him."

17 So when Jesus came, He found that he had already been in the tomb four days. ¹⁸Now Bethany was near Jerusalem, about two miles off; ¹⁹and many of the Jews had come to Martha and Mary, to console them concerning *their* brother. ²⁰Martha therefore, when she heard that Jesus was coming, went to meet Him, but Mary stayed at the house. ²¹Martha then said to Jesus, "Lord, if You had been here, my brother would not have died. ²²Even now I know that whatever You ask of God, God will give You." ²³Jesus *said to her, "Your brother will rise again." ²⁴Martha *said to Him, "I know that he will rise again in the resurrection on the last day." ²⁵Jesus said to her, "I am the resurrection and the life; he who believes in Me will live even if he dies, ²⁶and everyone who lives and believes in Me will never die. Do you believe this?" ²⁷She *said to Him, "Yes, Lord; I have believed that You are the Christ, the Son of God, *even* He who comes into the world."

28 When she had said this, she went away and called Mary her sister, saying secretly, "The Teacher is here and is calling for you." ²⁹And when she heard it, she *got up quickly and was coming to Him.

30 Now Jesus had not yet come into the village, but was still in the place where Martha met Him. ³¹Then the Jews who were with her in the house, and consoling her, when they saw that Mary got up quickly and went out, they followed her, supposing that she was going to the tomb to weep there. ³²Therefore, when Mary came where Jesus was, she saw Him, and fell at His feet, saying to Him, "Lord, if You had been here, my brother would not have died." ³³When Jesus therefore saw her weeping, and the Jews who came with her *also* weeping, He was deeply moved in spirit and was troubled, ³⁴and said, "Where have you laid him?" They *said to Him, "Lord, come and see." ³⁵Jesus wept. ³⁶So the Jews were saying, "See how He loved him!" ³⁷But some of them said, "Could not this man, who opened the eyes of the blind man, have kept this man also from dying?"

38 So Jesus, again being deeply moved within, *came to the tomb. Now it was a cave, and a stone was lying against it. ³⁹Jesus *said, "Remove the stone." Martha, the sister of the deceased, *said to Him, "Lord, by this time there will be a stench, for he has been *dead* four days." ⁴⁰Jesus *said to her, "Did I not say to you that if you believe, you will see the glory of God?" ⁴¹So they removed the stone. Then Jesus raised His eyes, and said, "Father, I thank You that You have heard Me. ⁴²I knew that You always hear Me; but because of the people standing around I said it, so that they may believe

that You sent Me." ⁴³When He had said these things, He cried out with a loud voice, "Lazarus, come forth." ⁴⁴The man who had died came forth, bound hand and foot with wrappings, and his face was wrapped around with a cloth. Jesus *said to them, "Unbind him, and let him go."

45 Therefore many of the Jews who came to Mary, and saw what He had done, believed in Him. ⁴⁶But some of them went to the Pharisees and told them the things which Jesus had done.

Conspiracy to Kill Jesus

47 Therefore the chief priests and the Pharisees convened a council, and were saying, "What are we doing? For this man is performing many signs. ⁴⁸If we let Him *go on* like this, all men will believe in Him, and the Romans will come and take away both our place and our nation." ⁴⁹But one of them, Caiaphas, who was high priest that year, said to them, "You know nothing at all, ⁵⁰nor do you take into account that it is expedient for you that one man die for the people, and that the whole nation not perish." ⁵¹Now he did not say this on his own initiative, but being high priest that year, he prophesied that Jesus was going to die for the nation, ⁵²and not for the nation only, but in order that

He might also gather together into one the children of God who are scattered abroad. ⁵³So from that day on they planned together to kill Him.

54 Therefore Jesus no longer continued to walk publicly among the Jews, but went away from there to the country near the wilderness, into a city called Ephraim; and there He stayed with the disciples.

55 Now the Passover of the Jews was near, and many went up to Jerusalem out of the country before the Passover to purify themselves. ⁵⁶So they were seeking for Jesus, and were saying to one another as they stood in the temple, "What do you think; that He will not come to the feast at all?" ⁵⁷Now the chief priests and the Pharisees had given orders that if anyone knew where He was, he was to report it, so that they might seize Him.

Mary Anoints Jesus

12 Jesus, therefore, six days before the Passover, came to Bethany where Lazarus was, whom Jesus had raised from the dead. ²So they made Him a supper there, and Martha was serving; but Lazarus was one of those reclining *at the table* with Him. ³Mary then took a pound of very costly perfume of pure nard, and anointed the feet of Jesus and wiped His feet with her hair; and the house was filled with the fragrance of the perfume. ⁴But Judas Iscariot, one of His disciples, who was intending to betray Him, *said, ⁵"Why was this perfume not sold for ᵃthree hundred denarii and given to poor *people?*" ⁶Now he said this, not because he was concerned about the poor, but because he was a thief, and as he had the money box, he used to pilfer what was put into it. ⁷Therefore Jesus said, "Let her alone, so that she may keep ᵇit for the day of My burial. ⁸For you always have the poor with you, but you do not always have Me."

9 The large crowd of the Jews then learned that He was there; and they came, not for Jesus' sake only, but that they might also see Lazarus, whom He raised from the dead. ¹⁰But the chief priests planned to put Lazarus to death also; ¹¹because on account of him many of the Jews were going away and were believing in Jesus.

Jesus Enters Jerusalem

12 On the next day the large crowd who had come to the feast, when they heard that Jesus was coming to Jerusalem, ¹³took the branches of the palm trees and went out to meet Him, and *began* to shout, "Hosanna! BLESSED IS HE WHO COMES IN THE NAME OF THE LORD, even the King of Israel."

ᵃ**12:5** Equivalent to 11 months' wages; ᵇ**12:7** I.e. the custom of preparing the body for burial

¹⁴Jesus, finding a young donkey, sat on it; as it is written, ¹⁵"FEAR NOT, DAUGHTER OF ZION; BEHOLD, YOUR KING IS COMING, SEATED ON A DONKEY'S COLT." ¹⁶These things His disciples did not understand at the first; but when Jesus was glorified, then they remembered that these things were written of Him, and that they had done these things to Him. ¹⁷So the people, who were with Him when He called Lazarus out of the tomb and raised him from the dead, continued to testify *about Him.* ¹⁸For this reason also the people went and met Him, because they heard that He had performed this sign. ¹⁹So the Pharisees said to one another, "You see that you are not doing any good; look, the world has gone after Him."

Greeks Seek Jesus

20 Now there were some Greeks among those who were going up to worship at the feast; ²¹these then came to Philip, who was from Bethsaida of Galilee, and *began to* ask him, saying, "Sir, we wish to see Jesus." ²²Philip *came and *told Andrew; Andrew and Philip *came and *told Jesus. ²³And Jesus *answered them, saying, "The hour has come for the Son of Man to be glorified. ²⁴Truly, truly, I say to you, unless a grain of wheat falls into the earth and dies, it remains alone; but if it dies, it bears much fruit. ²⁵He who loves his life loses it, and he who hates his life in this world will keep it to life eternal. ²⁶If anyone serves Me, he must follow Me; and where I am, there My servant will be also; if anyone serves Me, the Father will honor him.

Jesus Foretells His Death

27 "Now My soul has become troubled; and what shall I say, 'Father, save Me from this hour'? But for this purpose I came to this hour. ²⁸Father, glorify Your name." Then a voice came out of heaven: "I have both glorified it, and will glorify it again." ²⁹So the crowd *of people* who stood by and heard it were saying that it had thundered; others were saying, "An angel has spoken to Him." ³⁰Jesus answered and said, "This voice has not come for My sake, but for your sakes. ³¹Now judgment is upon this world; now the ruler of this world will be cast out. ³²And I, if I am lifted up from the earth, will draw all men to Myself." ³³But He was saying this to indicate the kind of death by which He was to die. ³⁴The crowd then answered Him, "We have heard out of the Law that the Christ is to remain forever; and how can You say, 'The Son of Man must be lifted up'? Who is this Son of Man?" ³⁵So Jesus said to them, "For a little while longer the Light is among you. Walk while you have the Light, so that darkness will not overtake you; he who walks in the darkness does not know where he goes. ³⁶While you have the Light, believe in the Light, so that you may become sons of Light."

These things Jesus spoke, and He went away and hid Himself from them. ³⁷But though He had performed so many signs before them, *yet* they were not believing in Him. ³⁸*This was* to fulfill the word of Isaiah the prophet which he spoke: "LORD, WHO HAS BELIEVED OUR REPORT? AND TO WHOM HAS THE ARM OF THE LORD BEEN REVEALED?" ³⁹For this reason they could not believe, for Isaiah said again, ⁴⁰"HE HAS BLINDED THEIR EYES AND HE HARDENED THEIR HEART, SO THAT THEY WOULD NOT SEE WITH THEIR EYES AND PERCEIVE WITH THEIR HEART, AND BE CONVERTED AND I HEAL THEM." ⁴¹These things Isaiah said because he saw His glory, and he spoke of Him. ⁴²Nevertheless many even of the rulers believed in Him, but because of the Pharisees they were not confessing *Him,* for fear that they would be put out of the synagogue; ⁴³for they loved the approval of men rather than the approval of God.

44 And Jesus cried out and said, "He who believes in Me, does not believe in Me but in Him who sent Me. ⁴⁵He who sees Me sees the One who sent Me. ⁴⁶I have come *as* Light into the world, so that everyone who believes in Me will not remain in darkness. ⁴⁷If anyone hears My sayings and does not keep them, I do not judge him; for I did not come to judge the world, but to save the world. ⁴⁸He who rejects Me and does not receive My sayings, has one who judges him; the word I spoke is what will judge him at the last day. ⁴⁹For I did not speak on My own initiative, but the Father Himself who sent Me has given Me a commandment *as to* what to say and what to speak. ⁵⁰I know that His commandment is eternal life; therefore the things I speak, I speak just as the Father has told Me."

The Lord's Supper

13 Now before the Feast of the Passover, Jesus knowing that His hour had come that He would depart out of this world to the Father, having loved His own who were in the world, He loved them to the end. ²During supper, the devil having already put into the heart of Judas Iscariot, *the son* of Simon, to betray Him, ³*Jesus,* knowing that the Father had given all things into His hands, and that He had come forth from God and was going back to God, ⁴*got up from supper, and *laid aside His garments; and taking a towel, He girded Himself.

Jesus Washes the Disciples' Feet

[5]Then He *poured water into the basin, and began to wash the disciples' feet and to wipe them with the towel with which He was girded. [6]So He *came to Simon Peter. He *said to Him, "Lord, do You wash my feet?" [7]Jesus answered and said to him, "What I do you do not realize now, but you will understand hereafter." [8]Peter *said to Him, "Never shall You wash my feet!" Jesus answered him, "If I do not wash you, you have no part with Me." [9]Simon Peter *said to Him, "Lord, *then wash* not only my feet, but also my hands and my head." [10]Jesus *said to him, "He who has bathed needs only to wash his feet, but is completely clean; and you are clean, but not all *of you.*" [11]For He knew the one who was betraying Him; for this reason He said, "Not all of you are clean."

[12] So when He had washed their feet, and taken His garments and reclined *at the table* again, He said to them, "Do you know what I have done to you? [13]You call Me Teacher and Lord; and you are right, for *so* I am. [14]If I then, the Lord and the Teacher, washed your feet, you also ought to wash one another's feet. [15]For I gave you an example

that you also should do as I did to you. [16]Truly, truly, I say to you, a slave is not greater than his master, nor *is* one who is sent greater than the one who sent him. [17]If you know these things, you are blessed if you do them. [18]I do not speak of all of you. I know the ones I have chosen; but *it is* that the Scripture may be fulfilled, 'HE WHO EATS MY BREAD HAS LIFTED UP HIS HEEL AGAINST ME.' [19]From now on I am telling you before *it* comes to pass, so that when it does occur, you may believe that I am *He.* [20]Truly, truly, I say to you, he who receives whomever I send receives Me; and he who receives Me receives Him who sent Me."

Jesus Predicts His Betrayal

[21] When Jesus had said this, He became troubled in spirit, and testified and said, "Truly, truly, I say to you, that one of you will betray Me." [22]The disciples *began* looking at one another, at a loss *to know* of which one He was speaking. [23]There was reclining on Jesus' bosom one of His disciples, whom Jesus loved. [24]So Simon Peter *gestured to him, and *said to him, "Tell *us* who it is of whom He is speaking." [25]He, leaning back thus on Jesus' bosom, *said to Him, "Lord, who is it?" [26]Jesus then *answered, "That is the one for whom I shall dip the morsel and give it to him." So when He had dipped

the morsel, He *took and *gave it to Judas, *the son* of Simon Iscariot. ²⁷After the morsel, Satan then entered into him. Therefore Jesus *said to him, "What you do, do quickly." ²⁸Now no one of those reclining *at the table* knew for what purpose He had said this to him. ²⁹For some were supposing, because Judas had the money box, that Jesus was saying to him, "Buy the things we have need of for the feast"; or else, that he should give something to the poor. ³⁰So after receiving the morsel he went out immediately; and it was night.

31 Therefore when he had gone out, Jesus *said, "Now is the Son of Man glorified, and God is glorified in Him; ³²if God is glorified in Him, God will also glorify Him in Himself, and will glorify Him immediately. ³³Little children, I am with you a little while longer. You will seek Me; and as I said to the Jews, now I also say to you, 'Where I am going, you cannot come.' ³⁴A new commandment I give to you, that you love one another, even as I have loved you, that you also love one another. ³⁵By this all men will know that you are My disciples, if you have love for one another."

36 Simon Peter *said to Him, "Lord, where are You going?" Jesus answered, "Where I go, you cannot follow Me now; but you will

follow later." ³⁷Peter *said to Him, "Lord, why can I not follow You right now? I will lay down my life for You." ³⁸Jesus *answered, "Will you lay down your life for Me? Truly, truly, I say to you, a rooster will not crow until you deny Me three times.

Jesus Comforts His Disciples

14"Do not let your heart be troubled; ᵃbelieve in God, believe also in Me. ²In My Father's house are many dwelling places; if it were not so, I would have told you; for I go to prepare a place for you. ³If I go and prepare a place for you, I will come again and receive you to Myself, that where I am, *there* you may be also. ⁴And you know the way where I am going." ⁵Thomas *said to Him, "Lord, we do not know where You are going, how do we know the way?" ⁶Jesus *said to him, "I am the way, and the truth, and the life; no one comes to the Father but through Me.

Oneness with the Father

⁷If you had known Me, you would have known My Father also; from now on you know Him, and have seen Him."

8 Philip *said to Him, "Lord, show us the Father, and it is enough for us." ⁹Jesus *said to him, "Have I been so long with you, and *yet* you have not come to know Me, Philip?

*14:1 Or you believe in God

He who has seen Me has seen the Father; how *can* you say, 'Show us the Father'? ¹⁰Do you not believe that I am in the Father, and the Father is in Me? The words that I say to you I do not speak on My own initiative, but the Father abiding in Me does His works. ¹¹Believe Me that I am in the Father and the Father is in Me; otherwise believe because of the works themselves. ¹²Truly, truly, I say to you, he who believes in Me, the works that I do, he will do also; and greater *works* than these he will do; because I go to the Father. ¹³Whatever you ask in My name, that will I do, so that the Father may be glorified in the Son. ¹⁴If you ask Me anything in My name, I will do *it*.

15 "If you love Me, you will keep My commandments.

Role of the Spirit

¹⁶I will ask the Father, and He will give you another Helper, that He may be with you forever; ¹⁷*that is* the Spirit of truth, whom the world cannot receive, because it does not see Him or know Him, *but* you know Him because He abides with you and will be in you.

18 "I will not leave you as orphans; I will come to you. ¹⁹After a little while the world will no longer see Me, but you *will* see Me; because I live, you will live also. ²⁰In that day you will know that I am in My Father, and you in Me, and I in you. ²¹He who has My commandments and keeps them is the one who loves Me; and he who loves Me will be loved by My Father, and I will love him and will disclose Myself to him." ²²Judas (not Iscariot) *said to Him, "Lord, what then has happened that You are going to disclose Yourself to us and not to the world?" ²³Jesus answered and said to him, "If anyone loves Me, he will keep My word; and My Father will love him, and We will come to him and make Our abode with him. ²⁴He who does not love Me does not keep My words; and the word which you hear is not Mine, but the Father's who sent Me.

25 "These things I have spoken to you while abiding with you. ²⁶But the Helper, the Holy Spirit, whom the Father will send in My name, He will teach you all things, and bring to your remembrance all that I said to you. ²⁷Peace I leave with you; My peace I give to you; not as the world gives do I give to you. Do not let your heart be troubled, nor let it be fearful. ²⁸You heard that I said to you, 'I go away, and I will come to you.' If you loved Me, you would have rejoiced because I go to the Father, for the Father is greater than I. ²⁹Now I have told you before it happens, so that when it happens, you may believe. ³⁰I will not speak much more with you, for the ruler of the world is coming, and he has nothing in Me; ³¹but so that the world may know that I love the Father, I do exactly as the Father commanded Me. Get up, let us go from here.

Jesus Is the Vine—
Followers Are Branches

15 "I am the true vine, and My Father is the vinedresser. ²Every branch in Me that does not bear fruit, He takes away; and every *branch* that bears fruit, He ᵃprunes it so that it may bear more fruit. ³You are already clean because of the word which I have spoken to you. ⁴Abide in Me, and I in you. As the branch cannot bear fruit of itself unless it abides in the vine, so neither *can* you unless you abide in Me. ⁵I am the vine, you are the branches; he who abides in Me and I in him, he bears much fruit, for apart from Me you can do nothing. ⁶If anyone does not abide in Me, he is thrown away as a branch and dries up; and they gather them, and cast them into the fire and they are burned. ⁷If you abide in Me, and My words abide in you, ask whatever you wish, and it will be done for you. ⁸My Father is glorified by this, that you bear much fruit, and *so* prove to be My disciples. ⁹Just as the Father has loved Me, I have also

loved you; abide in My love. ¹⁰If you keep My commandments, you will abide in My love; just as I have kept My Father's commandments and abide in His love. ¹¹These things I have spoken to you so that My joy may be in you, and *that* your joy may be made full.

Disciples' Relation to
Each Other

12 "This is My commandment, that you love one another, just as I have loved you. ¹³Greater love has no one than this, that one lay down his life for his friends. ¹⁴You are My friends if you do what I command you. ¹⁵No longer do I call you slaves, for the slave does not know what his master is doing; but I have called you friends, for all things that I have heard from My Father I have made known to you. ¹⁶You did not choose Me but I chose you, and appointed you that you would go and bear fruit, and *that* your fruit would remain, so that whatever you ask of the Father in My name He may give to you. ¹⁷This I command you, that you love one another.

Disciples' Relation to the World

18 "If the world hates you, you know that it has hated Me before *it hated* you. ¹⁹If you were of the world, the world would love its own; but because you are not of the world, but I chose you out

---

ᵃ**15:2** Lit *cleans*; used to describe pruning

of the world, because of this the world hates you. ²⁰Remember the word that I said to you, 'A slave is not greater than his master.' If they persecuted Me, they will also persecute you; if they kept My word, they will keep yours also. ²¹But all these things they will do to you for My name's sake, because they do not know the One who sent Me. ²²If I had not come and spoken to them, they would not have sin, but now they have no excuse for their sin. ²³He who hates Me hates My Father also. ²⁴If I had not done among them the works which no one else did, they would not have sin; but now they have both seen and hated Me and My Father as well. ²⁵But *they have done this* to fulfill the word that is written in their Law, 'THEY HATED ME WITHOUT A CAUSE.'

26 "When the Helper comes, whom I will send to you from the Father, *that is* the Spirit of truth who proceeds from the Father, He will testify about Me, ²⁷and you *will* testify also, because you have been with Me from the beginning.

Jesus' Warning

16 "These things I have spoken to you so that you may be kept from stumbling. ²They will make you outcasts from the synagogue, but an hour is coming for everyone who kills you to think that he is offering service to God. ³These things they will do because they have not known the Father or Me. ⁴But these things I have spoken to you, so that when their hour comes, you may remember that I told you of them. These things I did not say to you at the beginning, because I was with you.

The Holy Spirit Promised

5 "But now I am going to Him who sent Me; and none of you asks Me, 'Where are You going?' ⁶But because I have said these things to you, sorrow has filled your heart. ⁷But I tell you the truth, it is to your advantage that I go away; for if I do not go away, the Helper will not come to you; but if I go, I will send Him to you. ⁸And He, when He comes, will convict the world concerning sin and righteousness and judgment; ⁹concerning sin, because they do not believe in Me; ¹⁰and concerning righteousness, because I go to the Father and you no longer see Me; ¹¹and concerning judgment, because the ruler of this world has been judged.

12 "I have many more things to say to you, but you cannot bear *them* now. ¹³But when He, the Spirit of truth, comes, He will guide you into all the truth; for He will not speak on His own initiative, but whatever He hears, He will speak; and He will disclose to you what

is to come. [14]He will glorify Me, for He will take of Mine and will disclose *it* to you. [15]All things that the Father has are Mine; therefore I said that He takes of Mine and will disclose *it* to you.

Jesus' Death and Resurrection Foretold

[16] "A little while, and you will no longer see Me; and again a little while, and you will see Me." [17]*Some* of His disciples then said to one another, "What is this thing He is telling us, 'A little while, and you will not see Me; and again a little while, and you will see Me'; and, 'because I go to the Father'?" [18]So they were saying, "What is this that He says, 'A little while'? We do not know what He is talking about." [19]Jesus knew that they wished to question Him, and He said to them, "Are you deliberating together about this, that I said, 'A little while, and you will not see Me, and again a little while, and you will see Me'? [20]Truly, truly, I say to you, that you will weep and lament, but the world will rejoice; you will grieve, but your grief will be turned into joy. [21]Whenever a woman is in labor she has pain, because her hour has come; but when she gives birth to the child, she no longer remembers the anguish because of the joy that a child has been born into the world. [22]Therefore you too have grief now; but I will see you again, and your heart will rejoice, and no one *will* take your joy away from you.

Prayer Promises

[23]In that day you will not question Me about anything. Truly, truly, I say to you, if you ask the Father for anything in My name, He will give it to you. [24]Until now you have asked for nothing in My name; ask and you will receive, so that your joy may be made full.

[25] "These things I have spoken to you in figurative language; an hour is coming when I will no longer speak to you in figurative language, but will tell you plainly of the Father. [26]In that day you will ask in My name, and I do not say to you that I will request of the Father on your behalf; [27]for the Father Himself loves you, because you have loved Me and have believed that I came forth from the Father. [28]I came forth from the Father and have come into the world; I am leaving the world again and going to the Father."

[29] His disciples *said, "Lo, now You are speaking plainly and are not using a figure of speech. [30]Now we know that You know all things, and have no need for anyone to question You; by this we believe that You came from God."

³¹Jesus answered them, "Do you now believe? ³²Behold, an hour is coming, and has *already* come, for you to be scattered, each to his own *home,* and to leave Me alone; and *yet* I am not alone, because the Father is with Me. ³³These things I have spoken to you, so that in Me you may have peace. In the world you have tribulation, but take courage; I have overcome the world."

The High Priestly Prayer

17 Jesus spoke these things; and lifting up His eyes to heaven, He said, "Father, the hour has come; glorify Your Son, that the Son may glorify You, ²even as You gave Him authority over all flesh, that to all whom You have given Him, He may give eternal life. ³This is eternal life, that they may know You, the only true God, and Jesus Christ whom You have sent. ⁴I glorified You on the earth, having accomplished the work which You have given Me to do. ⁵Now, Father, glorify Me together with Yourself, with the glory which I had with You before the world was.

6 "I have manifested Your name to the men whom You gave Me out of the world; they were Yours and You gave them to Me, and they have kept Your word. ⁷Now they have come to know that everything You have given Me is from You; ⁸for the words which You gave Me I have given to them; and they received *them* and truly understood that I came forth from You, and they believed that You sent Me. ⁹I ask on their behalf; I do not ask on behalf of the world, but of those whom You have given Me; for they are Yours; ¹⁰and all things that are Mine are Yours, and Yours are Mine; and I have been glorified in them. ¹¹I am no longer in the world; and *yet* they themselves are in the world, and I come to You. Holy Father, keep them in Your name, *the name* which You have given Me, that they may be one even as We *are.* ¹²While I was with them, I was keeping them in Your name which You have given Me; and I guarded them and not one of them perished but the son of perdition, so that the Scripture would be fulfilled.

The Disciples in the World

¹³But now I come to You; and these things I speak in the world so that they may have My joy made full in themselves. ¹⁴I have given them Your word; and the world has hated them, because they are not of the world, even as I am not of the world. ¹⁵I do not ask You to take them out of the world, but to keep them from the evil *one.* ¹⁶They are not of the world, even as I am not of the world. ¹⁷Sanctify them in the

truth; Your word is truth. ¹⁸As You sent Me into the world, I also have sent them into the world. ¹⁹For their sakes I sanctify Myself, that they themselves also may be sanctified in truth.

20 "I do not ask on behalf of these alone, but for those also who believe in Me through their word; ²¹that they may all be one; even as You, Father, *are* in Me and I in You, that they also may be in Us, so that the world may believe that You sent Me.

Their Future Glory

²²The glory which You have given Me I have given to them, that they may be one, just as We are one; ²³I in them and You in Me, that they may be perfected in unity, so that the world may know that You sent Me, and loved them, even as You have loved Me. ²⁴Father, I desire that they also, whom You have given Me, be with Me where I am, so that they may see My glory which You have given Me, for You loved Me before the foundation of the world.

25 "O righteous Father, although the world has not known You, yet I have known You; and these have known that You sent Me; ²⁶and I have made Your name known to them, and will make it known, so that the love with which You

loved Me may be in them, and I in them."

Judas Betrays Jesus

18When Jesus had spoken these words, He went forth with His disciples over the ravine of the Kidron, where there was a garden, in which He entered with His disciples. ²Now Judas also, who was betraying Him, knew the place, for Jesus had often met there with His disciples. ³Judas then, having received the *Roman* cohort and officers from the chief priests and the Pharisees, *came there with lanterns and torches and weapons. ⁴So Jesus, knowing all the things that were coming upon Him, went forth and *said to them, "Whom do you seek?" ⁵They answered Him, "Jesus the Nazarene." He *said to them, "I am *He*." And Judas also, who was betraying Him, was standing with them. ⁶So when He said to them, "I am *He*," they drew back and fell to the ground. ⁷Therefore He again asked them, "Whom do you seek?" And they said, "Jesus the Nazarene." ⁸Jesus answered, "I told you that I am *He*; so if you seek Me, let these go their way," ⁹to fulfill the word which He spoke, "Of those whom You have given Me I lost not one." ¹⁰Simon Peter then, having a sword, drew it and struck the high priest's slave, and cut off his right ear; and the slave's name was Malchus. [11]So Jesus said to Peter, "Put the sword into the sheath; the cup which the Father has given Me, shall I not drink it?"

Jesus before the Priests

12 So the *Roman* cohort and the commander and the officers of the Jews, arrested Jesus and bound Him, [13]and led Him to Annas first; for he was father-in-law of Caiaphas, who was high priest that year. [14]Now Caiaphas was the one who had advised the Jews that it was expedient for one man to die on behalf of the people.

15 Simon Peter was following Jesus, and *so was* another disciple. Now that disciple was known to the high priest, and entered with Jesus into the court of the high priest, [16]but Peter was standing at the door outside. So the other disciple, who was known to the high priest, went out and spoke to the doorkeeper, and brought Peter in. [17]Then the slave-girl who kept the door *said to Peter, "You are not also *one* of this man's disciples, are you?" He *said, "I am not." [18]Now the slaves and the officers were standing *there,* having made a charcoal fire, for it was cold and they were warming themselves; and Peter was also with them, standing and warming himself.

19 The high priest then questioned Jesus about His disciples, and about His teaching. [20]Jesus answered him, "I have spoken openly to the world; I always taught in synagogues and in the temple, where all the Jews come together; and I spoke nothing in secret. [21]Why do you question Me? Question those who have heard what I spoke to them; they know what I said." [22]When He had said this, one of the officers standing nearby struck Jesus, saying, "Is that the way You answer the high priest?" [23]Jesus answered him, "If I have spoken wrongly, testify of the wrong; but if rightly, why do you strike Me?" [24]So Annas sent Him bound to Caiaphas the high priest.

Peter's Denial of Jesus

25 Now Simon Peter was standing and warming himself. So they said to him, "You are not also *one* of His disciples, are you?" He denied *it,* and said, "I am not." [26]One of the slaves of the high priest, being a relative of the one whose ear Peter cut off, *said, "Did I not see you in the garden with Him?" [27]Peter then denied *it* again, and immediately a rooster crowed.

Jesus before Pilate

28 Then they *led Jesus from Caiaphas into the [a]Praetorium, and it was early; and they themselves did not enter into the

---

[a]**18:28** I.e. governor's official residence

Praetorium so that they would not be defiled, but might eat the Passover. [29]Therefore Pilate went out to them and *said, "What accusation do you bring against this Man?" [30]They answered and said to him, "If this Man were not an evildoer, we would not have delivered Him to you." [31]So Pilate said to them, "Take Him yourselves, and judge Him according to your law." The Jews said to him, "We are not permitted to put anyone to death," [32]to fulfill the word of Jesus which He spoke, signifying by what kind of death He was about to die.

33 Therefore Pilate entered again into the Praetorium, and summoned Jesus and said to Him, "Are You the King of the Jews?" [34]Jesus answered, "Are you saying this on your own initiative, or did others tell you about Me?" [35]Pilate answered, "I am not a Jew, am I? Your own nation and the chief priests delivered You to me; what have You done?" [36]Jesus answered, "My kingdom is not of this world. If My kingdom were of this world, then My servants would be fighting so that I would not be handed over to the Jews; but as it is, My kingdom is not ªof this realm." [37]Therefore Pilate said to Him, "So You are a king?" Jesus answered, "You say correctly that I am a king. For this I have been born, and for this I have come into the world, to testify

ª**18:36** Lit from here

to the truth. Everyone who is of the truth hears My voice." [38]Pilate *said to Him, "What is truth?"

And when he had said this, he went out again to the Jews and *said to them, "I find no guilt in Him. [39]But you have a custom that I release someone for you at the Passover; do you wish then that I release for you the King of the Jews?" [40]So they cried out again, saying, "Not this Man, but Barabbas." Now Barabbas was a robber.

The Crown of Thorns

19 Pilate then took Jesus and scourged Him. [2]And the soldiers twisted together a crown of thorns and put it on His head, and put a purple robe on Him; [3]and they began to come up to Him and say, "Hail, King of the Jews!" and to give Him slaps in the face. [4]Pilate came out again and *said to them, "Behold, I am bringing Him out to you so that you may know that I find no guilt in Him." [5]Jesus then came out, wearing the crown of thorns and the purple robe. Pilate *said to them, "Behold, the Man!" [6]So when the chief priests and the officers saw Him, they cried out saying, "Crucify, crucify!" Pilate *said to them, "Take Him yourselves and crucify Him, for I find no guilt in Him." [7]The Jews answered him, "We have a law, and by that law He ought to die because He made Himself out *to be* the Son of God."

8 Therefore when Pilate heard this statement, he was *even* more afraid; [9]and he entered into the [a]Praetorium again and *said to Jesus, "Where are You from?" But Jesus gave him no answer. [10]So Pilate *said to Him, "You do not speak to me? Do You not know that I have authority to release You, and I have authority to crucify You?" [11]Jesus answered, "You would have no authority over Me, unless it had been given you from above; for this reason he who delivered Me to you has *the* greater sin." [12]As a result of this Pilate made efforts to release Him, but the Jews cried out saying, "If you release this Man, you are no friend of Caesar; everyone who makes himself out *to be* a king opposes Caesar."

13 Therefore when Pilate heard these words, he brought Jesus out, and sat down on the judgment seat at a place called The Pavement, but in Hebrew, Gabbatha. [14]Now it was the day of preparation for the Passover; it was about the [a]sixth hour. And he *said to the Jews, "Behold, your King!" [15]So they cried out, "Away with *Him,* away with *Him,* crucify Him!" Pilate *said to them, "Shall I crucify your King?" The chief priests answered, "We have no king but Caesar."

The Crucifixion

[16]So he then handed Him over to them to be crucified.

17 They took Jesus, therefore, and He went out, bearing His own cross, to the place called the Place of a Skull, which is called in Hebrew, Golgotha. [18]There they crucified Him, and with Him two other men, one on either side, and Jesus in between. [19]Pilate also wrote an inscription and put it on the cross. It was written, "JESUS THE NAZARENE, THE KING OF THE JEWS." [20]Therefore many of the Jews read this inscription, for the place where Jesus was crucified was near the city; and it was written in Hebrew, Latin *and* in Greek. [21]So the chief priests of the Jews were saying to Pilate, "Do not write, 'The King of the Jews'; but that He said, 'I am King of the Jews.' " [22]Pilate answered, "What I have written I have written."

23 Then the soldiers, when they had crucified Jesus, took His outer garments and made four parts, a part to every soldier and *also* the [c]tunic; now the tunic was seamless, woven in one piece. [24]So they said to one another, "Let us not tear it, but cast lots for it, *to decide* whose it shall be"; *this was* to fulfill the Scripture: "THEY DIVIDED MY OUTER GARMENTS AMONG THEM, AND

[a]**19:9** I.e. governor's official residence; [b]**19:14** Perhaps 6 a.m.; [c]**19:23** Gr *khiton,* the garment worn next to the skin

FOR MY CLOTHING THEY CAST LOTS." ²⁵Therefore the soldiers did these things.

But standing by the cross of Jesus were His mother, and His mother's sister, Mary the *wife* of Clopas, and Mary Magdalene. ²⁶When Jesus then saw His mother, and the disciple whom He loved standing nearby, He *said to His mother, "Woman, behold, your son!" ²⁷Then He *said to the disciple, "Behold, your mother!" From that hour the disciple took her into his own *household*.

28 After this, Jesus, knowing that all things had already been accomplished, to fulfill the Scripture, *said, "I am thirsty." ²⁹A jar full of sour wine was standing there; so they put a sponge full of the sour wine upon *a branch of* hyssop and brought it up to His mouth. ³⁰Therefore when Jesus had received the sour wine, He said, "It is finished!" And He bowed His head and gave up His spirit.

Care of the Body of Jesus

31 Then the Jews, because it was the day of preparation, so that the bodies would not remain on the cross on the Sabbath (for that Sabbath was a high day), asked Pilate that their legs might be broken, and *that* they might be taken away. ³²So the soldiers came, and broke the legs of the first man and of the other who was crucified with Him; ³³but coming to Jesus, when they saw that He was already dead, they did not break His legs. ³⁴But one of the soldiers pierced His side with a spear, and immediately blood and water came out. ³⁵And he who has seen has testified, and his testimony is true; and he knows that he is telling the truth, so that you also may believe. ³⁶For these things came to pass to fulfill the Scripture, "NOT A BONE OF HIM SHALL BE BROKEN." ³⁷And again another Scripture says, "THEY SHALL LOOK ON HIM WHOM THEY PIERCED."

38 After these things Joseph of Arimathea, being a disciple of Jesus, but a secret *one* for fear of the Jews, asked Pilate that he might take away the body of Jesus; and Pilate granted permission. So he came and took away His body. ³⁹Nicodemus, who had first come to Him by night, also came, bringing a mixture of myrrh and aloes, about a hundred pounds *weight*. ⁴⁰So they took the body of Jesus and bound it in linen wrappings with the spices, as is the burial custom of the Jews. ⁴¹Now in the place where He was crucified there was a garden, and in the garden a new tomb in which no one had yet been laid. ⁴²Therefore because of the Jewish day of preparation, since the tomb was nearby, they laid Jesus there.

The Empty Tomb

20 Now on the first *day* of the week Mary Magdalene *came early to the tomb, while it *was still dark, and *saw the stone *already* taken away from the tomb. ²So she *ran and *came to Simon Peter and to the other disciple whom Jesus loved, and *said to them, "They have taken away the Lord out of the tomb, and we do not know where they have laid Him." ³So Peter and the other disciple went forth, and they were going to the tomb. ⁴The two were running together; and the other disciple ran ahead faster than Peter and came to the tomb first; ⁵and stooping and looking in, he *saw the linen wrappings lying *there;* but he did not go in. ⁶And so Simon Peter also *came, following him, and entered the tomb; and he *saw the linen wrappings lying *there,* ⁷and the face-cloth which had been on His head, not lying with the linen wrappings, but rolled up in a place by itself. ⁸So the other disciple who had first come to the tomb then also entered, and he saw and believed. ⁹For as yet they did not understand the Scripture, that He must rise again from the dead. ¹⁰So the disciples went away again to their own homes.

11 But Mary was standing outside the tomb weeping; and so, as she wept, she stooped and looked into the tomb; ¹²and she *saw two angels in white sitting, one at the head and one at the feet, where the body of Jesus had been lying. ¹³And they *said to her, "Woman, why are you weeping?" She *said to them, "Because they have taken away my Lord, and I do not know where they have laid Him." ¹⁴When she had said this, she turned around and *saw Jesus standing *there,* and did not know that it was Jesus. ¹⁵Jesus *said to her, "Woman, why are you weeping? Whom are you seeking?" Supposing Him to be the gardener, she *said to Him, "Sir, if you have carried Him away, tell me where you have laid Him, and I will take Him away." ¹⁶Jesus *said to her, "Mary!" She turned and *said to Him in Hebrew, "Rabboni!" (which means, Teacher). ¹⁷Jesus *said to her, "Stop clinging to Me, for I have not yet ascended to the Father; but go to My brethren and say to them, 'I ascend to My Father and your Father, and My God and your God.' " ¹⁸Mary Magdalene *came, announcing to the disciples, "I have seen the Lord," and *that* He had said these things to her.

Jesus among His Disciples

19 So when it was evening on that

day, the first *day* of the week, and when the doors were shut where the disciples were, for fear of the Jews, Jesus came and stood in their midst and *said to them, "Peace *be* with you." ²⁰And when He had said this, He showed them both His hands and His side. The disciples then rejoiced when they saw the Lord. ²¹So Jesus said to them again, "Peace *be* with you; as the Father has sent Me, I also send you." ²²And when He had said this, He breathed on them and *said to them, "Receive the Holy Spirit. ²³If you forgive the sins of any, *their sins* have been forgiven them; if you retain the *sins* of any, they have been retained."

24 But Thomas, one of the twelve, called Didymus, was not with them when Jesus came. ²⁵So the other disciples were saying to him, "We have seen the Lord!" But he said to them, "Unless I see in His hands the imprint of the nails, and put my finger into the place of the nails, and put my hand into His side, I will not believe."

26 After eight days His disciples were again inside, and Thomas with them. Jesus *came, the doors having been shut, and stood in their midst and said, "Peace *be* with you." ²⁷Then He *said to Thomas, "Reach here with your finger, and see My hands; and reach here your hand and put it into My side; and do not be unbelieving, but believing." ²⁸Thomas answered and said to Him, "My Lord and my God!" ²⁹Jesus *said to him, "Because you have seen Me, have you believed? Blessed *are* they who did not see, and *yet* believed."

Why This Gospel Was Written

30 Therefore many other signs Jesus also performed in the presence of the disciples, which are not written in this book; ³¹but these have been written so that you may believe that Jesus is the Christ, the Son of God; and that believing you may have life in His name.

Jesus Appears at the Sea of Galilee

21 After these things Jesus manifested Himself again to the disciples at the Sea of Tiberias, and He manifested *Himself* in this way. ²Simon Peter, and Thomas called Didymus, and Nathanael of Cana in Galilee, and the *sons* of Zebedee, and two others of His disciples were together. ³Simon Peter *said to them, "I am going fishing." They *said to him, "We will also come with you." They went out and got into the boat; and that night they caught nothing.

4 But when the day was now breaking, Jesus stood on the beach; yet

the disciples did not know that it was Jesus. [5]So Jesus *said to them, "Children, you do not have any fish, do you?" They answered Him, "No." [6]And He said to them, "Cast the net on the right-hand side of the boat and you will find *a catch.*" So they cast, and then they were not able to haul it in because of the great number of fish. [7]Therefore that disciple whom Jesus loved *said to Peter, "It is the Lord." So when Simon Peter heard that it was the Lord, he put his outer garment on (for he was stripped *for work*), and threw himself into the sea. [8]But the other disciples came in the little boat, for they were not far from the land, but about one hundred yards away, dragging the net *full* of fish.

[9] So when they got out on the land, they *saw a charcoal fire *already* laid and fish placed on it, and bread. [10]Jesus *said to them, "Bring some of the fish which you have now caught." [11]Simon Peter went up and drew the net to land, full of large fish, a hundred and fifty-three; and although there were so many, the net was not torn.

Jesus Provides

[12]Jesus *said to them, "Come *and* have breakfast." None of the disciples ventured to question Him, "Who are You?" knowing that it was the Lord. [13]Jesus *came and *took the bread and *gave *it* to them, and the fish likewise. [14]This is now the third time that Jesus was manifested to the disciples, after He was raised from the dead.

The Love Motivation

[15] So when they had finished breakfast, Jesus *said to Simon Peter, "Simon, *son* of John, do you love Me more than these?" He *said to Him, "Yes, Lord; You know that I love You." He *said to him, "Tend My lambs." [16]He *said to him again a second time, "Simon, *son* of John, do you love Me?" He *said to Him, "Yes, Lord; You know that I love You." He *said to him, "Shepherd My sheep." [17]He *said to him the third time, "Simon, *son* of John, do you love Me?" Peter was grieved because He said to him the third time, "Do you love Me?" And he said to Him, "Lord, You know all things; You know that I love You." Jesus *said to him, "Tend My sheep.

Our Times Are in His Hand

[18]Truly, truly, I say to you, when you were younger, you used to gird yourself and walk wherever you wished; but when you grow old, you will stretch out your hands and someone else will gird you, and bring you where you do not wish to *go.*" [19]Now this He said, signifying by what kind of death he would glorify God. And when He

had spoken this, He *said to him, "Follow Me!"

20 Peter, turning around, *saw the disciple whom Jesus loved following *them;* the one who also had leaned back on His bosom at the supper and said, "Lord, who is the one who betrays You?" ²¹So Peter seeing him *said to Jesus, "Lord, and what about this man?" ²²Jesus *said to him, "If I want him to remain until I come, what *is that* to you? You follow Me!" ²³Therefore this saying went out among the brethren that that disciple would not die; yet Jesus did not say to him that he would not die, but *only,* "If I want him to remain until I come, what *is that* to you?"

24 This is the disciple who is testifying to these things and wrote these things, and we know that his testimony is true.

25 And there are also many other things which Jesus did, which if they *were written in detail, I suppose that even the world itself *would not contain the books that *would be written.

ACTS

Introduction

1 The first account I composed, Theophilus, about all that Jesus began to do and teach, ²until the day when He was taken up *to heaven,* after He had by the Holy Spirit given orders to the apostles whom He had chosen. ³To these He also presented Himself alive after His suffering, by many convincing proofs, appearing to them over *a period of* forty days and speaking of the things concerning the kingdom of God. ⁴Gathering them together, He commanded them not to leave Jerusalem, but to wait for what the Father had promised, "Which," He said, "you heard of from Me; ⁵for John baptized with water, but you will be baptized with the Holy Spirit not many days from now."

6 So when they had come together, they were asking Him, saying, "Lord, is it at this time You are restoring the kingdom to Israel?" ⁷He said to them, "It is not for you to know times or epochs which the Father has fixed by His own authority; [8]but you will receive power when the Holy Spirit has come upon you; and you shall be My witnesses both in Jerusalem, and in all Judea and Samaria, and even to the remotest part of the earth."

The Ascension

[9]And after He had said these things, He was lifted up while they were looking on, and a cloud received Him out of their sight. [10]And as they were gazing intently into the sky while He was going, behold, two men in white clothing stood beside them. [11]They also said, "Men of Galilee, why do you stand looking into the sky? This Jesus, who has been taken up from you into heaven, will come in just the same way as you have watched Him go into heaven."

The Upper Room

12 Then they returned to Jerusalem from the mount called Olivet, which is near Jerusalem, a Sabbath day's journey away. [13]When they had entered *the city,* they went up to the upper room where they were staying; that is, Peter and John and James and Andrew, Philip and Thomas, Bartholomew and Matthew, James *the son* of Alphaeus, and Simon the Zealot, and Judas *the son* of James. [14]These all with one mind were continually devoting themselves

to prayer, along with *the* women, and Mary the mother of Jesus, and with His brothers.

15 At this time Peter stood up in the midst of the brethren (a gathering of about one hundred and twenty persons was there together), and said, [16]"Brethren, the Scripture had to be fulfilled, which the Holy Spirit foretold by the mouth of David concerning Judas, who became a guide to those who arrested Jesus. [17]For he was counted among us and received his share in this ministry." [18](Now this man acquired a field with the price of his wickedness, and falling headlong, he burst open in the middle and all his intestines gushed out. [19]And it became known to all who were living in Jerusalem; so that in their own language that field was called Hakeldama, that is, Field of Blood.) [20]"For it is written in the book of Psalms,

'LET HIS HOMESTEAD BE MADE DESOLATE,
AND LET NO ONE DWELL IN IT';

and,

'LET ANOTHER MAN TAKE HIS OFFICE.'

[21]Therefore it is necessary that of the men who have accompanied us all the time that the Lord Jesus went in and out among us— [22]beginning with the baptism of John until the day that He was taken up from us—one of these *must* become a

witness with us of His resurrection." ²³So they put forward two men, Joseph called Barsabbas (who was also called Justus), and Matthias. ²⁴And they prayed and said, "You, Lord, who know the hearts of all men, show which one of these two You have chosen ²⁵to occupy this ministry and apostleship from which Judas turned aside to go to his own place." ²⁶And they drew lots for them, and the lot fell to Matthias; and he was added to the eleven apostles.

The Day of Pentecost

2 When the day of Pentecost had come, they were all together in one place. ²And suddenly there came from heaven a noise like a violent rushing wind, and it filled the whole house where they were sitting. ³And there appeared to them tongues as of fire distributing themselves, and they rested on each one of them. ⁴And they were all filled with the Holy Spirit and began to speak with other tongues, as the Spirit was giving them utterance.

5 Now there were Jews living in Jerusalem, devout men from every nation under heaven. ⁶And when this sound occurred, the crowd came together, and were bewildered because each one of them was hearing them speak in his own language. ⁷They were amazed and astonished, saying, "Why, are not all these who are speaking Galileans? ⁸And how is it that we each hear *them* in our own language to which we were born? ⁹Parthians and Medes and Elamites, and residents of Mesopotamia, Judea and Cappadocia, Pontus and Asia, ¹⁰Phrygia and Pamphylia, Egypt and the districts of Libya around Cyrene, and visitors from Rome, both Jews and ᵃproselytes, ¹¹Cretans and Arabs— we hear them in our *own* tongues speaking of the mighty deeds of God." ¹²And they all continued in amazement and great perplexity, saying to one another, "What does this mean?" ¹³But others were mocking and saying, "They are full of sweet wine."

Peter's Sermon

14 But Peter, taking his stand with the eleven, raised his voice and declared to them: "Men of Judea and all you who live in Jerusalem, let this be known to you and give heed to my words. ¹⁵For these men are not drunk, as you suppose, for it is *only* the ᵇthird hour of the day; ¹⁶but this is what was spoken of through the prophet Joel:

¹⁷'AND IT SHALL BE IN THE
    LAST DAYS,' God says,
'THAT I WILL POUR FORTH
    OF MY SPIRIT ON ALL
    MANKIND;
AND YOUR SONS AND YOUR

ᵃ**2:10** I.e. Gentile converts to Judaism; ᵇ**2:15** I.e. 9 a.m.

DAUGHTERS SHALL PROPHESY,

AND YOUR YOUNG MEN SHALL SEE VISIONS,

AND YOUR OLD MEN SHALL DREAM DREAMS;

18EVEN ON MY BONDSLAVES, BOTH MEN AND WOMEN,

I WILL IN THOSE DAYS POUR FORTH OF MY SPIRIT

And they shall prophesy.

19'AND I WILL GRANT WONDERS IN THE SKY ABOVE

AND SIGNS ON THE EARTH BELOW,

BLOOD, AND FIRE, AND VAPOR OF SMOKE.

20'THE SUN WILL BE TURNED INTO DARKNESS

AND THE MOON INTO BLOOD, BEFORE THE GREAT AND GLORIOUS DAY OF THE LORD SHALL COME.

21'AND IT SHALL BE THAT EVERYONE WHO CALLS ON THE NAME OF THE LORD WILL BE SAVED.'

22 "Men of Israel, listen to these words: Jesus the Nazarene, a man attested to you by God with miracles and wonders and signs which God performed through Him in your midst, just as you yourselves know— 23this *Man,* delivered over by the predetermined plan and foreknowledge of God, you nailed to a cross by the hands of godless men and put *Him* to death. 24But God raised Him up again, putting an end to the agony of death, since it was impossible for Him to be held in its power. 25For David says of Him,

'I SAW THE LORD ALWAYS IN MY PRESENCE;

FOR HE IS AT MY RIGHT HAND, SO THAT I WILL NOT BE SHAKEN.

26'THEREFORE MY HEART WAS GLAD AND MY TONGUE EXULTED;

MOREOVER MY FLESH ALSO WILL LIVE IN HOPE;

27BECAUSE YOU WILL NOT ABANDON MY SOUL TO HADES,

NOR ALLOW YOUR HOLY ONE TO UNDERGO DECAY.

28'YOU HAVE MADE KNOWN TO ME THE WAYS OF LIFE;

YOU WILL MAKE ME FULL OF GLADNESS WITH YOUR PRESENCE.'

29 "Brethren, I may confidently say to you regarding the patriarch David that he both died and was buried, and his tomb is with us to this day. 30And so, because he was a prophet and knew that GOD HAD SWORN TO HIM WITH AN OATH TO SEAT *one* OF HIS DESCENDANTS ON HIS THRONE, 31he looked ahead and spoke of the resurrection of athe Christ, that HE WAS NEITHER ABANDONED TO HADES, NOR DID His flesh SUFFER DECAY. 32This Jesus God raised up again, to which we are

a**2:31** I.e. the Messiah

all witnesses. [33]Therefore having been exalted to the right hand of God, and having received from the Father the promise of the Holy Spirit, He has poured forth this which you both see and hear. [34]For it was not David who ascended into heaven, but he himself says:
'THE LORD SAID TO MY LORD,
"SIT AT MY RIGHT HAND,
[35]UNTIL I MAKE YOUR ENE-
    MIES A FOOTSTOOL FOR
    YOUR FEET." '
[36]Therefore let all the house of Israel know for certain that God has made Him both Lord and Christ—this Jesus whom you crucified."

The Ingathering

[37] Now when they heard *this,* they were pierced to the heart, and said to Peter and the rest of the apostles, "Brethren, what shall we do?" [38]Peter *said* to them, "Repent, and each of you be baptized in the name of Jesus Christ for the forgiveness of your sins; and you will receive the gift of the Holy Spirit. [39]For the promise is for you and your children and for all who are far off, as many as the Lord our God will call to Himself." [40]And with many other words he solemnly testified and kept on exhorting them, saying, "Be saved from this perverse generation!" [41]So then, those who had received his word were baptized; and that day there were added about three thousand [a]souls. [42]They were continually devoting themselves to the apostles' teaching and to fellowship, to the breaking of bread and to prayer.

[43] Everyone kept feeling a sense of awe; and many wonders and signs were taking place through the apostles. [44]And all those who had believed [b]were together and had all things in common; [45]and they *began* selling their property and possessions and were sharing them with all, as anyone might have need. [46]Day by day continuing with one mind in the temple, and breaking bread from house to house, they were taking their meals together with gladness and sincerity of heart, [47]praising God and having favor with all the people. And the Lord was adding to their number day by day those who were being saved.

Healing the Lame Beggar

3 Now Peter and John were going up to the temple at the [c]ninth *hour,* the hour of prayer. [2]And a man who had been lame from his mother's womb was being carried along, whom they used to set down every day at the gate of the temple which is called Beautiful, in order to beg [d]alms of those who were entering the temple. [3]When he saw Peter and John about to go into the temple, he *began* asking

[a]**2:41** I.e. persons; [b]**2:44** One early ms does not contain *were* and *and;* [c]**3:1** I.e. 3 p.m.; [d]**3:2** Or *a gift of charity*

to receive alms. ⁴But Peter, along with John, fixed his gaze on him and said, "Look at us!" ⁵And he *began* to give them his attention, expecting to receive something from them. ⁶But Peter said, "I do not possess silver and gold, but what I do have I give to you: In the name of Jesus Christ the Nazarene—walk!" ⁷And seizing him by the right hand, he raised him up; and immediately his feet and his ankles were strengthened. ⁸With a leap he stood upright and *began* to walk; and he entered the temple with them, walking and leaping and praising God. ⁹And all the people saw him walking and praising God; ¹⁰and they were taking note of him as being the one who used to sit at the Beautiful Gate of the temple to *beg* alms, and they were filled with wonder and amazement at what had happened to him.

Peter's Second Sermon

11 While he was clinging to Peter and John, all the people ran together to them at the so-called portico of Solomon, full of amazement. ¹²But when Peter saw *this,* he replied to the people, "Men of Israel, why are you amazed at this, or why do you gaze at us, as if by our own power or piety we had made him walk? ¹³The God of Abraham, Isaac and Jacob, the God of our fathers, has glorified His servant Jesus, *the one* whom you delivered and disowned in the presence of Pilate, when he had decided to release Him. ¹⁴But you disowned the Holy and Righteous One and asked for a murderer to be granted to you, ¹⁵but put to death the Prince of life, *the one* whom God raised from the dead, *a fact* to which we are witnesses. ¹⁶And on the basis of faith in His name, *it is* the name of Jesus which has strengthened this man whom you see and know; and the faith which *comes* through Him has given him this perfect health in the presence of you all.

17 "And now, brethren, I know that you acted in ignorance, just as your rulers did also. ¹⁸But the things which God announced beforehand by the mouth of all the prophets, that His Christ would suffer, He has thus fulfilled. ¹⁹Therefore repent and return, so that your sins may be wiped away, in order that times of refreshing may come from the presence of the Lord; ²⁰and that He may send Jesus, the Christ appointed for you, ²¹whom heaven must receive until *the* period of restoration of all things about which God spoke by the mouth of His holy prophets from ancient time. ²²Moses said, 'THE LORD GOD WILL RAISE UP FOR YOU A PROPHET LIKE ME FROM YOUR BRETHREN; TO

HIM YOU SHALL GIVE HEED to everything He says to you. ²³And it will be that every soul that does not heed that prophet shall be utterly destroyed from among the people.' ²⁴And likewise, all the prophets who have spoken, from Samuel and *his* successors onward, also announced these days. ²⁵It is you who are the sons of the prophets and of the covenant which God made with your fathers, saying to Abraham, 'AND IN YOUR SEED ALL THE FAMILIES OF THE EARTH SHALL BE BLESSED.' ²⁶For you first, God raised up His Servant and sent Him to bless you by turning every one *of you* from your wicked ways."

Peter and John Arrested

4 As they were speaking to the people, the priests and the captain of the temple *guard* and the Sadducees came up to them, ²being greatly disturbed because they were teaching the people and proclaiming in Jesus the resurrection from the dead. ³And they laid hands on them and put them in jail until the next day, for it was already evening. ⁴But many of those who had heard the message believed; and the number of the men came to be about five thousand.

5 On the next day, their rulers and elders and scribes were gathered together in Jerusalem; ⁶and Annas the high priest *was there*, and Caiaphas and John and Alexander, and all who were of high-priestly descent. ⁷When they had placed them in the center, they *began to* inquire, "By what power, or in what name, have you done this?" ⁸Then Peter, filled with the Holy Spirit, said to them, "Rulers and elders of the people, ⁹if we are on trial today for a benefit done to a sick man, as to how this man has been made well, ¹⁰let it be known to all of you and to all the people of Israel, that by the name of Jesus Christ the Nazarene, whom you crucified, whom God raised from the dead—by this *name* this man stands here before you in good health. ¹¹He is the STONE WHICH WAS REJECTED by you, THE BUILDERS, *but* WHICH BECAME THE CHIEF CORNER *stone*. ¹²And there is salvation in no one else; for there is no other name under heaven that has been given among men by which we must be saved."

Threat and Release

13 Now as they observed the confidence of Peter and John and understood that they were uneducated and untrained men, they were amazed, and *began* to recognize them as having been with Jesus. ¹⁴And seeing the man who had been healed standing with them, they had nothing to say in reply. ¹⁵But when they had ordered them to leave the Council, they *began* to confer with one another, [16]saying, "What shall we do with these men? For the fact that a noteworthy miracle has taken place through them is apparent to all who live in Jerusalem, and we cannot deny it. [17]But so that it will not spread any further among the people, let us warn them to speak no longer to any man in this name." [18]And when they had summoned them, they commanded them not to speak or teach at all in the name of Jesus. [19]But Peter and John answered and said to them, "Whether it is right in the sight of God to give heed to you rather than to God, you be the judge; [20]for we cannot stop speaking about what we have seen and heard." [21]When they had threatened them further, they let them go (finding no basis on which to punish them) on account of the people, because they were all glorifying God for what had happened; [22]for the man was more than forty years old on whom this miracle of healing had been performed.

23 When they had been released, they went to their own *companions* and reported all that the chief priests and the elders had said to them. [24]And when they heard *this,* they lifted their voices to God with one accord and said, "O Lord, it is You who MADE THE HEAVEN AND THE EARTH AND THE SEA, AND ALL THAT IS IN THEM, [25]who by the Holy Spirit, *through* the mouth of our father David Your servant, said,

'WHY DID THE [a]GENTILES RAGE,
AND THE PEOPLES DEVISE FUTILE THINGS?
[26]'THE KINGS OF THE EARTH TOOK THEIR STAND,
AND THE RULERS WERE GATHERED TOGETHER
AGAINST THE LORD AND AGAINST HIS CHRIST.'

[27]For truly in this city there were gathered together against Your holy servant Jesus, whom You anointed, both Herod and Pontius Pilate, along with the Gentiles and the peoples of Israel, [28]to do whatever Your hand and Your purpose predestined to occur. [29]And now, Lord, take note of their threats, and grant that Your bond-servants may speak Your word with all confidence, [30]while You extend Your hand to heal, and signs and wonders take place through the name of Your holy servant Jesus." [31]And when they had prayed, the place where they had gathered together was shaken, and they were all filled with the Holy Spirit and *began* to speak the word of God with boldness.

Sharing among Believers

32 And the congregation of those

---

who believed were of one heart and soul; and not one *of them* claimed that anything belonging to him was his own, but all things were common property to them. ³³And with great power the apostles were giving testimony to the resurrection of the Lord Jesus, and abundant grace was upon them all. ³⁴For there was not a needy person among them, for all who were owners of land or houses would sell them and bring the proceeds of the sales ³⁵and lay them at the apostles' feet, and they would be distributed to each as any had need.

36 Now Joseph, a Levite of Cyprian birth, who was also called Barnabas by the apostles (which translated means Son of Encouragement), ³⁷and who owned a tract of land, sold it and brought the money and laid it at the apostles' feet.

Fate of Ananias and Sapphira

5 But a man named Ananias, with his wife Sapphira, sold a piece of property, ²and kept back *some* of the price for himself, with his wife's full knowledge, and bringing a portion of it, he laid it at the apostles' feet. ³But Peter said, "Ananias, why has Satan filled your heart to lie to the Holy Spirit and to keep back *some* of the price of the land? ⁴While it remained *unsold,* did it not remain your own? And after it was sold, was it not under your control? Why is it that you have conceived this deed in your heart? You have not lied to men but to God." ⁵And as he heard these words, Ananias fell down and breathed his last; and great fear came over all who heard of it. ⁶The young men got up and covered him up, and after carrying him out, they buried him.

7 Now there elapsed an interval of about three hours, and his wife came in, not knowing what had happened. ⁸And Peter responded to her, "Tell me whether you sold the land for such and such a price?" And she said, "Yes, that was the price." ⁹Then Peter *said* to her, "Why is it that you have agreed together to put the Spirit of the Lord to the test? Behold, the feet of those who have buried your husband are at the door, and they will carry you out *as well.*" ¹⁰And immediately she fell at his feet and breathed her last, and the young men came in and found her dead, and they carried her out and buried her beside her husband. ¹¹And great fear came over the whole church, and over all who heard of these things.

12 At the hands of the apostles many signs and wonders were taking place among the people; and they were all with one accord in

Solomon's portico. ¹³But none of the rest dared to associate with them; however, the people held them in high esteem. ¹⁴And all the more believers in the Lord, multitudes of men and women, were constantly added to *their number,* ¹⁵to such an extent that they even carried the sick out into the streets and laid them on cots and pallets, so that when Peter came by at least his shadow might fall on any one of them. ¹⁶Also the people from the cities in the vicinity of Jerusalem were coming together, bringing people who were sick ᵃor afflicted with unclean spirits, and they were all being healed.

Imprisonment and Release

17 But the high priest rose up, along with all his associates (that is the sect of the Sadducees), and they were filled with jealousy. ¹⁸They laid hands on the apostles and put them in a public jail. ¹⁹But during the night an angel of the Lord opened the gates of the prison, and taking them out he said, ²⁰"Go, stand and speak to the people in the temple the whole message of this Life." ²¹Upon hearing *this,* they entered into the temple about daybreak and *began* to teach.

Now when the high priest and his associates came, they called the Council together, even all the Senate of the sons of Israel, and sent *orders* to the prison house for them to be brought. ²²But the officers who came did not find them in the prison; and they returned and reported back, ²³saying, "We found the prison house locked quite securely and the guards standing at the doors; but when we had opened up, we found no one inside." ²⁴Now when the captain of the temple *guard* and the chief priests heard these words, they were greatly perplexed about them as to what would come of this. ²⁵But someone came and reported to them, "The men whom you put in prison are standing in the temple and teaching the people!" ²⁶Then the captain went along with the officers and *proceeded* to bring them *back* without violence (for they were afraid of the people, that they might be stoned).

27 When they had brought them, they stood them before the Council. The high priest questioned them, ²⁸saying, "We gave you strict orders not to continue teaching in this name, and yet, you have filled Jerusalem with your teaching and intend to bring this man's blood upon us." ²⁹But Peter and the apostles answered, "We must obey God rather than men. ³⁰The God of our fathers raised up Jesus, whom you had put to death by hanging Him on a cross. ³¹He is the one whom

ᵃ**5:16** Lit *and*

God exalted to His right hand as a Prince and a Savior, to grant repentance to Israel, and forgiveness of sins. [32]And we are witnesses [a]of these things; and *so is* the Holy Spirit, whom God has given to those who obey Him."

Gamaliel's Counsel

33 But when they heard this, they were cut to the quick and intended to kill them. [34]But a Pharisee named Gamaliel, a teacher of the Law, respected by all the people, stood up in the Council and gave orders to put the men outside for a short time. [35]And he said to them, "Men of Israel, take care what you propose to do with these men. [36]For some time ago Theudas rose up, claiming to be somebody, and a group of about four hundred men joined up with him. But he was killed, and all who followed him were dispersed and came to nothing. [37]After this man, Judas of Galilee rose up in the days of the census and drew away *some* people after him; he too perished, and all those who followed him were scattered. [38]So in the present case, I say to you, stay away from these men and let them alone, for if this plan or action is of men, it will be overthrown; [39]but if it is of God, you will not be able to overthrow them; or else you may even be found fighting against God."

[40]They took his advice; and after calling the apostles in, they flogged them and ordered them not to speak in the name of Jesus, and *then* released them. [41]So they went on their way from the presence of the Council, rejoicing that they had been considered worthy to suffer shame for *His* name. [42]And every day, in the temple and from house to house, they kept right on teaching and preaching Jesus *as* the Christ.

Choosing of the Seven

6Now at this time while the disciples were increasing *in number,* a complaint arose on the part of the [b]Hellenistic *Jews* against the *native* Hebrews, because their widows were being overlooked in the daily serving *of food.* [2]So the twelve summoned the congregation of the disciples and said, "It is not desirable for us to neglect the word of God in order to serve tables. [3]Therefore, brethren, select from among you seven men of good reputation, full of the Spirit and of wisdom, whom we may put in charge of this task. [4]But we will devote ourselves to prayer and to the ministry of the word." [5]The statement found approval with the whole congregation; and they chose Stephen, a man full of faith and of the Holy Spirit, and Philip, Prochorus, Nicanor, Timon, Parmenas and Nicolas, a [c]proselyte

[a]**5:32** One early ms adds *in Him;* [b]**6:1** Jews who adopted the Gr language and much of Gr culture through acculturation; [c]**6:5** a Gentile convert to Judaism

from Antioch. ⁶And these they brought before the apostles; and after praying, they laid their hands on them.

7 The word of God kept on spreading; and the number of the disciples continued to increase greatly in Jerusalem, and a great many of the priests were becoming obedient to the faith.

8 And Stephen, full of grace and power, was performing great wonders and signs among the people. ⁹But some men from what was called the Synagogue of the Freedmen, *including* both Cyrenians and Alexandrians, and some from Cilicia and Asia, rose up and argued with Stephen. ¹⁰But they were unable to cope with the wisdom and the Spirit with which he was speaking. ¹¹Then they secretly induced men to say, "We have heard him speak blasphemous words against Moses and *against* God." ¹²And they stirred up the people, the elders and the scribes, and they came up to him and dragged him away and brought him before the Council. ¹³They put forward false witnesses who said, "This man incessantly speaks against this holy place and the Law; ¹⁴for we have heard him say that this Nazarene, Jesus, will destroy this place and alter the customs which Moses handed down to us." ¹⁵And

ᵃ**7:7** Or *worship*

fixing their gaze on him, all who were sitting in the Council saw his face like the face of an angel.

Stephen's Defense

7 The high priest said, "Are these things so?"

2 And he said, "Hear me, brethren and fathers! The God of glory appeared to our father Abraham when he was in Mesopotamia, before he lived in Haran, ³and said to him, 'LEAVE YOUR COUNTRY AND YOUR RELATIVES, AND COME INTO THE LAND THAT I WILL SHOW YOU.' ⁴Then he left the land of the Chaldeans and settled in Haran. From there, after his father died, *God* had him move to this country in which you are now living. ⁵But He gave him no inheritance in it, not even a foot of ground, and *yet,* even when he had no child, He promised that HE WOULD GIVE IT TO HIM AS A POSSESSION, AND TO HIS DESCENDANTS AFTER HIM. ⁶But God spoke to this effect, that his DESCENDANTS WOULD BE ALIENS IN A FOREIGN LAND, AND THAT THEY WOULD BE ENSLAVED AND MISTREATED FOR FOUR HUNDRED YEARS. ⁷ 'AND WHATEVER NATION TO WHICH THEY WILL BE IN BONDAGE I MYSELF WILL JUDGE,' said God, 'AND AFTER THAT THEY WILL COME OUT AND ᵃSERVE ME IN

THIS PLACE.' [8]And He gave him the covenant of circumcision; and so *Abraham* became the father of Isaac, and circumcised him on the eighth day; and Isaac *became the father of* Jacob, and Jacob *of* the twelve patriarchs.

"The patriarchs became jealous of Joseph and sold him into Egypt. *Yet* God was with him, [10]and rescued him from all his afflictions, and granted him favor and wisdom in the sight of Pharaoh, king of Egypt, and he made him governor over Egypt and all his household.

11 "Now a famine came over all Egypt and Canaan, and great affliction *with it,* and our fathers could find no food. [12]But when Jacob heard that there was grain in Egypt, he sent our fathers *there* the first time. [13]On the second *visit* Joseph made himself known to his brothers, and Joseph's family was disclosed to Pharaoh. [14]Then Joseph sent *word* and invited Jacob his father and all his relatives to come to him, seventy-five persons *in all.* [15]And Jacob went down to Egypt and *there* he and our fathers died. [16]*From there* they were removed to Shechem and laid in the tomb which Abraham had purchased for a sum of money from the sons of Hamor in Shechem.

17 "But as the time of the promise was approaching which God had assured to Abraham, the people increased and multiplied in Egypt, [18]until THERE AROSE ANOTHER KING OVER EGYPT WHO KNEW NOTHING ABOUT JOSEPH. [19]It was he who took shrewd advantage of our race and mistreated our fathers so that they would expose their infants and they would not survive. [20]It was at this time that Moses was born; and he was lovely in the sight of God, and he was nurtured three months in his father's home. [21]And after he had been set outside, Pharaoh's daughter took him away and nurtured him as her own son. [22]Moses was educated in all the learning of the Egyptians, and he was a man of power in words and deeds. [23]But when he was approaching the age of forty, it entered his mind to visit his brethren, the sons of Israel. [24]And when he saw one *of them* being treated unjustly, he defended him and took vengeance for the oppressed by striking down the Egyptian. [25]And he supposed that his brethren understood that God was granting them deliverance through him, but they did not understand. [26]On the following day he appeared to them as they were fighting together, and he tried to reconcile them in peace, saying, 'Men, you are brethren, why do you injure one another?' [27]But the one who was injuring his neighbor pushed him away, saying, 'WHO MADE YOU A RULER AND JUDGE OVER US? [28]YOU DO NOT MEAN TO KILL ME AS YOU KILLED THE EGYPTIAN YESTERDAY, DO YOU?' [29]At this remark, MOSES FLED AND BECAME AN ALIEN IN THE LAND OF MIDIAN, where he became the father of two sons.

30 "After forty years had passed, AN ANGEL APPEARED TO HIM IN THE WILDERNESS OF MOUNT Sinai, IN THE FLAME OF A BURNING THORN BUSH. [31]When Moses saw it, he marveled at the sight; and as he approached to look *more* closely, there came the voice of the Lord: [32]'I AM THE GOD OF YOUR FATHERS, THE GOD OF ABRAHAM AND ISAAC AND JACOB.' Moses shook with fear and would not venture to look. [33]BUT THE LORD SAID TO HIM, 'TAKE OFF THE SANDALS FROM YOUR FEET, FOR THE PLACE ON WHICH YOU ARE STANDING IS HOLY GROUND. [34]I HAVE CERTAINLY SEEN THE OPPRESSION OF MY PEOPLE IN EGYPT AND HAVE HEARD THEIR GROANS, AND I HAVE COME DOWN TO RESCUE THEM; COME NOW, AND I WILL SEND YOU TO EGYPT.'

35 "This Moses whom they disowned, saying, 'WHO MADE YOU A RULER AND A JUDGE?' is the one whom God sent *to be* both a ruler and a deliverer with the help of the angel who appeared to him in the thorn bush. [36]This man led them out, performing wonders and signs in the land of Egypt and in the Red Sea and in the wilderness for forty years. [37]This is the Moses who said to the sons of Israel, 'GOD WILL RAISE UP FOR YOU A PROPHET LIKE ME FROM YOUR BRETHREN.' [38]This is the one who was in the congregation in the wilderness together with the angel who was speaking to him on Mount Sinai, and *who was* with our fathers; and he received living oracles to pass on to you. [39]Our fathers were unwilling to be obedient to him, but repudiated him and in their hearts turned back to Egypt, [40]SAYING TO AARON, 'MAKE FOR US GODS WHO WILL GO BEFORE US; FOR THIS MOSES WHO LED US OUT OF THE LAND OF EGYPT—WE DO NOT KNOW WHAT HAPPENED TO HIM.' [41]At that time they made a calf and brought a sacrifice to the idol, and were rejoicing in the works of their hands. [42]But God turned away and delivered them up to serve the host of heaven; as it is written in the book of the prophets, 'IT WAS NOT TO ME THAT YOU OFFERED VICTIMS AND SACRIFICES FORTY YEARS IN THE WILDERNESS, WAS IT,

O HOUSE OF ISRAEL? ⁴³YOU ALSO TOOK ALONG THE TABERNACLE OF MOLOCH AND THE STAR OF THE GOD ROMPHA, THE IMAGES WHICH YOU MADE TO WORSHIP. I ALSO WILL REMOVE YOU BEYOND BABYLON.'

44 "Our fathers had the tabernacle of testimony in the wilderness, just as He who spoke to Moses directed *him* to make it according to the pattern which he had seen. ⁴⁵And having received it in their turn, our fathers brought it in with Joshua upon dispossessing the nations whom God drove out before our fathers, until the time of David. ⁴⁶*David* found favor in God's sight, and asked that he might find a dwelling place for the ªGod of Jacob. ⁴⁷But it was Solomon who built a house for Him. ⁴⁸However, the Most High does not dwell in *houses* made by *human* hands; as the prophet says:

⁴⁹'HEAVEN IS MY THRONE,
AND EARTH IS THE FOOTSTOOL OF MY FEET;
WHAT KIND OF HOUSE WILL YOU BUILD FOR ME?' says the Lord,
'OR WHAT PLACE IS THERE FOR MY REPOSE?
⁵⁰'WAS IT NOT MY HAND WHICH MADE ALL THESE THINGS?'

51 "You men who are stiff-necked and uncircumcised in heart and ears are always resisting the Holy Spirit; you are doing just as your fathers did. ⁵²Which one of the prophets did your fathers not persecute? They killed those who had previously announced the coming of the Righteous One, whose betrayers and murderers you have now become; ⁵³you who received the law as ordained by angels, and *yet* did not keep it."

Stephen Put to Death

54 Now when they heard this, they were cut to the quick, and they *began* gnashing their teeth at him. ⁵⁵But being full of the Holy Spirit, he gazed intently into heaven and saw the glory of God, and Jesus standing at the right hand of God; ⁵⁶and he said, "Behold, I see the heavens opened up and the Son of Man standing at the right hand of God." ⁵⁷But they cried out with a loud voice, and covered their ears and rushed at him with one impulse. ⁵⁸When they had driven him out of the city, they *began* stoning *him;* and the witnesses laid aside their robes at the feet of a young man named Saul. ⁵⁹They went on stoning Stephen as he called on *the Lord* and said, "Lord Jesus, receive my spirit!" ⁶⁰Then falling on his knees, he cried out with a loud voice, "Lord, do not hold this sin against them!" Having said this, he fell asleep.

ª**7:46** The earliest mss read *house* instead of *God*; the Septuagint reads God

Saul Persecutes the Church

8 Saul was in hearty agreement with putting him to death.

And on that day a great persecution began against the church in Jerusalem, and they were all scattered throughout the regions of Judea and Samaria, except the apostles. [2]*Some* devout men buried Stephen, and made loud lamentation over him. [3]But Saul *began* ravaging the church, entering house after house, and dragging off men and women, he would put them in prison.

Philip in Samaria

4 Therefore, those who had been scattered went about preaching the word. [5]Philip went down to the city of Samaria and *began* proclaiming Christ to them. [6]The crowds with one accord were giving attention to what was said by Philip, as they heard and saw the signs which he was performing. [7]For *in the case of* many who had unclean spirits, they were coming out *of them* shouting with a loud voice; and many who had been paralyzed and lame were healed. [8]So there was much rejoicing in that city.

9 Now there was a man named Simon, who formerly was practicing magic in the city and astonishing the people of Samaria, claiming to be someone great; [10]and they all, from smallest to greatest, were giving attention to him, saying, "This man is what is called the Great Power of God." [11]And they were giving him attention because he had for a long time astonished them with his magic arts. [12]But when they believed Philip preaching the good news about the kingdom of God and the name of Jesus Christ, they were being baptized, men and women alike. [13]Even Simon himself believed; and after being baptized, he continued on with Philip, and as he observed signs and great miracles taking place, he was constantly amazed.

14 Now when the apostles in Jerusalem heard that Samaria had received the word of God, they sent them Peter and John, [15]who came down and prayed for them that they might receive the Holy Spirit. [16]For He had not yet fallen upon any of them; they had simply been baptized in the name of the Lord Jesus. [17]Then they *began* laying their hands on them, and they were receiving the Holy Spirit. [18]Now when Simon saw that the Spirit was bestowed through the laying on of the apostles' hands, he offered them money, [19]saying, "Give this authority to me as well, so that everyone on whom I lay my hands may receive the Holy

Spirit." ²⁰But Peter said to him, "May your silver perish with you, because you thought you could obtain the gift of God with money! ²¹You have no part or portion in this matter, for your heart is not right before God. ²²Therefore repent of this wickedness of yours, and pray the Lord that, if possible, the intention of your heart may be forgiven you. ²³For I see that you are in the gall of bitterness and in the bondage of iniquity." ²⁴But Simon answered and said, "Pray to the Lord for me yourselves, so that nothing of what you have said may come upon me."

An Ethiopian Receives Christ

25 So, when they had solemnly testified and spoken the word of the Lord, they started back to Jerusalem, and were preaching the gospel to many villages of the Samaritans.

26 But an angel of the Lord spoke to Philip saying, "Get up and go south to the road that descends from Jerusalem to Gaza." (This is a desert *road*.) ²⁷So he got up and went; and there was an Ethiopian eunuch, a court official of Candace, queen of the Ethiopians, who was in charge of all her treasure; and he had come to Jerusalem to worship, ²⁸and he was returning and sitting in his chariot, and was reading the prophet Isaiah. ²⁹Then

*8:37 Early mss do not contain this v

the Spirit said to Philip, "Go up and join this chariot." ³⁰Philip ran up and heard him reading Isaiah the prophet, and said, "Do you understand what you are reading?" ³¹And he said, "Well, how could I, unless someone guides me?" And he invited Philip to come up and sit with him. ³²Now the passage of Scripture which he was reading was this:

"HE WAS LED AS A SHEEP TO
    SLAUGHTER;
AND AS A LAMB BEFORE ITS
    SHEARER IS SILENT,
SO HE DOES NOT OPEN HIS
    MOUTH.
³³"IN HUMILIATION HIS JUDG-
    MENT WAS TAKEN AWAY;
WHO   WILL   RELATE   HIS
    GENERATION?
FOR HIS LIFE IS REMOVED
    FROM THE EARTH."

³⁴The eunuch answered Philip and said, "Please *tell me,* of whom does the prophet say this? Of himself or of someone else?" ³⁵Then Philip opened his mouth, and beginning from this Scripture he preached Jesus to him. ³⁶As they went along the road they came to some water; and the eunuch *said, "Look! Water! What prevents me from being baptized?" ^{37a}[And Philip said, "If you believe with all your heart, you may." And he answered and said, "I believe that Jesus Christ is the Son of God."] ³⁸And he ordered the chariot to stop; and they both

went down into the water, Philip as well as the eunuch, and he baptized him. ³⁹When they came up out of the water, the Spirit of the Lord snatched Philip away; and the eunuch no longer saw him, but went on his way rejoicing. ⁴⁰But Philip found himself at Azotus, and as he passed through he kept preaching the gospel to all the cities until he came to Caesarea.

The Conversion of Saul

9 Now Saul, still breathing threats and murder against the disciples of the Lord, went to the high priest, ²and asked for letters from him to the synagogues at Damascus, so that if he found any belonging to the Way, both men and women, he might bring them bound to Jerusalem. ³As he was traveling, it happened that he was approaching Damascus, and suddenly a light from heaven flashed around him; ⁴and he fell to the ground and heard a voice saying to him, "Saul, Saul, why are you persecuting Me?" ⁵And he said, "Who are You, Lord?" And He *said*, "I am Jesus whom you are persecuting, ⁶but get up and enter the city, and it will be told you what you must do." ⁷The men who traveled with him stood speechless, hearing the voice but seeing no one. ⁸Saul got up from the ground, and though his eyes were open, he could see nothing; and leading him by the hand,

they brought him into Damascus. ⁹And he was three days without sight, and neither ate nor drank.

10 Now there was a disciple at Damascus named Ananias; and the Lord said to him in a vision, "Ananias." And he said, "Here I am, Lord." ¹¹And the Lord *said* to him, "Get up and go to the street called Straight, and inquire at the house of Judas for a man from Tarsus named Saul, for he is praying, ¹²and he has seen ªin a vision a man named Ananias come in and lay his hands on him, so that he might regain his sight." ¹³But Ananias answered, "Lord, I have heard from many about this man, how much harm he did to Your saints at Jerusalem; ¹⁴and here he has authority from the chief priests to bind all who call on Your name." ¹⁵But the Lord said to him, "Go, for he is a chosen ᵇinstrument of Mine, to bear My name before the Gentiles and kings and the sons of Israel; ¹⁶for I will show him how much he must suffer for My name's sake." ¹⁷So Ananias departed and entered the house, and after laying his hands on him said, "Brother Saul, the Lord Jesus, who appeared to you on the road by which you were coming, has sent me so that you may regain your sight and be filled with the Holy Spirit." ¹⁸And immediately there fell from his

ª**9:12** A few early mss do not contain *in a vision;* ᵇ**9:15** Or *vessel* eyes something like scales, and he regained his sight, and he got up and was baptized; [19]and he took food and was strengthened.

Saul Begins to Preach Christ

Now for several days he was with the disciples who were at Damascus, [20]and immediately he *began* to proclaim Jesus in the synagogues, saying, "He is the Son of God." [21]All those hearing him continued to be amazed, and were saying, "Is this not he who in Jerusalem destroyed those who called on this name, and *who* had come here for the purpose of bringing them bound before the chief priests?" [22]But Saul kept increasing in strength and confounding the Jews who lived at Damascus by proving that this *Jesus* is the Christ.

[23] When many days had elapsed, the Jews plotted together to do away with him, [24]but their plot became known to Saul. They were also watching the gates day and night so that they might put him to death; [25]but his disciples took him by night and let him down through *an opening in* the wall, lowering him in a large basket.

[26] When he came to Jerusalem, he was trying to associate with the disciples; but they were all afraid of him, not believing that he was a disciple. [27]But Barnabas took hold of him and brought him to the apostles and described to them how he had seen the Lord on the road, and that He had talked to him, and how at Damascus he had spoken out boldly in the name of Jesus. [28]And he was with them, moving about freely in Jerusalem, speaking out boldly in the name of the Lord. [29]And he was talking and arguing with the Hellenistic *Jews;* but they were attempting to put him to death. [30]But when the brethren learned *of it,* they brought him down to Caesarea and sent him away to Tarsus.

[31] So the church throughout all Judea and Galilee and Samaria enjoyed peace, being built up; and going on in the fear of the Lord and in the comfort of the Holy Spirit, it continued to increase.

Peter's Ministry

[32] Now as Peter was traveling through all *those regions,* he came down also to the saints who lived at Lydda. [33]There he found a man named Aeneas, who had been bedridden eight years, for he was paralyzed. [34]Peter said to him, "Aeneas, Jesus Christ heals you; get up and make your bed." Immediately he got up. [35]And all who lived at Lydda and Sharon saw him, and they turned to the Lord.

36 Now in Joppa there was a disciple named Tabitha (which translated *in Greek* is called Dorcas); this woman was abounding with deeds of kindness and charity which she continually did. ³⁷And it happened at that time that she fell sick and died; and when they had washed her body, they laid it in an upper room. ³⁸Since Lydda was near Joppa, the disciples, having heard that Peter was there, sent two men to him, imploring him, "Do not delay in coming to us." ³⁹So Peter arose and went with them. When he arrived, they brought him into the upper room; and all the widows stood beside him, weeping and showing all the ᵃtunics and garments that Dorcas used to make while she was with them. ⁴⁰But Peter sent them all out and knelt down and prayed, and turning to the body, he said, "Tabitha, arise." And she opened her eyes, and when she saw Peter, she sat up. ⁴¹And he gave her his hand and raised her up; and calling the saints and widows, he presented her alive. ⁴²It became known all over Joppa, and many believed in the Lord. ⁴³And Peter stayed many days in Joppa with a tanner *named* Simon.

Cornelius's Vision

10 Now *there was* a man at Caesarea named Cornelius, a centurion of what was called the Italian ᵇcohort, ²a devout man and one who feared God with all his household, and gave many ᶜalms to the *Jewish* people and prayed to God continually. ³About the ᵈninth hour of the day he clearly saw in a vision an angel of God who had *just* come in and said to him, "Cornelius!" ⁴And fixing his gaze on him and being much alarmed, he said, "What is it, Lord?" And he said to him, "Your prayers and ᵉalms have ascended as a memorial before God. ⁵Now dispatch *some* men to Joppa and send for a man *named* Simon, who is also called Peter; ⁶he is staying with a tanner *named* Simon, whose house is by the sea." ⁷When the angel who was speaking to him had left, he summoned two of his servants and a devout soldier of those who were his personal attendants, ⁸and after he had explained everything to them, he sent them to Joppa.

9 On the next day, as they were on their way and approaching the city, Peter went up on the housetop about the ᶠsixth hour to pray. ¹⁰But he became hungry and was desiring to eat; but while they were making preparations, he fell into a trance; ¹¹and he *saw the sky opened up, and an ᵍobject like a great sheet coming down, lowered by four corners to the ground, ¹²and there were in it all *kinds of* four-footed animals and

ᵃ**9:39** Or *inner garments*; ᵇ**10:1** Or *battalion*; ᶜ**10:2** Or *gifts of charity*; ᵈ**10:3** I.e. 3 p.m.; ᵉ**10:4** Or *deeds of charity*; ᶠ**10:9** I.e. noon; ᵍ**10:11** Or *vessel* ᵃcrawling creatures of the earth and birds of the air. ¹³A voice came to him, "Get up, Peter, kill and eat!" ¹⁴But Peter said, "By no means, Lord, for I have never eaten anything unholy and unclean." ¹⁵Again a voice *came* to him a second time, "What God has cleansed, no *longer* consider unholy." ¹⁶This happened three times, and immediately the object was taken up into the sky.

17 Now while Peter was greatly perplexed in mind as to what the vision which he had seen might be, behold, the men who had been sent by Cornelius, having asked directions for Simon's house, appeared at the gate; ¹⁸and calling out, they were asking whether Simon, who was also called Peter, was staying there. ¹⁹While Peter was reflecting on the vision, the Spirit said to him, "Behold, three men are looking for you. ²⁰But get up, go downstairs and accompany them without misgivings, for I have sent them Myself." ²¹Peter went down to the men and said, "Behold, I am the one you are looking for; what is the reason for which you have come?" ²²They said, "Cornelius, a centurion, a righteous and God-fearing man well spoken of by the entire nation of the Jews, was *divinely* directed by a holy angel to send for you *to come* to his house and hear

a message from you." ²³So he invited them in and gave them lodging.

Peter at Caesarea

And on the next day he got up and went away with them, and some of the brethren from Joppa accompanied him. ²⁴On the following day he entered Caesarea. Now Cornelius was waiting for them and had called together his relatives and close friends. ²⁵When Peter entered, Cornelius met him, and fell at his feet and worshiped *him*. ²⁶But Peter raised him up, saying, "Stand up; I too am *just* a man." ²⁷As he talked with him, he entered and *found many people assembled. ²⁸And he said to them, "You yourselves know how unlawful it is for a man who is a Jew to associate with a foreigner or to visit him; and *yet* God has shown me that I should not call any man unholy or unclean. ²⁹That is why I came without even raising any objection when I was sent for. So I ask for what reason you have sent for me."

30 Cornelius said, "Four days ago to this hour, I was praying in my house during the ᵇninth hour; and behold, a man stood before me in shining garments, ³¹and he *said, 'Cornelius, your prayer has been heard and your alms have been remembered before God. ³²Therefore send to Joppa and invite

ᵃ**10:12** Or *reptiles;* ᵇ**10:30** I.e. 3 to 4 p.m.

Simon, who is also called Peter, to come to you; he is staying at the house of Simon *the* tanner by the sea.' ³³So I sent for you immediately, and you have been kind enough to come. Now then, we are all here present before God to hear all that you have been commanded by the Lord."

Gentiles Hear Good News

34 Opening his mouth, Peter said:

"I most certainly understand *now* that God is not one to show partiality, ³⁵but in every nation the man who fears Him and does what is right is welcome to Him. ³⁶The word which He sent to the sons of Israel, preaching peace through Jesus Christ (He is Lord of all)— ³⁷you yourselves know the thing which took place throughout all Judea, starting from Galilee, after the baptism which John proclaimed. ³⁸*You know of* Jesus of Nazareth, how God anointed Him with the Holy Spirit and with power, and *how* He went about doing good and healing all who were oppressed by the devil, for God was with Him. ³⁹We are witnesses of all the things He did both in the land of the Jews and in Jerusalem. They also put Him to death by hanging Him on a cross. ⁴⁰God raised Him up on the third day and granted that He become visible, ⁴¹not to all the people, but to

witnesses who were chosen beforehand by God, *that is,* to us who ate and drank with Him after He arose from the dead. ⁴²And He ordered us to preach to the people, and solemnly to testify that this is the One who has been appointed by God as Judge of the living and the dead. ⁴³Of Him all the prophets bear witness that through His name everyone who believes in Him receives forgiveness of sins."

44 While Peter was still speaking these words, the Holy Spirit fell upon all those who were listening to the message. ⁴⁵All the circumcised believers who came with Peter were amazed, because the gift of the Holy Spirit had been poured out on the Gentiles also. ⁴⁶For they were hearing them speaking with tongues and exalting God. Then Peter answered, ⁴⁷"Surely no one can refuse the water for these to be baptized who have received the Holy Spirit just as we *did,* can he?" ⁴⁸And he ordered them to be baptized in the name of Jesus Christ. Then they asked him to stay on for a few days.

Peter Reports at Jerusalem

11 Now the apostles and the brethren who were throughout Judea heard that the Gentiles also had received the word of God. ²And when Peter came up to Jerusalem, those who were

circumcised took issue with him, [3]saying, "You went to uncircumcised men and ate with them." [4]But Peter began *speaking* and *proceeded* to explain to them in orderly sequence, saying, [5]"I was in the city of Joppa praying; and in a trance I saw a vision, an object coming down like a great sheet lowered by four corners from the sky; and it came right down to me, [6]and when I had fixed my gaze on it and was observing it I saw the four-footed animals of the earth and the wild beasts and the [a]crawling creatures and the birds of the air. [7]I also heard a voice saying to me, 'Get up, Peter; kill and eat.' [8]But I said, 'By no means, Lord, for nothing unholy or unclean has ever entered my mouth.' [9]But a voice from heaven answered a second time, 'What God has cleansed, no longer consider unholy.' [10]This happened three times, and everything was drawn back up into the sky. [11]And behold, at that moment three men appeared at the house in which we were *staying*, having been sent to me from Caesarea. [12]The Spirit told me to go with them without misgivings. These six brethren also went with me and we entered the man's house. [13]And he reported to us how he had seen the angel standing in his house, and saying, 'Send to Joppa and have Simon, who is also called Peter, brought here; [14]and

he will speak words to you by which you will be saved, you and all your household.' [15]And as I began to speak, the Holy Spirit fell upon them just as *He did* upon us at the beginning. [16]And I remembered the word of the Lord, how He used to say, 'John baptized with water, but you will be baptized with the Holy Spirit.' [17]Therefore if God gave to them the same gift as *He gave* to us also after believing in the Lord Jesus Christ, who was I that I could stand in God's way?" [18]When they heard this, they quieted down and glorified God, saying, "Well then, God has granted to the Gentiles also the repentance *that leads* to life."

The Church at Antioch

19 So then those who were scattered because of the persecution that occurred in connection with Stephen made their way to Phoenicia and Cyprus and Antioch, speaking the word to no one except to Jews alone. [20]But there were some of them, men of Cyprus and Cyrene, who came to Antioch and *began* speaking to the [b]Greeks also, preaching the Lord Jesus. [21]And the hand of the Lord was with them, and a large number who believed turned to the Lord. [22]The news about them reached the ears of the church at Jerusalem, and they sent Barnabas off to Antioch. [23]Then when he arrived

[a]**11:6** Or *reptiles;* [b]**11:20** Lit Hellenists; people who lived by Greek customs and culture

and witnessed the grace of God, he rejoiced and *began* to encourage them all with resolute heart to remain *true* to the Lord; ²⁴for he was a good man, and full of the Holy Spirit and of faith. And considerable numbers were brought to the Lord. ²⁵And he left for Tarsus to look for Saul; ²⁶and when he had found him, he brought him to Antioch. And for an entire year they met with the church and taught considerable numbers; and the disciples were first called Christians in Antioch.

27 Now at this time some prophets came down from Jerusalem to Antioch. ²⁸One of them named Agabus stood up and *began* to indicate by the Spirit that there would certainly be a great famine all over the world. And this took place in the *reign* of Claudius. ²⁹And in the proportion that any of the disciples had means, each of them determined to send *a contribution* for the relief of the brethren living in Judea. ³⁰And this they did, sending it in charge of Barnabas and Saul to the elders.

Peter's Arrest and Deliverance

12 Now about that time Herod the king laid hands on some who belonged to the church in order to mistreat them. ²And he had James the brother of John put to death with a sword. ³When he saw that it pleased the Jews, he proceeded to arrest Peter also. Now it was during the days of Unleavened Bread. ⁴When he had seized him, he put him in prison, delivering him to four squads of soldiers to guard him, intending after the Passover to bring him out before the people. ⁵So Peter was kept in the prison, but prayer for him was being made fervently by the church to God.

6 On the very night when Herod was about to bring him forward, Peter was sleeping between two soldiers, bound with two chains, and guards in front of the door were watching over the prison. ⁷And behold, an angel of the Lord suddenly appeared and a light shone in the cell; and he struck Peter's side and woke him up, saying, "Get up quickly." And his chains fell off his hands. ⁸And the angel said to him, "Gird yourself and put on your sandals." And he did so. And he *said to him, "Wrap your cloak around you and follow me." ⁹And he went out and continued to follow, and he did not know that what was being done by the angel was real, but thought he was seeing a vision. ¹⁰When they had passed the first and second guard, they came to the iron gate that leads into the city, which opened for them by itself; and they went out and went along one street, and immediately

the angel departed from him. [11]When Peter came to himself, he said, "Now I know for sure that the Lord has sent forth His angel and rescued me from the hand of Herod and from all that the Jewish people were expecting." [12]And when he realized *this,* he went to the house of Mary, the mother of John who was also called Mark, where many were gathered together and were praying. [13]When he knocked at the door of the gate, a servant-girl named Rhoda came to answer. [14]When she recognized Peter's voice, because of her joy she did not open the gate, but ran in and announced that Peter was standing in front of the gate. [15]They said to her, "You are out of your mind!" But she kept insisting that it was so. They kept saying, "It is his angel." [16]But Peter continued knocking; and when they had opened *the door,* they saw him and were amazed. [17]But motioning to them with his hand to be silent, he described to them how the Lord had led him out of the prison. And he said, "Report these things to James and the brethren." Then he left and went to another place.

[18] Now when day came, there was no small disturbance among the soldiers *as to* what could have become of Peter. [19]When Herod had searched for him and had not found him, he examined the guards and ordered that they be led away *to execution.* Then he went down from Judea to Caesarea and was spending time there.

Death of Herod

[20] Now he was very angry with the people of Tyre and Sidon; and with one accord they came to him, and having won over Blastus the king's chamberlain, they were asking for peace, because their country was fed by the king's country. [21]On an appointed day Herod, having put on his royal apparel, took his seat on the rostrum and *began* delivering an address to them. [22]The people kept crying out, "The voice of a god and not of a man!" [23]And immediately an angel of the Lord struck him because he did not give God the glory, and he was eaten by worms and died.

[24] But the word of the Lord continued to grow and to be multiplied.

[25] And Barnabas and Saul returned from Jerusalem when they had fulfilled their mission, taking along with *them* John, who was also called Mark.

First Missionary Journey

13 Now there were at Antioch, in the church that was *there,* prophets and teachers: Barnabas, and Simeon who was called Niger, and Lucius of Cyrene, and

Manaen who had been brought up with Herod the tetrarch, and Saul. ²While they were ministering to the Lord and fasting, the Holy Spirit said, "Set apart for Me Barnabas and Saul for the work to which I have called them." ³Then, when they had fasted and prayed and laid their hands on them, they sent them away.

4 So, being sent out by the Holy Spirit, they went down to Seleucia and from there they sailed to Cyprus. ⁵When they reached Salamis, they *began* to proclaim the word of God in the synagogues of the Jews; and they also had John as their helper. ⁶When they had gone through the whole island as far as Paphos, they found a magician, a Jewish false prophet whose name was Bar-Jesus, ⁷who was with the proconsul, Sergius Paulus, a man of intelligence. This man summoned Barnabas and Saul and sought to hear the word of God. ⁸But Elymas the magician (for so his name is translated) was opposing them, seeking to turn the proconsul away from the faith. ⁹But Saul, who was also *known as* Paul, filled with the Holy Spirit, fixed his gaze on him, ¹⁰and said, "You who are full of all deceit and fraud, you son of the devil, you enemy of all righteousness, will you not cease to make crooked the straight ways of the Lord? ¹¹Now, behold, the hand of the Lord is upon you, and you will be blind and not see the sun for a time." And immediately a mist and a darkness fell upon him, and he went about seeking those who would lead him by the hand. ¹²Then the proconsul believed when he saw what had happened, being amazed at the teaching of the Lord.

13 Now Paul and his companions put out to sea from Paphos and came to Perga in Pamphylia; but John left them and returned to Jerusalem. ¹⁴But going on from Perga, they arrived at Pisidian Antioch, and on the Sabbath day they went into the synagogue and sat down. ¹⁵After the reading of the Law and the Prophets the synagogue officials sent to them, saying, "Brethren, if you have any word of exhortation for the people, say it." ¹⁶Paul stood up, and motioning with his hand said,

"Men of Israel, and you who fear God, listen: ¹⁷The God of this people Israel chose our fathers and made the people great during their stay in the land of Egypt, and with an uplifted arm He led them out from it. ¹⁸For a period of about forty years He put up with them in the wilderness. ¹⁹When He had destroyed seven nations in the land of Canaan, He distributed their land as an inheritance—*all of which took* about four hundred and fifty years. ²⁰After these things He gave *them* judges until Samuel the prophet. ²¹Then they asked for a king, and God gave them Saul the son of Kish, a man of the tribe of Benjamin, for forty years. ²²After He had removed him, He raised up David to be their king, concerning whom He also testified and said, 'I HAVE FOUND DAVID the son of Jesse, A MAN AFTER MY HEART, who will do all My will.' ²³From the descendants of this man, according to promise, God has brought to Israel a Savior, Jesus, ²⁴after John had proclaimed before His coming a baptism of repentance to all the people of Israel. ²⁵And while John was completing his course, he kept saying, 'What do you suppose that I am? I am not *He*. But behold, one is coming after me the sandals of whose feet I am not worthy to untie.'

26 "Brethren, sons of Abraham's family, and those among you who fear God, to us the message of this salvation has been sent. ²⁷For those who live in Jerusalem, and their rulers, recognizing neither Him nor the utterances of the prophets which are read every Sabbath, fulfilled *these* by condemning *Him*. ²⁸And though they found no ground for *putting Him to* death, they asked Pilate

that He be executed. ²⁹When they had carried out all that was written concerning Him, they took Him down from the cross and laid Him in a tomb. ³⁰But God raised Him from the dead; ³¹and for many days He appeared to those who came up with Him from Galilee to Jerusalem, the very ones who are now His witnesses to the people. ³²And we preach to you the good news of the promise made to the fathers, ³³that God has fulfilled this *promise* to our children in that He raised up Jesus, as it is also written in the second Psalm, 'YOU ARE MY SON; TODAY I HAVE BEGOTTEN YOU.' ³⁴*As for the fact* that He raised Him up from the dead, no longer to return to decay, He has spoken in this way: 'I WILL GIVE YOU THE HOLY *and* SURE *blessings* OF DAVID.' ³⁵Therefore He also says in another *Psalm,* 'YOU WILL NOT ALLOW YOUR HOLY ONE TO UNDERGO DECAY.' ³⁶For David, after he had served the purpose of God in his own generation, fell asleep, and was laid among his fathers and underwent decay; ³⁷but He whom God raised did not undergo decay. ³⁸Therefore let it be known to you, brethren, that through Him forgiveness of sins is proclaimed to you, ³⁹and through Him everyone who believes is freed from all things, from which you could not be freed through the Law of

Moses. [40]Therefore take heed, so that the thing spoken of in the Prophets may not come upon *you:*
[41]'BEHOLD, YOU SCOFFERS, AND MARVEL, AND PERISH;
FOR I AM ACCOMPLISHING A WORK IN YOUR DAYS,
A WORK WHICH YOU WILL NEVER BELIEVE, THOUGH SOMEONE SHOULD DESCRIBE IT TO YOU.' "

[42] As Paul and Barnabas were going out, the people kept begging that these things might be spoken to them the next Sabbath. [43]Now when *the meeting of* the synagogue had broken up, many of the Jews and of the God-fearing proselytes followed Paul and Barnabas, who, speaking to them, were urging them to continue in the grace of God.

Paul Turns to the Gentiles

[44] The next Sabbath nearly the whole city assembled to hear the word of the Lord. [45]But when the Jews saw the crowds, they were filled with jealousy and *began* contradicting the things spoken by Paul, and were blaspheming. [46]Paul and Barnabas spoke out boldly and said, "It was necessary that the word of God be spoken to you first; since you repudiate it and judge yourselves unworthy of eternal life, behold, we are turning to the Gentiles. [47]For so the Lord has commanded us,

'I HAVE PLACED YOU AS A LIGHT FOR THE GENTILES,
THAT YOU MAY BRING SALVATION TO THE END OF THE EARTH.' "

[48] When the Gentiles heard this, they *began* rejoicing and glorifying the word of the Lord; and as many as had been appointed to eternal life believed. [49]And the word of the Lord was being spread through the whole region. [50]But the Jews incited the devout women of prominence and the leading men of the city, and instigated a persecution against Paul and Barnabas, and drove them out of their district. [51]But they shook off the dust of their feet *in protest* against them and went to Iconium. [52]And the disciples were continually filled with joy and with the Holy Spirit.

Acceptance and Opposition

14In Iconium they entered the synagogue of the Jews together, and spoke in such a manner that a large number of people believed, both of Jews and of Greeks. [2]But the Jews who disbelieved stirred up the minds of the Gentiles and embittered them against the brethren. [3]Therefore they spent a long time *there* speaking boldly *with reliance* upon the Lord, who was testifying to the word of His grace, granting that signs and wonders be done by their hands. [4]But the people of the city were divided; and some sided with the Jews, and some with the apostles. ⁵And when an attempt was made by both the Gentiles and the Jews with their rulers, to mistreat and to stone them, ⁶they became aware of it and fled to the cities of Lycaonia, Lystra and Derbe, and the surrounding region; ⁷and there they continued to preach the gospel.

8 At Lystra a man was sitting who had no strength in his feet, lame from his mother's womb, who had never walked. ⁹This man was listening to Paul as he spoke, who, when he had fixed his gaze on him and had seen that he had faith to be made well, ¹⁰said with a loud voice, "Stand upright on your feet." And he leaped up and *began* to walk. ¹¹When the crowds saw what Paul had done, they raised their voice, saying in the Lycaonian language, "The gods have become like men and have come down to us." ¹²And they *began* calling Barnabas, Zeus, and Paul, Hermes, because he was the chief speaker. ¹³The priest of Zeus, whose *temple* was just outside the city, brought oxen and garlands to the gates, and wanted to offer sacrifice with the crowds. ¹⁴But when the apostles Barnabas and Paul heard of it, they tore their robes and rushed out into the crowd, crying out ¹⁵and saying, "Men, why are you doing these

things? We are also men of the same nature as you, and preach the gospel to you that you should turn from these ᵃvain things to a living God, WHO MADE THE HEAVEN AND THE EARTH AND THE SEA AND ALL THAT IS IN THEM. ¹⁶In the generations gone by He permitted all the nations to go their own ways; ¹⁷and yet He did not leave Himself without witness, in that He did good and gave you rains from heaven and fruitful seasons, satisfying your hearts with food and gladness." ¹⁸*Even* saying these things, with difficulty they restrained the crowds from offering sacrifice to them.

19 But Jews came from Antioch and Iconium, and having won over the crowds, they stoned Paul and dragged him out of the city, supposing him to be dead. ²⁰But while the disciples stood around him, he got up and entered the city. The next day he went away with Barnabas to Derbe. ²¹After they had preached the gospel to that city and had made many disciples, they returned to Lystra and to Iconium and to Antioch, ²²strengthening the souls of the disciples, encouraging them to continue in the faith, and *saying*, "Through many tribulations we must enter the kingdom of God." ²³When they had appointed elders for them in every church,

ᵃ**14:15** I.e. idols

having prayed with fasting, they commended them to the Lord in whom they had believed.

24 They passed through Pisidia and came into Pamphylia. ²⁵When they had spoken the word in Perga, they went down to Attalia. ²⁶From there they sailed to Antioch, from which they had been commended to the grace of God for the work that they had accomplished. ²⁷When they had arrived and gathered the church together, they *began* to report all things that God had done with them and how He had opened a door of faith to the Gentiles. ²⁸And they spent a long time with the disciples.

The Council at Jerusalem

15 Some men came down from Judea and *began* teaching the brethren, "Unless you are circumcised according to the custom of Moses, you cannot be saved." ²And when Paul and Barnabas had great dissension and debate with them, *the brethren* determined that Paul and Barnabas and some others of them should go up to Jerusalem to the apostles and elders concerning this issue. ³Therefore, being sent on their way by the church, they were passing through both Phoenicia and Samaria, describing in detail the conversion of the Gentiles, and were bringing great joy to all the brethren.

⁴When they arrived at Jerusalem, they were received by the church and the apostles and the elders, and they reported all that God had done with them. ⁵But some of the sect of the Pharisees who had believed stood up, saying, "It is necessary to circumcise them and to direct them to observe the Law of Moses."

6 The apostles and the elders came together to look into this matter. ⁷After there had been much debate, Peter stood up and said to them, "Brethren, you know that in the early days God made a choice among you, that by my mouth the Gentiles would hear the word of the gospel and believe. ⁸And God, who knows the heart, testified to them giving them the Holy Spirit, just as He also did to us; ⁹and He made no distinction between us and them, cleansing their hearts by faith. ¹⁰Now therefore why do you put God to the test by placing upon the neck of the disciples a yoke which neither our fathers nor we have been able to bear? ¹¹But we believe that we are saved through the grace of the Lord Jesus, in the same way as they also are."

12 All the people kept silent, and they were listening to Barnabas and Paul as they were relating what signs and wonders God

had done through them among the Gentiles.

James's Judgment

¹³After they had stopped speaking, James answered, saying, "Brethren, listen to me. ¹⁴Simeon has related how God first concerned Himself about taking from among the Gentiles a people for His name. ¹⁵With this the words of the Prophets agree, just as it is written,

¹⁶'AFTER THESE THINGS I will return,
AND I WILL REBUILD THE TABERNACLE OF DAVID WHICH HAS FALLEN,
AND I WILL REBUILD ITS RUINS,
AND I WILL RESTORE IT,
¹⁷SO THAT THE REST OF MANKIND MAY SEEK THE LORD,
AND ALL THE GENTILES WHO ARE CALLED BY MY NAME,'
¹⁸SAYS THE LORD, WHO MAKES THESE THINGS KNOWN FROM LONG AGO.

¹⁹Therefore it is my judgment that we do not trouble those who are turning to God from among the Gentiles, ²⁰but that we write to them that they abstain from things contaminated by idols and from fornication and from what is strangled and from blood. ²¹For Moses from ancient generations has in every city those who preach him, since he is read in the synagogues every Sabbath."

²²Then it seemed good to the apostles and the elders, with the whole church, to choose men from among them to send to Antioch with Paul and Barnabas—Judas called Barsabbas, and Silas, leading men among the brethren, ²³and they sent this letter by them,

"The apostles and the brethren who are elders, to the brethren in Antioch and Syria and Cilicia who are from the Gentiles, greetings.

²⁴"Since we have heard that some of our number to whom we gave no instruction have disturbed you with *their* words, unsettling your souls, ²⁵it seemed good to us, having become of one mind, to select men to send to you with our beloved Barnabas and Paul, ²⁶men who have risked their lives for the name of our Lord Jesus Christ.

²⁷"Therefore we have sent Judas and Silas, who themselves will also report the same things by word *of mouth.* ²⁸"For it seemed good to the Holy Spirit and to us to lay upon you no greater burden than these essentials: ²⁹that you abstain from things sacrificed to idols and from blood and from things strangled and from fornication; if you keep yourselves free from such things, you will do well. Farewell."

30 So when they were sent away, they went down to Antioch; and having gathered the congregation together, they delivered the letter. [31]When they had read it, they rejoiced because of its encouragement. [32]Judas and Silas, also being prophets themselves, encouraged and strengthened the brethren with a lengthy message. [33]After they had spent time *there,* they were sent away from the brethren in peace to those who had sent them out. [34a][But it seemed good to Silas to remain there.] [35]But Paul and Barnabas stayed in Antioch, teaching and preaching with many others also, the word of the Lord.

Second Missionary Journey

36 After some days Paul said to Barnabas, "Let us return and visit the brethren in every city in which we proclaimed the word of the Lord, *and see* how they are." [37]Barnabas wanted to take John, called Mark, along with them also. [38]But Paul kept insisting that they should not take him along who had deserted them in Pamphylia and had not gone with them to the work. [39]And there occurred such a sharp disagreement that they separated from one another, and Barnabas took Mark with him and sailed away to Cyprus. [40]But Paul chose Silas and left, being committed by the brethren to the grace of the Lord. [41]And he was traveling through Syria and Cilicia, strengthening the churches.

The Macedonian Vision

16 Paul came also to Derbe and to Lystra. And a disciple was there, named Timothy, the son of a Jewish woman who was a believer, but his father was a Greek, [2]and he was well spoken of by the brethren who were in Lystra and Iconium. [3]Paul wanted this man to go with him; and he took him and circumcised him because of the Jews who were in those parts, for they all knew that his father was a Greek. [4]Now while they were passing through the cities, they were delivering the decrees which had been decided upon by the apostles and elders who were in Jerusalem, for them to observe. [5]So the churches were being strengthened in the faith, and were increasing in number daily.

6 They passed through the Phrygian and Galatian region, having been forbidden by the Holy Spirit to speak the word in Asia; [7]and after they came to Mysia, they were trying to go into Bithynia, and the Spirit of Jesus did not permit them; [8]and passing by Mysia, they came down to Troas. [9]A vision appeared to Paul in the night: a man of Macedonia was standing and appealing to him, and saying,

*15:34 Early mss do not contain this v

"Come over to Macedonia and help us." [10]When he had seen the vision, immediately we sought to go into Macedonia, concluding that God had called us to preach the gospel to them.

11 So putting out to sea from Troas, we ran a straight course to Samothrace, and on the day following to Neapolis; [12]and from there to Philippi, which is a leading city of the district of Macedonia, a *Roman* colony; and we were staying in this city for some days. [13]And on the Sabbath day we went outside the gate to a riverside, where we were supposing that there would be a place of prayer; and we sat down and began speaking to the women who had assembled.

First Convert in Europe

[14]A woman named Lydia, from the city of Thyatira, a seller of purple fabrics, a worshiper of God, was listening; and the Lord opened her heart to respond to the things spoken by Paul. [15]And when she and her household had been baptized, she urged us, saying, "If you have judged me to be faithful to the Lord, come into my house and stay." And she prevailed upon us.

16 It happened that as we were going to the place of prayer, a slave-girl having a spirit of divination met us, who was bringing her masters much profit by fortune-telling. [17]Following after Paul and us, she kept crying out, saying, "These men are bond-servants of the Most High God, who are proclaiming to you the way of salvation." [18]She continued doing this for many days. But Paul was greatly annoyed, and turned and said to the spirit, "I command you in the name of Jesus Christ to come out of her!" And it came out at that very moment.

19 But when her masters saw that their hope of profit was gone, they seized Paul and Silas and dragged them into the market place before the authorities, [20]and when they had brought them to the chief magistrates, they said, "These men are throwing our city into confusion, being Jews, [21]and are proclaiming customs which it is not lawful for us to accept or to observe, being Romans."

Paul and Silas Imprisoned

[22]The crowd rose up together against them, and the chief magistrates tore their robes off them and proceeded to order *them* to be beaten with rods. [23]When they had struck them with many blows, they threw them into prison, commanding the jailer to guard them securely; [24]and he, having received such a command, threw them into

the inner prison and fastened their feet in the stocks.

25 But about midnight Paul and Silas were praying and singing hymns of praise to God, and the prisoners were listening to them; ²⁶and suddenly there came a great earthquake, so that the foundations of the prison house were shaken; and immediately all the doors were opened and everyone's chains were unfastened. ²⁷When the jailer awoke and saw the prison doors opened, he drew his sword and was about to kill himself, supposing that the prisoners had escaped. ²⁸But Paul cried out with a loud voice, saying, "Do not harm yourself, for we are all here!" ²⁹And he called for lights and rushed in, and trembling with fear he fell down before Paul and Silas, ³⁰and after he brought them out, he said, "Sirs, what must I do to be saved?"

The Jailer Converted

³¹They said, "Believe in the Lord Jesus, and you will be saved, you and your household." ³²And they spoke the word of the Lord to him together with all who were in his house. ³³And he took them that *very* hour of the night and washed their wounds, and immediately he was baptized, he and all his *household*. ³⁴And he brought them into his house and set food before them, and rejoiced greatly, having believed in God with his whole household.

35 Now when day came, the chief magistrates sent their policemen, saying, "Release those men." ³⁶And the jailer reported these words to Paul, *saying*, "The chief magistrates have sent to release you. Therefore come out now and go in peace." ³⁷But Paul said to them, "They have beaten us in public without trial, men who are Romans, and have thrown us into prison; and now are they sending us away secretly? No indeed! But let them come themselves and bring us out." ³⁸The policemen reported these words to the chief magistrates. They were afraid when they heard that they were Romans, ³⁹and they came and appealed to them, and when they had brought them out, they kept begging them to leave the city. ⁴⁰They went out of the prison and entered *the house of* Lydia, and when they saw the brethren, they encouraged them and departed.

Paul at Thessalonica

17 Now when they had traveled through Amphipolis and Apollonia, they came to Thessalonica, where there was a synagogue of the Jews. ²And according to Paul's custom, he went to them, and for three Sabbaths reasoned with them from the Scriptures, [3]explaining and giving evidence that the Christ had to suffer and rise again from the dead, and *saying*, "This Jesus whom I am proclaiming to you is the Christ." [4]And some of them were persuaded and joined Paul and Silas, along with a large number of the God-fearing Greeks and a number of the leading women. [5]But the Jews, becoming jealous and taking along some wicked men from the market place, formed a mob and set the city in an uproar; and attacking the house of Jason, they were seeking to bring them out to the people. [6]When they did not find them, they *began* dragging Jason and some brethren before the city authorities, shouting, "These men who have upset [a]the world have come here also; [7]and Jason has welcomed them, and they all act contrary to the decrees of Caesar, saying that there is another king, Jesus." [8]They stirred up the crowd and the city authorities who heard these things. [9]And when they had received a pledge from Jason and the others, they released them.

Paul at Berea

10 The brethren immediately sent Paul and Silas away by night to Berea, and when they arrived, they went into the synagogue of the Jews. [11]Now these were more noble-minded than those in Thessalonica, for they received the word with great eagerness, examining the Scriptures daily *to see* whether these things were so. [12]Therefore many of them believed, along with a number of prominent Greek women and men. [13]But when the Jews of Thessalonica found out that the word of God had been proclaimed by Paul in Berea also, they came there as well, agitating and stirring up the crowds. [14]Then immediately the brethren sent Paul out to go as far as the sea; and Silas and Timothy remained there. [15]Now those who escorted Paul brought him as far as Athens; and receiving a command for Silas and Timothy to come to him as soon as possible, they left.

Paul at Athens

16 Now while Paul was waiting for them at Athens, his spirit was being provoked within him as he was observing the city full of idols. [17]So he was reasoning in the synagogue with the Jews and the God-fearing *Gentiles*, and in the market place every day with those who happened to be present. [18]And also some of the Epicurean and Stoic philosophers were conversing with him. Some were saying, "What would this idle babbler wish to say?" Others, "He seems to be a proclaimer of strange deities,"— because he was preaching Jesus

and the resurrection. ¹⁹And they took him and brought him to the Areopagus, saying, "May we know what this new teaching is which you are proclaiming? ²⁰For you are bringing some strange things to our ears; so we want to know what these things mean." ²¹(Now all the Athenians and the strangers visiting there used to spend their time in nothing other than telling or hearing something new.)

Sermon on Mars Hill

22 So Paul stood in the midst of the Areopagus and said, "Men of Athens, I observe that you are very religious in all respects. ²³For while I was passing through and examining the objects of your worship, I also found an altar with this inscription, 'TO AN UNKNOWN GOD.' Therefore what you worship in ignorance, this I proclaim to you. ²⁴The God who made the world and all things in it, since He is Lord of heaven and earth, does not dwell in temples made with hands; ²⁵nor is He served by human hands, as though He needed anything, since He Himself gives to all *people* life and breath and all things; ²⁶and He made from one *man* every nation of mankind to live on all the face of the earth, having determined *their* appointed times and the boundaries of their habitation, ²⁷that they would seek God, if perhaps they might grope for Him and find Him, though He is not far from each one of us; ²⁸for in Him we live and move and exist, as even some of your own poets have said, 'For we also are His children.' ²⁹Being then the children of God, we ought not to think that the Divine Nature is like gold or silver or stone, an image formed by the art and thought of man. ³⁰Therefore having overlooked the times of ignorance, God is now declaring to men that all *people* everywhere should repent, ³¹because He has fixed a day in which He will judge the world in righteousness through a Man whom He has appointed, having furnished proof to all men by raising Him from the dead."

32 Now when they heard of the resurrection of the dead, some *began* to sneer, but others said, "We shall hear you again concerning this." ³³So Paul went out of their midst. ³⁴But some men joined him and believed, among whom also were Dionysius the Areopagite and a woman named Damaris and others with them.

Paul at Corinth

18After these things he left Athens and went to Corinth. ²And he found a Jew named Aquila, a native of Pontus, having recently come from Italy with his wife Priscilla, because Claudius had commanded all the Jews to leave Rome. He came to them, [3]and because he was of the same trade, he stayed with them and they were working, for by trade they were tent-makers. [4]And he was reasoning in the synagogue every Sabbath and trying to persuade Jews and Greeks.

5 But when Silas and Timothy came down from Macedonia, Paul *began* devoting himself completely to the word, solemnly testifying to the Jews that Jesus was the Christ. [6]But when they resisted and blasphemed, he shook out his garments and said to them, "Your blood *be* on your own heads! I am clean. From now on I will go to the Gentiles." [7]Then he left there and went to the house of a man named Titius Justus, a worshiper of God, whose house was next to the synagogue. [8]Crispus, the leader of the synagogue, believed in the Lord with all his household, and many of the Corinthians when they heard were believing and being baptized. [9]And the Lord said to Paul in the night by a vision, "Do not be afraid *any longer,* but go on speaking and do not be silent; [10]for I am with you, and no man will attack you in order to harm you, for I have many people in this city." [11]And he settled *there* a year and six months, teaching the word of God among them.

12 But while Gallio was proconsul of Achaia, the Jews with one accord rose up against Paul and brought him before the judgment seat, [13]saying, "This man persuades men to worship God contrary to the law." [14]But when Paul was about to open his mouth, Gallio said to the Jews, "If it were a matter of wrong or of vicious crime, O Jews, it would be reasonable for me to put up with you; [15]but if there are questions about words and names and your own law, look after it yourselves; I am unwilling to be a judge of these matters." [16]And he drove them away from the judgment seat. [17]And they all took hold of Sosthenes, the leader of the synagogue, and *began* beating him in front of the judgment seat. But Gallio was not concerned about any of these things.

18 Paul, having remained many days longer, took leave of the brethren and put out to sea for Syria, and with him were Priscilla and Aquila. In Cenchrea he had his hair cut, for he was keeping a vow. [19]They came to Ephesus, and he left them there. Now he himself entered the synagogue and reasoned with the Jews. [20]When they asked him to stay for a longer time, he did not consent, [21]but taking leave of them and saying, "I will return to you again if God wills," he set sail from Ephesus.

22 When he had landed at Caesarea, he went up and greeted the church, and went down to Antioch.

Third Missionary Journey

23 And having spent some time *there,* he left and passed successively through the Galatian region and Phrygia, strengthening all the disciples.

24 Now a Jew named Apollos, an Alexandrian by birth, an eloquent man, came to Ephesus; and he was mighty in the Scriptures. **25** This man had been instructed in the way of the Lord; and being fervent in spirit, he was speaking and teaching accurately the things concerning Jesus, being acquainted only with the baptism of John; **26** and he began to speak out boldly in the synagogue. But when Priscilla and Aquila heard him, they took him aside and explained to him the way of God more accurately. **27** And when he wanted to go across to Achaia, the brethren encouraged him and wrote to the disciples to welcome him; and when he had arrived, he greatly helped those who had believed through grace, **28** for he powerfully refuted the Jews in public, demonstrating by the Scriptures that Jesus was the Christ.

Paul at Ephesus

19 It happened that while Apollos was at Corinth, Paul passed through the upper country and came to Ephesus, and found some disciples. **2** He said to them, "Did you receive the Holy Spirit when you believed?" And they *said* to him, "No, we have not even heard whether there is a Holy Spirit." **3** And he said, "Into what then were you baptized?" And they said, "Into John's baptism." **4** Paul said, "John baptized with the baptism of repentance, telling the people to believe in Him who was coming after him, that is, in Jesus." **5** When they heard this, they were baptized in the name of the Lord Jesus. **6** And when Paul had laid his hands upon them, the Holy Spirit came on them, and they *began* speaking with tongues and prophesying. **7** There were in all about twelve men.

8 And he entered the synagogue and continued speaking out boldly for three months, reasoning and persuading *them* about the kingdom of God. **9** But when some were becoming hardened and disobedient, speaking evil of the Way before the people, he withdrew from them and took away the disciples, reasoning daily in the school of Tyrannus. **10** This took place for two years, so that all who lived in Asia heard the word of the Lord, both Jews and Greeks.

Miracles at Ephesus

11 God was performing extraordinary miracles by the hands of Paul, [12]so that handkerchiefs or aprons were even carried from his body to the sick, and the diseases left them and the evil spirits went out. [13]But also some of the Jewish exorcists, who went from place to place, attempted to name over those who had the evil spirits the name of the Lord Jesus, saying, "I adjure you by Jesus whom Paul preaches." [14]Seven sons of one Sceva, a Jewish chief priest, were doing this. [15]And the evil spirit answered and said to them, "I recognize Jesus, and I know about Paul, but who are you?" [16]And the man, in whom was the evil spirit, leaped on them and subdued all of them and overpowered them, so that they fled out of that house naked and wounded. [17]This became known to all, both Jews and Greeks, who lived in Ephesus; and fear fell upon them all and the name of the Lord Jesus was being magnified. [18]Many also of those who had believed kept coming, confessing and disclosing their practices. [19]And many of those who practiced magic brought their books together and *began* burning them in the sight of everyone; and they counted up the price of them and found it fifty thousand pieces of silver. [20]So the word of the Lord was growing mightily and prevailing.

21 Now after these things were finished, Paul purposed in the Spirit to go to Jerusalem after he had passed through Macedonia and Achaia, saying, "After I have been there, I must also see Rome." [22]And having sent into Macedonia two of those who ministered to him, Timothy and Erastus, he himself stayed in Asia for a while.

23 About that time there occurred no small disturbance concerning the Way. [24]For a man named Demetrius, a silversmith, who made silver shrines of Artemis, was bringing no little business to the craftsmen; [25]these he gathered together with the workmen of similar *trades,* and said, "Men, you know that our prosperity depends upon this business. [26]You see and hear that not only in Ephesus, but in almost all of Asia, this Paul has persuaded and turned away a considerable number of people, saying that gods made with hands are no gods *at all.* [27]Not only is there danger that this trade of ours fall into disrepute, but also that the temple of the great goddess Artemis be regarded as worthless and that she whom all of Asia and the

world worship will even be dethroned from her magnificence."

28 When they heard *this* and were filled with rage, they *began* crying out, saying, "Great is Artemis of the Ephesians!" ²⁹The city was filled with the confusion, and they rushed with one accord into the theater, dragging along Gaius and Aristarchus, Paul's traveling companions from Macedonia. ³⁰And when Paul wanted to go into the assembly, the disciples would not let him. ³¹Also some of the ᵃAsiarchs who were friends of his sent to him and repeatedly urged him not to venture into the theater. ³²So then, some were shouting one thing and some another, for the assembly was in confusion and the majority did not know for what reason they had come together. ³³Some of the crowd concluded *it was* Alexander, since the Jews had put him forward; and having motioned with his hand, Alexander was intending to make a defense to the assembly. ³⁴But when they recognized that he was a Jew, a *single* outcry arose from them all as they shouted for about two hours, "Great is Artemis of the Ephesians!" ³⁵After quieting the crowd, the town clerk *said, "Men of Ephesus, what man is there after all who does not know that the city of the Ephesians is guardian of the temple of the great Artemis and of

the *image* which fell down from heaven? ³⁶So, since these are undeniable facts, you ought to keep calm and to do nothing rash. ³⁷For you have brought these men *here* who are neither robbers of temples nor blasphemers of our goddess. ³⁸So then, if Demetrius and the craftsmen who are with him have a complaint against any man, the courts are in session and proconsuls are *available;* let them bring charges against one another. ³⁹But if you want anything beyond this, it shall be settled in the lawful assembly. ⁴⁰For indeed we are in danger of being accused of a riot in connection with today's events, since there is no *real* cause *for it,* and in this connection we will be unable to account for this disorderly gathering." ⁴¹After saying this he dismissed the assembly.

Paul in Macedonia and Greece

20 After the uproar had ceased, Paul sent for the disciples, and when he had exhorted them and taken his leave of them, he left to go to Macedonia. ²When he had gone through those districts and had given them much exhortation, he came to Greece. ³And *there* he spent three months, and when a plot was formed against him by the Jews as he was about to set sail for Syria, he decided to return through Macedonia. ⁴And he was accompanied by Sopater

ᵃ**19:31** I.e. political or religious officials of the province of Asia of Berea, *the son* of Pyrrhus, and by Aristarchus and Secundus of the Thessalonians, and Gaius of Derbe, and Timothy, and Tychicus and Trophimus of Asia. ⁵But these had gone on ahead and were waiting for us at Troas. ⁶We sailed from Philippi after the days of Unleavened Bread, and came to them at Troas within five days; and there we stayed seven days.

7 On the first day of the week, when we were gathered together to break bread, Paul *began* talking to them, intending to leave the next day, and he prolonged his message until midnight. ⁸There were many lamps in the upper room where we were gathered together. ⁹And there was a young man named Eutychus sitting on the window sill, sinking into a deep sleep; and as Paul kept on talking, he was overcome by sleep and fell down from the third floor and was picked up dead. ¹⁰But Paul went down and fell upon him, and after embracing him, he said, "Do not be troubled, for his life is in him." ¹¹When he had gone *back* up and had broken the bread and eaten, he talked with them a long while until daybreak, and then left. ¹²They took away the boy alive, and were greatly comforted.

Troas to Miletus

13 But we, going ahead to the ship, set sail for Assos, intending from there to take Paul on board; for so he had arranged it, intending himself to go by land. ¹⁴And when he met us at Assos, we took him on board and came to Mitylene. ¹⁵Sailing from there, we arrived the following day opposite Chios; and the next day we crossed over to Samos; and the day following we came to Miletus. ¹⁶For Paul had decided to sail past Ephesus so that he would not have to spend time in Asia; for he was hurrying to be in Jerusalem, if possible, on the day of Pentecost.

Farewell to Ephesus

17 From Miletus he sent to Ephesus and called to him the elders of the church. ¹⁸And when they had come to him, he said to them, "You yourselves know, from the first day that I set foot in Asia, how I was with you the whole time, ¹⁹serving the Lord with all humility and with tears and with trials which came upon me through the plots of the Jews; ²⁰how I did not shrink from declaring to you anything that was profitable, and teaching you publicly and from house to house, ²¹solemnly testifying to both Jews and Greeks of repentance toward God and faith in our Lord Jesus Christ. ²²And now, behold, bound by the Spirit, I am on my way to Jerusalem, not knowing what will happen to

me there, [23]except that the Holy Spirit solemnly testifies to me in every city, saying that bonds and afflictions await me. [24]But I do not consider my life of any account as dear to myself, so that I may finish my course and the ministry which I received from the Lord Jesus, to testify solemnly of the gospel of the grace of God.

[25] "And now, behold, I know that all of you, among whom I went about preaching the kingdom, will no longer see my face. [26]Therefore, I testify to you this day that I am innocent of the blood of all men. [27]For I did not shrink from declaring to you the whole purpose of God. [28]Be on guard for yourselves and for all the flock, among which the Holy Spirit has made you overseers, to shepherd the church of God which He purchased with His own blood. [29]I know that after my departure savage wolves will come in among you, not sparing the flock; [30]and from among your own selves men will arise, speaking perverse things, to draw away the disciples after them. [31]Therefore be on the alert, remembering that night and day for a period of three years I did not cease to admonish each one with tears. [32]And now I commend you to God and to the word of His grace, which is able to build *you* up and to give *you* the inheritance among all those who

are sanctified. [33]I have coveted no one's silver or gold or clothes. [34]You yourselves know that these hands ministered to my *own* needs and to the men who were with me. [35]In everything I showed you that by working hard in this manner you must help the weak and remember the words of the Lord Jesus, that He Himself said, 'It is more blessed to give than to receive.'"

[36] When he had said these things, he knelt down and prayed with them all. [37]And they *began* to weep aloud and embraced Paul, and repeatedly kissed him, [38]grieving especially over the word which he had spoken, that they would not see his face again. And they were accompanying him to the ship.

Paul Sails from Miletus

21 When we had parted from them and had set sail, we ran a straight course to Cos and the next day to Rhodes and from there to Patara; [2]and having found a ship crossing over to Phoenicia, we went aboard and set sail. [3]When we came in sight of Cyprus, leaving it on the left, we kept sailing to Syria and landed at Tyre; for there the ship was to unload its cargo. [4]After looking up the disciples, we stayed there seven days; and they kept telling Paul through the Spirit not to set foot in Jerusalem. [5]When our days there were ended, we left and started on our journey, while they all, with wives and children, escorted us until *we were* out of the city. After kneeling down on the beach and praying, we said farewell to one another. [6]Then we went on board the ship, and they returned home again.

7 When we had finished the voyage from Tyre, we arrived at Ptolemais, and after greeting the brethren, we stayed with them for a day. [8]On the next day we left and came to Caesarea, and entering the house of Philip the evangelist, who was one of the seven, we stayed with him. [9]Now this man had four virgin daughters who were prophetesses. [10]As we were staying there for some days, a prophet named Agabus came down from Judea. [11]And coming to us, he took Paul's belt and bound his own feet and hands, and said, "This is what the Holy Spirit says: 'In this way the Jews at Jerusalem will bind the man who owns this belt and deliver him into the hands of the Gentiles.' " [12]When we had heard this, we as well as the local residents *began* begging him not to go up to Jerusalem. [13]Then Paul answered, "What are you doing, weeping and breaking my heart? For I am ready not only to be bound, but even to die at Jerusalem for the name of the Lord Jesus." [14]And since he

would not be persuaded, we fell silent, remarking, "The will of the Lord be done!"

Paul at Jerusalem

15 After these days we got ready and started on our way up to Jerusalem. [16]*Some* of the disciples from Caesarea also came with us, taking us to Mnason of Cyprus, a disciple of long standing with whom we were to lodge.

17 After we arrived in Jerusalem, the brethren received us gladly. [18]And the following day Paul went in with us to James, and all the elders were present. [19]After he had greeted them, he *began* to relate one by one the things which God had done among the Gentiles through his ministry. [20]And when they heard it they *began* glorifying God; and they said to him, "You see, brother, how many thousands there are among the Jews of those who have believed, and they are all zealous for the Law; [21]and they have been told about you, that you are teaching all the Jews who are among the Gentiles to forsake Moses, telling them not to circumcise their children nor to walk according to the customs. [22]What, then, is *to be done?* They will certainly hear that you have come. [23]Therefore do this that we tell you. We have four men who are under a [24]
them and

with them, and pay their expenses so that they may shave their heads; and all will know that there is nothing to the things which they have been told about you, but that you yourself also walk orderly, keeping the Law. ²⁵But concerning the Gentiles who have believed, we wrote, having decided that they should abstain from meat sacrificed to idols and from blood and from what is strangled and from fornication." ²⁶Then Paul took the men, and the next day, purifying himself along with them, went into the temple giving notice of the completion of the days of purification, until the sacrifice was offered for each one of them.

Paul Seized in the Temple

27 When the seven days were almost over, the Jews from Asia, upon seeing him in the temple, *began* to stir up all the crowd and laid hands on him, ²⁸crying out, "Men of Israel, come to our aid! This is the man who preaches to all men everywhere against our people and the Law and this place; and besides he has even brought Greeks into the temple and has defiled this holy place." ²⁹For they had previously seen Trophimus the Ephesian in the city with him, and they supposed that Paul had brought him in the temple. ³⁰Then all the people took hold of

Paul they dragged him out of the temple, and immediately the doors were shut. ³¹While they were seeking to kill him, a report came up to the ^acommander of the *Roman* cohort that all Jerusalem was in confusion. ³²At once he took along *some* soldiers and centurions and ran down to them; and when they saw the commander and the soldiers, they stopped beating Paul. ³³Then the commander came up and took hold of him, and ordered him to be bound with two chains; and he *began* asking who he was and what he had done. ³⁴But among the crowd some were shouting one thing *and* some another, and when he could not find out the facts because of the uproar, he ordered him to be brought into the barracks. ³⁵When he got to the stairs, he was carried by the soldiers because of the violence of the mob; ³⁶for the multitude of the people kept following them, shouting, "Away with him!"

37 As Paul was about to be brought into the barracks, he said to the commander, "May I say something to you?" And he *said, "Do you know Greek? ³⁸Then you are not the Egyptian who some time ago stirred up a revolt and led the four thousand men of the Assassins out into the wilderness?" ³⁹But Paul said, "I am a Jew of Tarsus in Cilicia, a citizen of no insignificant city; and I beg you, allow me to speak to the people." ⁴⁰When he had given him permission, Paul, standing on the stairs, motioned to the people with his hand; and when there was a great hush, he spoke to them in the Hebrew dialect, saying,

Paul's Defense before the Jews

22 "Brethren and fathers, hear my defense which I now *offer* to you."

2 And when they heard that he was addressing them in the Hebrew dialect, they became even more quiet; and he *said,

3 "I am a Jew, born in Tarsus of Cilicia, but brought up in this city, educated under Gamaliel, strictly according to the law of our fathers, being zealous for God just as you all are today. ⁴I persecuted this Way to the death, binding and putting both men and women into prisons, ⁵as also the high priest and all the Council of the elders can testify. From them I also received letters to the brethren, and started off for Damascus in order to bring even those who were there to Jerusalem as prisoners to be punished.

6 "But it happened that as I was on my way, approaching Damascus about noontime, a very bright light suddenly flashed from heaven all around me, ⁷and I fell to the ground and heard a voice saying to me, 'Saul, Saul, why are you persecuting Me?' ⁸And I answered, 'Who are You, Lord?' And He said to me, 'I am Jesus the Nazarene, whom you are persecuting.' ⁹And those who were with me saw the light, to be sure, but did not understand the voice of the One who was speaking to me. ¹⁰And I said, 'What shall I do, Lord?' And the Lord said to me, 'Get up and go on into Damascus, and there you will be told of all that has been appointed for you to do.' ¹¹But since I could not see because of the brightness of that light, I was led by the hand by those who were with me and came into Damascus.

12 "A certain Ananias, a man who was devout by the standard of the Law, *and* well spoken of by all the Jews who lived there, ¹³came to me, and standing near said to me, 'Brother Saul, receive your sight!' And at that very time I looked up at him. ¹⁴And he said, 'The God of our fathers has appointed you to know His will and to see the Righteous One and to hear an utterance from His mouth. ¹⁵For you will be a witness for Him to all men of what you have seen and heard. ¹⁶Now why do you delay? Get up and be baptized, and wash away your sins, calling on His name.'

17 "It happened when I returned to Jerusalem and was praying in the temple, that I fell into a trance, [18]and I saw Him saying to me, 'Make haste, and get out of Jerusalem quickly, because they will not accept your testimony about Me.' [19]And I said, 'Lord, they themselves understand that in one synagogue after another I used to imprison and beat those who believed in You. [20]And when the blood of Your witness Stephen was being shed, I also was standing by approving, and watching out for the coats of those who were slaying him.' [21]And He said to me, 'Go! For I will send you far away to the Gentiles.'"

22 They listened to him up to this statement, and *then* they raised their voices and said, "Away with such a fellow from the earth, for he should not be allowed to live!" [23]And as they were crying out and throwing off their cloaks and tossing dust into the air, [24]the ᵃcommander ordered him to be brought into the barracks, stating that he should be examined by scourging so that he might find out the reason why they were shouting against him that way. [25]But when they stretched him out with thongs, Paul said to the centurion who was standing by, "Is it lawful for you to scourge a man who is a Roman and uncondemned?"

[26]When the centurion heard *this,* he went to the commander and told him, saying, "What are you about to do? For this man is a Roman." [27]The commander came and said to him, "Tell me, are you a Roman?" And he said, "Yes." [28]The commander answered, "I acquired this citizenship with a large sum of money." And Paul said, "But I was actually born *a citizen.*" [29]Therefore those who were about to examine him immediately let go of him; and the commander also was afraid when he found out that he was a Roman, and because he had put him in chains.

30 But on the next day, wishing to know for certain why he had been accused by the Jews, he released him and ordered the chief priests and all the Council to assemble, and brought Paul down and set him before them.

Paul before the Council

23 Paul, looking intently at the Council, said, "Brethren, I have lived my life with a perfectly good conscience before God up to this day." [2]The high priest Ananias commanded those standing beside him to strike him on the mouth. [3]Then Paul said to him, "God is going to strike you, you whitewashed wall! Do you sit to try me according to the Law, and in violation of the Law order me to be

ᵃ**22:24** I.e. chiliarch, in command of one thousand troops struck?" [4]But the bystanders said, "Do you revile God's high priest?" [5]And Paul said, "I was not aware, brethren, that he was high priest; for it is written, 'YOU SHALL NOT SPEAK EVIL OF A RULER OF YOUR PEOPLE.' "

[6] But perceiving that one group were Sadducees and the other Pharisees, Paul *began* crying out in the Council, "Brethren, I am a Pharisee, a son of Pharisees; I am on trial for the hope and resurrection of the dead!" [7]As he said this, there occurred a dissension between the Pharisees and Sadducees, and the assembly was divided. [8]For the Sadducees say that there is no resurrection, nor an angel, nor a spirit, but the Pharisees acknowledge them all. [9]And there occurred a great uproar; and some of the scribes of the Pharisaic party stood up and *began* to argue heatedly, saying, "We find nothing wrong with this man; suppose a spirit or an angel has spoken to him?" [10]And as a great dissension was developing, the [a]commander was afraid Paul would be torn to pieces by them and ordered the troops to go down and take him away from them by force, and bring him into the barracks.

[11] But on the night *immediately* following, the Lord stood at his side and said, "Take courage; for as you have solemnly witnessed to My cause at Jerusalem, so you must witness at Rome also."

A Conspiracy to Kill Paul

[12] When it was day, the Jews formed a conspiracy and bound themselves under an oath, saying that they would neither eat nor drink until they had killed Paul. [13]There were more than forty who formed this plot. [14]They came to the chief priests and the elders and said, "We have bound ourselves under a solemn oath to taste nothing until we have killed Paul. [15]Now therefore, you and the Council notify the commander to bring him down to you, as though you were going to determine his case by a more thorough investigation; and we for our part are ready to slay him before he comes near *the place*."

[16] But the son of Paul's sister heard of their ambush, and he came and entered the barracks and told Paul. [17]Paul called one of the centurions to him and said, "Lead this young man to the commander, for he has something to report to him." [18]So he took him and led him to the commander and *said, "Paul the prisoner called me to him and asked me to lead this young man to you since he has something to tell you." [19]The commander took him by the hand and stepping

[a]23:10 I.e. chiliarch, in command of one thousand troops

aside, *began* to inquire of him privately, "What is it that you have to report to me?" ²⁰And he said, "The Jews have agreed to ask you to bring Paul down tomorrow to the Council, as though they were going to inquire somewhat more thoroughly about him. ²¹So do not listen to them, for more than forty of them are lying in wait for him who have bound themselves under a curse not to eat or drink until they slay him; and now they are ready and waiting for the promise from you." ²²So the commander let the young man go, instructing him, "Tell no one that you have notified me of these things."

Paul Moved to Caesarea

²³And he called to him two of the centurions and said, "Get two hundred soldiers ready by the ^athird hour of the night to proceed to Caesarea, with seventy horsemen and two hundred spearmen." ²⁴*They were* also to provide mounts to put Paul on and bring him safely to Felix the governor. ²⁵And he wrote a letter having this form:

26 "Claudius Lysias, to the most excellent governor Felix, greetings.

27 "When this man was arrested by the Jews and was about to be slain by them, I came up to them with the troops and rescued him, having learned that he was a Roman.

²⁸"And wanting to ascertain the charge for which they were accusing him, I brought him down to their Council;

²⁹and I found him to be accused over questions about their Law, but under no accusation deserving death or imprisonment.

30 "When I was informed that there would be a plot against the man, I sent him to you at once, also instructing his accusers to bring charges against him before you."

31 So the soldiers, in accordance with their orders, took Paul and brought him by night to Antipatris. ³²But the next day, leaving the horsemen to go on with him, they returned to the barracks. ³³When these had come to Caesarea and delivered the letter to the governor, they also presented Paul to him. ³⁴When he had read it, he asked from what province he was, and when he learned that he was from Cilicia, ³⁵he said, "I will give you a hearing after your accusers arrive also," giving orders for him to be kept in Herod's ^bPraetorium.

Paul before Felix

24 After five days the high priest Ananias came down with some elders, with an attorney *named* Tertullus, and they

^a**23:23** I.e. 9 p.m.; ^b**23:35** I.e. governor's official residence

brought charges to the governor against Paul. [2]After *Paul* had been summoned, Tertullus began to accuse him, saying *to the governor,* "Since we have through you attained much peace, and since by your providence reforms are being carried out for this nation, [3]we acknowledge *this* in every way and everywhere, most excellent Felix, with all thankfulness. [4]But, that I may not weary you any further, I beg you to grant us, by your kindness, a brief hearing. [5]For we have found this man a real pest and a fellow who stirs up dissension among all the Jews throughout [a]the world, and a ringleader of the sect of the Nazarenes. [6]And he even tried to desecrate the temple; and then we arrested him. [b][We wanted to judge him according to our own Law. [7]But Lysias the commander came along, and with much violence took him out of our hands, [8]ordering his accusers to come before you.] By examining him yourself concerning all these matters you will be able to ascertain the things of which we accuse him." [9]The Jews also joined in the attack, asserting that these things were so.

10 When the governor had nodded for him to speak, Paul responded: "Knowing that for many years you have been a judge to this nation, I cheerfully make my defense, [11]since you can take note of the fact that no more than twelve days ago I went up to Jerusalem to worship. [12]Neither in the temple, nor in the synagogues, nor in the city *itself* did they find me carrying on a discussion with anyone or causing a riot. [13]Nor can they prove to you *the charges* of which they now accuse me. [14]But this I admit to you, that according to the Way which they call a sect I do serve the God of our fathers, believing everything that is in accordance with the Law and that is written in the Prophets; [15]having a hope in God, which these men cherish themselves, that there shall certainly be a resurrection of both the righteous and the wicked. [16]In view of this, I also do my best to maintain always a blameless conscience *both* before God and before men. [17]Now after several years I came to bring [c]alms to my nation and to present offerings; [18]in which they found me *occupied* in the temple, having been purified, without *any* crowd or uproar. But *there were* some Jews from Asia— [19]who ought to have been present before you and to make accusation, if they should have anything against me. [20]Or else let these men themselves tell what misdeed they found when I stood before the Council, [21]other than for this one statement which I shouted out while standing

[a]**24:5** Lit *the inhabited earth;* [b]**24:6** The early mss do not contain the remainder of v 6, v 7, nor the first part of v 8; [c]**24:17** Or *gifts to charity*

among them, 'For the resurrection of the dead I am on trial before you today.' "

22 But Felix, having a more exact knowledge about the Way, put them off, saying, "When Lysias the ᵃcommander comes down, I will decide your case." ²³Then he gave orders to the centurion for him to be kept in custody and *yet* have *some* freedom, and not to prevent any of his friends from ministering to him.

24 But some days later Felix arrived with Drusilla, his wife who was a Jewess, and sent for Paul and heard him *speak* about faith in Christ Jesus. ²⁵But as he was discussing righteousness, self-control and the judgment to come, Felix became frightened and said, "Go away for the present, and when I find time I will summon you." ²⁶At the same time too, he was hoping that money would be given him by Paul; therefore he also used to send for him quite often and converse with him. ²⁷But after two years had passed, Felix was succeeded by Porcius Festus, and wishing to do the Jews a favor, Felix left Paul imprisoned.

Paul before Festus

25 Festus then, having arrived in the province, three days later went up to Jerusalem from Caesarea. ²And the chief priests and the leading men of the Jews brought charges against Paul, and they were urging him, ³requesting a concession against Paul, that he might have him brought to Jerusalem (*at the same time,* setting an ambush to kill him on the way). ⁴Festus then answered that Paul was being kept in custody at Caesarea and that he himself was about to leave shortly. ⁵"Therefore," he *said, "let the influential men among you go there with me, and if there is anything wrong about the man, let them prosecute him."

6 After he had spent not more than eight or ten days among them, he went down to Caesarea, and on the next day he took his seat on the tribunal and ordered Paul to be brought. ⁷After Paul arrived, the Jews who had come down from Jerusalem stood around him, bringing many and serious charges against him which they could not prove, ⁸while Paul said in his own defense, "I have committed no offense either against the Law of the Jews or against the temple or against Caesar." ⁹But Festus, wishing to do the Jews a favor, answered Paul and said, "Are you willing to go up to Jerusalem and stand trial before me on these *charges?*" ¹⁰But Paul said, "I am standing before Caesar's tribunal, where I ought to be tried. I have

ᵃ**24:22** I.e. chiliarch, in command of one thousand troops done no wrong to *the* Jews, as you also very well know. [11]If, then, I am a wrongdoer and have committed anything worthy of death, I do not refuse to die; but if none of those things is *true* of which these men accuse me, no one can hand me over to them. I appeal to Caesar." [12]Then when Festus had conferred with his council, he answered, "You have appealed to Caesar, to Caesar you shall go."

[13] Now when several days had elapsed, King Agrippa and Bernice arrived at Caesarea and paid their respects to Festus. [14]While they were spending many days there, Festus laid Paul's case before the king, saying, "There is a man who was left as a prisoner by Felix; [15]and when I was at Jerusalem, the chief priests and the elders of the Jews brought charges against him, asking for a sentence of condemnation against him. [16]I answered them that it is not the custom of the Romans to hand over any man before the accused meets his accusers face to face and has an opportunity to make his defense against the charges. [17]So after they had assembled here, I did not delay, but on the next day took my seat on the tribunal and ordered the man to be brought before me. [18]When the accusers stood up, they *began* bringing charges against him not of such crimes as

I was expecting, [19]but they *simply* had some points of disagreement with him about their own religion and about a dead man, Jesus, whom Paul asserted to be alive. [20]Being at a loss how to investigate such matters, I asked whether he was willing to go to Jerusalem and there stand trial on these matters. [21]But when Paul appealed to be held in custody for [b]the Emperor's decision, I ordered him to be kept in custody until I send him to Caesar." [22]Then Agrippa *said* to Festus, "I also would like to hear the man myself." "Tomorrow," he *said, "you shall hear him."

Paul before Agrippa

[23] So, on the next day when Agrippa came together with Bernice amid great pomp, and entered the auditorium accompanied by the commanders and the prominent men of the city, at the command of Festus, Paul was brought in. [24]Festus *said, "King Agrippa, and all you gentlemen here present with us, you see this man about whom all the people of the Jews appealed to me, both at Jerusalem and here, loudly declaring that he ought not to live any longer. [25]But I found that he had committed nothing worthy of death; and since he himself appealed to the Emperor, I decided to send him. [26]Yet I have nothing definite about him to write to my lord. Therefore I have brought him

[a]24:22 I.e. chiliarch, in command of one thousand troops; [b]25:21 Lit *the Augustus's* (in this case Nero); [c]25:23 Lit *and with*

before you *all* and especially before you, King Agrippa, so that after the investigation has taken place, I may have something to write. ²⁷For it seems absurd to me in sending a prisoner, not to indicate also the charges against him."

Paul's Defense before Agrippa

26 Agrippa said to Paul, "You are permitted to speak for yourself." Then Paul stretched out his hand and *proceeded* to make his defense:

2 "In regard to all the things of which I am accused by the Jews, I consider myself fortunate, King Agrippa, that I am about to make my defense before you today; ³especially because you are an expert in all customs and questions among *the* Jews; therefore I beg you to listen to me patiently.

4 "So then, all Jews know my manner of life from my youth up, which from the beginning was spent among my *own* nation and at Jerusalem; ⁵since they have known about me for a long time, if they are willing to testify, that I lived *as* a Pharisee according to the strictest sect of our religion. ⁶And now I am standing trial for the hope of the promise made by God to our fathers; ⁷*the promise* to which our twelve tribes hope to attain, as they earnestly serve *God* night and day. And for this hope, O King, I am being accused by Jews. ⁸Why is it considered incredible among you *people* if God does raise the dead?

9 "So then, I thought to myself that I had to do many things hostile to the name of Jesus of Nazareth. ¹⁰And this is just what I did in Jerusalem; not only did I lock up many of the saints in prisons, having received authority from the chief priests, but also when they were being put to death I cast my vote against them. ¹¹And as I punished them often in all the synagogues, I tried to force them to blaspheme; and being furiously enraged at them, I kept pursuing them even to foreign cities.

12 "While so engaged as I was journeying to Damascus with the authority and commission of the chief priests, ¹³at midday, O King, I saw on the way a light from heaven, brighter than the sun, shining all around me and those who were journeying with me. ¹⁴And when we had all fallen to the ground, I heard a voice saying to me in the Hebrew dialect, 'Saul, Saul, why are you persecuting Me? It is hard for you to kick against the goads.' ¹⁵And I said, 'Who are You, Lord?' And the Lord said, 'I am Jesus whom you are persecuting. ¹⁶But get up and stand on your feet; for this purpose I have appeared to you, to appoint you a minister and a witness not only to the things which you have seen, but also to the things in which I will appear to you; [17]rescuing you from the *Jewish* people and from the Gentiles, to whom I am sending you, [18]to open their eyes so that they may turn from darkness to light and from the dominion of Satan to God, that they may receive forgiveness of sins and an inheritance among those who have been sanctified by faith in Me.'

[19] "So, King Agrippa, I did not prove disobedient to the heavenly vision, [20]but *kept* declaring both to those of Damascus first, and *also* at Jerusalem and *then* throughout all the region of Judea, and *even* to the Gentiles, that they should repent and turn to God, performing deeds appropriate to repentance. [21]For this reason *some* Jews seized me in the temple and tried to put me to death. [22]So, having obtained help from God, I stand to this day testifying both to small and great, stating nothing but what the Prophets and Moses said was going to take place; [23]that the Christ was to suffer, *and* that by reason of *His* resurrection from the dead He would be the first to proclaim light both to the *Jewish* people and to the Gentiles."

[24] While *Paul* was saying this in his defense, Festus *said in a loud voice, "Paul, you are out of your mind! *Your* great learning is driving you mad." [25]But Paul *said, "I am not out of my mind, most excellent Festus, but I utter words of sober truth. [26]For the king knows about these matters, and I speak to him also with confidence, since I am persuaded that none of these things escape his notice; for this has not been done in a corner. [27]King Agrippa, do you believe the Prophets? I know that you do." [28]Agrippa *replied* to Paul, "In a short time you will persuade me to become a Christian." [29]And Paul *said*, "I would wish to God, that whether in a short or long time, not only you, but also all who hear me this day, might become such as I am, except for these chains."

[30] The king stood up and the governor and Bernice, and those who were sitting with them, [31]and when they had gone aside, they *began* talking to one another, saying, "This man is not doing anything worthy of death or imprisonment." [32]And Agrippa said to Festus, "This man might have been set free if he had not appealed to Caesar."

Paul Is Sent to Rome

27 When it was decided that we would sail for Italy, they proceeded to deliver Paul and some other prisoners to a centurion of the Augustan [a]cohort named Julius. [2]And embarking in an Adramyttian ship, which was about to sail to the regions along the coast of Asia, we put out to sea accompanied by Aristarchus, a Macedonian of Thessalonica. [3]The next day we put in at Sidon; and Julius treated Paul with consideration and allowed him to go to his friends and receive care. [4]From there we put out to sea and sailed under the shelter of Cyprus because the winds were contrary. [5]When we had sailed through the sea along the coast of Cilicia and Pamphylia, we landed at Myra in Lycia. [6]There the centurion found an Alexandrian ship sailing for Italy, and he put us aboard it. [7]When we had sailed slowly for a good many days, and with difficulty had arrived off Cnidus, since the wind did not permit us *to go* farther, we sailed under the shelter of Crete, off Salmone; [8]and with difficulty sailing past it we came to a place called Fair Havens, near which was the city of Lasea.

[9] When considerable time had passed and the voyage was now dangerous, since even the [b]fast was already over, Paul *began* to admonish them, [10]and said to them, "Men, I perceive that the voyage will certainly be with damage and great loss, not only of the cargo and the ship, but also of our lives." [11]But the centurion was more persuaded by the pilot and the captain of the ship than by what was being said by Paul. [12]Because the harbor was not suitable for wintering, the majority reached a decision to put out to sea from there, if somehow they could reach Phoenix, a harbor of Crete, facing southwest and northwest, and spend the winter *there*.

[13] When a moderate south wind came up, supposing that they had attained their purpose, they weighed anchor and *began* sailing along Crete, close *inshore*.

Shipwreck

[14]But before very long there rushed down from the land a violent wind, called [c]Euraquilo; [15]and when the ship was caught *in it* and could not face the wind, we gave way *to it* and let ourselves be driven along. [16]Running under the shelter of a small island called Clauda, we were scarcely able to get the *ship's* boat under control. [17]After they had hoisted it up, they used supporting cables in undergirding the ship; and fearing that they might run aground on *the shallows* of Syrtis, they let down the sea anchor and in this way let themselves be driven along. [18]The next day as we were

[a]**27:1** Or *battalion;* [b]**27:9** I.e. Day of Atonement in September or October, which was a dangerous time of year for navigation; [c]**27:14** a northeaster

being violently storm-tossed, they began to jettison the cargo; [19]and on the third day they threw the ship's tackle overboard with their own hands. [20]Since neither sun nor stars appeared for many days, and no small storm was assailing *us,* from then on all hope of our being saved was gradually abandoned.

21 When they had gone a long time without food, then Paul stood up in their midst and said, "Men, you ought to have followed my advice and not to have set sail from Crete and incurred this damage and loss. [22]*Yet* now I urge you to keep up your courage, for there will be no loss of life among you, but *only* of the ship. [23]For this very night an angel of the God to whom I belong and whom I serve stood before me, [24]saying, 'Do not be afraid, Paul; you must stand before Caesar; and behold, God has granted you all those who are sailing with you.' [25]Therefore, keep up your courage, men, for I believe God that it will turn out exactly as I have been told. [26]But we must run aground on a certain island."

27 But when the fourteenth night came, as we were being driven about in the Adriatic Sea, about midnight the sailors *began* to surmise that they were approaching some land. [28]They took soundings and found *it to be* twenty fathoms; and a little farther on they took another sounding and found *it to be* fifteen fathoms. [29]Fearing that we might run aground somewhere on the rocks, they cast four anchors from the stern and wished for daybreak. [30]But as the sailors were trying to escape from the ship and had let down the *ship's* boat into the sea, on the pretense of intending to lay out anchors from the bow, [31]Paul said to the centurion and to the soldiers, "Unless these men remain in the ship, you yourselves cannot be saved." [32]Then the soldiers cut away the ropes of the *ship's* boat and let it fall away.

33 Until the day was about to dawn, Paul was encouraging them all to take some food, saying, "Today is the fourteenth day that you have been constantly watching and going without eating, having taken nothing. [34]Therefore I encourage you to take some food, for this is for your preservation, for not a hair from the head of any of you will perish." [35]Having said this, he took bread and gave thanks to God in the presence of all, and he broke it and began to eat. [36]All of them were encouraged and they themselves also took food. [37]All of us in the ship were two hundred and seventy-six persons. [38]When they had eaten enough, they *began* to lighten the ship by throwing out the wheat into the sea.

39 When day came, they could not recognize the land; but they did observe a bay with a beach, and they resolved to drive the ship onto it if they could. ⁴⁰And casting off the anchors, they left them in the sea while at the same time they were loosening the ropes of the rudders; and hoisting the foresail to the wind, they were heading for the beach. ⁴¹But striking a reef where two seas met, they ran the vessel aground; and the prow stuck fast and remained immovable, but the stern *began* to be broken up by the force *of the waves.* ⁴²The soldiers' plan was to kill the prisoners, so that none *of them* would swim away and escape; ⁴³but the centurion, wanting to bring Paul safely through, kept them from their intention, and commanded that those who could swim should jump overboard first and get to land, ⁴⁴and the rest *should follow,* some on planks, and others on various things from the ship. And so it happened that they all were brought safely to land.

Safe at Malta

28^{When} they had been brought safely through, then we found out that the island was called Malta. ²The natives showed us extraordinary kindness; for because of the rain that had set in and because of the cold, they kindled a fire and received us all. ³But when Paul had gathered a bundle of sticks and laid them on the fire, a viper came out because of the heat and fastened itself on his hand. ⁴When the natives saw the creature hanging from his hand, they *began* saying to one another, "Undoubtedly this man is a murderer, and though he has been saved from the sea, justice has not allowed him to live." ⁵However he shook the creature off into the fire and suffered no harm. ⁶But they were expecting that he was about to swell up or suddenly fall down dead. But after they had waited a long time and had seen nothing unusual happen to him, they changed their minds and *began* to say that he was a god.

7 Now in the neighborhood of that place were lands belonging to the leading man of the island, named Publius, who welcomed us and entertained us courteously three days. ⁸And it happened that the father of Publius was lying *in bed* afflicted with *recurrent* fever and dysentery; and Paul went in *to see* him and after he had prayed, he laid his hands on him and healed him. ⁹After this had happened, the rest of the people on the island who had diseases were coming to him and getting cured.

[10]They also honored us with many marks of respect; and when we were setting sail, they supplied *us* with all we needed.

Paul Arrives at Rome

11 At the end of three months we set sail on an Alexandrian ship which had wintered at the island, and which had the Twin Brothers for its figurehead. [12]After we put in at Syracuse, we stayed there for three days. [13]From there we sailed around and arrived at Rhegium, and a day later a south wind sprang up, and on the second day we came to Puteoli. [14]There we found *some* brethren, and were invited to stay with them for seven days; and thus we came to Rome. [15]And the brethren, when they heard about us, came from there as far as the Market of Appius and Three Inns to meet us; and when Paul saw them, he thanked God and took courage.

16 When we entered Rome, Paul was allowed to stay by himself, with the soldier who was guarding him.

17 After three days Paul called together those who were the leading men of the Jews, and when they came together, he *began* saying to them, "Brethren, though I had done nothing against our people or the customs of our fathers, yet I was delivered as a prisoner from Jerusalem into the hands of the Romans. [18]And when they had examined me, they were willing to release me because there was no ground for putting me to death. [19]But when the Jews objected, I was forced to appeal to Caesar, not that I had any accusation against my nation. [20]For this reason, therefore, I requested to see you and to speak with you, for I am wearing this chain for the sake of the hope of Israel." [21]They said to him, "We have neither received letters from Judea concerning you, nor have any of the brethren come here and reported or spoken anything bad about you. [22]But we desire to hear from you what your views are; for concerning this sect, it is known to us that it is spoken against everywhere."

23 When they had set a day for Paul, they came to him at his lodging in large numbers; and he was explaining to them by solemnly testifying about the kingdom of God and trying to persuade them concerning Jesus, from both the Law of Moses and from the Prophets, from morning until evening. [24]Some were being persuaded by the things spoken, but others would not believe. [25]And when they did not agree with one another, they *began* leaving after Paul had spoken one *parting* word, "The Holy Spirit rightly

spoke through Isaiah the prophet to your fathers, ²⁶saying,
'GO TO THIS PEOPLE AND SAY,
"YOU WILL KEEP ON HEARING, BUT WILL NOT UNDERSTAND;
AND YOU WILL KEEP ON SEEING, BUT WILL NOT PERCEIVE;
²⁷FOR THE HEART OF THIS PEOPLE HAS BECOME DULL,
AND WITH THEIR EARS THEY SCARCELY HEAR,
AND THEY HAVE CLOSED THEIR EYES;
OTHERWISE THEY MIGHT SEE WITH THEIR EYES,
AND HEAR WITH THEIR EARS,
AND UNDERSTAND WITH THEIR HEART AND RETURN,
AND I WOULD HEAL THEM." '
²⁸Therefore let it be known to you that this salvation of God has been sent to the Gentiles; they will also listen." ²⁹ᵃ[When he had spoken these words, the Jews departed, having a great dispute among themselves.]

30 And he stayed two full years in his own rented quarters and was welcoming all who came to him, ³¹preaching the kingdom of God and teaching concerning the Lord Jesus Christ with all openness, unhindered.

ROMANS

The Gospel Exalted

1 Paul, a bond-servant of Christ Jesus, called *as* an apostle, set apart for the gospel of God, ²which He promised beforehand through His prophets in the holy Scriptures, ³concerning His Son, who was born of a descendant of David according to the flesh, ⁴who was declared the Son of God with power ᵇby the resurrection from the dead, according to the Spirit of holiness, Jesus Christ our Lord, ⁵through whom we have received grace and apostleship to bring about *the* obedience of faith among all the Gentiles for His name's sake, ⁶among whom you also are the called of Jesus Christ;

7 to all who are beloved of God in Rome, called *as* saints: Grace to you and peace from God our Father and the Lord Jesus Christ.

8 First, I thank my God through Jesus Christ for you all, because your faith is being proclaimed throughout the whole world. ⁹For God, whom I serve in my spirit in the

ᵃ**28:29** Early mss do not contain this v; ᵇ**1:4** Or *as a result of* *preaching of the* gospel of His Son, is my witness *as to* how unceasingly I make mention of you, [10]always in my prayers making request, if perhaps now at last by the will of God I may succeed in coming to you. [11]For I long to see you so that I may impart some spiritual gift to you, that you may be established; [12]that is, that I may be encouraged together with you *while* among you, each of us by the other's faith, both yours and mine. [13]I do not want you to be unaware, brethren, that often I have planned to come to you (and have been prevented so far) so that I may obtain some fruit among you also, even as among the rest of the Gentiles. [14]I am [a]under obligation both to Greeks and to barbarians, both to the wise and to the foolish. [15]So, for my part, I am eager to preach the gospel to you also who are in Rome.

16 For I am not ashamed of the gospel, for it is the power of God for salvation to everyone who believes, to the Jew first and also to the Greek. [17]For in it *the* righteousness of God is revealed from faith to faith; as it is written, "BUT THE RIGHTEOUS *man* SHALL LIVE BY FAITH."

Unbelief and Its Consequences

18 For the wrath of God is revealed from heaven against all ungodliness and unrighteousness of men who suppress the truth in unrighteousness, [19]because that which is known about God is evident within them; for God made it evident to them. [20]For since the creation of the world His invisible attributes, His eternal power and divine nature, have been clearly seen, being understood through what has been made, so that they are without excuse. [21]For even though they knew God, they did not [b]honor Him as God or give thanks, but they became futile in their speculations, and their foolish heart was darkened. [22]Professing to be wise, they became fools, [23]and exchanged the glory of the incorruptible God for an image in the form of corruptible man and of birds and four-footed animals and [c]crawling creatures.

24 Therefore God gave them over in the lusts of their hearts to impurity, so that their bodies would be dishonored among them. [25]For they exchanged the truth of God for a lie, and worshiped and served the creature rather than the Creator, who is blessed forever. Amen.

26 For this reason God gave them over to degrading passions; for their women exchanged the natural function for that which is unnatural, [27]and in the same way also the men abandoned the natural function of the woman and

[a]**1:14** Lit *debtor*; [b]**1:21** Lit *glorify*; [c]**1:23** Or *reptiles*

burned in their desire toward one another, men with men committing indecent acts and receiving in their own persons the due penalty of their error.

28 And just as they did not see fit to acknowledge God any longer, God gave them over to a depraved mind, to do those things which are not proper, [29]being filled with all unrighteousness, wickedness, greed, evil; full of envy, murder, strife, deceit, malice; *they are* gossips, [30]slanderers, haters of God, insolent, arrogant, boastful, inventors of evil, disobedient to parents, [31]without understanding, untrustworthy, unloving, unmerciful; [32]and although they know the ordinance of God, that those who practice such things are worthy of death, they not only do the same, but also give hearty approval to those who practice them.

The Impartiality of God

2 Therefore you have no excuse, everyone of you who passes judgment, for in that which you judge another, you condemn yourself; for you who judge practice the same things. [2]And we know that the judgment of God rightly falls upon those who practice such things. [3]But do you suppose this, O man, when you pass judgment on those who practice such things and do the same *yourself,* that you will escape the judgment of God? [4]Or do you think lightly of the riches of His kindness and tolerance and patience, not knowing that the kindness of God leads you to repentance? [5]But because of your stubbornness and unrepentant heart you are storing up wrath for yourself in the day of wrath and revelation of the righteous judgment of God, [6]who WILL RENDER TO EACH PERSON ACCORDING TO HIS DEEDS: [7]to those who by perseverance in doing good seek for glory and honor and immortality, eternal life; [8]but to those who are selfishly ambitious and do not obey the truth, but obey unrighteousness, wrath and indignation. [9]*There will be* tribulation and distress for every soul of man who does evil, of the Jew first and also of the Greek, [10]but glory and honor and peace to everyone who does good, to the Jew first and also to the Greek. [11]For there is no partiality with God.

12 For all who have sinned without the Law will also perish without the Law, and all who have sinned under the Law will be judged by the Law; [13]for *it is* not the hearers of the Law *who* are just before God, but the doers of the Law will be justified. [14]For when Gentiles who do not have the Law do instinctively the things of the

Law, these, not having the Law, are a law to themselves, [15]in that they show the work of the Law written in their hearts, their conscience bearing witness and their thoughts alternately accusing or else defending them, [16]on the day when, according to my gospel, God will judge the secrets of men through Christ Jesus.

The Jew Is Condemned
by the Law

17 But if you bear the name "Jew" and rely upon the Law and boast in God, [18]and know *His* will and approve the things that are essential, being instructed out of the Law, [19]and are confident that you yourself are a guide to the blind, a light to those who are in darkness, [20]a corrector of the foolish, a teacher of the immature, having in the Law the embodiment of knowledge and of the truth, [21]you, therefore, who teach another, do you not teach yourself? You who preach that one shall not steal, do you steal? [22]You who say that one should not commit adultery, do you commit adultery? You who abhor idols, do you rob temples? [23]You who boast in the Law, through your breaking the Law, do you dishonor God? [24]For "THE NAME OF GOD IS BLASPHEMED AMONG THE GENTILES BECAUSE OF YOU," just as it is written.

25 For indeed circumcision is of value if you practice the Law; but if you are a transgressor of the Law, your circumcision has become uncircumcision. [26]So if the uncircumcised man keeps the requirements of the Law, will not his uncircumcision be regarded as circumcision? [27]And he who is physically uncircumcised, if he keeps the Law, will he not judge you who though having the letter *of the Law* and circumcision are a transgressor of the Law? [28]For he is not a Jew who is one outwardly, nor is circumcision that which is outward in the flesh. [29]But he is a Jew who is one inwardly; and circumcision is that which is of the heart, by the Spirit, not by the letter; and his praise is not from men, but from God.

All the World Guilty

3 Then what advantage has the Jew? Or what is the benefit of circumcision? [2]Great in every respect. First of all, that they were entrusted with the oracles of God. [3]What then? If some did not believe, their unbelief will not nullify the faithfulness of God, will it? [4]May it never be! Rather, let God be found true, though every man *be found* a liar, as it is written,

"THAT YOU MAY BE JUSTIFIED
    IN YOUR WORDS,
AND PREVAIL WHEN YOU ARE
    JUDGED."

⁵But if our unrighteousness demonstrates the righteousness of God, what shall we say? The God who inflicts wrath is not unrighteous, is He? (I am speaking in human terms.) ⁶May it never be! For otherwise, how will God judge the world? ⁷But if through my lie the truth of God abounded to His glory, why am I also still being judged as a sinner? ⁸And why not *say* (as we are slanderously reported and as some claim that we say), "Let us do evil that good may come"? Their condemnation is just.

9 What then? Are we better than they? Not at all; for we have already charged that both Jews and Greeks are all under sin; ¹⁰as it is written,

"THERE IS NONE RIGHTEOUS,
    NOT EVEN ONE;
¹¹THERE   IS   NONE   WHO
    UNDERSTANDS,
THERE IS NONE WHO SEEKS
    FOR GOD;
¹²ALL HAVE TURNED ASIDE,
    TOGETHER THEY HAVE BE-
    COME USELESS;
THERE IS NONE WHO DOES
    GOOD,
THERE IS NOT EVEN ONE."
¹³"THEIR THROAT IS AN OPEN
    GRAVE,
WITH THEIR TONGUES THEY
    KEEP DECEIVING,"
"THE   POISON   OF   ASPS   IS

UNDER THEIR LIPS";
¹⁴"WHOSE MOUTH IS FULL
    OF   CURSING   AND
    BITTERNESS";
¹⁵"THEIR FEET ARE SWIFT TO
    SHED BLOOD,
¹⁶DESTRUCTION AND MISERY
    ARE IN THEIR PATHS,
¹⁷AND THE PATH OF PEACE
    THEY HAVE NOT KNOWN."
¹⁸"THERE IS NO FEAR OF GOD
    BEFORE THEIR EYES."

19 Now we know that whatever the Law says, it speaks to those who are under the Law, so that every mouth may be closed and all the world may become accountable to God; ²⁰because by the works of the Law no flesh will be justified in His sight; for through the Law *comes* the knowledge of sin.

Justification by Faith

21 But now apart from the Law *the* righteousness of God has been manifested, being witnessed by the Law and the Prophets, ²²even *the* righteousness of God through faith in Jesus Christ for all those who believe; for there is no distinction; ²³for all have sinned and fall short of the glory of God, ²⁴being justified as a gift by His grace through the redemption which is in Christ Jesus; ²⁵whom God displayed publicly as a propitiation in His blood through faith. *This was* to demonstrate His righteousness, because in the forbearance of God

He passed over the sins previously committed; [26]for the demonstration, *I say*, of His righteousness at the present time, so that He would be just and the justifier of the one who has faith in Jesus.

27 Where then is boasting? It is excluded. By what kind of law? Of works? No, but by a law of faith. [28]For we maintain that a man is justified by faith apart from works of the Law. [29]Or is God *the God* of Jews only? Is He not *the God* of Gentiles also? Yes, of Gentiles also, [30]since indeed God who will justify the circumcised by faith and the uncircumcised through faith is one.

31 Do we then nullify the Law through faith? May it never be! On the contrary, we establish the Law.

Justification by Faith Evidenced in Old Testament

4 What then shall we say that Abraham, our forefather according to the flesh, has found? [2]For if Abraham was justified by works, he has something to boast about, but not before God. [3]For what does the Scripture say? "ABRAHAM BELIEVED GOD, AND IT WAS CREDITED TO HIM AS RIGHTEOUSNESS." [4]Now to the one who works, his wage is not credited as a favor, but as what is due. [5]But to the one who does not work, but believes in Him who justifies the ungodly, his faith is credited as righteousness, [6]just as David also speaks of the blessing on the man to whom God credits righteousness apart from works:

[7]"BLESSED ARE THOSE WHOSE LAWLESS DEEDS HAVE BEEN FORGIVEN,

AND WHOSE SINS HAVE BEEN COVERED.

[8]"BLESSED IS THE MAN WHOSE SIN THE LORD WILL NOT TAKE INTO ACCOUNT."

9 Is this blessing then on the circumcised, or on the uncircumcised also? For we say, "FAITH WAS CREDITED TO ABRAHAM AS RIGHTEOUSNESS." [10]How then was it credited? While he was circumcised, or uncircumcised? Not while circumcised, but while uncircumcised; [11]and he received the sign of circumcision, a seal of the righteousness of the faith which he had while uncircumcised, so that he might be the father of all who believe without being circumcised, that righteousness might be credited to them, [12]and the father of circumcision to those who not only are of the circumcision, but who also follow in the steps of the faith of our father Abraham which he had while uncircumcised.

13 For the promise to Abraham or to his descendants that he

would be heir of the world was not through the Law, but through the righteousness of faith. [14]For if those who are of the Law are heirs, faith is made void and the promise is nullified; [15]for the Law brings about wrath, but where there is no law, there also is no violation.

16 For this reason *it is* by faith, in order that *it may be* in accordance with grace, so that the promise will be guaranteed to all the descendants, not only to those who are of the Law, but also to those who are of the faith of Abraham, who is the father of us all, [17](as it is written, "A FATHER OF MANY NATIONS HAVE I MADE YOU") in the presence of Him whom he believed, *even* God, who gives life to the dead and calls into being that which does not exist. [18]In hope against hope he believed, so that he might become a father of many nations according to that which had been spoken, "SO SHALL YOUR DESCENDANTS BE." [19]Without becoming weak in faith he contemplated his own body, now as good as dead since he was about a hundred years old, and the deadness of Sarah's womb; [20]yet, with respect to the promise of God, he did not waver in unbelief but grew strong in faith, giving glory to God, [21]and being fully assured that what God

had promised, He was able also to perform. [22]Therefore IT WAS ALSO CREDITED TO HIM AS RIGHTEOUSNESS. [23]Now not for his sake only was it written that it was credited to him, [24]but for our sake also, to whom it will be credited, as those who believe in Him who raised Jesus our Lord from the dead, [25]*He* who was delivered over because of our transgressions, and was raised because of our justification.

Results of Justification

5Therefore, having been justified by faith, we have peace with God through our Lord Jesus Christ, [2]through whom also we have obtained our introduction by faith into this grace in which we stand; and we exult in hope of the glory of God. [3]And not only this, but we also exult in our tribulations, knowing that tribulation brings about perseverance; [4]and perseverance, proven character; and proven character, hope; [5]and hope does not disappoint, because the love of God has been poured out within our hearts through the Holy Spirit who was given to us.

6 For while we were still helpless, at the right time Christ died for the ungodly. [7]For one will hardly die for a righteous man; though perhaps for the good man someone would dare even to die. **⁸But God demonstrates His own love toward us, in that while we were yet sinners, Christ died for us.** ⁹Much more then, having now been justified by His blood, we shall be saved from the wrath *of God* through Him. ¹⁰For if while we were enemies we were reconciled to God through the death of His Son, much more, having been reconciled, we shall be saved by His life. ¹¹And not only this, but we also exult in God through our Lord Jesus Christ, through whom we have now received the reconciliation.

¹² Therefore, just as through one man sin entered into the world, and death through sin, and so death spread to all men, because all sinned— ¹³for until the Law sin was in the world, but sin is not imputed when there is no law. ¹⁴Nevertheless death reigned from Adam until Moses, even over those who had not sinned in the likeness of the offense of Adam, who is a ªtype of Him who was to come.

¹⁵ But the free gift is not like the transgression. For if by the transgression of the one the many died, much more did the grace of God and the gift by the grace of the one Man, Jesus Christ, abound to the many. ¹⁶The gift is not like *that which came* through the one

ª**5:14** Or foreshadowing

who sinned; for on the one hand the judgment *arose* from one *transgression* resulting in condemnation, but on the other hand the free gift *arose* from many transgressions resulting in justification. ¹⁷For if by the transgression of the one, death reigned through the one, much more those who receive the abundance of grace and of the gift of righteousness will reign in life through the One, Jesus Christ.

18 So then as through one transgression there resulted condemnation to all men, even so through one act of righteousness there resulted justification of life to all men. ¹⁹For as through the one man's disobedience the many were made sinners, even so through the obedience of the One the many will be made righteous. ²⁰The Law came in so that the transgression would increase; but where sin increased, grace abounded all the more, ²¹so that, as sin reigned in death, even so grace would reign through righteousness to eternal life through Jesus Christ our Lord.

Believers Are Dead to Sin, Alive to God

6What shall we say then? Are we to continue in sin so that grace may increase? ²May it never be! How shall we who died to sin still live in it? ³Or do you not know that all of us who have been baptized into Christ Jesus have been baptized into His death? [4]Therefore we have been buried with Him through baptism into death, so that as Christ was raised from the dead through the glory of the Father, so we too might walk in newness of life. [5]For if we have become united with *Him* in the likeness of His death, certainly we shall also be *in the likeness* of His resurrection, [6]knowing this, that our old self was crucified with *Him,* in order that our body of sin might be done away with, so that we would no longer be slaves to sin; [7]for he who has died is freed from sin.

[8] Now if we have died with Christ, we believe that we shall also live with Him, [9]knowing that Christ, having been raised from the dead, is never to die again; death no longer is master over Him. [10]For the death that He died, He died to sin once for all; but the life that He lives, He lives to God. [11]Even so consider yourselves to be dead to sin, but alive to God in Christ Jesus.

[12] Therefore do not let sin reign in your mortal body so that you obey its lusts, [13]and do not go on presenting the members of your body to sin *as* instruments of unrighteousness; but present yourselves to God as those alive from the dead, and your members *as* instruments of righteousness to God. [14]For sin shall not be master over you, for you are not under law but under grace.

[15] What then? Shall we sin because we are not under law but under grace? May it never be! [16]Do you not know that when you present yourselves to someone *as* slaves for obedience, you are slaves of the one whom you obey, either of sin resulting in death, or of obedience resulting in righteousness? [17]But thanks be to God that though you were slaves of sin, you became obedient from the heart to that form of teaching to which you were committed, [18]and having been freed from sin, you became slaves of righteousness. [19]I am speaking in human terms because of the weakness of your flesh. For just as you presented your members as slaves to impurity and to lawlessness, resulting in *further* lawlessness, so now present your members as slaves to righteousness, resulting in sanctification.

[20] For when you were slaves of sin, you were free in regard to righteousness. [21]Therefore what benefit were you then deriving from the things of which you are now ashamed? For the outcome of those things is death. [22]But now having been freed from sin and enslaved to God, you derive your benefit, resulting in sanctification, and the outcome, eternal life.

²³For the wages of sin is death, but the free gift of God is eternal life in Christ Jesus our Lord.

Believers United to Christ

7Or do you not know, brethren (for I am speaking to those who know the law), that the law has jurisdiction over a person as long as he lives? ²For the married woman is bound by law to her husband while he is living; but if her husband dies, she is released from the law concerning the husband. ³So then, if while her husband is living she is joined to another man, she shall be called an adulteress; but if her husband dies, she is free from the law, so that she is not an adulteress though she is joined to another man.

4 Therefore, my brethren, you also were made to die to the Law through the body of Christ, so that you might be joined to another, to Him who was raised from the dead, in order that we might bear fruit for God. ⁵For while we were in the flesh, the sinful passions, which were *aroused* by the Law, were at work in the members of our body to bear fruit for death. ⁶But now we have been released from the Law, having died to that by which we were bound, so that we serve in newness of the ᵃSpirit and not in oldness of the letter.

7 What shall we say then? Is the Law sin? May it never be! On the contrary, I would not have come to know sin except through the Law; for I would not have known about coveting if the Law had not said, "YOU SHALL NOT COVET." ⁸But sin, taking opportunity through the commandment, produced in me coveting of every kind; for apart from the Law sin *is* dead. ⁹I was once alive apart from the Law; but when the commandment came, sin became alive and I died; ¹⁰and this commandment, which was to result in life, proved to result in death for me; ¹¹for sin, taking an opportunity through the commandment, deceived me and through it killed me. ¹²So then, the Law is holy, and the commandment is holy and righteous and good.

13 Therefore did that which is good become *a cause of* death for me? May it never be! Rather it was sin, in order that it might be shown to be sin by effecting my death through that which is good, so that through the commandment sin would become utterly sinful.

The Conflict of Two Natures

14 For we know that the Law is spiritual, but I am of flesh, sold into bondage to sin. ¹⁵For what I am doing, I do not understand; for I am not practicing what I

ᵃ**7:6** Or spirit

would like to *do,* but I am doing the very thing I hate. [16]But if I do the very thing I do not want *to do,* I agree with the Law, *confessing* that the Law is good. [17]So now, no longer am I the one doing it, but sin which dwells in me. [18]For I know that nothing good dwells in me, that is, in my flesh; for the willing is present in me, but the doing of the good *is* not. [19]For the good that I want, I do not do, but I practice the very evil that I do not want. [20]But if I am doing the very thing I do not want, I am no longer the one doing it, but sin which dwells in me.

21 I find then the principle that evil is present in me, the one who wants to do good. [22]For I joyfully concur with the law of God in the inner man, [23]but I see a different law in the members of my body, waging war against the law of my mind and making me a prisoner of the law of sin which is in my members. [24]Wretched man that I am! Who will set me free from the body of this death? [25]Thanks be to God through Jesus Christ our Lord! So then, on the one hand I myself with my mind am serving the law of God, but on the other, with my flesh the law of sin.

Deliverance from Bondage

8 Therefore there is now no condemnation for those who are in Christ Jesus. [2]For the law of the Spirit of life in Christ Jesus has set you free from the law of sin and of death. [3]For what the Law could not do, weak as it was through the flesh, God *did:* sending His own Son in the likeness of sinful flesh and *as an offering* for sin, He condemned sin in the flesh, [4]so that the requirement of the Law might be fulfilled in us, who do not walk according to the flesh but according to the Spirit. [5]For those who are according to the flesh set their minds on the things of the flesh, but those who are according to the Spirit, the things of the Spirit. [6]For the mind set on the flesh is death, but the mind set on the Spirit is life and peace, [7]because the mind set on the flesh is hostile toward God; for it does not subject itself to the law of God, for it is not even able *to do so,* [8]and those who are in the flesh cannot please God.

9 However, you are not in the flesh but in the Spirit, if indeed the Spirit of God dwells in you. But if anyone does not have the Spirit of Christ, he does not belong to Him. [10]If Christ is in you, though the body is dead because of sin, yet the spirit is alive because of righteousness. [11]But if the Spirit of Him who raised Jesus from the dead dwells in you, He who raised Christ Jesus from the dead will also give life to your mortal bodies ªthrough His Spirit who dwells in you.

12 So then, brethren, we are under obligation, not to the flesh, to live according to the flesh— 13for if you are living according to the flesh, you must die; but if by the Spirit you are putting to death the deeds of the body, you will live. 14For all who are being led by the Spirit of God, these are sons of God. 15For you have not received a spirit of slavery leading to fear again, but you have received a spirit of adoption as sons by which we cry out, "Abba! Father!" 16The Spirit Himself testifies with our spirit that we are children of God, 17and if children, heirs also, heirs of God and fellow heirs with Christ, if indeed we suffer with *Him* so that we may also be glorified with *Him*.

18 For I consider that the sufferings of this present time are not worthy to be compared with the glory that is to be revealed to us. 19For the anxious longing of the creation waits eagerly for the revealing of the sons of God. 20For the creation was subjected to futility, not willingly, but because of Him who subjected it, ᵇin hope 21that the creation itself also will be set free from its slavery to corruption into the freedom of the glory of the children of God. 22For we know that the whole creation groans and suffers the pains of childbirth together until now. 23And not only this, but also we ourselves, having the first fruits of the Spirit, even we ourselves groan within ourselves, waiting eagerly for *our* adoption as sons, the redemption of our body. 24For in hope we have been saved, but hope that is seen is not hope; for who hopes for what he *already* sees? 25But if we hope for what we do not see, with perseverance we wait eagerly for it.

Our Victory in Christ

26 In the same way the Spirit also helps our weakness; for we do not know how to pray as we should, but the Spirit Himself intercedes for *us* with groanings too deep for words; 27and He who searches the hearts knows what the mind of the Spirit is, because He intercedes for the saints according to *the will of* God.

28 And we know that ᶜGod causes all things to work together for good to those who love God, to those who are called according to *His* purpose. 29For those whom He foreknew, He also predestined *to become* conformed to the image of His Son, so that He would be the firstborn among many brethren; 30and these whom He predestined, He also called; and these whom He called, He also

ª**8:11** One early ms reads *because of;* ᵇ**8:20** Or *in hope; because the creation;* ᶜ**8:28** One early ms reads *all things work together for good* justified; and these whom He justified, He also glorified.

31 What then shall we say to these things? If God *is* for us, who *is* against us? ³²He who did not spare His own Son, but delivered Him over for us all, how will He not also with Him freely give us all things? ³³Who will bring a charge against God's elect? God is the one who justifies; ³⁴who is the one who condemns? Christ Jesus is He who died, yes, rather who was ªraised, who is at the right hand of God, who also intercedes for us. ³⁵Who will separate us from the love of ᵇChrist? Will tribulation, or distress, or persecution, or famine, or nakedness, or peril, or sword? ³⁶Just as it is written,

"FOR YOUR SAKE WE ARE BE-
    ING PUT TO DEATH ALL
    DAY LONG;
WE   WERE   CONSIDERED
    AS   SHEEP   TO   BE
    SLAUGHTERED."

³⁷But in all these things we overwhelmingly conquer through Him who loved us. ³⁸For I am convinced that neither death, nor life, nor angels, nor principalities, nor things present, nor things to come, nor powers, ³⁹nor height, nor depth, nor any other created thing, will be able to separate us from the love of God, which is in Christ Jesus our Lord.

Solicitude for Israel

9 I am telling the truth in Christ, I am not lying, my conscience testifies with me in the Holy Spirit, ²that I have great sorrow and unceasing grief in my heart. ³For I could wish that I myself were accursed, *separated* from Christ for the sake of my brethren, my kinsmen according to the flesh, ⁴who are Israelites, to whom belongs the adoption as sons, and the glory and the covenants and the giving of the Law and the *temple* service and the promises, ⁵whose are the fathers, and from whom is the Christ according to the flesh, who is over all, God blessed forever. Amen.

6 But *it is* not as though the word of God has failed. For they are not all Israel who are *descended* from Israel; ⁷nor are they all children because they are Abraham's descendants, but: "THROUGH ISAAC YOUR DESCENDANTS WILL BE NAMED." ⁸That is, it is not the children of the flesh who are children of God, but the children of the promise are regarded as descendants. ⁹For this is the word of promise: "AT THIS TIME I WILL COME, AND SARAH SHALL HAVE A SON." ¹⁰And not only this, but there was Rebekah also, when she had conceived *twins* by one man, our father Isaac; ¹¹for though *the twins* were not

ª**8:34** One early ms reads *raised from the dead*; ᵇ**8:35** Two early mss read *God* yet born and had not done anything good or bad, so that God's purpose according to *His* choice would stand, not because of works but because of Him who calls, [12]it was said to her, "THE OLDER WILL SERVE THE YOUNGER." [13]Just as it is written, "JACOB I LOVED, BUT ESAU I HATED."

14 What shall we say then? There is no injustice with God, is there? May it never be! [15]For He says to Moses, "I WILL HAVE MERCY ON WHOM I HAVE MERCY, AND I WILL HAVE COMPASSION ON WHOM I HAVE COMPASSION." [16]So then it *does* not *depend* on the man who wills or the man who runs, but on God who has mercy. [17]For the Scripture says to Pharaoh, "FOR THIS VERY PURPOSE I RAISED YOU UP, TO DEMONSTRATE MY POWER IN YOU, AND THAT MY NAME MIGHT BE PROCLAIMED THROUGHOUT THE WHOLE EARTH." [18]So then He has mercy on whom He desires, and He hardens whom He desires.

19 You will say to me then, "Why does He still find fault? For who resists His will?" [20]On the contrary, who are you, O man, who answers back to God? The thing molded will not say to the molder, "Why did you make me like this," will it? [21]Or does not the potter have a right over the clay, to make from the same lump one vessel for honorable use and another for common use? [22]What if God, although willing to demonstrate His wrath and to make His power known, endured with much patience vessels of wrath prepared for destruction? [23]And *He did so* to make known the riches of His glory upon vessels of mercy, which He prepared beforehand for glory, [24]*even* us, whom He also called, not from among Jews only, but also from among Gentiles. [25]As He says also in Hosea,

"I WILL CALL THOSE WHO
     WERE NOT MY PEOPLE, 'MY
     PEOPLE,'
AND HER WHO WAS NOT BE-
     LOVED, 'BELOVED.' "
[26]"AND IT SHALL BE THAT IN
     THE PLACE WHERE IT WAS
     SAID TO THEM, 'YOU ARE
     NOT MY PEOPLE,'
THERE THEY SHALL BE CALLED
     SONS OF THE LIVING GOD."
27 Isaiah cries out concerning Israel, "THOUGH THE NUMBER OF THE SONS OF ISRAEL BE LIKE THE SAND OF THE SEA, IT IS THE REMNANT THAT WILL BE SAVED; [28]FOR THE LORD WILL EXECUTE HIS WORD ON THE EARTH, THOROUGHLY AND QUICKLY." [29]And just as Isaiah foretold,

"UNLESS THE LORD OF SA-
     BAOTH HAD LEFT TO US A

POSTERITY,
WE WOULD HAVE BECOME LIKE
SODOM, AND WOULD HAVE
RESEMBLED GOMORRAH."

30 What shall we say then? That Gentiles, who did not pursue righteousness, attained righteousness, even the righteousness which is by faith; [31]but Israel, pursuing a law of righteousness, did not arrive at *that* law. [32]Why? Because *they did* not *pursue it* by faith, but as though *it were* by works. They stumbled over the stumbling stone, [33]just as it is written,

"BEHOLD, I LAY IN ZION A
STONE OF STUMBLING AND
A ROCK OF OFFENSE,
AND HE WHO BELIEVES
IN HIM WILL NOT BE
DISAPPOINTED."

The Word of Faith Brings Salvation

10 Brethren, my heart's desire and my prayer to God for them is for *their* salvation. [2]For I testify about them that they have a zeal for God, but not in accordance with knowledge. [3]For not knowing about God's righteousness and seeking to establish their own, they did not subject themselves to the righteousness of God. [4]For Christ is the end of the law for righteousness to everyone who believes.

5 For Moses writes that the man who practices the righteousness which is based on law shall live by that righteousness. [6]But the righteousness based on faith speaks as follows: "DO NOT SAY IN YOUR HEART, 'WHO WILL ASCEND INTO HEAVEN?' (that is, to bring Christ down), [7]or 'WHO WILL DESCEND INTO THE ABYSS?' (that is, to bring Christ up from the dead)." [8]But what does it say? "THE WORD IS NEAR YOU, IN YOUR MOUTH AND IN YOUR HEART"—that is, the word of faith which we are preaching, [9]that if you confess with your mouth Jesus *as* Lord, and believe in your heart that God raised Him from the dead, you will be saved; [10]for with the heart a person believes, resulting in righteousness, and with the mouth he confesses, resulting in salvation. [11]For the Scripture says, "WHOEVER BELIEVES IN HIM WILL NOT BE DISAPPOINTED." [12]For there is no distinction between Jew and Greek; for the same Lord is Lord of all, abounding in riches for all who call on Him; [13]for "WHOEVER WILL CALL ON THE NAME OF THE LORD WILL BE SAVED."

14 How then will they call on Him in whom they have not believed? How will they believe in Him whom they have not heard? And how will they hear without a preacher? [15]How will they preach unless they are sent? Just as it is written, "HOW BEAUTIFUL ARE THE FEET OF THOSE WHO BRING GOOD NEWS OF GOOD THINGS!"

16 However, they did not all heed the good news; for Isaiah says, "LORD, WHO HAS BELIEVED OUR REPORT?" [17]So faith *comes* from hearing, and hearing by the word of Christ.

18 But I say, surely they have never heard, have they? Indeed they have;

"THEIR VOICE HAS GONE OUT
    INTO ALL THE EARTH,
AND THEIR WORDS TO THE
    ENDS OF THE WORLD."

[19]But I say, surely Israel did not know, did they? First Moses says,

"I WILL MAKE YOU JEALOUS
    BY THAT WHICH IS NOT A
    NATION,
BY A NATION WITHOUT UN-
    DERSTANDING   WILL   I
    ANGER YOU."

[20]And Isaiah is very bold and says,

"I WAS FOUND BY THOSE WHO
    DID NOT SEEK ME,
I BECAME MANIFEST TO THOSE
    WHO DID NOT ASK FOR ME."

[21]But as for Israel He says, "ALL THE DAY LONG I HAVE STRETCHED OUT MY HANDS TO A DISOBEDIENT AND OBSTI-NATE PEOPLE."

Israel Is Not Cast Away

11 I say then, God has not re-jected His people, has He? May it never be! For I too am an Israelite, a descendant of Abra-ham, of the tribe of Benjamin. [2]God has not rejected His people whom He foreknew. Or do you not know what the Scripture says in *the passage about* Elijah, how he pleads with God against Isra-el? [3]"Lord, THEY HAVE KILLED YOUR PROPHETS, THEY HAVE TORN DOWN YOUR ALTARS, AND I ALONE AM LEFT, AND THEY ARE SEEKING MY LIFE." [4]But what is the divine response to him? "I HAVE KEPT for Myself SEVEN THOUSAND MEN WHO HAVE NOT BOWED THE KNEE TO BAAL." [5]In the same way then, there has also come to be at the present time a remnant according to *God's* gracious choice. [6]But if it is by grace, it is no longer on the basis of works, otherwise grace is no longer grace.

7 What then? What Israel is seek-ing, it has not obtained, but those who were chosen obtained it, and the rest were hardened; [8]just as it is written,

"GOD GAVE THEM A SPIRIT OF
    STUPOR,
EYES TO SEE NOT AND EARS TO
    HEAR NOT,
DOWN TO THIS VERY DAY."

[9]And David says,

"LET THEIR TABLE BECOME A
    SNARE AND A TRAP,
AND A STUMBLING BLOCK AND
    A RETRIBUTION TO THEM.
¹⁰"LET THEIR EYES BE DARK-
    ENED TO SEE NOT,
AND BEND THEIR BACKS
    FOREVER."

11 I say then, they did not stumble so as to fall, did they? May it never be! But by their transgression salvation *has* come to the Gentiles, to make them jealous. ¹²Now if their transgression is riches for the world and their failure is riches for the Gentiles, how much more will their fulfillment be! ¹³But I am speaking to you who are Gentiles. Inasmuch then as I am an apostle of Gentiles, I magnify my ministry, ¹⁴if somehow I might move to jealousy my fellow countrymen and save some of them. ¹⁵For if their rejection is the reconciliation of the world, what will *their* acceptance be but life from the dead? ¹⁶If the first piece *of dough* is holy, the lump is also; and if the root is holy, the branches are too.

17 But if some of the branches were broken off, and you, being a wild olive, were grafted in among them and became partaker with them of the rich root of the olive tree, ¹⁸do not be arrogant toward the branches; but if you are arrogant, *remember that* it is not you who supports the root, but

the root *supports* you. ¹⁹You will say then, "Branches were broken off so that I might be grafted in." ²⁰Quite right, they were broken off for their unbelief, but you stand by your faith. Do not be conceited, but fear; ²¹for if God did not spare the natural branches, He will not spare you, either. ²²Behold then the kindness and severity of God; to those who fell, severity, but to you, God's kindness, if you continue in His kindness; otherwise you also will be cut off. ²³And they also, if they do not continue in their unbelief, will be grafted in, for God is able to graft them in again. ²⁴For if you were cut off from what is by nature a wild olive tree, and were grafted contrary to nature into a cultivated olive tree, how much more will these who are the natural *branches* be grafted into their own olive tree?

25 For I do not want you, brethren, to be uninformed of this mystery—so that you will not be wise in your own estimation—that a partial hardening has happened to Israel until the fullness of the Gentiles has come in; ²⁶and so all Israel will be saved; just as it is written,

"THE DELIVERER WILL COME
    FROM ZION,
HE WILL REMOVE UNGODLI-
    NESS FROM JACOB."
²⁷"THIS IS MY COVENANT

WITH THEM,
WHEN I TAKE AWAY THEIR SINS."
²⁸From the standpoint of the gospel they are enemies for your sake, but from the standpoint of *God's* choice they are beloved for the sake of the fathers; ²⁹for the gifts and the calling of God are irrevocable. ³⁰For just as you once were disobedient to God, but now have been shown mercy because of their disobedience, ³¹so these also now have been disobedient, that because of the mercy shown to you they also may now be shown mercy. ³²For God has shut up all in disobedience so that He may show mercy to all.

33 Oh, the depth of the riches both of the wisdom and knowledge of God! How unsearchable are His judgments and unfathomable His ways! ³⁴For WHO HAS KNOWN THE MIND OF THE LORD, OR WHO BECAME HIS COUNSELOR? ³⁵Or WHO HAS FIRST GIVEN TO HIM THAT IT MIGHT BE PAID BACK TO HIM AGAIN? ³⁶For from Him and through Him and to Him are all things. To Him *be* the glory forever. Amen.

Dedicated Service

12 Therefore I urge you, brethren, by the mercies of God, to present your bodies a living and holy sacrifice, acceptable to God, *which is* your spiritual service of worship. ²And do not be conformed to this world, but be transformed by the renewing of your mind, so that you may prove what the will of God is, that which is good and acceptable and perfect.

3 For through the grace given to me I say to everyone among you not to think more highly of himself than he ought to think; but to think so as to have sound judgment, as God has allotted to each a measure of faith. ⁴For just as we have many members in one body and all the members do not have the same function, ⁵so we, who are many, are one body in Christ, and individually members one of another. ⁶Since we have gifts that differ according to the grace given to us, *each of us is to exercise them accordingly:* if prophecy, according to the proportion of his faith; ⁷if service, in his serving; or he who teaches, in his teaching; ⁸or he who exhorts, in his exhortation; he who gives, with ªliberality; he who leads, with diligence; he who shows mercy, with cheerfulness.

9 *Let* love *be* without hypocrisy. Abhor what is evil; cling to what is good. ¹⁰*Be* devoted to one another in brotherly love; give preference to one another in honor; ¹¹not lagging behind in diligence, fervent in spirit, serving the Lord; ¹²rejoicing in hope, persevering

ª**12:8** Or *simplicity*

in tribulation, devoted to prayer, [13]contributing to the needs of the saints, practicing hospitality.

[14] Bless those who persecute [a]you; bless and do not curse. [15]Rejoice with those who rejoice, and weep with those who weep. [16]Be of the same mind toward one another; do not be haughty in mind, but associate with the lowly. Do not be wise in your own estimation. [17]Never pay back evil for evil to anyone. Respect what is right in the sight of all men. [18]If possible, so far as it depends on you, be at peace with all men. [19]Never take your own revenge, beloved, but leave room for the wrath *of God,* for it is written, "VENGEANCE IS MINE, I WILL REPAY," says the Lord. [20]"BUT IF YOUR ENEMY IS HUNGRY, FEED HIM, AND IF HE IS THIRSTY, GIVE HIM A DRINK; FOR IN SO DOING YOU WILL HEAP BURNING COALS ON HIS HEAD." [21]Do not be overcome by evil, but overcome evil with good.

Be Subject to Government

13 Every person is to be in subjection to the governing authorities. For there is no authority except from God, and those which exist are established by God. [2]Therefore whoever resists authority has opposed the ordinance of God; and they who have

opposed will receive condemnation upon themselves. [3]For rulers are not a cause of fear for good behavior, but for evil. Do you want to have no fear of authority? Do what is good and you will have praise from the same; [4]for it is a minister of God to you for good. But if you do what is evil, be afraid; for it does not bear the sword for nothing; for it is a minister of God, an avenger who brings wrath on the one who practices evil. [5]Therefore it is necessary to be in subjection, not only because of wrath, but also for conscience' sake. [6]For because of this you also pay taxes, for *rulers* are servants of God, devoting themselves to this very thing. [7]Render to all what is due them: tax to whom tax *is due;* custom to whom custom; fear to whom fear; honor to whom honor.

[8] Owe nothing to anyone except to love one another; for he who loves his neighbor has fulfilled *the* law. [9]For this, "YOU SHALL NOT COMMIT ADULTERY, YOU SHALL NOT MURDER, YOU SHALL NOT STEAL, YOU SHALL NOT COVET," and if there is any other commandment, it is summed up in this saying, "YOU SHALL LOVE YOUR NEIGHBOR AS YOURSELF." [10]Love does no wrong to a neighbor; therefore love is the fulfillment of *the* law.

11 *Do* this, knowing the time, that it is already the hour for you to awaken from sleep; for now [a]salvation is nearer to us than when we believed. **12**The night is almost gone, and the day is near. Therefore let us lay aside the deeds of darkness and put on the armor of light. **13**Let us behave properly as in the day, not in carousing and drunkenness, not in sexual promiscuity and sensuality, not in strife and jealousy. **14**But put on the Lord Jesus Christ, and make no provision for the flesh in regard to *its* lusts.

Principles of Conscience

14 Now accept the one who is weak in faith, *but* not for *the purpose of* passing judgment on his opinions. **2**One person has faith that he may eat all things, but he who is weak eats vegetables *only.* **3**The one who eats is not to regard with contempt the one who does not eat, and the one who does not eat is not to judge the one who eats, for God has accepted him. **4**Who are you to judge the servant of another? To his own master he stands or falls; and he will stand, for the Lord is able to make him stand.

5 One person regards one day above another, another regards every day *alike.* Each person must be fully convinced in his own mind.

6He who observes the day, observes it for the Lord, and he who eats, does so for the Lord, for he gives thanks to God; and he who eats not, for the Lord he does not eat, and gives thanks to God. **7**For not one of us lives for himself, and not one dies for himself; **8**for if we live, we live for the Lord, or if we die, we die for the Lord; therefore whether we live or die, we are the Lord's. **9**For to this end Christ died and lived again, that He might be Lord both of the dead and of the living.

10 But you, why do you judge your brother? Or you again, why do you regard your brother with contempt? For we will all stand before the judgment seat of God. **11**For it is written,

"AS I LIVE, SAYS THE LORD, EVERY KNEE SHALL BOW TO ME,

AND EVERY TONGUE SHALL GIVE PRAISE TO GOD."

12So then each one of us will give an account of himself to God.

13 Therefore let us not judge one another anymore, but rather determine this—not to put an obstacle or a stumbling block in a brother's way. **14**I know and am convinced in the Lord Jesus that nothing is unclean in itself; but to him who thinks anything to be unclean, to him it is unclean. **15**For if because

[a]**13:11** Or *our salvation is nearer than when*

of food your brother is hurt, you are no longer walking according to love. Do not destroy with your food him for whom Christ died. [16]Therefore do not let what is for you a good thing be spoken of as evil; [17]for the kingdom of God is not eating and drinking, but righteousness and peace and joy in the Holy Spirit. [18]For he who in this *way* serves Christ is acceptable to God and approved by men. [19]So then [a]we pursue the things which make for peace and the building up of one another. [20]Do not tear down the work of God for the sake of food. All things indeed are clean, but they are evil for the man who eats and gives offense. [21]It is good not to eat meat or to drink wine, or *to do anything* by which your brother stumbles. [22]The faith which you have, have as your own conviction before God. Happy is he who does not condemn himself in what he approves. [23]But he who doubts is condemned if he eats, because *his eating is* not from faith; and whatever is not from faith is sin.

Self-denial on Behalf of Others

15 Now we who are strong ought to bear the weaknesses of those without strength and not *just* please ourselves. [2]Each of us is to please his neighbor for his good, to his edification. [3]For even Christ did not please

[a]14:19 Later mss read *let us pursue*

Himself; but as it is written, "THE REPROACHES OF THOSE WHO REPROACHED YOU FELL ON ME." [4]For whatever was written in earlier times was written for our instruction, so that through perseverance and the encouragement of the Scriptures we might have hope. [5]Now may the God who gives perseverance and encouragement grant you to be of the same mind with one another according to Christ Jesus, [6]so that with one accord you may with one voice glorify the God and Father of our Lord Jesus Christ.

7 Therefore, accept one another, just as Christ also accepted us to the glory of God. [8]For I say that Christ has become a servant to the circumcision on behalf of the truth of God to confirm the promises *given* to the fathers, [9]and for the Gentiles to glorify God for His mercy; as it is written,

"THEREFORE I WILL GIVE
    PRAISE TO YOU AMONG
    THE GENTILES,
AND I WILL SING TO YOUR
    NAME."

[10]Again he says,

"REJOICE, O GENTILES, WITH
    HIS PEOPLE."

[11]And again,

"PRAISE THE LORD ALL YOU
    GENTILES,
AND LET ALL THE PEOPLES
    PRAISE HIM."

¹²Again Isaiah says,

"THERE SHALL COME THE
    ROOT OF JESSE,
AND HE WHO ARISES TO RULE
    OVER THE GENTILES,
IN HIM SHALL THE GENTILES
    HOPE."

¹³Now may the God of hope fill you with all joy and peace in believing, so that you will abound in hope by the power of the Holy Spirit.

14 And concerning you, my brethren, I myself also am convinced that you yourselves are full of goodness, filled with all knowledge and able also to admonish one another. ¹⁵But I have written very boldly to you on some points so as to remind you again, because of the grace that was given me from God, ¹⁶to be a minister of Christ Jesus to the Gentiles, ministering as a priest the gospel of God, so that *my* offering of the Gentiles may become acceptable, sanctified by the Holy Spirit. ¹⁷Therefore in Christ Jesus I have found reason for boasting in things pertaining to God. ¹⁸For I will not presume to speak of anything except what Christ has accomplished through me, resulting in the obedience of the Gentiles by word and deed, ¹⁹in the power of signs and wonders, in the power of the Spirit; so that from Jerusalem and round about as far as Illyricum I have fully preached the gospel of Christ. ²⁰And thus I aspired to preach the gospel, not where Christ was *already* named, so that I would not build on another man's foundation; ²¹but as it is written,

"THEY WHO HAD NO NEWS OF
    HIM SHALL SEE,
AND THEY WHO HAVE
    NOT HEARD SHALL
    UNDERSTAND."

22 For this reason I have often been prevented from coming to you; ²³but now, with no further place for me in these regions, and since I have had for many years a longing to come to you ²⁴whenever I go to Spain—for I hope to see you in passing, and to be helped on my way there by you, when I have first enjoyed your company for a while— ²⁵but now, I am going to Jerusalem serving the saints. ²⁶For Macedonia and Achaia have been pleased to make a contribution for the poor among the saints in Jerusalem. ²⁷Yes, they were pleased *to do so,* and they are indebted to them. For if the Gentiles have shared in their spiritual things, they are indebted to minister to them also in material things. ²⁸Therefore, when I have finished this, and have put my seal on this fruit of theirs, I will go on by way of you to Spain. ²⁹I know that when I come to you, I will come in the fullness of the blessing of Christ.

30 Now I urge you, brethren, by our Lord Jesus Christ and by the love of the Spirit, to strive together with me in your prayers to God for me, **31**that I may be rescued from those who are disobedient in Judea, and *that* my service for Jerusalem may prove acceptable to the saints; **32**so that I may come to you in joy by the will of God and find *refreshing* rest in your company. **33**Now the God of peace be with you all. Amen.

Greetings and Love Expressed

16 I commend to you our sister Phoebe, who is a servant of the church which is at Cenchrea; **2**that you receive her in the Lord in a manner worthy of the saints, and that you help her in whatever matter she may have need of you; for she herself has also been a helper of many, and of myself as well.

3 Greet Prisca and Aquila, my fellow workers in Christ Jesus, **4**who for my life risked their own necks, to whom not only do I give thanks, but also all the churches of the Gentiles; **5**also *greet* the church that is in their house. Greet Epaenetus, my beloved, who is the first convert to Christ from Asia. **6**Greet Mary, who has worked hard for you. **7**Greet Andronicus and Junias, my kinsmen and my fellow prisoners, who are outstanding among the apostles, who also were in Christ before me. **8**Greet Ampliatus, my beloved in the Lord. **9**Greet Urbanus, our fellow worker in Christ, and Stachys my beloved. **10**Greet Apelles, the approved in Christ. Greet those who are of the *household* of Aristobulus. **11**Greet Herodion, my kinsman. Greet those of the *household* of Narcissus, who are in the Lord. **12**Greet Tryphaena and Tryphosa, workers in the Lord. Greet Persis the beloved, who has worked hard in the Lord. **13**Greet Rufus, a choice man in the Lord, also his mother and mine. **14**Greet Asyncritus, Phlegon, Hermes, Patrobas, Hermas and the brethren with them. **15**Greet Philologus and Julia, Nereus and his sister, and Olympas, and all the saints who are with them. **16**Greet one another with a holy kiss. All the churches of Christ greet you.

17 Now I urge you, brethren, keep your eye on those who cause dissensions and hindrances contrary to the teaching which you learned, and turn away from them. **18**For such men are slaves, not of our Lord Christ but of their own appetites; and by their smooth and flattering speech they deceive the hearts of the unsuspecting. **19**For the report of your obedience has reached to all; therefore I am rejoicing over you, but I want you to be wise in what is good and innocent in what is evil. [20]The God of peace will soon crush Satan under your feet. The grace of our Lord Jesus be with you.

[21] Timothy my fellow worker greets you, and *so do* Lucius and Jason and Sosipater, my kinsmen.

[22] I, Tertius, who write this letter, greet you in the Lord.

[23] Gaius, host to me and to the whole church, greets you. Erastus, the city treasurer greets you, and Quartus, the brother. [24a][The grace of our Lord Jesus Christ be with you all. Amen.]

[25] Now to Him who is able to establish you according to my gospel and the preaching of Jesus Christ, according to the revelation of the mystery which has been kept secret for long ages past, [26]but now is manifested, and by the Scriptures of the prophets, according to the commandment of the eternal God, has been made known to all the nations, *leading* to obedience of faith; [27]to the only wise God, through Jesus Christ, be the glory forever. Amen.

1 CORINTHIANS

Appeal to Unity

1 Paul, called *as* an apostle of Jesus Christ by the will of God, and Sosthenes our brother,

[2] To the church of God which is at Corinth, to those who have been sanctified in Christ Jesus, saints by calling, with all who in every place call on the name of our Lord Jesus Christ, their *Lord* and ours:

[3] Grace to you and peace from God our Father and the Lord Jesus Christ.

[4] I thank [b]my God always concerning you for the grace of God which was given you in Christ Jesus, [5]that in everything you were enriched in Him, in all speech and all knowledge, [6]even as the testimony concerning Christ was confirmed in you, [7]so that you are not lacking in any gift, awaiting eagerly the revelation of our Lord Jesus Christ, [8]who will also confirm you to the end, blameless in the day of our Lord Jesus Christ. [9]God is faithful, through whom you were

[a]**16:24** Early mss do not contain this; [b]**1:4** Two early mss do not contain *my*

called into fellowship with His Son, Jesus Christ our Lord.

10 Now I exhort you, brethren, by the name of our Lord Jesus Christ, that you all agree and that there be no divisions among you, but that you be made complete in the same mind and in the same judgment. [11]For I have been informed concerning you, my brethren, by Chloe's *people,* that there are quarrels among you. [12]Now I mean this, that each one of you is saying, "I am of Paul," and "I of Apollos," and "I of Cephas," and "I of Christ." [13]Has Christ been divided? Paul was not crucified for you, was he? Or were you baptized in the name of Paul? [14a]I thank God that I baptized none of you except Crispus and Gaius, [15]so that no one would say you were baptized in my name. [16]Now I did baptize also the household of Stephanas; beyond that, I do not know whether I baptized any other. [17]For Christ did not send me to baptize, but to preach the gospel, not in cleverness of speech, so that the cross of Christ would not be made void.

The Wisdom of God

18 For the word of the cross is foolishness to those who are perishing, but to us who are being saved it is the power of God. [19]For it is written,

"I WILL DESTROY THE WISDOM OF THE WISE,
AND THE CLEVERNESS OF THE CLEVER I WILL SET ASIDE."
[20]Where is the wise man? Where is the scribe? Where is the debater of this age? Has not God made foolish the wisdom of the world? [21]For since in the wisdom of God the world through its wisdom did not *come to* know God, God was well-pleased through the foolishness of the message preached to save those who believe. [22]For indeed Jews ask for signs and Greeks search for wisdom; [23]but we preach [b]Christ crucified, to Jews a stumbling block and to Gentiles foolishness, [24]but to those who are the called, both Jews and Greeks, Christ the power of God and the wisdom of God. [25]Because the foolishness of God is wiser than men, and the weakness of God is stronger than men.

26 For consider your calling, brethren, that there were not many wise according to the flesh, not many mighty, not many noble; [27]but God has chosen the foolish things of the world to shame the wise, and God has chosen the weak things of the world to shame the things which are strong, [28]and the base things of the world and the despised God has chosen, the things that are not, so that He may nullify the things that are, [29]so that no man may boast before God. [30]But

---

[a]**1:14** Two early mss read *I give thanks that;* [b]**1:23** I.e. Messiah

by His doing you are in Christ Jesus, who became to us wisdom from God, and righteousness and sanctification, and redemption, [31]so that, just as it is written, "LET HIM WHO BOASTS, BOAST IN THE LORD."

Paul's Reliance upon the Spirit

2 And when I came to you, brethren, I did not come with superiority of speech or of wisdom, proclaiming to you the [a]testimony of God. [2]For I determined to know nothing among you except Jesus Christ, and Him crucified. [3]I was with you in weakness and in fear and in much trembling, [4]and my message and my preaching were not in persuasive words of wisdom, but in demonstration of the Spirit and of power, [5]so that your faith would not rest on the wisdom of men, but on the power of God.

6 Yet we do speak wisdom among those who are mature; a wisdom, however, not of this age nor of the rulers of this age, who are passing away; [7]but we speak God's wisdom in a mystery, the hidden *wisdom* which God predestined before the ages to our glory; [8]*the wisdom* which none of the rulers of this age has understood; for if they had understood it they would not have crucified the Lord of glory; [9]but just as it is written,

"THINGS WHICH EYE HAS NOT
    SEEN AND EAR HAS NOT
    HEARD,
AND *which* HAVE NOT ENTERED
    THE HEART OF MAN,
ALL THAT GOD HAS PREPARED
    FOR THOSE WHO LOVE
    HIM."

[10b]For to us God revealed *them* through the Spirit; for the Spirit searches all things, even the depths of God. [11]For who among men knows the *thoughts* of a man except the spirit of the man which is in him? Even so the *thoughts* of God no one knows except the Spirit of God. [12]Now we have received, not the spirit of the world, but the Spirit who is from God, so that we may know the things freely given to us by God, [13]which things we also speak, not in words taught by human wisdom, but in those taught by the Spirit, combining spiritual *thoughts* with spiritual *words*.

14 But a natural man does not accept the things of the Spirit of God, for they are foolishness to him; and he cannot understand them, because they are spiritually appraised. [15]But he who is spiritual appraises all things, yet he himself is appraised by no one. [16]For WHO HAS KNOWN THE MIND OF THE LORD, THAT HE WILL INSTRUCT HIM? But we have the mind of Christ.

2:1 One early ms reads mystery; **2:10** One early ms reads *But*

Foundations for Living

3 And I, brethren, could not speak to you as to spiritual men, but as to men of flesh, as to infants in Christ. [2]I gave you milk to drink, not solid food; for you were not yet able *to receive it.* Indeed, even now you are not yet able, [3]for you are still fleshly. For since there is jealousy and strife among you, are you not fleshly, and are you not walking like mere men? [4]For when one says, "I am of Paul," and another, "I am of Apollos," are you not *mere* men?

5 What then is Apollos? And what is Paul? Servants through whom you believed, even as the Lord gave *opportunity* to each one. [6]I planted, Apollos watered, but God was causing the growth. [7]So then neither the one who plants nor the one who waters is anything, but God who causes the growth. [8]Now he who plants and he who waters are one; but each will receive his own reward according to his own labor. [9]For we are God's fellow workers; you are God's field, God's building.

10 According to the grace of God which was given to me, like a wise master builder I laid a foundation, and another is building on it. But each man must be careful how he builds on it. [11]For no man can lay a foundation other than the one which is laid, which is Jesus Christ. [12]Now if any man builds on the foundation with gold, silver, precious stones, wood, hay, straw, [13]each man's work will become evident; for the day will show it because it is *to be* revealed with fire, and the fire itself will test the quality of each man's work. [14]If any man's work which he has built on it remains, he will receive a reward. [15]If any man's work is burned up, he will suffer loss; but he himself will be saved, yet so as through fire.

16 Do you not know that you are a temple of God and *that* the Spirit of God dwells in you? [17]If any man destroys the temple of God, God will destroy him, for the temple of God is holy, and that is what you are.

18 Let no man deceive himself. If any man among you thinks that he is wise in this age, he must become foolish, so that he may become wise. [19]For the wisdom of this world is foolishness before God. For it is written, "*He is* THE ONE WHO CATCHES THE WISE IN THEIR CRAFTINESS"; [20]and again, "THE LORD KNOWS THE REASONINGS of the wise, THAT THEY ARE USELESS." [21]So then let no one boast in men. For all things belong to you, [22]whether Paul or Apollos or Cephas or the world or life or death or things present or things to come; all things belong to you, ²³and you belong to Christ; and Christ belongs to God.

Servants of Christ

4 Let a man regard us in this manner, as servants of Christ and stewards of the mysteries of God. ²In this case, moreover, it is required of stewards that one be found trustworthy. ³But to me it is a very small thing that I may be examined by you, or by *any* human court; in fact, I do not even examine myself. ⁴For I am conscious of nothing against myself, yet I am not by this acquitted; but the one who examines me is the Lord. ⁵Therefore do not go on passing judgment before ^athe time, *but wait* until the Lord comes who will both bring to light the things hidden in the darkness and disclose the motives of *men's* hearts; and then each man's praise will come to him from God.

6 Now these things, brethren, I have figuratively applied to myself and Apollos for your sakes, so that in us you may learn not to exceed what is written, so that no one of you will become arrogant in behalf of one against the other. ⁷For who regards you as superior? What do you have that you did not receive? And if you did receive it,

^a**4:5** I.e. the appointed time of judgment

why do you boast as if you had not received it?

8 You are already filled, you have already become rich, you have become kings without us; and indeed, *I* wish that you had become kings so that we also might reign with you. ⁹For, I think, God has exhibited us apostles last of all, as men condemned to death; because we have become a spectacle to the world, both to angels and to men. ¹⁰We are fools for Christ's sake, but you are prudent in Christ; we are weak, but you are strong; you are distinguished, but we are without honor. ¹¹To this present hour we are both hungry and thirsty, and are poorly clothed, and are roughly treated, and are homeless; ¹²and we toil, working with our own hands; when we are reviled, we bless; when we are persecuted, we endure; ¹³when we are slandered, we try to conciliate; we have become as the scum of the world, the dregs of all things, *even* until now.

14 I do not write these things to shame you, but to admonish you as my beloved children. ¹⁵For if you were to have countless tutors in Christ, yet *you would* not *have* many fathers, for in Christ Jesus I became your father through the gospel. ¹⁶Therefore I exhort you, be imitators of me. ¹⁷For this reason I have sent to you Timothy, who is my beloved and faithful child in the Lord, and he will remind you of my ways which are in Christ, just as I teach everywhere in every church. [18]Now some have become arrogant, as though I were not coming to you. [19]But I will come to you soon, if the Lord wills, and I shall find out, not the words of those who are arrogant but their power. [20]For the kingdom of God does not consist in words but in power. [21]What do you desire? Shall I come to you with a rod, or with love and a spirit of gentleness?

Immorality Rebuked

5 It is actually reported that there is immorality among you, and immorality of such a kind as does not exist even among the Gentiles, that someone has his father's wife. [2]You have become arrogant and have not mourned instead, so that the one who had done this deed would be removed from your midst.

[3] For I, on my part, though absent in body but present in spirit, have already judged him who has so committed this, as though I were present. [4]In the name of our Lord Jesus, when you are assembled, and I with you in spirit, with the power of our Lord Jesus, [5]*I have decided* to deliver such a one to Satan for the destruction of his flesh,

[a]**5:5** Two early mss do not contain *Jesus*

so that his spirit may be saved in the day of the Lord a*Jesus*.

6 Your boasting is not good. Do you not know that a little leaven leavens the whole lump *of dough?* [7]Clean out the old leaven so that you may be a new lump, just as you are *in fact* unleavened. For Christ our Passover also has been sacrificed. [8]Therefore let us celebrate the feast, not with old leaven, nor with the leaven of malice and wickedness, but with the unleavened bread of sincerity and truth.

9 I wrote you in my letter not to associate with immoral people; [10]I *did* not at all *mean* with the immoral people of this world, or with the covetous and swindlers, or with idolaters, for then you would have to go out of the world. [11]But actually, I wrote to you not to associate with any so-called brother if he is an immoral person, or covetous, or an idolater, or a reviler, or a drunkard, or a swindler—not even to eat with such a one. [12]For what have I to do with judging outsiders? Do you not judge those who are within *the church?* [13]But those who are outside, God judges. REMOVE THE WICKED MAN FROM AMONG YOURSELVES.

Lawsuits Discouraged

6 Does any one of you, when he has a case against his

neighbor, dare to go to law before the unrighteous and not before the saints? [2]Or do you not know that the saints will judge the world? If the world is judged by you, are you not competent *to constitute* the smallest law courts? [3]Do you not know that we will judge angels? How much more matters of this life? [4]So if you have law courts dealing with matters of this life, do you appoint them as judges who are of no account in the church? [5]I say *this* to your shame. *Is it so, that* there is not among you one wise man who will be able to decide between his brethren, [6]but brother goes to law with brother, and that before unbelievers?

[7]Actually, then, it is already a defeat for you, that you have lawsuits with one another. Why not rather be wronged? Why not rather be defrauded? [8]On the contrary, you yourselves wrong and defraud. *You do* this even to *your* brethren.

[9]Or do you not know that the unrighteous will not inherit the kingdom of God? Do not be deceived; neither fornicators, nor idolaters, nor adulterers, nor [a]effeminate, nor homosexuals, [10]nor thieves, nor *the* covetous, nor drunkards, nor revilers, nor swindlers, will inherit the kingdom of God. [11]Such were some of you; but you were washed, but you were

sanctified, but you were justified in the name of the Lord Jesus Christ and in the Spirit of our God.

The Body Is the Lord's

[12]All things are lawful for me, but not all things are profitable. All things are lawful for me, but I will not be mastered by anything. [13]Food is for the stomach and the stomach is for food, but God will do away with both of them. Yet the body is not for immorality, but for the Lord, and the Lord is for the body. [14]Now God has not only raised the Lord, but will also raise us up through His power. [15]Do you not know that your bodies are members of Christ? Shall I then take away the members of Christ and make them members of a prostitute? May it never be! [16]Or do you not know that the one who joins himself to a prostitute is one body *with her*? For He says, "THE TWO SHALL BECOME ONE FLESH." [17]But the one who joins himself to the Lord is one spirit *with Him*. [18]Flee immorality. Every *other* sin that a man commits is outside the body, but the immoral man sins against his own body. [19]Or do you not know that your body is a temple of the Holy Spirit who is in you, whom you have from God, and that you are not your own? [20]For you have been bought with a price: therefore glorify God in your body.

[a]**6:9** I.e. effeminate by perversion

Teaching on Marriage

7 Now concerning the things about which you wrote, it is good for a man not to touch a woman. ²But because of immoralities, each man is to have his own wife, and each woman is to have her own husband. ³The husband must fulfill his duty to his wife, and likewise also the wife to her husband. ⁴The wife does not have authority over her own body, but the husband *does;* and likewise also the husband does not have authority over his own body, but the wife *does.* ⁵Stop depriving one another, except by agreement for a time, so that you may devote yourselves to prayer, and come together again so that Satan will not tempt you because of your lack of self-control. ⁶But this I say by way of concession, not of command. ⁷ᵃYet I wish that all men were even as I myself am. However, each man has his own gift from God, one in this manner, and another in that.

8 But I say to the unmarried and to widows that it is good for them if they remain even as I. ⁹But if they do not have self-control, let them marry; for it is better to marry than to burn *with passion.*

10 But to the married I give instructions, not I, but the Lord, that the wife should not leave her husband ¹¹(but if she does leave, she must remain unmarried, or else be reconciled to her husband), and that the husband should not divorce his wife.

12 But to the rest I say, not the Lord, that if any brother has a wife who is an unbeliever, and she consents to live with him, he must not divorce her. ¹³And a woman who has an unbelieving husband, and he consents to live with her, she must not send her husband away. ¹⁴For the unbelieving husband is sanctified through his wife, and the unbelieving wife is sanctified through her believing husband; for otherwise your children are unclean, but now they are holy. ¹⁵Yet if the unbelieving one leaves, let him leave; the brother or the sister is not under bondage in such *cases,* but God has called ᵇus to peace. ¹⁶For how do you know, O wife, whether you will save your husband? Or how do you know, O husband, whether you will save your wife?

17 Only, as the Lord has assigned to each one, as God has called each, in this manner let him walk. And so I direct in all the churches. ¹⁸Was any man called *when he was already* circumcised? He is not to become uncircumcised. Has anyone been called in uncircumcision? He is not to be circumcised.

ᵃ**7:7** One early ms reads *For*; ᵇ**7:15** One early ms reads *you*

¹⁹Circumcision is nothing, and uncircumcision is nothing, but *what matters is* the keeping of the commandments of God. ²⁰Each man must remain in that condition in which he was called.

21 Were you called while a slave? Do not worry about it; but if you are able also to become free, rather do that. ²²For he who was called in the Lord while a slave, is the Lord's freedman; likewise he who was called while free, is Christ's slave. ²³You were bought with a price; do not become slaves of men. ²⁴Brethren, each one is to remain with God in that *condition* in which he was called.

25 Now concerning virgins I have no command of the Lord, but I give an opinion as one who by the mercy of the Lord is trustworthy. ²⁶I think then that this is good in view of the present distress, that it is good for a man to remain as he is. ²⁷Are you bound to a wife? Do not seek to be released. Are you released from a wife? Do not seek a wife. ²⁸But if you marry, you have not sinned; and if a virgin marries, she has not sinned. Yet such will have trouble in this life, and I am trying to spare you. ²⁹But this I say, brethren, the time has been shortened, so that from now on those who have wives should be as though they had none; ³⁰and those who weep, as though they did not weep; and those who rejoice, as though they did not rejoice; and those who buy, as though they did not possess; ³¹and those who use the world, as though they did not make full use of it; for the form of this world is passing away.

32 But I want you to be free from concern. One who is unmarried is concerned about the things of the Lord, how he may please the Lord; ³³but one who is married is concerned about the things of the world, how he may please his wife, ³⁴and *his interests* are divided. The woman who is unmarried, and the virgin, is concerned about the things of the Lord, that she may be holy both in body and spirit; but one who is married is concerned about the things of the world, how she may please her husband. ³⁵This I say for your own benefit; not to put a restraint upon you, but to promote what is appropriate and *to secure* undistracted devotion to the Lord.

36 But if any man thinks that he is acting unbecomingly toward his virgin *daughter*, if she is past her youth, and if it must be so, let him do what he wishes, he does not sin; let her marry. ³⁷But he who stands firm in his heart, being under no constraint, but has authority over his own will, and has decided this in his own heart, to keep his own virgin *daughter,* he will do well. [38]So then both he who gives his own virgin *daughter* in marriage does well, and he who does not give her in marriage will do better.

39 A wife is bound as long as her husband lives; but if her husband is dead, she is free to be married to whom she wishes, only in the Lord. [40]But in my opinion she is happier if she remains as she is; and I think that I also have the Spirit of God.

Take Care with Your Liberty

8 Now concerning things sacrificed to idols, we know that we all have knowledge. Knowledge makes arrogant, but love edifies. [2]If anyone supposes that he knows anything, he has not yet known as he ought to know; [3]but if anyone loves God, he is known by Him.

4 Therefore concerning the eating of things sacrificed to idols, we know that [a]there is no such thing as an idol in the world, and that there is no God but one. [5]For even if there are so-called gods whether in heaven or on earth, as indeed there are many gods and many lords, [6]yet for us there is *but* one God, the Father, from whom are all things and we *exist* for Him; and one Lord, Jesus Christ, by whom are all things, and we *exist* through Him.

7 However not all men have this knowledge; but some, being accustomed to the idol until now, eat *food* as if it were sacrificed to an idol; and their conscience being weak is defiled. [8]But food will not commend us to God; we are neither the worse if we do not eat, nor the better if we do eat. [9]But take care that this liberty of yours does not somehow become a stumbling block to the weak. [10]For if someone sees you, who have knowledge, dining in an idol's temple, will not his conscience, if he is weak, be strengthened to eat things sacrificed to idols? [11]For through your knowledge he who is weak is ruined, the brother for whose sake Christ died. [12]And so, by sinning against the brethren and wounding their conscience when it is weak, you sin against Christ. [13]Therefore, if food causes my brother to stumble, I will never eat meat again, so that I will not cause my brother to stumble.

Paul's Use of Liberty

9 Am I not free? Am I not an apostle? Have I not seen Jesus our Lord? Are you not my work in the Lord? [2]If to others I am not an apostle, at least I am to you; for you are the seal of my apostleship in the Lord.

3 My defense to those who examine me is this: [4]Do we not have

---

[a]**8:4** Lit *nothing is an idol in the world;* i.e. an idol has no real existence

a right to eat and drink? ⁵Do we not have a right to take along a believing wife, even as the rest of the apostles and the brothers of the Lord and Cephas? ⁶Or do only Barnabas and I not have a right to refrain from working? ⁷Who at any time serves as a soldier at his own expense? Who plants a vineyard and does not eat the fruit of it? Or who tends a flock and does not use the milk of the flock?

8 I am not speaking these things according to human judgment, am I? Or does not the Law also say these things? ⁹For it is written in the Law of Moses, "YOU SHALL NOT MUZZLE THE OX WHILE HE IS THRESHING." God is not concerned about oxen, is He? ¹⁰Or is He speaking altogether for our sake? Yes, for our sake it was written, because the plowman ought to plow in hope, and the thresher *to thresh* in hope of sharing *the crops.* ¹¹If we sowed spiritual things in you, is it too much if we reap material things from you? ¹²If others share the right over you, do we not more? Nevertheless, we did not use this right, but we endure all things so that we will cause no hindrance to the gospel of Christ. ¹³Do you not know that those who perform sacred services eat the *food* of the temple, *and* those who attend regularly to the altar have their share from the altar? ¹⁴So also the Lord directed those who proclaim the gospel to get their living from the gospel.

15 But I have used none of these things. And I am not writing these things so that it will be done so in my case; for it would be better for me to die than have any man make my boast an empty one. ¹⁶For if I preach the gospel, I have nothing to boast of, for I am under compulsion; for woe is me if I do not preach the gospel. ¹⁷For if I do this voluntarily, I have a reward; but if against my will, I have a stewardship entrusted to me. ¹⁸What then is my reward? That, when I preach the gospel, I may offer the gospel without charge, so as not to make full use of my right in the gospel.

19 For though I am free from all *men,* I have made myself a slave to all, so that I may win more. ²⁰To the Jews I became as a Jew, so that I might win Jews; to those who are under the Law, as under the Law though not being myself under the Law, so that I might win those who are under the Law; ²¹to those who are without law, as without law, though not being without the law of God but under the law of Christ, so that I might win those who are without law. ²²To the weak I became weak, that I might win the weak; I have become all things to all men, so that I may by all means

save some. ²³I do all things for the sake of the gospel, so that I may become a fellow partaker of it.

24 Do you not know that those who run in a race all run, but *only* one receives the prize? Run in such a way that you may win. ²⁵Everyone who competes in the games exercises self-control in all things. They then *do it* to receive a perishable wreath, but we an imperishable. ²⁶Therefore I run in such a way, as not without aim; I box in such a way, as not beating the air; ²⁷but I discipline my body and make it my slave, so that, after I have preached to others, I myself will not be disqualified.

Avoid Israel's Mistakes

10 For I do not want you to be unaware, brethren, that our fathers were all under the cloud and all passed through the sea; ²and all were baptized into Moses in the cloud and in the sea; ³and all ate the same spiritual food; ⁴and all drank the same spiritual drink, for they were drinking from a spiritual rock which followed them; and the rock was Christ. ⁵Nevertheless, with most of them God was not well-pleased; for they were laid low in the wilderness.

6 Now these things happened as examples for us, so that we would not crave evil things as they also craved. ⁷Do not be idolaters, as some of them were; as it is written, "THE PEOPLE SAT DOWN TO EAT AND DRINK, AND STOOD UP TO PLAY." ⁸Nor let us act immorally, as some of them did, and twenty-three thousand fell in one day. ⁹Nor let us try the Lord, as some of them did, and were destroyed by the serpents. ¹⁰Nor grumble, as some of them did, and were destroyed by the destroyer. ¹¹Now these things happened to them as an example, and they were written for our instruction, upon whom the ends of the ages have come. ¹²Therefore let him who thinks he stands take heed that he does not fall. ¹³No temptation has overtaken you but such as is common to man; and God is faithful, who will not allow you to be tempted beyond what you are able, but with the temptation will provide the way of escape also, so that you will be able to endure it.

14 Therefore, my beloved, flee from idolatry. ¹⁵I speak as to wise men; you judge what I say. ¹⁶Is not the cup of blessing which we bless a sharing in the blood of Christ? Is not the bread which we break a sharing in the body of Christ? ¹⁷Since there is one bread, we who are many are one body; for we all partake of the one bread. ¹⁸Look at the nation Israel; are not those who eat the sacrifices sharers in the altar? [19]What do I mean then? That a thing sacrificed to idols is anything, or that an idol is anything? [20]*No*, but *I say* that the things which the Gentiles sacrifice, they sacrifice to demons and not to God; and I do not want you to become sharers in demons. [21]You cannot drink the cup of the Lord and the cup of demons; you cannot partake of the table of the Lord and the table of demons. [22]Or do we provoke the Lord to jealousy? We are not stronger than He, are we?

[23] All things are lawful, but not all things are profitable. All things are lawful, but not all things edify. [24]Let no one seek his own *good*, but that of his neighbor. [25]Eat anything that is sold in the meat market without asking questions for conscience' sake; [26]FOR THE EARTH IS THE LORD'S, AND ALL IT CONTAINS. [27]If one of the unbelievers invites you and you want to go, eat anything that is set before you without asking questions for conscience' sake. [28]But if anyone says to you, "This is meat sacrificed to idols," do not eat *it*, for the sake of the one who informed *you*, and for conscience' sake; [29]I mean not your own conscience, but the other *man's*; for why is my freedom judged by another's conscience? [30]If I partake with thankfulness, why am I slandered concerning that for which I give thanks?

[31] Whether, then, you eat or drink or whatever you do, do all to the glory of God. [32]Give no offense either to Jews or to Greeks or to the church of God; [33]just as I also please all men in all things, not seeking my own profit but the *profit* of the many, so that they may be saved.

Christian Order

11 Be imitators of me, just as I also am of Christ.

[2] Now I praise you because you remember me in everything and hold firmly to the traditions, just as I delivered them to you. [3]But I want you to understand that Christ is the head of every man, and the man is the head of a woman, and God is the head of Christ. [4]Every man who has some*thing* on his head while praying or prophesying disgraces his head. [5]But every woman who has her head uncovered while praying or prophesying disgraces her head, for she is one and the same as the woman whose head is shaved. [6]For if a woman does not cover her head, let her also have her hair cut off; but if it is disgraceful for a woman to have her hair cut off or her head shaved, let her cover her head. [7]For a man ought not to

have his head covered, since he is the image and glory of God; but the woman is the glory of man. [8]For man does not originate from woman, but woman from man; [9]for indeed man was not created for the woman's sake, but woman for the man's sake. [10]Therefore the woman ought to have *a symbol of* authority on her head, because of the angels. [11]However, in the Lord, neither is woman independent of man, nor is man independent of woman. [12]For as the woman originates from the man, so also the man *has his birth* through the woman; and all things originate from God. [13]Judge for yourselves: is it proper for a woman to pray to God *with her head* uncovered? [14]Does not even nature itself teach you that if a man has long hair, it is a dishonor to him, [15]but if a woman has long hair, it is a glory to her? For her hair is given to her for a covering. [16]But if one is inclined to be contentious, we have no other practice, nor have the churches of God.

[17] But in giving this instruction, I do not praise you, because you come together not for the better but for the worse. [18]For, in the first place, when you come together as a church, I hear that divisions exist among you; and in part I believe it. [19]For there must also be factions among you, so that those who are approved may become evident among you. [20]Therefore when you meet together, it is not to eat the Lord's Supper, [21]for in your eating each one takes his own supper first; and one is hungry and another is drunk. [22]What! Do you not have houses in which to eat and drink? Or do you despise the church of God and shame those who have nothing? What shall I say to you? Shall I praise you? In this I will not praise you.

The Lord's Supper

23 For I received from the Lord that which I also delivered to you, that the Lord Jesus in the night in which He was betrayed took bread; [24]and when He had given thanks, He broke it and said, "This is My body, which is for you; do this in remembrance of Me." [25]In the same way *He took* the cup also after supper, saying, "This cup is the new covenant in My blood; do this, as often as you drink *it,* in remembrance of Me." [26]For as often as you eat this bread and drink the cup, you proclaim the Lord's death until He comes.

27 Therefore whoever eats the bread or drinks the cup of the Lord in an unworthy manner, shall be guilty of the body and the blood of the Lord. [28]But a man must examine himself, and in so doing he is to eat of the bread and drink of the

cup. ²⁹For he who eats and drinks, eats and drinks judgment to himself if he does not judge the body rightly. ³⁰For this reason many among you are weak and sick, and a number sleep. ³¹But if we judged ourselves rightly, we would not be judged. ³²But when we are judged, we are disciplined by the Lord so that we will not be condemned along with the world.

33 So then, my brethren, when you come together to eat, wait for one another. ³⁴If anyone is hungry, let him eat at home, so that you will not come together for judgment. The remaining matters I will arrange when I come.

The Use of Spiritual Gifts

12 Now concerning spiritual *gifts*, brethren, I do not want you to be unaware. ²You know that when you were pagans, *you were* led astray to the mute idols, however you were led. ³Therefore I make known to you that no one speaking by the Spirit of God says, "Jesus is accursed"; and no one can say, "Jesus is Lord," except by the Holy Spirit.

4 Now there are varieties of gifts, but the same Spirit. ⁵And there are varieties of ministries, and the same Lord. ⁶There are varieties of effects, but the same God who works all things in all *persons*. ⁷But

to each one is given the manifestation of the Spirit for the common good. ⁸For to one is given the word of wisdom through the Spirit, and to another the word of knowledge according to the same Spirit; ⁹to another faith by the same Spirit, and to another gifts of healing by the one Spirit, ¹⁰and to another the effecting of miracles, and to another prophecy, and to another the distinguishing of spirits, to another *various* kinds of tongues, and to another the interpretation of tongues. ¹¹But one and the same Spirit works all these things, distributing to each one individually just as He wills.

12 For even as the body is one and *yet* has many members, and all the members of the body, though they are many, are one body, so also is Christ. ¹³For by one Spirit we were all baptized into one body, whether Jews or Greeks, whether slaves or free, and we were all made to drink of one Spirit.

14 For the body is not one member, but many. ¹⁵If the foot says, "Because I am not a hand, I am not *a part* of the body," it is not for this reason any the less *a part* of the body. ¹⁶And if the ear says, "Because I am not an eye, I am not *a part* of the body," it is not for this reason any the less *a part* of the body. ¹⁷If the whole body were an

eye, where would the hearing be? If the whole were hearing, where would the sense of smell be? [18]But now God has placed the members, each one of them, in the body, just as He desired. [19]If they were all one member, where would the body be? [20]But now there are many members, but one body. [21]And the eye cannot say to the hand, "I have no need of you"; or again the head to the feet, "I have no need of you." [22]On the contrary, it is much truer that the members of the body which seem to be weaker are necessary; [23]and those *members* of the body which we deem less honorable, on these we bestow more abundant honor, and our less presentable members become much more presentable, [24]whereas our more presentable members have no need *of it*. But God has *so* composed the body, giving more abundant honor to that *member* which lacked, [25]so that there may be no division in the body, but *that* the members may have the same care for one another. [26]And if one member suffers, all the members suffer with it; if *one* member is honored, all the members rejoice with it.

[27] Now you are Christ's body, and individually members of it. [28]And God has appointed in the church, first apostles, second prophets, third teachers, then miracles, then gifts of healings, helps, administrations, *various* kinds of tongues. [29]All are not apostles, are they? All are not prophets, are they? All are not teachers, are they? All are not *workers of* miracles, are they? [30]All do not have gifts of healings, do they? All do not speak with tongues, do they? All do not interpret, do they? [31]But earnestly desire the greater gifts. And I show you a still more excellent way.

The Excellence of Love

13 If I speak with the tongues of men and of angels, but do not have love, I have become a noisy gong or a clanging cymbal. [2]If I have *the gift of* prophecy, and know all mysteries and all knowledge; and if I have all faith, so as to remove mountains, but do not have love, I am nothing. [3]And if I give all my possessions to feed *the poor*, and if I surrender my body [a]to be burned, but do not have love, it profits me nothing.

[4] Love is patient, love is kind *and* is not jealous; love does not brag *and* is not arrogant, [5]does not act unbecomingly; it does not seek its own, is not provoked, does not take into account a wrong *suffered*, [6]does not rejoice in unrighteousness, but rejoices with the truth; [7]bears all things, believes all

[a]13:3 Early mss read *that I may boast*

things, hopes all things, endures all things.

8 Love never fails; but if *there are gifts of* prophecy, they will be done away; if *there are* tongues, they will cease; if *there is* knowledge, it will be done away. ⁹For we know in part and we prophesy in part; ¹⁰but when the perfect comes, the partial will be done away. ¹¹When I was a child, I used to speak like a child, think like a child, reason like a child; when I became a man, I did away with childish things. ¹²For now we see in a mirror dimly, but then face to face; now I know in part, but then I will know fully just as I also have been fully known. ¹³But now faith, hope, love, abide these three; but the greatest of these is love.

Prophecy a Superior Gift

14 Pursue love, yet desire earnestly spiritual *gifts,* but especially that you may prophesy. ²For one who speaks in a tongue does not speak to men but to God; for no one understands, but in *his* spirit he speaks mysteries. ³But one who prophesies speaks to men for edification and exhortation and consolation. ⁴One who speaks in a tongue edifies himself; but one who prophesies edifies the church. ⁵Now I wish that you all spoke in tongues, but *even* more that you would prophesy; and greater is one who prophesies than one who speaks in tongues, unless he interprets, so that the church may receive edifying.

6 But now, brethren, if I come to you speaking in tongues, what will I profit you unless I speak to you either by way of revelation or of knowledge or of prophecy or of teaching? ⁷Yet *even* lifeless things, either flute or harp, in producing a sound, if they do not produce a distinction in the tones, how will it be known what is played on the flute or on the harp? ⁸For if the bugle produces an indistinct sound, who will prepare himself for battle? ⁹So also you, unless you utter by the tongue speech that is clear, how will it be known what is spoken? For you will be speaking into the air. ¹⁰There are, perhaps, a great many kinds of languages in the world, and no *kind* is without meaning. ¹¹If then I do not know the meaning of the language, I will be to the one who speaks a barbarian, and the one who speaks will be a barbarian to me. ¹²So also you, since you are zealous of spiritual *gifts,* seek to abound for the edification of the church.

13 Therefore let one who speaks in a tongue pray that he may interpret. ¹⁴For if I pray in a tongue, my spirit prays, but my mind is unfruitful. ¹⁵What is *the outcome* then? I will pray with the spirit and I will pray with the mind also; I will sing with the spirit and I will sing with the mind also. [16]Otherwise if you bless in the spirit *only,* how will the one who fills the place of the ungifted say the "Amen" at your giving of thanks, since he does not know what you are saying? [17]For you are giving thanks well enough, but the other person is not edified. [18]I thank God, I speak in tongues more than you all; [19]however, in the church I desire to speak five words with my mind so that I may instruct others also, rather than ten thousand words in a tongue.

Instruction for the Church

20 Brethren, do not be children in your thinking; yet in evil be infants, but in your thinking be mature. [21]In the Law it is written, "BY MEN OF STRANGE TONGUES AND BY THE LIPS OF STRANGERS I WILL SPEAK TO THIS PEOPLE, AND EVEN SO THEY WILL NOT LISTEN TO ME," says the Lord. [22]So then tongues are for a sign, not to those who believe but to unbelievers; but prophecy *is for a sign,* not to unbelievers but to those who believe. [23]Therefore if the whole church assembles together and all speak in tongues, and ungifted men or unbelievers enter, will they not say that you are mad? [24]But if all

prophesy, and an unbeliever or an ungifted man enters, he is convicted by all, he is called to account by all; [25]the secrets of his heart are disclosed; and so he will fall on his face and worship God, declaring that God is certainly among you.

26 What is *the outcome* then, brethren? When you assemble, each one has a psalm, has a teaching, has a revelation, has a tongue, has an interpretation. Let all things be done for edification. [27]If anyone speaks in a tongue, *it should be* by two or at the most three, and *each* in turn, and one must interpret; [28]but if there is no interpreter, he must keep silent in the church; and let him speak to himself and to God. [29]Let two or three prophets speak, and let the others pass judgment. [30]But if a revelation is made to another who is seated, the first one must keep silent. [31]For you can all prophesy one by one, so that all may learn and all may be exhorted; [32]and the spirits of prophets are subject to prophets; [33]for God is not *a God* of confusion but of peace, as in all the churches of the saints.

34 The women are to keep silent in the churches; for they are not permitted to speak, but are to subject themselves, just as the Law also says. [35]If they desire to learn anything, let them ask their own

husbands at home; for it is improper for a woman to speak in church. [36]Was it from you that the word of God *first* went forth? Or has it come to you only?

37 If anyone thinks he is a prophet or spiritual, let him recognize that the things which I write to you are the Lord's commandment. [38]But if anyone does not recognize *this,* he [a]is not recognized.

39 Therefore, my brethren, desire earnestly to prophesy, and do not forbid to speak in tongues. [40]But all things must be done properly and in an orderly manner.

The Fact of Christ's Resurrection

15 Now I make known to you, brethren, the gospel which I preached to you, which also you received, in which also you stand, [2]by which also you are saved, if you hold fast the word which I preached to you, unless you believed in vain.

3 For I delivered to you as of first importance what I also received, that Christ died for our sins according to the Scriptures, [4]and that He was buried, and that He was raised on the third day according to the Scriptures, [5]and that He appeared to Cephas, then to the twelve. [6]After that He appeared to more than five hundred brethren at one time, most of whom remain until now, but some have fallen asleep; [7]then He appeared to James, then to all the apostles; [8]and last of all, as to one untimely born, He appeared to me also. [9]For I am the least of the apostles, and not fit to be called an apostle, because I persecuted the church of God. [10]But by the grace of God I am what I am, and His grace toward me did not prove vain; but I labored even more than all of them, yet not I, but the grace of God with me. [11]Whether then *it was* I or they, so we preach and so you believed.

12 Now if Christ is preached, that He has been raised from the dead, how do some among you say that there is no resurrection of the dead? [13]But if there is no resurrection of the dead, not even Christ has been raised; [14]and if Christ has not been raised, then our preaching is vain, your faith also is vain. [15]Moreover we are even found *to be* false witnesses of God, because we testified against God that He raised [b]Christ, whom He did not raise, if in fact the dead are not raised. [16]For if the dead are not raised, not even Christ has been raised; [17]and if Christ has not been raised, your faith is worthless; you are still in your sins. [18]Then those also who have fallen asleep in Christ have perished. [19]If we have

---

[a]**14:38** Two early mss read *is not to be recognized;* [b]**14:38** I.e. the Messiah

hoped in Christ in this life only, we are of all men most to be pitied.

The Order of Resurrection

20 But now Christ has been raised from the dead, the first fruits of those who are asleep. ²¹For since by a man *came* death, by a man also *came* the resurrection of the dead. ²²For as in Adam all die, so also in Christ all will be made alive. ²³But each in his own order: Christ the first fruits, after that those who are Christ's at His coming, ²⁴then *comes* the end, when He hands over the kingdom to the God and Father, when He has abolished all rule and all authority and power. ²⁵For He must reign until He has put all His enemies under His feet. ²⁶The last enemy that will be abolished is death. ²⁷For HE HAS PUT ALL THINGS IN SUBJECTION UNDER HIS FEET. But when He says, "All things are put in subjection," it is evident that He is excepted who put all things in subjection to Him. ²⁸When all things are subjected to Him, then the Son Himself also will be subjected to the One who subjected all things to Him, so that God may be all in all.

29 Otherwise, what will those do who are baptized for the dead? If the dead are not raised at all, why then are they baptized for them? ³⁰Why are we also in danger every hour? ³¹I affirm, brethren, by the boasting in you which I have in Christ Jesus our Lord, I die daily. ³²If from human motives I fought with wild beasts at Ephesus, what does it profit me? If the dead are not raised, LET US EAT AND DRINK, FOR TOMORROW WE DIE. ³³Do not be deceived: "Bad company corrupts good morals." ³⁴Become sober-minded as you ought, and stop sinning; for some have no knowledge of God. I speak *this* to your shame.

35 But someone will say, "How are the dead raised? And with what kind of body do they come?" ³⁶You fool! That which you sow does not come to life unless it dies; ³⁷and that which you sow, you do not sow the body which is to be, but a bare grain, perhaps of wheat or of something else. ³⁸But God gives it a body just as He wished, and to each of the seeds a body of its own. ³⁹All flesh is not the same flesh, but there is one *flesh* of men, and another flesh of beasts, and another flesh of birds, and another of fish. ⁴⁰There are also heavenly bodies and earthly bodies, but the glory of the heavenly is one, and the *glory* of the earthly is another. ⁴¹There is one glory of the sun, and another glory of the moon, and another glory of the stars; for star differs from star in glory.

42 So also is the resurrection of the dead. It is sown a perishable *body*, it is raised an imperishable *body*; ⁴³it is sown in dishonor, it is raised in glory; it is sown in weakness, it is raised in power; ⁴⁴it is sown a natural body, it is raised a spiritual body. If there is a natural body, there is also a spiritual *body*. ⁴⁵So also it is written, "The first MAN, Adam, BECAME A LIVING SOUL." The last Adam *became* a life-giving spirit. ⁴⁶However, the spiritual is not first, but the natural; then the spiritual. ⁴⁷The first man is from the earth, earthy; the second man is from heaven. ⁴⁸As is the earthy, so also are those who are earthy; and as is the heavenly, so also are those who are heavenly. ⁴⁹Just as we have borne the image of the earthy, ^awe will also bear the image of the heavenly.

The Mystery of Resurrection

50 Now I say this, brethren, that flesh and blood cannot inherit the kingdom of God; nor does the perishable inherit the imperishable. ⁵¹Behold, I tell you a mystery; we will not all sleep, but we will all be changed, ⁵²in a moment, in the twinkling of an eye, at the last trumpet; for the trumpet will sound, and the dead will be raised imperishable, and we will be changed. ⁵³For this perishable must put on the imperishable, and this mortal must put

^a**15:49** Two early mss read *let us also*

on immortality. ⁵⁴But when this perishable will have put on the imperishable, and this mortal will have put on immortality, then will come about the saying that is written, "DEATH IS SWALLOWED UP in victory. ⁵⁵O DEATH, WHERE IS YOUR VICTORY? O DEATH, WHERE IS YOUR STING?" ⁵⁶The sting of death is sin, and the power of sin is the law; ⁵⁷but thanks be to God, who gives us the victory through our Lord Jesus Christ.

58 Therefore, my beloved brethren, be steadfast, immovable, always abounding in the work of the Lord, knowing that your toil is not *in* vain in the Lord.

Instructions and Greetings

16 Now concerning the collection for the saints, as I directed the churches of Galatia, so do you also. ²On the first day of every week each one of you is to put aside and save, as he may prosper, so that no collections be made when I come. ³When I arrive, whomever you may approve, I will send them with letters to carry your gift to Jerusalem; ⁴and if it is fitting for me to go also, they will go with me.

5 But I will come to you after I go through Macedonia, for I am going through Macedonia; ⁶and perhaps I will stay with you, or even spend the winter, so that you may send me on my way wherever I may go. [7]For I do not wish to see you now *just* in passing; for I hope to remain with you for some time, if the Lord permits. [8]But I will remain in Ephesus until Pentecost; [9]for a wide door for effective *service* has opened to me, and there are many adversaries.

10 Now if Timothy comes, see that he is with you without cause to be afraid, for he is doing the Lord's work, as I also am. [11]So let no one despise him. But send him on his way in peace, so that he may come to me; for I expect him with the brethren.

12 But concerning Apollos our brother, I encouraged him greatly to come to you with the brethren; and it was not at all *his* desire to come now, but he will come when he has opportunity.

13 Be on the alert, stand firm in the faith, act like men, be strong. [14]Let all that you do be done in love.

15 Now I urge you, brethren (you know the household of Stephanas, that they were the first fruits of Achaia, and that they have devoted themselves for ministry to the saints), [16]that you also be in subjection to such men and to everyone who helps in the work and labors. [17]I rejoice over the coming of Stephanas and Fortunatus and Achaicus, because they have supplied what was lacking on your part. [18]For they have refreshed my spirit and yours. Therefore acknowledge such men.

19 The churches of Asia greet you. Aquila and Prisca greet you heartily in the Lord, with the church that is in their house. [20]All the brethren greet you. Greet one another with a holy kiss.

21 The greeting is in my own hand—Paul. [22]If anyone does not love the Lord, he is to be accursed. Maranatha. [23]The grace of the Lord Jesus be with you. [24]My love be with you all in Christ Jesus. Amen.

2 CORINTHIANS

Introduction

1 Paul, an apostle of Christ Jesus by the will of God, and Timothy *our* brother, To the church of God which is at Corinth with all the saints who are throughout Achaia:

2 Grace to you and peace from God our Father and the Lord Jesus Christ.

3 Blessed *be* the God and Father of our Lord Jesus Christ, the Father of mercies and God of all comfort, ⁴who comforts us in all our affliction so that we will be able to comfort those who are in any affliction with the comfort with which we ourselves are comforted by God. ⁵For just as the sufferings of Christ are ours in abundance, so also our comfort is abundant through Christ. ⁶But if we are afflicted, it is for your comfort and salvation; or if we are comforted, it is for your comfort, which is effective in the patient enduring of the same sufferings which we also suffer; ⁷and our hope for you is firmly grounded, knowing that as you are sharers of our sufferings, so also you are *sharers* of our comfort.

8 For we do not want you to be unaware, brethren, of our affliction which came *to us* in Asia, that we were burdened excessively, beyond our strength, so that we despaired even of life; ⁹indeed, we had the sentence of death within ourselves so that we would not trust in ourselves, but in God who raises the dead; ¹⁰who delivered us from so great a *peril of* death, and will deliver *us*, He on whom we have set our hope. And He will yet deliver us, ¹¹you also joining in helping us through your prayers, so that thanks may be given by many persons on our behalf for the favor bestowed on us through *the prayers of* many.

Paul's Integrity

12 For our proud confidence is this: the testimony of our conscience, that in holiness and godly sincerity, not in fleshly wisdom but in the grace of God, we have conducted ourselves in the world, and especially toward you. ¹³For we write nothing else to you than what you read and understand, and I hope you will understand until the end; ¹⁴just as you also partially did understand us, that we are your reason to be proud as you also are ours, in the day of our Lord Jesus.

15 In this confidence I intended at first to come to you, so that you might twice receive a blessing; [16]that is, to pass your way into Macedonia, and again from Macedonia to come to you, and by you to be helped on my journey to Judea. [17]Therefore, I was not vacillating when I intended to do this, was I? Or what I purpose, do I purpose according to the flesh, so that with me there will be yes, yes and no, no *at the same time?* [18]But as God is faithful, our word to you is not yes and no. [19]For the Son of God, Christ Jesus, who was preached among you by us—by me and Silvanus and Timothy—was not yes and no, but is yes in Him. [20]For as many as are the promises of God, in Him they are yes; therefore also through Him is our Amen to the glory of God through us. [21]Now He who establishes us with you in Christ and anointed us is God, [22]who also sealed us and gave *us* the Spirit in our hearts as a pledge.

23 But I call God as witness to my soul, that to spare you I did not come again to Corinth. [24]Not that we lord it over your faith, but are workers with you for your joy; for in your faith you are standing firm.

Reaffirm Your Love

2 But I determined this for my own sake, that I would not come to you in sorrow again. [2]For if I cause you sorrow, who then makes me glad but the one whom I made sorrowful? [3]This is the very thing I wrote you, so that when I came, I would not have sorrow from those who ought to make me rejoice; having confidence in you all that my joy would be *the joy* of you all. [4]For out of much affliction and anguish of heart I wrote to you with many tears; not so that you would be made sorrowful, but that you might know the love which I have especially for you.

5 But if any has caused sorrow, he has caused sorrow not to me, but in some degree—in order not to say too much—to all of you. [6]Sufficient for such a one is this punishment which *was inflicted by* the majority, [7]so that on the contrary you should rather forgive and comfort *him,* otherwise such a one might be overwhelmed by excessive sorrow. [8]Wherefore I urge you to reaffirm *your* love for him. [9]For to this end also I wrote, so that I might put you to the test, whether you are obedient in all things. [10]But one whom you forgive anything, I *forgive* also; for indeed what I have forgiven, if I have forgiven anything, *I did it* for your sakes in the presence of Christ,

[11]so that no advantage would be taken of us by Satan, for we are not ignorant of his schemes.

12 Now when I came to Troas for the gospel of Christ and when a door was opened for me in the Lord, [13]I had no rest for my spirit, not finding Titus my brother; but taking my leave of them, I went on to Macedonia.

14 But thanks be to God, who always leads us in triumph in Christ, and manifests through us the sweet aroma of the knowledge of Him in every place. [15]For we are a fragrance of Christ to God among those who are being saved and among those who are perishing; [16]to the one an aroma from death to death, to the other an aroma from life to life. And who is adequate for these things? [17]For we are not like many, [a]peddling the word of God, but as from sincerity, but as from God, we speak in Christ in the sight of God.

Ministers of a New Covenant

3 Are we beginning to commend ourselves again? Or do we need, as some, letters of commendation to you or from you? [2]You are our letter, written in our hearts, known and read by all men; [3]being manifested that you are a letter of Christ, cared for by us, written not with ink but with the Spirit of the living God, not on tablets of stone but on tablets of human hearts.

4 Such confidence we have through Christ toward God. [5]Not that we are adequate in ourselves to consider anything as *coming* from ourselves, but our adequacy is from God, [6]who also made us adequate as servants of a new covenant, not of the letter but of the Spirit; for the letter kills, but the Spirit gives life.

7 But if the ministry of death, in letters engraved on stones, came with glory, so that the sons of Israel could not look intently at the face of Moses because of the glory of his face, fading *as* it was, [8]how will the ministry of the Spirit fail to be even more with glory? [9]For if the ministry of condemnation has glory, much more does the ministry of righteousness abound in glory. [10]For indeed what had glory, in this case has no glory because of the glory that surpasses *it.* [11]For if that which fades away *was* with glory, much more that which remains *is* in glory.

12 Therefore having such a hope, we use great boldness in *our* speech, [13]and *are* not like Moses, *who* used to put a veil over

---

[a]**2:17** Or *corrupting*

his face so that the sons of Israel would not look intently at the end of what was fading away. [14]But their minds were hardened; for until this very day at the reading of the old covenant the same veil remains unlifted, because it is removed in Christ. [15]But to this day whenever Moses is read, a veil lies over their heart; [16]but whenever a person turns to the Lord, the veil is taken away. [17]Now the Lord is the Spirit, and where the Spirit of the Lord is, *there* is liberty. [18]But we all, with unveiled face, beholding as in a mirror the glory of the Lord, are being transformed into the same image from glory to glory, just as from the Lord, the Spirit.

Paul's Apostolic Ministry

4 Therefore, since we have this ministry, as we received mercy, we do not lose heart, [2]but we have renounced the things hidden because of shame, not walking in craftiness or adulterating the word of God, but by the manifestation of truth commending ourselves to every man's conscience in the sight of God. [3]And even if our gospel is veiled, it is veiled to those who are perishing, [4]in whose case the god of this world has blinded the minds of the unbelieving so that they might not see the light of the gospel of the glory of Christ, who is the image of God. [5]For we do not preach ourselves but Christ Jesus as Lord, and ourselves as your bond-servants for Jesus' sake. [6]For God, who said, "Light shall shine out of darkness," is the One who has shone in our hearts to give the Light of the knowledge of the glory of God in the face of Christ.

7 But we have this treasure in earthen vessels, so that the surpassing greatness of the power will be of God and not from ourselves; [8]*we are* afflicted in every way, but not crushed; perplexed, but not despairing; [9]persecuted, but not forsaken; struck down, but not destroyed; [10]always carrying about in the body the dying of Jesus, so that the life of Jesus also may be manifested in our body. [11]For we who live are constantly being delivered over to death for Jesus' sake, so that the life of Jesus also may be manifested in our mortal flesh. [12]So death works in us, but life in you.

13 But having the same spirit of faith, according to what is written, "I BELIEVED, THEREFORE I SPOKE," we also believe, therefore we also speak, [14]knowing that He who raised the Lord Jesus will raise us also with Jesus and will present us with you. [15]For all things *are* for your sakes, so that the grace which is spreading to more and more people may cause

the giving of thanks to abound to the glory of God.

16 Therefore we do not lose heart, but though our outer man is decaying, yet our inner man is being renewed day by day. [17]For momentary, light affliction is producing for us an eternal weight of glory far beyond all comparison, [18]while we look not at the things which are seen, but at the things which are not seen; for the things which are seen are temporal, but the things which are not seen are eternal.

The Temporal and Eternal

5 For we know that if the earthly tent which is our house is torn down, we have a building from God, a house not made with hands, eternal in the heavens. [2]For indeed in this *house* we groan, longing to be clothed with our dwelling from heaven, [3]inasmuch as we, having put it on, will not be found naked. [4]For indeed while we are in this tent, we groan, being burdened, because we do not want to be unclothed but to be clothed, so that what is mortal will be swallowed up by life. [5]Now He who prepared us for this very purpose is God, who gave to us the Spirit as a pledge.

6 Therefore, being always of good courage, and knowing that while we are at home in the body we are absent from the Lord— [7]for we walk by faith, not by sight— [8]we are of good courage, I say, and prefer rather to be absent from the body and to be at home with the Lord. [9]Therefore we also have as our ambition, whether at home or absent, to be pleasing to Him. [10]For we must all appear before the judgment seat of Christ, so that each one may be recompensed for his deeds in the body, according to what he has done, whether good or bad.

11 Therefore, knowing the fear of the Lord, we persuade men, but we are made manifest to God; and I hope that we are made manifest also in your consciences. [12]We are not again commending ourselves to you but *are* giving you an occasion to be proud of us, so that you will have *an answer* for those who take pride in appearance and not in heart. [13]For if we are beside ourselves, it is for God; if we are of sound mind, it is for you. [14]For the love of Christ controls us, having concluded this, that one died for all, therefore all died; [15]and He died for all, so that they who live might no longer live for themselves, but for Him who died and rose again on their behalf.

16 Therefore from now on we recognize no one according to the flesh; even though we have known

Christ according to the flesh, yet now we know *Him in this way* no longer. ¹⁷Therefore if anyone is in Christ, *he is* a new creature; the old things passed away; behold, new things have come. ¹⁸Now all *these* things are from God, who reconciled us to Himself through Christ and gave us the ministry of reconciliation, ¹⁹namely, that God was in Christ reconciling the world to Himself, not counting their trespasses against them, and He has committed to us the word of reconciliation.

20 Therefore, we are ambassadors for Christ, as though God were making an appeal through us; we beg you on behalf of Christ, be reconciled to God. ²¹He made Him who knew no sin *to be* sin on our behalf, so that we might become the righteousness of God in Him.

Their Ministry Commended

6And working together *with Him*, we also urge you not to receive the grace of God in vain— ²for He says,

"AT THE ACCEPTABLE TIME I LISTENED TO YOU,
AND ON THE DAY OF SALVATION I HELPED YOU."

Behold, now is "THE ACCEPTABLE TIME," behold, now is "THE DAY OF SALVATION"— ³giving no cause for offense in anything, so that the ministry will not be discredited, ⁴but in everything commending ourselves as servants of God, in much endurance, in afflictions, in hardships, in distresses, ⁵in beatings, in imprisonments, in tumults, in labors, in sleeplessness, in hunger, ⁶in purity, in knowledge, in patience, in kindness, in the Holy Spirit, in genuine love, ⁷in the word of truth, in the power of God; by the weapons of righteousness for the right hand and the left, ⁸by glory and dishonor, by evil report and good report; *regarded* as deceivers and yet true; ⁹as unknown yet well-known, as dying yet behold, we live; as punished yet not put to death, ¹⁰as sorrowful yet always rejoicing, as poor yet making many rich, as having nothing yet possessing all things.

11 Our mouth has spoken freely to you, O Corinthians, our heart is opened wide. ¹²You are not restrained by us, but you are restrained in your own affections. ¹³Now in a like exchange—I speak as to children—open wide *to us* also.

14 Do not be bound together with unbelievers; for what partnership have righteousness and lawlessness, or what fellowship has light with darkness? ¹⁵Or what harmony has Christ with Belial, or what has a believer in common with an unbeliever? [16]Or what agreement has the temple of God with idols? For we are the temple of the living God; just as God said,

"I WILL DWELL IN THEM AND WALK AMONG THEM;

AND I WILL BE THEIR GOD, AND THEY SHALL BE MY PEOPLE.

[17]"Therefore, COME OUT FROM THEIR MIDST AND BE SEPARATE," says the Lord.

"AND DO NOT TOUCH WHAT IS UNCLEAN;

And I will welcome you.

[18]"And I will be a father to you, And you shall be sons and daughters to Me,"

Says the Lord Almighty.

Paul Reveals His Heart

7Therefore, having these promises, beloved, let us cleanse ourselves from all defilement of flesh and spirit, perfecting holiness in the fear of God.

2 Make room for us *in your hearts;* we wronged no one, we corrupted no one, we took advantage of no one. [3]I do not speak to condemn you, for I have said before that you are in our hearts to die together and to live together. [4]Great is my confidence in you; great is my boasting on your behalf. I am filled with comfort; I am overflowing with joy in all our affliction.

5 For even when we came into Macedonia our flesh had no rest, but we were afflicted on every side: conflicts without, fears within. [6]But God, who comforts the depressed, comforted us by the coming of Titus; [7]and not only by his coming, but also by the comfort with which he was comforted in you, as he reported to us your longing, your mourning, your zeal for me; so that I rejoiced even more. [8]For though I caused you sorrow by my letter, I do not regret it; though I did regret it—*for* I see that that letter caused you sorrow, though only for a while— [9]I now rejoice, not that you were made sorrowful, but that you were made sorrowful to *the point of* repentance; for you were made sorrowful according to *the will of* God, so that you might not suffer loss in anything through us. [10]For the sorrow that is according to *the will of* God produces a repentance without regret, *leading* to salvation, but the sorrow of the world produces death. [11]For behold what earnestness this very thing, this godly sorrow, has produced in you: what vindication of yourselves, what indignation, what fear, what longing, what zeal, what avenging of wrong! In everything you demonstrated yourselves to be innocent in the matter. [12]So although I wrote to you, *it was* not for the sake of the offender nor for the sake of the one offended, but that your earnestness on our behalf might be made known to you in the sight of God. ¹³For this reason we have been comforted.

And besides our comfort, we rejoiced even much more for the joy of Titus, because his spirit has been refreshed by you all. ¹⁴For if in anything I have boasted to him about you, I was not put to shame; but as we spoke all things to you in truth, so also our boasting before Titus proved to be *the* truth. ¹⁵His affection abounds all the more toward you, as he remembers the obedience of you all, how you received him with fear and trembling. ¹⁶I rejoice that in everything I have confidence in you.

Great Generosity

8 Now, brethren, we *wish to* make known to you the grace of God which has been given in the churches of Macedonia, ²that in a great ordeal of affliction their abundance of joy and their deep poverty overflowed in the wealth of their liberality. ³For I testify that according to their ability, and beyond their ability, *they gave* of their own accord, ⁴begging us with much urging for the favor of participation in the support of the saints, ⁵and *this,* not as we had expected, but they first gave themselves to the Lord and to us by the

will of God. ⁶So we urged Titus that as he had previously made a beginning, so he would also complete in you this gracious work as well.

7 But just as you abound in everything, in faith and utterance and knowledge and in all earnestness and in the ªlove we inspired in you, *see* that you abound in this gracious work also. ⁸I am not speaking *this* as a command, but as proving through the earnestness of others the sincerity of your love also. ⁹For you know the grace of our Lord Jesus Christ, that though He was rich, yet for your sake He became poor, so that you through His poverty might become rich. ¹⁰I give *my* opinion in this matter, for this is to your advantage, who were the first to begin a year ago not only to do *this,* but also to desire *to do it.* ¹¹But now finish doing it also, so that just as *there was* the readiness to desire it, so *there may be* also the completion of it by your ability. ¹²For if the readiness is present, it is acceptable according to what *a person* has, not according to what he does not have. ¹³For *this* is not for the ease of others *and* for your affliction, but by way of equality— ¹⁴at this present time your abundance *being a supply* for their need, so that their abundance also may become *a supply* for your need,

ª**8:7** Lit love *from us in you;* one early ms reads *your love for us* that there may be equality; [15]as it is written, "HE WHO *gathered* MUCH DID NOT HAVE TOO MUCH, AND HE WHO *gathered* LITTLE HAD NO LACK."

16 But thanks be to God who puts the same earnestness on your behalf in the heart of Titus. [17]For he not only accepted our appeal, but being himself very earnest, he has gone to you of his own accord. [18]We have sent along with him the brother whose fame in *the things of* the gospel *has spread* through all the churches; [19]and not only *this,* but he has also been appointed by the churches to travel with us in this gracious work, which is being administered by us for the glory of the Lord Himself, and *to show* our readiness, [20]taking precaution so that no one will discredit us in our administration of this generous gift; [21]for we have regard for what is honorable, not only in the sight of the Lord, but also in the sight of men. [22]We have sent with them our brother, whom we have often tested and found diligent in many things, but now even more diligent because of *his* great confidence in you. [23]As for Titus, *he is* my partner and fellow worker among you; as for our brethren, *they are* messengers of the churches, a glory to Christ. [24]Therefore openly before the churches, show them the proof of your love and of our reason for boasting about you.

God Gives Most

9 For it is superfluous for me to write to you about this ministry to the saints; [2]for I know your readiness, of which I boast about you to the Macedonians, *namely,* that Achaia has been prepared since last year, and your zeal has stirred up most of them. [3]But I have sent the brethren, in order that our boasting about you may not be made empty in this case, so that, as I was saying, you may be prepared; [4]otherwise if any Macedonians come with me and find you unprepared, we—not to speak of you—will be put to shame by this confidence. [5]So I thought it necessary to urge the brethren that they would go on ahead to you and arrange beforehand your previously promised bountiful gift, so that the same would be ready as a bountiful gift and not affected by covetousness.

6 Now this *I say,* he who sows sparingly will also reap sparingly, and he who sows bountifully will also reap bountifully. [7]Each one *must do* just as he has purposed in his heart, not grudgingly or under compulsion, for God loves a cheerful giver. [8]And God is able to make all grace abound to you, so that always having all sufficiency in everything, you may have an abundance for every good deed; [9]as it is written,

"HE SCATTERED ABROAD, HE GAVE TO THE POOR,
HIS RIGHTEOUSNESS ENDURES FOREVER."

[10]Now He who supplies seed to the sower and bread for food will supply and multiply your seed for sowing and increase the harvest of your righteousness; [11]you will be enriched in everything for all liberality, which through us is producing thanksgiving to God. [12]For the ministry of this service is not only fully supplying the needs of the saints, but is also overflowing through many thanksgivings to God. [13]Because of the proof given by this ministry, they will glorify God for *your* obedience to your confession of the gospel of Christ and for the liberality of your contribution to them and to all, [14]while they also, by prayer on your behalf, yearn for you because of the surpassing grace of God in you. [15]Thanks be to God for His indescribable gift!

Paul Describes Himself

10Now I, Paul, myself urge you by the meekness and gentleness of Christ—I who am meek when face to face with you, but bold toward you when absent! [2]I ask that when I am present I *need* not be bold with the confidence

with which I propose to be courageous against some, who regard us as if we walked according to the flesh. [3]For though we walk in the flesh, we do not war according to the flesh, [4]for the weapons of our warfare are not of the flesh, but divinely powerful for the destruction of fortresses. [5]*We are* destroying speculations and every lofty thing raised up against the knowledge of God, and *we are* taking every thought captive to the obedience of Christ, [6]and we are ready to punish all disobedience, whenever your obedience is complete.

[7] You are looking at things as they are outwardly. If anyone is confident in himself that he is Christ's, let him consider this again within himself, that just as he is Christ's, so also are we. [8]For even if I boast somewhat further about our authority, which the Lord gave for building you up and not for destroying you, I will not be put to shame, [9]for I do not wish to seem as if I would terrify you by my letters. [10]For they say, "His letters are weighty and strong, but his personal presence is unimpressive and his speech contemptible." [11]Let such a person consider this, that what we are in word by letters when absent, such persons *we are* also in deed when present.

[12] For we are not bold to class or

compare ourselves with some of those who commend themselves; but when they measure themselves by themselves and compare themselves with themselves, they are without understanding. [13]But we will not boast beyond *our* measure, but within the measure of the sphere which God apportioned to us as a measure, to reach even as far as you. [14]For we are not over-extending ourselves, as if we did not reach to you, for we were the first to come even as far as you in the gospel of Christ; [15]not boasting beyond *our* measure, *that is,* in other men's labors, but with the hope that as your faith grows, we will be, within our sphere, enlarged even more by you, [16]so as to preach the gospel even to the regions beyond you, *and* not to boast in what has been accomplished in the sphere of another. [17]But HE WHO BOASTS IS TO BOAST IN THE LORD. [18]For it is not he who commends himself that is approved, but he whom the Lord commends.

Paul Defends His Apostleship

11 I wish that you would bear with me in a little foolishness; but indeed you are bearing with me. [2]For I am jealous for you with a godly jealousy; for I betrothed you to one husband, so that to Christ I might present you *as* a pure virgin. [3]But I am afraid that, as the serpent deceived Eve by his craftiness, your minds will be led astray from the simplicity and purity *of devotion* to Christ. [4]For if one comes and preaches another Jesus whom we have not preached, or you receive a different spirit which you have not received, or a different gospel which you have not accepted, you bear *this* beautifully. [5]For I consider myself not in the least inferior to the most eminent apostles. [6]But even if I am unskilled in speech, yet I am not *so* in knowledge; in fact, in every way we have made *this* evident to you in all things.

[7] Or did I commit a sin in humbling myself so that you might be exalted, because I preached the gospel of God to you without charge? [8]I robbed other churches by taking wages *from them* to serve you; [9]and when I was present with you and was in need, I was not a burden to anyone; for when the brethren came from Macedonia they fully supplied my need, and in everything I kept myself from being a burden to you, and will continue to do so. [10]As the truth of Christ is in me, this boasting of mine will not be stopped in the regions of Achaia. [11]Why? Because I do not love you? God knows *I do!*

[12] But what I am doing I will continue to do, so that I may cut off

opportunity from those who desire an opportunity to be regarded just as we are in the matter about which they are boasting. ¹³For such men are false apostles, deceitful workers, disguising themselves as apostles of Christ. ¹⁴No wonder, for even Satan disguises himself as an angel of light. ¹⁵Therefore it is not surprising if his servants also disguise themselves as servants of righteousness, whose end will be according to their deeds.

16 Again I say, let no one think me foolish; but if *you do,* receive me even as foolish, so that I also may boast a little. ¹⁷What I am saying, I am not saying as the Lord would, but as in foolishness, in this confidence of boasting. ¹⁸Since many boast according to the flesh, I will boast also. ¹⁹For you, being *so* wise, tolerate the foolish gladly. ²⁰For you tolerate it if anyone enslaves you, anyone devours you, anyone takes advantage of you, anyone exalts himself, anyone hits you in the face. ²¹To *my* shame I *must* say that we have been weak *by comparison.*

But in whatever respect anyone *else* is bold—I speak in foolishness—I am just as bold myself. ²²Are they Hebrews? So am I. Are they Israelites? So am I. Are they descendants of Abraham? So am I. ²³Are they servants of Christ?—I speak as if insane—I more so; in far more labors, in far more imprisonments, beaten times without number, often in danger of death. ²⁴Five times I received from the Jews thirty-nine *lashes.* ²⁵Three times I was beaten with rods, once I was stoned, three times I was shipwrecked, a night and a day I have spent in the deep. ²⁶*I have been* on frequent journeys, in dangers from rivers, dangers from robbers, dangers from *my* countrymen, dangers from the Gentiles, dangers in the city, dangers in the wilderness, dangers on the sea, dangers among false brethren; ²⁷*I have been* in labor and hardship, through many sleepless nights, in hunger and thirst, often without food, in cold and exposure. ²⁸Apart from *such* external things, there is the daily pressure on me *of* concern for all the churches. ²⁹Who is weak without my being weak? Who is led into sin without my intense concern?

30 If I have to boast, I will boast of what pertains to my weakness. ³¹The God and Father of the Lord Jesus, He who is blessed forever, knows that I am not lying. ³²In Damascus the ethnarch under Aretas the king was guarding the city of the Damascenes in order to seize me, ³³and I was let down in a basket through a window in the wall, and *so* escaped his hands.

Paul's Vision

12 Boasting is necessary, though it is not profitable; but I will go on to visions and revelations of the Lord. [2]I know a man in Christ who fourteen years ago—whether in the body I do not know, or out of the body I do not know, God knows—such a man was caught up to the third heaven. [3]And I know how such a man—whether in the body or apart from the body I do not know, God knows— [4]was caught up into Paradise and heard inexpressible words, which a man is not permitted to speak. [5]On behalf of such a man I will boast; but on my own behalf I will not boast, except in regard to *my* weaknesses. [6]For if I do wish to boast I will not be foolish, for I will be speaking the truth; but I refrain *from this,* so that no one will credit me with more than he sees *in* me or hears from me.

A Thorn in the Flesh

[7]Because of the surpassing greatness of the revelations, for this reason, to keep me from exalting myself, there was given me a thorn in the flesh, a messenger of Satan to torment me—to keep me from exalting myself! [8]Concerning this I implored the Lord three times that it might leave me. [9]And He has said to me, "My grace is sufficient for you, for power is perfected in weakness." Most gladly, therefore, I will rather boast about my weaknesses, so that the power of Christ may dwell in me. [10]Therefore I am well content with weaknesses, with insults, with distresses, with persecutions, with difficulties, for Christ's sake; for when I am weak, then I am strong.

11 I have become foolish; you yourselves compelled me. Actually I should have been commended by you, for in no respect was I inferior to the most eminent apostles, even though I am a nobody. [12]The signs of a true apostle were performed among you with all perseverance, by signs and wonders and miracles. [13]For in what respect were you treated as inferior to the rest of the churches, except that I myself did not become a burden to you? Forgive me this wrong!

14 Here for this third time I am ready to come to you, and I will not be a burden to you; for I do not seek what is yours, but you; for children are not responsible to save up for *their* parents, but parents for *their* children. [15]I will most gladly spend and be expended for your souls. If I love you more, am I to be loved less? [16]But

be that as it may, I did not burden you myself; nevertheless, crafty fellow that I am, I took you in by deceit. ¹⁷Certainly I have not taken advantage of you through any of those whom I have sent to you, have I? ¹⁸I urged Titus *to go,* and I sent the brother with him. Titus did not take any advantage of you, did he? Did we not conduct ourselves in the same spirit *and walk* in the same steps?

19 All this time you have been thinking that we are defending ourselves to you. *Actually,* it is in the sight of God that we have been speaking in Christ; and all for your upbuilding, beloved. ²⁰For I am afraid that perhaps when I come I may find you to be not what I wish and may be found by you to be not what you wish; that perhaps *there will be* strife, jealousy, angry tempers, disputes, slanders, gossip, arrogance, disturbances; ²¹I am afraid that when I come again my God may humiliate me before you, and I may mourn over many of those who have sinned in the past and not repented of the impurity, immorality and sensuality which they have practiced.

Examine Yourselves

13 This is the third time I am coming to you. EVERY FACT IS TO BE CONFIRMED BY THE TESTIMONY OF TWO OR THREE WITNESSES. ²I have previously said when present the second time, and though now absent I say in advance to those who have sinned in the past and to all the rest *as well,* that if I come again I will not spare *anyone,* ³since you are seeking for proof of the Christ who speaks in me, and who is not weak toward you, but mighty in you. ⁴For indeed He was crucified because of weakness, yet He lives because of the power of God. For we also are weak ^ain Him, yet we will live with Him because of the power of God *directed* toward you.

5 Test yourselves *to see* if you are in the faith; examine yourselves! Or do you not recognize this about yourselves, that Jesus Christ is in you—unless indeed you fail the test? ⁶But I trust that you will realize that we ourselves do not fail the test. ⁷Now we pray to God that you do no wrong; not that we ourselves may appear approved, but that you may do what is right, even though we may appear unapproved. ⁸For we can do nothing against the truth, but *only* for the truth. ⁹For we rejoice when we ourselves are weak but you are strong; this we also pray for, that you be made complete. ¹⁰For this reason I am writing these things while absent, so that when present I *need* not use severity, in accordance with the authority which

^a**13:4** One early ms reads *with Him*

the Lord gave me for building up and not for tearing down.

11 Finally, brethren, rejoice, be made complete, be comforted, be like-minded, live in peace; and the God of love and peace will be with you. ¹²Greet one another with a holy kiss. ¹³All the saints greet you.

14 The grace of the Lord Jesus Christ, and the love of God, and the fellowship of the Holy Spirit, be with you all.

GALATIANS

Introduction

1 Paul, an apostle (not *sent* from men nor through the agency of man, but through Jesus Christ and God the Father, who raised Him from the dead), ²and all the brethren who are with me, To the churches of Galatia:

3 Grace to you and peace from God our Father and the Lord Jesus Christ, ⁴who gave Himself for our sins so that He might rescue us from this present evil age, according to the will of our God and Father, ⁵to whom *be* the glory forevermore. Amen.

Perversion of the Gospel

6 I am amazed that you are so quickly deserting Him who called you by the grace of Christ, for a different gospel; ⁷which is *really* not another; only there are some who are disturbing you and want to distort the gospel of Christ. ⁸But even if we, or an angel from heaven, should preach to you a gospel contrary to what we have preached to you, he is to be accursed! ⁹As we have said before, so I say again now, if any man is preaching to you a gospel contrary to what you received, he is to be accursed!

10 For am I now seeking the favor of men, or of God? Or am I striving to please men? If I were still trying to please men, I would not be a bond-servant of Christ.

Paul Defends His Ministry

11 For I would have you know, brethren, that the gospel which was preached by me is not according to man. ¹²For I neither received it from man, nor was I taught it, but *I received it* through a revelation of Jesus Christ.

13 For you have heard of my former manner of life in Judaism, how

I used to persecute the church of God beyond measure and tried to destroy it; [14]and I was advancing in Judaism beyond many of my contemporaries among my countrymen, being more extremely zealous for my ancestral traditions. [15]But when God, who had set me apart *even* from my mother's womb and called me through His grace, was pleased [16]to reveal His Son in me so that I might preach Him among the Gentiles, I did not immediately consult with flesh and blood, [17]nor did I go up to Jerusalem to those who were apostles before me; but I went away to Arabia, and returned once more to Damascus.

[18] Then three years later I went up to Jerusalem to become acquainted with Cephas, and stayed with him fifteen days. [19]But I did not see any other of the apostles except James, the Lord's brother. [20](Now in what I am writing to you, I assure you before God that I am not lying.) [21]Then I went into the regions of Syria and Cilicia. [22]I was *still* unknown by sight to the churches of Judea which were in Christ; [23]but only, they kept hearing, "He who once persecuted us is now preaching the faith which he once tried to destroy." [24]And they were glorifying God because of me.

The Council at Jerusalem

2 Then after an interval of fourteen years I went up again to Jerusalem with Barnabas, taking Titus along also. [2]It was because of a revelation that I went up; and I submitted to them the gospel which I preach among the Gentiles, but *I did so* in private to those who were of reputation, for fear that I might be running, or had run, in vain. [3]But not even Titus, who was with me, though he was a Greek, was compelled to be circumcised. [4]But *it was* because of the false brethren secretly brought in, who had sneaked in to spy out our liberty which we have in Christ Jesus, in order to bring us into bondage. [5]But we did not yield in subjection to them for even an hour, so that the truth of the gospel would remain with you. [6]But from those who were of high reputation (what they were makes no difference to me; God shows no partiality)—well, those who were of reputation contributed nothing to me. [7]But on the contrary, seeing that I had been entrusted with the gospel to the uncircumcised, just as Peter *had been* to the circumcised [8](for He who effectually worked for Peter in *his* apostleship to the circumcised effectually worked for me also to the Gentiles), [9]and recognizing the grace that had been given to me, James and Cephas and John, who

were reputed to be pillars, gave to me and Barnabas the right hand of fellowship, so that we *might go* to the Gentiles and they to the circumcised. ¹⁰*They* only *asked* us to remember the poor—the very thing I also was eager to do.

Peter (Cephas) Opposed by Paul

11 But when Cephas came to Antioch, I opposed him to his face, because he stood condemned. ¹²For prior to the coming of certain men from James, he used to eat with the Gentiles; but when they came, he *began* to withdraw and hold himself aloof, fearing the party of the circumcision. ¹³The rest of the Jews joined him in hypocrisy, with the result that even Barnabas was carried away by their hypocrisy. ¹⁴But when I saw that they were not straightforward about the truth of the gospel, I said to Cephas in the presence of all, "If you, being a Jew, live like the Gentiles and not like the Jews, how *is it that* you compel the Gentiles to live like Jews?

15 "We *are* Jews by nature and not sinners from among the Gentiles; ¹⁶nevertheless knowing that a man is not justified by the works of the Law but through faith in Christ Jesus, even we have believed in Christ Jesus, so that we may be justified by faith in Christ and not by the works of the Law;

since by the works of the Law no flesh will be justified. ¹⁷But if, while seeking to be justified in Christ, we ourselves have also been found sinners, is Christ then a minister of sin? May it never be! ¹⁸For if I rebuild what I have *once* destroyed, I prove myself to be a transgressor. ¹⁹For through the Law I died to the Law, so that I might live to God. ²⁰I have been crucified with Christ; and it is no longer I who live, but Christ lives in me; and the *life* which I now live in the flesh I live by faith in the Son of God, who loved me and gave Himself up for me. ²¹I do not nullify the grace of God, for if righteousness *comes* through the Law, then Christ died needlessly."

Faith Brings Righteousness

3 You foolish Galatians, who has bewitched you, before whose eyes Jesus Christ was publicly portrayed *as* crucified? ²This is the only thing I want to find out from you: did you receive the Spirit by the works of the Law, or by hearing with faith? ³Are you so foolish? Having begun by the Spirit, are you now being perfected by the flesh? ⁴Did you suffer so many things in vain—if indeed it was in vain? ⁵So then, does He who provides you with the Spirit and works miracles among you, do it by the works of the Law, or by hearing with faith?

6 Even so Abraham BELIEVED GOD, AND IT WAS RECKONED TO HIM AS RIGHTEOUSNESS. [7]Therefore, be sure that it is those who are of faith who are sons of Abraham. [8]The Scripture, foreseeing that God would justify the Gentiles by faith, preached the gospel beforehand to Abraham, *saying,* "ALL THE NATIONS WILL BE BLESSED IN YOU." [9]So then those who are of faith are blessed with Abraham, the believer.

10 For as many as are of the works of the Law are under a curse; for it is written, "CURSED IS EVERYONE WHO DOES NOT ABIDE BY ALL THINGS WRITTEN IN THE BOOK OF THE LAW, TO PERFORM THEM." [11]Now that no one is justified by the Law before God is evident; for, "THE RIGHTEOUS MAN SHALL LIVE BY FAITH." [12]However, the Law is not of faith; on the contrary, "HE WHO PRACTICES THEM SHALL LIVE BY THEM." [13]Christ redeemed us from the curse of the Law, having become a curse for us—for it is written, "CURSED IS EVERYONE WHO HANGS ON A TREE"— [14]in order that in Christ Jesus the blessing of Abraham might come to the Gentiles, so that we would receive the promise of the Spirit through faith.

Intent of the Law

15 Brethren, I speak in terms of human relations: even though it is *only* a man's covenant, yet when it has been ratified, no one sets it aside or adds conditions to it. [16]Now the promises were spoken to Abraham and to his seed. He does not say, "And to seeds," as *referring* to many, but *rather* to one, "And to your seed," that is, Christ. [17]What I am saying is this: the Law, which came four hundred and thirty years later, does not invalidate a covenant previously ratified by God, so as to nullify the promise. [18]For if the inheritance is based on law, it is no longer based on a promise; but God has granted it to Abraham by means of a promise.

19 Why the Law then? It was added because of transgressions, having been ordained through angels by the agency of a mediator, until the seed would come to whom the promise had been made. [20]Now a mediator is not for one *party only;* whereas God is *only* one. [21]Is the Law then contrary to the promises of God? May it never be! For if a law had been given which was able to impart life, then righteousness would indeed have been based on law. [22]But the Scripture has shut up everyone under sin, so that the promise by faith in Jesus Christ might be given to those who believe.

23 But before faith came, we were kept in custody under the law, being shut up to the faith which was later to be revealed. **24**Therefore the Law has become our tutor *to lead us* to Christ, so that we may be justified by faith. **25**But now that faith has come, we are no longer under a tutor. **26**For you are all sons of God through faith in Christ Jesus. **27**For all of you who were baptized into Christ have clothed yourselves with Christ. **28**There is neither Jew nor Greek, there is neither slave nor free man, there is neither male nor female; for you are all one in Christ Jesus. **29**And if you belong to Christ, then you are Abraham's descendants, heirs according to promise.

Sonship in Christ

4 Now I say, as long as the heir is a child, he does not differ at all from a slave although he is owner of everything, **2**but he is under guardians and managers until the date set by the father. **3**So also we, while we were children, were held in bondage under the elemental things of the world. **4**But when the fullness of the time came, God sent forth His Son, born of a woman, born under the Law, **5**so that He might redeem those who were under the Law, that we might receive the adoption as sons. **6**Because you are sons, God has sent forth the Spirit of His Son into our hearts, crying, "Abba! Father!" **7**Therefore you are no longer a slave, but a son; and if a son, then an heir through God.

8 However at that time, when you did not know God, you were slaves to those which by nature are no gods. **9**But now that you have come to know God, or rather to be known by God, how is it that you turn back again to the weak and worthless elemental things, to which you desire to be enslaved all over again? **10**You observe days and months and seasons and years. **11**I fear for you, that perhaps I have labored over you in vain.

12 I beg of you, brethren, become as I *am,* for I also *have become* as you *are.* You have done me no wrong; **13**but you know that it was because of a bodily illness that I preached the gospel to you the first time; **14**and that which was a trial to you in my bodily condition you did not despise or loathe, but you received me as an angel of God, as Christ Jesus *Himself.* **15**Where then is that sense of blessing you had? For I bear you witness that, if possible, you would have plucked out your eyes and given them to me. **16**So have I become your enemy by telling you the truth? **17**They eagerly seek you, not commendably, but they wish to shut you out so that you will seek them. [18]But it is good always to be eagerly sought in a commendable manner, and not only when I am present with you. [19]My children, with whom I am again in labor until Christ is formed in you— [20]but I could wish to be present with you now and to change my tone, for I am perplexed about you.

Bond and Free

21 Tell me, you who want to be under law, do you not listen to the law? [22]For it is written that Abraham had two sons, one by the bondwoman and one by the free woman. [23]But the son by the bondwoman was born according to the flesh, and the son by the free woman through the promise. [24]This is allegorically speaking, for these *women* are two covenants: one *proceeding* from Mount Sinai bearing children who are to be slaves; she is Hagar. [25]Now this Hagar is Mount Sinai in Arabia and corresponds to the present Jerusalem, for she is in slavery with her children. [26]But the Jerusalem above is free; she is our mother. [27]For it is written,

"REJOICE, BARREN WOMAN
    WHO DOES NOT BEAR;
BREAK FORTH AND SHOUT,
    YOU WHO ARE NOT IN
    LABOR;
FOR MORE NUMEROUS ARE
    THE CHILDREN OF THE

DESOLATE
THAN OF THE ONE WHO HAS A
    HUSBAND."

[28]And you brethren, like Isaac, are children of promise. [29]But as at that time he who was born according to the flesh persecuted him *who was born* according to the Spirit, so it is now also. [30]But what does the Scripture say? "CAST OUT THE BONDWOMAN
    AND HER SON,
FOR THE SON OF THE BOND-
    WOMAN SHALL NOT BE AN
    HEIR WITH THE SON OF
    THE FREE WOMAN."

[31]So then, brethren, we are not children of a bondwoman, but of the free woman.

Walk by the Spirit

5 It was for freedom that Christ set us free; therefore keep standing firm and do not be subject again to a yoke of slavery.

2 Behold I, Paul, say to you that if you receive circumcision, Christ will be of no benefit to you. [3]And I testify again to every man who receives circumcision, that he is under obligation to keep the whole Law. [4]You have been severed from Christ, you who are seeking to be justified by law; you have fallen from grace. [5]For we through the Spirit, by faith, are waiting for the hope of righteousness. [6]For in Christ Jesus neither circumcision nor uncircumcision means anything, but faith working through love.

7 You were running well; who hindered you from obeying the truth? [8]This persuasion *did* not *come* from Him who calls you. [9]A little leaven leavens the whole lump *of dough.* [10]I have confidence in you in the Lord that you will adopt no other view; but the one who is disturbing you will bear his judgment, whoever he is. [11]But I, brethren, if I still preach circumcision, why am I still persecuted? Then the stumbling block of the cross has been abolished. [12]I wish that those who are troubling you would even mutilate themselves.

13 For you were called to freedom, brethren; only *do* not *turn* your freedom into an opportunity for the flesh, but through love serve one another. [14]For the whole Law is fulfilled in one word, in the *statement,* "YOU SHALL LOVE YOUR NEIGHBOR AS YOURSELF." [15]But if you bite and devour one another, take care that you are not consumed by one another.

16 But I say, walk by the Spirit, and you will not carry out the desire of the flesh. [17]For the flesh sets its desire against the Spirit, and the Spirit against the flesh; for these are in opposition to one another, so that you may not do the things that you please. [18]But if you are led by the Spirit, you are not under the Law. [19]Now the deeds of the flesh are evident, which are: immorality, impurity, sensuality, [20]idolatry, sorcery, enmities, strife, jealousy, outbursts of anger, disputes, dissensions, factions, [21]envying, drunkenness, carousing, and things like these, of which I forewarn you, just as I have forewarned you, that those who practice such things will not inherit the kingdom of God. [22]But the fruit of the Spirit is love, joy, peace, patience, kindness, goodness, faithfulness, [23]gentleness, self-control; against such things there is no law. [24]Now those who belong to Christ Jesus have crucified the flesh with its passions and desires.

25 If we live by the Spirit, let us also walk by the Spirit. [26]Let us not become boastful, challenging one another, envying one another.

Bear One Another's Burdens

6 Brethren, even if anyone is caught in any trespass, you who are spiritual, restore such a one in a spirit of gentleness; *each one* looking to yourself, so that you too will not be tempted. [2]Bear one another's burdens, and thereby fulfill the law of Christ. [3]For if anyone thinks he is something when he is nothing, he deceives himself. [4]But each one must examine his own work, and then he will have *reason for* boasting in regard to himself alone, and not in regard to another. [5]For each one will bear his own load.

6 The one who is taught the word is to share all good things with the one who teaches *him*. [7]Do not be deceived, God is not mocked; for whatever a man sows, this he will also reap. [8]For the one who sows to his own flesh will from the flesh reap corruption, but the one who sows to the Spirit will from the Spirit reap eternal life. [9]Let us not lose heart in doing good, for in due time we will reap if we do not grow weary. [10]So then, while we have opportunity, let us do good to all people, and especially to those who are of the household of the faith.

11 See with what large letters I am writing to you with my own hand.

[12]Those who desire to make a good showing in the flesh try to compel you to be circumcised, simply so that they will not be persecuted for the cross of Christ. [13]For those who [a]are circumcised do not even keep the Law themselves, but they desire to have you circumcised so that they may boast in your flesh. [14]But may it never be that I would boast, except in the cross of our Lord Jesus Christ, through which the world has been crucified to me, and I to the world. [15]For neither is circumcision anything, nor uncircumcision, but a new creation. [16]And those who will walk by this rule, peace and mercy *be* upon them, and upon the Israel of God.

17 From now on let no one cause trouble for me, for I bear on my body the brand-marks of Jesus.

18 The grace of our Lord Jesus Christ be with your spirit, brethren. Amen.

EPHESIANS

The Blessings of Redemption

1 Paul, an apostle of Christ Jesus by the will of God, To the saints who are at [b]Ephesus and *who are* faithful in Christ Jesus; [2]Grace to you and peace from God our Father and the Lord Jesus Christ.

[a]**6:13** Two early mss read *have been;* [b]**1:1** Three early mss do not contain *at Ephesus*

3 Blessed *be* the God and Father of our Lord Jesus Christ, who has blessed us with every spiritual blessing in the heavenly *places* in Christ, [4]just as He chose us in Him before the foundation of the world, that we would be holy and blameless before [a]Him. In love [5]He predestined us to adoption as sons through Jesus Christ to Himself, according to the kind intention of His will, [6]to the praise of the glory of His grace, which He freely bestowed on us in the Beloved. [7]In Him we have redemption through His blood, the forgiveness of our trespasses, according to the riches of His grace [8]which He lavished on us. In all wisdom and insight [9]He made known to us the mystery of His will, according to His kind intention which He purposed in Him [10]with a view to an administration suitable to the fullness of the times, *that is,* the summing up of all things in Christ, things in the heavens and things on the earth. In Him [11]also we have obtained an inheritance, having been predestined according to His purpose who works all things after the counsel of His will, [12]to the end that we who were the first to hope in [b]Christ would be to the praise of His glory. [13]In Him, you also, after listening to the message of truth, the gospel of your salvation—having also believed, you were sealed in Him with the Holy Spirit of promise, [14]who is given as a pledge of our inheritance, with a view to the redemption of *God's own* possession, to the praise of His glory.

15 For this reason I too, having heard of the faith in the Lord Jesus which *exists* among you and [c]your love for all the saints, [16]do not cease giving thanks for you, while making mention *of you* in my prayers; [17]that the God of our Lord Jesus Christ, the Father of glory, may give to you a spirit of wisdom and of revelation in the knowledge of Him. [18]*I pray that* the eyes of your heart may be enlightened, so that you will know what is the hope of His calling, what are the riches of the glory of His inheritance in the saints, [19]and what is the surpassing greatness of His power toward us who believe. *These are* in accordance with the working of the strength of His might [20]which He brought about in Christ, when He raised Him from the dead and seated Him at His right hand in the heavenly *places,* [21]far above all rule and authority and power and dominion, and every name that is named, not only in this age but also in the one to come. [22]And He put all things in subjection under His feet, and gave Him as head over all things to the church, [23]which is His body, the fullness of Him who fills all in all.

[a]**1:4** Or *Him, in love;* [b]**1:12** the Messiah; [c]**1:15** Three early mss do not contain *your love*

Made Alive in Christ

2 And you were dead in your trespasses and sins, [2]in which you formerly walked according to the course of this world, according to the prince of the power of the air, of the spirit that is now working in the sons of disobedience. [3]Among them we too all formerly lived in the lusts of our flesh, indulging the desires of the flesh and of the mind, and were by nature children of wrath, even as the rest. [4]But God, being rich in mercy, because of His great love with which He loved us, [5]even when we were dead in our transgressions, made us alive together *with Christ (by grace you have been saved), [6]and raised us up with Him, and seated us with Him in the heavenly *places* in Christ Jesus, [7]so that in the ages to come He might show the surpassing riches of His grace in kindness toward us in Christ Jesus. [8]For by grace you have been saved through faith; and that not of yourselves, *it is* the gift of God; [9]not as a result of works, so that no one may boast. [10]For we are His workmanship, created in Christ Jesus for good works, which God prepared beforehand so that we would walk in them.

[11] Therefore remember that formerly you, the Gentiles in the flesh, who are called "Uncircumcision" by the so-called "Circumcision," *which is* performed in the flesh by human hands— [12]*remember* that you were at that time separate from Christ, excluded from the commonwealth of Israel, and strangers to the covenants of promise, having no hope and without God in the world. [13]But now in Christ Jesus you who formerly were far off have been brought near by the blood of Christ. [14]For He Himself is our peace, who made both *groups into* one and broke down the barrier of the dividing wall, [15]by abolishing in His flesh the enmity, *which is* the Law of commandments *contained* in ordinances, so that in Himself He might make the two into one new man, *thus* establishing peace, [16]and might reconcile them both in one body to God through the cross, by it having put to death the enmity. [17]AND HE CAME AND PREACHED PEACE TO YOU WHO WERE FAR AWAY, AND PEACE TO THOSE WHO WERE NEAR; [18]for through Him we both have our access in one Spirit to the Father. [19]So then you are no longer strangers and aliens, but you are fellow citizens with the saints, and are of God's household, [20]having been built on the foundation of the apostles and prophets, Christ Jesus Himself being the corner *stone,* [21]in whom the whole building, being fitted together, is growing into a holy temple in the

*2:5 Two early mss read *in Christ*

Lord, [22]in whom you also are being built together into a dwelling of God in the Spirit.

Paul's Stewardship

3 For this reason I, Paul, the prisoner of Christ Jesus for the sake of you Gentiles— [2]if indeed you have heard of the stewardship of God's grace which was given to me for you; [3]that by revelation there was made known to me the mystery, as I wrote before in brief. [4]By referring to this, when you read you can understand my insight into the mystery of Christ, [5]which in other generations was not made known to the sons of men, as it has now been revealed to His holy apostles and prophets in the Spirit; [6]*to be specific,* that the Gentiles are fellow heirs and fellow members of the body, and fellow partakers of the promise in Christ Jesus through the gospel, [7]of which I was made a minister, according to the gift of God's grace which was given to me according to the working of His power. [8]To me, the very least of all saints, this grace was given, to preach to the Gentiles the unfathomable riches of Christ, [9]and to bring to light what is the administration of the mystery which for ages has been hidden in God who created all things; [10]so that the manifold wisdom of God might now be made known through the church to the rulers and the authorities in the heavenly *places.* [11]*This was* in accordance with the eternal purpose which He carried out in Christ Jesus our Lord, [12]in whom we have boldness and confident access through faith in Him. [13]Therefore I ask you not to lose heart at my tribulations on your behalf, for they are your glory.

14 For this reason I bow my knees before the Father, [15]from whom every family in heaven and on earth derives its name, [16]that He would grant you, according to the riches of His glory, to be strengthened with power through His Spirit in the inner man, [17]so that Christ may dwell in your hearts through faith; *and* that you, being rooted and grounded in love, [18]may be able to comprehend with all the saints what is the breadth and length and height and depth, [19]and to know the love of Christ which surpasses knowledge, that you may be filled up to all the fullness of God.

20 Now to Him who is able to do far more abundantly beyond all that we ask or think, according to the power that works within us, [21]to Him *be* the glory in the church and in Christ Jesus to all generations forever and ever. Amen.

4

Unity of the Spirit

4 Therefore I, the prisoner of the Lord, implore you to walk in a manner worthy of the calling with which you have been called, [2]with all humility and gentleness, with patience, showing tolerance for one another in love, [3]being diligent to preserve the unity of the Spirit in the bond of peace. [4]*There is* one body and one Spirit, just as also you were called in one hope of your calling; [5]one Lord, one faith, one baptism, [6]one God and Father of all who is over all and through all and in all.

[7] But to each one of us grace was given according to the measure of Christ's gift. [8]Therefore it says,

"WHEN HE ASCENDED ON HIGH,

HE LED CAPTIVE A HOST OF CAPTIVES,

AND HE GAVE GIFTS TO MEN."

[9](Now this *expression,* "He ascended," what does it mean except that He also had descended into the lower parts of the earth? [10]He who descended is Himself also He who ascended far above all the heavens, so that He might fill all things.) [11]And He gave some *as* apostles, and some *as* prophets, and some *as* evangelists, and some *as* pastors and teachers, [12]for the equipping of the saints for the work of service, to the building up of the body of Christ; [13]until we all attain to the unity of the faith, and of the knowledge of the Son of God, to a mature man, to the measure of the stature which belongs to the fullness of Christ. [14]As a result, we are no longer to be children, tossed here and there by waves and carried about by every wind of doctrine, by the trickery of men, by craftiness in deceitful scheming; [15]but speaking the truth in love, we are to grow up in all *aspects* into Him who is the head, *even* Christ, [16]from whom the whole body, being fitted and held together by what every joint supplies, according to the proper working of each individual part, causes the growth of the body for the building up of itself in love.

The Christian's Walk

[17] So this I say, and affirm together with the Lord, that you walk no longer just as the Gentiles also walk, in the futility of their mind, [18]being darkened in their understanding, excluded from the life of God because of the ignorance that is in them, because of the hardness of their heart; [19]and they, having become callous, have given themselves over to sensuality for the practice of every kind of impurity with greediness. [20]But you did not learn Christ in this way, [21]if indeed you have heard Him and have been taught in Him, just as truth is in Jesus, [22]that, in reference to

your former manner of life, you lay aside the old self, which is being corrupted in accordance with the lusts of deceit, [23]and that you be renewed in the spirit of your mind, [24]and put on the new self, which in *the likeness of* God has been created in righteousness and holiness of the truth.

25 Therefore, laying aside falsehood, SPEAK TRUTH EACH ONE *of you* WITH HIS NEIGHBOR, for we are members of one another. [26]BE ANGRY, AND *yet* DO NOT SIN; do not let the sun go down on your anger, [27]and do not give the devil an opportunity. [28]He who steals must steal no longer; but rather he must labor, performing with his own hands what is good, so that he will have *something* to share with one who has need. [29]Let no unwholesome word proceed from your mouth, but only such *a word* as is good for edification according to the need *of the moment,* so that it will give grace to those who hear. [30]Do not grieve the Holy Spirit of God, by whom you were sealed for the day of redemption. [31]Let all bitterness and wrath and anger and clamor and slander be put away from you, along with all malice. [32]Be kind to one another, tender-hearted, forgiving each other, just as God in Christ also has forgiven [a]you.

Be Imitators of God

5 Therefore be imitators of God, as beloved children; [2]and walk in love, just as Christ also loved [b]you and gave Himself up for us, an offering and a sacrifice to God as a fragrant aroma.

3 But immorality or any impurity or greed must not even be named among you, as is proper among saints; [4]and *there must be no* filthiness and silly talk, or coarse jesting, which are not fitting, but rather giving of thanks. [5]For this you know with certainty, that no immoral or impure person or covetous man, who is an idolater, has an inheritance in the kingdom of Christ and God.

6 Let no one deceive you with empty words, for because of these things the wrath of God comes upon the sons of disobedience. [7]Therefore do not be partakers with them; [8]for you were formerly darkness, but now you are Light in the Lord; walk as children of Light [9](for the fruit of the Light *consists* in all goodness and righteousness and truth), [10]trying to learn what is pleasing to the Lord. [11]Do not participate in the unfruitful deeds of darkness, but instead even expose them; [12]for it is disgraceful even to speak of the things which are done by them in secret. [13]But all things become visible when

---

[a]**4:32** Two early mss read *us;* [b]**5:2** One early ms reads *us*

they are exposed by the light, for everything that becomes visible is light. [14]For this reason it says,

"Awake, sleeper,
And arise from the dead,
And Christ will shine on you."

15 Therefore be careful how you walk, not as unwise men but as wise, [16]making the most of your time, because the days are evil. [17]So then do not be foolish, but understand what the will of the Lord is. [18]And do not get drunk with wine, for that is dissipation, but be filled with the Spirit, [19]speaking to one another in psalms and hymns and spiritual songs, singing and making melody with your heart to the Lord; [20]always giving thanks for all things in the name of our Lord Jesus Christ to God, even the Father; [21]and be subject to one another in the fear of Christ.

Marriage Like Christ and the Church

22 Wives, *be subject* to your own husbands, as to the Lord. [23]For the husband is the head of the wife, as Christ also is the head of the church, He Himself *being* the Savior of the body. [24]But as the church is subject to Christ, so also the wives *ought to be* to their husbands in everything.

25 Husbands, love your wives, just as Christ also loved the church and gave Himself up for her, [26]so that He might sanctify her, having cleansed her by the washing of water with the word, [27]that He might present to Himself the church in all her glory, having no spot or wrinkle or any such thing; but that she would be holy and blameless. [28]So husbands ought also to love their own wives as their own bodies. He who loves his own wife loves himself; [29]for no one ever hated his own flesh, but nourishes and cherishes it, just as Christ also *does* the church, [30]because we are members of His body. [31]FOR THIS REASON A MAN SHALL LEAVE HIS FATHER AND MOTHER AND SHALL BE JOINED TO HIS WIFE, AND THE TWO SHALL BECOME ONE FLESH. [32]This mystery is great; but I am speaking with reference to Christ and the church. [33]Nevertheless, each individual among you also is to love his own wife even as himself, and the wife must *see to it* that she respects her husband.

Family Relationships

6 Children, obey your parents in the Lord, for this is right. [2]HONOR YOUR FATHER AND MOTHER (which is the first commandment with a promise), [3]SO THAT IT MAY BE WELL WITH YOU, AND THAT YOU MAY LIVE LONG ON THE EARTH.

4 Fathers, do not provoke your

children to anger, but bring them up in the discipline and instruction of the Lord.

5 Slaves, be obedient to those who are your masters according to the flesh, with fear and trembling, in the sincerity of your heart, as to Christ; [6]not by way of eyeservice, as men-pleasers, but as slaves of Christ, doing the will of God from the heart. [7]With good will render service, as to the Lord, and not to men, [8]knowing that whatever good thing each one does, this he will receive back from the Lord, whether slave or free.

9 And masters, do the same things to them, and give up threatening, knowing that both their Master and yours is in heaven, and there is no partiality with Him.

The Armor of God

10 Finally, be strong in the Lord and in the strength of His might. [11]Put on the full armor of God, so that you will be able to stand firm against the schemes of the devil. [12]For our struggle is not against flesh and blood, but against the rulers, against the powers, against the world forces of this darkness, against the spiritual *forces* of wickedness in the heavenly *places*. [13]Therefore, take up the full armor of God, so that you will be able to resist in the evil day, and

having done everything, to stand firm. [14]Stand firm therefore, HAVING GIRDED YOUR LOINS WITH TRUTH, and HAVING PUT ON THE BREASTPLATE OF RIGHTEOUSNESS, [15]and having shod YOUR FEET WITH THE PREPARATION OF THE GOSPEL OF PEACE; [16]in addition to all, taking up the shield of faith with which you will be able to extinguish all the flaming arrows of the evil *one*. [17]And take THE HELMET OF SALVATION, and the sword of the Spirit, which is the word of God.

18 With all prayer and petition pray at all times in the Spirit, and with this in view, be on the alert with all perseverance and petition for all the saints, [19]and *pray* on my behalf, that utterance may be given to me in the opening of my mouth, to make known with boldness the mystery of the gospel, [20]for which I am an ambassador in chains; that [b]in *proclaiming* it I may speak boldly, as I ought to speak.

21 But that you also may know about my circumstances, how I am doing, Tychicus, the beloved brother and faithful minister in the Lord, will make everything known to you. [22]I have sent him to you for this very purpose, so that you may know about us, and that he may comfort your hearts.

6:20 Two early mss read *I may speak it boldly*

23 Peace be to the brethren, and love with faith, from God the Father and the Lord Jesus Christ. [24]Grace be with all those who love our Lord Jesus Christ with incorruptible *love*.

PHILIPPIANS

Thanksgiving

1 Paul and Timothy, bond-servants of Christ Jesus,

To all the saints in Christ Jesus who are in Philippi, including the overseers and deacons: [2]Grace to you and peace from God our Father and the Lord Jesus Christ.

3 I thank my God in all my remembrance of you, [4]always offering prayer with joy in my every prayer for you all, [5]in view of your participation in the gospel from the first day until now. [6]*For I am* confident of this very thing, that He who began a good work in you will perfect it until the day of Christ Jesus. [7]For it is only right for me to feel this way about you all, because I have you in my heart, since both in my imprisonment and in the defense and confirmation of the gospel, you all are

partakers of grace with me. [8]For God is my witness, how I long for you all with the affection of Christ Jesus. [9]And this I pray, that your love may abound still more and more in real knowledge and all discernment, [10]so that you may approve the things that are excellent, in order to be sincere and blameless until the day of Christ; [11]having been filled with the fruit of righteousness which *comes* through Jesus Christ, to the glory and praise of God.

The Gospel Is Preached

12 Now I want you to know, brethren, that my circumstances have turned out for the greater progress of the gospel, [13]so that my imprisonment in *the cause of* Christ has become well known throughout the whole [a]praetorian guard and to everyone else, [14]and that most of the brethren, trusting in

[a]**1:13** Or *governor's palace*

the Lord because of my imprisonment, have far more courage to speak the word of God without fear. ¹⁵Some, to be sure, are preaching Christ even from envy and strife, but some also from good will; ¹⁶the latter *do it* out of love, knowing that I am appointed for the defense of the gospel; ¹⁷the former proclaim Christ out of selfish ambition rather than from pure motives, thinking to cause me distress in my imprisonment. ¹⁸What then? Only that in every way, whether in pretense or in truth, Christ is proclaimed; and in this I rejoice.

Yes, and I will rejoice, ¹⁹for I know that this will turn out for my deliverance through your prayers and the provision of the Spirit of Jesus Christ, ²⁰according to my earnest expectation and hope, that I will not be put to shame in anything, but *that* with all boldness, Christ will even now, as always, be exalted in my body, whether by life or by death.

To Live Is Christ

²¹For to me, to live is Christ and to die is gain. ²²But if I *am* to live *on* in the flesh, this *will mean* fruitful labor for me; and I do not know which to choose. ²³But I am hard-pressed from both *directions,* having the desire to depart and be with Christ, for *that* is very much

better; ²⁴yet to remain on in the flesh is more necessary for your sake. ²⁵Convinced of this, I know that I will remain and continue with you all for your progress and joy in the faith, ²⁶so that your proud confidence in me may abound in Christ Jesus through my coming to you again.

27 Only conduct yourselves in a manner worthy of the gospel of Christ, so that whether I come and see you or remain absent, I will hear of you that you are standing firm in one spirit, with one mind striving together for the faith of the gospel; ²⁸in no way alarmed by *your* opponents—which is a sign of destruction for them, but of salvation for you, and that *too,* from God. ²⁹For to you it has been granted for Christ's sake, not only to believe in Him, but also to suffer for His sake, ³⁰experiencing the same conflict which you saw in me, and now hear *to be* in me.

Be Like Christ

2 Therefore if there is any encouragement in Christ, if there is any consolation of love, if there is any fellowship of the Spirit, if any affection and compassion, ²make my joy complete by being of the same mind, maintaining the same love, united in spirit, intent on one purpose. ³Do nothing from selfishness or empty conceit,

but with humility of mind regard one another as more important than yourselves; [4]do not *merely* look out for your own personal interests, but also for the interests of others. [5]Have this attitude in yourselves which was also in Christ Jesus, [6]who, although He existed in the form of God, did not regard equality with God a thing to be grasped, [7]but [a]emptied Himself, taking the form of a bond-servant, *and* being made in the likeness of men. [8]Being found in appearance as a man, He humbled Himself by becoming obedient to the point of death, even death on a cross. [9]For this reason also, God highly exalted Him, and bestowed on Him the name which is above every name, [10]so that at the name of Jesus EVERY KNEE WILL BOW, of those who are in heaven and on earth and under the earth, [11]and that every tongue will confess that Jesus Christ is Lord, to the glory of God the Father.

[12] So then, my beloved, just as you have always obeyed, not as in my presence only, but now much more in my absence, work out your salvation with fear and trembling; [13]for it is God who is at work in you, both to will and to work for *His* good pleasure.

[14] Do all things without grumbling or disputing; [15]so that you

will prove yourselves to be blameless and innocent, children of God above reproach in the midst of a crooked and perverse generation, among whom you appear as lights in the world, [16]holding fast the word of life, so that in the day of Christ I will have reason to glory because I did not run in vain nor toil in vain. [17]But even if I am being poured out as a drink offering upon the sacrifice and service of your faith, I rejoice and share my joy with you all. [18]You too, *I urge you,* rejoice in the same way and share your joy with me.

Timothy and Epaphroditus

[19] But I hope in the Lord Jesus to send Timothy to you shortly, so that I also may be encouraged when I learn of your condition. [20]For I have no one *else* of kindred spirit who will genuinely be concerned for your welfare. [21]For they all seek after their own interests, not those of Christ Jesus. [22]But you know of his proven worth, that he served with me in the furtherance of the gospel like a child *serving* his father. [23]Therefore I hope to send him immediately, as soon as I see how things *go* with me; [24]and I trust in the Lord that I myself also will be coming shortly. [25]But I thought it necessary to send to you Epaphroditus, my brother and fellow worker and fellow soldier, who is also your messenger and minister

[a]**2:7** I.e. laid aside His privileges

to my need; [26]because he was long-ing *for you all and was distressed because you had heard that he was sick. [27]For indeed he was sick to the point of death, but God had mercy on him, and not on him only but also on me, so that I would not have sorrow upon sorrow. [28]Therefore I have sent him all the more eagerly so that when you see him again you may rejoice and I may be less concerned *about you.* [29]Receive him then in the Lord with all joy, and hold men like him in high regard; [30]because he came close to death for the work of Christ, risking his life to complete what was deficient in your service to me.

The Goal of Life

3 Finally, my brethren, rejoice in the Lord. To write the same things *again* is no trouble to me, and it is a safeguard for you.

2 Beware of the dogs, beware of the evil workers, beware of the false circumcision; [3]for we are the *true* circumcision, who worship in the Spirit of God and glory in Christ Jesus and put no confidence in the flesh, [4]although I myself might have confidence even in the flesh. If anyone else has a mind to put confidence in the flesh, I far more: [5]circumcised the eighth day, of the nation of Israel, of the tribe of Benjamin, a Hebrew of Hebrews; as to the Law, a Pharisee; [6]as to

zeal, a persecutor of the church; as to the righteousness which is in the Law, found blameless.

7 But whatever things were gain to me, those things I have counted as loss for the sake of Christ. [8]More than that, I count all things to be loss in view of the surpassing value of knowing Christ Jesus my Lord, for whom I have suffered the loss of all things, and count them but rubbish so that I may gain Christ, [9]and may be found in Him, not having a righteousness of my own derived from *the* Law, but that which is through faith in Christ, the righteousness which *comes* from God on the basis of faith, [10]that I may know Him and the power of His resurrection and the fellowship of His sufferings, being conformed to His death; [11]in order that I may attain to the resurrection from the dead.

12 Not that I have already obtained *it* or have already become perfect, but I press on so that I may lay hold of that for which also I was laid hold of by Christ Jesus. [13]Brethren, I do not regard myself as having laid hold of *it* yet; but one thing *I do:* forgetting what *lies* behind and reaching forward to what *lies* ahead, [14]I press on toward the goal for the prize of the upward call of God in Christ Jesus. [15]Let us therefore, as many as are

---

*2:26 One early ms reads *to see you all*

perfect, have this attitude; and if in anything you have a different attitude, God will reveal that also to you; [16]however, let us keep living by that same *standard* to which we have attained.

17 Brethren, join in following my example, and observe those who walk according to the pattern you have in us. [18]For many walk, of whom I often told you, and now tell you even weeping, *that they are* enemies of the cross of Christ, [19]whose end is destruction, whose god is *their* appetite, and *whose* glory is in their shame, who set their minds on earthly things. [20]For our citizenship is in heaven, from which also we eagerly wait for a Savior, the Lord Jesus Christ; [21]who will transform the body of our humble state into conformity with the body of His glory, by the exertion of the power that He has even to subject all things to Himself.

Think of Excellence

4 Therefore, my beloved brethren whom I long *to see,* my joy and crown, in this way stand firm in the Lord, my beloved.

2 I urge Euodia and I urge Syntyche to live in harmony in the Lord. [3]Indeed, true companion, I ask you also to help these women who have shared my struggle in *the cause of* the gospel, together with Clement also and the rest of my fellow workers, whose names are in the book of life.

4 Rejoice in the Lord always; again I will say, rejoice! [5]Let your gentle *spirit* be known to all men. The Lord is near. [6]Be anxious for nothing, but in everything by prayer and supplication with thanksgiving let your requests be made known to God. [7]And the peace of God, which surpasses all comprehension, will guard your hearts and your minds in Christ Jesus.

8 Finally, brethren, whatever is true, whatever is honorable, whatever is right, whatever is pure, whatever is lovely, whatever is of good repute, if there is any excellence and if anything worthy of praise, dwell on these things. [9]The things you have learned and received and heard and seen in me, practice these things, and the God of peace will be with you.

God's Provisions

10 But I rejoiced in the Lord greatly, that now at last you have revived your concern for me; indeed, you were concerned *before,* but you lacked opportunity. [11]Not that I speak from want, for I have learned to be content in whatever circumstances I am. [12]I know how to get along with humble

means, and I also know how to live in prosperity; in any and every circumstance I have learned the secret of being filled and going hungry, both of having abundance and suffering need. [13]I can do all things through Him who strengthens me. [14]Nevertheless, you have done well to share *with me* in my affliction.

15 You yourselves also know, Philippians, that at the first preaching of the gospel, after I left Macedonia, no church shared with me in the matter of giving and receiving but you alone; [16]for even in Thessalonica you sent *a gift* more than once for my needs. [17]Not that I seek the gift itself, but I seek for the profit which increases to your account. [18]But I have received everything in full and have an abundance; I am amply supplied, having received from Epaphroditus what you have sent, a fragrant aroma, an acceptable sacrifice, well-pleasing to God. [19]And my God will supply all your needs according to His riches in glory in Christ Jesus. [20]Now to our God and Father *be* the glory forever and ever. Amen.

21 Greet every saint in Christ Jesus. The brethren who are with me greet you. [22]All the saints greet you, especially those of Caesar's household.
23 The grace of the Lord Jesus Christ be with your spirit.

COLOSSIANS

Thankfulness for Spiritual Attainments

1 Paul, an apostle of Jesus Christ by the will of God, and Timothy our brother,

2 To the saints and faithful brethren in Christ *who are* at Colossae: Grace to you and peace from God our Father.

3 We give thanks to God, the Father of our Lord Jesus Christ, praying always for you, [4]since we heard of your faith in Christ Jesus and the love which you have for all the saints; [5]because of the hope laid up for you in heaven, of which you previously heard in the word of truth, the gospel [6]which has come to you, just as in all the world also it is constantly bearing

fruit and increasing, even as *it has been doing* in you also since the day you heard *of it* and understood the grace of God in truth; [7]just as you learned *it* from Epaphras, our beloved fellow bond-servant, who is a faithful servant of Christ on our behalf, [8]and he also informed us of your love in the Spirit.

9 For this reason also, since the day we heard *of it*, we have not ceased to pray for you and to ask that you may be filled with the knowledge of His will in all spiritual wisdom and understanding, [10]so that you will walk in a manner worthy of the Lord, to please *Him* in all respects, bearing fruit in every good work and increasing in the knowledge of God; [11]strengthened with all power, according to His glorious might, for the attaining of all steadfastness and patience; joyously [12]giving thanks to the Father, who has qualified us to share in the inheritance of the saints in Light.

The Incomparable Christ

[13]For He rescued us from the domain of darkness, and transferred us to the kingdom of His beloved Son, [14]in whom we have redemption, the forgiveness of sins.

15 He is the image of the invisible God, the firstborn of all creation. [16]For by Him all things were created, *both* in the heavens and on earth, visible and invisible, whether thrones or dominions or rulers or authorities—all things have been created through Him and for Him. [17]He is before all things, and in Him all things hold together. [18]He is also head of the body, the church; and He is the beginning, the firstborn from the dead, so that He Himself will come to have first place in everything. [19]For it was the *Father's* good pleasure for all the fullness to dwell in Him, [20]and through Him to reconcile all things to Himself, having made peace through the blood of His cross; through Him, *I say,* whether things on earth or things in heaven.

21 And although you were formerly alienated and hostile in mind, *engaged* in evil deeds, [22]yet He has now reconciled you in His fleshly body through death, in order to present you before Him holy and blameless and beyond reproach— [23]if indeed you continue in the faith firmly established and steadfast, and not moved away from the hope of the gospel that you have heard, which was proclaimed in all creation under heaven, and of which I, Paul, was made a minister.

24 Now I rejoice in my sufferings for your sake, and in my flesh I do

my share on behalf of His body, which is the church, in filling up what is lacking in Christ's afflictions. [25]Of *this church* I was made a minister according to the stewardship from God bestowed on me for your benefit, so that I might fully carry out the *preaching of* the word of God, [26]*that is,* the mystery which has been hidden from the *past* ages and generations, but has now been manifested to His saints, [27]to whom God willed to make known what is the riches of the glory of this mystery among the Gentiles, which is Christ in you, the hope of glory. [28]We proclaim Him, admonishing every man and teaching every man with all wisdom, so that we may present every man complete in Christ. [29]For this purpose also I labor, striving according to His power, which mightily works within me.

You Are Built Up in Christ

2 For I want you to know how great a struggle I have on your behalf and for those who are at Laodicea, and for all those who have not personally seen my face, [2]that their hearts may be encouraged, having been knit together in love, and *attaining* to all the wealth that comes from the full assurance of understanding, *resulting* in a true knowledge of God's mystery, *that is,* Christ *Himself*, [3]in whom are hidden all the treasures of wisdom

and knowledge. [4]I say this so that no one will delude you with persuasive argument. [5]For even though I am absent in body, nevertheless I am with you in spirit, rejoicing to see your good discipline and the stability of your faith in Christ.

6 Therefore as you have received Christ Jesus the Lord, *so* walk in Him, [7]having been firmly rooted *and now* being built up in Him and established [a]in your faith, just as you were instructed, *and* overflowing with gratitude.

8 See to it that no one takes you captive through philosophy and empty deception, according to the tradition of men, according to the elementary principles of the world, rather than according to Christ. [9]For in Him all the fullness of Deity dwells in bodily form, [10]and in Him you have been made complete, and He is the head over all rule and authority; [11]and in Him you were also circumcised with a circumcision made without hands, in the removal of the body of the flesh by the circumcision of Christ; [12]having been buried with Him in baptism, in which you were also raised up with Him through faith in the working of God, who raised Him from the dead. [13]When you were dead in your transgressions

[a]**2:7** Or by

and the uncircumcision of your flesh, He made you alive together with Him, having forgiven us all our transgressions, [14]having canceled out the certificate of debt consisting of decrees against us, which was hostile to us; and He has taken it out of the way, having nailed it to the cross. [15]When He had disarmed the rulers and authorities, He made a public display of them, having triumphed over them through Him.

[16] Therefore no one is to act as your judge in regard to food or drink or in respect to a festival or a new moon or a Sabbath day— [17]things which are a *mere* shadow of what is to come; but the substance belongs to Christ. [18]Let no one keep defrauding you of your prize by delighting in self-abasement and the worship of the angels, taking his stand on *visions* he has seen, inflated without cause by his fleshly mind, [19]and not holding fast to the head, from whom the entire body, being supplied and held together by the joints and ligaments, grows with a growth which is from God.

[20] If you have died with Christ to the elementary principles of the world, why, as if you were living in the world, do you submit yourself to decrees, such as, [21]"Do not handle, do not taste, do not touch!"

[22](which all *refer to* things destined to perish with use)—in accordance with the commandments and teachings of men? [23]These are matters which have, to be sure, the appearance of wisdom in self-made religion and self-abasement and severe treatment of the body, *but are* of no value against fleshly indulgence.

Put On the New Self

3 Therefore if you have been raised up with Christ, keep seeking the things above, where Christ is, seated at the right hand of God. [2]Set your mind on the things above, not on the things that are on earth. [3]For you have died and your life is hidden with Christ in God. [4]When Christ, who is our life, is revealed, then you also will be revealed with Him in glory.

[5] Therefore consider the members of your earthly body as dead to immorality, impurity, passion, evil desire, and greed, which amounts to idolatry. [6]For it is because of these things that the wrath of God will come [b]upon the sons of disobedience, [7]and in them you also once walked, when you were living in them. [8]But now you also, put them all aside: anger, wrath, malice, slander, *and* abusive speech from your mouth. [9]Do not lie to one another, since you laid aside the old self with its *evil* practices,

[a]**3:6** Two early mss do not contain *upon the sons of disobedience*

[10]and have put on the new self who is being renewed to a true knowledge according to the image of the One who created him— [11]*a renewal* in which there is no *distinction between* Greek and Jew, circumcised and uncircumcised, [a]barbarian, Scythian, slave and freeman, but Christ is all, and in all.

[12] So, as those who have been chosen of God, holy and beloved, put on a heart of compassion, kindness, humility, gentleness and patience; [13]bearing with one another, and forgiving each other, whoever has a complaint against anyone; just as the Lord forgave you, so also should you. [14]Beyond all these things *put on* love, which is the perfect bond of unity. [15]Let the peace of Christ rule in your hearts, to which indeed you were called in one body; and be thankful. [16]Let the word of [b]Christ richly dwell within you, with all wisdom teaching and admonishing one another with psalms *and* hymns *and* spiritual songs, singing with thankfulness in your hearts to God. [17]Whatever you do in word or deed, *do* all in the name of the Lord Jesus, giving thanks through Him to God the Father.

Family Relations

[18] Wives, be subject to your husbands, as is fitting in the Lord. [19]Husbands, love your wives and do not be embittered against them. [20]Children, be obedient to your parents in all things, for this is well-pleasing to the Lord. [21]Fathers, do not exasperate your children, so that they will not lose heart.

[22] Slaves, in all things obey those who are your masters on earth, not with external service, as those who *merely* please men, but with sincerity of heart, fearing the Lord. [23]Whatever you do, do your work heartily, as for the Lord rather than for men, [24]knowing that from the Lord you will receive the reward of the inheritance. It is the Lord Christ whom you serve. [25]For he who does wrong will receive the consequences of the wrong which he has done, and that without partiality.

Fellow Workers

4 Masters, grant to your slaves justice and fairness, knowing that you too have a Master in heaven.

[2] Devote yourselves to prayer, keeping alert in it with *an attitude of* thanksgiving; [3]praying at the same time for us as well, that God will open up to us a door for the word, so that we may speak forth the mystery of Christ, for which I have also been imprisoned; [4]that I may make it clear in the way I ought to speak.

---

[a]**3:11** I.e. those who were not Greeks, either by birth or by culture; [b]**3:16** One early ms reads *the Lord*

5 Conduct yourselves with wisdom toward outsiders, making the most of the opportunity. ⁶Let your speech always be with grace, *as though* seasoned with salt, so that you will know how you should respond to each person.

7 As to all my affairs, Tychicus, *our* beloved brother and faithful servant and fellow bond-servant in the Lord, will bring you information. ⁸*For* I have sent him to you for this very purpose, that you may know about our circumstances and that he may encourage your hearts; ⁹and with him Onesimus, *our* faithful and beloved brother, who is one of your *number.* They will inform you about the whole situation here.

10 Aristarchus, my fellow prisoner, sends you his greetings; and *also* Barnabas's cousin Mark (about whom you received instructions; if he comes to you, welcome him); ¹¹and *also* Jesus who is called Justus; these are the only fellow workers for the kingdom of God who are from the circumcision, and they have proved to be an encouragement to me. ¹²Epaphras, who is one of your number, a bondslave of Jesus Christ, sends you his greetings, always laboring earnestly for you in his prayers, that you may stand perfect and fully assured in all the will of God. ¹³For I testify for him that he has a deep concern for you and for those who are in Laodicea and Hierapolis. ¹⁴Luke, the beloved physician, sends you his greetings, and *also* Demas. ¹⁵Greet the brethren who are in Laodicea and also ªNympha and the church that is in her house. ¹⁶When this letter is read among you, have it also read in the church of the Laodiceans; and you, for your part read my letter *that is coming* from Laodicea. ¹⁷Say to Archippus, "Take heed to the ministry which you have received in the Lord, that you may fulfill it."

18 I, Paul, write this greeting with my own hand. Remember my imprisonment. Grace be with you.

ª**4:15** Or *Nymphas* (masc)

1 THESSALONIANS

Thanksgiving for These Believers

1 Paul and Silvanus and Timothy,
To the church of the Thessalonians in God the Father and the Lord Jesus Christ: Grace to you and peace.

2 We give thanks to God always for all of you, making mention *of you* in our prayers; [3]constantly bearing in mind your work of faith and labor of love and steadfastness of hope in our Lord Jesus Christ in the presence of our God and Father, [4]knowing, brethren beloved by God, *His* choice of you; [5]for our gospel did not come to you in word only, but also in power and in the Holy Spirit and with full conviction; just as you know what kind of men we proved to be among you for your sake. [6]You also became imitators of us and of the Lord, having received the word in much tribulation with the joy of the Holy Spirit, [7]so that you became an example to all the believers in Macedonia and in Achaia. [8]For the word of the Lord has sounded forth from you, not only in Macedonia and Achaia, but also in every place your faith toward God has gone forth, so that we have no need to say anything.

[9]For they themselves report about us what kind of a reception we had with you, and how you turned to God from idols to serve a living and true God, [10]and to wait for His Son from heaven, whom He raised from the dead, *that is* Jesus, who rescues us from the wrath to come.

Paul's Ministry

2 For you yourselves know, brethren, that our coming to you was not in vain, [2]but after we had already suffered and been mistreated in Philippi, as you know, we had the boldness in our God to speak to you the gospel of God amid much opposition. [3]For our exhortation does not *come* from error or impurity or by way of deceit; [4]but just as we have been approved by God to be entrusted with the gospel, so we speak, not as pleasing men, but God who examines our hearts. [5]For we never came with flattering speech, as you know, nor with a pretext for greed—God is witness— [6]nor did we seek glory from men, either from you or from others, even though as apostles of Christ we might have asserted our authority. [7]But we proved to be [a]gentle among

[a]**2:7** Three early mss read *babes*

you, as a nursing *mother* tenderly cares for her own children. [8]Having so fond an affection for you, we were well-pleased to impart to you not only the gospel of God but also our own lives, because you had become very dear to us.

9 For you recall, brethren, our labor and hardship, *how* working night and day so as not to be a burden to any of you, we proclaimed to you the gospel of God. [10]You are witnesses, and *so is* God, how devoutly and uprightly and blamelessly we behaved toward you believers; [11]just as you know how we *were* exhorting and encouraging and imploring each one of you as a father *would* his own children, [12]so that you would walk in a manner worthy of the God who calls you into His own kingdom and glory.

13 For this reason we also constantly thank God that when you received the word of God which you heard from us, you accepted *it* not *as* the word of men, but *for* what it really is, the word of God, which also performs its work in you who believe. [14]For you, brethren, became imitators of the churches of God in Christ Jesus that are in Judea, for you also endured the same sufferings at the hands of your own countrymen, even as they *did* from the Jews,

2:16 *Or forever or altogether; lit to the end*

[15]who both killed the Lord Jesus and the prophets, and drove us out. They are not pleasing to God, but hostile to all men, [16]hindering us from speaking to the Gentiles so that they may be saved; with the result that they always fill up the measure of their sins. But wrath has come upon them ªto the utmost.

17 But we, brethren, having been taken away from you for a short while—in person, not in spirit—were all the more eager with great desire to see your face. [18]For we wanted to come to you—I, Paul, more than once—and *yet* Satan hindered us. [19]For who is our hope or joy or crown of exultation? Is it not even you, in the presence of our Lord Jesus at His coming? [20]For you are our glory and joy.

Encouragement of Timothy's Visit

3 Therefore when we could endure *it* no longer, we thought it best to be left behind at Athens alone, [2]and we sent Timothy, our brother and God's fellow worker in the gospel of Christ, to strengthen and encourage you as to your faith, [3]so that no one would be disturbed by these afflictions; for you yourselves know that we have been destined for this. [4]For indeed when we were with you, we *kept* telling you in advance that we were going to suffer affliction; and so it came to pass, as you know. [5]For this reason, when I could endure *it* no longer, I also sent to find out about your faith, for fear that the tempter might have tempted you, and our labor would be in vain.

[6] But now that Timothy has come to us from you, and has brought us good news of your faith and love, and that you always think kindly of us, longing to see us just as we also long to see you, [7]for this reason, brethren, in all our distress and affliction we were comforted about you through your faith; [8]for now we *really* live, if you stand firm in the Lord. [9]For what thanks can we render to God for you in return for all the joy with which we rejoice before our God on your account, [10]as we night and day keep praying most earnestly that we may see your face, and may complete what is lacking in your faith?

[11] Now may our God and Father Himself and Jesus our Lord direct our way to you; [12]and may the Lord cause you to increase and abound in love for one another, and for all people, just as we also *do* for you; [13]so that He may establish your hearts without blame in holiness before our God and Father at the coming of our Lord Jesus with all His saints.

Sanctification and Love

4 Finally then, brethren, we request and exhort you in the Lord Jesus, that as you received from us *instruction* as to how you ought to walk and please God (just as you actually do [a]walk), that you excel still more. [2]For you know what commandments we gave you [b]by *the authority of* the Lord Jesus. [3]For this is the will of God, your sanctification; *that is,* that you abstain from sexual immorality; [4]that each of you know how to possess his own [c]vessel in sanctification and honor, [5]not in lustful passion, like the Gentiles who do not know God; [6]*and* that no man transgress and defraud his brother in the matter because the Lord is *the* avenger in all these things, just as we also told you before and solemnly warned *you.* [7]For God has not called us for the purpose of impurity, but in sanctification. [8]So, he who rejects *this* is not rejecting man but the God who gives His Holy Spirit to you.

[9] Now as to the love of the brethren, you have no need for *anyone* to write to you, for you yourselves are taught by God to love one another; [10]for indeed you do practice it toward all the brethren who are in all Macedonia. But we urge you, brethren, to excel still more, [11]and to make it your ambition to lead a quiet life and attend to your

[a]**4:1** Or *conduct yourselves;* [b]**4:2** Lit *through the Lord;* [c]**4:4** I.e. body; or wife

own business and work with your hands, just as we commanded you, [12]so that you will behave properly toward outsiders and not be in any need.

Those Who Died in Christ

13 But we do not want you to be uninformed, brethren, about those who are asleep, so that you will not grieve as do the rest who have no hope. [14]For if we believe that Jesus died and rose again, even so God will bring with Him those who have fallen asleep in Jesus. [15]For this we say to you by the word of the Lord, that we who are alive and remain until the coming of the Lord, will not precede those who have fallen asleep. [16]For the Lord Himself will descend from heaven with a shout, with the voice of *the* archangel and with the trumpet of God, and the dead in Christ will rise first. [17]Then we who are alive and remain will be caught up together with them in the clouds to meet the Lord in the air, and so we shall always be with the Lord. [18]Therefore comfort one another with these words.

The Day of the Lord

5 Now as to the times and the epochs, brethren, you have no need of anything to be written to you. [2]For you yourselves know full well that the day of the Lord will come just like a thief in the night.

[3]While they are saying, "Peace and safety!" then destruction will come upon them suddenly like labor pains upon a woman with child, and they will not escape. [4]But you, brethren, are not in darkness, that the day would overtake you like a thief; [5]for you are all sons of light and sons of day. We are not of night nor of darkness; [6]so then let us not sleep as others do, but let us be alert and [a]sober. [7]For those who sleep do their sleeping at night, and those who get drunk get drunk at night. [8]But since we are of *the* day, let us be [b]sober, having put on the breastplate of faith and love, and as a helmet, the hope of salvation. [9]For God has not destined us for wrath, but for obtaining salvation through our Lord Jesus Christ, [10]who died for us, so that whether we are awake or asleep, we will live together with Him. [11]Therefore encourage one another and build up one another, just as you also are doing.

Christian Conduct

12 But we request of you, brethren, that you appreciate those who diligently labor among you, and have charge over you in the Lord and give you instruction, [13]and that you esteem them very highly in love because of their work. Live in peace with one another. [14]We urge you, brethren, admonish the

[a]**5:6** Or *self-controlled*; [b]**5:8** Or *self-controlled*

unruly, encourage the fainthearted, help the weak, be patient with everyone. [15]See that no one repays another with evil for evil, but always seek after that which is good for one another and for all people. [16]Rejoice always; [17]pray without ceasing; [18]in everything give thanks; for this is God's will for you in Christ Jesus. [19]Do not quench the Spirit; [20]do not despise prophetic [a]utterances. [21]But examine everything *carefully;* hold fast to that which is good; [22]abstain from every [b]form of evil.

[23] Now may the God of peace Himself sanctify you entirely; and may your spirit and soul and body be preserved complete, without blame at the coming of our Lord Jesus Christ. [24]Faithful is He who calls you, and He also will bring it to pass.

[25] Brethren, pray for us[c].

[26] Greet all the brethren with a holy kiss. [27]I adjure you by the Lord to have this letter read to all the brethren.

[28] The grace of our Lord Jesus Christ be with you.

2 THESSALONIANS

Thanksgiving for Faith and Perseverance

1 Paul and Silvanus and Timothy,

To the church of the Thessalonians in God our Father and the Lord Jesus Christ: [2]Grace to you and peace from God the Father and the Lord Jesus Christ.

[3] We ought always to give thanks to God for you, brethren, as is *only* fitting, because your faith is greatly enlarged, and the love of each one of you toward one another grows *ever* greater; [4]therefore, we ourselves speak proudly of you among the churches of God for your perseverance and faith in the midst of all your persecutions and afflictions which you endure. [5]This is a plain indication of God's righteous judgment so that you will be considered worthy of the kingdom of God, for which indeed you are suffering. [6]For after all it is *only* just for God to repay with affliction those who afflict you, [7]and *to give*

relief to you who are afflicted and to us as well when the Lord Jesus will be revealed from heaven with His mighty angels in flaming fire, [8]dealing out retribution to those who do not know God and to those who do not obey the gospel of our Lord Jesus. [9]These will pay the penalty of eternal destruction, away from the presence of the Lord and from the glory of His power, [10]when He comes to be glorified in His saints on that day, and to be marveled at among all who have believed—for our testimony to you was believed. [11]To this end also we pray for you always, that our God will count you worthy of your calling, and fulfill every desire for goodness and the work of faith with power, [12]so that the name of our Lord Jesus will be glorified in you, and you in Him, according to the grace of our God and *the* Lord Jesus Christ.

Man of Lawlessness

2 Now we request you, brethren, with regard to the coming of our Lord Jesus Christ and our gathering together to Him, [2]that you not be quickly shaken from your composure or be disturbed either by a spirit or a message or a letter as if from us, to the effect that the day of the Lord has come. [3]Let no one in any way deceive you, for *it will not come* unless the [a]apostasy comes first, and the man of lawlessness is revealed, the son of destruction, [4]who opposes and exalts himself above every so-called god or object of worship, so that he takes his seat in the temple of God, displaying himself as being God. [5]Do you not remember that while I was still with you, I was telling you these things? [6]And you know what restrains him now, so that in his time he will be revealed. [7]For the mystery of lawlessness is already at work; only he who now restrains *will do so* until he is taken out of the way. [8]Then that lawless one will be revealed whom the Lord will slay with the breath of His mouth and bring to an end by the appearance of His coming; [9]*that is,* the one whose coming is in accord with the activity of Satan, with all power and signs and false wonders, [10]and with all the deception of wickedness for those who perish, because they did not receive the love of the truth so as to be saved. [11]For this reason God will send upon them a deluding influence so that they will believe what is false, [12]in order that they all may be judged who did not believe the truth, but took pleasure in wickedness.

13 But we should always give thanks to God for you, brethren beloved by the Lord, because God has chosen you [b]from the beginning for salvation through

[a]**2:3** Or *falling away* from the faith; [b]**2:13** One early ms reads *first fruits*

sanctification by the Spirit and faith in the truth. [14]It was for this He called you through our gospel, that you may gain the glory of our Lord Jesus Christ. [15]So then, brethren, stand firm and hold to the traditions which you were taught, whether by word *of mouth* or by letter from us.

16 Now may our Lord Jesus Christ Himself and God our Father, who has loved us and given us eternal comfort and good hope by grace, [17]comfort and strengthen your hearts in every good work and word.

Exhortation

3 Finally, brethren, pray for us that the word of the Lord will spread rapidly and be glorified, just as *it did* also with you; [2]and that we will be rescued from perverse and evil men; for not all have faith. [3]But the Lord is faithful, and He will strengthen and protect you from the evil *one.* [4]We have confidence in the Lord concerning you, that you are doing and will *continue to* do what we command. [5]May the Lord direct your hearts into the love of God and into the steadfastness of Christ.

6 Now we command you, brethren, in the name of our Lord Jesus Christ, that you keep away from every brother who leads an unruly life and not according to the tradition which you received from us. [7]For you yourselves know how you ought to follow our example, because we did not act in an undisciplined manner among you, [8]nor did we eat anyone's bread without paying for it, but with labor and hardship we *kept* working night and day so that we would not be a burden to any of you; [9]not because we do not have the right *to this,* but in order to offer ourselves as a model for you, so that you would follow our example. [10]For even when we were with you, we used to give you this order: if anyone is not willing to work, then he is not to eat, either. [11]For we hear that some among you are leading an undisciplined life, doing no work at all, but acting like busybodies. [12]Now such persons we command and exhort in the Lord Jesus Christ to work in quiet fashion and eat their own bread. [13]But as for you, brethren, do not grow weary of doing good.

14 If anyone does not obey our instruction in this letter, take special note of that person and do not associate with him, so that he will be put to shame. [15]*Yet* do not regard him as an enemy, but admonish him as a brother.

16 Now may the Lord of peace Himself continually grant you peace in every circumstance. The Lord be with you all!

17 I, Paul, write this greeting with my own hand, and this is a distinguishing mark in every letter; this is the way I write. **18**The grace of our Lord Jesus Christ be with you all.

1 TIMOTHY

Misleadings in Doctrine and Living

1 Paul, an apostle of Christ Jesus according to the commandment of God our Savior, and of Christ Jesus, *who is* our hope,

2 To Timothy, *my* true child in *the* faith: Grace, mercy *and* peace from God the Father and Christ Jesus our Lord.

3 As I urged you upon my departure for Macedonia, remain on at Ephesus so that you may instruct certain men not to teach strange doctrines, ⁴nor to pay attention to myths and endless genealogies, which give rise to mere speculation rather than *furthering* the administration of God which is by faith. ⁵But the goal of our instruction is love from a pure heart and a good conscience and a sincere faith. ⁶For some men, straying from these things, have turned aside to fruitless discussion, ⁷wanting to be teachers of the Law, even though they do not understand either what they are saying or the matters about which they make confident assertions.

8 But we know that the Law is good, if one uses it lawfully, ⁹realizing the fact that law is not made for a righteous person, but for those who are lawless and rebellious, for the ungodly and sinners, for the unholy and profane, for those who kill their fathers or mothers, for murderers ¹⁰and immoral men and homosexuals and kidnappers and liars and perjurers, and whatever else is contrary to sound teaching, [11]according to the glorious gospel of the blessed God, with which I have been entrusted.

12 I thank Christ Jesus our Lord, who has strengthened me, because He considered me faithful, putting me into service, [13]even though I was formerly a blasphemer and a persecutor and a violent aggressor. Yet I was shown mercy because I acted ignorantly in unbelief; [14]and the grace of our Lord was more than abundant, with the faith and love which are *found* in Christ Jesus. [15]It is a trustworthy statement, deserving full acceptance, that Christ Jesus came into the world to save sinners, among whom I am foremost *of all.* [16]Yet for this reason I found mercy, so that in me as the foremost, Jesus Christ might demonstrate His perfect patience as an example for those who would believe in Him for eternal life. [17]Now to the King eternal, immortal, invisible, the only God, *be* honor and glory forever and ever. Amen.

18 This command I entrust to you, Timothy, *my* son, in accordance with the prophecies previously made concerning you, that by them you fight the good fight, [19]keeping faith and a good conscience, which some have rejected and suffered shipwreck in regard to their faith. [20]Among these are Hymenaeus and Alexander, whom I have handed over to Satan, so that they will be taught not to blaspheme.

A Call to Prayer

2 First of all, then, I urge that entreaties *and* prayers, petitions *and* thanksgivings, be made on behalf of all men, [2]for kings and all who are in authority, so that we may lead a tranquil and quiet life in all godliness and dignity. [3]This is good and acceptable in the sight of God our Savior, [4]who desires all men to be saved and to come to the knowledge of the truth. [5]For there is one God, *and* one mediator also between God and men, *the* man Christ Jesus, [6]who gave Himself as a ransom for all, the testimony *given* at the proper time. [7]For this I was appointed a preacher and an apostle (I am telling the truth, I am not lying) as a teacher of the Gentiles in faith and truth.

8 Therefore I want the men in every place to pray, lifting up holy hands, without wrath and dissension.

Women Instructed

[9]Likewise, *I want* women to adorn themselves with proper clothing, modestly and discreetly, not with

braided hair and gold or pearls or costly garments, ¹⁰but rather by means of good works, as is proper for women making a claim to godliness. ¹¹A woman must quietly receive instruction with entire submissiveness. ¹²But I do not allow a woman to teach or exercise authority over a man, but to remain quiet. ¹³For it was Adam who was first created, *and* then Eve. ¹⁴And *it was* not Adam *who* was deceived, but the woman being deceived, fell into transgression. ¹⁵But *women* will be preserved through the bearing of children if they continue in faith and love and sanctity with self-restraint.

Overseers and Deacons

3 It is a trustworthy statement: if any man aspires to the office of overseer, it is a fine work he desires *to do.* ²An overseer, then, must be above reproach, the husband of one wife, temperate, prudent, respectable, hospitable, able to teach, ³not addicted to wine or pugnacious, but gentle, peaceable, free from the love of money. ⁴*He must be* one who manages his own household well, keeping his children under control with all dignity ⁵(but if a man does not know how to manage his own household, how will he take care of the church of God?), ⁶and not a new convert, so that he will not become conceited and fall into the condemnation

incurred by the devil. ⁷And he must have a good reputation with those outside *the church,* so that he will not fall into reproach and the snare of the devil.

8 Deacons likewise *must be* men of dignity, not double-tongued, or addicted to much wine or fond of sordid gain, ⁹*but* holding to the mystery of the faith with a clear conscience. ¹⁰These men must also first be tested; then let them serve as deacons if they are beyond reproach. ¹¹Women *must* likewise *be* dignified, not malicious gossips, but temperate, faithful in all things. ¹²Deacons must be husbands of *only* one wife, *and* good managers of *their* children and their own households. ¹³For those who have served well as deacons obtain for themselves a high standing and great confidence in the faith that is in Christ Jesus.

14 I am writing these things to you, hoping to come to you before long; ¹⁵but in case I am delayed, *I write* so that you will know how one ought to conduct himself in the household of God, which is the church of the living God, the pillar and support of the truth. ¹⁶By common confession, great is the mystery of godliness:

He who was revealed in the flesh,
Was vindicated in the Spirit,
Seen by angels,

Proclaimed among the nations,
Believed on in the world,
Taken up in glory.

Apostasy

4But the Spirit explicitly says that in later times some will fall away from the faith, paying attention to deceitful spirits and doctrines of demons, ²by means of the hypocrisy of liars seared in their own conscience as with a branding iron, ³*men* who forbid marriage *and advocate* abstaining from foods which God has created to be gratefully shared in by those who believe and know the truth. ⁴For everything created by God is good, and nothing is to be rejected if it is received with gratitude; ⁵for it is sanctified by means of the word of God and prayer.

A Good Minister's Discipline

6 In pointing out these things to the brethren, you will be a good servant of Christ Jesus, *constantly* nourished on the words of the faith and of the sound doctrine which you have been following. ⁷But have nothing to do with worldly fables fit only for old women. On the other hand, discipline yourself for the purpose of godliness; ⁸for bodily discipline is only of little profit, but godliness is profitable for all things, since it holds promise for the present life and *also* for the *life* to come. ⁹It is a trustworthy statement deserving full acceptance. ¹⁰For it is for this we labor and strive, because we have fixed our hope on the living God, who is the Savior of all men, especially of believers.

11 Prescribe and teach these things. ¹²Let no one look down on your youthfulness, but *rather* in speech, conduct, love, faith *and* purity, show yourself an example of those who believe. ¹³Until I come, give attention to the *public* reading *of Scripture*, to exhortation and teaching. ¹⁴Do not neglect the spiritual gift within you, which was bestowed on you through prophetic utterance with the laying on of hands by the presbytery. ¹⁵Take pains with these things; be *absorbed* in them, so that your progress will be evident to all. ¹⁶Pay close attention to yourself and to your teaching; persevere in these things, for as you do this you will ensure salvation both for yourself and for those who hear you.

Honor Widows

5Do not sharply rebuke an older man, but *rather* appeal to *him* as a father, *to* the younger men as brothers, ²the older women as mothers, *and* the younger women as sisters, in all purity.

3 Honor widows who are widows indeed; ⁴but if any widow has children or grandchildren, they must first learn to practice piety in regard to their own family and to make some return to their parents; for this is acceptable in the sight of God. ⁵Now she who is a widow indeed and who has been left alone, has fixed her hope on God and continues in entreaties and prayers night and day. ⁶But she who gives herself to wanton pleasure is dead even while she lives. ⁷Prescribe these things as well, so that they may be above reproach. ⁸But if anyone does not provide for his own, and especially for those of his household, he has denied the faith and is worse than an unbeliever.

9 A widow is to be put on the list only if she is not less than sixty years old, *having been* the wife of one man, ¹⁰having a reputation for good works; *and* if she has brought up children, if she has shown hospitality to strangers, if she has washed the saints' feet, if she has assisted those in distress, *and* if she has devoted herself to every good work. ¹¹But refuse *to put* younger widows *on the list,* for when they feel sensual desires in disregard of Christ, they want to get married, ¹²*thus* incurring condemnation, because they have set aside their previous pledge. ¹³At the same time they also learn *to be* idle, as they go around from house to house; and not merely idle, but also gossips and busybodies, talking about things not proper *to mention.* ¹⁴Therefore, I want younger *widows* to get married, bear children, keep house, *and* give the enemy no occasion for reproach; ¹⁵for some have already turned aside to follow Satan. ¹⁶If any woman who is a believer has *dependent* widows, she must assist them and the church must not be burdened, so that it may assist those who are widows indeed.

Concerning Elders

17 The elders who rule well are to be considered worthy of double honor, especially those who work hard at preaching and teaching. ¹⁸For the Scripture says, "YOU SHALL NOT MUZZLE THE OX WHILE HE IS THRESHING," and "The laborer is worthy of his wages." ¹⁹Do not receive an accusation against an elder except on the basis of two or three witnesses. ²⁰Those who continue in sin, rebuke in the presence of all, so that the rest also will be fearful *of sinning.* ²¹I solemnly charge you in the presence of God and of Christ Jesus and of *His* chosen angels, to maintain these *principles* without bias, doing nothing in a *spirit of* partiality. ²²Do not lay hands upon anyone *too* hastily and thereby share *responsibility for* the sins of others; keep yourself free from sin.

23 No longer drink water *exclusively,* but use a little wine for the sake of your stomach and your frequent ailments.

24 The sins of some men are quite evident, going before them to judgment; for others, their *sins* follow after. [25]Likewise also, deeds that are good are quite evident, and those which are otherwise cannot be concealed.

Instructions to Those Who Minister

6All who are under the yoke as slaves are to regard their own masters as worthy of all honor so that the name of God and *our* doctrine will not be spoken against. [2]Those who have believers as their masters must not be disrespectful to them because they are brethren, but must serve them all the more, because those who partake of the benefit are believers and beloved. Teach and preach these *principles.*

3 If anyone advocates a different doctrine and does not agree with sound words, those of our Lord Jesus Christ, and with the doctrine conforming to godliness, [4]he is conceited *and* understands nothing; but he has a morbid interest in controversial questions and disputes about words, out of which arise envy, strife, abusive language, evil suspicions, [5]and constant friction between men of depraved mind and deprived of the truth, who suppose that godliness is a means of gain. [6]But godliness *actually* is a means of great gain when accompanied by contentment. [7]For we have brought nothing into the world, so we cannot take anything out of it either. [8]If we have food and covering, with these we shall be content. [9]But those who want to get rich fall into temptation and a snare and many foolish and harmful desires which plunge men into ruin and destruction. [10]For the love of money is a root of all sorts of evil, and some by longing for it have wandered away from the faith and pierced themselves with many griefs.

11 But flee from these things, you man of God, and pursue righteousness, godliness, faith, love, perseverance *and* gentleness. [12]Fight the good fight of faith; take hold of the eternal life to which you were called, and you made the good confession in the presence of many witnesses. [13]I charge you in the presence of God, who gives life to all things, and of Christ Jesus, who testified the good confession before Pontius Pilate, [14]that you keep the commandment without stain or reproach until the appearing of our Lord Jesus Christ, [15]which He will bring about at the proper time—He who is the blessed and only Sovereign, the King of kings and Lord of lords, [16]who alone possesses immortality and dwells in unapproachable light, whom no man has seen or can see. To Him *be* honor and eternal dominion! Amen.

17 Instruct those who are rich in this present world not to be conceited or to fix their hope on the uncertainty of riches, but on God, who richly supplies us with all things to enjoy. [18]*Instruct them* to do good, to be rich in good works, to be generous and ready to share, [19]storing up for themselves the treasure of a good foundation for the future, so that they may take hold of that which is life indeed.

20 O Timothy, guard what has been entrusted to you, avoiding worldly *and* empty chatter *and* the opposing arguments of what is falsely called "knowledge"— [21]which some have professed and thus gone astray from the faith.

Grace be with you.

2 TIMOTHY

Timothy Charged to Guard His Trust

1 Paul, an apostle of Christ Jesus by the will of God, according to the promise of life in Christ Jesus,

2 To Timothy, my beloved son: Grace, mercy *and* peace from God the Father and Christ Jesus our Lord.

3 I thank God, whom I serve with a clear conscience the way my forefathers did, as I constantly remember you in my prayers night and day, [4]longing to see you, even as I recall your tears, so that I may be filled with joy. [5]For I am mindful of the sincere faith within you, which first dwelt in your grandmother Lois and your mother Eunice, and I am sure that *it is* in you as well. [6]For this reason I remind you to kindle afresh the gift of God which is in you through the laying on of my hands. [7]For God has not given us a spirit of timidity, but of power and love and discipline.

8 Therefore do not be ashamed of the testimony of our Lord or of me His prisoner, but join with *me* in suffering for the gospel according to the power of God, ⁹who has saved us and called us with a holy calling, not according to our works, but according to His own purpose and grace which was granted us in Christ Jesus from all eternity, ¹⁰but now has been revealed by the appearing of our Savior Christ Jesus, who abolished death and brought life and immortality to light through the gospel, ¹¹for which I was appointed a preacher and an apostle and a teacher. ¹²For this reason I also suffer these things, but I am not ashamed; for I know whom I have believed and I am convinced that He is able to guard what I have entrusted to Him until that day. ¹³Retain the standard of sound words which you have heard from me, in the faith and love which are in Christ Jesus. ¹⁴Guard, through the Holy Spirit who dwells in us, the treasure which has been entrusted to *you*.

15 You are aware of the fact that all who are in Asia turned away from me, among whom are Phygelus and Hermogenes. ¹⁶The Lord grant mercy to the house of Onesiphorus, for he often refreshed me and was not ashamed of my chains; ¹⁷but when he was in Rome, he eagerly searched for me and found me— ¹⁸the Lord grant to him to find mercy from the Lord on that day—and you know very well what services he rendered at Ephesus.

Be Strong

2 You therefore, my son, be strong in the grace that is in Christ Jesus. ²The things which you have heard from me in the presence of many witnesses, entrust these to faithful men who will be able to teach others also. ³Suffer hardship with *me*, as a good soldier of Christ Jesus. ⁴No soldier in active service entangles himself in the affairs of everyday life, so that he may please the one who enlisted him as a soldier. ⁵Also if anyone competes as an athlete, he does not win the prize unless he competes according to the rules. ⁶The hard-working farmer ought to be the first to receive his share of the crops. ⁷Consider what I say, for the Lord will give you understanding in everything.

8 Remember Jesus Christ, risen from the dead, descendant of David, according to my gospel, ⁹for which I suffer hardship even to imprisonment as a criminal; but the word of God is not imprisoned. ¹⁰For this reason I endure all things for the sake of those who are chosen, so that they also

may obtain the salvation which is in Christ Jesus *and* with *it* eternal glory. [11]It is a trustworthy statement:
For if we died with Him, we will also live with Him;
[12]If we endure, we will also reign with Him;
If we deny Him, He also will deny us;
[13]If we are faithless, He remains faithful, for He cannot deny Himself.

An Unashamed Workman

14 Remind *them* of these things, and solemnly charge *them* in the presence of God not to wrangle about words, which is useless *and leads* to the ruin of the hearers. [15]Be diligent to present yourself approved to God as a workman who does not need to be ashamed, accurately handling the word of truth. [16]But avoid worldly *and* empty chatter, for it will lead to further ungodliness, [17]and their talk will spread like [a]gangrene. Among them are Hymenaeus and Philetus, [18]*men* who have gone astray from the truth saying that the resurrection has already taken place, and they upset the faith of some. [19]Nevertheless, the firm foundation of God stands, having this seal, "The Lord knows those who are His," and, "Everyone who names the name of the Lord is to abstain from wickedness."

[a]**2:17** Or *cancer*

20 Now in a large house there are not only gold and silver vessels, but also vessels of wood and of earthenware, and some to honor and some to dishonor. [21]Therefore, if anyone cleanses himself from these *things,* he will be a vessel for honor, sanctified, useful to the Master, prepared for every good work. [22]Now flee from youthful lusts and pursue righteousness, faith, love *and* peace, with those who call on the Lord from a pure heart. [23]But refuse foolish and ignorant speculations, knowing that they produce quarrels. [24]The Lord's bond-servant must not be quarrelsome, but be kind to all, able to teach, patient when wronged, [25]with gentleness correcting those who are in opposition, if perhaps God may grant them repentance leading to the knowledge of the truth, [26]and they may come to their senses *and escape* from the snare of the devil, having been held captive by him to do his will.

"Difficult Times Will Come"

3 But realize this, that in the last days difficult times will come. [2]For men will be lovers of self, lovers of money, boastful, arrogant, revilers, disobedient to parents, ungrateful, unholy, [3]unloving, irreconcilable, malicious gossips, without self-control, brutal, haters of good, [4]treacherous, reckless, conceited, lovers of pleasure rather than lovers of God, ⁵holding to a form of godliness, although they have denied its power; Avoid such men as these. ⁶For among them are those who enter into households and captivate weak women weighed down with sins, led on by various impulses, ⁷always learning and never able to come to the knowledge of the truth. ⁸Just as Jannes and Jambres opposed Moses, so these *men* also oppose the truth, men of depraved mind, rejected in regard to the faith. ⁹But they will not make further progress; for their folly will be obvious to all, just as Jannes's and Jambres's folly was also.

10 Now you followed my teaching, conduct, purpose, faith, patience, love, perseverance, ¹¹persecutions, *and* sufferings, such as happened to me at Antioch, at Iconium *and* at Lystra; what persecutions I endured, and out of them all the Lord rescued me! ¹²Indeed, all who desire to live godly in Christ Jesus will be persecuted. ¹³But evil men and impostors will proceed *from bad* to worse, deceiving and being deceived. ¹⁴You, however, continue in the things you have learned and become convinced of, knowing from whom you have learned *them,* ¹⁵and that from childhood you have known the sacred writings which are able to give you

the wisdom that leads to salvation through faith which is in Christ Jesus. ¹⁶All Scripture is inspired by God and profitable for teaching, for reproof, for correction, for training in righteousness; ¹⁷so that the man of God may be adequate, equipped for every good work.

"Preach the Word"

4 I solemnly charge *you* in the presence of God and of Christ Jesus, who is to judge the living and the dead, and by His appearing and His kingdom: ²preach the word; be ready in season *and* out of season; reprove, rebuke, exhort, with great patience and instruction. ³For the time will come when they will not endure sound doctrine; but *wanting* to have their ears tickled, they will accumulate for themselves teachers in accordance to their own desires, ⁴and will turn away their ears from the truth and will turn aside to myths. ⁵But you, be sober in all things, endure hardship, do the work of an evangelist, fulfill your ministry.

6 For I am already being poured out as a drink offering, and the time of my departure has come. ⁷I have fought the good fight, I have finished the course, I have kept the faith; ⁸in the future there is laid up for me the crown of righteousness, which the Lord, the righteous Judge, will award to me on that day; and not only to me, but also to all who have loved His appearing.

Personal Concerns

9 Make every effort to come to me soon; [10]for Demas, having loved this present world, has deserted me and gone to Thessalonica; Crescens *has gone* to Galatia, Titus to Dalmatia. [11]Only Luke is with me. Pick up Mark and bring him with you, for he is useful to me for service. [12]But Tychicus I have sent to Ephesus. [13]When you come bring the cloak which I left at Troas with Carpus, and the books, especially the parchments. [14]Alexander the coppersmith did me much harm; the Lord will repay him according to his deeds. [15]Be on guard against him yourself, for he vigorously opposed our teaching.

16 At my first defense no one supported me, but all deserted me; may it not be counted against them. [17]But the Lord stood with me and strengthened me, so that through me the proclamation might be fully accomplished, and that all the Gentiles might hear; and I was rescued out of the lion's mouth. [18]The Lord will rescue me from every evil deed, and will bring me safely to His heavenly kingdom; to Him *be* the glory forever and ever. Amen.

19 Greet Prisca and Aquila, and the household of Onesiphorus. [20]Erastus remained at Corinth, but Trophimus I left sick at Miletus. [21]Make every effort to come before winter. Eubulus greets you, also Pudens and Linus and Claudia and all the brethren.

22 The Lord be with your spirit. Grace be with you.

TITUS

Salutation

1 Paul, a bond-servant of God and an apostle of Jesus Christ, for the faith of those chosen of God and the knowledge of the truth which is according to godliness, [2]in the hope of eternal life, which God, who cannot lie, promised long ages ago, [3]but at the proper time manifested, *even* His word, in the proclamation with which I was entrusted according to the commandment of God our Savior,

4 To Titus, my true child in a common faith: Grace and peace from God the Father and Christ Jesus our Savior.

Qualifications of Elders

5 For this reason I left you in Crete, that you would set in order what remains and appoint elders in every city as I directed you, ⁶*namely,* if any man is above reproach, the husband of one wife, having children who believe, not accused of dissipation or rebellion. ⁷For the overseer must be above reproach as God's steward, not self-willed, not quick-tempered, not addicted to wine, not pugnacious, not fond of sordid gain, ⁸but hospitable, loving what is good, sensible, just, devout, self-controlled, ⁹holding fast the faithful word which is in accordance with the teaching, so that he will be able both to exhort in sound doctrine and to refute those who contradict.

10 For there are many rebellious men, empty talkers and deceivers, especially those of the circumcision, ¹¹who must be silenced because they are upsetting whole families, teaching things they should not *teach* for the sake of sordid gain. ¹²One of themselves, a prophet of their own, said, "Cretans are always liars, evil beasts, lazy gluttons." ¹³This testimony is true. For this reason reprove them severely so that they may be sound in the faith, ¹⁴not paying attention to Jewish myths and commandments of men who turn away from the truth. ¹⁵To the pure, all things are pure; but to those who are defiled and unbelieving, nothing is pure, but both their mind and their conscience are defiled. ¹⁶They profess to know God, but by *their* deeds they deny *Him,* being detestable and disobedient and worthless for any good deed.

Duties of the Older and Younger

2 But as for you, speak the things which are fitting for sound doctrine. ²Older men are to be temperate, dignified, sensible, sound in faith, in love, in perseverance.

3 Older women likewise are to be reverent in their behavior, not malicious gossips nor enslaved to much wine, teaching what is good, ⁴so that they may encourage the young women to love their husbands, to love their children, ⁵*to be* sensible, pure, workers at home, kind, being subject to their own husbands, so that the word of God will not be dishonored.

6 Likewise urge the young men to be sensible; ⁷in all things show

yourself to be an example of good deeds, *with* purity in doctrine, dignified, [8]sound *in* speech which is beyond reproach, so that the opponent will be put to shame, having nothing bad to say about us.

9 *Urge* bondslaves to be subject to their own masters in everything, to be well-pleasing, not argumentative, [10]not pilfering, but showing all good faith so that they will adorn the doctrine of God our Savior in every respect.

11 For the grace of God has appeared, bringing salvation to all men, [12]instructing us to deny ungodliness and worldly desires and to live sensibly, righteously and godly in the present age, [13]looking for the blessed hope and the appearing of the glory of our great God and Savior, Christ Jesus, [14]who gave Himself for us to redeem us from every lawless deed, and to purify for Himself a people for His own possession, zealous for good deeds.

15 These things speak and exhort and reprove with all authority. Let no one disregard you.

Godly Living

3 Remind them to be subject to rulers, to authorities, to be obedient, to be ready for every good deed, [2]to malign no one, to be peaceable, gentle, showing every consideration for all men. [3]For we also once were foolish ourselves, disobedient, deceived, enslaved to various lusts and pleasures, spending our life in malice and envy, hateful, hating one another. [4]But when the kindness of God our Savior and *His* love for mankind appeared, [5]He saved us, not on the basis of deeds which we have done in righteousness, but according to His mercy, by the washing of regeneration and renewing by the Holy Spirit, [6]whom He poured out upon us richly through Jesus Christ our Savior, [7]so that being justified by His grace we would be made heirs according to *the* hope of eternal life. [8]This is a trustworthy statement; and concerning these things I want you to speak confidently, so that those who have believed God will be careful to engage in good deeds. These things are good and profitable for men. [9]But avoid foolish controversies and genealogies and strife and disputes about the Law, for they are unprofitable and worthless. [10]Reject a factious man after a first and second warning, [11]knowing that such a man is perverted and is sinning, being self-condemned.

Personal Concerns

12 When I send Artemas or Tychicus to you, make every effort to come to me at Nicopolis, for I have decided to spend the winter there. ¹³Diligently help Zenas the lawyer and Apollos on their way so that nothing is lacking for them. ¹⁴Our people must also learn to engage in good deeds to meet pressing needs, so that they will not be unfruitful.

15 All who are with me greet you. Greet those who love us in *the* faith.

Grace be with you all.

PHILEMON

Salutation

1 Paul, a prisoner of Christ Jesus, and Timothy our brother,

To Philemon our beloved *brother* and fellow worker, ²and to Apphia our sister, and to Archippus our fellow soldier, and to the church in your house: ³Grace to you and peace from God our Father and the Lord Jesus Christ.

Philemon's Love and Faith

4 I thank my God always, making mention of you in my prayers, ⁵because I hear of your love and of the faith which you have toward the Lord Jesus and toward all the saints; ⁶*and I pray* that the fellowship of your faith may become effective ªthrough the knowledge of every good thing which is in you

for Christ's sake. ⁷For I have come to have much joy and comfort in your love, because the hearts of the saints have been refreshed through you, brother.

8 Therefore, though I have enough confidence in Christ to order you *to do* what is proper, ⁹yet for love's sake I rather appeal *to you*—since I am such a person as Paul, the aged, and now also a prisoner of Christ Jesus—

Plea for Onesimus, a Free Man

¹⁰I appeal to you for my child ᵇOnesimus, whom I have begotten in my imprisonment, ¹¹who formerly was useless to you, but now is useful both to you and to me. ¹²I have sent him back to you in person, that is, *sending* my very heart,

ª**1:6** Or in; ᵇ**1:10** I.e. useful

¹³whom I wished to keep with me, so that on your behalf he might minister to me in my imprisonment for the gospel; ¹⁴but without your consent I did not want to do anything, so that your goodness would not be, in effect, by compulsion but of your own free will. ¹⁵For perhaps he was for this reason separated *from you* for a while, that you would have him back forever, ¹⁶no longer as a slave, but more than a slave, a beloved brother, especially to me, but how much more to you, both in the flesh and in the Lord.

17 If then you regard me a partner, accept him as *you would* me. ¹⁸But if he has wronged you in any way or owes you anything, charge that to my account; ¹⁹I, Paul, am writing this with my own hand, I will repay it (not to mention to you that you owe to me even your own self as well). ²⁰Yes, brother, let me benefit from you in the Lord; refresh my heart in Christ.

21 Having confidence in your obedience, I write to you, since I know that you will do even more than what I say.

22 At the same time also prepare me a lodging, for I hope that through your prayers I will be given to you.

23 Epaphras, my fellow prisoner in Christ Jesus, greets you, ²⁴*as do* Mark, Aristarchus, Demas, Luke, my fellow workers.

25 The grace of the Lord Jesus Christ be with your spirit^a.

HEBREWS

God's Final Word in His Son

1 God, after He spoke long ago to the fathers in the prophets in many portions and in many ways, ²in these last days has spoken to us in His Son, whom He appointed heir of all things, through whom also He made the world. ³And He is the radiance of His glory and the exact representation of His nature, and upholds all things by the word of His power. When He had made purification of sins, He sat down at the right hand of the Majesty on high, ⁴having become as much better than the angels, as

ª1:25 One early ms adds *Amen*

He has inherited a more excellent name than they.

5 For to which of the angels did He ever say,

"YOU ARE MY SON,
TODAY I HAVE BEGOTTEN YOU"?

And again,

"I WILL BE A FATHER TO HIM
AND HE SHALL BE A SON TO ME"?

[6]And when He again brings the firstborn into the world, He says,

"AND LET ALL THE ANGELS OF GOD WORSHIP HIM."

[7]And of the angels He says,

"WHO MAKES HIS ANGELS WINDS,
AND HIS MINISTERS A FLAME OF FIRE."

[8]But of the Son *He says,*

"YOUR THRONE, O GOD, IS FOR-EVER AND EVER,
AND THE RIGHTEOUS SCEP-TER IS THE SCEPTER OF [a]HIS KINGDOM.
[9]"YOU HAVE LOVED RIGH-TEOUSNESS AND HATED LAWLESSNESS;
THEREFORE GOD, YOUR GOD, HAS ANOINTED YOU
WITH THE OIL OF GLADNESS ABOVE YOUR COMPANIONS."

[10]And,

"YOU, LORD, IN THE BEGINNING LAID THE FOUNDATION OF THE EARTH,
AND THE HEAVENS ARE THE WORKS OF YOUR HANDS;
[11]THEY WILL PERISH, BUT YOU REMAIN;
AND THEY ALL WILL BECOME OLD LIKE A GARMENT,
[12]AND LIKE A MANTLE YOU WILL ROLL THEM UP;
LIKE A GARMENT THEY WILL ALSO BE CHANGED.
BUT YOU ARE THE SAME,
AND YOUR YEARS WILL NOT COME TO AN END."

[13]But to which of the angels has He ever said,

"SIT AT MY RIGHT HAND,
UNTIL I MAKE YOUR ENEMIES A FOOTSTOOL FOR YOUR FEET"?

[14]Are they not all ministering spir-its, sent out to render service for the sake of those who will inherit salvation?

Give Heed

2 For this reason we must pay much closer attention to what we have heard, so that we do not drift away *from it.* [2]For if the word spoken through angels proved unalterable, and every transgres-sion and disobedience received a just penalty, [3]how will we escape if we neglect so great a salvation? After it was at the first spoken through the Lord, it was con-firmed to us by those who heard, [4]God also testifying with them, both by signs and wonders and by various miracles and by gifts of

[a]1:8 Late mss read *Your*

the Holy Spirit according to His own will.

Earth Subject to Man

5 For He did not subject to angels the world to come, concerning which we are speaking. ⁶But one has testified somewhere, saying,

"WHAT IS MAN, THAT YOU REMEMBER HIM?
OR THE SON OF MAN, THAT YOU ARE CONCERNED ABOUT HIM?
⁷"YOU HAVE MADE HIM FOR A LITTLE WHILE LOWER THAN THE ANGELS;
YOU HAVE CROWNED HIM WITH GLORY AND HONOR,
ªAND HAVE APPOINTED HIM OVER THE WORKS OF YOUR HANDS;
⁸YOU HAVE PUT ALL THINGS IN SUBJECTION UNDER HIS FEET."

For in subjecting all things to him, He left nothing that is not subject to him. But now we do not yet see all things subjected to him.

Jesus Briefly Humbled

⁹But we do see Him who was made for a little while lower than the angels, *namely,* Jesus, because of the suffering of death crowned with glory and honor, so that by the grace of God He might taste death for everyone.

10 For it was fitting for Him, for

whom are all things, and through whom are all things, in bringing many sons to glory, to perfect the author of their salvation through sufferings. ¹¹For both He who sanctifies and those who are sanctified are all from one *Father;* for which reason He is not ashamed to call them brethren, ¹²saying,

"I WILL PROCLAIM YOUR NAME TO MY BRETHREN,
IN THE MIDST OF THE CONGREGATION I WILL SING YOUR PRAISE."

¹³And again,

"I WILL PUT MY TRUST IN HIM."
And again,

"BEHOLD, I AND THE CHILDREN WHOM GOD HAS GIVEN ME."

14 Therefore, since the children share in flesh and blood, He Himself likewise also partook of the same, that through death He might render powerless him who had the power of death, that is, the devil, ¹⁵and might free those who through fear of death were subject to slavery all their lives. ¹⁶For assuredly He does not give help to angels, but He gives help to the descendant of Abraham. ¹⁷Therefore, He had to be made like His brethren in all things, so that He might become a merciful and faithful high priest in things pertaining to God, to make propitiation for the sins of the people. ¹⁸For since He Himself

was tempted in that which He has suffered, He is able to come to the aid of those who are tempted.

Jesus Our High Priest

3 Therefore, holy brethren, partakers of a heavenly calling, consider Jesus, the Apostle and High Priest of our confession; ²He was faithful to Him who appointed Him, as Moses also was in all His house. ³For He has been counted worthy of more glory than Moses, by just so much as the builder of the house has more honor than the house. ⁴For every house is built by someone, but the builder of all things is God. ⁵Now Moses was faithful in all His house as a servant, for a testimony of those things which were to be spoken later; ⁶but Christ *was faithful* as a Son over His house—whose house we are, if we hold fast our confidence and the boast of our hope firm until the end.

7 Therefore, just as the Holy Spirit says,
"TODAY IF YOU HEAR HIS VOICE,
⁸DO NOT HARDEN YOUR HEARTS AS WHEN THEY PROVOKED ME,
AS IN THE DAY OF TRIAL IN THE WILDERNESS,
⁹WHERE YOUR FATHERS TRIED *Me* BY TESTING *Me*,
AND SAW MY WORKS FOR FORTY YEARS.
¹⁰"THEREFORE I WAS ANGRY WITH THIS GENERATION,
AND SAID, 'THEY ALWAYS GO ASTRAY IN THEIR HEART,
AND THEY DID NOT KNOW MY WAYS';
¹¹AS I SWORE IN MY WRATH, 'THEY SHALL NOT ENTER MY REST.'"

The Peril of Unbelief

¹²Take care, brethren, that there not be in any one of you an evil, unbelieving heart that falls away from the living God. ¹³But encourage one another day after day, as long as it is *still* called "Today," so that none of you will be hardened by the deceitfulness of sin. ¹⁴For we have become partakers of Christ, if we hold fast the beginning of our assurance firm until the end, ¹⁵while it is said,
"TODAY IF YOU HEAR HIS VOICE,
DO NOT HARDEN YOUR HEARTS, AS WHEN THEY PROVOKED ME."
¹⁶For who provoked *Him* when they had heard? Indeed, did not all those who came out of Egypt *led* by Moses? ¹⁷And with whom was He angry for forty years? Was it not with those who sinned, whose bodies fell in the wilderness? ¹⁸And to whom did He swear that they would not enter His rest, but to those who were disobedient?

¹⁹*So* we see that they were not able to enter because of unbelief.

The Believer's Rest

4 Therefore, let us fear if, while a promise remains of entering His rest, any one of you may seem to have come short of it. ²For indeed we have had good news preached to us, just as they also; but the word they heard did not profit them, because it was not united by faith in those who heard. ³For we who have believed enter that rest, just as He has said,

"AS I SWORE IN MY WRATH,
THEY SHALL NOT ENTER MY
    REST,"

although His works were finished from the foundation of the world. ⁴For He has said somewhere concerning the seventh *day:* "AND GOD RESTED ON THE SEVENTH DAY FROM ALL HIS WORKS"; ⁵and again in this *passage,* "THEY SHALL NOT ENTER MY REST." ⁶Therefore, since it remains for some to enter it, and those who formerly had good news preached to them failed to enter because of disobedience, ⁷He again fixes a certain day, "Today," saying through David after so long a time just as has been said before,

"TODAY IF YOU HEAR HIS
    VOICE,
DO NOT HARDEN YOUR
    HEARTS."

⁸For if Joshua had given them rest, He would not have spoken of another day after that. ⁹So there remains a Sabbath rest for the people of God. ¹⁰For the one who has entered His rest has himself also rested from his works, as God did from His. ¹¹Therefore let us be diligent to enter that rest, so that no one will fall, through *following* the same example of disobedience. ¹²For the word of God is living and active and sharper than any two-edged sword, and piercing as far as the division of soul and spirit, of both joints and marrow, and able to judge the thoughts and intentions of the heart. ¹³And there is no creature hidden from His sight, but all things are open and laid bare to the eyes of Him with whom we have to do.

14 Therefore, since we have a great high priest who has passed through the heavens, Jesus the Son of God, let us hold fast our confession. ¹⁵For we do not have a high priest who cannot sympathize with our weaknesses, but One who has been tempted in all things as *we are,* *yet* without sin. ¹⁶Therefore let us draw near with confidence to the throne of grace, so that we may receive mercy and find grace to help in time of need.

The Perfect High Priest

5 For every high priest taken from among men is appointed on behalf of men in things pertaining to God, in order to offer both gifts and sacrifices for sins; [2]he can deal gently with the ignorant and misguided, since he himself also is beset with weakness; [3]and because of it he is obligated to offer *sacrifices* for sins, as for the people, so also for himself. [4]And no one takes the honor to himself, but *receives it* when he is called by God, even as Aaron was.

[5] So also Christ did not glorify Himself so as to become a high priest, but He who said to Him,
"YOU ARE MY SON,
TODAY I HAVE BEGOTTEN YOU";
[6]just as He says also in another *passage,*
"YOU ARE A PRIEST FOREVER ACCORDING TO THE ORDER OF MELCHIZEDEK."
[7]In the days of His flesh, He offered up both prayers and supplications with loud crying and tears to the One able to save Him from death, and He was heard because of His piety. [8]Although He was a Son, He learned obedience from the things which He suffered. [9]And having been made perfect, He became to all those who obey Him the source of eternal salvation, [10]being designated by God as a high priest according to the order of Melchizedek.

[11] Concerning [a]him we have much to say, and *it is* hard to explain, since you have become dull of hearing. [12]For though by this time you ought to be teachers, you have need again for someone to teach you the elementary principles of the oracles of God, and you have come to need milk and not solid food. [13]For everyone who partakes *only* of milk is not accustomed to the word of righteousness, for he is an infant. [14]But solid food is for the mature, who because of practice have their senses trained to discern good and evil.

The Peril of Falling Away

6Therefore leaving the elementary teaching about the Christ, let us press on to maturity, not laying again a foundation of repentance from dead works and of faith toward God, [2]of instruction about washings and laying on of hands, and the resurrection of the dead and eternal judgment. [3]And this we will do, if God permits. [4]For in the case of those who have once been enlightened and have tasted of the heavenly gift and have been made partakers of the Holy Spirit, [5]and have tasted the good word of God and the powers of the age to come, [6]and *then* have fallen away, it is impossible to renew them again to repentance, since they again crucify to themselves the Son of God and put Him to open shame.

⁷For ground that drinks the rain which often falls on it and brings forth vegetation useful to those for whose sake it is also tilled, receives a blessing from God; ⁸but if it yields thorns and thistles, it is worthless and close to being cursed, and it ends up being burned.

Better Things for You

9 But, beloved, we are convinced of better things concerning you, and things that accompany salvation, though we are speaking in this way. ¹⁰For God is not unjust so as to forget your work and the love which you have shown toward His name, in having ministered and in still ministering to the saints. ¹¹And we desire that each one of you show the same diligence so as to realize the full assurance of hope until the end, ¹²so that you will not be sluggish, but imitators of those who through faith and patience inherit the promises.

13 For when God made the promise to Abraham, since He could swear by no one greater, He swore by Himself, ¹⁴saying, "I WILL SURELY BLESS YOU AND I WILL SURELY MULTIPLY YOU." ¹⁵And so, having patiently waited, he obtained the promise. ¹⁶For men swear by one greater *than themselves,* and with them an oath *given* as confirmation is an end of every dispute. ¹⁷In the same

way God, desiring even more to show to the heirs of the promise the unchangeableness of His purpose, interposed with an oath, ¹⁸so that by two unchangeable things in which it is impossible for God to lie, we who have taken refuge would have strong encouragement to take hold of the hope set before us. ¹⁹This hope we have as an anchor of the soul, a *hope* both sure and steadfast and one which enters within the veil, ²⁰where Jesus has entered as a forerunner for us, having become a high priest forever according to the order of Melchizedek.

Melchizedek's Priesthood Like Christ's

7 For this Melchizedek, king of Salem, priest of the Most High God, who met Abraham as he was returning from the slaughter of the kings and blessed him, ²to whom also Abraham apportioned a tenth part of all *the spoils,* was first of all, by the translation *of his name,* king of righteousness, and then also king of Salem, which is king of peace. ³Without father, without mother, without genealogy, having neither beginning of days nor end of life, but made like the Son of God, he remains a priest perpetually.

4 Now observe how great this man was to whom Abraham,

the patriarch, gave a tenth of the choicest spoils. ⁵And those indeed of the sons of Levi who receive the priest's office have commandment in the Law to collect a tenth from the people, that is, from their brethren, although these are descended from Abraham. ⁶But the one whose genealogy is not traced from them collected a tenth from Abraham and blessed the one who had the promises. ⁷But without any dispute the lesser is blessed by the greater. ⁸In this case mortal men receive tithes, but in that case one *receives them,* of whom it is witnessed that he lives on. ⁹And, so to speak, through Abraham even Levi, who received tithes, paid tithes, ¹⁰for he was still in the loins of his father when Melchizedek met him.

11 Now if perfection was through the Levitical priesthood (for on the basis of it the people received the Law), what further need *was there* for another priest to arise according to the order of Melchizedek, and not be designated according to the order of Aaron? ¹²For when the priesthood is changed, of necessity there takes place a change of law also. ¹³For the one concerning whom these things are spoken belongs to another tribe, from which no one has officiated at the altar. ¹⁴For it is evident that our Lord was descended from Judah,

a tribe with reference to which Moses spoke nothing concerning priests. ¹⁵And this is clearer still, if another priest arises according to the likeness of Melchizedek, ¹⁶who has become *such* not on the basis of a law of physical requirement, but according to the power of an indestructible life. ¹⁷For it is attested *of Him,*

"YOU ARE A PRIEST FOREVER ACCORDING TO THE ORDER OF MELCHIZEDEK."

¹⁸For, on the one hand, there is a setting aside of a former commandment because of its weakness and uselessness ¹⁹(for the Law made nothing perfect), and on the other hand there is a bringing in of a better hope, through which we draw near to God. ²⁰And inasmuch as *it was* not without an oath ²¹(for they indeed became priests without an oath, but He with an oath through the One who said to Him,

"THE LORD HAS SWORN
AND WILL NOT CHANGE HIS MIND,
'YOU ARE A PRIEST FOREVER'");
²²so much the more also Jesus has become the guarantee of a better covenant.

23 The *former* priests, on the one hand, existed in greater numbers because they were prevented by death from continuing, ²⁴but Jesus, on the other hand, because He continues forever, holds His priesthood permanently. ²⁵Therefore He is able also to save forever those who draw near to God through Him, since He always lives to make intercession for them.

26 For it was fitting for us to have such a high priest, holy, innocent, undefiled, separated from sinners and exalted above the heavens; ²⁷who does not need daily, like those high priests, to offer up sacrifices, first for His own sins and then for the *sins* of the people, because this He did once for all when He offered up Himself. ²⁸For the Law appoints men as high priests who are weak, but the word of the oath, which came after the Law, *appoints* a Son, made perfect forever.

A Better Ministry

8 Now the main point in what has been said *is this:* we have such a high priest, who has taken His seat at the right hand of the throne of the Majesty in the heavens, ²a minister in the sanctuary and in the true tabernacle, which the Lord pitched, not man. ³For every high priest is appointed to offer both gifts and sacrifices; so it is necessary that this *high priest* also have something to offer. ⁴Now if He were on earth, He would not be a priest at all, since there are those who offer the gifts according to the Law;

⁵who serve a copy and shadow of the heavenly things, just as Moses was warned *by God* when he was about to erect the tabernacle; for, "SEE," He says, "THAT YOU MAKE all things ACCORDING TO THE PATTERN WHICH WAS SHOWN YOU ON THE MOUNTAIN." ⁶But now He has obtained a more excellent ministry, by as much as He is also the mediator of a better covenant, which has been enacted on better promises.

A New Covenant

⁷For if that first *covenant* had been faultless, there would have been no occasion sought for a second. ⁸For finding fault with them, He says,

"BEHOLD, DAYS ARE COMING,
    SAYS THE LORD,
WHEN I WILL EFFECT A NEW
    COVENANT
WITH THE HOUSE OF ISRAEL
    AND WITH THE HOUSE OF
    JUDAH;
⁹NOT LIKE THE COVENANT
    WHICH I MADE WITH
    THEIR FATHERS
ON THE DAY WHEN I TOOK
    THEM BY THE HAND
TO LEAD THEM OUT OF THE
    LAND OF EGYPT;
FOR THEY DID NOT CONTIN-
    UE IN MY COVENANT,
AND I DID NOT CARE FOR
    THEM, SAYS THE LORD.
¹⁰"FOR THIS IS THE COVENANT

THAT I WILL MAKE WITH
THE HOUSE OF ISRAEL
AFTER THOSE DAYS, SAYS THE
LORD:
I WILL PUT MY LAWS INTO
THEIR MINDS,
AND I WILL WRITE THEM ON
THEIR HEARTS.
AND I WILL BE THEIR GOD,
AND THEY SHALL BE MY
PEOPLE.
[11]"AND THEY SHALL NOT
TEACH EVERYONE HIS FEL-
LOW CITIZEN,
AND EVERYONE HIS BROTHER,
SAYING, 'KNOW THE LORD,'
FOR ALL WILL KNOW ME,
FROM THE LEAST TO THE
GREATEST OF THEM.
[12]"FOR I WILL BE MERCIFUL TO
THEIR INIQUITIES,
AND I WILL REMEMBER THEIR
SINS NO MORE."
[13]When He said, "A new *cov-enant*," He has made the first obsolete. But whatever is becoming obsolete and growing old is ready to disappear.

The Old and the New

9 Now even the first *covenant* had regulations of divine worship and the earthly sanctuary. [2]For there was a tabernacle prepared, the outer one, in which *were* the lampstand and the table and the sacred bread; this is called the holy place. [3]Behind the second veil there was a tabernacle which

is called the Holy of Holies, [4]having a golden altar of incense and the ark of the covenant covered on all sides with gold, in which was a golden jar holding the manna, and Aaron's rod which budded, and the tables of the covenant; [5]and above it *were* the cherubim of glory overshadowing the mercy seat; but of these things we cannot now speak in detail.

6 Now when these things have been so prepared, the priests are continually entering the outer tabernacle performing the divine worship, [7]but into the second, only the high priest *enters* once a year, not without *taking* blood, which he offers for himself and for the sins of the people committed in ignorance. [8]The Holy Spirit *is* signifying this, that the way into the holy place has not yet been disclosed while the outer tabernacle is still standing, [9]which *is* a symbol for the present time. Accordingly both gifts and sacrifices are offered which cannot make the worshiper perfect in conscience, [10]since they *relate* only to food and drink and various washings, regulations for the body imposed until a time of reformation.

11 But when Christ appeared *as* a high priest of the good things [a]to come, *He entered* through the greater and more perfect

[a]9:11 Two early mss read *that have come*

tabernacle, not made with hands, that is to say, not of this creation; [12]and not through the blood of goats and calves, but through His own blood, He entered the holy place once for all, having obtained eternal redemption. [13]For if the blood of goats and bulls and the ashes of a heifer sprinkling those who have been defiled sanctify for the cleansing of the flesh, [14]how much more will the blood of Christ, who through the eternal Spirit offered Himself without blemish to God, cleanse your conscience from dead works to serve the living God?

15 For this reason He is the mediator of a new covenant, so that, since a death has taken place for the redemption of the transgressions that were *committed* under the first covenant, those who have been called may receive the promise of the eternal inheritance. [16]For where a covenant is, there must of necessity be the death of the one who made it. [17]For a covenant is valid *only* when men are dead, [a]for it is never in force while the one who made it lives. [18]Therefore even the first *covenant* was not inaugurated without blood. [19]For when every commandment had been spoken by Moses to all the people according to the Law, he took the blood of the calves and the goats, with water and scarlet wool and hyssop, and sprinkled both the book itself and all the people, [20]saying, "THIS IS THE BLOOD OF THE COVENANT WHICH GOD COMMANDED YOU." [21]And in the same way he sprinkled both the tabernacle and all the vessels of the ministry with the blood. [22]And according to the Law, *one may* almost *say,* all things are cleansed with blood, and without shedding of blood there is no forgiveness.

23 Therefore it was necessary for the copies of the things in the heavens to be cleansed with these, but the heavenly things themselves with better sacrifices than these. [24]For Christ did not enter a holy place made with hands, a *mere* copy of the true one, but into heaven itself, now to appear in the presence of God for us; [25]nor was it that He would offer Himself often, as the high priest enters the holy place year by year with blood that is not his own. [26]Otherwise, He would have needed to suffer often since the foundation of the world; but now once at the consummation of the ages He has been manifested to put away sin by the sacrifice of Himself. [27]And inasmuch as it is appointed for men to die once and after this *comes* judgment, [28]so Christ also, having been offered once to bear the sins of many, will appear a second time for salvation without *reference to* sin, to those who eagerly await Him.

One Sacrifice of Christ Is Sufficient

10 For the Law, since it has *only* a shadow of the good things to come *and* not the very form of things, [a]can never, by the same sacrifices which they offer continually year by year, make perfect those who draw near. [2]Otherwise, would they not have ceased to be offered, because the worshipers, having once been cleansed, would no longer have had consciousness of sins? [3]But in those *sacrifices* there is a reminder of sins year by year. [4]For it is impossible for the blood of bulls and goats to take away sins. [5]Therefore, when He comes into the world, He says,

"SACRIFICE AND OFFERING YOU HAVE NOT DESIRED,
BUT A BODY YOU HAVE PREPARED FOR ME;
[6]IN WHOLE BURNT OFFERINGS AND *sacrifices* FOR SIN YOU HAVE TAKEN NO PLEASURE.
[7]"THEN I SAID, 'BEHOLD, I HAVE COME
(IN THE SCROLL OF THE BOOK IT IS WRITTEN OF ME)
TO DO YOUR WILL, O GOD.' "
[8]After saying above, "SACRIFICES AND OFFERINGS AND WHOLE BURNT OFFERINGS AND *sacrifices* FOR SIN YOU HAVE NOT

DESIRED, NOR HAVE YOU TAKEN PLEASURE *in them*" (which are offered according to the Law), [9]then He said, "BEHOLD, I HAVE COME TO DO YOUR WILL." He takes away the first in order to establish the second. [10]By this will we have been sanctified through the offering of the body of Jesus Christ once for all.

[11] Every priest stands daily ministering and offering time after time the same sacrifices, which can never take away sins; [12]but He, having offered one sacrifice for sins for all time, SAT DOWN AT THE RIGHT HAND OF GOD, [13]waiting from that time onward UNTIL HIS ENEMIES BE MADE A FOOTSTOOL FOR HIS FEET. [14]For by one offering He has perfected for all time those who are sanctified. [15]And the Holy Spirit also testifies to us; for after saying,
[16]"THIS IS THE COVENANT THAT I WILL MAKE WITH THEM
AFTER THOSE DAYS, SAYS THE LORD:
I WILL PUT MY LAWS UPON THEIR HEART,
AND ON THEIR MIND I WILL WRITE THEM,"
He then says,
[17]"AND THEIR SINS AND THEIR LAWLESS DEEDS
I WILL REMEMBER NO MORE."
[18]Now where there is forgiveness

[a]**10:1** Two early mss read *they can*

of these things, there is no longer *any* offering for sin.

A New and Living Way

19 Therefore, brethren, since we have confidence to enter the holy place by the blood of Jesus, ²⁰by a new and living way which He inaugurated for us through the veil, that is, His flesh, ²¹and since *we have* a great priest over the house of God, ²²let us draw near with a sincere heart in full assurance of faith, having our hearts sprinkled *clean* from an evil conscience and our bodies washed with pure water. ²³Let us hold fast the confession of our hope without wavering, for He who promised is faithful; ²⁴and let us consider how to stimulate one another to love and good deeds, ²⁵not forsaking our own assembling together, as is the habit of some, but encouraging *one another;* and all the more as you see the day drawing near.

Christ or Judgment

26 For if we go on sinning willfully after receiving the knowledge of the truth, there no longer remains a sacrifice for sins, ²⁷but a terrifying expectation of judgment and THE FURY OF A FIRE WHICH WILL CONSUME THE ADVERSARIES. ²⁸Anyone who has set aside the Law of Moses dies without mercy on *the testimony of* two or three witnesses. ²⁹How much severer punishment do you think he will deserve who has trampled under foot the Son of God, and has regarded as unclean the blood of the covenant by which he was sanctified, and has insulted the Spirit of grace? ³⁰For we know Him who said, "VENGEANCE IS MINE, I WILL REPAY." And again, "THE LORD WILL JUDGE HIS PEOPLE." ³¹It is a terrifying thing to fall into the hands of the living God.

32 But remember the former days, when, after being enlightened, you endured a great conflict of sufferings, ³³partly by being made a public spectacle through reproaches and tribulations, and partly by becoming sharers with those who were so treated. ³⁴For you showed sympathy to the prisoners and accepted joyfully the seizure of your property, knowing that you have for yourselves a better possession and a lasting one. ³⁵Therefore, do not throw away your confidence, which has a great reward. ³⁶For you have need of endurance, so that when you have done the will of God, you may receive what was promised. ³⁷FOR YET IN A VERY LITTLE WHILE,

HE WHO IS COMING WILL COME, AND WILL NOT DELAY.
³⁸BUT MY RIGHTEOUS ONE SHALL LIVE BY FAITH;

AND IF HE SHRINKS BACK, MY
   SOUL HAS NO PLEASURE
   IN HIM.
[39]But we are not of those who
shrink back to destruction, but of
those who have faith to the pre-
serving of the soul.

The Triumphs of Faith

11 Now faith is the assurance
of *things* hoped for, the conviction of things not seen. [2]For by
it the men of old gained approval.

3 By faith we understand that the
worlds were prepared by the word
of God, so that what is seen was not
made out of things which are visible. [4]By faith Abel offered to God a
better sacrifice than Cain, through
which he obtained the testimony
that he was righteous, God testifying about his gifts, and through
faith, though he is dead, he still
speaks. [5]By faith Enoch was taken
up so that he would not see death;
AND HE WAS NOT FOUND BE-
CAUSE GOD TOOK HIM UP; for
he obtained the witness that before
his being taken up he was pleasing to God. [6]And without faith it
is impossible to please *Him,* for he
who comes to God must believe
that He is and *that* He is a rewarder
of those who seek Him. [7]By faith
Noah, being warned *by God* about
things not yet seen, in reverence
prepared an ark for the salvation
of his household, by which he

condemned the world, and became an heir of the righteousness
which is according to faith.

8 By faith Abraham, when he was
called, obeyed by going out to a
place which he was to receive for
an inheritance; and he went out,
not knowing where he was going.
[9]By faith he lived as an alien in the
land of promise, as in a foreign
land, dwelling in tents with Isaac
and Jacob, fellow heirs of the same
promise; [10]for he was looking for
the city which has foundations,
whose architect and builder is
God. [11]By faith even Sarah herself
received ability to conceive, even
beyond the proper time of life,
since she considered Him faithful who had promised. [12]Therefore
there was born even of one man,
and him as good as dead at that, *as
many descendants* AS THE STARS
OF HEAVEN IN NUMBER, AND
INNUMERABLE AS THE SAND
WHICH IS BY THE SEASHORE.

13 All these died in faith, without
receiving the promises, but having
seen them and having welcomed
them from a distance, and having
confessed that they were strangers
and exiles on the earth. [14]For those
who say such things make it clear
that they are seeking a country of
their own. [15]And indeed if they
had been thinking of that *country*
from which they went out, they

would have had opportunity to return. ¹⁶But as it is, they desire a better *country,* that is, a heavenly one. Therefore God is not ashamed to be called their God; for He has prepared a city for them.

17 By faith Abraham, when he was tested, offered up Isaac, and he who had received the promises was offering up his only begotten *son;* ¹⁸*it was he* to whom it was said, "IN ISAAC YOUR DESCENDANTS SHALL BE CALLED." ¹⁹He considered that God is able to raise *people* even from the dead, from which he also received him back as a type. ²⁰By faith Isaac blessed Jacob and Esau, even regarding things to come. ²¹By faith Jacob, as he was dying, blessed each of the sons of Joseph, and worshiped, *leaning* on the top of his staff. ²²By faith Joseph, when he was dying, made mention of the exodus of the sons of Israel, and gave orders concerning his bones.

23 By faith Moses, when he was born, was hidden for three months by his parents, because they saw he was a beautiful child; and they were not afraid of the king's edict. ²⁴By faith Moses, when he had grown up, refused to be called the son of Pharaoh's daughter, ²⁵choosing rather to endure ill-treatment with the people of God than to enjoy the passing

pleasures of sin, ²⁶considering the reproach of Christ greater riches than the treasures of Egypt; for he was looking to the reward. ²⁷By faith he left Egypt, not fearing the wrath of the king; for he endured, as seeing Him who is unseen. ²⁸By faith he kept the Passover and the sprinkling of the blood, so that he who destroyed the firstborn would not touch them. ²⁹By faith they passed through the Red Sea as though *they were passing* through dry land; and the Egyptians, when they attempted it, were drowned.

30 By faith the walls of Jericho fell down after they had been encircled for seven days. ³¹By faith Rahab the harlot did not perish along with those who were disobedient, after she had welcomed the spies in peace.

32 And what more shall I say? For time will fail me if I tell of Gideon, Barak, Samson, Jephthah, of David and Samuel and the prophets, ³³who by faith conquered kingdoms, performed *acts of* righteousness, obtained promises, shut the mouths of lions, ³⁴quenched the power of fire, escaped the edge of the sword, from weakness were made strong, became mighty in war, put foreign armies to flight. ³⁵Women received *back* their dead by resurrection; and others were tortured, not accepting their release, so that they might obtain a better resurrection; [36]and others experienced mockings and scourgings, yes, also chains and imprisonment. [37]They were stoned, they were sawn in two, [a]they were tempted, they were put to death with the sword; they went about in sheepskins, in goatskins, being destitute, afflicted, ill-treated [38](*men* of whom the world was not worthy), wandering in deserts and mountains and caves and holes in the ground.

[39] And all these, having gained approval through their faith, did not receive what was promised, [40]because God had provided something better for us, so that apart from us they would not be made perfect.

Jesus, the Example

12 Therefore, since we have so great a cloud of witnesses surrounding us, let us also lay aside every encumbrance and the sin which so easily entangles us, and let us run with endurance the race that is set before us, [2]fixing our eyes on Jesus, the author and perfecter of faith, who for the joy set before Him endured the cross, despising the shame, and has sat down at the right hand of the throne of God.

[3] For consider Him who has endured such hostility by sinners against Himself, so that you will not grow weary and lose heart.

A Father's Discipline

[4]You have not yet resisted to the point of shedding blood in your striving against sin; [5]and you have forgotten the exhortation which is addressed to you as sons,

"MY SON, DO NOT REGARD
    LIGHTLY THE DISCIPLINE
    OF THE LORD,
NOR FAINT WHEN YOU ARE RE-
    PROVED BY HIM;
[6]FOR THOSE WHOM THE LORD
    LOVES HE DISCIPLINES,
AND HE SCOURGES EVERY SON
    WHOM HE RECEIVES."

[7]It is for discipline that you endure; God deals with you as with sons; for what son is there whom *his* father does not discipline? [8]But if you are without discipline, of which all have become partakers, then you are illegitimate children and not sons. [9]Furthermore, we had earthly fathers to discipline us, and we respected them; shall we not much rather be subject to the Father of spirits, and live? [10]For they disciplined us for a short time as seemed best to them, but He *disciplines us* for *our* good, so that we may share His holiness. [11]All discipline for the moment seems not to be joyful, but sorrowful; yet to those who

---

[a]**11:37** One early ms does not contain *they were tempted*

have been trained by it, afterwards it yields the peaceful fruit of righteousness.

12 Therefore, strengthen the hands that are weak and the knees that are feeble, [13]and make straight paths for your feet, so that *the limb* which is lame may not be put out of joint, but rather be healed.

14 Pursue peace with all men, and the sanctification without which no one will see the Lord. [15]See to it that no one comes short of the grace of God; that no root of bitterness springing up causes trouble, and by it many be defiled; [16]that *there be* no immoral or godless person like Esau, who sold his own birthright for a *single* meal. [17]For you know that even afterwards, when he desired to inherit the blessing, he was rejected, for he found no place for repentance, though he sought for it with tears.

Contrast of Sinai and Zion

18 For you have not come to *a mountain* that can be touched and to a blazing fire, and to darkness and gloom and whirlwind, [19]and to the blast of a trumpet and the sound of words which *sound was such that* those who heard begged that no further word be spoken to them. [20]For they could not bear the command, "IF EVEN A BEAST TOUCHES THE MOUNTAIN, IT WILL BE STONED." [21]And so terrible was the sight, *that* Moses said, "I AM FULL OF FEAR and trembling." [22]But you have come to Mount Zion and to the city of the living God, the heavenly Jerusalem, and to myriads of angels, [23]to the general assembly and church of the firstborn who are enrolled in heaven, and to God, the Judge of all, and to the spirits of *the* righteous made perfect, [24]and to Jesus, the mediator of a new covenant, and to the sprinkled blood, which speaks better than *the blood* of Abel.

The Unshaken Kingdom

25 See to it that you do not refuse Him who is speaking. For if those did not escape when they refused him who warned *them* on earth, much less *will* we *escape* who turn away from Him who *warns* from heaven. [26]And His voice shook the earth then, but now He has promised, saying, "YET ONCE MORE I WILL SHAKE NOT ONLY THE EARTH, BUT ALSO THE HEAVEN." [27]This *expression,* "Yet once more," denotes the removing of those things which can be shaken, as of created things, so that those things which cannot be shaken may remain. [28]Therefore, since we receive a kingdom which cannot be shaken, let us show gratitude, by which we may offer to God an acceptable service with reverence and awe; [29]for our God is a consuming fire.

The Changeless Christ

13 Let love of the brethren continue. [2]Do not neglect to show hospitality to strangers, for by this some have entertained angels without knowing it. [3]Remember the prisoners, as though in prison with them, *and* those who are ill-treated, since you yourselves also are in the body. [4]Marriage *is to be held* in honor among all, and the *marriage* bed *is to be* undefiled; for fornicators and adulterers God will judge. [5]*Make sure that* your character is free from the love of money, being content with what you have; for He Himself has said, "I WILL NEVER DESERT YOU, NOR WILL I EVER FORSAKE YOU," [6]so that we confidently say,

"THE LORD IS MY HELPER, I
    WILL NOT BE AFRAID.
WHAT WILL MAN DO TO ME?"
[7] Remember those who led you, who spoke the word of God to you; and considering the result of their conduct, imitate their faith. [8]Jesus Christ *is* the same yesterday and today and forever. [9]Do not be carried away by varied and strange teachings; for it is good for the heart to be strengthened by grace, not by foods, through which those who were so occupied were not benefited. [10]We have an altar from which those who serve the tabernacle have no right to eat. [11]For the bodies of those animals whose blood is brought into the holy place by the high priest *as an offering* for sin, are burned outside the camp. [12]Therefore Jesus also, that He might sanctify the people through His own blood, suffered outside the gate. [13]So, let us go out to Him outside the camp, bearing His reproach. [14]For here we do not have a lasting city, but we are seeking *the city* which is to come.

God-pleasing Sacrifices

[15]Through Him then, let us continually offer up a sacrifice of praise to God, that is, the fruit of lips that give thanks to His name. [16]And do not neglect doing good and sharing, for with such sacrifices God is pleased.

[17] Obey your leaders and submit *to them,* for they keep watch over your souls as those who will give an account. Let them do this with joy and not with grief, for this would be unprofitable for you.

[18] Pray for us, for we are sure that we have a good conscience, desiring to conduct ourselves honorably in all things. [19]And I urge *you* all the more to do this, so that I may be restored to you the sooner.

Benediction

20 Now the God of peace, who brought up from the dead the great Shepherd of the sheep through the blood of the eternal covenant, *even* Jesus our Lord, [21]equip you in every good thing to do His will, working in us that which is pleasing in His sight, through Jesus Christ, to whom *be* the glory forever and ever. Amen.

22 But I urge you, brethren, bear with this word of exhortation, for I have written to you briefly. [23]Take notice that our brother Timothy has been released, with whom, if he comes soon, I will see you. [24]Greet all of your leaders and all the saints. Those from Italy greet you.

25 Grace be with you all.

JAMES

Testing Your Faith

1 James, a bond-servant of God and of the Lord Jesus Christ,

To the twelve tribes who are dispersed abroad: Greetings.

2 Consider it all joy, my brethren, when you encounter various trials, [3]knowing that the testing of your faith produces endurance. [4]And let endurance have *its* perfect result, so that you may be perfect and complete, lacking in nothing.

5 But if any of you lacks wisdom, let him ask of God, who gives to all generously and without reproach, and it will be given to him. [6]But he must ask in faith without any doubting, for the one who doubts is like the surf of the sea, driven and tossed by the wind. [7]For that man ought not to expect that he will receive anything from the Lord, [8]*being* a double-minded man, unstable in all his ways.

9 But the brother of humble circumstances is to glory in his high position; [10]and the rich man *is to glory* in his humiliation, because like flowering grass he will pass away. [11]For the sun rises with a scorching wind and withers the grass; and its flower falls off and the beauty of its appearance is destroyed; so too the rich man in the midst of his pursuits will fade away.

12 Blessed is a man who perseveres under trial; for once he has been approved, he will receive the crown of life which *the Lord* has promised to those who love Him. [13]Let no one say when he is tempted, "I am being tempted by God"; for God cannot be tempted by evil, and He Himself does not tempt anyone. [14]But each one is tempted when he is carried away and enticed by his own lust. [15]Then when lust has conceived, it gives birth to sin; and when sin is accomplished, it brings forth death. [16]Do not be deceived, my beloved brethren. [17]Every good thing given and every perfect gift is from above, coming down from the Father of lights, with whom there is no variation or shifting shadow. [18]In the exercise of His will He brought us forth by the word of truth, so that we would be a kind of first fruits among His creatures.

19 [a]*This* you know, my beloved brethren. But everyone must be quick to hear, slow to speak *and* slow to anger; [20]for the anger of man does not achieve the righteousness of God. [21]Therefore, putting aside all filthiness and *all* that remains of wickedness, in humility receive the word implanted, which is able to save your souls. [22]But prove yourselves doers of the word, and not merely hearers who delude themselves. [23]For if anyone is a hearer of the word and not a doer, he is like a man who looks at his natural face in a mirror; [24]for *once* he has looked at himself and gone away, he has immediately forgotten what kind of person he was. [25]But one who looks intently at the perfect law, the *law* of liberty, and abides by it, not having become a forgetful hearer but an effectual doer, this man will be blessed in what he does.

26 If anyone thinks himself to be religious, and yet does not bridle his tongue but deceives his *own* heart, this man's religion is worthless. [27]Pure and undefiled religion in the sight of *our* God and Father is this: to visit orphans and widows in their distress, *and* to keep oneself unstained by the world.

The Sin of Partiality

2 My brethren, do not hold your faith in our glorious Lord Jesus Christ with *an attitude of* personal favoritism. [2]For if a man comes into your assembly with a gold ring and dressed in fine clothes, and there also comes in a poor man in dirty clothes, [3]and you pay special attention to the one who is wearing the fine clothes, and say, "You sit here in a good place," and you say to the poor man, "You stand over there, or sit down by my footstool," [4]have you not made distinctions among yourselves, and become judges with evil motives? [5]Listen, my beloved brethren: did not God choose the poor of this world *to be* rich in faith and heirs of the kingdom which He promised to those who love Him? [6]But you have dishonored the poor man. Is it not the rich who oppress you and personally drag you into court? [7]Do they not blaspheme the fair name by which you have been called?

[8]If, however, you are fulfilling the royal law according to the Scripture, "YOU SHALL LOVE YOUR NEIGHBOR AS YOURSELF," you are doing well. [9]But if you show partiality, you are committing sin *and* are convicted by the law as transgressors. [10]For whoever keeps the whole law and yet stumbles in one *point,* he has become guilty of all. [11]For He who said, "DO NOT COMMIT ADULTERY," also said, "DO NOT COMMIT MURDER." Now if you do not commit adultery, but do commit murder, you have become a transgressor of the law. [12]So speak and so act as those who are to be judged by *the* law of liberty. [13]For judgment *will be* merciless to one who has shown no mercy; mercy triumphs over judgment.

Faith and Works

[14]What use is it, my brethren, if someone says he has faith but he has no works? Can that faith save him? [15]If a brother or sister is without clothing and in need of daily food, [16]and one of you says to them, "Go in peace, be warmed and be filled," and yet you do not give them what is necessary for *their* body, what use is that? [17]Even so faith, if it has no works, is dead, *being* by itself.

[18]But someone may *well* say, "You have faith and I have works; show me your faith without the works, and I will show you my faith by my works." [19]You believe that ªGod is one. You do well; the demons also believe, and shudder. [20]But are you willing to recognize, you foolish fellow, that faith without works is useless? [21]Was not Abraham our father justified by works when he offered up Isaac his son on the altar? [22]You see that faith was working with his works, and as a result of the works, faith was perfected; [23]and the Scripture was fulfilled which says, "AND ABRAHAM BELIEVED GOD, AND IT WAS RECKONED TO HIM AS RIGHTEOUSNESS," and he was called the friend of God. [24]You see that a man is justified by works and not by faith alone. [25]In the same way, was not Rahab the harlot also justified by works when she received the messengers and sent them out by another way? [26]For just as the body without *the* spirit

ª**2:19** One early ms reads *there is one God*

is dead, so also faith without works is dead.

The Tongue Is a Fire

3 Let not many *of you* become teachers, my brethren, knowing that as such we will incur a stricter judgment. ²For we all stumble in many *ways*. If anyone does not stumble in what he says, he is a perfect man, able to bridle the whole body as well. ³Now if we put the bits into the horses' mouths so that they will obey us, we direct their entire body as well. ⁴Look at the ships also, though they are so great and are driven by strong winds, are still directed by a very small rudder wherever the inclination of the pilot desires. ⁵So also the tongue is a small part of the body, and *yet* it boasts of great things.

See how great a forest is set aflame by such a small fire! ⁶And the tongue is a fire, the *very* world of iniquity; the tongue is set among our members as that which defiles the entire body, and sets on fire the course of *our* life, and is set on fire by hell. ⁷For every species of beasts and birds, of reptiles and creatures of the sea, is tamed and has been tamed by the human race. ⁸But no one can tame the tongue; *it is* a restless evil *and* full of deadly poison. ⁹With it we bless *our* Lord and Father, and with it we curse men, who have been made in the likeness of God; ¹⁰from the same mouth come *both* blessing and cursing. My brethren, these things ought not to be this way. ¹¹Does a fountain send out from the same opening *both* fresh and bitter *water*? ¹²Can a fig tree, my brethren, produce olives, or a vine produce figs? Nor *can* salt water produce fresh.

Wisdom from Above

13 Who among you is wise and understanding? Let him show by his good behavior his deeds in the gentleness of wisdom. ¹⁴But if you have bitter jealousy and selfish ambition in your heart, do not be arrogant and *so* lie against the truth. ¹⁵This wisdom is not that which comes down from above, but is earthly, natural, demonic. ¹⁶For where jealousy and selfish ambition exist, there is disorder and every evil thing. ¹⁷But the wisdom from above is first pure, then peaceable, gentle, reasonable, full of mercy and good fruits, unwavering, without hypocrisy. ¹⁸And the seed whose fruit is righteousness is sown in peace by those who make peace.

Things to Avoid

4 What is the source of quarrels and conflicts among you? Is not the source your pleasures that wage war in your members? ²You lust and do not have; *so* you commit murder. You are envious and cannot obtain; *so* you fight and quarrel. You do not have because you do not ask. ³You ask and do not receive, because you ask with wrong motives, so that you may spend *it* on your pleasures. ⁴You adulteresses, do you not know that friendship with the world is hostility toward God? Therefore whoever wishes to be a friend of the world makes himself an enemy of God. ⁵Or do you think that the Scripture speaks to no purpose: "ᵃHe jealously desires the Spirit which He has made to dwell in us"? ⁶But He gives a greater grace. Therefore *it* says, "GOD IS OPPOSED TO THE PROUD, BUT GIVES GRACE TO THE HUMBLE." ⁷Submit therefore to God. Resist the devil and he will flee from you. ⁸Draw near to God and He will draw near to you. Cleanse your hands, you sinners; and purify your hearts, you double-minded. ⁹Be miserable and mourn and weep; let your laughter be turned into mourning and your joy to gloom. ¹⁰Humble yourselves in the presence of the Lord, and He will exalt you.

11 Do not speak against one another, brethren. He who speaks against a brother or judges his brother, speaks against the law and judges the law; but if you judge the law, you are not a doer of the law but a judge *of it.* ¹²There is *only* one Lawgiver and Judge, the One who is able to save and to destroy; but who are you who judge your neighbor?

13 Come now, you who say, "Today or tomorrow we will go to such and such a city, and spend a year there and engage in business and make a profit." ¹⁴Yet you do not know what your life will be like tomorrow. You are *just* a vapor that appears for a little while and then vanishes away. ¹⁵Instead, *you ought* to say, "If the Lord wills, we will live and also do this or that." ¹⁶But as it is, you boast in your arrogance; all such boasting is evil. ¹⁷Therefore, to one who knows *the* right thing to do and does not do it, to him it is sin.

Misuse of Riches

5 Come now, you rich, weep and howl for your miseries which are coming upon you. ²Your riches have rotted and your garments have become moth-eaten. ³Your gold and your silver have rusted; and their rust will be a witness against you and will consume your flesh like fire. It is in the last days that you have stored up your treasure! ⁴Behold, the pay of the laborers who mowed your fields, *and* which has been withheld by you, cries out *against you;* and the outcry of those who did the

---

ᵃ4:5 Or The spirit which He has made to dwell in us lusts with envy harvesting has reached the ears of the Lord of Sabaoth. [5]You have lived luxuriously on the earth and led a life of wanton pleasure; you have fattened your hearts in a day of slaughter. [6]You have condemned and put to death the righteous *man*; he does not resist you.

Exhortation

[7] Therefore be patient, brethren, until the coming of the Lord. The farmer waits for the precious produce of the soil, being patient about it, until it gets the early and late rains. [8]You too be patient; strengthen your hearts, for the coming of the Lord is near. [9]Do not complain, brethren, against one another, so that you yourselves may not be judged; behold, the Judge is standing right at the door. [10]As an example, brethren, of suffering and patience, take the prophets who spoke in the name of the Lord. [11]We count those blessed who endured. You have heard of the endurance of Job and have seen the outcome of the Lord's dealings, that the Lord is full of compassion and *is* merciful.

[12] But above all, my brethren, do not swear, either by heaven or by earth or with any other oath; but your yes is to be yes, and your no, no, so that you may not fall under judgment.

[a]**5:15** Or *save*

[13] Is anyone among you suffering? *Then* he must pray. Is anyone cheerful? He is to sing praises. [14]Is anyone among you sick? *Then* he must call for the elders of the church and they are to pray over him, anointing him with oil in the name of the Lord; [15]and the prayer offered in faith will [a]restore the one who is sick, and the Lord will raise him up, and if he has committed sins, they will be forgiven him. [16]Therefore, confess your sins to one another, and pray for one another so that you may be healed. The effective prayer of a righteous man can accomplish much. [17]Elijah was a man with a nature like ours, and he prayed earnestly that it would not rain, and it did not rain on the earth for three years and six months. [18]Then he prayed again, and the sky poured rain and the earth produced its fruit.

[19] My brethren, if any among you strays from the truth and one turns him back, [20]let him know that he who turns a sinner from the error of his way will save his soul from death and will cover a multitude of sins.

1 PETER

A Living Hope, and
a Sure Salvation

1 Peter, an apostle of Jesus Christ,

To those who reside as aliens, scattered throughout Pontus, Galatia, Cappadocia, Asia, and Bithynia, who are chosen ²according to the foreknowledge of God the Father, by the sanctifying work of the Spirit, to obey Jesus Christ and be sprinkled with His blood: May grace and peace be yours in the fullest measure.

3 Blessed be the God and Father of our Lord Jesus Christ, who according to His great mercy has caused us to be born again to a living hope through the resurrection of Jesus Christ from the dead, ⁴to *obtain* an inheritance *which is* imperishable and undefiled and will not fade away, reserved in heaven for you, ⁵who are protected by the power of God through faith for a salvation ready to be revealed in the last time. ⁶In this you greatly rejoice, even though now for a little while, if necessary, you have been distressed by various trials, ⁷so that the proof of your faith, *being* more precious than gold which is perishable, even though tested by fire, may be found to result in praise and glory and honor at the revelation of Jesus Christ; ⁸and though you have not seen Him, you love Him, and though you do not see Him now, but believe in Him, you greatly rejoice with joy inexpressible and full of glory, ⁹obtaining as the outcome of your faith the salvation of ᵃyour souls.

10 As to this salvation, the prophets who prophesied of the grace that *would come* to you made careful searches and inquiries, ¹¹seeking to know what person or time the Spirit of Christ within them was indicating as He predicted the sufferings of Christ and the glories to follow. ¹²It was revealed to them that they were not serving themselves, but you, in these things which now have been announced to you through those who preached the gospel to you by the Holy Spirit sent from heaven—things into which angels long to look.

13 Therefore, prepare your minds for action, keep sober *in spirit*, fix your hope completely on the grace to be brought to you at the revelation of Jesus Christ. ¹⁴As

---

ᵃ**1:9** One early ms does not contain *your*

obedient children, do not be conformed to the former lusts *which were yours* in your ignorance, [15]but like the Holy One who called you, be holy yourselves also in all *your* behavior; [16]because it is written, "YOU SHALL BE HOLY, FOR I AM HOLY."

17 If you address as Father the One who impartially judges according to each one's work, conduct yourselves in fear during the time of your stay *on earth;* [18]knowing that you were not redeemed with perishable things like silver or gold from your futile way of life inherited from your forefathers, [19]but with precious blood, as of a lamb unblemished and spotless, *the blood* of Christ. [20]For He was foreknown before the foundation of the world, but has appeared in these last times for the sake of you [21]who through Him are believers in God, who raised Him from the dead and gave Him glory, so that your faith and hope are in God.

22 Since you have in obedience to the truth purified your souls for a sincere love of the brethren, fervently love one another from [a]the heart, [23]for you have been born again not of seed which is perishable but imperishable, *that is,* through the living and enduring word of God. [24]For,
"ALL FLESH IS LIKE GRASS,

AND ALL ITS GLORY LIKE THE
    FLOWER OF GRASS.
THE GRASS WITHERS,
AND THE FLOWER FALLS OFF,
[25]BUT THE WORD OF THE LORD
    ENDURES FOREVER."
And this is the word which was preached to you.

As Newborn Babes

2 Therefore, putting aside all malice and all deceit and hypocrisy and envy and all slander, [2]like newborn babies, long for the pure milk of the word, so that by it you may grow in respect to salvation, [3]if you have tasted the kindness of the Lord.

As Living Stones

4 And coming to Him as to a living stone which has been rejected by men, but is choice and precious in the sight of God, [5]you also, as living stones, are being built up as a spiritual house for a holy priesthood, to offer up spiritual sacrifices acceptable to God through Jesus Christ. [6]For *this* is contained in Scripture:
"BEHOLD, I LAY IN ZION A
    CHOICE STONE, A PRE-
    CIOUS CORNER *stone,*
AND HE WHO BELIEVES
    IN HIM WILL NOT BE
    DISAPPOINTED."
[7]This precious value, then, is for you who believe; but for those who disbelieve,

[a]1:22 Two early mss read *a clean heart*

"THE STONE WHICH THE
    BUILDERS REJECTED,
THIS BECAME THE VERY COR-
    NER *stone*,"
[8]and,
"A STONE OF STUMBLING AND
    A ROCK OF OFFENSE";
for they stumble because they
are disobedient to the word,
and to this *doom* they were also
appointed.

9 But you are A CHOSEN RACE,
A royal PRIESTHOOD, A HOLY
NATION, A PEOPLE FOR *God's*
OWN POSSESSION, so that you
may proclaim the excellencies
of Him who has called you out
of darkness into His marvelous
light; [10]for you once were NOT
A PEOPLE, but now you are THE
PEOPLE OF GOD; you had NOT
RECEIVED MERCY, but now you
have RECEIVED MERCY.

11 Beloved, I urge you as aliens and
strangers to abstain from fleshly
lusts which wage war against the
soul. [12]Keep your behavior excellent among the Gentiles, so that
in the thing in which they slander
you as evildoers, they may because
of your good deeds, as they observe *them*, glorify God in the day
of [a]visitation.

Honor Authority

13 Submit yourselves for the Lord's
sake to every human institution,
whether to a king as the one in authority, [14]or to governors as sent by
him for the punishment of evildoers and the praise of those who do
right. [15]For such is the will of God
that by doing right you may silence
the ignorance of foolish men. [16]*Act*
as free men, and do not use your
freedom as a covering for evil, but
use it as bondslaves of God. [17]Hon-
or all people, love the brotherhood,
fear God, honor the king.

18 Servants, be submissive to your
masters with all respect, not only
to those who are good and gentle,
but also to those who are unrea-
sonable. [19]For this *finds* favor, if
for the sake of conscience toward
God a person bears up under
sorrows when suffering unjustly.
[20]For what credit is there if, when
you sin and are harshly treated,
you endure it with patience? But
if when you do what is right and
suffer *for it* you patiently endure it,
this *finds* favor with God.

Christ Is Our Example

[21]For you have been called for this
purpose, since Christ also suffered
for you, leaving you an example for you to follow in His steps,
[22]WHO COMMITTED NO SIN,
NOR WAS ANY DECEIT FOUND
IN HIS MOUTH; [23]and while be
ing reviled, He did not revile in
return; while suffering, He uttered
no threats, but kept entrusting

[a]**2:12** I.e. Christ's coming again in judgment

Himself to Him who judges righteously; ²⁴and He Himself bore our sins in His body on the cross, so that we might die to sin and live to righteousness; for by His wounds you were healed. ²⁵For you were continually straying like sheep, but now you have returned to the Shepherd and Guardian of your souls.

Godly Living

3 In the same way, you wives, be submissive to your own husbands so that even if any *of them* are disobedient to the word, they may be won without a word by the behavior of their wives, ²as they observe your chaste and respectful behavior. ³Your adornment must not be *merely* external—braiding the hair, and wearing gold jewelry, or putting on dresses; ⁴but *let it be* the hidden person of the heart, with the imperishable quality of a gentle and quiet spirit, which is precious in the sight of God. ⁵For in this way in former times the holy women also, who hoped in God, used to adorn themselves, being submissive to their own husbands; ⁶just as Sarah obeyed Abraham, calling him lord, and you have become her children if you do what is right without being frightened by any fear.

7 You husbands in the same way, live with *your wives* in an understanding way, as with someone weaker, since she is a woman; and show her honor as a fellow heir of the grace of life, so that your prayers will not be hindered.

8 To sum up, all of you be harmonious, sympathetic, brotherly, kindhearted, and humble in spirit; ⁹not returning evil for evil or insult for insult, but giving a blessing instead; for you were called for the very purpose that you might inherit a blessing. ¹⁰For,

"THE ONE WHO DESIRES LIFE,
    TO LOVE AND SEE GOOD
    DAYS,
MUST KEEP HIS TONGUE FROM
    EVIL AND HIS LIPS FROM
    SPEAKING DECEIT.
¹¹HE MUST TURN AWAY FROM
    EVIL AND DO GOOD;
HE MUST SEEK PEACE AND
    PURSUE IT.
¹²FOR THE EYES OF THE
    LORD ARE TOWARD THE
    RIGHTEOUS,
AND HIS EARS ATTEND TO
    THEIR PRAYER,
BUT THE FACE OF THE LORD IS
    AGAINST THOSE WHO DO
    EVIL."

13 Who is there to harm you if you prove zealous for what is good? ¹⁴But even if you should suffer for the sake of righteousness, you are blessed. AND DO NOT FEAR THEIR INTIMIDATION, AND DO NOT BE TROUBLED, ¹⁵but

^asanctify Christ as Lord in your hearts, always *being* ready to make a defense to everyone who asks you to give an account for the hope that is in you, yet with gentleness and reverence; ¹⁶and keep a good conscience so that in the thing in which you are slandered, those who revile your good behavior in Christ will be put to shame. ¹⁷For it is better, if God should will it so, that you suffer for doing what is right rather than for doing what is wrong. ¹⁸For Christ also died for sins once for all, *the* just for *the* unjust, so that He might bring us to God, having been put to death in the flesh, but made alive in the spirit; ¹⁹in which also He went and made proclamation to the spirits *now* in prison, ²⁰who once were disobedient, when the patience of God kept waiting in the days of Noah, during the construction of the ark, in which a few, that is, eight persons, were brought safely through *the* water. ²¹Corresponding to that, baptism now saves you—not the removal of dirt from the flesh, but an appeal to God for a good conscience—through the resurrection of Jesus Christ, ²²who is at the right hand of God, having gone into heaven, after angels and authorities and powers had been subjected to Him.

Keep Fervent in Your Love

4Therefore, since Christ has ^bsuffered in the flesh, arm yourselves also with the same purpose, because he who has suffered in the flesh has ceased from sin, ²so as to live the rest of the time in the flesh no longer for the lusts of men, but for the will of God. ³For the time already past is sufficient *for you* to have carried out the desire of the Gentiles, having pursued a course of sensuality, lusts, drunkenness, carousing, drinking parties and abominable idolatries. ⁴In *all* this, they are surprised that you do not run with *them* into the same excesses of dissipation, and they malign *you;* ⁵but they will give account to Him who is ready to judge the living and the dead. ⁶For the gospel has for this purpose been preached even to those who are dead, that though they are judged in the flesh as men, they may live in the spirit according to *the will of* God.

7 The end of all things is near; therefore, be of sound judgment and sober *spirit* for the purpose of prayer. ⁸Above all, keep fervent in your love for one another, because love covers a multitude of sins. ⁹Be hospitable to one another without complaint. ¹⁰As each one has received a *special* gift, employ it in serving one another as good stewards of the manifold grace of

^a**3:15** l.e. set apart; ^b**4:1** l.e. suffered death

God. [11]Whoever speaks, *is to do so* as one who is speaking the utterances of God; whoever serves *is to do so* as one who is serving by the strength which God supplies; so that in all things God may be glorified through Jesus Christ, to whom belongs the glory and dominion forever and ever. Amen.

Share the Sufferings of Christ

12 Beloved, do not be surprised at the fiery ordeal among you, which comes upon you for your testing, as though some strange thing were happening to you; [13]but to the degree that you share the sufferings of Christ, keep on rejoicing, so that also at the revelation of His glory you may rejoice with exultation. [14]If you are reviled for the name of Christ, you are blessed, because the Spirit of glory and of God rests on you. [15]Make sure that none of you suffers as a murderer, or thief, or evildoer, or a troublesome meddler; [16]but if *anyone suffers* as a Christian, he is not to be ashamed, but is to glorify God in this name. [17]For *it is* time for judgment to begin with the household of God; and if *it begins* with us first, what *will be* the outcome for those who do not obey the gospel of God? [18]AND IF IT IS WITH DIFFICULTY THAT THE RIGHTEOUS IS SAVED, WHAT WILL BECOME OF THE GODLESS MAN AND THE SINNER? [19]Therefore, those also who suffer according to the will of God shall entrust their souls to a faithful Creator in doing what is right.

Serve God Willingly

5 Therefore, I exhort the elders among you, as *your* fellow elder and witness of the sufferings of Christ, and a partaker also of the glory that is to be revealed, [2]shepherd the flock of God among you, exercising oversight not under compulsion, but voluntarily, according to *the will of* God; and not for sordid gain, but with eagerness; [3]nor yet as lording it over those allotted to your charge, but proving to be examples to the flock. [4]And when the Chief Shepherd appears, you will receive the unfading crown of glory. [5]You younger men, likewise, be subject to *your* elders; and all of you, clothe yourselves with humility toward one another, for GOD IS OPPOSED TO THE PROUD, BUT GIVES GRACE TO THE HUMBLE.

6 Therefore humble yourselves under the mighty hand of God, that He may exalt you at the proper time, [7]casting all your anxiety on Him, because He cares for you. [8]Be of sober *spirit,* be on the alert. Your adversary, the devil, prowls around like a roaring lion, seeking someone to devour. [9]But resist him, firm in *your* faith, knowing

that the same experiences of suffering are being accomplished by your brethren who are in the world. ¹⁰After you have suffered for a little while, the God of all grace, who called you to His eternal glory in Christ, will Himself perfect, confirm, strengthen *and* establish you. ¹¹To Him *be* dominion forever and ever. Amen.

12 Through Silvanus, our faithful brother (for so I regard *him*), I have written to you briefly, exhorting and testifying that this is the true grace of God. Stand firm in it! ¹³She who is in Babylon, chosen together with you, sends you greetings, and *so does* my son, Mark. ¹⁴Greet one another with a kiss of love.

Peace be to you all who are in Christ.

2 PETER

Growth in Christian Virtue

1 Simon Peter, a bond-servant and apostle of Jesus Christ,

To those who have received a faith of the same kind as ours, by the righteousness of our God and Savior, Jesus Christ: ²Grace and peace be multiplied to you in the knowledge of God and of Jesus our Lord; ³seeing that His divine power has granted to us everything pertaining to life and godliness, through the true knowledge of Him who called us by His own glory and excellence. ⁴For by these He has granted to us His precious and magnificent promises, so that by them you may become partakers of *the* divine nature, having escaped the corruption that is in the world by lust. ⁵Now for this very reason also, applying all diligence, in your faith supply moral excellence, and in *your* moral excellence, knowledge, ⁶and in *your* knowledge, self-control, and in *your* self-control, perseverance, and in *your* perseverance, godliness, ⁷and in *your* godliness, brotherly kindness, and in *your* brotherly kindness, love. ⁸For if these *qualities* are yours and are increasing, they render you neither useless nor unfruitful in the true knowledge of our Lord Jesus Christ. ⁹For he who lacks these *qualities* is blind *or* short-sighted, having forgotten *his* purification from his former sins. ¹⁰Therefore, brethren, be all the more diligent to make certain about His calling and choosing you; for as long as you practice these things, you will never stumble; ¹¹for in this way the entrance into the eternal kingdom of our Lord and Savior Jesus Christ will be abundantly supplied to you.

12 Therefore, I will always be ready to remind you of these things, even though you *already* know *them,* and have been established in the truth which is present with *you.* ¹³I consider it right, as long as I am in this *earthly* dwelling, to stir you up by way of reminder, ¹⁴knowing that the laying aside of my *earthly* dwelling is imminent, as also our Lord Jesus Christ has made clear to me. ¹⁵And I will also be diligent that at any time after my departure you will be able to call these things to mind.

Eyewitnesses

16 For we did not follow cleverly devised tales when we made known to you the power and coming of our Lord Jesus Christ, but we were eyewitnesses of His majesty. ¹⁷For when He received honor and glory from God the Father, such an utterance as this was made to Him by the Majestic Glory, "This is My beloved Son with whom I am well-pleased"— ¹⁸and we ourselves heard this utterance made from heaven when we were with Him on the holy mountain.

19 *So* we have the prophetic word *made* more sure, to which you do well to pay attention as to a lamp shining in a dark place, until the day dawns and the morning star arises in your hearts. ²⁰But know this first of all, that no prophecy of Scripture is *a matter* of one's own interpretation, ²¹for no prophecy was ever made by an act of human will, but men moved by the Holy Spirit spoke from God.

The Rise of False Prophets

2 But false prophets also arose among the people, just as there will also be false teachers among you, who will secretly introduce destructive heresies, even denying the Master who bought them, bringing swift destruction upon themselves. ²Many will follow their sensuality, and because of them the way of the truth will be maligned; ³and in *their* greed they will exploit you with false words; their judgment from long ago is not idle, and their destruction is not asleep.

4 For if God did not spare angels when they sinned, but cast them into hell and committed them to pits of darkness, reserved

for judgment; ⁵and did not spare the ancient world, but preserved Noah, a preacher of righteousness, with seven others, when He brought a flood upon the world of the ungodly; ⁶and *if* He condemned the cities of Sodom and Gomorrah to destruction by reducing *them* to ashes, having made them an example to those who would live ungodly *lives* thereafter; ⁷and *if* He rescued righteous Lot, oppressed by the sensual conduct of unprincipled men ⁸(for by what he saw and heard *that* righteous man, while living among them, felt *his* righteous soul tormented day after day by *their* lawless deeds), ⁹*then* the Lord knows how to rescue the godly from temptation, and to keep the unrighteous under punishment for the day of judgment, ¹⁰and especially those who indulge the flesh in *its* corrupt desires and despise authority.

Daring, self-willed, they do not tremble when they revile angelic majesties, ¹¹whereas angels who are greater in might and power do not bring a reviling judgment against them before the Lord. ¹²But these, like unreasoning animals, born as creatures of instinct to be captured and killed, reviling where they have no knowledge, will in the destruction of those creatures also be destroyed,

¹³suffering wrong as the wages of doing wrong. They count it a pleasure to revel in the daytime. They are stains and blemishes, reveling in their ᵃdeceptions, as they carouse with you, ¹⁴having eyes full of adultery that never cease from sin, enticing unstable souls, having a heart trained in greed, accursed children; ¹⁵forsaking the right way, they have gone astray, having followed the way of Balaam, the *son* of Beor, who loved the wages of unrighteousness; ¹⁶but he received a rebuke for his own transgression, *for* a mute donkey, speaking with a voice of a man, restrained the madness of the prophet.

17 These are springs without water and mists driven by a storm, for whom the black darkness has been reserved. ¹⁸For speaking out arrogant *words* of vanity they entice by fleshly desires, by sensuality, those who barely escape from the ones who live in error, ¹⁹promising them freedom while they themselves are slaves of corruption; for by what a man is overcome, by this he is enslaved. ²⁰For if, after they have escaped the defilements of the world by the knowledge of the Lord and Savior Jesus Christ, they are again entangled in them and are overcome, the last state has become worse for them than the first. ²¹For it would be better

ᵃ**2:13** One early ms reads *love feasts*

for them not to have known the way of righteousness, than having known it, to turn away from the holy commandment handed on to them. [22]It has happened to them according to the true proverb, "A DOG RETURNS TO ITS OWN VOMIT," and, "A sow, after washing, *returns* to wallowing in the mire."

Purpose of This Letter

3 This is now, beloved, the second letter I am writing to you in which I am stirring up your sincere mind by way of reminder, [2]that you should remember the words spoken beforehand by the holy prophets and the commandment of the Lord and Savior *spoken* by your apostles.

The Coming Day of the Lord

[3]Know this first of all, that in the last days mockers will come with *their* mocking, following after their own lusts, [4]and saying, "Where is the promise of His coming? For *ever* since the fathers fell asleep, all continues just as it was from the beginning of creation." [5]For when they maintain this, it escapes their notice that by the word of God *the* heavens existed long ago and *the* earth was formed out of water and by water, [6]through which the world at that time was destroyed, being flooded with water. [7]But by His word the present heavens and earth are being reserved for fire, kept for the day of judgment and destruction of ungodly men.

8 But do not let this one *fact* escape your notice, beloved, that with the Lord one day is like a thousand years, and a thousand years like one day. [9]The Lord is not slow about His promise, as some count slowness, but is patient toward you, not wishing for any to perish but for all to come to repentance.

A New Heaven and Earth

[10]But the day of the Lord will come like a thief, in which the heavens will pass away with a roar and the elements will be destroyed with intense heat, and the earth and its works will be [a]burned up.

11 Since all these things are to be destroyed in this way, what sort of people ought you to be in holy conduct and godliness, [12]looking for and hastening the coming of the day of God, because of which the heavens will be destroyed by burning, and the elements will melt with intense heat! [13]But according to His promise we are looking for new heavens and a new earth, in which righteousness dwells.

14 Therefore, beloved, since you look for these things, be diligent to be found by Him in peace, spotless

---

[a]**3:10** Two early mss read *discovered*

and blameless, ¹⁵and regard the patience of our Lord *as* salvation; just as also our beloved brother Paul, according to the wisdom given him, wrote to you, ¹⁶as also in all *his* letters, speaking in them of these things, in which are some things hard to understand, which the untaught and unstable distort, as *they do* also the rest of the Scriptures, to their own destruction.

¹⁷You therefore, beloved, knowing this beforehand, be on your guard so that you are not carried away by the error of unprincipled men and fall from your own steadfastness, ¹⁸but grow in the grace and knowledge of our Lord and Savior Jesus Christ. To Him *be* the glory, both now and to the day of eternity. Amen.

1 JOHN

Introduction, The Incarnate Word

1 What was from the beginning, what we have heard, what we have seen with our eyes, what we have looked at and touched with our hands, concerning the Word of Life— ²and the life was manifested, and we have seen and testify and proclaim to you the eternal life, which was with the Father and was manifested to us— ³what we have seen and heard we proclaim to you also, so that you too may have fellowship with us; and indeed our fellowship is with the Father, and with His Son Jesus Christ. ⁴These things we write, so that our joy may be made complete.

God Is Light

5 This is the message we have heard from Him and announce to you, that God is Light, and in Him there is no darkness at all. ⁶If we say that we have fellowship with Him and *yet* walk in the darkness, we lie and do not practice the truth; ⁷but if we walk in the Light as He Himself is in the Light, we have fellowship with one another, and the blood of Jesus His Son cleanses us from all sin. ⁸If we say that we have no sin, we are deceiving ourselves and the truth is not in us. ⁹If we confess our sins, He is faithful and righteous to forgive us our sins and to cleanse us from all unrighteousness. ¹⁰If we say that we have not sinned, we make Him a liar and His word is not in us.

Christ Is Our Advocate

2 My little children, I am writing these things to you so that you may not sin. And if anyone sins, we have an ªAdvocate with the Father, Jesus Christ the righteous; ²and He Himself is the propitiation for our sins; and not for ours only, but also for *those of* the whole world.

3 By this we know that we have come to know Him, if we keep His commandments. ⁴The one who says, "I have come to know Him," and does not keep His commandments, is a liar, and the truth is not in him; ⁵but whoever keeps His word, in him the love of God has truly been perfected. By this we know that we are in Him: ⁶the one who says he abides in Him ought himself to walk in the same manner as He walked.

7 Beloved, I am not writing a new commandment to you, but an old commandment which you have had from the beginning; the old commandment is the word which you have heard. ⁸On the other hand, I am writing a new commandment to you, which is true in Him and in you, because the darkness is passing away and the true Light is already shining.

⁹The one who says he is in the Light and *yet* hates his brother is in the darkness until now. ¹⁰The one who loves his brother abides in the Light and there is no cause for stumbling in him. ¹¹But the one who hates his brother is in the darkness and walks in the darkness, and does not know where he is going because the darkness has blinded his eyes.

12 I am writing to you, little children, because your sins have been forgiven you for His name's sake. ¹³I am writing to you, fathers, because you know Him who has been from the beginning. I am writing to you, young men, because you have overcome the evil one. I have written to you, children, because you know the Father. ¹⁴I have written to you, fathers, because you know Him who has been from the beginning. I have written to you, young men, because you are strong, and the word of God abides in you, and you have overcome the evil one.

Do Not Love the World

15 Do not love the world nor the things in the world. If anyone loves the world, the love of the Father is not in him. ¹⁶For all that is in the world, the lust of the flesh and the lust of the eyes and the boastful pride of life, is not from the Father, but is from the world. ¹⁷The world is passing away, and

ª**2:1** Gr *Paracletos*, one called alongside to help; or *Intercessor* *also* its lusts; but the one who does the will of God lives forever.

18 Children, it is the last hour; and just as you heard that antichrist is coming, even now many antichrists have appeared; from this we know that it is the last hour. [19]They went out from us, but they were not *really* of us; for if they had been of us, they would have remained with us; but *they went out,* so that it would be shown that they all are not of us. [20]But you have an anointing from the Holy One, and you all know. [21]I have not written to you because you do not know the truth, but because you do know it, and because no lie is of the truth. [22]Who is the liar but the one who denies that Jesus is the Christ? This is the antichrist, the one who denies the Father and the Son. [23]Whoever denies the Son does not have the Father; the one who confesses the Son has the Father also. [24]As for you, let that abide in you which you heard from the beginning. If what you heard from the beginning abides in you, you also will abide in the Son and in the Father.

The Promise Is Eternal Life

[25]This is the promise which He Himself made to us: eternal life.

26 These things I have written to you concerning those who are trying to deceive you. [27]As for you, the anointing which you received from Him abides in you, and you have no need for anyone to teach you; but as His anointing teaches you about all things, and is true and is not a lie, and just as it has taught you, you abide in Him.

28 Now, little children, abide in Him, so that when He appears, we may have confidence and not shrink away from Him in shame at His coming. [29]If you know that He is righteous, you know that everyone also who practices righteousness is born of Him.

Children of God Love One Another

3 See how great a love the Father has bestowed on us, that we would be called children of God; and *such* we are. For this reason the world does not know us, because it did not know Him. [2]Beloved, now we are children of God, and it has not appeared as yet what we will be. We know that when He appears, we will be like Him, because we will see Him just as He is. [3]And everyone who has this hope *fixed* on Him purifies himself, just as He is pure.

4 Everyone who practices sin also practices lawlessness; and sin is lawlessness. [5]You know that He appeared in order to take away sins; and in Him there is no sin. [6]No one who abides in Him sins; no one who sins has seen Him or knows Him. [7]Little children, make sure no one deceives you; the one who practices righteousness is righteous, just as He is righteous; [8]the one who practices sin is of the devil; for the devil has sinned from the beginning. The Son of God appeared for this purpose, to destroy the works of the devil. [9]No one who is born of God practices sin, because His seed abides in him; and he cannot sin, because he is born of God. [10]By this the children of God and the children of the devil are obvious: anyone who does not practice righteousness is not of God, nor the one who does not love his brother.

11 For this is the message which you have heard from the beginning, that we should love one another; [12]not as Cain, *who* was of the evil one and slew his brother. And for what reason did he slay him? Because his deeds were evil, and his brother's were righteous.

13 Do not be surprised, brethren, if the world hates you. [14]We know that we have passed out of death into life, because we love the brethren. He who does not love abides in death. [15]Everyone who hates his brother is a murderer; and you know that no murderer

has eternal life abiding in him. [16]We know love by this, that He laid down His life for us; and we ought to lay down our lives for the brethren. [17]But whoever has the world's goods, and sees his brother in need and closes his heart against him, how does the love of God abide in him? [18]Little children, let us not love with word or with tongue, but in deed and truth. [19]We will know by this that we are of the truth, and will assure our heart before Him [20]in whatever our heart condemns us; for God is greater than our heart and knows all things. [21]Beloved, if our heart does not condemn us, we have confidence before God; [22]and whatever we ask we receive from Him, because we keep His commandments and do the things that are pleasing in His sight.

23 This is His commandment, that we believe in the name of His Son Jesus Christ, and love one another, just as He commanded us. [24]The one who keeps His commandments abides in Him, and He in him. We know by this that He abides in us, by the Spirit whom He has given us.

Testing the Spirits

4 Beloved, do not believe every spirit, but test the spirits to see whether they are from God, because many false prophets have gone out into the world. ²By this you know the Spirit of God: every spirit that confesses that Jesus Christ has come in the flesh is from God; ³and every spirit that does not confess Jesus is not from God; this is the *spirit* of the antichrist, of which you have heard that it is coming, and now it is already in the world. ⁴You are from God, little children, and have overcome them; because greater is He who is in you than he who is in the world. ⁵They are from the world; therefore they speak *as* from the world, and the world listens to them. ⁶We are from God; he who knows God listens to us; he who is not from God does not listen to us. By this we know the spirit of truth and the spirit of error.

God Is Love

7 Beloved, let us love one another, for love is from God; and everyone who loves is born of God and knows God. ⁸The one who does not love does not know God, for God is love. ⁹By this the love of God was manifested in us, that God has sent His only begotten Son into the world so that we might live through Him. ¹⁰In this is love, not that we loved God, but that He loved us and sent His Son *to be* the propitiation for our sins. ¹¹Beloved, if God so loved us, we also ought to love one another.

¹²No one has seen God at any time; if we love one another, God abides in us, and His love is perfected in us. ¹³By this we know that we abide in Him and He in us, because He has given us of His Spirit. ¹⁴We have seen and testify that the Father has sent the Son *to be* the Savior of the world.

15 Whoever confesses that Jesus is the Son of God, God abides in him, and he in God. ¹⁶We have come to know and have believed the love which God has for us. God is love, and the one who abides in love abides in God, and God abides in him. ¹⁷By this, love is perfected with us, so that we may have confidence in the day of judgment; because as He is, so also are we in this world. ¹⁸There is no fear in love; but perfect love casts out fear, because fear involves punishment, and the one who fears is not perfected in love. ¹⁹We love, because He first loved us. ²⁰If someone says, "I love God," and hates his brother, he is a liar; for the one who does not love his brother whom he has seen, cannot love God whom he has not seen. ²¹And this commandment we have from Him, that the one who loves God should love his brother also.

Overcoming the World

5 Whoever believes that Jesus is the ^aChrist is born of God, and whoever loves the Father loves the *child* born of Him. ²By this we know that we love the children of God, when we love God and observe His commandments. ³For this is the love of God, that we keep His commandments; and His commandments are not burdensome. ⁴For whatever is born of God overcomes the world; and this is the victory that has overcome the world—our faith.

5 Who is the one who overcomes the world, but he who believes that Jesus is the Son of God? ⁶This is the One who came by water and blood, Jesus Christ; not with the water only, but with the water and with the blood. It is the Spirit who testifies, because the Spirit is the truth. ⁷For there are three that testify: ^{8b}the Spirit and the water and the blood; and the three are in agreement. ⁹If we receive the testimony of men, the testimony of God is greater; for the testimony of God is this, that He has testified concerning His Son. ¹⁰The one who believes in the Son of God has the testimony in himself; the one who does not believe God has made Him a liar, because he has not believed in the testimony that God has given concerning His Son. ¹¹And the testimony is this, that God has given us eternal life, and this life is in His Son. ¹²He who has the Son has the life; he who does not have the Son of God does not have the life.

This Is Written That You May Know

13 These things I have written to you who believe in the name of the Son of God, so that you may know that you have eternal life. ¹⁴This is the confidence which we have before Him, that, if we ask anything according to His will, He hears us. ¹⁵And if we know that He hears us *in* whatever we ask, we know that we have the requests which we have asked from Him.

16 If anyone sees his brother committing a sin not *leading* to death, he shall ask and *God* will for him give life to those who commit sin not *leading* to death. There is a sin *leading* to death; I do not say that he should make request for this. ¹⁷All unrighteousness is sin, and there is a sin not *leading* to death.

18 We know that no one who is born of God sins; but He who was born of God keeps him, and the evil one does not touch him. ¹⁹We know that we are of God, and that the whole world lies in *the power of* the evil one. ²⁰And we know that the Son of God has come, and

^a**5:1** I.e. Messiah; ^a**5:8** A few late mss add ...*in heaven, the Father, the Word, and the Holy Spirit, and these three are one. And there are three that testify on earth, the Spirit*

has given us understanding so that we may know Him who is true; and we are in Him who is true, in His Son Jesus Christ. This is the true God and eternal life.

21 Little children, guard yourselves from idols.

2 JOHN

Walk According to His Commandments

1 The elder to the chosen lady and her children, whom I love in truth; and not only I, but also all who know the truth, ²for the sake of the truth which abides in us and will be with us forever: ³Grace, mercy *and* peace will be with us, from God the Father and from Jesus Christ, the Son of the Father, in truth and love.

4 I was very glad to find *some* of your children walking in truth, just as we have received commandment *to do* from the Father. ⁵Now I ask you, lady, not as though I *were* writing to you a new commandment, but the one which we have had from the beginning, that we love one another. ⁶And this is love, that we walk according to His commandments. This is the commandment, just as you have heard from the beginning, that you should walk in it.

7 For many deceivers have gone out into the world, those who do not acknowledge Jesus Christ *as* coming in the flesh. This is the deceiver and the antichrist. ⁸Watch yourselves, that you do not lose what we have accomplished, but that you may receive a full reward. ⁹Anyone who goes too far and does not abide in the teaching of Christ, does not have God; the one who abides in the teaching, he has both the Father and the Son. ¹⁰If anyone comes to you and does not bring this teaching, do not receive him into *your* house, and do not give him a greeting; ¹¹for the one who gives him a greeting participates in his evil deeds.

12 Though I have many things to write to you, I do not want to *do so* with paper and ink; but I hope to come to you and speak face to face, so that your joy may be made full.

13 The children of your chosen sister greet you.

3 JOHN

You Walk in the Truth

1 The elder to the beloved Gaius, whom I love in truth.

2 Beloved, I pray that in all respects you may prosper and be in good health, just as your soul prospers. ³For I was very glad when brethren came and testified to your truth, *that is,* how you are walking in truth. ⁴I have no greater joy than this, to hear of my children walking in the truth.

5 Beloved, you are acting faithfully in whatever you accomplish for the brethren, and especially *when they are* strangers; ⁶and they have testified to your love before the church. You will do well to send them on their way in a manner worthy of God. ⁷For they went out for the sake of the Name, accepting nothing from the Gentiles. ⁸Therefore we ought to support such men, so that we may be fellow workers with the truth.

9 I wrote something to the church; but Diotrephes, who loves to be first among them, does not accept what we say. ¹⁰For this reason, if I come, I will call attention to his deeds which he does, unjustly accusing us with wicked words; and not satisfied with this, he himself does not receive the brethren, either, and he forbids those who desire *to do so* and puts *them* out of the church.

11 Beloved, do not imitate what is evil, but what is good. The one who does good is of God; the one who does evil has not seen God. ¹²Demetrius has received a *good* testimony from everyone, and from the truth itself; and we add our testimony, and you know that our testimony is true.

13 I had many things to write to you, but I am not willing to write *them* to you with pen and ink; ¹⁴but I hope to see you shortly, and we will speak face to face.

15 Peace *be* to you. The friends greet you. Greet the friends by name.

JUDE

The Warnings of History to the Ungodly

1 Jude, a bond-servant of Jesus Christ, and brother of James,

To those who are the called, beloved in God the Father, and kept for Jesus Christ: ²May mercy and peace and love be multiplied to you.

3 Beloved, while I was making every effort to write you about our common salvation, I felt the necessity to write to you appealing that you contend earnestly for the faith which was once for all handed down to the saints. ⁴For certain persons have crept in unnoticed, those who were long beforehand marked out for this condemnation, ungodly persons who turn the grace of our God into licentiousness and deny our only Master and Lord, Jesus Christ.

5 Now I desire to remind you, though you know all things once for all, that ªthe Lord, after saving a people out of the land of Egypt, subsequently destroyed those who did not believe. ⁶And angels who did not keep their own domain, but abandoned their proper abode, He has kept in eternal bonds under darkness for the judgment of the great day, ⁷just as Sodom and Gomorrah and the cities around them, since they in the same way as these indulged in gross immorality and went after strange flesh, are exhibited as an example in undergoing the punishment of eternal fire.

8 Yet in the same way these men, also by dreaming, defile the flesh, and reject authority, and revile angelic majesties. ⁹But Michael the archangel, when he disputed with the devil and argued about

ª**1:5** Two early mss read *Jesus*

the body of Moses, did not dare pronounce against him a railing judgment, but said, "The Lord rebuke you!" [10]But these men revile the things which they do not understand; and the things which they know by instinct, like unreasoning animals, by these things they are destroyed. [11]Woe to them! For they have gone the way of Cain, and for pay they have rushed headlong into the error of Balaam, and perished in the rebellion of Korah. [12]These are the men who are hidden reefs in your love feasts when they feast with you without fear, caring for themselves; clouds without water, carried along by winds; autumn trees without fruit, doubly dead, uprooted; [13]wild waves of the sea, casting up their own shame like foam; wandering stars, for whom the black darkness has been reserved forever.

[14]*It was* also about these men *that* Enoch, *in* the seventh *generation* from Adam, prophesied, saying, "Behold, the Lord came with many thousands of His holy ones, [15]to execute judgment upon all, and to convict all the ungodly of all their ungodly deeds which they have done in an ungodly way, and of all the harsh things which ungodly sinners have spoken against Him." [16]These are grumblers, finding fault, following after their *own* lusts; they speak arrogantly, flattering people for the sake of *gaining an* advantage.

Keep Yourselves in the Love of God

[17]But you, beloved, ought to remember the words that were spoken beforehand by the apostles of our Lord Jesus Christ, [18]that they were saying to you, "In the last time there will be mockers, following after their own ungodly lusts." [19]These are the ones who cause divisions, worldly-minded, devoid of the Spirit. [20]But you, beloved, building yourselves up on your most holy faith, praying in the Holy Spirit, [21]keep yourselves in the love of God, waiting anxiously for the mercy of our Lord Jesus Christ to eternal life. [22]And have mercy on some, who are doubting; [23]save others, snatching them out of the fire; and on some have mercy with fear, hating even the garment polluted by the flesh.

[24]Now to Him who is able to keep you from stumbling, and to make you stand in the presence of His glory blameless with great joy, [25]to the only God our Savior, through Jesus Christ our Lord, *be* glory, majesty, dominion and authority, before all time and now and forever. Amen.

REVELATION

The Revelation of Jesus Christ

1 The Revelation of Jesus Christ, which God gave Him to show to His bond-servants, the things which must soon take place; and He sent and communicated *it* by His angel to His bond-servant John, [2]who testified to the word of God and to the testimony of Jesus Christ, *even* to all that he saw. [3]Blessed is he who reads and those who hear the words of the prophecy, and heed the things which are written in it; for the time is near.

Message to the Seven Churches

4 John to the seven churches that are in Asia: Grace to you and peace, from Him who is and who was and who is to come, and from the seven Spirits who are before His throne, [5]and from Jesus Christ, the faithful witness, the firstborn of the dead, and the ruler of the kings of the earth. To Him who loves us and released us from our sins by His blood— [6]and He has made us *to be* a kingdom, priests to His God and Father—to Him *be* the glory and the dominion forever and ever. Amen [7]BEHOLD, HE IS COMING WITH THE CLOUDS, and every eye will see Him, even those who pierced

Him; and all the tribes of the earth will mourn over Him. So it is to be. Amen.

8 "I am the Alpha and the Omega," says the Lord God, "who is and who was and who is to come, the Almighty."

The Patmos Vision

9 I, John, your brother and fellow partaker in the tribulation and kingdom and perseverance *which are* in Jesus, was on the island called Patmos because of the word of God and the testimony of Jesus. [10]I was ªin the Spirit on the Lord's day, and I heard behind me a loud voice like *the sound* of a trumpet, [11]saying, "Write in a book what you see, and send *it* to the seven churches: to Ephesus and to Smyrna and to Pergamum and to Thyatira and to Sardis and to Philadelphia and to Laodicea."

12 Then I turned to see the voice that was speaking with me. And having turned I saw seven golden lampstands; [13]and in the middle of the lampstands *I saw* one like ᵇa son of man, clothed in a robe reaching to the feet, and girded across His chest with a golden sash.

ª**1:10** *Or in spirit;* ᵇ**1:13** *Or the Son of Man*

¹⁴His head and His hair were white like white wool, like snow; and His eyes were like a flame of fire. ¹⁵His feet *were* like burnished bronze, when it has been made to glow in a furnace, and His voice *was* like the sound of many waters. ¹⁶In His right hand He held seven stars, and out of His mouth came a sharp two-edged sword; and His face was like the sun shining in its strength.

17 When I saw Him, I fell at His feet like a dead man. And He placed His right hand on me, saying, "Do not be afraid; I am the first and the last, ¹⁸and the living One; and I was dead, and behold, I am alive forevermore, and I have the keys of death and of Hades. ¹⁹Therefore write the things which you have seen, and the things which are, and the things which will take place after these things. ²⁰As for the mystery of the seven stars which you saw in My right hand, and the seven golden lampstands: the seven stars are the angels of the seven churches, and the seven lampstands are the seven churches.

Message to Ephesus

2 "To the angel of the church in Ephesus write:

The One who holds the seven stars in His right hand, the One who walks among the seven golden lampstands, says this:

2 'I know your deeds and your toil and perseverance, and that you cannot tolerate evil men, and you put to the test those who call themselves apostles, and they are not, and you found them *to be* false; ³and you have perseverance and have endured for My name's sake, and have not grown weary. ⁴But I have *this* against you, that you have left your first love. ⁵Therefore remember from where you have fallen, and repent and do the deeds you did at first; or else I am coming to you and will remove your lampstand out of its place—unless you repent. ⁶Yet this you do have, that you hate the deeds of the Nicolaitans, which I also hate. ⁷He who has an ear, let him hear what the Spirit says to the churches. To him who overcomes, I will grant to eat of the tree of life which is in the Paradise of God.'

Message to Smyrna

8 "And to the angel of the church in Smyrna write:

The first and the last, who was dead, and has come to life, says this:

9 'I know your tribulation and your poverty (but you are rich), and the blasphemy by those who say they are Jews and are not, but are a synagogue of Satan. ¹⁰Do not fear what you are about to suffer. Behold, the devil is about to cast some of you into prison, so that you will be tested, and you will have tribulation for ten days. Be faithful until death, and I will give you the crown of life. [11]He who has an ear, let him hear what the Spirit says to the churches. He who overcomes will not be hurt by the second death.'

Message to Pergamum

12 "And to the angel of the church in Pergamum write:

The One who has the sharp two-edged sword says this:

13 'I know where you dwell, where Satan's throne is; and you hold fast My name, and did not deny My faith even in the days of Antipas, My witness, My faithful one, who was killed among you, where Satan dwells. [14]But I have a few things against you, because you have there some who hold the teaching of Balaam, who kept teaching Balak to put a stumbling block before the sons of Israel, to eat things sacrificed to idols and to commit *acts of* immorality. [15]So you also have some who in the same way hold the teaching of the Nicolaitans. [16]Therefore repent; or else I am coming to you quickly, and I will make war against them with the sword of My mouth. [17]He

who has an ear, let him hear what the Spirit says to the churches. To him who overcomes, to him I will give *some* of the hidden manna, and I will give him a white stone, and a new name written on the stone which no one knows but he who receives it.'

Message to Thyatira

18 "And to the angel of the church in Thyatira write:

The Son of God, who has eyes like a flame of fire, and His feet are like burnished bronze, says this:

19 'I know your deeds, and your love and faith and service and perseverance, and that your deeds of late are greater than at first. [20]But I have *this* against you, that you tolerate the woman Jezebel, who calls herself a prophetess, and she teaches and leads My bond-servants astray so that they commit *acts of* immorality and eat things sacrificed to idols. [21]I gave her time to repent, and she does not want to repent of her immorality. [22]Behold, I will throw her on a bed *of sickness,* and those who commit adultery with her into great tribulation, unless they repent of [a]her deeds. [23]And I will kill her children with pestilence, and all the churches will know that I am He who searches the minds and hearts; and I will give to each one of you according to your deeds. ²⁴But I say to you, the rest who are in Thyatira, who do not hold this teaching, who have not known the deep things of Satan, as they call them—I place no other burden on you. ²⁵Nevertheless what you have, hold fast until I come. ²⁶He who overcomes, and he who keeps My deeds until the end, TO HIM I WILL GIVE AUTHORITY OVER THE NATIONS; ²⁷AND HE SHALL RULE THEM WITH A ROD OF IRON, AS THE VESSELS OF THE POTTER ARE BROKEN TO PIECES, as I also have received *authority* from My Father; ²⁸and I will give him the morning star. ²⁹He who has an ear, let him hear what the Spirit says to the churches.'

Message to Sardis

3 "To the angel of the church in Sardis write:

He who has the seven Spirits of God and the seven stars, says this: 'I know your deeds, that you have a name that you are alive, but you are dead. ²Wake up, and strengthen the things that remain, which were about to die; for I have not found your deeds completed in the sight of My God. ³So remember what you have received and heard; and keep *it,* and repent. Therefore if you do not wake up, I will come like a thief, and you will not know at what hour I will come to you. ⁴But you have a few people in Sardis who have not soiled their garments; and they will walk with Me in white, for they are worthy. ⁵He who overcomes will thus be clothed in white garments; and I will not erase his name from the book of life, and I will confess his name before My Father and before His angels. ⁶He who has an ear, let him hear what the Spirit says to the churches.'

Message to Philadelphia

7 "And to the angel of the church in Philadelphia write:

He who is holy, who is true, who has the key of David, who opens and no one will shut, and who shuts and no one opens, says this:

8 'I know your ªdeeds. Behold, I have put before you an open door which no one can shut, because you have a little power, and have kept My word, and have not denied My name. ⁹Behold, I will cause *those* of the synagogue of Satan, who say that they are Jews and are not, but lie—I will make them come and bow down at your feet, and *make them* know that I have loved you. ¹⁰Because you have kept the word of My perseverance, I also will keep you from the hour of testing, that *hour* which is about to come upon the whole

ª**3:8** Or *deeds (behold...shut), that you have*

world, to test those who dwell on the earth. [11]I am coming quickly; hold fast what you have, so that no one will take your crown. [12]He who overcomes, I will make him a pillar in the temple of My God, and he will not go out from it anymore; and I will write on him the name of My God, and the name of the city of My God, the new Jerusalem, which comes down out of heaven from My God, and My new name. [13]He who has an ear, let him hear what the Spirit says to the churches.'

Message to Laodicea

14 "To the angel of the church in Laodicea write:

The Amen, the faithful and true Witness, the [a]Beginning of the creation of God, says this:

15 'I know your deeds, that you are neither cold nor hot; I wish that you were cold or hot. [16]So because you are lukewarm, and neither hot nor cold, I will spit you out of My mouth. [17]Because you say, "I am rich, and have become wealthy, and have need of nothing," and you do not know that you are wretched and miserable and poor and blind and naked, [18]I advise you to buy from Me gold refined by fire so that you may become rich, and white garments so that you may clothe yourself, and *that* the shame

of your nakedness will not be revealed; and eye salve to anoint your eyes so that you may see. [19]Those whom I love, I reprove and discipline; therefore be zealous and repent. [20]Behold, I stand at the door and knock; if anyone hears My voice and opens the door, I will come in to him and will dine with him, and he with Me. [21]He who overcomes, I will grant to him to sit down with Me on My throne, as I also overcame and sat down with My Father on His throne. [22]He who has an ear, let him hear what the Spirit says to the churches.' "

Scene in Heaven

4 After these things I looked, and behold, a door *standing* open in heaven, and the first voice which I had heard, like *the sound* of a trumpet speaking with me, said, "Come up here, and I will show you what must take place after these things." [2]Immediately I was [b]in the Spirit; and behold, a throne was standing in heaven, and One sitting on the throne. [3]And He who was sitting *was* like a jasper stone and a sardius in appearance; and *there was* a rainbow around the throne, like an emerald in appearance. [4]Around the throne *were* twenty-four thrones; and upon the thrones *I saw* twenty-four elders sitting, clothed in white garments, and golden crowns on their heads.

[a]**3:14** I.e. Origin or Source; [b]**4:2** Or *in spirit*

The Throne and Worship of the Creator

[5]Out from the throne come flashes of lightning and sounds and peals of thunder. And *there were* seven lamps of fire burning before the throne, which are the seven Spirits of God; [6]and before the throne *there was something* like a sea of glass, like crystal; and in the center and around the throne, four living creatures full of eyes in front and behind. [7]The first creature *was* like a lion, and the second creature like a calf, and the third creature had a face like that of a man, and the fourth creature *was* like a flying eagle. [8]And the four living creatures, each one of them having six wings, are full of eyes around and within; and day and night they do not cease to say, "HOLY, HOLY, HOLY *is* THE LORD GOD, THE ALMIGHTY, WHO WAS AND WHO IS AND WHO IS TO COME." [9]And when the living creatures give glory and honor and thanks to Him who sits on the throne, to Him who lives forever and ever, [10]the twenty-four elders will fall down before Him who sits on the throne, and will worship Him who lives forever and ever, and will cast their crowns before the throne, saying,

[11]"Worthy are You, our Lord and our God, to receive glory and honor and power; for You created all things, and because

of Your will they existed, and were created."

The Book with Seven Seals

[5]I saw in the right hand of Him who sat on the throne a book written inside and on the back, sealed up with seven seals. [2]And I saw a strong angel proclaiming with a loud voice, "Who is worthy to open the book and to break its seals?" [3]And no one in heaven or on the earth or under the earth was able to open the book or to look into it. [4]Then I *began* to weep greatly because no one was found worthy to open the book or to look into it; [5]and one of the elders *said to me, "Stop weeping; behold, the Lion that is from the tribe of Judah, the Root of David, has overcome so as to open the book and its seven seals."

[6] And I saw [a]between the throne (with the four living creatures) and the elders a Lamb standing, as if slain, having seven horns and seven eyes, which are the seven Spirits of God, sent out into all the earth. [7]And He came and took the book out of the right hand of Him who sat on the throne. [8]When He had taken the book, the four living creatures and the twenty-four elders fell down before the Lamb, each one holding a harp and golden bowls full of incense, which are the prayers of the saints. [9]And they

[a]**5:6** Lit in the middle of the throne and of the four living creatures, and in the middle of the elders

*sang a new song, saying, "Worthy are You to take the book and to break its seals; for You were slain, and purchased for God with Your blood *men* from every tribe and tongue and people and nation. ¹⁰"You have made them *to be* a kingdom and priests to our God; and they will reign upon the earth."

Angels Exalt the Lamb

11 Then I looked, and I heard the voice of many angels around the throne and the living creatures and the elders; and the number of them was myriads of myriads, and thousands of thousands, ¹²saying with a loud voice, "Worthy is the Lamb that was slain to receive power and riches and wisdom and might and honor and glory and blessing." ¹³And every created thing which is in heaven and on the earth and under the earth and on the sea, and all things in them, I heard saying, "To Him who sits on the throne, and to the Lamb, *be* blessing and honor and glory and dominion forever and ever." ¹⁴And the four living creatures kept saying, "Amen." And the elders fell down and worshiped.

The First Seal—
Rider on White Horse

6 Then I saw when the Lamb broke one of the seven seals, and I heard one of the four living creatures saying as with a voice of thunder, "Come." ²I looked, and behold, a white horse, and he who sat on it had a bow; and a crown was given to him, and he went out conquering and to conquer.

The Second Seal—War

3 When He broke the second seal, I heard the second living creature saying, "Come." ⁴And another, a red horse, went out; and to him who sat on it, it was granted to take peace from the earth, and that *men* would slay one another; and a great sword was given to him.

The Third Seal—Famine

5 When He broke the third seal, I heard the third living creature saying, "Come." I looked, and behold, a black horse; and he who sat on it had a pair of scales in his hand. ⁶And I heard *something* like a voice in the center of the four living creatures saying, "A ᵃquart of wheat for a denarius, and three quarts of barley for a denarius; and do not damage the oil and the wine."

The Fourth Seal—Death

7 When the Lamb broke the fourth seal, I heard the voice of the fourth living creature saying, "Come." ⁸I looked, and behold, an ashen horse; and he who sat on it had the name Death; and Hades was following with him. Authority was given to them over a fourth

ᵃ**6:6** Gr *choenix*; i.e. a dry measure almost equal to a qt of the earth, to kill with sword and with famine and with pestilence and by the wild beasts of the earth.

The Fifth Seal—Martyrs

9 When the Lamb broke the fifth seal, I saw underneath the altar the souls of those who had been slain because of the word of God, and because of the testimony which they had maintained; [10]and they cried out with a loud voice, saying, "How long, O Lord, holy and true, will You refrain from judging and avenging our blood on those who dwell on the earth?" [11]And there was given to each of them a white robe; and they were told that they should rest for a little while longer, until *the number of* their fellow servants and their brethren who were to be killed even as they had been, would be completed also.

The Sixth Seal—Terror

12 I looked when He broke the sixth seal, and there was a great earthquake; and the sun became black as sackcloth *made* of hair, and the whole moon became like blood; [13]and the stars of the sky fell to the earth, as a fig tree casts its unripe figs when shaken by a great wind. [14]The sky was split apart like a scroll when it is rolled up, and every mountain and island were moved out of their places. [15]Then the kings of the earth and the great men and the [a]commanders and

the rich and the strong and every slave and free man hid themselves in the caves and among the rocks of the mountains; [16]and they *said to the mountains and to the rocks, "Fall on us and hide us from the presence of Him who sits on the throne, and from the wrath of the Lamb; [17]for the great day of their wrath has come, and who is able to stand?"

An Interlude

7 After this I saw four angels standing at the four corners of the earth, holding back the four winds of the earth, so that no wind would blow on the earth or on the sea or on any tree. [2]And I saw another angel ascending from the rising of the sun, having the seal of the living God; and he cried out with a loud voice to the four angels to whom it was granted to harm the earth and the sea, [3]saying, "Do not harm the earth or the sea or the trees until we have sealed the bond-servants of our God on their foreheads."

The 144,000

4 And I heard the number of those who were sealed, one hundred and forty-four thousand sealed from every tribe of the sons of Israel: [5]from the tribe of Judah, twelve thousand *were* sealed, from the tribe of Reuben twelve thousand, from the tribe of

6:15 I.e. chiliarchs, in command of one thousand troops

Gad twelve thousand,
[6]from the tribe of Asher twelve thousand, from the tribe of Naphtali twelve thousand, from the tribe of Manasseh twelve thousand,
[7]from the tribe of Simeon twelve thousand, from the tribe of Levi twelve thousand, from the tribe of Issachar twelve thousand,
[8]from the tribe of Zebulun twelve thousand, from the tribe of Joseph twelve thousand, from the tribe of Benjamin, twelve thousand *were* sealed.

A Multitude from the Tribulation

9 After these things I looked, and behold, a great multitude which no one could count, from every nation and *all* tribes and peoples and tongues, standing before the throne and before the Lamb, clothed in white robes, and palm branches *were* in their hands; [10]and they cry out with a loud voice, saying,

"Salvation to our God who sits on the throne, and to the Lamb." [11]And all the angels were standing around the throne and *around* the elders and the four living creatures; and they fell on their faces before the throne and worshiped God, [12]saying,

"Amen, blessing and glory and wisdom and thanksgiving and honor and power and might, *be* to our God forever and ever. Amen."

13 Then one of the elders answered, saying to me, "These who are clothed in the white robes, who are they, and where have they come from?" [14]I said to him, "My lord, you know." And he said to me, "These are the ones who come out of the great tribulation, and they have washed their robes and made them white in the blood of the Lamb. [15]For this reason, they are before the throne of God; and they serve Him day and night in His temple; and He who sits on the throne will spread His tabernacle over them. [16]They will hunger no longer, nor thirst anymore; nor will the sun beat down on them, nor any heat; [17]for the Lamb in the center of the throne will be their shepherd, and will guide them to springs of the water of life; and God will wipe every tear from their eyes."

The Seventh Seal—the Trumpets

8 When the Lamb broke the seventh seal, there was silence in heaven for about half an hour. [2]And I saw the seven angels who stand before God, and seven trumpets were given to them.

3 Another angel came and stood at the altar, holding a golden censer; and much incense was given to him, so that he might add it to the prayers of all the saints on the golden altar which was before the throne. ⁴And the smoke of the incense, with the prayers of the saints, went up before God out of the angel's hand. ⁵Then the angel took the censer and filled it with the fire of the altar, and threw it to the earth; and there followed peals of thunder and sounds and flashes of lightning and an earthquake.

6 And the seven angels who had the seven trumpets prepared themselves to sound them.

7 The first sounded, and there came hail and fire, mixed with blood, and they were thrown to the earth; and a third of the earth was burned up, and a third of the trees were burned up, and all the green grass was burned up.

8 The second angel sounded, and *something* like a great mountain burning with fire was thrown into the sea; and a third of the sea became blood, ⁹and a third of the creatures which were in the sea and had life, died; and a third of the ships were destroyed.

10 The third angel sounded, and a great star fell from heaven, burning like a torch, and it fell on a third of the rivers and on the springs of waters. ¹¹The name of the star is called Wormwood; and a third of the waters became wormwood, and many men died from the waters, because they were made bitter.

12 The fourth angel sounded, and a third of the sun and a third of the moon and a third of the stars were struck, so that a third of them would be darkened and the day would not shine for a third of it, and the night in the same way.

13 Then I looked, and I heard an eagle flying in midheaven, saying with a loud voice, "Woe, woe, woe to those who dwell on the earth, because of the remaining blasts of the trumpet of the three angels who are about to sound!"

The Fifth Trumpet—
the Bottomless Pit

9 Then the fifth angel sounded, and I saw a star from heaven which had fallen to the earth; and the key of the bottomless pit was given to him. ²He opened the bottomless pit, and smoke went up out of the pit, like the smoke of a great furnace; and the sun and the air were darkened by the smoke of the pit. ³Then out of the smoke came locusts upon the earth, and power was given them, as the

scorpions of the earth have power. [4]They were told not to hurt the grass of the earth, nor any green thing, nor any tree, but only the men who do not have the seal of God on their foreheads. [5]And they were not permitted to kill anyone, but to torment for five months; and their torment was like the torment of a scorpion when it stings a man. [6]And in those days men will seek death and will not find it; they will long to die, and death flees from them.

7 The appearance of the locusts was like horses prepared for battle; and on their heads appeared to be crowns like gold, and their faces were like the faces of men. [8]They had hair like the hair of women, and their teeth were like *the teeth* of lions. [9]They had breastplates like breastplates of iron; and the sound of their wings was like the sound of chariots, of many horses rushing to battle. [10]They have tails like scorpions, and stings; and in their tails is their power to hurt men for five months. [11]They have as king over them, the angel of the abyss; his name in Hebrew is [a]Abaddon, and in the Greek he has the name Apollyon.

12 The first woe is past; behold, two woes are still coming after these things.

The Sixth Trumpet—
Army from the East

13 Then the sixth angel sounded, and I heard a voice from the [b]four horns of the golden altar which is before God, [14]one saying to the sixth angel who had the trumpet, "Release the four angels who are bound at the great river Euphrates." [15]And the four angels, who had been prepared for the hour and day and month and year, were released, so that they would kill a third of mankind. [16]The number of the armies of the horsemen was two hundred million; I heard the number of them. [17]And this is how I saw in the vision the horses and those who sat on them: *the riders* had breastplates *the color* of fire and of hyacinth and of brimstone; and the heads of the horses are like the heads of lions; and out of their mouths proceed fire and smoke and brimstone. [18]A third of mankind was killed by these three plagues, by the fire and the smoke and the brimstone which proceeded out of their mouths. [19]For the power of the horses is in their mouths and in their tails; for their tails are like serpents and have heads, and with them they do harm.

20 The rest of mankind, who were not killed by these plagues, did not repent of the works of their hands, so as not to worship demons, and

[a]**9:11** I.e. destruction; [b]**9:13** Two early mss do not contain *four*

the idols of gold and of silver and of brass and of stone and of wood, which can neither see nor hear nor walk; ²¹and they did not repent of their murders nor of their sorceries nor of their immorality nor of their thefts.

The Angel and the Little Book

10 I saw another strong angel coming down out of heaven, clothed with a cloud; and the rainbow was upon his head, and his face was like the sun, and his feet like pillars of fire; ²and he had in his hand a little book which was open. He placed his right foot on the sea and his left on the land; ³and he cried out with a loud voice, as when a lion roars; and when he had cried out, the seven peals of thunder uttered their voices. ⁴When the seven peals of thunder had spoken, I was about to write; and I heard a voice from heaven saying, "Seal up the things which the seven peals of thunder have spoken and do not write them." ⁵Then the angel whom I saw standing on the sea and on the land lifted up his right hand to heaven, ⁶and swore by Him who lives forever and ever, WHO CREATED HEAVEN AND THE THINGS IN IT, AND THE EARTH AND THE THINGS IN IT, AND THE SEA AND THE THINGS IN IT, that there will be delay no longer, ⁷but in the days of the voice of the seventh angel, when he is about to sound, then the mystery of God is finished, as He preached to His servants the prophets.

8 Then the voice which I heard from heaven, *I heard* again speaking with me, and saying, "Go, take the book which is open in the hand of the angel who stands on the sea and on the land." ⁹So I went to the angel, telling him to give me the little book. And he *said to me, "Take it and eat it; it will make your stomach bitter, but in your mouth it will be sweet as honey." ¹⁰I took the little book out of the angel's hand and ate it, and in my mouth it was sweet as honey; and when I had eaten it, my stomach was made bitter. ¹¹And they *said to me, "You must prophesy again concerning many peoples and nations and tongues and kings."

The Two Witnesses

11 Then there was given me a measuring rod like a staff; and someone said, "Get up and measure the temple of God and the altar, and those who worship in it. ²Leave out the court which is outside the temple and do not measure it, for it has been given to the nations; and they will tread under foot the holy city for forty-two months. ³And I will grant *authority* to my two witnesses, and they will prophesy for twelve hundred and sixty days, clothed in sackcloth." [4]These are the two olive trees and the two lampstands that stand before the Lord of the earth. [5]And if anyone wants to harm them, fire flows out of their mouth and devours their enemies; so if anyone wants to harm them, he must be killed in this way. [6]These have the power to shut up the sky, so that rain will not fall during the days of their prophesying; and they have power over the waters to turn them into blood, and to strike the earth with every plague, as often as they desire.

[7] When they have finished their testimony, the beast that comes up out of the abyss will make war with them, and overcome them and kill them. [8]And their dead bodies *will lie* in the street of the great city which [a]mystically is called Sodom and Egypt, where also their Lord was crucified. [9]Those from the peoples and tribes and tongues and nations *will* look at their dead [b]bodies for three and a half days, and will not permit their dead bodies to be laid in a tomb. [10]And those who dwell on the earth *will* rejoice over them and celebrate; and they will send gifts to one another, because these two prophets tormented those who dwell on the earth.

[11] But after the three and a half days, the breath of life from God came into them, and they stood on their feet; and great fear fell upon those who were watching them. [12]And they heard a loud voice from heaven saying to them, "Come up here." Then they went up into heaven in the cloud, and their enemies watched them. [13]And in that hour there was a great earthquake, and a tenth of the city fell; seven thousand people were killed in the earthquake, and the rest were terrified and gave glory to the God of heaven.

[14] The second woe is past; behold, the third woe is coming quickly.

The Seventh Trumpet—
Christ's Reign Foreseen

[15] Then the seventh angel sounded; and there were loud voices in heaven, saying,

"The kingdom of the world has become *the kingdom* of our Lord and of His [c]Christ; and He will reign forever and ever." [16]And the twenty-four elders, who sit on their thrones before God, fell on their faces and worshiped God, [17]saying,

"We give You thanks, O Lord God, the Almighty, who are and who were, because You have taken Your great power and have begun to reign. [18]And the nations were enraged, and Your wrath came, and the time *came* for the dead to

[a]11:8 Lit *spiritually*; [b]11:9 Lit *body*; [c]11:15 I.e. Messiah

be judged, and *the time* to reward Your bond-servants the prophets and the saints and those who fear Your name, the small and the great, and to destroy those who destroy the earth."

19 And the temple of God which is in heaven was opened; and the ark of His covenant appeared in His temple, and there were flashes of lightning and sounds and peals of thunder and an earthquake and a great hailstorm.

The Woman, Israel

12 A great sign appeared in heaven: a woman clothed with the sun, and the moon under her feet, and on her head a crown of twelve stars; ²and she was with child; and she *cried out, being in labor and in pain to give birth.

The Red Dragon, Satan

³Then another sign appeared in heaven: and behold, a great red dragon having seven heads and ten horns, and on his heads *were* seven diadems. ⁴And his tail *swept away a third of the stars of heaven and threw them to the earth. And the dragon stood before the woman who was about to give birth, so that when she gave birth he might devour her child.

The Male Child, Christ

⁵And she gave birth to a son, a male *child,* who is to rule all the nations with a rod of iron; and her child was caught up to God and to His throne. ⁶Then the woman fled into the wilderness where she *had a place prepared by God, so that there she would be nourished for one thousand two hundred and sixty days.

The Angel, Michael

7 And there was war in heaven, Michael and his angels waging war with the dragon. The dragon and his angels waged war, ⁸and they were not strong enough, and there was no longer a place found for them in heaven. ⁹And the great dragon was thrown down, the serpent of old who is called the devil and Satan, who deceives the whole world; he was thrown down to the earth, and his angels were thrown down with him. ¹⁰Then I heard a loud voice in heaven, saying,

"Now the salvation, and the power, and the kingdom of our God and the authority of His Christ have come, for the accuser of our brethren has been thrown down, he who accuses them before our God day and night. ¹¹And they overcame him because of the blood of the Lamb and because of the word of their testimony, and they did not love their life even when faced with death. ¹²For this reason, rejoice, O heavens and you who dwell in them. Woe to the earth and the sea, because the devil has come down to you, having great wrath, knowing that he has *only* a short time."

13 And when the dragon saw that he was thrown down to the earth, he persecuted the woman who gave birth to the male *child*. [14]But the two wings of the great eagle were given to the woman, so that she could fly into the wilderness to her place, where she *was nourished for a time and times and half a time, from the presence of the serpent. [15]And the serpent poured water like a river out of his mouth after the woman, so that he might cause her to be swept away with the flood. [16]But the earth helped the woman, and the earth opened its mouth and drank up the river which the dragon poured out of his mouth. [17]So the dragon was enraged with the woman, and went off to make war with the rest of her children, who keep the commandments of God and hold to the testimony of Jesus.

The Beast from the Sea

13 And the dragon stood on the sand of the seashore.

Then I saw a beast coming up out of the sea, having ten horns and seven heads, and on his horns *were* ten diadems, and on his heads *were* blasphemous names. [2]And the beast which I saw was like a leopard, and his feet were like *those* of a bear, and his mouth like the mouth of a lion. And the dragon gave him his power and his throne and great authority. [3]*I saw* one of his heads as if it had been slain, and his fatal wound was healed. And the whole earth was amazed *and followed* after the beast; [4]they worshiped the dragon because he gave his authority to the beast; and they worshiped the beast, saying, "Who is like the beast, and who is able to wage war with him?" [5]There was given to him a mouth speaking arrogant words and blasphemies, and authority to act for forty-two months was given to him. [6]And he opened his mouth in blasphemies against God, to blaspheme His name and His tabernacle, *that is,* those who dwell in heaven.

7 It was also given to him to make war with the saints and to overcome them, and authority over every tribe and people and tongue and nation was given to him. [8]All who dwell on the earth will worship him, *everyone* whose name has not been [a]written from the foundation of the world in the book of life of the Lamb who has been slain. [9]If anyone has an ear, let him hear. [10]If anyone [b]*is destined* for captivity, to captivity

[a]**13:8** Or written in the book...slain from the foundation of the world; [b]**13:10** Or written in the book...slain from the foundation of the world

he goes; if anyone kills with the sword, with the sword he must be killed. Here is the perseverance and the faith of the saints.

The Beast from the Earth

11 Then I saw another beast coming up out of the earth; and he had two horns like a lamb and he spoke as a dragon. [12]He exercises all the authority of the first beast in his presence. And he makes the earth and those who dwell in it to worship the first beast, whose fatal wound was healed. [13]He performs great signs, so that he even makes fire come down out of heaven to the earth in the presence of men. [14]And he deceives those who dwell on the earth because of the signs which it was given him to perform in the presence of the beast, telling those who dwell on the earth to make an image to the beast who *had the wound of the sword and has come to life. [15]And it was given to him to give breath to the image of the beast, so that the image of the beast would even aspeak and cause as many as do not worship the image of the beast to be killed. [16]And he causes all, the small and the great, and the rich and the poor, and the free men and the slaves, to be given a mark on their right hand or on their forehead, [17]and he provides that no one will be able to buy or to sell, except the one who has the mark, either the name of the beast or the number of his name. [18]Here is wisdom. Let him who has understanding calculate the number of the beast, for the number is that of a man; and his number is bsix hundred and sixty-six.

The Lamb and the 144,000 on Mount Zion

14 Then I looked, and behold, the Lamb was standing on Mount Zion, and with Him one hundred and forty-four thousand, having His name and the name of His Father written on their foreheads. [2]And I heard a voice from heaven, like the sound of many waters and like the sound of loud thunder, and the voice which I heard was like the sound of harpists playing on their harps. [3]And they *sang a new song before the throne and before the four living creatures and the elders; and no one could learn the song except the one hundred and forty-four thousand who had been purchased from the earth. [4]These are the ones who have not been defiled with women, for they chave kept themselves chaste. These are the ones who follow the Lamb wherever He goes. These were purchased from among men as first fruits to God and to the Lamb. [5]And no lie was found in their mouth; they are blameless.

---

a**13:15** One early ms reads speak, and he will cause; b**13:18** One early ms reads 616; c**14:4** Lit are chaste men

Vision of the Angel
with the Gospel

6 And I saw another angel flying in midheaven, having an eternal gospel to preach to those who live on the earth, and to every nation and tribe and tongue and people; [7]and he said with a loud voice, "Fear God, and give Him glory, because the hour of His judgment has come; worship Him who made the heaven and the earth and sea and springs of waters."

8 And another angel, a second one, followed, saying, "Fallen, fallen is Babylon the great, she who has made all the nations drink of the wine of the passion of her immorality."

Doom for Worshipers
of the Beast

9 Then another angel, a third one, followed them, saying with a loud voice, "If anyone worships the beast and his image, and receives a mark on his forehead or on his hand, [10]he also will drink of the wine of the wrath of God, which is mixed in full strength in the cup of His anger; and he will be tormented with fire and brimstone in the presence of the holy angels and in the presence of the Lamb. [11]And the smoke of their torment goes up forever and ever; they have no rest day and night, those who worship the beast and his image, and whoever receives the mark of his name." [12]Here is the perseverance of the saints who keep the commandments of God and their faith in Jesus.

13 And I heard a voice from heaven, saying, "Write, 'Blessed are the dead who die in the Lord from now on!' " "Yes," says the Spirit, "so that they may rest from their labors, for their deeds follow with them."

The Reapers

14 Then I looked, and behold, a white cloud, and sitting on the cloud was one like ªa son of man, having a golden crown on His head and a sharp sickle in His hand. [15]And another angel came out of the temple, crying out with a loud voice to Him who sat on the cloud, "Put in your sickle and reap, for the hour to reap has come, because the harvest of the earth is ripe." [16]Then He who sat on the cloud swung His sickle over the earth, and the earth was reaped.

17 And another angel came out of the temple which is in heaven, and he also had a sharp sickle. [18]Then another angel, the one who has power over fire, came out from the altar; and he called with a loud voice to him who had the sharp sickle, saying, "Put in your sharp sickle and gather the clusters from

the vine of the earth, because her grapes are ripe." [19]So the angel swung his sickle to the earth and gathered *the clusters from* the vine of the earth, and threw them into the great wine press of the wrath of God. [20]And the wine press was trodden outside the city, and blood came out from the wine press, up to the horses' bridles, for a distance of [a]two hundred miles.

A Scene of Heaven

15Then I saw another sign in heaven, great and marvelous, seven angels who had seven plagues, *which are* the last, because in them the wrath of God is finished.

[2] And I saw something like a sea of glass mixed with fire, and those who had been victorious over the beast and his image and the number of his name, standing on the sea of glass, holding harps of God. [3]And they *sang the song of Moses, the bond-servant of God, and the song of the Lamb, saying,

"Great and marvelous are Your works,

O Lord God, the Almighty;

Righteous and true are Your ways,

King of the [b]nations!

[4]"Who will not fear, O Lord, and glorify Your name?

For You alone are holy;

For ALL THE NATIONS WILL COME AND WORSHIP BEFORE YOU,

FOR YOUR RIGHTEOUS ACTS HAVE BEEN REVEALED."

[5] After these things I looked, and the temple of the tabernacle of testimony in heaven was opened, [6]and the seven angels who had the seven plagues came out of the temple, clothed in [c]linen, clean *and* bright, and girded around their chests with golden sashes. [7]Then one of the four living creatures gave to the seven angels seven golden bowls full of the wrath of God, who lives forever and ever. [8]And the temple was filled with smoke from the glory of God and from His power; and no one was able to enter the temple until the seven plagues of the seven angels were finished.

Six Bowls of Wrath

16Then I heard a loud voice from the temple, saying to the seven angels, "Go and pour out on the earth the seven bowls of the wrath of God."

[2] So the first *angel* went and poured out his bowl on the earth; and it became a loathsome and malignant sore on the people who had the mark of the beast and who worshiped his image.

[3] The second *angel* poured out his bowl into the sea, and it became blood like *that* of a dead

man; and every living ᵃthing in the sea died.

4 Then the third *angel* poured out his bowl into the rivers and the springs of waters; and they became blood. ⁵And I heard the angel of the waters saying, "Righteous are You, who are and who were, O Holy One, because You judged these things; ⁶for they poured out the blood of saints and prophets, and You have given them blood to drink. They deserve it." ⁷And I heard the altar saying, "Yes, O Lord God, the Almighty, true and righteous are Your judgments."

8 The fourth *angel* poured out his bowl upon the sun, and it was given to it to scorch men with fire. ⁹Men were scorched with fierce heat; and they blasphemed the name of God who has the power over these plagues, and they did not repent so as to give Him glory.

10 Then the fifth *angel* poured out his bowl on the throne of the beast, and his kingdom became darkened; and they gnawed their tongues because of pain, ¹¹and they blasphemed the God of heaven because of their pains and their sores; and they did not repent of their deeds.

12 The sixth *angel* poured out his bowl on the great river, the Euphrates; and its water was dried up, so that the way would be prepared for the kings from the east.

Armageddon

¹³And I saw *coming* out of the mouth of the dragon and out of the mouth of the beast and out of the mouth of the false prophet, three unclean spirits like frogs; ¹⁴for they are spirits of demons, performing signs, which go out to the kings of the whole world, to gather them together for the war of the great day of God, the Almighty. ¹⁵("Behold, I am coming like a thief. Blessed is the one who stays awake and keeps his clothes, so that he will not walk about naked and men will not see his shame.") ¹⁶And they gathered them together to the place which in Hebrew is called ᵃHar-Magedon.

Seventh Bowl of Wrath

17 Then the seventh *angel* poured out his bowl upon the air, and a loud voice came out of the temple from the throne, saying, "It is done." ¹⁸And there were flashes of lightning and sounds and peals of thunder; and there was a great earthquake, such as there had not been since man came to be upon the earth, so great an earthquake *was it, and* so mighty. ¹⁹The great city was split into three parts, and the cities of the nations fell. Babylon the great was remembered

ᵃ**16:3** Lit *soul*; ᵇ**16:16** Two early mss read *Armagedon* before God, to give her the cup of the wine of His fierce wrath. ²⁰And every island fled away, and the mountains were not found. ²¹And huge hailstones, about ^aone hundred pounds each, *came down from heaven upon men; and men blasphemed God because of the plague of the hail, because its plague *was extremely severe.

The Doom of Babylon

17 Then one of the seven angels who had the seven bowls came and spoke with me, saying, "Come here, I will show you the judgment of the great harlot who sits on many waters, ²with whom the kings of the earth committed *acts of* immorality, and those who dwell on the earth were made drunk with the wine of her immorality." ³And he carried me away ^bin the Spirit into a wilderness; and I saw a woman sitting on a scarlet beast, full of blasphemous names, having seven heads and ten horns. ⁴The woman was clothed in purple and scarlet, and adorned with gold and precious stones and pearls, having in her hand a gold cup full of abominations and of the unclean things of her immorality, ⁵and on her forehead a name *was* written, a mystery, "BABYLON THE GREAT, THE MOTHER OF HARLOTS AND OF THE ABOMINATIONS OF THE EARTH." ⁶And I saw the woman drunk with the blood of the saints, and with the blood of the witnesses of Jesus. When I saw her, I wondered greatly. ⁷And the angel said to me, "Why do you wonder? I will tell you the mystery of the woman and of the beast that carries her, which has the seven heads and the ten horns.

8 "The beast that you saw was, and is not, and is about to come up out of the abyss and ^cgo to destruction. And those who dwell on the earth, whose name has not been written in the book of life from the foundation of the world, will wonder when they see the beast, that he was and is not and will come. ⁹Here is the mind which has wisdom. The seven heads are seven mountains on which the woman sits, ¹⁰and they are seven kings; five have fallen, one is, the other has not yet come; and when he comes, he must remain a little while. ¹¹The beast which was and is not, is himself also an eighth and is *one* of the seven, and he goes to destruction. ¹²The ten horns which you saw are ten kings who have not yet received a kingdom, but they receive authority as kings with the beast for one hour. ¹³These have one purpose, and they give their power and authority to the beast.

Victory for the Lamb

¹⁴These will wage war against the Lamb, and the Lamb will

^a**16:21** Lit the weight of a talent; ^b**17:3** Or *in spirit*; ^c**17:8** One early ms reads *is going*

overcome them, because He is Lord of lords and King of kings, and those who are with Him *are the* called and chosen and faithful."

15 And he *said to me, "The waters which you saw where the harlot sits, are peoples and multitudes and nations and tongues. ^16And the ten horns which you saw, and the beast, these will hate the harlot and will make her desolate and naked, and will eat her flesh and will burn her up with fire. ^17For God has put it in their hearts to execute His purpose by having a common purpose, and by giving their kingdom to the beast, until the words of God will be fulfilled. ^18The woman whom you saw is the great city, which reigns over the kings of the earth."

Babylon Is Fallen

18 After these things I saw another angel coming down from heaven, having great authority, and the earth was illumined with his glory. ^2And he cried out with a mighty voice, saying, "Fallen, fallen is Babylon the great! She has become a dwelling place of demons and a prison of every unclean spirit, and a prison of every unclean and hateful bird. ^3For all the nations ^ahave drunk of the wine of the passion of her immorality, and the kings of the earth have committed *acts of* immorality

^a**18:3** Two early ancient mss read *have fallen by*

with her, and the merchants of the earth have become rich by the wealth of her sensuality."

4 I heard another voice from heaven, saying, "Come out of her, my people, so that you will not participate in her sins and receive of her plagues; ^5for her sins have piled up as high as heaven, and God has remembered her iniquities. ^6Pay her back even as she has paid, and give back *to her* double according to her deeds; in the cup which she has mixed, mix twice as much for her. ^7To the degree that she glorified herself and lived sensuously, to the same degree give her torment and mourning; for she says in her heart, 'I SIT *as* A QUEEN AND I AM NOT A WIDOW, and will never see mourning.' ^8For this reason in one day her plagues will come, pestilence and mourning and famine, and she will be burned up with fire; for the Lord God who judges her is strong.

Lament for Babylon

9 "And the kings of the earth, who committed *acts of* immorality and lived sensuously with her, will weep and lament over her when they see the smoke of her burning, ^10standing at a distance because of the fear of her torment, saying, 'Woe, woe, the great city, Babylon, the strong city! For in one hour your judgment has come.'

11 "And the merchants of the earth weep and mourn over her, because no one buys their cargoes any more— 12cargoes of gold and silver and precious stones and pearls and fine linen and purple and silk and scarlet, and every *kind of* citron wood and every article of ivory and every article *made* from very costly wood and bronze and iron and marble, 13and cinnamon and spice and incense and perfume and frankincense and wine and olive oil and fine flour and wheat and cattle and sheep, and *cargoes* of horses and chariots and slaves and human lives. 14The fruit you long for has gone from you, and all things that were luxurious and splendid have passed away from you and *men* will no longer find them. 15The merchants of these things, who became rich from her, will stand at a distance because of the fear of her torment, weeping and mourning, 16saying, 'Woe, woe, the great city, she who was clothed in fine linen and purple and scarlet, and adorned with gold and precious stones and pearls; 17for in one hour such great wealth has been laid waste!' And every shipmaster and every passenger and sailor, and as many as make their living by the sea, stood at a distance, 18and were crying out as they saw the smoke of her burning, saying, 'What *city* is like the great city?' 19And they threw dust on their heads and were crying out, weeping and mourning, saying, 'Woe, woe, the great city, in which all who had ships at sea became rich by her wealth, for in one hour she has been laid waste!' 20Rejoice over her, O heaven, and you saints and apostles and prophets, because God has pronounced judgment for you against her."

21 Then a strong angel took up a stone like a great millstone and threw it into the sea, saying, "So will Babylon, the great city, be thrown down with violence, and will not be found any longer. 22And the sound of harpists and musicians and flute-players and trumpeters will not be heard in you any longer; and no craftsman of any craft will be found in you any longer; and the sound of a mill will not be heard in you any longer; 23and the light of a lamp will not shine in you any longer; and the voice of the bridegroom and bride will not be heard in you any longer; for your merchants were the great men of the earth, because all the nations were deceived by your sorcery. 24And in her was found the blood of prophets and of saints and of all who have been slain on the earth."

The Fourfold Hallelujah

19 After these things I heard something like a loud voice of a great multitude in heaven, saying,

"Hallelujah! Salvation and glory and glory and power belong to our God; [2]BECAUSE HIS JUDGMENTS ARE TRUE AND RIGHTEOUS; for He has judged the great harlot who was corrupting the earth with her immorality, and HE HAS AVENGED THE BLOOD OF HIS BOND-SERVANTS ON HER." [3]And a second time they said, "Hallelujah! HER SMOKE RISES UP FOREVER AND EVER." [4]And the twenty-four elders and the four living creatures fell down and worshiped God who sits on the throne saying, "Amen. Hallelujah!" [5]And a voice came from the throne, saying,

"Give praise to our God, all you His bond-servants, you who fear Him, the small and the great." [6]Then I heard *something* like the voice of a great multitude and like the sound of many waters and like the sound of mighty peals of thunder, saying,

"Hallelujah! For the Lord our God, the Almighty, reigns.

Marriage of the Lamb

[7]Let us rejoice and be glad and give the glory to Him, for the marriage of the Lamb has come and His bride has made herself ready."

[8]It was given to her to clothe herself in fine linen, bright *and* clean; for the fine linen is the righteous acts of the saints.

[9] Then he *said to me, "Write, 'Blessed are those who are invited to the marriage supper of the Lamb.' " And he *said to me, "These are true words of God." [10]Then I fell at his feet to worship him. But he *said to me, "Do not do that; I am a fellow servant of yours and your brethren who hold the testimony of Jesus; worship God. For the testimony of Jesus is the spirit of prophecy."

The Coming of Christ

[11] And I saw heaven opened, and behold, a white horse, and He who sat on it *is* called Faithful and True, and in righteousness He judges and wages war. [12]His eyes *are* a flame of fire, and on His head *are* many diadems; and He has a name written *on Him* which no one knows except Himself. [13]*He is* clothed with a robe dipped in blood, and His name is called The Word of God. [14]And the armies which are in heaven, clothed in fine linen, white *and* clean, were following Him on white horses. [15]From His mouth comes a sharp sword, so that with it He may strike down the nations, and He will rule them with a rod of iron; and He treads the wine press of

the fierce wrath of God, the Almighty. ¹⁶And on His robe and on His thigh He has a name written, "KING OF KINGS, AND LORD OF LORDS."

17 Then I saw an angel standing in the sun, and he cried out with a loud voice, saying to all the birds which fly in midheaven, "Come, assemble for the great supper of God, ¹⁸so that you may eat the flesh of kings and the flesh of ªcommanders and the flesh of mighty men and the flesh of horses and of those who sit on them and the flesh of all men, both free men and slaves, and small and great."

19 And I saw the beast and the kings of the earth and their armies assembled to make war against Him who sat on the horse and against His army.

Doom of the Beast and False Prophet

²⁰And the beast was seized, and with him the false prophet who performed the signs in his presence, by which he deceived those who had received the mark of the beast and those who worshiped his image; these two were thrown alive into the lake of fire which burns with brimstone. ²¹And the rest were killed with the sword which came from the mouth of Him who sat on the horse, and

all the birds were filled with their flesh.

Satan Bound

20Then I saw an angel coming down from heaven, holding the key of the abyss and a great chain in his hand. ²And he laid hold of the dragon, the serpent of old, who is the devil and Satan, and bound him for a thousand years; ³and he threw him into the abyss, and shut *it* and sealed *it* over him, so that he would not deceive the nations any longer, until the thousand years were completed; after these things he must be released for a short time.

4 Then I saw thrones, and they sat on them, and judgment was given to them. And I *saw* the souls of those who had been beheaded because of their testimony of Jesus and because of the word of God, and those who had not worshiped the beast or his image, and had not received the mark on their forehead and on their hand; and they came to life and reigned with Christ for a thousand years. ⁵The rest of the dead did not come to life until the thousand years were completed. This is the first resurrection. ⁶Blessed and holy is the one who has a part in the first resurrection; over these the second death has no power, but they will be priests of God and of Christ

and will reign with Him for a thousand years.

Satan Freed, Doomed

7 When the thousand years are completed, Satan will be released from his prison, [8]and will come out to deceive the nations which are in the four corners of the earth, Gog and Magog, to gather them together for the war; the number of them is like the sand of the seashore. [9]And they came up on the broad plain of the earth and surrounded the camp of the saints and the beloved city, and fire came down from heaven and devoured them. [10]And the devil who deceived them was thrown into the lake of fire and brimstone, where the beast and the false prophet are also; and they will be tormented day and night forever and ever.

Judgment at the Throne of God

11 Then I saw a great white throne and Him who sat upon it, from whose presence earth and heaven fled away, and no place was found for them. [12]And I saw the dead, the great and the small, standing before the throne, and books were opened; and another book was opened, which is *the book* of life; and the dead were judged from the things which were written in the books, according to their deeds. [13]And the sea gave up the dead which were in it, and

death and Hades gave up the dead which were in them; and they were judged, every one *of them* according to their deeds. [14]Then death and Hades were thrown into the lake of fire. This is the second death, the lake of fire. [15]And if anyone's name was not found written in the book of life, he was thrown into the lake of fire.

The New Heaven and Earth

21 Then I saw a new heaven and a new earth; for the first heaven and the first earth passed away, and there is no longer *any* sea. [2]And I saw the holy city, new Jerusalem, coming down out of heaven from God, made ready as a bride adorned for her husband. [3]And I heard a loud voice from the throne, saying, "Behold, the tabernacle of God is among men, and He will dwell among them, and they shall be His people, and God Himself will be among them[a], [4]and He will wipe away every tear from their eyes; and there will no longer be *any* death; there will no longer be *any* mourning, or crying, or pain; the first things have passed away."

5 And He who sits on the throne said, "Behold, I am making all things new." And He *said, "Write, for these words are faithful and true." [6]Then He said to me, "It is done. I am the Alpha and the

---

[a]**21:3** One early ms reads, *and be their God*

Omega, the beginning and the end. I will give to the one who thirsts from the spring of the water of life without cost. ⁷He who overcomes will inherit these things, and I will be his God and he will be My son. ⁸But for the cowardly and unbelieving and abominable and murderers and immoral persons and sorcerers and idolaters and all liars, their part *will be* in the lake that burns with fire and brimstone, which is the second death."

9 Then one of the seven angels who had the seven bowls full of the seven last plagues came and spoke with me, saying, "Come here, I will show you the bride, the wife of the Lamb."

The New Jerusalem

¹⁰And he carried me away ᵃin the Spirit to a great and high mountain, and showed me the holy city, Jerusalem, coming down out of heaven from God, ¹¹having the glory of God. Her brilliance was like a very costly stone, as a stone of crystal-clear jasper. ¹²It had a great and high wall, with twelve gates, and at the gates twelve angels; and names *were* written on them, which are *the names* of the twelve tribes of the sons of Israel. ¹³*There were* three gates on the east and three gates on the north and three gates on the south and three gates on the west. ¹⁴And the wall of the city had twelve foundation stones, and on them *were* the twelve names of the twelve apostles of the Lamb.

15 The one who spoke with me had a gold measuring rod to measure the city, and its gates and its wall. ¹⁶The city is laid out as a square, and its length is as great as the width; and he measured the city with the rod, ᵇfifteen hundred miles; its length and width and height are equal. ¹⁷And he measured its wall, ᶜseventy-two yards, *according to* human measurements, which are *also* angelic *measurements.* ¹⁸The material of the wall was jasper; and the city was pure gold, like clear glass. ¹⁹The foundation stones of the city wall were adorned with every kind of precious stone. The first foundation stone was jasper; the second, sapphire; the third, chalcedony; the fourth, emerald; ²⁰the fifth, sardonyx; the sixth, sardius; the seventh, chrysolite; the eighth, beryl; the ninth, topaz; the tenth, chrysoprase; the eleventh, jacinth; the twelfth, amethyst. ²¹And the twelve gates were twelve pearls; each one of the gates was a single pearl. And the street of the city was pure gold, like transparent glass.

22 I saw no temple in it, for the Lord God the Almighty and the Lamb are its temple. ²³And the city has no need of the sun or of

---

ᵃ**21:10** Or *in spirit;* ᵇ**21:16** Lit *twelve thousand stadia;* a stadion was approx 600 ft; ᶜ**21:17** Lit *one hundred forty-four cubits* the moon to shine on it, for the glory of God has illumined it, and its lamp *is* the Lamb. ²⁴The nations will walk by its light, and the kings of the earth will bring their glory into it. ²⁵In the daytime (for there will be no night there) its gates will never be closed; ²⁶and they will bring the glory and the honor of the nations into it; ²⁷and nothing unclean, and no one who practices abomination and lying, shall ever come into it, but only those whose names are written in the Lamb's book of life.

The River and the Tree of Life

22 Then he showed me a river of the water of life, clear as crystal, coming from the throne of God and of the ᵃLamb, ²in the middle of its street. On either side of the river was the tree of life, bearing twelve ᵇ*kinds of* fruit, yielding its fruit every month; and the leaves of the tree were for the healing of the nations. ³There will no longer be any curse; and the throne of God and of the Lamb will be in it, and His bond-servants will serve Him; ⁴they will see His face, and His name *will be* on their foreheads. ⁵And there will no longer be *any* night; and they will not have need of the light of a lamp nor the light of the sun, because the Lord God will illumine them; and they will reign forever and ever.

6 And he said to me, "These words are faithful and true"; and the Lord, the God of the spirits of the prophets, sent His angel to show to His bond-servants the things which must soon take place.

7 "And behold, I am coming quickly. Blessed is he who heeds the words of the prophecy of this book."

8 I, John, am the one who heard and saw these things. And when I heard and saw, I fell down to worship at the feet of the angel who showed me these things. ⁹But he *said to me, "Do not do that. I am a fellow servant of yours and of your brethren the prophets and of those who heed the words of this book. Worship God."

The Final Message

10 And he *said to me, "Do not seal up the words of the prophecy of this book, for the time is near. ¹¹Let the one who does wrong, still do wrong; and the one who is filthy, still be filthy; and let the one who is righteous, still practice righteousness; and the one who is holy, still keep himself holy."

12 "Behold, I am coming quickly, and My reward *is* with Me, to render to every man according to what he has done. ¹³I am the Alpha and the Omega, the first

ᵃ**22:1** Or the Lamb. In the middle of its street, and on either side of the river, was; ᵇ**22:2** Or crops of fruit and the last, the beginning and the end."

14 Blessed are those who wash their robes, so that they may have the right to the tree of life, and may enter by the gates into the city. ¹⁵Outside are the dogs and the sorcerers and the immoral persons and the murderers and the idolaters, and everyone who loves and practices lying.

16 "I, Jesus, have sent My angel to testify to you these things for the churches. I am the root and the descendant of David, the bright morning star."

17 The Spirit and the bride say, "Come." And let the one who hears say, "Come." And let the one who is thirsty come; let the one who wishes take the water of life without cost.

18 I testify to everyone who hears the words of the prophecy of this book: if anyone adds to them, God will add to him the plagues which are written in this book; ¹⁹and if anyone takes away from the words of the book of this prophecy, God will take away his part from the tree of life and from the holy city, which are written in this book.

20 He who testifies to these things says, "Yes, I am coming quickly." Amen. Come, Lord Jesus.

21 The grace of the Lord Jesus be with all. Amen.

YOUR NEW LIFE IN CHRIST

A CALL TO DISCIPLESHIP

time to revive

- For Additional Resources -
www.timetorevive.com
1-877-265-1605

DISCIPLES

NEW IN CHRIST

Therefore, if anyone is in Christ, he is a new creature; the old things have passed away; behold, new things have come. 2 Corinthians 5:17

The Bible says you are a "new creature." You may feel different. You may not. Emotions often follow or indicate a change of heart. However, it is God's Word and the Holy Spirit that give the assurance that you belong to Him (Romans 8:16).

Your sins have been forgiven through faith in Jesus Christ and all He has done. You have His free gift of salvation and eternal life. You have been set free from the "old things" (sin) to live this new life in Christ. You have a new heart and a new Spirit living in you. Thousands of years ago, one of God's prophets of the Old Testament described what God would do for you. Ezekiel 36:26-27 says:

And I will give you a new heart, and a new spirit I will put within you. And I will remove the heart of stone from your flesh and give you a heart of flesh. And I will put My Spirit within you, and cause you to walk in My statutes and be careful to obey My rules.

God's Word and the Holy Spirit give you everything you need to become more

 THE HOLY SPIRIT

He is a member of the Godhead: The Father, Son, and Holy Spirit. Each member is distinct, yet all together are one God (Deuteronomy 6:4). The Holy Spirit lives in every believer (1 Corinthians 3:16). He has many different roles in your life:

Comforter
(Acts 9:31)
Helper
(John 14:16; Romans 8:26)
Teacher
(Luke 12:12)
Giver of Spiritual Gifts
(1 Corinthians 12)

like Jesus. He now lives within you. That may be hard to comprehend right now, but it will become clearer with time and the understanding He will give you.

God loves you and desires to lead your life as you seek to follow Him. A disciple in Christ abandons an "old" life to embrace a "new" life in Him.

6

DISCIPLES

GROW IN CHRIST

So then, those who had received his [Peter's] word were baptized; and that day there were added about three thousand souls. They were continually devoting themselves to the apostles' teaching and to fellowship, to the breaking of bread and to prayer. Acts 2:41-42

As a new disciple in Christ, God has given you everything you need to grow in Christ through the Holy Spirit, the Bible, prayer, and by being in community with other disciples of Christ Jesus.

 Community was incredibly important to Jesus' first disciples, who we call the "apostles." These first followers of Jesus walked with Him on earth, saw Him die, spent time with Him after His resurrection from the dead, and watched as He ascended into heaven. They show us how important it is for new believers to study the Bible together, pray with each other and fellowship. You can grow in your new life in Christ individually, but it is important to walk with others by joining a Bible study group or local church.

You will meet other believers and enjoy fellowship with new friends who will love you simply because Jesus loves them (1 John 4:19). The Holy Spirit living in you and every believer allows us to love one another and help each other through good and bad times. The Bible describes the Church like a human body. Each person in Christ has a necessary part to make the whole work together properly (1 Corinthians 12:12-26). You need the support of other believers, and they need you too.

 As Jesus commanded, the apostles baptized every new disciple with water (Matthew 28:19; Acts 3:41). Baptism shows what has taken place in every believer in Jesus Christ. You have died to your old life – your sins have been washed away through the sacrifice of Jesus and you are raised to new life in Him. Romans 6:4 says:

We have been buried with Him through baptism into death, so that as Christ was raised from the dead through the glory of the Father, so we too might walk in newness of life.

Studying The Bible is something you should do with other believers, but also in your daily individual life with Jesus. If you don't know what to read, the book of John is a great place to start. You will learn more of who Jesus is and what He wants to teach you.

Prayer is another important aspect of walking with Jesus. It is something the apostles devoted themselves to. Prayer is talking with God and also letting Him speak to you. In a local church or Bible study, you will learn to pray with and for others, and let others pray for you.

If you need help getting connected to a church or would like to be baptized, contact the one who introduced you to Jesus or contact Time to Revive (855-CALL-TTR).

DISCIPLES

SHARE CHRIST

And Jesus came up and spoke to them, saying, "All authority has been given to Me in heaven and on earth. Go therefore and make disciples of all the nations, baptizing them in the name of the Father and the Son and the Holy Spirit, teaching them to observe all that I commanded you; and lo, I am with you always, even to the end of the age." Matthew 28:18-20

All of Jesus' disciples are called to make disciples by telling others about Him. Chances are, you heard about Jesus because someone introduced you to Him. It is now your calling to tell others about the new life in Christ you are growing in.

Jesus said, "As the Father has sent Me, even so I am sending you" (John 20:21). As His disciple, you have been sent by Jesus and entrusted with the message of life: the death, burial and resurrection of Jesus.

 Tell others what God has done for you, how you repented of your sins and are forgiven because of Jesus' sacrifice on the cross. Tell them how Jesus died for your sin, but rose again so that you can have new life in Him. Tell others in love, with words and with your deeds (Matthew 5:13-16).

You can tell your family, friends, or even strangers about Jesus. You might be afraid and tempted not to share with someone. This fear doesn't come from God, but from the enemy, satan, who convinced man to disobey God in the beginning (Genesis 3). Second Timothy 1:7 says, "For God has not given us a spirit of timidity (fear), but of power and love and discipline." Remember, the Holy Spirit living in you will teach you what to say (Luke 12:12) and He will always be with you (Matthew 28:20b).

Go. Share. Make New Disciples in Christ.

Who will you go and share Christ with?

_____

_____

_____